Guide to Linux®
Installation and
Administration

Nicholas Wells

with Michael Jang

COURSE
TECHNOLOGY

Thomson Learning™

ONE MAIN STREET, CAMBRIDGE, MA 02142

Australia • Canada • Denmark • Japan • Mexico • New Zealand • Philippines
Puerto Rico • Singapore • South Africa • Spain • United Kingdom • United States

Guide to Linux® Installation and Administration is published by Course Technology.

Product Manager:	Lisa Ayers Egan
Senior Acquisitions Editor:	Stephen Solomon
Development Editor:	Ann Shaffer
Production Editor:	Lisa Auer
Associate Product Manager:	Laura Hildebrand
Editorial Assistant:	Elizabeth Wessen
Composition House:	GEX, Inc.
Text Designer:	GEX, Inc.
Cover Designer:	Efrat Reis
Marketing Manager:	Susan Ogar

Trademarks

Linux is a registered trademark of Linus Torvalds and Linux International.

Disclaimer

Course Technology reserves the right to revise this publication and make changes from time to time in its content without notice.

Linux Penguin created by Larry Ewing, lewing@isc.tamu.edu
The Web addresses in this book are subject to change from time to time as necessary without notice.

For more information, contact Course Technology, One Main Street, Cambridge, MA 02142;
or find us on the World Wide Web at *www.course.com*.

For permission to use material from this text or product, contact us by

- Web: *www.thomsonrights.com*
- Phone: 1-800-730-2214
- Fax: 1-800-730-2215

ISBN 0-619-00097-x

Printed in Canada
4 5 WC 03 02

BRIEF CONTENTS

TABLE OF CONTENTS

CHAPTER FOUR
Running a Linux System

CHAPTER NINE
Hardware Redundancy and Fault Tolerance   **319**

CHAPTER TEN
Managing System Resources   **363**

CHAPTER THIRTEEN
The Printing System   **473**

Preface

The growth of Linux as an accepted and widely used operating system is the most important event to occur in the computer industry since the rise of the Internet. Many new Linux-focused companies are appearing, and most major hardware and software vendors are now moving rapidly to support Linux. Thus, it's essential that computer professionals become familiar with Linux technologies and applications. This book guides you through the process of learning Linux. It begins by introducing many basic concepts that may be unfamiliar to you and then explains the installation and use of a Linux-based computer from the point of view of a system administrator.

After you have become familiar with the tools and processes related to installing and administering a Linux system, you may need to demonstrate that knowledge by passing a Linux certification exam. After all, organizations are increasingly relying on such exams as a means of assessing technical skills. The world of Linux professional certification is still fairly new. As of this writing, two high-quality certification programs are available: the Linux Professional Institute (LPI) certification (see *www.lpi.org*) and the Sair & GNU Linux certification, called LCA, for Linux Certified Administrator (see *www.linuxcertification.org*).

LPI is sponsored by numerous major Linux vendors, including Caldera Systems, LinuxCare, and SuSE Linux. It is a nonprofit organization that operates with a board of directors who gather input from members of the Linux community to develop overall certification goals, testing objectives, and future plans. LPI has planned a three-level certification program. The first level, addressed by this book, consists of two tests aimed at basic Linux proficiency. One of these tests is a vendor-specific test and allows you to focus your training efforts on the Linux product that you expect to use most, such as Red Hat Linux, TurboLinux, Debian Linux, or others.

The Sair & GNU Linux certification effort was started by Tobin Maginnis, a professor at the University of Mississippi. With cooperation from leading free software enthusiasts, his organization created the LCA testing objectives and testing program. To obtain LCA certification, you must pass a series of four tests. The first two of these tests are addressed by this book. The third and fourth LCA exams are covered in *Guide to Linux Networking and Security,* (ISBN 0-619-00094-5), also published by Course Technology. The Sair & GNU Linux program is entirely vendor neutral, though it tends to focus somewhat on the Debian distribution.

Appendix A provides the most current information about the LPI and LCA certification objectives available at this writing. Both the LPI and LCA certification programs require you to take and pass multiple tests. To prepare for the LPI tests, you should master the material presented in this book and also in the companion book *Guide to Linux Networking and Security*. To prepare for the first two LCA tests, use this book; to prepare for the third and fourth LCA tests, use the companion book.

The chapters in this book discuss the following topics:

Chapter 1 introduces the term OpenSource as it applies to the Linux operating system and describes the history of the Linux project.

Chapters 2 and 3 help you compile the hardware information you need in order to install Linux. They explain concepts related to installation and then walk you through the process of installing Linux on a computer.

Chapter 4 introduces many concepts related to how a Linux operating system functions. It explains how to work at the command line and how the system is initialized. It also introduces essential Linux commands.

Chapter 5 presents the Linux graphical systems in detail, explaining how to configure and troubleshoot the graphical environment.

Chapter 6 includes more information about using the shell, or command-line environment, to complete work in Linux.

Chapter 7 introduces Linux system administration. It describes the work of a system administrator, some concepts that Linux system administrators should know, and a few key system administration commands.

Chapter 8 focuses on three key areas of Linux system administration: managing user accounts, managing file systems, and managing processes (programs).

Chapter 9 describes how to safeguard information on a Linux-based computer against hardware failure. It explains concepts such as redundancy and introduces you to the Linux tools you can use to protect your data.

Chapter 10 explains how to manage the performance of a Linux-based computer using standard Linux command-line and graphical utilities. It explains how to expand the file system, manage memory, and work with benchmarks to track system performance.

Chapter 11 is dedicated to system logging. It teaches you why logs are important, where they are located, and how you can use the information they contain to manage a Linux system.

Chapter 12 explains how to write scripts in Linux and then use those scripts to schedule tasks for execution at any time.

Chapter 13 focuses on printing from a Linux system. You learn about the printing system in general, the utilities used to print files and manage printers, and how to print to network-accessible printers.

Chapter 14 explains how to back up data using standard Linux utilities and popular hardware devices such as optical drives and tape drives.

The three appendices at the end of this book serve as references for the Linux professional. Appendix A provides a list of the certification objectives for the LPI and LCA certification programs. Review these objectives to test your knowledge and readiness before attempting to pass the certification exams. Be sure to check the Web sites mentioned earlier in the Preface to ensure you are using the most current certification objectives. Appendix B and Appendix C contain reference information about Linux command-line utilities and Linux graphical administration tools, respectively.

THE INTENDED AUDIENCE

This book is intended to serve the needs of readers who plan to work as Linux system administrators and who may also plan to take one or more certification tests as part of their professional preparation. The text and pedagogical features are designed to provide a truly interactive learning experience, preparing you for the challenges of the dynamic Linux industry. In addition to the information presented in the text, each chapter includes hands-on projects that take you through various tasks step by step. Each chapter also contains case projects that summarize a real-life situation in which you must use the knowledge gained in the chapter to address a specific problem.

FEATURES

To aid you in fully understanding the concepts related to Linux installation and system administration, this book includes the following features:

- ♦ **Chapter Objectives.** Each chapter in this book begins with a detailed list of the concepts or procedures to be mastered within that chapter. This list provides you with a quick reference to the contents of that chapter, as well as a useful study aid.

- ♦ **Illustrations and Tables.** Numerous figures of utility screens and conceptual diagrams help you visualize Linux tools and concepts. In addition, many tables provide detailed utility information, summaries of options, or comparisons of both practical and theoretical information.

- ♦ **Chapter Summaries.** Each chapter's text is followed by a summary of the concepts and tools introduced in the chapter. These summaries provide a helpful way to recap and revisit the ideas covered in each chapter.

- ♦ **Key Terms.** All of the terms within the chapter that were introduced with boldfaced text are gathered together in the Key Terms list at the end of the chapter. This provides you with a method of checking your understanding of all the terms introduced.

- ♦ **Review Questions.** End-of-chapter assessment begins with a set of review questions that reinforce the ideas introduced in each chapter. These questions are written to ensure that you have mastered the concepts presented.

- ♦ **Hands-on Projects.** Although it is important to understand the concepts behind the Linux operating system, nothing can match the value of real-world experience. To this end, each chapter provides hands-on projects aimed at providing you with a step-by-step guide to implementing real-world solutions.

- ♦ **Case Projects.** Located at the end of each chapter are several case-oriented questions. In answering these questions, you must describe how you would use the skills and knowledge gained in the chapter in real design and implementation scenarios.

TEXT AND GRAPHIC CONVENTIONS

Wherever appropriate, additional information and exercises have been added to this book to help you better understand what is being discussed in the chapter. Icons throughout the text alert you to additional materials. The icons used in this textbook are described below.

 The Tip icon is used to present additional helpful material related to the subject being described. Many of the tips are drawn from the author's experience to help you better understand the concept or utility being described.

 Each hands-on activity in this book is preceded by the Hands-On icon and a description of the exercise that follows.

 The cautions are included to help you anticipate potential mistakes or problems so you can prevent them from happening.

RED HAT 6.0 CD

This book includes a copy of the Publisher's Edition of Red Hat Linux from Red Hat, Inc., which you may use in accordance with the license agreements accompanying the software. The Official Red Hat Linux, which you may purchase from Red Hat, includes the complete Official Red Hat Linux distribution, Red Hat's documentation, and may include technical support for Official Red Hat Linux. You also may purchase technical support from Red Hat. You may purchase Official Red Hat Linux and technical support from Red Hat Software through the company's web site (*www.redhat.com*) or its toll-free number 1-888-REDHAT1.

SYSTEM REQUIREMENTS

To install Red Hat Linux 6, your computer must meet the following minimum requirements:

- Intel 486 processor
- 16 MB of RAM
- 500 MB free hard disk space
- 3.5-inch floppy drive
- CD-ROM drive

To access a Linux host on a local area network to which your computer is connected, you need the following software and information:

- Telnet program
- Either the IP address or the host and domain name of the Linux system

To access a Linux host via the Internet, you need the following software and information:

♦ Dial-up connection to an Internet Service Provider

♦ Telnet program

♦ Either the IP address or the host and domain name of the Linux system

INSTRUCTORS' MATERIALS

The following supplemental materials are available when this book is used in a classroom setting. All of the supplements available with this book are provided to the instructor on a single CD-ROM.

Electronic Instructor's Manual. The instructor's manual that accompanies this textbook includes:

♦ Additional instructional material to assist in class preparation, including suggestions for lecture topics, suggested lab activities, and sample syllabi.

♦ Solutions to all end-of-chapter materials, including the hands-on projects and case projects.

Course Test Manager 1.3. Accompanying this book is a powerful assessment tool known as the Course Test Manager. Designed by Course Technology, this cutting-edge, Windows-based testing software helps instructors design and administer tests and pretests. In addition to generating tests that can be printed and administered, this full-featured program has an online testing component that allows students to take tests at the computer and have their exams automatically graded.

PowerPoint Presentations. A complete set of Microsoft PowerPoint slides is available for each chapter. These can be used as a teaching aid for classroom presentation, as an online resource for chapter review, or as printed material for classroom distribution. Instructors are at liberty to add their own slides for additional topics introduced to the class.

DEDICATION

This book is dedicated to my favorite teacher, Quentin sT. Wells. Thanks, Dad.

ACKNOWLEDGMENTS

Preparing a book of this type requires the cooperation and coordination of many talented people. I felt privileged to work with them in creating this book together. Stephen Solomon at Course Technology started me on the road to this project and acted as a guide in the rapidly evolving world of Linux certification. Lisa Egan kept me on track during the many revisions and reviews required to prepare a book that we can all be proud of. She handled her job with humor and aplomb. A special thank-you is due to Ann Shaffer, the book's development editor, who showed me by her attentive and professional efforts that the craft of writing need not be diminished even when working in a fast-moving technical field. I trust that each reader will benefit from her attention as much as I did. Many other people at Course Technology contributed to the review, testing, and layout of this book, including Lisa Auer, the Production Editor, John Bosco, Manuscript Quality Assurance Manager, and the other members of the testing team. Other reviewers located around the country were willing to spend time reviewing the book before it was in a usable state. I thank all of these individuals for their patience and assistance:

Allan Collard	St. Clair County Community College
David Klann	Berbee Information Networks
Juliet Lauders	Rogue Community College
Guy Reams	Mount San Jacinto College
Philip Reid	Cleveland Community College
Vickee Stedham	St. Petersburgh Junior College
Neal Stenlund	Piedmont Community College
Sudharshan Vazhkudai	University of Mississippi

Those who are working to make Linux certification a powerful force for professional training and acceptance of Linux in large organizations deserve the thanks of everyone who works professionally with Linux. Dan York and others on the board of the Linux Professional Institute, and Tobin Maginnis, who founded the Sair & GNU Linux certification effort (now owned by Wave Technologies), both deserve mention.

Finally, I thank my wife Anne, who remains ever supportive during the sometimes tedious and always time-consuming process of writing a book. It couldn't be done without her.

1

INTRODUCING LINUX

**After reading this chapter and completing the exercises,
you will be able to:**

♦ Explain how an operating system works

♦ Explain how and why Linux was created

♦ Describe some benefits of using Linux

♦ Locate additional information about Linux commands and features

In this chapter you learn what an operating system is and how the Linux operating system compares to others that you may have already used. You learn about the unusual background of Linux and why many people feel so strongly about the way it continues to be developed. Finally, you learn about where you can find additional information regarding Linux.

UNDERSTANDING OPERATING SYSTEMS

If you are like most computer users, your experience is limited to working on one of the popular graphical computers such as an Apple Macintosh or a computer running Microsoft Windows 95, Windows 98, or Windows 2000. These platforms are popular and easy to use, but they aren't right for every computing need. Linux arose as an alternative choice for people whose computing needs require something other than the platforms most people are familiar with.

To appreciate the value of Linux, you must understand what an operating system is in relation to the computer itself and the programs (or applications) that you run on the computer. Then you can also understand the features and benefits that the Linux operating system offers.

Defining an Operating System

When computers were first created 40 or so years ago, everything the computer needed to do was **hard wired**, meaning that the instructions were arranged in the wires and other components that made up the computer. Because of this, a computer was able to complete only a single task—the one that it was hard wired to perform. For example, a computer

1

might be designed to add or subtract two numbers, but not have any other capability. As more powerful computer hardware became available, programmers began to demand more flexibility. The result was software. The term **software** refers to the programs that control the physical computer components, providing instructions for completing a task. Unlike a hard-wired system, software can be changed without disassembling the computer itself. Obviously, this was real progress.

Early software contained everything the computer needed to complete a task. Before long, however, programmers decided it was more efficient to create one kind of software that provided core functionality, and then to create applications that built upon those basic functions. An **application** is a program that provides a service to a person using the computer, rather than simply managing the computer's resources. For example, word processors and accounting software are applications. The core functionality was designed to send instructions to the hardware. Applications could then use the core functionality for more specific tasks. For example, one core function might be the ability to print characters on the monitor. An application could then use this functionality to print specific characters for a spreadsheet, a word processor, or other programs.

We call this set of core functionality the operating system. Although operating systems have advanced a great deal in the last 30 years, the basic purpose remains the same: an **operating system** is the program that contains a set of core functionality for other programs, providing both the interface between other programs and the hardware, and the interface between other programs and the user sitting at the computer. Figure 1-1 shows the relationship of the user, the application software, the operating system, and the computer hardware.

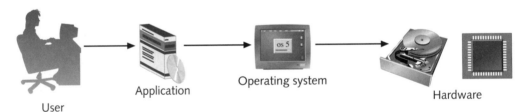

User   Application   Operating system   Hardware

Figure 1-1   Relationship between the user, applications, operating system, and hardware

Operating System Functions

Today you can choose from many operating systems. Although they vary in appearance and functionality, they do have many similarities. For instance, all applications rely on the operating system for basic services; the operating system in turn controls the computer hardware, doling out resources for applications as necessary. At its most basic, an operating system will usually do the following:

- Initialize (or prepare) the computer hardware so that the operating system and other programs can function correctly
- Allocate system resources, such as memory and processing time, to the programs that are using the operating system

- Keep track of multiple programs running at the same time
- Provide an organized method for all programs to use system devices (such as the hard disk, printer, and keyboard)

The effectiveness with which an operating system handles these basic tasks determines its power. These tasks are controlled by the core of an operating system, called the kernel. When we think of an operating system, however, we normally think of the kernel plus some additional components. These major parts of an operating system include:

- **Kernel**: the core of the operating system, which schedules when programs can use computer resources and interfaces directly with core components of the computer hardware, such as memory and hard disks
- **Device drivers**: special software that provides access to additional hardware, beyond core device support provided by the kernel
- **Utility programs**: special software that helps manage the hardware and operating system features (as opposed to doing other types of work such as word processing)
- **Graphical interface**: the program that provides mouse-driven applications with menu bars, buttons, and so forth

Commonly Used Operating Systems

Some of the better known operating systems that are or have been used around the world are described here. Many other operating systems besides those mentioned here are still in use. This section only summarizes a few key steps in the last 40 years of operating system development as they relate to the emergence of Linux.

The **UNIX** operating system was created at AT&T Bell Labs (now part of Lucent Technologies) about 30 years ago by Ken Thompson and Dennis Ritchie. It was designed to control networked computers being shared by many users. UNIX development has continued since it was first introduced, and the operating system is currently sold by dozens of large companies, such as IBM, Hewlett-Packard, and Sun Microsystems. The Internet was developed on UNIX and is still based around the UNIX operating system.

The Disk Operating System (**DOS**) was created in about 1980. Despite very limited functionality, it gained widespread acceptance when IBM introduced the first personal computer, the IBM PC, in August 1981. DOS was designed to make efficient use of very limited hardware resources for a single user on one computer.

Neither UNIX nor DOS included a graphical interface of any kind. The operating system provided only character-based screens, which required the user to type a series of commands. After a time, several graphical interfaces were developed for each operating system. These graphical interfaces provided additional core functionality that other programs could draw upon. The leading graphical interface for UNIX was called the **X Window System**. This system is still in use today and is also used for graphical displays on the Linux operating system. The leading graphical interface for DOS became **Microsoft Windows**.

In 1984 Apple Computer introduced the **Macintosh** system, which integrated the operating system and the graphical interface so that users remained essentially unaware of the operating system. Rather than having to type complicated text commands, users saw only the graphical interface. The Macintosh was designed to make new users feel comfortable. Although the popularity of the Macintosh never equaled that of Microsoft Windows (perhaps because Macintosh computers were much more expensive than IBM-compatible PCs), the idea of hiding the operating system from novice users took root. In August 1995 Microsoft introduced the Windows 95 operating system, which integrated a copy of DOS and a copy of Windows (both updated many times since earlier versions). In this new version of Windows, the user had no need to know about the operating system that provided the functionality for all the Windows programs running on the system.

While all this was happening in the world of personal computers, businesses continued to use UNIX systems and other specialized operating systems. These operating systems were much more powerful than DOS, Windows, or Macintosh systems, but they were also very expensive and only ran on costly computer hardware.

Microsoft continued development of its operating systems by creating a business-oriented product called **Windows NT**. Unlike the earlier version of Windows, Windows NT did not include DOS as an underlying operating system. Instead, Windows NT was built on the VMS operating system, a business-oriented operating system that had been used for years on expensive minicomputers. (A minicomputer, which is a multiuser computer midway between a personal computer and a mainframe, cost between about $20,000 and $100,000 in the early 1990s.) Windows NT developers sought to include UNIX features to capture the market of business users who wanted more power than a Macintosh or Windows 98 system provided.

The Arrival of Linux

Into this fray, Linux arrived as a relative newcomer with a strange background. In 1991 a college student in Helsinki, Finland, named **Linus Torvalds**, began to create an operating system kernel as a school project. He wanted to use a UNIX-like operating system (UNIX has always been popular on many college and university campuses), but he couldn't afford his own UNIX system. Instead he began to clone, or duplicate, the functionality of a UNIX kernel for his IBM-compatible PC. This in itself would not be different from the efforts of many other students working to create something useful to save a few dollars. But the efforts of Linus Torvalds blossomed into something much bigger because of the work of many people with goals similar to his. (For a photograph of Torvalds, see Figure 1-2.)

The next section describes how Torvalds and others working around the world were able to finish a complete clone of the UNIX operating system by about 1993, and why that operating system, dubbed Linux in honor of Linus, has had such a surprising impact in recent years.

Figure 1-2   Linus Torvalds, originator of the Linux kernel

THE SPIRIT OF LINUX

Several factors were working in favor of Linus Torvalds as he sought to create an operating system for his PC:

- Finland had (and has) excellent Internet access, especially on its college campuses. This gave Torvalds access to a worldwide network of people who could help him develop Linux.

- As a computer science student, Torvalds (and those who helped him) could draw on 40 years of shared experience with the UNIX operating system. All of the design and experimentation that had gone into creating UNIX could be implemented in the kernel that Torvalds created from scratch.

- Torvalds was working as an individual, with other individuals. Decisions about how to do things could be based on technical considerations rather than on market needs, a factor that often drives the actions of commercial software companies, sometimes to the detriment of those using the software.

- The most popular operating system at the time (that is, from 1991 to 1996) was Microsoft Windows. Many Windows users were becoming frustrated with some of its features and with its lack of stability. They were also frustrated by delays in Microsoft's promised upgrades to Windows.

- Torvalds decided to base the software license for the Linux kernel on a model used by Richard Stallman and the Free Software Foundation.

The last item in this list may surprise you. The fact that the license to a piece of software would be so important in its history is unusual and bears more explanation.

The Linux Software License

A **software license** is a legal definition of who can use the software and how it can be used. The programmer who develops a piece of software decides how the software will be licensed. Licenses for commercial software usually state that you can use one copy of the software (the one you paid for), that you may not copy the software, that the company is not responsible for how you use it, and so forth. The license for Linux is quite different, as you will learn in the following sections.

The Free Software Foundation and the GNU Project

In 1983 **Richard Stallman** at the Massachusetts Institute of Technology founded an organization called the **Free Software Foundation (FSF)**. Stallman's motivating idea was that software should be freely available, without restrictions on copying. He proposed that companies could make money by charging for services and customization, but that the software itself should not be restricted in its distribution by a standard commercial license agreement. To back up his opinions, Stallman and those working with the FSF created hundreds of utilities that run on the UNIX operating system and distributed them freely around the world. This effort was called the **GNU project**. The GNU project intended to create a completely free UNIX-like operating system. When almost the entire project was finished, Linus Torvalds appeared with the final, crucial piece: the kernel. The software created by the GNU project is still used by millions of people and is included with every Linux distribution.

One of the best known products of the GNU project is the C language compiler called **gcc**. This is a software program for converting C language programming instructions into code that a computer can execute. The gcc compiler is the most widely used, highly regarded compiler in the world.

The explanation given here for the work of the Free Software Foundation is necessarily simplistic. Much more information about both the philosophy of free software and the relationship between GNU and Linux is available at *www.fsf.org*.

The GNU General Public License (GPL)

The license that Richard Stallman designed for the programs created by the GNU project is called the **GNU General Public License**, often abbreviated as the GPL. Torvalds eventually released the Linux kernel under the GPL. The GPL allowed Linux to develop rapidly, but it is an unusual license in several ways. It includes the following points:

- A programmer who decides to license a piece of software under the GPL gives away the source code to the software. The **source code** is the set of human-readable programming instructions used to create the program. Normally, only the machine-readable **binary code** used to execute a program is distributed. Including the source code makes it possible for anyone to modify the original program.

- Anyone can distribute the software, charging money for it if he or she chooses. But distributors must also include the source code, and they cannot restrict the redistribution by anyone else.

- Anyone who makes modifications to the original program must freely give away those modifications, including the source code.

Almost from the beginning, the term *copyleft* was associated with the GPL. The legal process called *copyright* has always protected creative work by authors, artists, musicians, and others. A copyright lets the creator of a work control how that work is used, so that others cannot rob a creative person of his or her livelihood by using creative works without permission. Conversely, the GPL does not let an author (that is, a programmer) *control* a creative work; instead it lets the author maintain *credit* for a work, while letting everyone benefit without charge for what the author has done. The term **copyleft** is used ironically to describe this radical departure from the customary copyright arrangement. Legally, the author of a GPL program still maintains the program's copyright. By choosing to release software under the GPL, the author does not choose to give up the copyright; instead, he or she is simply stating who can use the software and how. The author's name always remains associated with the software that he or she created.

 TIP The name **OpenSource** is often used to refer to software licensed under the GPL. Although the FSF makes distinctions between the GPL and the term OpenSource, in practice they are used synonymously in the Linux industry.

The following list summarizes some results of the GPL for Linux in particular and the GNU project software in general:

- The code is very high quality (that is, it has few bugs, or problems, and it runs efficiently) because every programmer who wishes to can make improvements to the software. The process of refinement is more rigorous, with more people involved, than in almost any commercial software company. Developers who create software using the GPL must be open to accepting suggestions for improvements from other skilled programmers.

- A program can be developed very quickly because it can build upon similar software already in use. For example, if hardware driver software is needed for a new video card, the drivers for existing video cards can be used as a starting point. New or different features for the new video card are really just modifications to existing software. Adding to the speed of development is the fact that hundreds of interested developers from around the world might be working on a particular project.

- Because the GPL license does not permit companies or individuals to keep improvements to themselves, each developer's work benefits everyone else. Hence, qualified people are willing to spend time developing software for public use, because they know that other people are doing the same thing. Those who work on GPL software usually focus on something that is immediately useful in their own projects. They are willing to give their code away as a means of saying "thank you" for the work that others have given them.

 Developers who have created Linux include not only highly skilled young people, from high schools as well as universities, but also computer science professors, researchers, system administrators for large companies, and hundreds of others.

The GPL was not the first license to allow free redistribution of software. Nor was it the last. Other similar licenses are used for the Berkeley version of UNIX (called FreeBSD), the Apache Web server, the X Window System servers included with Linux, and many other programs. The real value of the GPL for Linux is that it requires source code to be included with each program. It also requires that enhancements be given away in the same manner (that is, the GPL applies to enhancements to a GPL program).

People are often confused about what is *not* licensed under the GPL. A program that becomes part of the Linux kernel must abide by the GPL, because Linux abides by the GPL. But a program that *runs* on Linux is not part of Linux itself. Thus, Linux applications do not need to be released under the GPL. IBM, Corel, and other companies have begun to sell Linux applications. They could not do this if all Linux applications were regulated by the GPL.

 Software called *system libraries* may be shared by both free programs and commercial programs operating in memory at the same time. The use of these libraries is covered by a version of the GPL called the Library GPL (or the **LGPL**) .

How Linux Is Developed

Linux kernel development follows the model of most GPL or OpenSource projects. To begin a project, a person identifies a need and then begins writing a program. At some point, the developer announces the work on the Internet. Developers who share an interest in that project respond, and soon they begin to work together on different parts of the project. This process works well and in fact is exactly how Linus Torvalds started to create the Linux kernel.

After a certain level of completion has been reached, the project's source code is released on the Internet. (Since the inception of Linux, the source code has been distributed via the Internet site *ftp://ftp.funet.fi*, based in Finland.) At this point, thousands of people download the source code and begin to try it out. Some of those people send back information about problems they have encountered (software bugs). The core team of developers tries to fix the bugs, occasionally working with other developers who have submitted bug fixes or specific enhancements to the software.

Linus Torvalds continues to work on the Linux kernel, along with a core group of developers who control what is included in Linux. Some commercial users of Linux have posed the unpleasant question of what will happen to Linux if something happens to Linus Torvalds. The answer is that another of the core developers on the Linux kernel team would simply take over. Each member of that team is a recognized expert in Linux. Torvalds leads them now, but he could conceivably retire from that position, leaving another qualified individual to continue the work.

Linux Distributions

The Linux kernel originally created by Linus Torvalds did not provide the functionality of a full-blown commercial operating system. To be really useful for the majority of organizations, Linux also requires:

- Networking utilities

- System administration utilities

- Documentation

- Installation tools

- Technical support information

- Hardware drivers

- A graphical environment (like the X Window System mentioned previously)

- Graphical tools

- Personal productivity applications such as word processors or spreadsheets

Given the way that Linux is developed (with developers all over the world creating and documenting its various parts), you might wonder how the many pieces of Linux could be combined into a complete operating system. Such a "productized" version of Linux, which includes many software components, installation tools, documentation, and so forth, is called a **Linux distribution**.

A Linux distribution has the Linux kernel at its core, along with hundreds or thousands of additional programs that run on Linux. Most of these are related to managing the Linux system—in other words, they are system utilities. These system utilities are drawn largely from the GNU project of the FSF. For this reason, many people refer to a Linux distribution as the GNU/Linux operating system. When taken as a whole, a Linux distribution makes it possible for nonprogrammers to install and use Linux.

Distributions in the Marketplace

Many new companies are attempting to meet the need for a Linux system that is ready to use. In accordance with the GPL, these companies include in their distributions the source code for the Linux kernel, as well as many other utilities. They can charge as much as they choose for their Linux distributions; because the software is freely available from other sources, the distributor essentially functions as a kind of packaging service that saves users the trouble of downloading a large number of files from the Internet. Thus distribution prices have generally been quite low—between $2 and $100. Because the Linux kernel and utilities offered by the many Linux vendors are practically identical, vendors often add commercial components or other software to make their distribution more attractive to consumers.

Table 1-1 lists several popular Linux distributions, along with the Web location where you can learn more about these products. Each company tends to focus on a specific type of customer. For example, Caldera seeks to provide a business-oriented product. TurboLinux is aimed at those requiring specialized Linux servers. SuSE is a distribution with an international background that attempts to include many software components.

Table 1-1   Popular Linux Distributions

Name	Comments	Web site
Red Hat Linux	The most widely used distribution in the world, from Red Hat Software.	www.redhat.com
OpenLinux	Produced by Caldera Systems. This distribution is aimed at business users.	www.calderasystems.com
Mandrake	Built on Red Hat Linux with additions.	www.linux-mandrake.com
Stampede	A distribution optimized for speed.	www.stampede.org
Debian	A noncommercial Linux distribution targeted specifically to free software enthusiasts. Debian does not have a company behind it. It is created and maintained by developers of free software.	www.debian.org
Slackware	One of the first Linux distributions; still maintained by its original creator, Patrick Volkerding. Distributed by Walnut Creek CDROM.	www.cdrom.com
SuSE	The leading German distribution. Now available in the United States.	www.SuSE.com

Distributions and the Future of Linux Development

Some Linux developers claim that commercial Linux distributions exploit the work of unpaid Linux developers solely for commercial profit. Most Linux developers, however, are glad to see their work widely distributed and enjoy the prestige that comes from having millions of people using their software. These developers also recognize that large organizations cannot afford to take the risk involved in using software that has been freely downloaded from the Internet—even if that software is reputedly of very high quality. Furthermore, Linux companies like Slackware, SuSE, and many others make using Linux a viable commercial option for large organizations; they contribute money and personnel toward developing and refining free software.

You should also keep in mind that, while individuals are free to download, install, and upgrade software at will, organizations with hundreds of networked computers have to take

1

a more systematic approach. Among other things, organizations require an entity through which they can acquire products with guarantees of upgrades, technical support contracts, and similar standard business services. Commercial Linux vendors fill this role.

The competition of the marketplace also pushes Linux vendors to make better, more powerful, and easier-to-use products. This benefits all Linux users. Because the technology is controlled solely by the developers, Linux vendors have less control over the prices of their products than do large vendors of proprietary software. Thus Linux users can be sure they are paying a fair price for a particular distribution. As a rule, prices remain low because the various distributions differ only slightly. If the price were to rise too high, users would choose to download the software for free; or else another company would create a new distribution at a lower price. (In the language of business schools, the barrier to entry as a new Linux vendor is fairly low—anyone can create his or her own Linux distribution using the free software on the Internet.)

Version Numbering

The version numbers of Linux can be confusing. First of all, keep in mind that each release of the Linux kernel is assigned a version number. At the same time, different version numbers are assigned to each component of a Linux distribution; these version numbers are assigned by the developer in charge of that component. The Linux distributions themselves also have version numbers, which are chosen arbitrarily or for marketing reasons, based on how often the distribution is revised and updated.

The version number of the Linux kernel includes three parts:

- A major version number, which changes very rarely. Currently Linux is in major version 2.

- A minor version number, which changes infrequently, perhaps every 10–18 months. Even-numbered minor versions are stable operating systems that are used for creating commercial Linux distributions. Odd-numbered minor versions are development versions of Linux that should not be used except by experienced Linux users because they may crash at any time. Development versions of Linux are used as interim releases while a new stable version of Linux (with additional features) is being created.

- A patch level, which changes very frequently for development versions of Linux, perhaps once per day or once per week. For stable versions of Linux, this number changes only a few times as problems are located and fixed to make the stable Linux kernel even more solid.

A version number for the Linux kernel might look like this: 2.2.10. This is a stable release of the kernel (as indicated by the second 2). It is also patch level 10, indicating that the 2.2 kernel has had several minor updates for stability or improvements in hardware support. Another Linux kernel version might look like this: 2.3.67. In this case the second number is odd, indicating that it is a development release of the kernel, which should not be used in a business environment. The 67 indicates that 67 versions of this release have occurred, each with fixes or enhancements added by the kernel developers. After a certain number of enhancements have been added and made stable, the kernel developers will decide to release a kernel version 2.4.0. The process then begins again as they work on adding new features with the 2.5 series of kernels.

 Don't run the development kernels on your servers unless you want to experiment with new features that might crash your system. Commercial Linux distributions always use stable Linux kernel releases.

Linux distributions created by companies such as Red Hat Software and Caldera Systems are composed of hundreds of programs. The version of the Linux kernel included with a product is important, but a separate version number for each component could also be mentioned, for example, the version number of the Apache Web server or the version of the gcc compiler. To avoid the need to specify which version of each component is included in a distribution, vendors of commercial Linux distributions assign a version number to the distribution as a whole. For example, Red Hat Linux 6.1 contains a 2.2.12 Linux kernel. The 6.1 designation for the distribution corresponds to the vendor's own numbering system, and has no real relation to the kernel number. The Linux distribution released by Caldera Systems about the same time was numbered 2.3, though it had almost the same set of software.

Don't worry much about the version number when comparing distributions. Instead, look at the versions for the individual components that matter most to you, including the Linux kernel, the graphical system, and specific services you need to use. You can get information about all these specific version numbers from the vendor that created a Linux distribution.

The Motivation of Free Software Developers

As Linux is discussed in business and computer publications, those unfamiliar with the software development model used by Linux and other free software ask the same question: "Why would so many people devote so much effort to something without expecting any reward? It just doesn't make sense."

Of course, the business world that asks these questions is driven by money, and when considering money alone, free software development does not make much sense. Linux developers, however, are driven by other motivations. After reading the first half of this chapter, you can probably compile a list of these motivations yourself. The following summarizes the forces that motivate many developers of Linux and other free software:

- Creating a piece of software often fills a developer's specific technical need. By creating the product as free software, the developer can effectively thank others for the free software that has already proven useful in his or her work.

- Within the free software community of developers, those who create the highest quality, most original work are regarded very highly by their peers. The respect of like-minded professionals whom you respect in turn is a powerful motivating factor. In addition, if you create a unique, powerful product, many people will use it, see your work, and thank you for it.

- The Linux community and other similar communities revolving around products like the Apache Web server are very popular in the news, with an increasing visibility and acceptance by major organizations. Participating in free software development gives a sense of contribution and community to developers, many of whom are not highly social, but nevertheless like the opportunity to be a part of something worthwhile. As the market strength of Linux continues to grow, participation in a well-known free software project is also a tremendous boost to a resume.

After reviewing this list, you might be thinking, "That's fine for some people, but I still need to earn a living." In that case, you'll be happy to learn that Linux can set you on the path toward a fulfilling and profitable career. Here is a list of occupations open to those with a strong understanding of Linux and its related technologies:

- Software engineer: many companies are using Linux as a development platform or Internet server and need qualified programmers to create software to run on Linux. The information in this book provides a good first step towards becoming a Linux developer.

- System administrator: each of the thousands of companies that uses Linux needs at least one qualified system administrator to keep the Linux server running smoothly, day after day. This book is designed to prepare you to be a Linux system administrator.

- Trainer: as more companies begin using Linux, they require training for both technical and nontechnical specialists who will be using Linux to complete their work. Trainers work in all types of companies, teaching people how to use Linux.

- Writer: if you are a good writer, you can share your knowledge about Linux with others. You might consider a career as a technical writer for a company, as a writer for a business-oriented computer publication, or some combination of these two. Keep in mind that new periodicals, books, and columns about Linux are appearing every month.

Even if you are not seeking a job in a field directly related to Linux, you should know that many companies now recognize Linux expertise as a sign of generally strong computer knowledge. Such companies list knowledge of Linux as a qualifying skill for many types of jobs, including training, marketing, sales, and technical management.

The following lists some Web sites that you can visit to research jobs related to Linux. To learn about Linux-related jobs, just search on the keyword *Linux* at any of these Web sites, or refine your search criteria further based on your specific interests. Each of these sites will give you a sense of the promising future that awaits students of Linux.

- *www.dice.com*

- *careers.wsj.com*

- *www.headhunter.net*

- *www.careermosaic.com*

THE STRENGTHS OF LINUX

In the previous sections you learned about the background of Linux and the license under which it is distributed. These are certainly contributing factors to the ongoing popularity of Linux. But the reason millions of people and many large organizations use Linux is not because it is free. They use Linux because it is a high-quality operating system. The next sections describe some features of Linux that make it so popular.

Stability

Linux has proven its stability in many organizations. Many businesses have run a Linux server continuously for more than a year at a time without any problems and without the need to reboot (restart) the system. This stability is in part due to the fact that Linux can end a program without affecting other programs or the operating system as a whole. Another reason for its stability is that the core functionality of Linux, such as how system memory is used, how the hard disk is accessed, and how programs share system resources, has been thoroughly tested by the thousands of people involved in each version of Linux.

Security

The same development process that yielded a highly stable operating system also yielded a very secure operating system. You might be tempted to conclude that an operating system with freely available source code could not possibly be secure. On the contrary, the fact that the source code is available to all, and released in a controlled manner by well-known, respected professionals, means that all interested developers can help identify and fix security problems.

Proponents of other operating systems may point to the fact that many security holes have been identified on Linux systems. In truth, these security problems almost always relate to programs running on Linux, such as the `sendmail` e-mail server program. And in any case, when users do discover security problems, Linux developers will create a software update to fix the problem within about 24 hours. These updates are posted on the Internet so that all Linux users can download them. In contrast, developers of other operating systems seek to create secure systems by hiding the security problems that have been identified. They do not generally provide open information and rapid software updates to fix potential problems.

 To learn more about security on computer systems, visit the Computer Emergency Response Team site at *www.cert.org*.

Speed

Linux was designed to use limited hardware resources efficiently. As a result, Linux makes better use of hardware resources than almost any other operating system. As recently as 1996, a complete Linux operating system could be run on a system with only 4 MB of system memory. The efficiency of Linux when operating with such limited resources translates into speed when more extensive resources are available. Given a certain piece of computer hardware (such as a Pentium computer running at 400 MHz with 64 MB of RAM), you will see better performance from Linux than from any other general-purpose operating system.

A Multitasking, Multiuser, Multiprocessing System

Linux is a true multitasking operating system, which means that it can run many programs at the same time. (A typical Linux system will have 20 to 50 programs running at the same time.) Although many operating systems can run multiple programs simultaneously, Linux does this very efficiently. What's more, a program can crash in Linux without affecting the other programs running on the system. This helps to create a stable system.

Linux manages multiple programs through a technology called **preemptive multitasking**, in which the Linux kernel controls which program runs at any given moment. Once a program has had a small time to work, the kernel intervenes and gives control to another program for a time. By contrast, some operating systems use **cooperative multitasking**, in which the kernel is forced to wait for a program to yield control. Cooperative multitasking can be problematic because it is possible for a poorly written program to crash before the kernel can regain control of the system, thus disabling all other programs running on the system.

Linux was also designed from the beginning as a **multiuser system**, which means that multiple users can log in to the same Linux system over a network connection and run programs, use the Internet, or complete other work. The programs run by one user do not affect the work of other users. A superuser, or administrative account, can configure and control all user accounts.

 TIP As a security feature, users must log in to a Linux system (using a valid username and password) before attempting to do any work.

Linux also supports multiple CPUs on the same computer, thanks to a technology called **symmetrical multiprocessing**. Systems with multiple processors perform faster than single-CPU systems because the processors can combine forces to work on one task at the same time. Linux (and some other operating systems) divide the components of a task between multiple processors via a technique called **multithreading**, in which a program is divided into parts, known as threads; the various threads of one program are then run simultaneously on multiple processors. Multithreading is found only in more advanced operating systems such as Linux, Windows NT, and UNIX. On commercial operating systems, using multiple processors adds significantly to the cost of the operating system. In contrast, all versions of

Linux provide multiprocessing capability. Figure 1–3 illustrates the concept of a multiuser, multitasking, multiprocessing operating system.

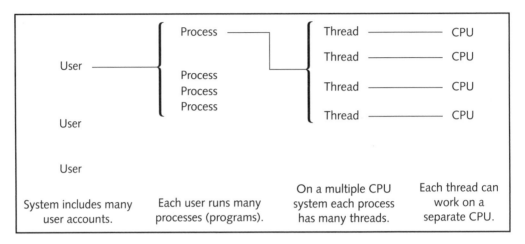

Figure 1-3   A multiuser, multitasking, multiprocessing operating system

Flexibility

Linux distributions are extremely flexible because they always include the source code to the operating system, allowing technically oriented system administrators and software developers to modify a system any way they want. More in-depth modifications may require outside help, but Linux developers are easily consulted via the Internet, and they are generally more than willing to help.

By comparison, operating systems that do not include source code offer little in the way of flexibility. With these systems, administrators are limited to asking the operating system manufacturer for an update that meets a specific need. And even then, the answer to such a request is usually, "Sorry, we can't do that."

Although you are free to modify a Linux system as much as you want, you certainly don't have to make changes to keep your system running smoothly. Linux is flexible enough to allow you to use old, stable technology that fulfills the job at hand, or to experiment with the latest advances and features. One Canadian retail organization that chose the first approach has been running a copy of the Linux kernel version 1.2.35 for years without a hitch and has no plans to upgrade to a new system.

Contributing to the flexibility of Linux is the fact that with only a few modifications, you can often run newer Linux applications on older versions of the kernel. With other operating systems, you would probably have to completely install a new version of the operating system before you could use the latest programs.

Some organizations might opt for a more restrictive, commercial operating system because they are intimidated by the flexibility of Linux and all the options it provides. But in fact, commercial Linux vendors such as SuSE and Red Hat Software provide the technical support commonly associated with commercial operating systems; thus, management teams can be confident that a Linux expert is only a phone call away. (Technically oriented individuals might prefer the Internet resources described later in this chapter.)

Applications

Years ago, Linux was used almost exclusively for developing UNIX software or for specialized Internet servers. Back then, critics of Linux might argue, "What good is an operating system that doesn't run the applications I need?"

Today that concern is unfounded. Although Linux still finds its greatest concentration of supporters among those running Internet servers and developing software, the number of applications available for Linux continues to grow rapidly and already includes the most prominent names in the software industry. Table 1-2 lists some of the programs currently available for Linux, as well as Web addresses where you can find more information.

Table 1-2   Common Linux Applications

Application	Description	Web site
WordPerfect for Linux	Complete, powerful word processor; from Corel	*linux.corel.com*
ApplixWare	Complete office suite	*www.applix.com*
StarOffice	Office suite and integrated Internet tools; attempts to imitate Microsoft Office	*www.sun.com/staroffice*
DB2	Powerful database package; from IBM	*www.ibm.com*
Oracle	The most widely used client/server database	*www.oracle.com*
Sybase	A popular client/server database package	*www.sybase.com*
Informix	A popular client/server database package	*www.informix.com*
UniCenter TNG	A graphical management console for very large networks; from Computer Associates	*www.cai.com*

LEARNING MORE ABOUT LINUX

This book contains an organized introduction to all the important topics you need to understand in order to use Linux effectively. You can explore additional Linux topics through a number of different venues, as described in the remainder of this chapter.

Reading Linux Documentation

Because the developers of Linux were working entirely via the Internet, they were forced to share descriptions of their software via electronic or online documentation. This documentation was typically incorporated into the various distributions. These days most Linux distributions include thousands of pages of online documentation. As you will see, this documentation can be quickly accessed using a few simple commands.

When you read Linux documentation, remember that much of it was written by developers, for developers. That is, these documents generally assume a high level of technical understanding. They contain a lot of useful details, but may be hard for a beginner to understand. As you begin investigating the world of Linux documentation, don't expect to understand everything all at once. Once you become more experienced with Linux, you'll find the documentation more useful.

The Linux Documentation Project

The **Linux Documentation Project (LDP)** was begun by Matt Welsh in the early 1990s, when Linux was just becoming well-known. The LDP was one of the first efforts to document how Linux works and continues to provide Linux documentation today in a variety of formats. The LDP currently contains about 6000 pages of documentation, all of which is available free of charge under a version of the GPL modified for use with documentation. The LDP consists of several types of documents. Some of these, such as the *Network Administrator's Guide* and the *kernel Hacker's Guide*, are complete online reference manuals.

Initially you will probably find the LDP's HOWTO documents most useful. The **HOWTOs** cover specific topics, such as sharing a system between Windows NT and Linux, or maintaining network security. (Figure 1-4 shows a sample HOWTO document.) Each document is written by one person, or a small group, with expertise in that topic. Documents called mini-HOWTOs focus on narrower subjects than do regular HOWTOs. HOWTO documents are usually written by software developers, but they are intended for all users, not just other developers.

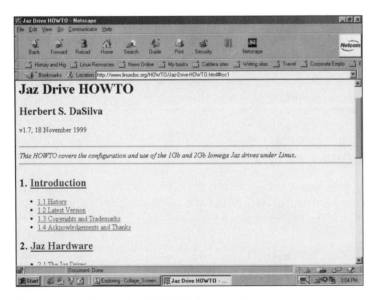

Figure 1-4   A sample HOWTO document

The LDP and all of the HOWTO documents are included with all Linux distributions. You can also read them on many Web sites. A good place to begin researching the documentation available as part of the LDP is *www.linuxhq.com/info.html*. The LDP is also available at *www.linuxdoc.org*. Table 1-3 lists some sample HOWTO documents.

Table 1-3 Sample Linux HOWTO Documents

Title	Description
CD Writing HOWTO	Using Linux with a writeable CD-ROM drive
Chinese HOWTO	Making Linux work effectively with Chinese characters
DOSEMU HOWTO	Using the DOS emulator in Linux to run DOS programs
Kernel HOWTO	Upgrading and modifying the Linux kernel
Laptop HOWTO	Installing and using Linux on a laptop computer
MP3 HOWTO	Downloading, playing, and creating MPEG3 audio files on Linux
Security HOWTO	Creating a more secure Linux system
Large Disk (mini-HOWTO)	Making optimal use of very large hard disks within Linux
ZIP Install (mini-HOWTO)	Installing an Iomega ZIP drive to be used in Linux

Linux Command Information

As you will learn in future chapters, Linux includes many different commands, each with numerous options. Few people memorize all of the commands and options, because they employ only a small percentage of them regularly. When you do need to use a new command, you can learn about it through the Linux command information available online. This information is provided in two formats. You can access online manual pages (called **man pages**) for most Linux commands by using the **man** command. For some Linux commands, the definitive source of information is an info page, which you can view using the **info** command. These commands will be described in detail in later chapters.

Documentation Included with Software Packages

Most of the software packages included with a Linux distribution provide at least some documentation. This documentation is installed on your system along with the software and you can usually view it in either a text editor or a Web browser. You will learn more about reviewing product or package documentation in future chapters.

Linux on the Internet

Linux was created on the Internet, and the Internet is still a great place to find out more about Linux. Every day on the Internet, developers release new software, companies make announcements about Linux products, and software documenters provide new or revised information. Table 1-4 lists some Web sites that you will find useful as you explore the world of Linux.

Table 1-4   Linux-Related Web Sites

Web site	Description
www.linuxjournal.com	A high-quality companion Web site to the monthly printed magazine; contains additional Linux links and information (mostly technically oriented)
www.linuxworld.com	A business-oriented online magazine with interviews, links, technical reports, and other up-to-date information
www.slashdot.org	An eclectic collection of news items related to free software and other topics (such as Star Wars, new music technologies, cryptography legislation, etc.) of interest to free software developers
www.linuxhq.com	A collection of information about work on the Linux kernel, with useful links to many other sites and Linux resources
www.linuxapps.com	Links to information about applications that run on Linux
www.lwn.net	Linux Weekly News, a collection of news items related to Linux and other free software

The Web sites for each of the Linux distributions (listed in Table 1-1) are also great resources for learning about Linux. You will learn about additional Web sites in later chapters.

CHAPTER SUMMARY

❐ An operating system provides an interface between the computer hardware and the applications run by the user. In its most basic form, an operating system manages the use of memory, CPU time, and other system resources. A complete operating system includes many other features that provide additional hardware support, such as a graphical environment and driver software.

❐ The Linux kernel was created by many talented individuals from around the world working under the leadership of Linus Torvalds, who continues to maintain the Linux kernel. The Free Software Foundation, led by Richard Stallman, created hundreds of software programs as part of its GNU project. These are included with the Linux kernel in each copy of a complete Linux operating system. The General Public License is responsible in large part for the phenomenal growth of Linux in the last few years.

❐ Various companies have created commercial products, called distributions, that are built around the Linux kernel and GNU software. Businesses are beginning to value knowledge of Linux highly as more people recognize the features that Linux offers, such as stability, speed, flexibility, and low cost.

❐ Information about Linux is available online as part of the Linux Documentation Project, which includes many HOWTO documents on specific topics. Online documentation for Linux commands is included with every copy of Linux. Many publications and Web sites maintain daily news updates about what is happening in the world of Linux and free software.

KEY TERMS

application — A program (such as a word processor or spreadsheet) that provides a service to a person using the computer, rather than simply managing the computer's resources.

binary code — Machine-readable instructions used to execute a program.

cooperative multitasking — A technique in which an operating system kernel must wait for a program to yield control to other programs.

copyleft — An ironic term that refers to the GNU General Public License (the GPL), signifying a radical departure from standard copyright.

device drivers — Software that provides access to additional hardware, beyond core device support provided by the kernel.

DOS — An operating system developed for personal computers in about 1980. It gained widespread acceptance when IBM introduced the first IBM PC.

Free Software Foundation (FSF) — An organization founded by Richard Stallman to promote his ideals of freely available software and to create and distribute that software.

gcc — A C language compiler. Probably the best known product of the GNU project.

GNU General Public License (GPL) — The free software license that Richard Stallman of the Free Software Foundation developed for the programs created by the GNU project.

GNU project — An effort by the Free Software Foundation to create a free UNIX-like operating system. Much of a Linux distribution comes from the GNU project.

graphical interface — Software that provides mouse-driven applications with menu bars, buttons, and so forth.

hard wired — Computer functionality that is arranged in the wires and other components that make up a computer. Hard-wired functionality cannot be easily altered.

HOWTOs — Documents within the Linux Documentation Project that cover specific topics.

kernel — The core of the operating system, which interacts directly with the computer hardware.

LGPL — A special version of the GNU General Public License intended to govern both free and commercial software use of software libraries.

Linux distribution — A Linux operating system product that includes the Linux kernel plus many software components, installation tools, documentation, and so forth.

Linux Documentation Project (LDP) — One of the first efforts to document how Linux is used. Started by Matt Welsh.

Macintosh — A computer developed by Apple Computer that integrated the operating system and the graphical interface.

man pages — Online manual pages for Linux commands. The man pages are accessed using the man command.

Microsoft Windows — The leading graphical interface for DOS.

multithreading — A technique used within multiprocessing operating systems to divide a larger task between multiple processors.

multiuser system — An operating system on which numerous users can log in to the same computer (usually over a network connection).

OpenSource — A trademarked name often used to refer to software licensed under the GPL.

operating system — Software that provides a set of core functionality for other programs to use in working with the computer hardware and interfacing with the user running the computer.

preemptive multitasking — A technique used by the Linux kernel to control which program is running from moment to moment.

software — Instructions that control the physical computer components, but which can be changed because they reside on a changeable media such as a hard disk.

software license — A legal definition of who can use a piece of software and how it can be used.

source code — A set of human-readable programming instructions used to create a piece of software.

Stallman, Richard — Founder of the Free Software Foundation and the GNU project.

symmetrical multiprocessing — A technique that allows an operating system to support multiple CPUs on the same computer.

Torvalds, Linus — Originator of the Linux kernel; formerly a student in Helsinki, Finland.

UNIX — An operating system created at AT&T Bell Labs (now part of Lucent Technologies) about 30 years ago by Ken Thompson and Dennis Ritchie. UNIX is still widely used, and it provided the technical basis for Linux.

utility programs — Software that provides assistance in managing the hardware and operating system features (as opposed to doing other types of work such as word processing).

Windows NT — A business-oriented operating system product developed by Microsoft. Windows NT is not based on DOS as an underlying operating system.

X Window System — A graphical software environment used by almost all UNIX and Linux operating systems.

REVIEW QUESTIONS

1. Explain the difference between a computer that is solely hard wired and one that uses an operating system.

2. An operating system does *not* do which of the following:

   a. Allocate system resources such as memory and CPU time

   b. Initialize computer hardware so it can be used by software running on the computer

   c. Keep track of multiple programs running at the same time

   d. Provide word processing features for users

3. The kernel of an operating system includes a graphical interface. True or False?

4. Which of the following operating systems included a graphical interface when first released?

   a. UNIX

   b. Macintosh

   c. Linux

   d. DOS

5. Linus Torvalds began to create Linux because:

   a. he was hired as an operating system consultant by a major corporation.

   b. he wanted a powerful operating system but could not afford one.

   c. his professor required that each student create a basic operating system.

   d. he felt it would be a good career move.

6. The Free Software Foundation is dedicated to the idea that:

   a. no company should be able to charge for any software.

   b. the real value of software was in customization, not in selling mass-produced copies.

   c. Richard Stallman's C compiler was the best in the world.

   d. Linux was an important development in operating systems.

7. The GNU project is important to Linux because:

   a. it provides the majority of the system utilities used by Linux.

   b. GNU software is the only software compatible with Linux.

   c. the media attention generated by the GNU project has made Linux popular.

   d. Richard Stallman is a strong supporter of the Linux movement.

8. The GPL includes all of the following *except*:

   a. GPL software must include source code.

   b. modifications to GPL software must be given away.

   c. software that runs on a GPL operating system must be given away.

   d. a company can charge money for GPL software.

9. Explain why the term "copyleft" came to be used as an ironic comparison to "copyright."

10. In general usage, the name OpenSource software is synonymous with software released under the GPL. True or False?

11. The fact that the use of Linux is governed by GPL means that:

   a. Linux is of high quality because everyone can review and improve the code.

   b. Linux is low cost because Linus Torvalds does not allow any commercial interference.

    c. Linux is low cost because most nations enforce the GPL commercial restrictions.

    d. Linux development advances quickly because people around the world participate in its growth.

12. Why might Linux provide better security than operating systems that do not provide source code to users?

13. Name five things that a Linux distribution vendor might add to the Linux kernel when creating a product to sell.

14. Market dynamics (competition) keep the price of Linux low because it can be freely downloaded. True or False?

15. In the Linux kernel version 2.4.10, the second digit, 4, indicates:

    a. a major kernel release number

    b. a minor kernel release number for a stable kernel

    c. a minor kernel release number for a development kernel

    d. a patch release number

16. Version numbers for Linux distributions generally match that of the Linux kernel itself. True or False?

17. Which of the following is not a likely motivating factor for those who develop free software?

    a. Greed

    b. Altruism or thanks

    c. Peer acceptance

    d. Desire for interesting work

18. Name five Linux distributions and comment on any specific purposes or background for each one.

19. Which of the following statements is *not* true?

    a. More businesses are using Linux and related products to run their businesses.

    b. Writing free software teaches marketable programming skills.

    c. Thousands of servers running Linux require competent system administrators.

    d. Linux is not based on any other operating system.

20. Linux systems have been known to run for months or years without crashing. True or False?

21. Compare preemptive multitasking to cooperative multitasking and multithreading.

22. Name five major applications that are available for Linux.

23. The use of a document produced as part of the Linux Documentation Project is governed by standard copyright notice. True or False?

24. The _____ and _____ commands provide information about Linux commands.

    a. HOWTO and mini-HOWTO

    b. man and info

    c. http and ftp

    d. GPL and LGPL

25. HOWTO documents discuss a variety of specific subjects but are only intended for very advanced users. True or False?

HANDS-ON PROJECTS

Project 1-1

In this project, you review several sources of documentation for Linux. You may want to save the results of this project for future use. To complete this project, you should have a computer with access to the Internet and a functioning Web browser.

1. Open your Web browser and connect to the Internet.

2. Go to the homepage of the Linux Documentation Project, at *www.linuxdoc.org*.

3. Click on the **LDP Mirrors** link to see a list of sites that also contain a copy of the LDP. Find the site that is physically closest to you. (If you have a reason to believe that you would have faster access to a different site, choose it instead.)

4. Note how frequently the mirror site is updated, and then click on your chosen mirror site link.

5. Save the information on your mirror site for future access. For example, choose the **Bookmark** option in your Web browser to record the Web address of the mirror site.

6. Review the home page of the LDP mirror site until you find the HOWTO link.

7. Explore the HOWTO documents. What different formats are available?

Project 1-2

In this project, you look at some of the different Linux HOWTOs. To complete this project, you should have a computer with access to the Internet and a functional Web browser.

1. Open your Web browser and connect to the Internet.

2. Go to the mirror site for the Linux Documentation Project that you selected in Project 1-1.

3. Browse the titles of the HOWTO documents.

4. Open up a HOWTO document that interests you. Review the table of contents.

5. Read one section of the HOWTO and summarize its main points.

Project 1-3

In this project, you review the Web sites for several Linux distributions. To complete this project, you should have a computer with access to the Internet and a functional Web browser.

1. Open your Web browser and connect to the Internet.

2. Visit the following Web sites: *www.debian.org*, *www.calderasystems.com*, *www.suse.com*, *www.redhat.com*.

3. For each Web site, answer the following questions:

   a. Can you determine the focus of the Linux distribution? To whom is the company trying to sell products?

   b. What key features of its distribution does each group highlight?

   c. What supporting documents (such as magazine articles) can you find on the Web site?

   d. Which Web site and distribution appeal most to you and why?

4. Locate information about signing up for an e-mail list on each Web site. What is the purpose of these mailing lists?

CASE PROJECTS

1. You work at ColTech Limited as a system administrator. Your boss is planning to purchase a new Web server, for which she is considering several platforms, including an IBM UNIX system, Windows NT, and Linux. You prefer Linux, but your manager hesitates because of concerns about the way Linux is developed. She asks you to explain why Linux is more stable and secure than other systems, and how the company can run the new Web server on free software. Write a brief report summarizing your thoughts on the matter. What useful information might you find on the vendor Web sites in Project 1-3? What concerns might remain unresolved?

2. Your manager has started to use Linux as the new Web server, and things are going well. You need to create a new piece of software to add a feature to your Web server. You are considering making it available to others under the GPL. What justification would you give your employer (who is paying you to write the software) that it should be given away to others under the GPL? What concerns might your employer have about doing that? Under what circumstances do you feel that a piece of software should not use the GPL?

3. Do you anticipate problems in the future as Linux becomes more commercial and popular? How might this affect the attitude of free software developers? How would you feel about the increasing popularity of Linux if you were participating in Linux development? What could commercial Linux vendors do to help alleviate potential problems?

CHAPTER

2

PLANNING YOUR SYSTEM

After reading this chapter and completing the exercises, you will be able to:

♦ Discuss hardware issues related to installing Linux

♦ Collect hardware and related information from several sources

♦ Prepare space for Linux on a system running Windows

I n the previous chapter you learned about the development of Linux, beginning with Linus Torvalds' school project and continuing with contributions from developers around the world. You learned about the license under which Linux is distributed and how that license affects the way people build businesses and careers on Linux.

In this chapter you learn about how Linux uses the hardware resources in your computer system. This information will help you plan your installation of Linux, so that you can make the right choices for your system.

PREPARING TO INSTALL LINUX

Most of the computer systems that you have used or purchased yourself probably had an operating system installed. As a result, you didn't have to think about how the operating system was installed on the computer's hard disk or how the operating system was configured to use other parts of the computer, such as the mouse, the video display capabilities, and so forth.

Although you can purchase computers with Linux preinstalled from companies like VA Linux Systems (*www.valinux.com*), you will learn a great deal about your computer system and about how Linux operates by installing the operating system yourself. Before you begin the installation of Linux in Chapter 3, you must decide a few things about how you want to install Linux. You must also compile information about your computer hardware so that you can answer questions that arise during the installation process.

As a general rule, Linux is not more difficult to install than other operating systems such as Windows. The difference is that you rarely install Windows—it comes preinstalled on most systems that you buy. But if you ever have to install Windows from scratch, you may find that it can be more difficult to install than Linux.

Understanding Computer Hardware

The design of the Linux operating system is based on the concept of the computer as a collection of devices. Information is stored on a hard disk device, output is written to a video card device, input is read from a keyboard device, and so forth. Linux must be configured to use all of the devices on the computer system in order to function correctly. Unfortunately, this is not always an easy task, as you will learn in the later sections of this chapter.

 Linux can be used on many types of computers, including those that use different types of microprocessors (CPUs), such as Alpha, SPARC, and PowerPC. The discussion in this chapter is devoted solely to computers using Intel and Intel-compatible microprocessors—in other words, standard PCs.

Different types of devices on a computer communicate with the operating system in different ways. This means that you must gather an array of information about your computer system before you can install Linux on that system. The section "Creating a System Inventory," later in this chapter, explains how to locate the information you need.

As you work with computer hardware, you should be familiar with a few common terms that describe that hardware. Space or capacity on a computer system is measured in bytes. A **byte** is enough space to store one character. Because computers store many characters, space is commonly measured in megabytes, abbreviated MB. One **megabyte** is 1,048,576 bytes, or enough space to store roughly 1 million characters. Another common term is gigabyte, abbreviated as GB. One **gigabyte** is 1024 MB, or roughly enough space to store 1 billion characters.

Storing Information

The electronic memory of a computer is called **random access memory**, or RAM. Information in RAM is only available when the computer is turned on. When you turn the computer off, everything stored in RAM is lost. RAM is normally measured in MB, with most computers having from 16 MB to 128 MB of RAM.

Another electronic component in a computer, called **read-only memory**, or ROM, stores information about how the computer starts and how the computer's devices are configured. Like RAM, ROM is stored on a computer chip, but information in ROM is not lost when the computer is turned off; it is permanent, or nonvolatile. One of the key things stored in ROM is the Basic Input/Output System, or **BIOS**, which provides instructions to the operating system for using the devices on the computer. The BIOS itself cannot be changed—it is permanent. But the ROM that contains the BIOS also contains parameters that control parts of the computer configuration. You can change these settings using a special BIOS utility.

2

Information in the BIOS might include the setting for the computer's clock, information about each disk drive, the settings used by the modem, a start-up password, and many other details.

You can usually access a menu to view and reconfigure settings related to the BIOS by pressing a key while the computer is starting. To find out which key, watch the screen during start-up for a message similar to "Press Del for Setup." You then have a few seconds during the system start-up to press the specified key, at which point the computer will display the BIOS configuration menus rather than starting the operating system. You will see example BIOS configuration menus later in this chapter.

The **hard disk** is a magnetic storage space for data, such as the operating system and data files that you create. You can think of magnetic storage as being like the stripe on the back of a credit card, except that a hard disk in a typical new computer holds from 3 billion to 10 billion characters (3 GB to 10 GB of data). Hard disk storage is not permanent—you can make changes to information on the hard disk—but it is also not volatile, meaning that storage on the hard disk remains intact when the computer is turned off. When you turn on your computer, the BIOS loads information from the hard disk into RAM for regular operations. When the computer is switched off, the information in RAM is discarded, but the data on the hard disk remains, ready to be reloaded the next time the computer is turned on. Table 2-1 highlights the differences between RAM, ROM (where the BIOS is stored), and the hard disk.

Table 2-1   Computer Storage Components

Component	Permanent (cannot be changed by a computer user)	Volatile (disappears when the power is turned off)
RAM	No	Yes
ROM	Yes	No
Hard disk space	No	No

A computer can have multiple hard disks. Each one is considered a separate device. In an operating system like Windows, two disk drives would be called C: and D:. The naming scheme is different in Linux, as you will see in Chapter 3.

TIP   When you see a reference to Windows in this chapter, the reference applies to Windows 95, Windows 98, Windows 2000, and Windows NT, unless otherwise noted.

Device Communications

Many computer devices communicate with the microprocessor and software programs via interrupt requests. An **interrupt request**, or IRQ, is a numbered channel of communication through which a device can ask the operating system to perform a specific action. A PC has a limited number of IRQs, ranging from 0 to 15. To configure some devices, such as Ethernet networking cards, you may have to know the IRQ that the device uses by default, or you may have to change the IRQ that it uses. Later in this chapter you will learn how to determine the IRQ used by a device.

Once a device sends an IRQ signal to the microprocessor, the device and the CPU can communicate data and status information between them. This is done using two methods: direct memory access and memory-mapped input/output.

A **direct memory access (DMA) channel** allows a device to read and write directly to the computer's RAM, without going through the microprocessor first. DMA allows a device such as a sound card to read and write information to memory much more quickly than if the microprocessor were involved in each data transaction.

Not all devices use DMA, however. Most use **memory-mapped input/output** (memory-mapped I/O)—a technique that assigns a range of memory addresses in the computer as a place for a device to send and receive data. Essentially, this kind of memory works like a post office box. The device places data in a specific memory location; then software programs retrieve the data from that memory location and place new data there. The device then retrieves the data placed by the software. For a device to use memory-mapped I/O, it must have a memory address assigned to it. Most devices can use several different addresses, so you can configure your computer to avoid a conflict between two devices that try to use the same address. The memory addresses used by a device for memory-mapped I/O are referred to as the **I/O ports** for the device. Some devices, such as sound cards, require both a DMA channel and an I/O port, but this is unusual.

To refer to an I/O port you use a computer memory address. These addresses use a different numbering system because of the way bytes store information. You may have heard of binary numbers, in which everything is represented by zeros and ones. Another commonly used system is called hexadecimal. **Hexadecimal** numbering is a base-16 counting system. It uses the letters *A* through *F* (usually capitalized) to count the numbers 10 through 15. Using hexadecimal (often called hex) numbers is strange at first. The important point is that when you encounter strange numbers that contain letters, be assured that they are simply hexadecimal numbers. Be certain to write them down and enter them in Linux using the format that you see them in, including all the letters.

Hexadecimal numbers are often written with a prefix of 0x to identify them as base-16 numbers. For example, you might see the number 0x220 used as an I/O port address. The 0x indicates that this is a hexadecimal number. You don't need to convert it to normal (decimal, or base-10) numbers. Just use it in Linux as it's written.

TIP   The range of IRQ numbers from 0 to 15 can all be represented by a single hexadecimal digit. The possible IRQ numbers in hex are 0, 1, 2, 3, 4, 5, 6, 7, 8, 9, A, B, C, D, E, F.

Hard Disk Devices

The hard disk in a computer must communicate with the microprocessor using an electronic interface that controls how data is sent and received. Two interfaces are used for hard disks in PCs: IDE (integrated drive electronics) and SCSI (small computer systems interface).

IDE is a low-cost, easy-to-manage interface used by most new computers to connect hard disks and CD-ROMs to the CPU. Standard new PCs always include one IDE hard disk. An **IDE controller** card is a device that handles communication between the hard disk and the microprocessor. (Sometimes the IDE controller is integrated into the system board rather than being a separate expansion card.) To use an IDE controller card to connect to the CPU, the hard disk must be compatible with the IDE interface. You will hear such hard disks referred to as IDE hard disks. Each IDE controller can be connected to two hard disks. Many computers come with two IDE controllers. The second IDE controller is used to communicate with a CD-ROM drive. Figure 2-1 shows how two IDE controllers, each with a separate cable, can be connected to hard disk and CD-ROM devices.

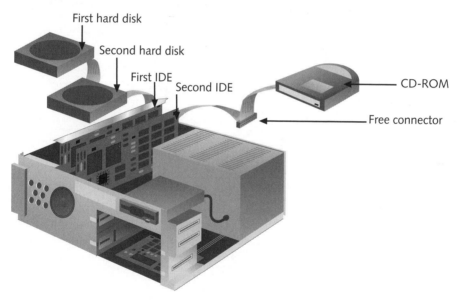

Figure 2-1   Hard disk and CD-ROM devices on multiple IDE interfaces

SCSI is a high-performance interface used by many types of devices to connect to a computer. SCSI is much faster than IDE, meaning that the flow of data between a hard disk or other device and the CPU is much more rapid. But SCSI devices are also much more expensive than IDE devices. As with IDE, a SCSI controller card provides the connection between

SCSI–compatible devices and the CPU of the computer. A single SCSI controller card can connect up to eight devices, each linked by a cable, as illustrated in Figure 2-2.

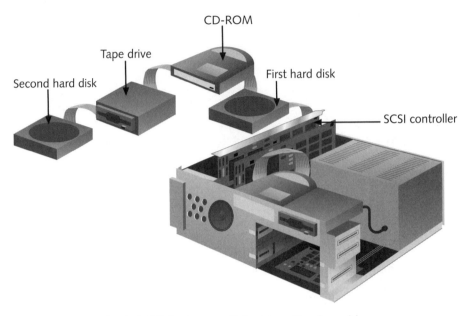

Figure 2-2   Multiple SCSI devices are linked together by cables

Supported Linux Hardware

Linux works with thousands of different hardware devices, from very old proprietary CD-ROM drives to the latest high-speed networking cards. But not all devices work with Linux. For example, Linux cannot accommodate the WinModem devices included with some new PCs.

You are likely to have trouble using Linux with very recently released hardware (such as a brand-new video card with many new features) and with very old equipment that uses standards that have since been discarded. The more information you have about the device in question, the more likely you can configure Linux to use the device, even if complete support for all of the device's features is not available.

Before installing Linux, you may want to check the Web site of your Linux vendor. The Web site may include a list of all supported hardware for that distribution. The hardware supported by all distributions is basically identical, so you can review the hardware compatibility list from any site as a starting place (for example, visit *http://www.calderasystems.com/support/hardware/*). Different versions of the Linux kernel, however, support slightly different hardware.

Understanding Networking

Many Linux systems are connected to networks so that they can communicate and share resources with other users connected to the network. In order to configure networking on

Linux, you will need some configuration information, as described later in this chapter. A basic knowledge of networking concepts will help you understand how to use that configuration information.

To communicate with each other effectively, computer systems use a **protocol**, which is an organized pattern of signals or words. Linux networking involves many different protocols. One protocol provides basic communication between network adapters. Another lets Web browsers communicate with Web servers. Altogether, Linux supports dozens of networking protocols, each one designed for a different purpose. Some of the most important protocols are discussed in the following sections.

IP Networking

The most important protocol in relation to Linux networking is called the Internet Protocol, or IP. **IP** is a networking protocol used to send packets of information across a network connection. IP is the basis on which most Linux networking is built. In order to use IP networking, each computer on the network must be assigned an identifying number, called an **IP address**. Each packet of data sent across the network includes two IP addresses: an address to identify the computer that the packet is coming from and one to identify the computer that the packet is going to.

IP addresses consist of four numbers, each separated by a period. For example, 207.29.12.1 is an IP address; so is 192.168.100.15. Each of the four numbers can be a value from 0 to 255. IP addresses are used all over the world, so to avoid the confusion that arises from duplicate IP addresses, you must use an IP address that has been assigned to the computer on which you install Linux. You may have to do some checking to find out what authority assigns the IP address for your computer. For instance, your Internet Service Provider (ISP) may have assigned a range of numbers to your system administrator, who would in turn assign a number to your computer as needed.

All of the IP addresses on a single network are related; for example, their first three numbers may be the same. Several special IP addresses are associated with setting up Linux networking so that packets can be passed around the network. These special IP addresses are listed here:

- A **network mask** tells the networking system in Linux how to identify IP numbers that are part of the local network, as opposed to IP numbers that are assigned to computers outside the local network.

- A **broadcast address** identifies a special IP address that will send a packet of data to all computers on the local network.

- A **gateway address** identifies the computer that can send packets of data outside the local network, to the Internet or to other networks in an organization.

A good Linux installation program can calculate some of the different IP addresses just described using the IP address of your computer. Still, your system administrator will probably give you each of the IP addresses needed for your computer and network.

Some networks use a special protocol designed to avoid the need to set up and track IP addresses on a network. This protocol, called the **Dynamic Host Configuration Protocol**

(DHCP), allows a computer to obtain an IP address dynamically from a network server at the time the computer is turned on. This can make it much easier for the system administrator to manage networking on a large system. A range of IP addresses and all the special addresses for the network are stored on a central server. Each computer is then configured to look for the DHCP server when it boots.

Rather than specifying an IP address, you may choose to use DHCP as you install Linux, depending on the configuration of your local network. You cannot use DHCP unless a DHCP server has been configured on your network. In addition, not all types of network services are well served by a computer that uses DHCP. For example, if you want to create a Web server on your Linux system, you should use an assigned IP address rather than relying on DHCP.

Domain Names and Hostnames

Transmitting data across a network would be difficult if you had to remember the IP address for every computer you wanted to access. To simplify matters, you can make use of a system of human-readable names for computers and networks. Each of these names is mapped to (is associated with) a specific IP address. As described in the next section, a special network server does the work of translating computer and network names into IP addresses, and vice versa.

A name assigned to a network is called a **domain name**. (Domain names are actually more all-encompassing than this definition implies, but equating a domain to a network is generally correct.) Some examples of domain names are *compaq.com, linux.org,* and *nasa.gov.* Domain names within a large organization may be longer than this. For example, within Compaq, you may find domains called *marketing.compaq.com, sales.compaq.com,* and *research.compaq.com.* The domain name is not limited to two words, but the ending portion of the domain name will always be one of the standard top-level (most generalized) domain names. Table 2-2 shows a few of the top-level domain names you are likely to see. Not all of the top-level domain names are listed, because each nation has a separate top-level domain name.

Table 2-2   Top-Level Domain Names

Name	Description
.com	Commercial/business entities
.org	Noncommercial organizations
.net	Organizations whose work relates to the Internet
.edu	Educational institutions, usually colleges and universities in the United States
.gov	U.S. government organizations
.mil	U.S. military organizations
.us	Generalized top-level domain for networks in the United States; used mostly for local governments and schools
.de	Top-level domain of Germany (Deutschland)
.uk	Top-level domain of the United Kingdom

Each computer in a domain is assigned a name. Computers involved in networking are often called **hosts**; so the name of a computer on the network is referred to as the computer's hostname. The **hostname** is a single word used to name a computer. Your system administrator may let you choose a hostname, or may assign one, such as lab13, or training01.

The hostname is combined with the domain name to create a **fully qualified domain name (FQDN)**. An example of an FQDN would be *lab13.myschool.edu*. Using the longer domain names given previously as examples, a sample FQDN might be *taco.research.compaq.com*. Web page addresses take the form of FQDNs. For example, the Web address *www.ibm.com* consists of a hostname (*www*) and a domain name (*ibm.com*). How can you tell that this is not simply a long domain name? By using a Web browser to successfully access a single system using that FQDN. (You can't tell by looking at the name.) In theory, IBM could have a domain named *www.ibm.com*. A host in that domain with a hostname such as *florida* would yield a FQDN of *florida.www.ibm.com*.

Domain Name Service (DNS)

The **Domain Name Service (DNS)** is the special network service devoted to the task of mapping human-readable domain names and hostnames to the IP addresses of specific networks and computers. A **DNS server** is the computer that actually performs this conversion. The process works like this: When you enter the address *www.ibm.com* in a Web browser, the browser must send a network packet to a DNS server asking for the IP address of *www.ibm.com*. Once that address is returned by the DNS server, the Web browser can establish a connection to the IBM Web server using the IP address (204.146.80.99 in this case).

Generally, you must provide the IP address of a DNS server as you configure Linux networking so that domain names and FQDNs can be converted to IP addresses. If you work on a small network that is not connected to the Internet, you can use a list of hostnames and IP addresses on your Linux system rather than a DNS server. Most networks employ a DNS server, however.

Creating a Shared System

Installing Linux on a system that already contains another operating system, such as Windows 98, allows you to experiment with Linux and take advantage of its features while relying on another operating system to support other needs, such as running applications that are not available for Linux. A shared system, also called a **dual-boot system**, is one that allows you to choose which operating system to start each time you boot (turn on) your computer. You can actually have numerous operating systems installed on one computer, not just two. The name dual-boot is commonly used to refer to any system with more than one operating system installed.

A program called a **boot manager** lets you select an operating system each time you boot the computer. **LILO (Linux Loader)** is the boot manager included with Linux. You can also use other commercial boot manager programs such as System Commander or BootMagic. Installing the LILO boot manager is part of every Linux installation, as you will learn in Chapter 3.

To create a dual-boot system, you must decide where on the computer's hard disks each operating system will reside. Two basic options are available:

- Store each operating system on a separate hard disk.

- Store multiple operating systems on the same hard disk.

The first option, using a different hard disk for each operating system, is preferable because all data from the different operating systems remains separate and installation is simpler. Of course, not many computer systems come with multiple hard disks, so this chapter focuses on how to store multiple operating systems on the same hard disk.

To use multiple operating systems on a single hard disk, you must decide how much space you will need for each operating system. The first operating system installed on the computer (often a version of Windows) probably takes up a lot of space already. You can determine the amount of hard disk space used on a Windows system as follows:

1. Double-click the **My Computer** icon on the Windows Desktop.

2. Right-click the icon for the hard disk. (This will normally have a name, followed by (C:), to indicate that it is drive C:.) A shortcut menu opens.

3. Click **Properties**. The Properties dialog box opens.

4. View the information on the General tab of the Properties dialog box, which is shown in Figure 2-3. This window shows the amount of used space and free space, as well as other information that will be covered later in this chapter.

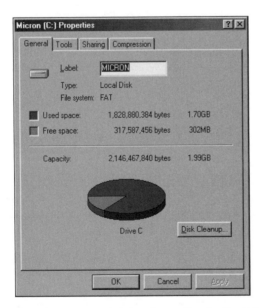

Figure 2-3   Hard disk information in the Windows Properties dialog box

5. Click **Cancel** to close the Properties dialog box.

Once you know how much space is available on the hard disk where Windows is stored, you can consider how much of the available free space you could use for your Linux operating system.

As with other operating systems, the exact components you need to install depend on what you intend to do with Linux. The more components you add, the more space you need on the hard disk. Each Linux distribution offers different standard installation options. Some distributions (such as Red Hat) let you select a Desktop system or a Server system; others (such as Caldera OpenLinux) let you choose a Web Server, Desktop System, Business Server, or Development Workstation (for use in developing software). Many distributions (including SuSE, Red Hat, and others) let you choose the exact software packages that you want to install. This is more time-consuming than just selecting a designation such as Web Server and letting the installation program choose what to install based on that selection. The sizes of a few standard options that you might see as you install different Linux distributions are shown in Table 2-3.

Table 2-3   Typical Linux Installation Options

Type of installation	Typical hard disk space required	Comments
Minimal installation without graphics support	40 MB	A specialized Linux system can use as little as 1 MB, but such specialized systems are not part of most Linux distributions.
Standard installation	400 MB to 600 MB	This generally includes a graphical system and numerous utilities.
Web server	300 MB	This includes all the networking utilities to run a Web server, but may not include graphical support.
Development workstation	500 MB	This allows you to develop Linux software.
Full (everything included with the distribution)	1.5 GB to 4 GB, depending on how many CD-ROMs are included with the distribution	

If you don't want to make a lot of decisions, choose one of the installation types shown in Table 2-3. At the other end of the spectrum, you could specify each and every option, a time-consuming process. As a compromise between these two options, you might consider a custom installation that lets you choose categories of packages. For example, in Red Hat Linux, you can choose a Custom installation option, then select packages from a list of about 20 categories.

Use the guidelines in Table 2-3 along with any documentation you have for your Linux distribution to determine how much space you need in order to install Linux.

In addition to space for the operating system, you must consider how much hard disk space you will want to have available *after* installing Linux to hold documents and other files that you create as you work in Linux. Depending on what you will do with Linux, you might need a lot of space for database files, Web server documents, programs that you download, or graphics files that you create. Add this amount to the amount of disk space for the operating system itself.

Don't let all the installation options presented so far confuse you. If you are just starting out with Linux, try to have about 1 GB of hard disk space to install Linux and work with Linux programs. This should be sufficient to get you started.

Graphical Systems

Setting up the video hardware that provides a graphical interface for Linux is undoubtedly the most challenging part of Linux configuration. A few old standards for video hardware exist, and these are still useful in configuring Linux. Newer video hardware uses proprietary technology that requires special software for each new product that becomes available. What's more, while video card vendors can be counted on to develop device drivers for Microsoft Windows, few vendors provide software support for Linux. At the same time, the vendor may refuse to release technical information about the video card, making it very difficult for Linux developers to provide their own support for the latest video cards.

On a positive note, when technical information is available, the graphical system in Linux can make full use of the features of all video hardware, without being restricted to the small number of standard modes that the vendor's Windows software supports.

The graphical environment in Linux is provided by the X Window System. Software from the **XFree86 Project** (another free software project) adds the X Window System to Linux. You can also use commercial software to add the X Window System to Linux, but the XFree86 software is included with all distributions of Linux and will be the focus of the graphical installation described in Chapter 3.

 You can read about the two major commercial X products for Linux by visiting Xi Graphics at *www.xig.com* and MetroLink at *www.metrolink.com*.

The Web page for the XFree86 Project contains a complete list of video cards supported by their software. New video cards are added regularly as new versions of XFree86 are released. Video card manufacturers are slowly beginning to recognize the fact that having support in XFree86 software helps to sell more video cards, and so they are becoming more open about providing technical information to the free software community.

In addition to knowing which video card your computer system uses, you might also be able to locate the name of the video chipset used. This is helpful because sometimes when the video card model is not listed in the Linux configuration options, the chipset used on that card is listed. The chipset information can then be used to configure the graphical environment.

Monitors and the Graphical System

Because the X Window System is flexible enough to use all the features of a video card, it may be able to produce better graphics than your monitor can display. This can cause a newer, powerful video card to send signals that damage older monitors. For example, if you have a video card that supports a high-resolution display of 1240 × 1024 pixels, but your monitor is not capable of displaying that resolution, the signal from the video card might damage the monitor.

The solution to this potential problem is to configure Linux with the correct information about your monitor's capabilities. Thus, Linux will calculate what the monitor can support and block any signals that the monitor cannot handle. In the example just given, a suitable lower resolution mode would be selected to display graphics.

Three specifications identify a monitor's capabilities:

- The number of screen redraws per second (called the refresh rate). This number is expressed in hertz, or Hz. New monitors often have a range of refresh rates, such as 50 to 90.

- The number of lines per second that can be redrawn. This number is expressed in kilohertz, or KHz.

- The clock speed of the monitor's electronics, which determines indirectly how many colors the monitor can support. This number is expressed in megahertz, or MHz.

When installing most Linux distributions, you will be asked for the first of these numbers, the Hz value.

CREATING A SYSTEM INVENTORY

Before you start installing Linux, you should gather all the information about your hardware that you might need to complete the installation. Table 2-4 lists the information you may need, with example values for each and a blank column where you can fill in your values. The following sections explain how to locate the necessary information.

> **TIP** Although the information in Table 2-4 is useful, it may not be strictly necessary in order to install Linux. The latest Linux installation programs attempt to make installation as easy as possible, automatically detecting many hardware components. This is especially true for newer computers with standard equipment such as IDE hard disks. Nevertheless, the information in Table 2-4 can be valuable *after* you have installed Linux and need to update configurations for the LILO boot manager, the graphical system, or other parts of the Linux operating system.

Table 2-4   Useful Hardware Information for Installing Linux

Hardware information	Sample value	Your system
Amount of RAM	64 MB	
Hard disk interface type	IDE	
Hard disk size	4.3 GB	
Serial port used by modem	COM1 (first serial port)	
IRQ used by modem	4	
Printer port	LPT1 (first parallel port)	
CD-ROM interface type	IDE	
Type of mouse	Microsoft serial	
Port used by mouse	COM2 (second serial port)	
Monitor make and model	NEC Multisync C400	
Monitor scan rate range	50–90	
Video card make and model	Starfighter AGP	
Video card chipset	Intel i740	
Amount of video RAM	8 MB	
SCSI card make and model (if you have one in your system)	Adaptec AIC-7850	
Network adapter make and model	3Com Fast Etherlink XL 10/100	
The IRQ used by the network adapter	11	
Sound card make and model	SoundBlaster	
The IRQ, DMA channel, and memory addresses used by the sound card	10, 3, 220	

In addition to information about your hardware, you may need to find the networking information listed in Table 2-5.

Table 2-5   Information Needed to Set Up Linux Networking

Network information	Sample value	Your system
Domain name	xmission.com	
Hostname	brighton	
DHCP server address	207.49.12.1	
Static IP address	192.168.100.13	
Network mask	255.255.255.0	
Broadcast address	192.168.100.255	
Gateway address	192.168.100.1	
DNS server address	192.168.100.1	
Secondary DNS server address	207.29.12.2	

Installations that use a network connection to access the installation data may also require that you provide the information in Table 2-6.

Table 2-6   Information Needed for a Networked Installation

Network installation information	Sample value	Your system
NFS or SMB server IP address	192.168.100.4	
Path to the installation files on the remote server	`/mnt/cdrom`	

You can get the information described in these tables from a variety of sources. It's probably easiest to ask a technician or system administrator who is familiar with the hardware you are working on. However, if you employ the methods described in the following sections, you will learn more about how your system functions and be better prepared to become a system administrator yourself.

Finding the Manuals

Nearly every computer system includes some type of printed manual that describes how to set up and use the system. Unfortunately, this documentation is usually filed in some forgotten corner minutes after the system is up and running. Although manuals seem to be getting smaller every year, yours probably contains at least a few key specifications for your system. Locate your computer's manual and do the following:

- Look in the index under the name of the hardware component you want to learn more about.

- Check the Table of Contents for a Specifications or a Troubleshooting section.

- Review the first few pages of the section about setting up the system, which may contain details about the hardware.

Most computers come with separate manuals for each component; each of these manuals is provided by a different manufacturer. (Sometimes these manuals are tucked inside a sleeve with a CD-ROM full of software for the device.) Look for separate manuals on the following items:

- Main system (the CPU)
- Monitor
- Mouse
- Video card
- Modem
- CD-ROM drive

If you can't locate the printed manuals, try going online. Visit the Web site for the manufacturer of your computer. Search under Products, Technical Support, or a related topic. Locating technical information on a huge Web site can be time-consuming, but this information is generally free. A sample Web page showing the specifications for a Toshiba laptop is shown in Figure 2-4.

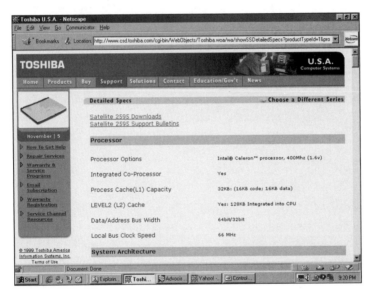

Figure 2-4   A sample Web-based specifications sheet

Reviewing BIOS Settings

Sometimes you can find information that is not evident in the printed or online documentation by reviewing the BIOS of the computer itself. Different systems use various methods of accessing the BIOS configuration menus, where you can learn about system status and devices. An on-screen message normally explains how to enter the Setup or BIOS information screen when you first boot the computer. Depending on your system, you might be asked to press F2, Del, Esc, or some other key to enter the BIOS menus. Review the system documentation if you don't see a message explaining how to enter the BIOS menus.

Exact steps for exploring the BIOS menus cannot be given because each manufacturer may use a different interface for configuring the BIOS. A sample screen for BIOS configuration is shown in Figure 2-5.

2

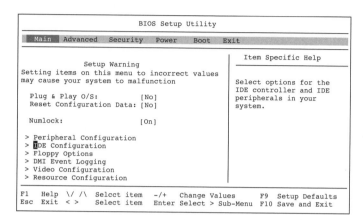

Figure 2-5   BIOS configuration menus

Keep the following points in mind as you examine the BIOS menus for hardware information:

- Some BIOS configurations include a number of options that are not relevant to installing Linux, such as how long to wait before entering a low-power mode and whether to include a power-on password. You can ignore these options and focus on locating the information in Table 2-4.

- Different levels of information may be provided in different menus. The details in Table 2-4 are often in the Advanced portion of the BIOS configuration, because most users don't need to know this information to use a system that is already up and running.

- You can make minor changes to the settings in the BIOS and save them as you exit the BIOS setup utility. Don't do this unless you have studied the system documentation and are familiar with the features you are altering. Watch carefully as you exit the BIOS menus to make sure you do not accidentally choose a Save and Exit option.

You may find any of the following pieces of information as you review your BIOS settings:

- Amount of RAM on the system.

- Hard disk interface type and size.

- Serial ports available on the system and the IRQ used by each one.

- IRQ numbers used by other devices that might conflict with devices such as a sound card or network adapter. (You usually can't see the IRQ used by these devices in the BIOS menus.)
- The SCSI card make and model.

Without accessing the BIOS, you can use a related method for locating system information: simply watch the screen carefully as the system starts. Many devices, especially SCSI cards and video cards, print identification messages to the screen as they are initialized at system boot time. You may have to power the system off and on several times to read the messages, but you can often gain much useful information from these small "advertisements" that the card prints on screen.

Studying Microsoft Windows

If your computer is already running a Windows operating system, you have an advantage in preparing for installation: the Windows operating system has already collected all of the hardware configuration information for you. Before installing Linux, you can start your computer in Windows and write down all the configuration information you'll need to use when installing Linux.

Device information in Windows is available from the Windows Control Panel, which you can view by clicking Start, pointing to Settings, and then double-clicking Control Panel. You can also double-click the My Computer icon on the Desktop, and then double-click the Control Panel icon. The Windows Control Panel (in large icon view) is shown in Figure 2-6. The icons on each Windows system vary slightly based on the hardware and software that you have installed; so your screen may vary slightly from the figure.

Figure 2-6   The Windows Control Panel

You can view device information in the Control Panel by double-clicking the System icon. Within the System Properties dialog box, the Device Manager tab shows a list of all the device categories on your system, such as disk drives, network adapters, and monitors. When you click the plus sign (+) to the left of an item, a more detailed list of information appears for that item. Figure 2-7 shows the Device Manager tab with several of the subsections opened for a more detailed view. As with the Control Panel, the information in this figure will differ slightly from what you see because different computer systems have different devices installed.

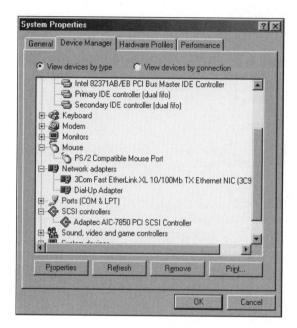

Figure 2-7   The Device Manager tab in the System Properties dialog box

In the list of devices, you may be able to see the manufacturer and model name for the device used on your system. Figure 2-7 shows a 3COM Fast Etherlink XL device as a network adapter and an Adaptec AIC-7850 as a SCSI controller. You can research additional information about your system's hardware by selecting a hardware device and choosing the Properties button at the bottom of the dialog box. (You can also double-click on any item in the list.) A separate dialog box will then appear for that device. Most of these device-specific dialog boxes include a tab labeled Resources.

The Resources tab for many devices shows the interrupt request number, the DMA channel, and the I/O port used by the device (labeled Input/Output Range in the dialog box). You can copy all of the information that you feel will be useful (based on what you have read so far) in setting up the Linux system. Not all of the information is necessary. For example, the keyboard device lists an IRQ and an input/output range, but the keyboard is automatically configured in Linux, so you won't need that information. Refer to Table 2-4 to review the hardware information you may need. Figure 2-8 shows a sample Resources tab for a device in the Device Manager.

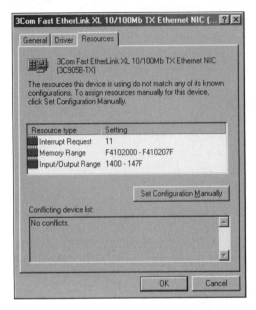

Figure 2-8   The Resources tab in the Properties dialog box of a selected device

You can also use Windows to find details about your networking configuration. Because a computer cannot run both Windows and Linux at the same time, you can normally use the same networking information for Linux that you use for Windows.

Within the Windows Control Panel, the Network icon leads to information about how networking is set up in Windows. The Identification tab in the Network dialog box includes a Computer name field with a name for your system. This name is associated with Windows networking, but you may want to use this as your hostname when you install Linux. Ask your system administrator for advice.

The Configuration tab of the Network dialog lists many different Windows networking components. One item is labeled TCP/IP, followed by the name of your networking device (this is usually an Ethernet networking adapter). Figure 2-9 shows a Network dialog box with the TCP/IP item selected.

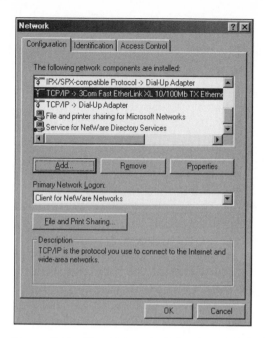

Figure 2-9   The Network dialog box in Windows

With the TCP/IP item selected, click the Properties button. This opens the TCP/IP Properties dialog box. In this dialog box you can collect the following information:

- On the IP Address tab, you see the IP Address field and the Subnet Mask field (which refers to the Network Mask field as described previously). The Obtain IP address automatically item indicates that the Windows system uses DHCP. If this option is selected in Windows, you can try to select DHCP as you install Linux.

- On the Gateway tab, the first item in the section, labeled Installed gateways provides the IP address that you should use as the gateway address when installing Linux.

- On the DNS Configuration tab, the DNS Server Search Order list contains at least one IP address. If multiple addresses are shown, you should make note of them all. The Host and Domain names above the DNS Server Search Order list are the hostname and domain name used for Windows networking. Unless directed otherwise, you should use these as the hostname and domain name when you install Linux. If the Disable DNS option is selected, the information in this dialog box may not be valid, or it may not be shown as described. In this case, ask your system administrator or ISP for the DNS-related information mentioned here.

Figure 2-10 shows the DNS Configuration tab in the TCP/IP Properties dialog box. The values shown differ on each system, based on the domain name and DNS servers used for each network.

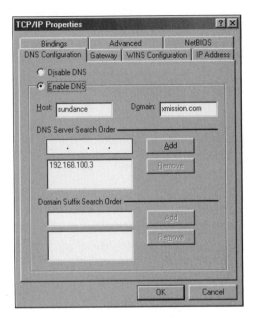

Figure 2-10   The DNS Configuration tab in the TCP/IP Properties dialog box

Exit all of the Windows dialog boxes described here by choosing the Cancel button. This prevents you from accidentally altering your Windows settings and causing problems with your hardware or networking configurations.

Asking Networking Questions

The only way to obtain some network settings is to ask the person (or organization) who assigns that setting. For instance, you cannot simply choose a network address, nor is the network address of your gateway or other servers something that you can guess. To get most of the networking information listed in Table 2-5 and Table 2-6, you will need to ask the authority who originally set up your network connection—that is, you need to consult either your system administrator or ISP.

In some cases, you will be allowed to select a hostname for your Linux installation. You can choose any brief name that you want for the hostname. System administrators often use a pattern of names for setting up multiple computers, such as the names of pets, cities, or something similar. The names are arbitrary, but you must provide the name to the person who manages the name server on your network so that e-mail and other services can be directed to your computer.

PREPARING YOUR HARD DISK

You must install Linux in a dedicated partition on the hard disk. A **partition** is a distinct area of a hard disk that has been prepared to store a particular type of data. For example, a computer that only contains Windows has one partition on its hard disk. That partition is marked as containing Windows data. To install Linux you must prepare another partition that is marked as containing Linux data. You must create a Linux partition whether you plan to establish a dual-boot system or install only Linux on the computer.

You can think of a partition as an empty space on the disk with a label attached to it. Before a partition can hold information, it must be formatted with a particular file system type. The term **file system** refers to the arrangement of information on a device such as a hard disk. The organization usually takes the form of files and directories. In theory, you could create a partition that was marked as holding a certain file system type, then format that partition with a different file system type than the partition specified. In practice, however, the operating system prevents this sort of mistake.

Figure 2-11 shows how two partitions might be arranged on a hard disk, with marks indicating the file system type and a file system format inside each partition. The default file system type for Linux is called **ext2** (extended file system version 2). The default file system type for Windows 98 systems is called **FAT32** (32-bit File Allocation Table). Windows NT uses a file system called **NTFS** (NT file system).

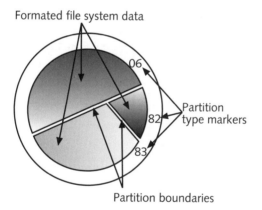

Figure 2-11   Partitions and file systems on a hard disk

Among all of the partitions on a hard disk, one can be marked as the active partition, or the bootable partition. The **active partition** is the one that the BIOS assumes contains the operating system to be started. The BIOS always attempts to start the boot manager program located at the beginning of the active partition.

In Chapter 3 you will learn in detail about the tools you can use to create Linux partitions. To use these tools, you must have free space available on your hard disk. For computers that will be dual-boot systems, you must prepare the free space for Linux before you start the Linux installation. For computer systems that will have only Linux installed, the partitions can be created during the installation. The information in the following sections will help you understand how to use the partitioning tools discussed in Chapter 3 and how to create free space on a Windows partition.

Booting the System

When you turn on a computer, the BIOS initializes the devices on the system, then starts the boot manager located on a small area of the first hard disk called the **Master Boot Record**, or MBR. The MBR contains a small program that decides how to start an operating system. Normally, the MBR passes control of the computer to the boot record of the active partition. The **boot record** is a small area on each partition that contains a boot manager program for launching the operating system on that partition. For partitions containing Linux, the boot record contains a copy of the LILO boot manager.

The boot manager can include instructions to pass control to other partitions, such as a partition containing a Windows operating system. This creates a dual-boot system in which you choose which operating system to start each time you turn on the computer.

Figure 2-12 shows how a hard disk is arranged to include an MBR and a boot record on multiple partitions, with one partition being marked as active. Sometimes the boot record is called the boot sector, or the root sector, of the partition.

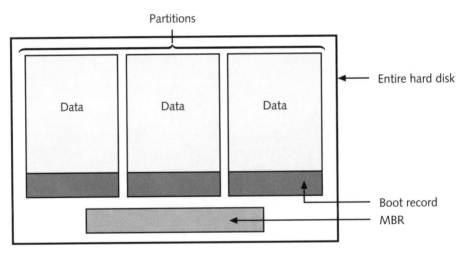

Figure 2-12   A hard disk with an MBR and boot records on each partition

Hard Disk Geometry

The operating system stored on a hard disk arranges information according to the file system used. Each operating system has a default file system. But the hard disk itself is designed to store information according to the physical characteristics of the hard disk. Sometimes you need to know something about the disk drive layout to configure the system properly.

A hard disk is composed of multiple flat platters that hold magnetic data. These platters are stacked together, with small reading devices moving between the platters to read the data on each platter. Each concentric circle on a platter is called a **track**. When you format a hard disk, each track is divided into multiple sectors. A **sector** is a unit of data storage on a hard disk. Normally a sector contains 512 bytes. Sectors are often grouped together into larger units called clusters or blocks. A default hard disk **block** in Linux is a unit of hard disk space that contains 1024 bytes, or two sectors. Figure 2-13 shows a single platter of a hard disk with the tracks, sectors, and blocks illustrated.

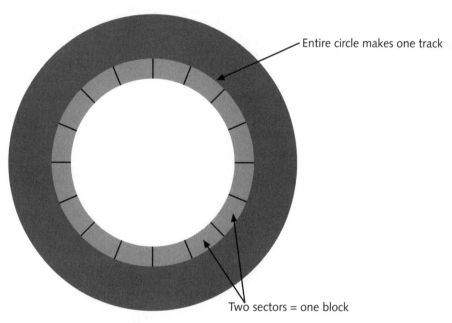

Entire circle makes one track

Two sectors = one block

Figure 2-13   Tracks, blocks, and sectors on a hard disk platter

Taken together, all of the tracks at the same position on each platter are called a cylinder. Put another way, a **cylinder** is a set of tracks at the same location on all the platters of a hard disk. Figure 2-14 illustrates this concept.

Note Figures 2-13 and 2-14 are somewhat deceptive. Keep in mind that a hard disk often has over 1000 cylinders, or concentric tracks, on each platter. This is an important point. Hard disks with many cylinders can cause special installation problems for Linux because of limitations in the BIOS of many computers. The next section explains this problem.

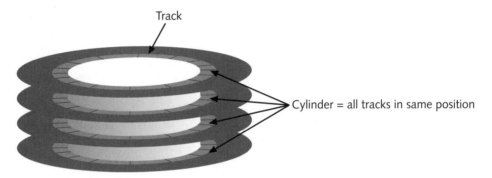

Figure 2-14   A cylinder on a hard disk

Using Big Disks

When installing Linux, the terms big disk or large disk refer to hard disks with more than 1024 cylinders. When you define partitions on your hard disk, you must define them on cylinder boundaries. That is, you cannot define a single cylinder as being partly in one partition and partly in another partition. Because of a limitation in the BIOS programming in many computers, the MBR cannot send control to a partition that includes cylinder numbers higher than 1024. The BIOS simply cannot handle larger numbers.

For example, suppose you define the partitions on your hard disk like this:

Windows: Cylinders 1–700
Linux: Cylinders 701–1400

Even if you mark the Linux partition as the active partition, the BIOS cannot pass control to the boot manager stored on the Linux partition because some of the cylinder numbers that make up the partition are too large for the BIOS to address. To deal with this strange problem, you sometimes must define your Linux system to include two partitions. First you define one small partition using smaller cylinder numbers; this partition can boot the operating system. Then you define a second, larger Linux partition that includes space on the hard disk beyond the 1024-cylinder boundary. Another operating system may reside in the space between the two Linux partitions. For example:

Linux start-up: Cylinders 1–200
Windows: Cylinders 700–1200
Linux: Cylinders 701–2000

The number of cylinders that you use for each partition depends on the amount of space you require for each operating system, but it also varies based on the total number of cylinders available on the hard disk. Most Linux installation programs will help you overcome the so-called big disk problem as you install Linux.

Swap Partitions

The Linux operating system and the files that you create in Linux are stored in a partition of type ext2. In addition to this partition, you must create a separate partition used as a swap partition for the Linux kernel's virtual memory. **Virtual memory** is a special area of the hard disk that the operating system treats as if it were RAM, storing programs there temporarily when they are not being used. The **swap partition** (also called swap space) is the designated area used as virtual memory by the Linux kernel. For example, you might start several programs in Linux, but if one of the programs is sitting idle and the RAM memory that the program uses is needed by another program, the Linux kernel will copy part of the program or its data to the swap partition. When the program is activated again, the program and data are moved back to RAM so they can continue operating.

Using a separate partition controlled by the Linux kernel allows the virtual memory feature to work very quickly, without interfering with other hard disk operations that read from or write to the `ext2` file system. A swap partition is normally from 32 MB to 256 MB in size, though it can be smaller or larger depending on how much hard disk space you have and how busy the Linux system will be. Some Linux systems limit a swap partition to 128 MB.

You create a swap partition just as you create a regular Linux partition. The partition is marked with an indicator that it will be used for Linux virtual memory.

Preparing a Shared Hard Disk

Dual-boot systems require that you either have a separate hard disk for Linux or that you use some of the hard disk space currently occupied by Windows to install Linux. If you choose the latter approach, you need to become familiar with **FIPS**—a program that lets you create two separate partitions from your existing Windows partition. During the Linux installation, you can delete the second, empty Windows partition and replace it with a Linux partition.

 Before using the FIPS program, you should back up any important data on your Windows system by copying it to disks, tape, or to a network server. FIPS is considered stable and safe, but altering hard disk partition information always puts your data at risk.

The FIPS program is a DOS program that is included with every Linux distribution, usually in a separate directory called `utils`, `dostools`, or something similar. Your Linux documentation will tell you where it is located on the CD-ROM. In order to use FIPS, you must first arrange all the data on the Windows partition so that it is together, leaving a contiguous area of free space at one end of the hard disk. In other words, you must defragment the Windows system. **Defragmenting** is a procedure that arranges each file in Windows so that the parts of the file are next to each other on the hard disk (as opposed to the parts of a file being fragmented, or spread across the hard disk). When you defragment a Windows system, all of the files are placed at the beginning of the hard disk. Figure 2-15 shows conceptually how a Windows partition is arranged before and after the defragmenting operation.

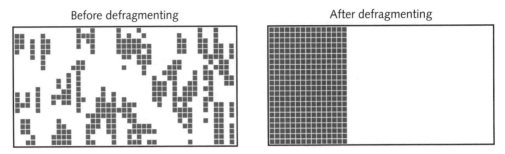

Figure 2-15   A Windows partition before and after defragmenting

Windows 98 includes a utility for defragmenting your Windows partitions. To defragment a Windows partition within Windows 98:

1. Double-click the **My Computer** icon.

2. Locate the hard disk on which you will later install Linux (this is normally C: in Windows).

3. Right-click the icon for that hard disk. A shortcut menu appears.

4. Click **Properties**. The Properties dialog box for the selected hard drive opens.

5. Click the **Tools** tab to display the options shown in Figure 2-16. The last item on the Tools tab is the Defragment utility.

Figure 2-16   The Tools tab for a Windows hard disk

6. Click the **Defragment Now** button. The Defragmentation program runs on the selected hard disk. You see a progress indicator as the program works.

7. Click **Show Details** in the progress indicator window to see how the Defragmentation program is rearranging data on the hard disk. Figure 2-17 shows the detailed screen as the program works.

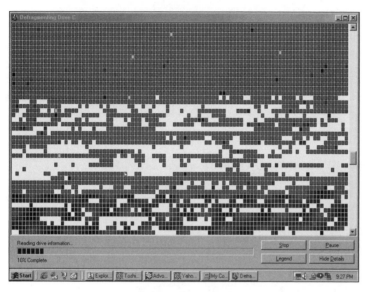

Figure 2-17   The Defragmentation details window

8. When the program finishes, click **Yes** to exit.

With the free space arranged on your Windows partition, you can run the FIPS program to split the Windows partition into two pieces. To run FIPS, follow these steps:

1. Obtain a floppy disk to use as a backup for your disk information.

2. Obtain a second floppy disk to hold the FIPS program.

3. Locate Fips.exe on the Linux installation CD (or among the Linux files that you have downloaded from the Internet). The CD may contain several copies of FIPS.exe in differnet folders. Use any copy that you find.

4. Copy Fips.exe to a floppy disk.

5. Click the **Start** button in Windows, click **Shut Down**, then click **Restart in MS-DOS mode**. After a moment, the DOS C:\ prompt appears.

6. Start the FIPS program using the command **FIPS** preceded by the drive letter for your floppy drive (for example, A:\FIPS). The CD-ROM drive is normally not available within the DOS mode, which is why you copied the FIPS program to a floppy disk.

7. Read the messages on screen, and then press a key to continue.

8. Using the floppy disk mentioned in Step 1, back up your disk information by following the instructions on screen. (Keep this disk until you have finished installing Linux and made certain that you can start both Windows and Linux.)

9. If you have multiple disk drives, select the one you want FIPS to alter.

10. The partition table for the hard disk is displayed. You can review this information, but you don't need to do anything about it. Press a key to continue.

11. FIPS presents you with two numbers showing the size of the current Windows partition (on the left) and the size of the new Windows partition (on the right). (Figure 2-18 shows a sample screen.) Use the Up and Down arrow keys to adjust the space on each partition. Because you are changing the point at which the partition will be split in two, one number goes up as the other goes down. The number on the right (shown in MB) should be large enough for your Linux partition and swap partition.

```
MS-DOS Prompt - FIPS
T  11 x 18

Number of FATs: 2
Number of rootdirectory entries: 0
Number of sectors (short): 0
Media descriptor byte: F8h
Sectors per FAT: 6003
Sectors per track: 63
Drive heads: 255
Hidden sectors: 63
Number of sectors (long): 6152832
Physical drive number: 80h
Signature: 29h

Checking boot sector ... OK
Checking FAT ... OK
Searching for free space ... OK

Do you want to make a backup copy of your root and boot sector before
proceeding (y/n)? n

Enter start cylinder for new partition (249 - 382):

Use the cursor keys to choose the cylinder, <enter> to continue

Old partition        Cylinder        New Partition
 1953.2 MB            249              1051.1 MB
```

Figure 2-18   FIPS during the process of resizing the Windows partition

 TIP   FIPS will not allow you to reduce the original Windows partition to a smaller size than is needed for the data residing on that Windows partition. If the number on the left for the size of the original Windows partition will not go low enough to allow space for Linux when the second Windows partition is deleted, you have not effectively moved all the data to the front of the Windows partition. Or the Windows partition may simply be too full to store Linux on the same computer.

12. Press **Enter** to accept your settings.

13. The partition table is displayed again as it will appear when updated by FIPS. If you are comfortable with the sizes shown, press **C** to confirm that you want to write this information to the hard disk. You can press **Ctrl+C** to exit FIPS without making any changes to your hard disk.

14. Reboot your computer immediately so that the updated hard disk information is reread into your system.

2

After using FIPS, you should have a smaller Windows partition containing the Windows operating system and your Windows data; you also have a second Windows partition that contains no data. During the Linux installation you will use a tool such as **fdisk** or the Disk Druid (discussed in Chapter 3) to delete this second, empty Windows partition and turn the resulting free space on the hard disk into the Linux partition and Linux swap partition.

In addition to FIPS, several commercial programs are available to help you prepare partitions for Linux. The most popular is called PartitionMagic, from PowerQuest (*www.powerquest.com*). PartitionMagic provides a graphical interface to create new partitions, and helps you back up data before altering the hard disk. However, PartitionMagic is commercial software that costs money. (The Caldera OpenLinux distribution includes a reduced version of PartitionMagic to help prepare a Windows system for a Linux installation.)

Chapter Summary

❑ Many Linux installation programs are designed to detect a computer's hardware. However, an understanding of basic computer hardware terminology will help you install Linux more smoothly, because it also allows you to compile additional information that may be needed to complete the Linux installation.

❑ To use Linux networking, you must assign an IP address to the system. Additional IP addresses give Linux the ability to work with other computers on the network and to convert domain names into IP addresses.

❑ You can compile a system inventory by referring to the computer documentation, a vendor's Web site, or by checking the settings in a copy of Windows that is already installed on the computer. Networking information is assigned by a system administrator or ISP.

❑ Before installing Linux, you must prepare the hard disk by creating partition that will hold the Linux file system. You also need to leave room for a swap partition. You can use the FIPS utility to create an empty Windows partition on a hard disk dedicated to Windows. You can then delete the empty partition and use the space for Linux.

Key Terms

active partition — The partition that receives control from the BIOS when the system is turned on.

BIOS (Basic Input/Output System) — Information stored in ROM that provides instructions to the operating system for using the devices on a computer.

block — A unit of hard disk space that contains 1024 bytes, or two sectors.

boot manager — A program that lets you select an operating system to use each time you boot the computer.

boot record — A small area on each partition that contains a program to launch the operating system on that partition.

broadcast address — A special IP address that sends a packet of data to all computers on the local network.

byte — Space within a computer system sufficient to store one character.

cylinder — A set of tracks at the same location on all the platters of a hard disk.

defragmenting — A procedure that arranges each file in Windows so that the parts of the file are next to each other on the hard disk (as opposed to the parts of a file being fragmented, or spread across the hard disk).

direct memory access (DMA) channel — A communication method within a computer that allows a device to read and write directly to the computer's RAM, without going through the microprocessor first.

DNS server — A computer that uses the DNS protocol to convert from domain name and hostname to IP address.

domain name — A name assigned to a network.

Domain Name Service (DNS) — A protocol that maps human-readable domain names and hostnames to IP addresses that correspond to networks and individual computers.

dual-boot system — A computer that allows a person to choose which operating system to start each time the computer is booted (turned on).

Dynamic Host Configuration Protocol (DHCP) — A protocol that allows a computer to obtain an IP address dynamically from a network server at the time the computer is turned on.

ext2 — The default file system type for Linux.

FAT32 — The default file system type for Windows 98.

file system — An organized arrangement of information on a device such as a hard disk.

FIPS — A program that creates two separate partitions from an existing Windows partition.

fully qualified domain name (FQDN) — The hostname of a computer and the domain name of the network to which the computer is attached.

gateway address — The IP address of the computer on a local network that can send packets of data outside that network.

gigabyte (GB) — A measure of space on computers equal to 1024 megabytes, or roughly enough space to store 1 billion characters.

hard disk — Magnetic storage space for data such as the operating system and data files.

hexadecimal (hex) — A numbering system using base-16. Hex uses 0 to 9, plus the letters A through F (usually capitalized) to count the numbers 10 through 15.

host — A computer attached to a network.

hostname — A single word used to name a computer.

IDE — A low-cost, easy-to-manage interface used by most new computers to connect hard disks and CD-ROM drives to the CPU.

IDE controller — A computer hardware component used to communicate between an IDE-compatible hard disk or other IDE device and the microprocessor.

interrupt request (IRQ) — A numbered channel of communication allowing a device to inform the system that some action needs to be taken for the device.

I/O ports — Memory addresses used by a device for memory-mapped I/O.

2

IP — A networking protocol used to send packets of information across a network connection.

IP address — An identifying number assigned to a computer or device that uses IP to communicate across a network.

LILO (Linux Loader) — The boot manager included with Linux.

Master Boot Record (MBR) — A small area of the first hard disk that contains a program to decide how to start an operating system.

megabyte (MB) — A measure of space on computers equal to 1,048,576 bytes, or enough space to store roughly 1 million characters.

memory-mapped input/output (memory-mapped I/O) — A technique that assigns a range of memory addresses in a computer as a place for a device to send and receive data.

network mask — A set of numbers that tells the networking system in Linux how to identify IP addresses that are part of the local network.

NTFS — The default file system type for Windows NT.

partition — A distinct area of a hard disk that has been prepared to store a particular type of data.

protocol — An organized pattern of signals or words used to communicate efficiently.

random access memory (RAM) — Volatile electronic storage within a computer.

read-only memory (ROM) — Nonvolatile electronic storage within a computer. Used to store information about how the computer starts and how the devices in the computer are configured.

SCSI — A high-performance interface used by many types of devices to connect to a computer.

sector — A unit of data storage on a hard disk. Normally a sector contains 512 bytes.

swap partition (also called swap space) — A designated area on a hard disk used as virtual memory by the Linux kernel.

tracks — The concentric circles on each platter of a hard disk.

virtual memory — A feature of the Linux kernel that allows Linux to treat a special area of the hard disk as if it were RAM, storing programs there temporarily when they are not being used.

XFree86 Project — A free software project that creates software to provide X Window System functionality to Linux.

REVIEW QUESTIONS

1. You can purchase computer systems with Linux preinstalled. True or False?

2. Why is Linux sometimes considered more difficult to install than other operating systems?

3. A byte is enough space to store:

   a. One character

   b. One hexadecimal digit

   c. One sector

   d. One megabyte

4. When you see a value in gigabytes, it probably refers to:

   a. An IRQ number

   b. A monitor refresh rate

   c. Hard disk size

   d. RAM size

5. Which of the following cannot be changed by a user?

   a. Magnetic data on a hard disk

   b. Electronic storage in RAM

   c. The configuration settings in the BIOS

   d. The BIOS stored in ROM

6. The BIOS configuration settings can be accessed using a special menu system provided with most computers. True or False?

7. Which of the following is *not* part of the configuration for most devices on a computer?

   a. IRQ

   b. FIPS

   c. I/O ports

   d. DMA channel

8. The _____ numbering system is often used to refer to information about computer hardware.

   a. hexadecimal

   b. MBR

   c. binary

   d. SCSI

9. Which of the following is *not* a valid hexadecimal digit?

   a. E

   b. D

   c. A

   d. H

2

10. The _____ interface is a high–cost, high–performance method of connecting hard disks to a computer.

   a. LILO

   b. SCSI

   c. IDE

   d. MBR

11. An IP address consists of four numbers from 0 to 999, each separated by a period.
True or False?

12. Name four items of information about the network that are required to complete a
Linux installation, and explain the purpose of each one.

13. By using DHCP, a Linux system can:

   a. Convert a domain name to an IP address

   b. Pass packets outside the local network to the Internet

   c. Send broadcast messages to all computers on the network

   d. Obtain an IP address from a network server

14. An FQDN includes:

   a. A hostname and an IP address

   b. A hostname and a domain name

   c. A domain name and an IP address

   d. The IP address provided by DHCP

15. A DNS server provides the following service to computers on the network:

   a. It converts domain names to IP addresses.

   b. It provides IP addresses when a computer is turned on.

   c. It sends data packets to the Internet.

   d. It configures independent file systems on the hard disk.

16. The most important monitor specification to obtain before installing Linux is:

   a. Refresh rate (given in Hz)

   b. Scan rate (given in KHz)

   c. Cylinder count

   d. Frequency (given in MHz)

17. Name four methods of obtaining system hardware specifications prior to
installing Linux.

18. The Windows _____ can provide many hardware details about a computer.

    a. Search dialog box

    b. FIPS program

    c. Start menu

    d. Control Panel

19. Networking information is not included in any Windows dialog boxes. True or False?

20. If you cannot find someone to assign an IP address to your computer, you can use any number temporarily. True or False?

21. A file system resides within a:

    a. Partition

    b. Track

    c. Block

    d. Sector

22. The BIOS has trouble booting Linux when:

    a. The boot record is on the active partition

    b. The Linux partition includes cylinder numbers beyond 1024

    c. The MBR refers to the active partition

    d. The IRQ of the BIOS is poorly chosen

23. Briefly define the purpose of a swap partition in Linux.

24. The FIPS program is used to split a Windows partition into two partitions. True or False?

25. When a file system is defragmented, the files are arranged so that:

    a. They are alphabetical in the directory structure.

    b. All parts of a file are next to each other on the hard disk.

    c. Compatible files are next to each other on the hard disk.

    d. Linux can easily use the files from Windows.

HANDS-ON PROJECTS

Project 2-1

In this activity you use the Windows Control Panel to find information about your hard disk. To complete this activity you need a computer with Windows installed. You can complete this activity as an exercise on a Windows computer even if you will not install Linux on the same computer later on.

1. Double-click the **My Computer** icon on the Windows Desktop. The My Computer window opens.

2. Double-click the **Control Panel** icon.

3. Double-click the **System** icon in the Control Panel window. The System Properties dialog box opens.

4. Click the **Device Manager** tab.

5. Locate the item in the Device Manager window list labeled Disk drives. Click the **+** to the left of the Disk drives label. Can you identify the interface used by the disk drives on your system based on what you see here? Does this dialog box appear to provide any information about how the partitions on the hard disk are set up?

6. Double-click the icon in the list representing a hard disk. The properties dialog box for the hard disk opens. Does the information in this dialog box help you learn about the partitions on the disk?

7. Click **Cancel** to close the hard disk properties dialog box.

8. Click **Cancel** to close the System Properties dialog box.

Project 2-2

In this activity you review the information provided on your Linux installation CD about the FIPS program. The documentation for FIPS includes information about how hard disks are organized and explains how to use FIPS. To complete this activity you need a CD containing a Linux distribution and a computer with a CD-ROM drive. This exercise assumes that you have a Red Hat Linux CD and a computer with Windows installed and a CD-ROM drive. Other types of Linux CDs can be used, but the location of the FIPS program on the CD will differ.

1. Insert your Linux CD into the CD-ROM drive.

2. Double-click the **My Computer** icon on the Windows Desktop.

3. Double-click the icon for the drive in which the Linux CD is located.

4. Double-click the **dosutils** icon.

5. Double-click the **fipsdocs** icon.

6. Double-click the **fips** document icon. (This icon may be labeled fips.doc, depending on your Windows configuration). The FIPS documentation appears in a word processing program.

7. Press **Alt+Tab** to switch back to the window showing the files in the `fipsdoc` directory.

8. Double-click on another document icon such as the techinfo (or techinfo.txt) icon.

9. Review the document files that you have opened to learn more about how FIPS operates. Open other files in the `fipsdoc` directory to learn additional information.

Project 2-3

In this activity you use the Windows Control Panel to gather information about how networking is set up on your computer. To complete this activity your computer must have Windows installed, and it must be connected to a network, either via a network adapter such as an Ethernet card, or via a modem. You can complete this activity as an exercise on a Windows computer even if you will not install Linux on the same computer later on.

1. Double-click the **My Computer** icon on the Windows Desktop. The My Computer window opens.

2. Double-click the **Control Panel** icon. The Control Panel window opens.

3. Double-click the **Network** icon.

4. Click the **Configuration** tab in the Network dialog box.

5. In the list of networking components in the Network dialog box, select the **TCP/IP** item.

6. Click **Properties** below the list of components. A TCP/IP Properties dialog box appears.

7. Click the **DNS Configuration** tab.

8. If Enable DNS is selected, write down the information in the Host, Domain, and DNS Server Search Order fields. Save this information to use when you install Linux.

9. Close all open dialog boxes without making any changes.

CASE PROJECTS

1. You have been asked to install Linux in a lab containing about 40 computers. Some of the computers are old; others are quite new. You have no experience with these particular machines, so you don't yet know anything about what they contain. Describe the steps you will take, in order, to quickly determine the different devices on which you must install Linux.

2. Assuming that some of the computers in the lab do not have any operating system installed, how does the process in Step 1 change? What resources outside of the lab might you draw on to help you identify the devices used in each computer? How might the vendors of the computers help you?

3. Now suppose you have finished studying the hardware in all of the lab's computers. Before you begin installing Linux, you have to decide which distribution of Linux to use. What would be the advantage of using the same Linux distribution on all the lab's computers? What factors might cause you to choose a different distribution, either before installation began or after you had begun to install Linux on multiple systems?

3

INSTALLING LINUX

After reading this chapter and completing the exercises, you will be able to:

♦ Discuss issues related to installing Linux

♦ Install a popular distribution of Linux

♦ Start using a new Linux system

♦ Troubleshoot problems with a Linux installation

In the previous chapter you learned how to gather information about hardware components and networking protocols as preparation for installing Linux. You also learned about preparing a computer running Microsoft Windows to be used as a dual-boot system with Linux.

In this chapter you will learn how to prepare for and install a new Linux operating system. Among other things, you will learn how to prepare Linux partitions, configure the system, and answer questions during the installation process. You will also learn what to do when the installation process doesn't work correctly. Finally, you will learn about starting Linux for the first time, after completing the installation.

UNDERSTANDING INSTALLATION ISSUES

The following sections review a few general issues related to installing Linux and explain how to answer the specific questions that arise during the installation process. Although the later parts of this chapter discuss installing the Red Hat Linux distribution included with this book, you may choose to install and use several different Linux products as you learn about Linux. Thus, this discussion concerns issues that are common to all versions of Linux.

Linux Distributions

People seem to like having favorites: one person insists that Ford trucks are better; another buys only Chevrolet. One person always drinks Coke; another chooses Pepsi every time. The differences between products may be slight, but the loyalty they inspire is not. Linux users often have similar feelings about the version or distribution they have chosen. One person insists that Debian Linux is the only reasonable choice; another uses Red Hat exclusively.

Although having a favorite is fine, remember that Linux distributions actually are very similar to each other. Each one takes the Linux kernel from the same location on the Internet, and each uses the same set of supporting utilities. Table 1-1 (in Chapter 1) names several of the better-known distributions. The list below highlights the major differences among Linux distributions. As this list indicates, you can choose a distribution with characteristics that fit your preferences.

- The installation program for each distribution is different. Linux vendors put a lot of time and money into designing their installation programs, in order to meet the needs of particular audiences. Thus, some installation programs focus on ease of use for those who are new to Linux; others focus on flexibility for users who are very familiar with Linux features.

- The arrangement of the files that make up a standard Linux system is fairly standard, but some variations are possible. Different vendors place certain configuration files in different locations. (These differences can be traced to the preferences of the software developers who assemble a particular distribution—each group of software developers has its own idea of the best way to arrange the files.) For example, Caldera OpenLinux places configuration files for the Samba network service in the directory `/etc/samba.d`, whereas Red Hat Linux places these files in the directory `/etc`. The variety of locations for configuration and initialization files makes moving from one Linux distribution to another a challenge. But overall, the differences are small compared to the total number of files installed for a typical Linux system.

- The default configuration values and the default services started on a new Linux system vary by distribution. One vendor might choose to start services or set up a user's environment slightly differently from another vendor. You can change these options after installing Linux.

- Some configuration tools used in a distribution are specifically developed by the vendor of that distribution. You will learn more about these tools in later chapters (beginning in Chapter 7). The text configuration files that control Linux are the same for all distributions, but the graphical utilities available for configuring these files are sometimes specific to one product. For example, only Red Hat Linux includes the LinuxConf utility; only Suse Linux includes the YAST utility.

- In general, each Linux vendor targets a certain type of customer. The intended customer might be very technical or very new to Linux; the customer might be business oriented or a home user; the customer might be in the United States or in another country. Linux vendors have wisely decided not to attempt to be all things to all people. Hence the distribution that you choose should match the type of customer you are (or that you intend to work for).

- Certain Linux vendors focus on creating products with the most recent versions of all software from the Internet, but they must sacrifice the time-consuming testing and documentation that other vendors choose to invest in. Having the very latest Linux features as soon as possible is a big concern for some Linux users; others prefer software that has been more thoroughly prepared for stable long-term use. For example, Debian Linux is generally considered to be dedicated to free software ideals; Red Hat Linux is usually the most current with recent Linux releases; Caldera OpenLinux is the most thoroughly tested and stable distribution; and SuSE Linux is the most suitable for international use.

Red Hat Linux

A few words about the Red Hat Linux distribution are in order here. Red Hat Linux is the most popular Linux distribution in the world (speaking of the number of people using the product). It has been around since about 1993. Red Hat was created for technical people who are actively following the Linux development community on the Internet, although more recently, Red Hat has been focusing on business users and ease of use. Some people prefer other distributions over Red Hat, but because of its popularity in the marketplace, Red Hat was selected for inclusion in this book as an installation example. Notes about installing other distributions are also included in this chapter.

The Red Hat Linux CD included with this book is the basis for the installation instructions provided in this chapter. You can, however, obtain a copy of several versions of Linux in any of the following ways:

- Use the CD provided with another book on Linux.

- Receive a free copy of Linux on CD at a trade show or other event sponsored by a Linux vendor.

- Purchase a Linux CD for less than $5 from a company such as Linux Mall (at *www.linuxmall.com*).

- Purchase a retail copy of Linux at a software store or bookstore. (Retail versions often include multiple CDs and a printed user manual.)

- Download Linux from the FTP site of a Linux vendor, such as *ftp.redhat.com*. (This option is free but takes a long time to download unless you have a very fast Internet connection.)

The Installation Process

Installing an operating system on a computer is different from installing an application like a word processor. When you install an application, the existing operating system takes control and provides a foundation for the installation process. When you install a new operating system, only the hardware is available—no other software can assist the installation process.

The new operating system must somehow initialize itself sufficiently to install itself on the computer.

You use a Linux installation utility to install Linux onto the hard disk of a computer. The general procedure is as follows:

1. Start the installation program from a CD, floppy disk, or other source.

2. Run a very small copy of Linux within the computer's RAM.

3. Determine (based on user input or by automatically probing the system) where the installation source data is located. (This is described in the next section.)

4. Determine (based on user input or by automatically probing the system) where the Linux operating system should be installed. A **target hard disk partition**, or target partition, is the location on the system's hard disk where Linux will be installed.

5. Collect user input to determine which software packages to install on the target partition.

6. Collect user input to determine configuration settings such as network addresses, preferred services to execute, keyboard settings, and so forth.

7. Copy the Linux software packages from the installation source to the target partition.

8. Finish setting up the software packages on the target partition so they are ready to use.

9. Configure the LILO boot manager and install it on the boot sector (or MBR) of a hard disk so that the computer's BIOS can launch Linux.

10. Restart the computer to launch the newly installed Linux operating system.

Some of the steps in the previous list are handled automatically by the installation program you use to install Linux; most steps require that you answer one or more questions about how the Linux system will be set up. More detailed information about these steps is presented later in this chapter. This information will help you understand how to answer the questions presented during a Linux installation.

Installation Source Options

The **installation source** is the set of files from which Linux is installed. In this book, it is assumed that your files are stored on a Linux CD and then copied to the hard disk in an orderly manner during the installation process. If your installation files are stored on another medium, you can specify the exact location as you install Linux. The following list summarizes the most common installation sources:

- Local CD-ROM: use the files from the CD-ROM drive attached to the system on which you are installing Linux.

- Local hard disk: use a copy of the CD-ROM files that has been stored on a hard disk within the system on which you are installing Linux. (This must be a hard disk partition or hard disk that is separate from the location where Linux will be installed.)

- Floppy disks: read a series of floppy disks in order to retrieve all the Linux installation source files during the installation process. This method is rarely used for standard Linux distributions because it would require over 100 disks for most installations. Also, CD-ROM drives are very commonly available now.

- Network installation: read the Linux installation source files from a server connected to the same network as the computer on which you are installing Linux. You can use the network to access installation data in a variety of formats, including FTP (a standard Internet format), SMB (used by Microsoft Windows servers), and NFS (the Network File System protocol, commonly available on all Linux and UNIX systems). Using a network installation requires some additional configuration on the server that will provide the installation source, but this method allows you, as a system administrator, to install multiple Linux systems from a single networked copy of the installation source.

A few specialized versions of Linux are completely contained on a single floppy disk. For information on one of these specialized products, visit the homepage of the Linux Router Project at *www.linuxrouter.org*.

When installing Linux from a network, be careful not to violate copyright restrictions by installing a Linux distribution on systems for which you do not have a software license. Many Linux products have no restrictions on installing the product on more than one system; some commercial versions of Linux, or software included with commercial versions of Linux, may only permit you to install the software on one computer for each copy you have purchased.

To use a networked installation source, you must prepare another computer to provide the installation data. Because this involves setting up networking services that are beyond the scope of this book, you should contact the system administrator of the networked server you want to use. To use a Microsoft Windows server for the Linux installation source, ask the system administrator of the Windows system to prepare a share containing the CD-ROM drive (or a hard disk onto which the CD data has been copied). To use the NFS protocol on a Linux or UNIX server, ask the system administrator to export the CD or hard disk directory containing the Linux installation source. Some Linux vendors provide FTP servers for installations that download files from the Internet as the product is installed. (If the version of Linux you are installing supports FTP-based installation, you will see an option for selecting FTP during the installation program.)

Red Hat Linux supports installation from CD-ROM or local hard disk, plus network-based installations from NFS, SMB, or FTP servers.

Starting the Installation

When you turn on a computer, the BIOS normally sends control to the MBR of the first hard disk so that the operating system on the hard disk can launch. To install Linux, however, you must pass control directly to the Linux installation program without first starting the operating system on the hard disk. In the past, this was normally accomplished by using a **boot disk** (a floppy disk that has a portion of the Linux installation program on it). But newer computer systems have bootable CD-ROM drives. A **bootable CD-ROM drive** is one that can launch an operating system (or other program) directly from a CD without accessing the hard disk.

Most Linux CDs (including the one provided with this book) are bootable CDs. To see if your CD-ROM drive is bootable, try inserting the installation CD into the CD-ROM drive and then restarting the computer. If the installation program launches, your CD-ROM drive is bootable.

 If the installation program does not start from the installation CD, it's possible that your CD-ROM drive is bootable, but that the BIOS is configured to start the operating system from the hard disk first. You can change the order in which devices are checked at boot time by reconfiguring the BIOS as described in Chapter 2.

Not all systems can boot directly from a CD. As a backup, virtually all systems can start the computer from a boot disk. (A boot disk is also called an **install disk** on some distributions of Linux.) After starting the system with a boot disk, the installation program locates the installation source on a CD or network server and proceeds with the installation. The CD containing the Linux installation source data also contains a copy of a boot disk in the form of a disk image. A **disk image** is a single file that contains an exact copy of a floppy disk. You can copy the disk image from the CD to a floppy disk by using the `rawrite` utility in DOS or Windows, or the `dd` utility on an existing Linux system.

Often you will need two disks to start the Linux installation because the necessary data will not fit on one disk. This is especially true if you are installing Linux on a laptop computer. Installing Linux on laptops is generally more challenging than installing it on a desktop system because laptops are more likely to contain unusual hardware components or components that are very new (and thus lack complete support in Linux). A great resource for information about installing Linux on various laptop models is the Linux on Laptops Web page, located at *www.cs.utexas.edu/users/kharker/linux-laptop/*.

Different distributions of Linux use different names for the disks used to start the Linux installation. One distribution calls the disks "Install" and "Modules," another calls them "boot" and "root." The Red Hat Linux CD included with this book uses the following three disk names. Each one is a file (with the file extension .img) located in the images subdirectory of the CD.:

- boot: used for standard installations from a CD.
- bootnet: used when the installation source is located on a network server (such as an NFS server).

- pcmcia: used to install Red Hat Linux on a laptop when the PCMCIA cards must be accessed to complete the installation. This occurs in two situations: when the device containing the installation source (such as a SCSI hard disk) is attached using a PCMCIA expansion card, or when installation is from a network server through a PCMCIA network adapter card. If neither of these situations applies, only the boot or bootnet disk is required.

To make a disk from a disk image on a CD in a Microsoft Windows computer, follow these steps. Note that these steps work for any Linux distribution, although the disk image names given in the steps are specific to the Red Hat Linux CD.

1. Insert the Red Hat Linux CD in a computer running Windows 95/98.

2. Use the Windows Explorer window to display the contents of the `dosutils` subdirectory on the CD. Note the drive letter associated with the CD-ROM drive (normally D: or E:).

3. Double-click the icon for the `rawrite` program. The program launches.

4. When you see the prompt for the name of a disk image file, enter the filename of the disk image you want to create. For example, if the CD–ROM drive is drive D: and you need to create the boot disk for Red Hat Linux, enter this:

`D:\images\boot.img`

5. You are now prompted for the drive letter of the floppy disk drive. Enter the letter for this disk drive (normally either A: or B:).

6. You are prompted to press Enter to begin creating the disk. Press Enter to do so. The process of copying the image file to disk may take several minutes. When the process is completed, the floppy disk drive stops rotating. You can then close the `rawrite` program window in Windows and remove the disk you created.

7. Label the disk you created as **Red Hat Boot Disk** and put it in a safe place, so you can use it to install Linux. (Labeling the disk is especially important if you must use more than one disk to start Linux; otherwise, you might attempt to begin the installation with the wrong disk.)

THE INSTALLATION PROCESS

When you begin the Linux installation program, you must respond to a series of questions about how to install and configure the new Linux system. These questions may appear on a graphical screen, as shown in Figure 3-1, or on a text-based screen, as shown in Figure 3-2. Each version of Linux uses a different installation program, though they all ask very similar questions to complete the installation process. Some installation programs (such as the one for Slackware Linux) assume you know a lot about your hardware and about Linux. They ask many questions that a new Linux user may not be prepared to answer. Other products, such as Red Hat Linux and Caldera OpenLinux, are intended for new Linux users. They automate many functions and ask you fewer questions as you install Linux. Although some users might prefer to answer as few questions as possible, others appreciate the customization options such questions imply.

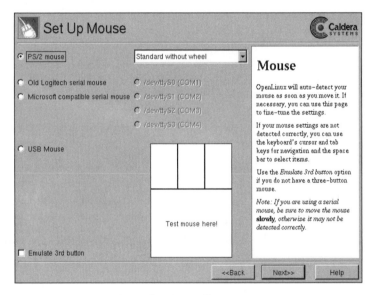

Figure 3-1 Typical graphical installation screen

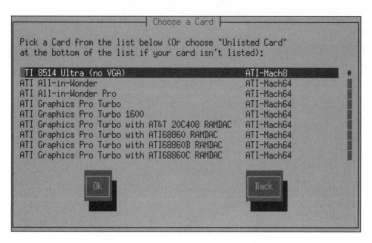

Figure 3-2   Typical text-based installation screen

As you install a Red Hat Linux distribution, you have several opportunities to enter information about your system and select which components of Linux you want to install, but overall, Red Hat Linux tries to minimize the information needed from the person completing the installation. Red Hat Linux also provides both a graphical installation and a text-based installation. The graphical installation is used by default, but on many systems you may encounter problems with the video card. For these systems you can use the text-based installation program.

The sections that follow explain some of the information that you must provide during a typical Linux installation, with specific comments related to the Red Hat Linux product included with this book.

 Projects 3-1 and 3-2, at the end of this chapter, provide step-by-step instructions for installing the version of Red Hat Linux provided with this book.

Answering Initial Questions

After you have started the installation program from a bootable CD-ROM or floppy drive, you need to answer questions about how to interact with the installation program. For example, you must choose a keyboard layout and a language for the installation. Depending on the version of Linux you are using, you might also be asked about your mouse, time zone, video card, or other details before selecting an installation source and target partition.

In many versions of Linux, you can back up to change your answer to previously asked questions. Because nothing is written to the hard disk of the computer until you have specified a target hard disk partition, you can also turn off the computer and restart the installation if you become concerned that you have not made correct selections. (Because nothing is written to hard disk in the early part of an installation, you can turn off the computer's power without the risk of losing data.)

Preparing Hard Disk Partitions

In Chapter 2 you learned how to prepare space on a Microsoft Windows computer so that you can install Linux on a hard disk where Windows is already installed. In this section you learn how to use that free space, or free hard disk space on any hard disk, to prepare for the installation of Linux.

The Linux installation program allows you to set up the partitions on your hard disk. Setting up Linux partitions involves the following steps, as you may recall from Chapter 2:

- Define a swap partition
- Define a Linux partition
- Mark the Linux partition as the active partition

Most Linux installation programs let you use a utility called **fdisk** (for *fixed disk*, meaning a hard disk). The **fdisk** utility is used to create partitions and configure how they are used. This utility is started from the installation program. (It can also be used after you have installed Linux to make changes in hard disk partitions.) Other utilities that have been developed by Linux vendors provide similar functionality, usually with an easier-to-use interface.

Hard Disk Specifications

Hard disks in Linux are identified by device names that resemble directory names. Later in this book you will learn more about how devices in Linux are accessed via the same directory structure as normal files. For now, you only need to know that certain names represent hard disk devices and partitions in Linux.

Hard disks that are attached to the computer using the IDE interface are identified as **/dev/hda** for the first hard disk, **/dev/hdb** for the second hard disk, and so forth, to **/dev/hdd** for the fourth hard disk. If you need to refer to a specific partition, you can add a partition number after the device name. For example, the first partition on the second IDE hard disk is represented as **/dev/hdb1**.

Hard disks that include the SCSI interface use a similar pattern of names, but with the letters *sd* instead of *hd*. For example, the first SCSI hard disk is **/dev/sda**. The second partition on the second SCSI hard disk is **/dev/sdb2**.

You will use these same device names to refer to a CD-ROM drive that is attached to the IDE or SCSI controller card on the system. For example, the CD-ROM drive is often attached as the third IDE device (the first device on the second IDE controller). Thus, the CD-ROM can be accessed by referring to **/dev/hdc**. (CD-ROMs do not have multiple partitions as hard disks do.)

Deciding on Mount Points

Unlike other operating systems, a Linux system does not use drive letters. Instead, different devices are accessed using subdirectories of a single directory structure. For example, in Windows, you might use the designations shown in Table 3-1.

Table 3-1 Typical Drive Letter Assignments in Windows

Drive	Description
A:	Floppy drive
C:	Main Windows hard disk partition
D:	Secondary Windows hard disk partition or second Windows hard disk
E:	CD-ROM drive
F:	Network server home directory

3

Instead of using drive letters, Linux defines a mount point for different file systems or devices that can contain data. A **mount point** is a subdirectory through which a set of data is accessed. Table 3-2 shows how the devices in Table 3-1 might be represented on a Linux system.

Table 3-2 Typical Subdirectory Mount Points Used to Access File Systems in Linux

Subdirectory (mount point)	Description
/mnt/floppy	Floppy drive
/	Main Linux hard disk partition
/opt	Secondary Linux hard disk partition or second Windows hard disk
/mnt/cdrom	CD-ROM drive
/remote_home	Network server home directory

The directory names used as mount points are arbitrary, but standard names are normally used for some devices, such as /mnt/floppy for the floppy disk drive. You will learn much more about setting up mount points in Linux in Chapter 8.

To complete the installation, you must be prepared to specify mount points for the new Linux system. The only mount point you *must* specify is the root partition, for the root directory, /. You must define which hard disk partition will hold this directory and its subdirectories. You can also define mount points for other hard disk partitions if you choose to. Because devices such as floppy disks and CD-ROM drives are not permanently available (you can insert and remove multiple disks as you work in Linux), these devices are not used during installation as mount points for installation files.

In Chapter 4 you will learn about the subdirectories that make up a standard Linux file system. One of the standard subdirectories is /home, where the home directory for each user account on the system is normally stored. For example, /home/nwells is a home directory for the user account nwells. During the installation you can place different subdirectories on different hard disk partitions by defining the subdirectory as a mount point.

When installing a very large Linux server supporting hundreds of users, it would be common to place the core operating system on one hard disk, all the user home directories on a second hard disk, and all the applications and data on a third hard disk. You would define this type of configuration during the installation as you set up the mount points for various directories. In this example, you might define the mount points listed in Table 3-3.

Table 3-3   Example Mount Points for a Multiple Partition Installation

Mount point	Device
/	/dev/hda2
/home	/dev/hdb1
/opt	/dev/hdb2

Your first few Linux installations shouldn't require anything but the / mount point for the main Linux system. The entire operating system will then be installed on a single partition. The following list gives a few reasons why you might want to use multiple partitions for a Linux installation as you become more experienced and work on larger and more complex Linux systems:

- Placing the core operating system files on a separate partition allows you to upgrade the operating system without disturbing user data files or applications.

- Placing the core operating system files on a separate partition prevents user data files or applications from filling all hard disk space that the operating system needs in order to continue functioning.

- Storing user data on a separate partition may make it easier to create backups of that data.

- Separating data onto multiple partitions and setting up different options for how each partition is accessed allows you to implement certain security features. (This is described in Chapter 8.)

- Having multiple hard disks working to retrieve data at the same time can improve performance.

Using fdisk

During the installation process you must prepare a target partition where Linux will be installed before the installation source files can be copied to that partition. The installation program often gives you the opportunity to start the fdisk utility to prepare a target partition. Using the fdisk utility within an installation program can be a little intimidating: the screen goes blank except for a single line with the text Command (m for help):, and if you make a mistake, you might erase everything on the hard disk.

When the installation program you are using starts fdisk, the utility reads the partition table from a hard disk. The **partition table** is the information that defines the size and location on the hard disk for each partition. You modify that partition information using commands within fdisk. Nothing is actually written to the hard disk until you tell fdisk to do so, at which point the partition information is updated on the hard disk.

Although `fdisk` doesn't provide much assistance to new users, you can always use the **m** command to list the available commands in `fdisk` and the **p** command to list the partitions currently defined for the hard disk. Figure 3-3 shows sample output for the **p** command.

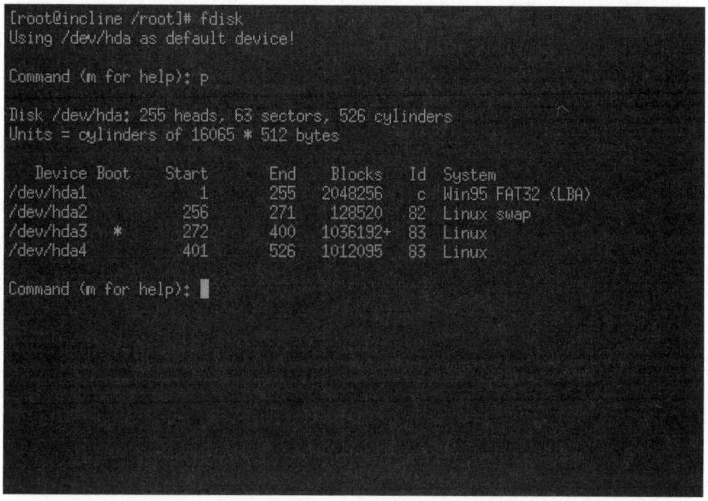

```
[root@incline /root]# fdisk
Using /dev/hda as default device!

Command (m for help): p

Disk /dev/hda: 255 heads, 63 sectors, 526 cylinders
Units = cylinders of 16065 * 512 bytes

   Device Boot    Start      End    Blocks   Id  System
/dev/hda1             1      255   2048256    c  Win95 FAT32 (LBA)
/dev/hda2           256      271    128520   82  Linux swap
/dev/hda3    *      272      400   1036192+  83  Linux
/dev/hda4           401      526   1012095   83  Linux

Command (m for help): 
```

Figure 3-3   The `fdisk` utility showing a command list and a partition table

The steps for using `fdisk` to create a Linux partition are given below in two sets of steps. The first creates a Linux swap partition, the second creates a Linux native partition. Review these for now, and be prepared to follow them if necessary later, when you complete the hands-on projects at the end of this chapter.

In these steps it is assumed that you have a single hard disk and want to place the swap partition and main Linux partition on that hard disk.

1. When you have indicated to the installation program that you need to work with partitions (you must explicitly select `fdisk` as well), the screen changes to a black background and the message `Command (m for help):` appears. Type **p** to list the partitions currently defined on the hard disk.

2. If you used the `FIPS` program in Chapter 2 to create two separate Windows partitions (the second one being empty), study the partition information listed by the **p** command to determine which partition contains Windows data and which is empty. Because the empty Windows partition is the space you will use for Linux, you must delete that empty Windows partition before creating a new Linux partition. Enter **d** to delete a partition. When prompted, enter the number of the partition you want to delete.

3. Enter **n** to begin creating a new partition.

4. Enter **p** for primary partition. (You can create more than four partitions on a hard disk using extended, or logical, partitions, but you shouldn't need to do this.)

5. Enter the partition number you are creating. For this value, enter the next free partition on the hard disk. (For example, if only one partition is defined, for Windows, then the next available partition number is 2.)

6. Begin to define the size of the new partition by entering its first cylinder as requested. The range of available cylinders on the hard disk is listed in parentheses, like this:

```
First cylinder (201-526, default 201):
```

Enter the first number in parentheses as the starting point for the new partition.

7. Enter a size for the ending point of the new partition. Enter **+128M** to create a swap partition of 128 MB. You can choose the appropriate size for your installation based on the amount of RAM on the system and the size of the hard disk.

8. Enter **t** to set the type of the new partition.

9. When prompted, enter the partition number of the new partition you just created.

10. Enter **82** as the partition type when prompted for it. This is the code number for the Linux swap partition.

11. Use the **p** command again to see how the new partition is defined.

TIP   The size you enter for the swap partition is rounded to the size of the nearest cylinder, so it may not be exactly the size that you specified.

Next, you will need to create a native Linux partition (on which the operating system will be stored). Once again, review the following steps, and be prepared to use them later if necessary.

1. Enter **n** to begin creating a new partition.

2. Enter **p** for primary partition.

3. Enter the partition number you are creating by referring to the output of the **p** command and using the next available number.

4. When the size is requested, the range of available cylinders on the hard disk is listed in parentheses, like this:

```
First cylinder (201-526, default 201):
```

Enter the first number you see in parentheses. (For example, if the system displays the text above, enter the number 201.) This number specifies the starting point for the new partition.

You cannot use cylinder number 1 as the first cylinder of a partition because that cylinder is reserved for storing the partition table. If something seems to be wrong with the `fdisk` program because of an entry such as cylinder number 1, press Ctrl+C to exit `fdisk` without making any changes, and then run the program again.

3

5. Enter the second number in parentheses. This second number that you enter specifies the ending point of the new partition. To use the rest of the hard disk space for Linux, use the second number (526 in the sample output). If you want to create a Linux partition of a specific size, enter that size now (just as you did earlier for the swap partition). For example, to create a 700 MB partition, enter **+700M**.

6. Next, you need to specify the type of the new partition. To specify the partition type, enter **t**, enter the partition number for the partition you just created, and then enter **83**. (83 is the code number for a Linux native partition.)

7. Enter **b** to define the bootable or active partition on the hard disk.

8. Enter the partition number of the Linux native partition that you just defined.

9. Use the **p** command to see how the new partitions are defined. You should see an asterisk (*) next to the Linux native partition, indicating that the partition is active.

10. If you are satisfied with the partition changes you have made, write them to the hard disk by entering **w** for write. This command also exits the `fdisk` utility. If you used the numbers described in the steps, as prompted by `fdisk`, the remaining space on the hard disk is used for a newly created Linux partition when you enter the **w** command.

You can also exit the `fdisk` utility without making any changes to your hard disk by entering **q** for quit.

You may be prompted by the installation program to restart the computer after changing the partition table with `fdisk`. By restarting the computer you ensure that the partition table is correctly read by the installation program.

Using Disk Druid

The Red Hat Linux installation program includes a tool called Disk Druid. You can use Disk Druid instead of `fdisk` to set up partitions on the hard disk. The installation program prompts you to use Disk Druid before the installation source can be copied to a target partition. The utility provides the same basic functionality as `fdisk`, but within an easier-to-use interface. In addition to creating partitions, Disk Druid defines the mount points for Linux subdirectories. If you have already used `fdisk` or a commercial partition management product to create the Linux partitions (swap and native Linux) needed for the installation, you only need to define which partition on the hard disk should act as a mount point for the installation source files. This is the same Linux partition that you created in `fdisk` or Disk Druid, but you must manually select the partition at this point in the installation process.

Figure 3-4 shows the Disk Druid utility. The bottom half of the screen lists hard disks on the system. (On most systems, only a single hard disk, /dev/hda, is listed.) The top half of the screen lists the partitions on the selected (or only) hard disk. For each partition, a column notes the type of file system assigned to that partition (such as Linux swap or Linux Native, ext2), the size, and the mount point (if applicable, for native Linux partitions).

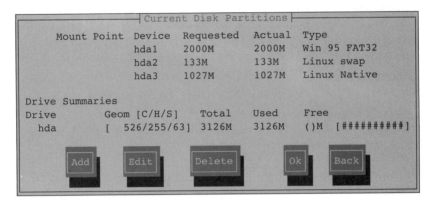

Figure 3-4 The Disk Druid utility in Red Hat Linux

Follow the next series of steps to set up new partitions in Disk Druid.

 TIP If you have not created a swap partition, create that partition first using these steps. The swap partition does not have a mount point because it is not accessed as part of the Linux directory structure.

1. Press the **Tab** key until the Add button is highlighted. The Add button begins the process of creating a new partition.

2. Press **Enter**. The Edit New Partition dialog box appears. Here, you can use the Tab and arrow keys to move to various fields.

3. Enter values for the mount point (this should be a forward slash, /), the file system type (this should be **ext2** to indicate a native Linux partition), and the partition size according to your preference.

4. If you want the partition size to use all remaining disk space, select the Grow to fill check box by pressing the Spacebar. (Don't use this option until you first create a swap partition.)

You may have created the necessary swap and native Linux partitions in another program such as **fdisk** or a commercial partitioning utility. In this case, you only need to follow these steps when Disk Druid starts:

1. Use the arrow keys to select the partition (in the top part of the Disk Druid window) that corresponds to the partition you want to use as the root of the Linux file system (the partition in which you want to install Linux).

2. Press **Tab** repeatedly until the Edit button is selected; then press **Enter**.

3. Enter **/** as the mount point for the partition.

4. Press **Tab** until the OK button is selected; then press **Enter**.

When you have created any necessary new partitions or, at a minimum, defined a partition that has **/** as a mount point, you can continue with the installation of Red Hat Linux.

Other Linux installation programs include their own specialized partitioning tools that are similar to Disk Druid. For example, Caldera OpenLinux provides a graphical tool that allows you to define partitions and mount points much as you do in Disk Druid. SuSE Linux uses the YAST configuration tool for setting up the target hard disk partition (and for selecting most other configuration options). Other versions of Linux use other tools.

Choosing What to Install

As you'll recall from Chapter 1, each Linux distribution comprises hundreds of different programs, including the Linux kernel, the Apache Web server, the GNU project system utilities, programming languages, compilers, graphical systems, games, and so forth. When installing Linux, you must decide which of these components to install, although the amount of freedom you have in making these choices varies by distribution.

Some distributions group the many possible components into a few different installation types. The **installation type** you choose determines which Linux software to install; the right installation type for your system depends on how the system will be used. For example, you might have a choice of installing a minimal system (which includes only the most basic components), installing a standard system (which includes the components the average user would be likely to use), or installing everything from the CD. Often, however, you will have more options regarding which software components you want to install.

Most Linux systems (including Red Hat, SuSE, Caldera, and Debian) gather many related files into a single software package. For example, all Linux products provide the Apache Web server, which is made up of dozens of files, as a software package. A **software package** is a single file that contains all the files needed to install and use an application or group of related applications. Special data formats are used to store many files in a software package. The Red Hat Package Manager format (abbreviated as `rpm`) is the most popular data storage format for creating software packages. Different data storage formats employed by Debian Linux also allow all of the files associated with an application to be stored in a single software package.

You will learn more about the `rpm` format in Chapter 4. Typical Linux products include between 400 and 1500 software packages. (To simplify matters, these packages are grouped into functional categories such as "text processing," "networking utilities," or "software development tool." Some Linux installations employ further generalizations based on a broad usage category for the Linux system. For example, a single selection such as "Web server installation" or "Desktop system" might define all of the categories, software packages, and files to install. During the installation you can specify which sets of packages or which type of system you want to install. Different Linux distributions allow different levels of detail in this selection process. Figure 3-5 illustrates the variety of groupings, from general installation types to specific files.

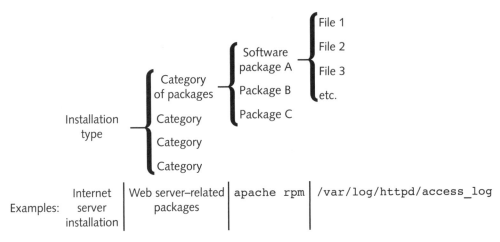

Figure 3-5   Files, software packages, categories of packages, and installation types

Red Hat Linux provides a few high-level installation types, such as Gnome Workstation, to create a desktop system using the Gnome graphical desktop. In addition, Red Hat Linux provides a Custom option that lets you select various categories of software packages according to your needs. The Custom option requires you to make decisions about 25 different categories of software packages. For each package, you need to decide whether to include or exclude it from the installation. Although it entails more work on your part, the Custom installation type is recommended for two reasons. First, it allows you to see the many options provided by the distribution you are installing. Second, it allows you to customize your installation to fit your needs. Table 3-4 shows the categories of packages (called Package Groups) that Red Hat Linux provides during a Custom Server installation.

Table 3-4   Package Groups in Red Hat Linux

Package Group	Description
Printer Support	Provides the ability to send documents to local or remote printers using standard Linux print server programs
X Window System	Provides the foundation for graphical applications in Linux. Required for the Gnome or KDE option
GNOME	Adds the Gnome graphical desktop interface to the system
KDE	Adds the KDE graphical desktop interface to the system
Mail/WWW/News Tools	Allows client access to the Internet for reading e-mail, browsing the Web, and reading newsgroups
DOS/Windows Connectivity	Includes programs that help you connect to DOS or Windows systems on the same network

3

Table 3-4   Package Groups in Red Hat Linux (continued)

Package Group	Description
Graphics Manipulation	Provides software for viewing and creating graphics files in various formats
Games	Adds a variety of Linux games to the system
Multimedia Support	Includes drivers and other software for using a sound card and playing video clips within Linux
Networked Workstation	Provides a collection of utilities considered useful if you are using Linux on a local network (such as an Ethernet or Token Ring network)
Dialup Workstation	Provides a collection of utilities considered useful if you are using Linux as a client that dials a modem to connect to a network
News Server	Provides Usenet newsgroup server capabilities
NFS Server	Provides the ability to make local file systems (hard disk partitions) available to users working on other computers
SMB (Samba) Server	Provides the ability to make local Linux resources available across the network to users working on Windows-based computers
IPX/NetWare Connectivity	Provides the ability to connect to NetWare servers located on the same network as the Linux system
Anonymous FTP Server	Lets Linux act as an FTP server to provide file downloads to networked users
Web Server	Installs and activates an Apache Web server on Linux
DNS Name Server	Allows Linux to act as a DNS server for other computers on the same network that need to convert domain names to IP addresses
Postgres (SQL) Server	Provides a complete client/server database on Linux (using the freely available Postgres program)
Network Management Workstation	Installs utilities considered useful for someone using the Linux system to manage other systems on a local network
TeX Document Formatting	Provides text-processing capabilities using the TeX document language (commonly used on UNIX systems)
Emacs	Installs the large and powerful Emacs text editor
Development	Provides software components needed to develop Linux software or compile Linux source code files
Kernel Development	Provides software components needed to change the Linux kernel after installation
Extra Documentation	Installs additional documentation files
Utilities	Installs additional useful Linux command-line and graphical utilities
Everything	Installs everything on the Red Hat Linux CD-ROM

TIP Red Hat Linux also allows you to select individual packages to install, but choosing among 600 or so packages takes more effort than most people can invest during the installation process. You'll find it easier to install package groups when installing Linux. Then you can easily add or remove individual software packages after completing the installation.

User Accounts

The Linux installation process creates an administrative user account named **root**, which is used for system management. Whoever has access to this account can control the entire system. During installation, you must specify a password for the **root** user account. Choose this password carefully and guard against anyone discovering the password. Because the **root** account is so powerful, you should only use it to complete system administration work.

For security purposes, you will not see the **root** password on screen as you type it. This prevents anyone from observing the password as you type. You will be prompted to enter the password a second time to make sure you typed it correctly.

The **root** account is created automatically—you only have to provide the password. In some distributions (including Red Hat Linux) you may also be prompted to create another user account besides **root**. If you are prompted to do so, choose a brief username of eight characters or less (such as nwells, thomasj, jane, or rms). Depending on your version of Linux, you may be prompted to enter a full name (your own complete name, such as Nicholas Wells), a password, or other information. You can use the commands described in Chapter 8 to change or add information to this user account after you have completed the installation.

Configuring the Graphical System

As mentioned in Chapter 2, configuring the graphical system (the video card) is the most challenging part of most Linux installations. The Linux installation program is designed to configure the video card for you, but you may need to enter some of the hardware information you gathered in Chapter 2 in order to complete the installation. If you are using the standard XFree86 graphical software included with all Linux distributions, you'll find the configuration file located at **/etc/X11/XF86Config** on a Red Hat Linux system, or **/etc/XF86Config** on some other Linux systems.

If the graphical configuration that you set up during the installation process does not appear to work correctly after starting the new Linux system, try entering one of the following commands (at a command line) to reconfigure the graphical system. (Keep in mind that not all of these commands are available on all Linux systems.) Note the upper- and lowercase letters used in each command name.

- **Xconfigurator**
- **lizardx**
- **XF86Setup**
- **xf86config**

Configuring the Boot Loader

During the Linux installation you will have the option of installing the Linux boot manager (LILO) in one of several locations. The option that you select depends on how you have configured the other operating systems on the computer and on how you want to start Linux. If you are uncertain, you can select the option that is preselected by the installation program. This option is based on the status of your system as determined by the installation program when it probes your hard disk. The following list explains reasons for choosing each of the possible locations for LILO:

- The Master Boot Record or MBR: this location ensures that Linux boots correctly after a new installation. When LILO is installed in the MBR, control passes from the BIOS of the computer directly to LILO, which can then start Linux directly. Many system administrators try to avoid writing LILO to the MBR because it may interfere with other operating systems used on the same computer, such as Windows NT.

- The boot sector of the partition on which Linux is being installed: this is the recommended location for LILO. When LILO is installed here, control passes from the BIOS to the MBR, to the copy of LILO stored on the boot sector of the active partition. LILO can then start Linux or pass control to another partition to start another operating system, such as Windows 2000. This method assumes that the partition on which Linux was installed is marked as the bootable or active partition. If it is not, control will pass from the BIOS to the MBR to the active (non-Linux) partition, and LILO will never be invoked (hence Linux cannot be started). If Linux is not installed on the active partition, the MBR or the active partition must contain a boot manager of some type (BootMagic, another copy of LILO, or another boot manager program) in order to have the option of starting Linux on the nonactive partition that you are installing.

- A floppy disk: this allows you to keep the MBR intact and leave another partition (such as one containing Windows) as the active partition while allowing you to start Linux from a floppy disk. When LILO is installed on a floppy disk, you can only start Linux by inserting that floppy disk into the computer. Then when you turn on the computer, control passes from the BIOS to the floppy disk containing LILO. LILO then starts Linux (or other operating systems if so configured). If the floppy disk is not inserted, the Linux operating system cannot be started and has no effect on other operating systems stored on the computer.

When you start a computer system, you see the word LILO appear very briefly on the screen as the LILO program is loaded and executed. Then a prompt appears at which you can enter the name of the operating system you want to start. The prompt used by LILO is boot:. When you see this prompt, you can press the Tab key to see a list of the operating system names that LILO recognizes. This list includes linux. It also includes either dos or win if you have a computer system on which Windows is also installed.

STARTING LINUX

After you have installed Linux, you can reboot the computer and begin using the operating system. The following sections describe how to begin working with the newly installed operating system.

Logging In

You cannot do anything on a Linux system until you have logged in using a valid username and password. The term **logging in** refers to the process of identifying yourself as a valid user who has been assigned a certain set of access rights. **Authentication** is another, more precise, term for logging in. Authentication also refers to entering a valid username and password, but it implies that the system has verified the identity of a user based on specific rules.

Although you should not use the administrative account, named `root`, for normal work, it may be the only account available on your system immediately after installation. In this case, use the username `root` and the password you entered during the installation to log in to your system, and immediately create another user account as described later in this chapter.

Depending on the configuration of your new Linux system, you might see a character-based login screen like the one shown in Figure 3-6, or a graphical login screen like the one shown in Figure 3-7. The character-based login screen starts a command-line interface after you log in; the graphical login screen starts a graphical desktop interface after you log in.

Figure 3-6   Character-based login screen

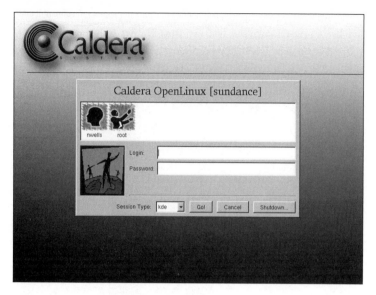

Figure 3-7   Graphical login screen

Starting the Graphical System

Linux systems that use a graphical login screen similar to the one shown in Figure 3-7 will change immediately to a graphical display after you enter a username and password. After logging in at a character-based screen, you can enter a command to start the graphical system. On most Linux systems you can use the following command (in all lowercase letters) to start the graphical system:

```
startx
```

Of course, in order to use this command you must have previously configured the graphical system. This is normally done during the installation process, although it is a challenging part of the installation and may require additional work after completing the installation.

Most recent Linux distributions provide a desktop graphical interface known as KDE. The desktop provided by Red Hat Linux is called Gnome. Figure 3-8 shows the Gnome desktop as it would appear after a new installation. Chapter 5 describes the graphical system in detail and explains how to configure it.

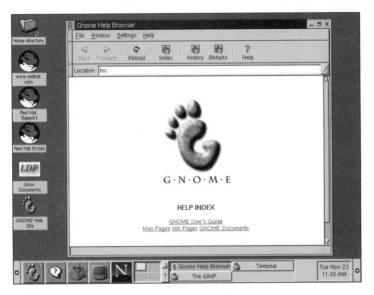

Figure 3-8   The Gnome desktop interface

Creating the First User Account

Many Linux distributions (including Red Hat Linux) create a regular user account during installation. A **regular user account** is a user account that is not used for system administration work (as the `root` account is). A regular user account has a name similar to a person's name, such as nwells, or georgew.

You should always use a regular user account to log in to Linux. If you did not define a regular user account during the installation, create one immediately after you log in to the new system as `root`. After creating a regular user account, use it for all work except system administration tasks. Note that you can only create a new user account when you are logged in as the `root` user.

Any one of several utilities will allow you to create a new user account. The most common command-line utility for creating user accounts is called either `useradd`, or `adduser` (depending on your system). On Red Hat Linux, you can create a new user account by combining the `useradd` command with a new user account name. For example, to create a new user account named `nwells`, you would log in as `root`, and then enter the following command:

```
useradd nwells
```

Managing user accounts is a large part of the work of a system administrator. Chapter 8 describes in detail how to set up user accounts with many different optional settings and how to manage those accounts on a busy Linux system.

Testing Network Connections

Networking is configured as part of the installation process. Many users will want to begin using the network connection immediately after installation, in order to send e-mail, browse the Web, or otherwise communicate with other networked users. Before using the connection, though, try a few simple commands to make sure it is correctly configured. Note that you do not have to be logged in as **root** to use the commands discussed in this section.

The **ping** command is used to test a network connection. To test your connection, begin by entering the following:

```
ping 127.0.0.1
```

You should see lines appear on screen once every second. Press Ctrl+C to stop the command. If no lines appear, networking is not configured or activated on your system. If the first **ping** command worked, try this next command, using the IP address that you entered for your system during the installation. (If you did not enter an IP address during installation, networking is not yet configured, and these tests do not apply.)

```
ping <IP address>
```

If you see lines appear once every second, your network adapter card has been configured. If no lines appear, see the following troubleshooting sections for suggestions on configuring your network adapter. Next, try to contact a remote site using an IP address. (You can use any IP address that corresponds to a real server on your local network or on the Internet, if you have an Internet connection.) For example, you might try the following command:

```
ping 207.49.12.1
```

If lines appear once every second, you have established a connection with another computer. Finally, try using a domain name with the **ping** command:

```
ping www.yahoo.com
```

If lines appear once every second, you are ready to use the network. If this last test fails (that is, if no lines appear), you need to configure your DNS server address. See the following troubleshooting sections.

To access the Internet using a Web browser, you may also need to configure your Web browser to use different server names or addresses for security purposes. Ask your system administrator or ISP if any configuration changes are required.

The preceding information outlines only the most basic network information. Complete details on configuring and using networking are beyond the scope of this book.

TROUBLESHOOTING A NEW INSTALLATION

Depending on your Linux distribution and your computer hardware, the installation process may go very smoothly, or you may have to overcome numerous obstacles. The following sections provide guidance on how to solve some common problems you might encounter during a difficult Linux installation. Not all possible problems are covered here, of course. In fact, some problems may not have solutions, because a system may have hardware that is not supported by Linux. (You would normally discover this while you gathered information about the computer before installation, as described in Chapter 2.) In addition, some troubleshooting requires knowledge far beyond what has been presented so far in this book. If your efforts don't succeed, ask a Linux expert for help.

The System Won't Boot

If the Linux installation program will not start, the problem may lie with the boot disk, which may not contain all the necessary files. You might also be trying to start the installation from a device that is not used by the BIOS during the system start-up. For example, if the BIOS is configured not to look at the floppy drive before booting from the hard disk, using a boot disk won't start the installation program. In this situation you must alter the BIOS configuration so that it checks the floppy drive before passing control to the hard disk.

Once you install Linux, you may have problems getting the newly installed Linux system to boot. (Or perhaps the computer will not boot at all.) In this situation, use the boot disk you created during the installation process to start the computer. The Red Hat Linux boot disk will search your hard disks for an existing Red Hat Linux installation and start that operating system after a few seconds.

After installing Linux and starting the system from a boot disk, you may also need to specify the partition on which the operating system is stored, via a boot parameter. A **boot parameter** is a piece of information that you can type in at the LILO prompt. The information you enter is sent to the Linux kernel as the system is being booted. These parameters are normally used to affect how Linux recognizes hardware devices, or which features of the operating system are enabled.

Each operating system that LILO can start has a label (a name) associated with it. When the LILO prompt (`boot:`) appears after you start the system, you can enter a label to start the corresponding operating system. For example, enter the label `linux` to start Linux. At this point you can also add a boot parameter to control the Linux kernel. One example of a boot parameter is `root=`, which designates the root partition for the operating system being booted. The `root=` parameter requires that you specify the partition to use as the root partition for Linux. This example shows what you could enter at the `boot:` prompt to use `/dev/hda1` as the root partition:

```
linux root=/dev/hda1
```

If you see only part of the word `LILO` (such as just the letters `LI`) as the computer system boots, and nothing else happens, the boot manager has been incorrectly installed (this is a rare occurrence). In this case, use the steps described in Chapter 4 to update the configuration of LILO after accessing the new Linux system from a boot disk.

The Graphical Interface Doesn't Work

Setting up the graphical system of Linux is often challenging—so challenging that an entire chapter of this book (Chapter 5) is devoted to the task. Before you can delve into the details of setting up the graphical system, you need to make sure your distribution supports the video card you want to use. Because virtually all Linux distributions use the XFree86 software to support the X Window System, you can check the version of XFree86 software included with your copy of Linux (ask the vendor if you don't have product literature to review), and then check the Web site *www.xfree86.org* to see if your video card is supported by that version of XFree86.

Some video cards are not supported by XFree86, but many of these cards are supported by commercial X Window System products that you can purchase and add to your Linux system. These products are available from Xi Graphics (see *www.xig.com*) and MetroLink (see *www.metrolink.com*).

Chapter 5 provides more explanation about how the graphical system works and how to configure the X Window System. You can always finish the installation of Linux without configuring graphics, then set them up afterwards. Even if your video card is listed as supported by XFree86, you may have trouble getting it correctly configured. In these cases, you may be able to find a Linux expert in your school or in a Linux user group who has experience with the video card you are trying to configure.

Some Hardware Isn't Available

Sometimes hardware that is included on the list of supported hardware on the Linux vendor's Web site is nevertheless not available after starting Linux. This is because the hardware is not correctly configured. As with a system that won't boot, the configuration can generally be corrected by adding a boot parameter when starting Linux. For example, some computers running Linux will not access the CD-ROM drive correctly unless the device name is added as a boot parameter, like this:

```
linux cdrom=/dev/hdc
```

Or Linux may not access all of the available system RAM because of limitations in the computer's BIOS. In this case, you can tell Linux the amount of RAM on the system using this format:

```
linux mem=<<amount of memory>>M
```

So to indicate 128 MB of RAM, you would use the following command:

```
linux mem=128M
```

Be sure to use the correct value for the amount of RAM on your computer, or Linux will crash as it tries to work with nonexistent memory.

You can also combine multiple boot parameters on a single line separated by spaces. For example:

```
linux cdrom=/dev/hdc mem=128M
```

The Boot Parameters HOWTO document provides details about how to add these parameters to make your hardware function correctly in Linux. (Chapter 1 describes how to access HOWTO documents on the Red Hat Linux CD or via the Internet.)

CHAPTER SUMMARY

❏ Different Linux distributions vary in how the Linux files are arranged, which installation programs are provided, and a few other areas; but at their core, all Linux distributions use the same set of software taken from the Internet. The installation programs used by different Linux vendors are also quite similar in the information that they request during the installation process.

❏ The process of installing Linux involves starting an installation program (normally from floppy disk or CD-ROM) and then answering questions about where Linux should be installed and how it should be configured. During the installation you prepare hard disk partitions for Linux using a tool such as **fdisk** or the Red Hat Disk Druid utility, assign a password to the **root** user account, and decide which types of software packages to install.

❏ After installing a new Linux system, you must log in using a valid user account name. You can then start the graphical system, check networking, and create an additional user account if necessary.

❏ Troubleshooting a Linux installation that is not going well may involve adding boot parameters, researching additional hardware information, or using configuration tools to finish setting up features such as the graphical environment or network access after the installation is otherwise complete.

KEY TERMS

authentication — The process of identifying a user to a computer system via some type of login procedure.

boot disk — A floppy disk containing a portion of the Linux installation program, which can be used to start the Linux installation program.

boot parameter — A piece of information passed directly to the Linux kernel as the system is being booted. These parameters are normally used to affect how Linux recognizes hardware devices or to enable certain features of the operating system.

bootable CD-ROM drive — A CD-ROM drive that can launch an operating system (or other program) directly from a CD without accessing the hard disk. (This feature of the CD-ROM drive must be enabled by the BIOS.)

disk image — A single file that contains an exact copy of a floppy disk.

fdisk — A utility used to create hard disk partitions and configure how they are used.

install disk — A disk used to start the Linux installation program on some distributions of Linux. *See* boot disk.

installation source — The set of files from which Linux is installed. These files are normally stored on a Linux CD.

3

installation type — A specification indicating which Linux software to install; the correct installation type depends on how the Linux system will be used.

logging in — The process of identifying yourself as a valid user who has been assigned a certain set of access rights.

mount point — A subdirectory through which a set of data is accessed.

partition table — Information that defines the size and location of each partition on a hard disk.

ping — A command used to test a network connection.

regular user account — A user account that, unlike the `root` account, is not used for system administration work. A regular user account has a name similar to a person's name.

software package — A single file that contains all the files needed to install and use an application or group of related applications. Special data formats are used to store many files in a single software package.

target hard disk partition — The location on the system's hard disk where Linux will be installed. Also known as *target partition*.

REVIEW QUESTIONS

1. Linux distributions vary greatly in the core functionality that they provide. True or False?

2. The installation program included with a Linux distribution is usually created by:

   a. The company, or vendor, that sells the Linux distribution

   b. A group of many vendors working together to create a common installation program

   c. The Gnu project of the Free Software Foundation

   d. Linus Torvalds, as part of the Linux kernel itself

3. Name two technical differences and two nontechnical (marketing related) differences between various Linux products.

4. Explain why installing a new Linux system is different from installing an application such as a spreadsheet or a database package.

5. The target hard disk partition is where:

   a. A dual-boot Windows system resides

   b. The Linux operating system will be installed

   c. Back-up data must be stored for Linux to access it

   d. The Linux installation program is stored

6. Possible locations for the installation source data do *not* include which of the following:

   a. The target hard disk partition

   b. A local CD-ROM

   c. A local hard disk

   d. A networked server using the SMB protocol

7. To start a networked installation you should contact:
   a. Red Hat software to obtain a different boot disk
   b. Your system administrator to obtain the target partition for the installation
   c. Your system administrator to determine whether your hard disk supports a network-based installation
   d. The network administrator of the server containing the installation source

8. When you turn on a computer, _____ sends control to the MBR of the first hard disk, or to another device such as a bootable CD-ROM drive or a floppy drive.
   a. Linux
   b. the `fdisk` utility
   c. LILO
   d. the BIOS

9. A boot disk used to start a Linux installation program may have different names on different distributions of Linux. True or False?

10. In which circumstance would you need a boot disk to start the Linux installation program?
    a. The computer does not have a bootable CD-ROM drive.
    b. When installing on a laptop.
    c. The root disk has become corrupted.
    d. When installing from a network installation source.

11. Name the tool used in Windows to copy a disk image to a floppy disk.

12. The `fdisk` utility is used to:
    a. Prepare partitions on a hard disk
    b. Create a boot disk from a disk image
    c. Start a Linux installation program from a boot disk
    d. Launch Linux from a Windows-based fixed disk (hard disk)

13. The device name `/dev/hda3` would refer to:
    a. The third partition on the first IDE hard disk
    b. The third partition on the first SCSI hard disk
    c. The third IDE hard disk
    d. The swap partition stored on a boot disk

14. Name three reasons why you might place different parts of the Linux file system on different hard disk partitions.

15. The _____ defines the size and location on the hard disk of each partition.
    a. MBR
    b. `fdisk` utility
    c. partition table
    d. Disk Druid utility

16. Most Linux distributions use a system of software packages to make managing software easier and more efficient. True or False?

17. Explain why you might choose to select groups of software packages rather than individual software packages during an installation.

18. The _____ user account is created as part of every Linux installation process.

   a. LILO

   b. installation source

   c. `useradd`

   d. `root`

19. Storing the LILO boot manager on a floppy disk allows you to:

   a. Start Linux only when the floppy disk is inserted in the computer

   b. Slow down the boot process to examine how it works

   c. Store user accounts along with LILO on the boot floppy

   d. Install Linux in a more secure manner

20. The _____ command normally starts the graphical system when working in a text-based Linux system.

   a. `startx`

   b. `GNOME`

   c. `KDE`

   d. `gnome`

21. The `ping` command is used to:

   a. Test a network connection

   b. Test the sound card configuration

   c. Test the integrity of a hard disk connector

   d. Send a small e-mail message to another system

22. Boot parameters can be used to pass additional information to the Linux kernel as the Linux installation program is started. True or False?

23. Name three programs that can be used to configure the X Window System after the Linux installation is completed.

24. Which of the following is *not* likely to cause hardware problems in Linux?

   a. The correct module supporting that hardware is not yet installed. '

   b. A parameter identifying the hardware was not entered correctly.

   c. Windows has disabled the hardware for use under Linux.

   d. The hardware is not supported by Linux.

25. The surest way to have LILO start Linux is to install LILO on:

   a. The MBR

   b. The boot sector of the active partition

   c. A floppy disk

   d. The installation source partition

HANDS-ON PROJECTS

Project 3-1

In this activity you create a boot disk to use when installing Red Hat Linux. To complete this activity you should have a computer with Windows 95 or 98 installed and both a CD-ROM drive and a floppy disk drive. You should also have a Red Hat Linux CD like the one included in this book and a blank floppy disk. For this project, it is assumed that you will install Red Hat Linux from a local CD-ROM drive rather than from a network connection and that you are not using a laptop.

1. Start Windows.

2. Insert the Red Hat Linux CD in the CD-ROM drive and a blank floppy disk in the floppy disk drive.

3. Double-click the **My Computer** icon on the Windows Desktop. A window opens showing you the contents of your computer.

4. Double-click the icon for the CD-ROM drive within the My Computer window. A window appears showing you the contents of the Red Hat Linux CD.

5. Double-click the **dosutils** folder within the CD-ROM drive window. A window appears showing you the contents of the Images folder.

6. Double-click the **rawrite** program within the Images folder window. An MS-DOS window appears in which the rawrite program is executed. The following text line is displayed:

   `Enter disk image source file name:`

7. Enter the name of the disk image that you are copying to a floppy disk. The exact text you enter depends on the drive letter for your CD-ROM drive in Windows. If your drive letter is E:, for example, enter this text: **E:\images\boot.img**. The following text line is displayed:

   `Enter target diskette drive:`

8. Enter the drive letter for the floppy disk drive on the Windows system. This is normally the letter *A*. The following text line is displayed. (The value **A:** varies based on the drive letter that you enter in this step.)

   `Please insert a formatted diskette into drive A: and press`
   `ENTER- :`

9. Check that the floppy disk is inserted, and then press **Enter**.

10. When the disk image has been copied from the CD to the floppy disk, the floppy disk drive stops turning (and the light on the front of the drive will turn off). Eject the floppy disk and close the MS-DOS window on the Windows Desktop. Leave the Red Hat CD in the CD-ROM drive.

11. Shut down the Windows computer.

Project 3-2

In this activity you install Red Hat Linux 6.0 from the CD included with this book. To complete this activity you should have the boot disk you created in Project 3-1, the Red Hat Linux CD included with this book, a second blank floppy disk to use during the installation, and a computer with sufficient resources to complete the installation (about 700 MB of hard disk space and 16 MB of RAM). To perform the steps that follow you must have sufficient free space on your hard disk so that you can use the Disk Druid tool to create a swap partition and a native Linux partition during the installation.

Installing Linux is a lengthy procedure, and there may be slight differences in some of the following steps because of differences in the hardware installed on your system. The steps given here along with the on-screen menus should guide you through the entire process. If your system has a SCSI adapter card, the dialog boxes and order of the steps may vary slightly on your computer. Because few standard PCs include SCSI adapter cards, these steps reflect an installation on an IDE hard disk.

1. Verify that the Red Hat Linux CD is still in the CD-ROM drive and that the boot disk that you created in Project 3-1 is inserted into the floppy drive, and then turn on the computer. After a few moments, several lines of text appear on a black background with the title `Welcome to Red Hat Linux` at the top of the screen.

2. Press **Enter** to continue. Messages display on the screen as different parts of the Linux installation program are loaded. (This loading process may take as much as three full minutes, depending on your computer's speed.)

3. When the installation program has finished loading, you see a blue screen with a welcome message. Review the message and press **Enter** to continue.

4. A list of language options appears, as shown in Figure 3-9. This same type of selection screen is used throughout the Red Hat Linux installation program.

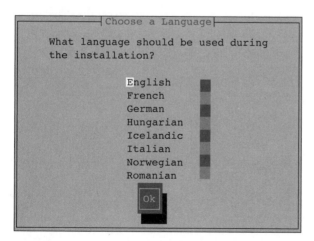

Figure 3-9   The `Language Selection` screen in the Red Hat Linux installation

5. Use the Up and Down arrow keys to select a language for the installation. (These steps are based on the English version.) Press **Enter** to continue. The `Keyboard Type` dialog box appears.

6. Use the Up and Down arrow keys to select the keyboard you are using from the list shown. (The items in the list are quite cryptic—the selection us is appropriate for most keyboards in the United States.) Press **Enter** to continue.

7. If PCMCIA laptop hardware is detected on your computer, a dialog box labeled `PCMCIA Support` appears. If you were installing Red Hat Linux on a laptop and required a connection via a PCMCIA expansion card to a network or SCSI adapter, you would need to choose `Yes` and use a special PCMCIA disk (created from the Red Hat Linux CD as in Project 3-1). Choose **No** to continue.

 Notice that a Back button appears at the bottom of most dialog boxes. You can return to a previous dialog box by pressing Tab repeatedly until the Back button is highlighted in white; then press Enter. To advance to the next screen, you can either press the F12 key or press Tab until the OK button is selected, and then press Enter.

8. The `Installation Method` dialog box appears. In this dialog box you can specify where the Red Hat Linux data files are located. Use the arrow keys to select `Local CDROM`, and then press **Enter** to continue.

9. A message box tells you to insert your Red Hat Linux CD into the CD-ROM drive. (If you followed Step 1 of this project, the CD should already be in the CD-ROM drive.) Press **Enter** to continue. A message tells you that the CD-ROM is being initialized.

10. The `Installation Path` dialog box appears. In this dialog box you select whether you want to install a new system or upgrade an existing Red Hat Linux system. The `Install` button is selected by default. Press **Enter** to continue.

11. The `Installation Class` dialog box appears. Use the arrow keys to select `Custom`. (Other options include `Workstation` and `Server`. The `Custom` option allows you flexibility later regarding which components you want to install.) Press **Enter** to continue. Depending on your system, the `SCSI Configuration` dialog box may appear next.

 You may see a different series of dialog boxes related to the process of configuring a SCSI card than described here.

12. If your system had a SCSI card, you would choose Yes and select the appropriate SCSI configuration from a list. No is selected by default because very few standard PCs have SCSI adapters. Make the correct selection, and press **Enter** to continue. The `Disk Setup` dialog box appears.

13. Make certain that the `Disk Druid` button is selected. (Use the Tab key if necessary to select it.) Press **Enter** to continue. The Disk Druid hard disk management utility appears, similar to the screen shown in Figure 3-4.

3

14. Review the Type column on the right side of the screen. If a Linux swap partition and a Linux native partition are not shown, press **Tab** until `Add` is highlighted in white, and then press **Enter** to begin creating the needed partitions for the installation. (These steps assume that the partitions have already been created using Disk Druid, `fdisk`, or another tool, but at this point in the installation process you can use the steps outlined in the chapter text to create new partitions on the hard disk.)

15. In the top part of the window, use the Up and Down arrow keys to select the partition on which you want to install Red Hat Linux. This partition must be labeled as "Linux native" in the Type column.

16. Press **Tab** repeatedly until the `Edit` button is highlighted in white.

17. Press **Enter** to open the `Edit Partition` dialog box.

18. In the Mount Point field, enter **/** (a single slash character) and press **Enter**. The `Edit Partition` dialog box closes, and you see the Disk Druid main screen again.

19. Press **F12** to continue the installation process. The `Active Swap Space` dialog box appears.

20. Make certain that the partition number you defined in Disk Druid as Linux swap space is marked with an asterisk, so that it can be formatted. Press the Spacebar if an asterisk does not appear to the left of the device name. (You don't need to select the `Check for bad blocks during format` option.) Press **Tab** until `OK` is selected, and then press **Enter** to continue. The `Partitions To Format` dialog box appears.

21. If you had selected multiple Linux native partitions with different mount points by using the Disk Druid tool in Steps 14 through 18, each one would be listed here. Here it is assumed you are using one partition for the entire installation, so a single partition (for the / directory) is listed in this dialog box. Make certain that the box to the left of the partition name contains an asterisk. (If it does not, press the Tab key repeatedly to select that line, and then press the Spacebar to add an asterisk.) You do not need to place an asterisk in front of the `Check for bad blocks during format` option unless you are concerned about the integrity of the hard disk on which you are installing Linux. Using this option adds significantly to the time required to prepare the partition for installation. Press **F12** to continue. The `Components to Install` dialog box appears.

22. Using the information provided in the chapter text and your own preferences, select the items you want to install by moving up and down the list with the arrow keys. Press the **Spacebar** to select or unselect each item as you highlight it. If you have sufficient hard disk space (more than 1 GB on the Linux partition), install as much as you can so you have more tools available to experiment with and learn about Linux. Don't select the option labeled `Select individual packages`. When you have finished, press **F12** to continue. The `Install log` dialog box appears.

23. Review the information in the `Install log` dialog box, which tells you that you can see information about the installation after it is completed by looking at the file `/tmp/install.log`. Press **F12** to continue. Message boxes inform you that the file system is being formatted and that packages are being installed. After a moment, the `Package Installation` screen appears. You don't need to do anything at this point.

24. Watch the packages being installed within the `Package Installation` screen. Note that the package names and sizes are shown as each one is installed. The total number of packages to be installed (based on your selection in Step 22) and the total size of all packages is shown in the middle of the screen. Read a few of the `Summary` lines as packages are installed. This part of the installation takes from 5 to 30 minutes depending on the speed of the computer system.

25. After the package installation is completed, a message box informs you of any mouse device that the installation was able to locate. Press **Enter** to continue. The `Configure Mouse` dialog box appears.

26. Select the type of mouse you have installed from the list shown by using the arrow keys. Press **Tab** to select the `Emulate 3 Buttons` item. Press the **Spacebar** to select that item. Then press **F12** to continue. The `Network Configuration` dialog box appears.

27. If you want to configure an Ethernet or other network adapter card, make certain that the **Yes** button is selected, and press **F12** to continue. (Most Linux systems are connected to networks, but you can choose to configure networking after the installation if you prefer.) A `Load module` dialog bo appears. If you prefer to choose No and configure networking after the installation is completed, skip to Step 31.

 TIP If the installation program detects a network card, you may not see some of the dialog boxes described here, or you may see different dialog boxes than described here.

28. In the `Load module` dialog box, use the arrow keys to select the module that corresponds to your network adapter card. If the installation program can detect a certain network card, the module for that card is selected by default. Press **Enter** when you have highlighted a module. If the module you select is not the correct one, you can return to this screen and try another module.

29. In the `Module options` dialog box, leave the `Autoprobe` option selected so that the installation program will attempt to autoconfigure the network card. You can also choose `Specify Options` and enter IRQ and I/O port numbers if the `Autoprobe` option is not successful.

 TIP You can install Red Hat Linux on a laptop using the CD included with this book. But because PCMCIA support is not part of the standard installation program, you will not be able to configure networking until you have completed the installation and rebooted the new Linux system. If you need to access the PCMCIA devices on the laptop in order to complete the installation via a network or SCSI connection, you must create a `bootnet` or `pcmcia` disk from the image files on the Red Hat Linux CD. See the documentation on the CD for more information.

30. After successfully installing the network adapter module, follow the on-screen instructions to enter the networking parameters specific to your local network.

3

31. The `Configure Timezones` dialog box appears. Use the arrow keys to select your time zone from the list shown. If your computer is only running Linux (and is not sharing a hard disk with Windows), select the option `Hardware clock set to GMT` by using the Tab key and pressing the Spacebar. Press **F12** to continue. The `Services` dialog box appears.

32. Use the arrow keys to highlight each service that you want to select or unselect, pressing the **Spacebar** to add or remove the asterisk next to each item in the list. In most cases, you can leave the services list configured as it is by default. Press **F12** to continue. The `Configure Printer` dialog box appears.

33. Use the **Tab** key to select **No**. (Printer configuration is discussed at length in Chapter 13.) Press **Enter** in the `Configure Printer` dialog box to continue. The `Root Password` dialog box appears.

34. Enter a root password in the `Password` field. Nothing appears as you type, though a flashing cursor is shown. Press **Tab** to return to the `Password` field, and reenter the password. Press **F12** to continue. You cannot continue until you have entered two matching passwords.

35. The `Authentication Configuration` dialog box appears. The default settings in this dialog box define how Red Hat Linux will store password information to protect it from intruders. Because the default settings provide good security, you can accept them by pressing **F12** to continue. (The `Enable NIS` check box is used if you are located on a network that uses the network information system protocol. Ask your network administrator if you think this might apply to the system you are installing.)

36. The `Bootdisk` dialog box appears. Insert your second blank floppy disk (mentioned at the beginning of this project). Yes is selected by default, so press **F12** to continue. A message box appears. Press **F12** a second time to begin creating the boot disk. A message box informs you that the disk is being created.

37. After the boot disk is created, the `Lilo Installation` dialog box appears. You see a list of possible locations where the LILO boot manager can be installed. If you have had problems getting Linux to boot after installation, choose the line containing `Master Boot Record`; otherwise, you can choose the line containing `First sector of boot partition`. Use the arrow keys to make your selection, and press **F12** to continue. A second `Lilo Installation` dialog box appears.

38. Some systems require boot parameters in order for Linux to work properly (as described in this chapter). The first time you install Linux you should not assume that these parameters are needed. If they were needed, you could enter them in this dialog box to activate them each time Linux was booted by LILO. Because they are generally not necessary, and should in any case only be added after trying an installation without them, press **F12** to continue.

39. The `Bootable Partitions` dialog box appears. It lists the Red Hat Linux partition and any other partitions containing other operating systems installed on your computer. A Default Boot label column indicates the name assigned to each one. If you need to change the information listed here so that you can use LILO to boot other operating systems, use the arrow keys to select a line containing a partition with another operating system, and then press **Tab** until the Edit button is highlighted. Press **Enter** to open the

Edit Boot Label dialog box. Enter a new label in the Boot label field. When the second LILO configuration dialog box appears again, press **F12** to continue. The Choose a Card dialog box appears.

If the installation program is able to detect information about your video card, you may not see some of the dialog boxes described here.

40. Use the arrow keys to select your video card from the list of hundreds of video cards. On the keyboard, press the first letter in the card's name to move to that point alphabetically in the list. The last item in the list is Unlisted Card, which you can select if the video card you need to configure is not listed. Press **F12** to continue. A message box informs you that the corresponding X server software is being installed on the system. The Monitor Setup dialog box then appears.

41. Select your monitor from the list of monitors shown. If your monitor model is not listed, choose Custom. (In this case, you will be prompted by additional screens to enter your monitor details.) On the keyboard, press a letter key to move to that letter position in the alphabetic listing of monitors. Laptop screens are listed under LCD Panel. When you have selected a monitor, press **F12** to continue. A Screen Configuration message box appears.

42. Review the information in the Screen Configuration message box. For most systems, you can choose Probe to determine your video hardware. When you press **Enter**, a message in a dialog box informs you that the probing is about to begin. Press **F12** to continue. The screen blinks a few times as the installation program searches for information about your video card. Finally, a new dialog box appears informing you that the probing process is finished.

43. Press the **Tab** key repeatedly until the Use Default button is highlighted in white. This causes the installation to use the values determined by probing the video card. Press **F12** to continue. The Starting X message box appears, informing you that the X Window System is about to be tested.

44. Press **F12** to try the X Window System. If the configuration of your video card was successful, you see a graphical message box asking you to click Yes with your mouse to indicate that the graphics mode worked. You can then choose to start your Red Hat Linux system in that graphical mode automatically by clicking Yes in a second graphical message box.

45. The Done dialog box appears, informing you that the installation is finished. Press **F12** to restart the computer in the new Red Hat Linux system.

If you have trouble with the graphical configuration because your video card or monitor is not listed, or the X Window System does not start successfully, choose the Skip option after the X Window System launch fails. You can configure and troubleshoot the graphical system using the information in Chapter 5.

Project 3-3

In this activity you begin to use the new Linux system that you installed in Project 3-2. To complete this activity you should have a newly installed Red Hat Linux system available.

1. Remove any CDs and floppy disks from the computer.

2. Restart the computer. When you see a prompt consisting of the text **boot:**, press **Tab** to see the available operating systems that are installed.

3. The installation program assigned a label (name) to Red Hat Linux during the installation. This label is normally **linux**, which you see when you press **Tab**. Enter this label used for the Red Hat Linux operating system. Review the messages that appear as the system boots.

4. When the boot process is finished, a login screen appears. (This may be a text-mode login screen or a graphical login screen depending on the selections you made in Project 3-2.) Enter the username that you created as a regular user account during the installation.

5. Enter the wrong password. What happens? Can you use the system without entering one of the valid usernames and the corresponding password?

6. Enter the correct username and password of the regular user account to log in to the system.

7. If you are using a text-based screen, enter the command **logout**, or choose **Logout** from the main menu of the graphical system if you have entered the graphical desktop automatically.

8. Log in again using the **root** account name and password. Do you see any differences in the appearance of the system when you log in as **root**?

CASE PROJECTS

1. Your friend manages a group of resorts known collectively as the Lakewood Resorts. The Lakewood company has recently started to expand its operations by promoting the resort to vacationers around the country. To support this expansion, they have installed a call center with about 100 computers to handle incoming requests for information and reservations. Each computer will be staffed by a representative who can answer questions and make reservations or send out a resort brochure. All of the computers will be running Linux and will be connected to a large reservations computer located in another office. You have been asked to install Linux on all of the systems. Based on the options you learned in this chapter, would you use a local CD-ROM drive to install each system or place the installation source files on a networked server? Explain your choice. Describe in detail the additional features (beyond those discussed explicitly in the chapter) you would like to see in a Linux distribution or installation program to support your work on this project. Visit the Web sites of several Linux vendors, and see what features you can find that fit your criteria.

2. Assuming you find the features you're looking for to ease the task of installing 100 new systems in a short time, would those features alone lead you to use one Linux distribution over another? What other technical or nontechnical features would be important to you as you prepare to install the call center's computers? Given the standard cost range of Linux distributions mentioned in the chapter, how important is the cost of the Linux product in making your decision?

3. Suppose all the call center's computers already have Microsoft Windows installed. You have been asked to make each one a dual-boot system, so that representatives can use Windows software occasionally if they need to. Does this change the Linux product you would choose? Conduct research on the Internet or through Linux vendors to locate commercial Windows software to help you install (or prepare to install) the Linux systems. Assuming that the Linux systems were already installed and you were later asked to add Windows to each system, how would your arrangement of the Linux partitions (and possibly multiple mount points) affect your ability to make the requested change to the systems? Are some possible future needs too costly to prepare for now?

# CHAPTER 4

RUNNING A LINUX SYSTEM

After reading this chapter and completing the exercises, you will be able to:

♦ Work with files and directories on a Linux system using basic commands

♦ Run programs and manage the corresponding software packages using popular data formats

♦ Add or remove features from the Linux kernel

♦ Review and change the initialization process that starts a Linux-based computer

In the previous chapter you learned about installing a new Linux system from a CD. You learned how to set up Linux hard disk partitions, how to answer configuration questions, and how to log in to a newly installed Linux system.

In this chapter you will learn about how to work with the files and directories on a Linux system and manage the software packages installed on the system. You will also learn about internal Linux operations, including the basics of the Linux kernel and the initialization process.

WORKING WITH LINUX FILES AND DIRECTORIES

From your work with computers, you know that manipulating files and directories is a large part of interacting with a computer. You search directories for a certain file, you open a file to review or change its contents, you save an updated version of a file, and so forth. Linux operates in much the same way as other operating systems: your data is stored in files; files are arranged in directories. Multiple directories are arranged in a branching treelike structure, in which one directory leads to other directories. Directories are also commonly represented by folders that can contain other folders (that is, other directories) and documents (or files). The directories contained within another directory are called subdirectories. Each subdirectory can in turn contain its own subdirectories.

Within Linux, every data file and device is part of one large directory structure. All directories in the Linux directory structure branch out from the root directory. The **root directory**, represented by a single forward slash (/), is the starting point for all access to Linux resources. All Linux configuration files are located in subdirectories of the root directory. All devices are also associated with a file located in a subdirectory of the root directory. (You may remember examples such as /dev/hda1 from previous chapters.) As a system administrator, much of the work that you do to maintain a Linux system consists of reviewing the contents of files, updating files, and otherwise managing the status, contents, and location of files and the directories that contain them.

 TIP The /root subdirectory is the home directory of the root user account. Don't confuse this with the root directory, /. For clarity, it's helpful to refer to the /root subdirectory as "slash-root," or "root's home directory."

By default, Linux includes a standard set of subdirectories that branch off the root directory. Table 4-1 lists these subdirectories and what they contain. Some versions of Linux may contain subdirectories of the root directory that are not listed here, but Table 4-1 contains those that are found on all Linux systems. You will become very familiar with all of these main subdirectories as you learn more about Linux.

Table 4-1   Standard Linux Subdirectories of the Root Directory

Directory	Contents
/etc	Configuration files.
/var	Variable (changing) information, including system log files (see Chapter 11), e-mail messages, and files being printed.
/home	Home directories for all regular user accounts.
/bin	Executable programs.
/sbin	Executable programs used only by the root user.
/usr	Files (data, programs, documentation) used by all regular users on the Linux system. This subdirectory contains many other files and subdirectories.
/tmp	Temporary files used by the system or regular users.
/root	Home directory of the root user (the superuser account).
/boot	Files used to initialize Linux when the system is booted.
/dev	Files used to access hardware resources (devices) on the computer system.
/lib	System libraries (described later in this chapter) used by many Linux programs.

On most Linux systems, the largest of the directories in Table 4-1 (that is, the one containing the most files and subdirectories), is the /usr subdirectory. This subdirectory contains nearly all of the programs you regularly use in Linux (such as the commands described in the following sections), the files for the graphical system, all the standard Linux online documentation, and many other types of files.

The names and arrangement of the Linux subdirectories may not be intuitive—the names are short and strange. But each one has a distinct purpose that has been refined over the years of UNIX and Linux development. This predefined directory arrangement ensures that a program can locate the files it needs (such as system configuration files) on any Linux system. The best way to become familiar with the arrangement and purpose of the hundreds of files included with a standard Linux distribution is to use the `cd` and `ls` commands (explained in "Linux File Commands") to explore your system's directory structure.

Working at a Command Line

After you log in (using a valid username and password), the system may be in a text-mode (also called character-mode or character-cell) environment, in which case you see a prompt where you can type commands. This environment is shown in Figure 4-1.

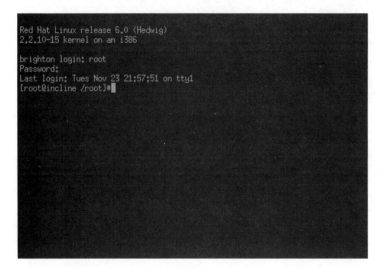

```
Red Hat Linux release 6.0 (Hedwig)
2.2.10-15 kernel on an i386

brighton login: root
Password:
Last login: Tues Nov 23 21:57:51 on tty1
[root@incline /root]#
```

Figure 4-1 A text-mode prompt

Instead of text mode, your system may start in a graphical environment, such as Gnome or KDE. (These graphical environments are discussed in detail in Chapter 5.) Within a graphical environment, you can open a **command-line window** that permits you to enter commands at the keyboard. The command-line environment is also called a **terminal emulator window** (or terminal window) because it resembles an old-fashioned dumb terminal connection to a large computer system. Within a graphical environment, a program call **xterm** (pronounced "ex-term") is sometimes used to provide a command-line window. Figure 4–2 shows a graphical environment with a command-line window open.

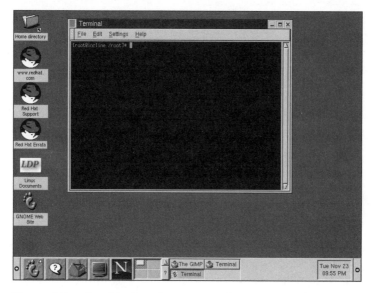

Figure 4-2   Graphical environment with a command-line window

To open a command-line window, choose the appropriate menu item within the graphical environment. For example, within the Gnome Desktop, click on the footprint icon in the lower-left corner of the window, point to Utilities, and then click Gnome Terminal. Within the KDE Desktop, click on the K icon in the lower-left corner of the window, point to Utilities, and then click Terminal.

At a command-line prompt, either in text mode or graphical mode, you can explore the Linux directory structure and learn how to use basic Linux commands.

Linux File Commands

When you first log in to Linux or open a command-line window, your working area is defined as your home directory. A **home directory** is the location where all of your personal files are stored. For the root user account, the home directory is /root. For regular users, the home directory is a subdirectory of the /home directory that matches your user account name. For example, if you log in as a user named nwells, your home directory will be /home/nwells. On some larger Linux systems, a different location is used for home directories, but this is rare.

In Linux, the command-line environment is called the **shell**. In Chapter 6 you will learn more details about the shell. For now you only need to know that after you type a command and press Enter, the shell will process the command. When you enter the **pwd** command, the shell displays your **current working directory** (that is, the directory in which you are working).The name **pwd** stands for *print working directory*.After you first log in, the **pwd** command will display your home directory.

All of the commands presented in this section must be entered in lowercase letters. Linux is case sensitive—entering the command PWD produces different results from the **pwd** command. All Linux commands are lowercase.

4

The **cd** command changes the current working directory to a directory you specify.To use the **cd** command, remember the following points:

- You specify the full directory name of the directory that you want to make your current working directory. For example, **cd /home/nwells**.

- If you prefer, you can specify only the name of a subdirectory to which you want to change. For example: **cd nwells**. Note that this command does not begin with a forward slash (/).

- You can enter **cd** without any directory name after it to change to your home directory.

- To change to a directory one level higher (one level closer to the root directory, /), use the directory name **..** (two periods).The directory that is one level above your current directory is called its **parent directory**. For example, **cd ..** will change to the parent directory of the directory you are working in.

In DOS and Windows systems you can use the command **cd..** (without a space between cd and ..) to switch to the parent directory. This command does not work in Linux. You must always include a space after the **cd** command.

Linux provides two additional commands related to directories.The **mkdir** command creates a new directory that is a subdirectory of the current working directory. For example, if you are in the home directory **/home/nwells**, the command **mkdir archive** creates a new subdirectory named **archive**. The full name of the new directory would then be **/home/nwells/archive**.The **rmdir** command removes (deletes) a directory. Note that a directory must be empty (it cannot contain any files) before you can delete it using the **rmdir** command.

The **ls** command lists the files in a directory.When used alone, the **ls** command only prints the names of files in a directory. But the **ls** command has dozens of options for printing additional information about files and directories. One commonly used option is **-l** (a hyphen followed by lowercase *l*). Entering the command **ls -l** prints a long list of details about each file, such as when the file was created and how many bytes it contains.

The **touch** command creates a new file with no data in it. If you use the **touch** command with a filename that already exists, the file is updated to show that the last time it was accessed was the moment in which the **touch** command was used. For example, if you enter the command **touch test**, a new file called **test** (containing zero bytes) is created. If you enter the command **touch test** a second time, the internal data about the **test** file is updated to show that the file was accessed at that moment. Information about the date and time when an event occurred is stored on a Linux system in the form of a **timestamp**. Linux maintains a set of timestamps for each file and directory that define when the file was created, when it was last modified, and when it was last accessed. The **touch** command updates a file's last accessed timestamp (that is, the date and time when the file was last accessed).

Often you will need to make a copy of a file, remove it, or change its name or location. Linux provides commands for all of these operations. The **cp** command copies a file or directory from one location to another. You can use the **cp** command to copy a file within the same directory using a different filename, such as **cp file1 file2**. You can also copy a file to another directory using the same name. For example, the command **cp file1 /tmp** makes a copy of the file named **file1** in the **/tmp** directory (using the same filename, **file1**).

To delete a file, use the **rm** command (for *remove*). Be very careful using the **rm** command. When you delete a file using **rm**, the file cannot be undeleted like files placed in a trash can or recycle bin on a graphical desktop. (Linux graphical desktops provide a trash can, but the **rm** command does not use the trash can—it permanently deletes files.)

In Linux the operations of moving and renaming a file are combined in one command, the **mv** command. The name **mv** is short for *move*, which makes sense if you keep in mind that, in essence, renaming a file is the same as *moving* it to a different filename. For example, if you have a file named **test**, you can change its name to **retest** using this command: **mv test retest**. This places the renamed file in the same directory as the original file. To move a file, you provide a different directory name and, optionally, a different filename. The command to move the **test** file to a subdirectory named **archive** is **mv test archive**. If a subdirectory named **archive** does not exist, the **test** file will be renamed as **archive**. To move and rename a file, give a new location and a new filename. For example, to move the **test** file to the **archive** directory under the name **retest**, use the command **mv test archive/retest**.

Linux provides several utilities for viewing the contents of a file. The simplest of these is the **cat** command, which prints the contents of a file to the screen. For example, the command **cat test** prints the contents of the **test** file to the screen. (The **cat** command is also used to concatenate, or combine, multiple files into one larger file. This is described in Chapter 6.) The **zcat** command prints the contents of a compressed file to the screen. If a file ends with the letters **gz**, indicating that the file is compressed, you can use the **zcat** command to view the contents of the file without first uncompressing it. Most files do not fit on one screen, in which case the **cat** command works too quickly—you will only see the last 20 or so lines of text in a file. To view a larger file, use the **less** command, which prints the contents of a file one screenful at a time. You can use the arrow keys or Page Up and Page Down keys to move to different areas of the file. The Q key exits the **less** command. For example, the command **less /etc/termcap** displays a large configuration file on screen. Press Q to exit this file.

The `less` command is similar to the **more** command, which is used to print the contents of a file one screenful at a time. The `less` command has more features than the **more** command, but you can use either one to view the contents of files. The `less` and **more** commands are only intended to display text files (with human-readable content). You can use the **file** command to determine what a file contains. The **file** command prints a summary of the type of data contained in a file. For example, the command `file /etc/printcap` will tell you that the `/etc/printcap` file is a text file. The command `file /sbin/lilo` will tell you that `/sbin/lilo` is a Linux-executable program. Before you try using the `less` and **more** commands on files that do not contain human-readable text, you can check their contents with the **file** command.

This section has described only a few of the Linux commands used to work with files and directories on a command line. Table 4-2 summarizes these commands. You will have the chance to practice using these commands in the hands-on projects at the end of this chapter. You will also learn many other Linux commands in the sections and chapters to come.

Table 4-2 Commands for Managing Files and Directories

Command	Description	Example
pwd	Print the current working directory.	pwd
cd	Change to a different directory.	cd /home/nwells
mkdir	Make (create) a new directory.	mkdir /home/nwells/ archive
rmdir	Remove (erase) an empty directory.	rmdir /home/nwells/archive
ls	List the contents of a directory.	ls
touch	Create a new, empty file, or update the timestamp of an existing file.	touch testfile
cp	Copy a file to a new location or filename.	cp testfile testfile.backup
rm	Remove (delete) a file.	rm testfile.old
mv	Rename a file or move a file to a new location (possibly under a new name as well).	mv testfile testfile.old
cat	Display the contents of a file on screen.	cat /etc/printcap
less	Display the contents of a file on screen, one screenful at a time.	less /etc/termcap
more	Display the contents of a file on screen, one screenful at a time.	more /etc/termcap
file	Display a description of what a file contains or is used for.	file /sbin/lilo
zcat	Displays the contents of a compressed file on screen.	zcat /tmp/report.gz

In the examples used with these commands (and in browsing through Linux), you may already have noticed a few things about Linux filenames and directory names:

- All filenames are case sensitive. In general, most filenames contain only lowercase, but if you type uppercase letters when naming a new file or directory, they are stored as uppercase, and you must use uppercase the next time you refer to that file or directory. Thus the filenames `test`, `Test`, and `TEST` are all distinct.

- Filenames can be long, up to 256 characters, and can contain periods, numbers, and punctuation marks in addition to upper- and lowercase letters. You should not, however, try to use a forward or backward slash within a filename. For clarity, if a filename contains unusual characters such as punctuation, you might need to enclose the filename in quotation marks when you refer to the file in a Linux command.

- Filenames in Linux often don't include file extensions used in some operating systems. For example, a Linux configuration file may not have any ending, or it may end with `.conf`, or some other file extension. (A **file extension** is the last part of the filename after a period.) The names of Linux program files don't include any file extensions (such as .EXE or .COM on other systems).

In future sections and chapters you will learn how to control the commands introduced here by adding options. You will also learn about many additional useful commands.

Linux Files on a Graphical Desktop

Modern graphical interfaces provided with Linux include file manager windows that make it easy to perform most of the tasks you would otherwise perform using the text commands described in the previous section. A **file manager window** is a graphical interface that displays the contents of a directory (usually as a collection of icons) and lets you work with the files and directories using menus, mouse clicks, and dialog boxes.

 The descriptions here refer to the Gnome Desktop interface, but the KDE Desktop provides almost identical functionality.

To open a file manager window in the Gnome Desktop, open the Gnome main menu by clicking on the footprint icon in the lower-left corner of the screen; then click `File Manager`. A file manager window appears like the one shown in Figure 4-3. (In KDE, choose `Home Directory` from the KDE main menu.)

The file manager window includes a list of directories on the left side. You can view the subdirectories within a directory by clicking on the small plus sign (+) to the left of a directory name. (If the directory contains no other directories, no plus sign is shown.) When you click on a directory in the list, the right side of the file manager window shows the files contained in that directory.

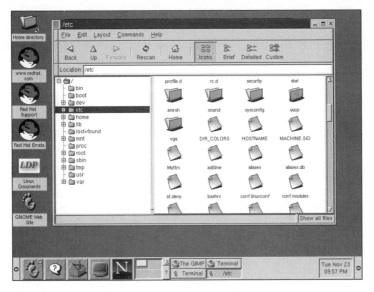

Figure 4-3   A Gnome file manager window

You can click on a file in the right side of a file manager window to perform operations on that file. For example, you can drag and drop a file's icon to another directory, either in the left side of the same file manager window or in another file manager window. You can also right-click on a file's icon to see a pop-up menu with a list of options, such as **Copy**, **Delete**, and **Move**. The **Properties** option in the pop-up menu opens a dialog box in which you can view status information about the file you selected. Figure 4-4 shows a Properties dialog box for a file within the Gnome Desktop. You will learn more about the other tabs in this dialog box later in this chapter.

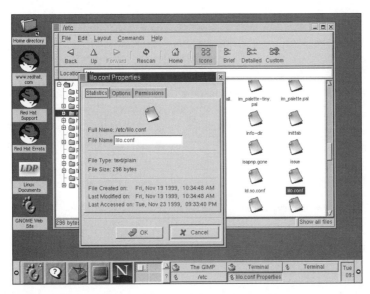

Figure 4-4   Properties dialog box viewed in the Gnome file manager

File Properties

Several properties are associated with each file in Linux. You learned earlier in this chapter about the timestamp values associated with a file, such as the date when the file was created and last accessed. (These values are visible in the Properties dialog box shown in Figure 4-4.) You can view other properties of a file or a directory using the `ls -l` command. The output of this command for two sample files is shown here:

```
-rwxr-xr-x   1 nwells    users     121024 Nov 18 14:36 newprogram
-rw-rw-rw-   1 nwells    users          0 Nov 18 15:22 test
```

Although the fields of information displayed by the `ls` command are not labeled, you should be able to recognize the username `nwells` in the sample output. Each file has a username associated with it. This user is the owner of the file. Whenever you create a new file or directory, your username is assigned as the owner of that file. Each file and each directory is also assigned a group; the group is then said to *own* that file. A **group** is a named account that consists of a collection of users. Each member of a group has access to files owned by that group. (You will learn about users and groups in detail in Chapter 8.) In the sample listing above from the `ls` command, the `users` group is assigned to the files. Depending on how your Linux distribution is configured, all of the regular user accounts on a Linux system might be members of the `users` group.

The `root` user can execute the **chown** command to change the ownership of a file or directory. To use this command, type `chown`, followed by the username and group (separated by a period) that you want to assign to the file or directory. Next, type the name of the file or directory. For example, the following command changes the owner of the file `test` to `jtaylor` and the group assigned to the file `test` to `managers`:

```
chown jtaylor.managers test
```

The user and group that you assign to a file must already exist on the Linux system, as described in Chapter 8.

The owner and group assigned to a file determine who can access the file. The term **file permissions** refers to the type of access that a user has to a file or directory on the Linux system. If you have used other operating systems, you may have heard terms such as *file rights* or *access permissions*. These terms are synonymous with file permissions. Linux file permissions provide adequate security to protect access to files and directories, but they are not as detailed as those provided by other operating systems. In Linux, only three different file permissions can be assigned: read, write, and execute.

- **Read permission** allows a user to read the contents of a file or browse the files in a directory. This permission is designated in file listings by a letter **r**.

- **Write permission** allows a user to add or change information in a file or create files within a directory. This permission is designated in file listings by a letter **w**.

- **Execute permission** allows a user to launch a file as a program or see files within a directory. This permission is designated in file listings by a letter **x**.

Each of these three possible permissions can be assigned in three different ways:

- **User permissions** always apply to the owner of a file or directory.

- **Group permissions** always apply to members of the group assigned to a file or directory.

- **Other permissions** always apply to all users on the Linux system who are not the owner of the file or directory in question and are not members of the group assigned to the file or directory.

The three permissions assigned in three ways create a total of nine permissions that can be assigned to any file or directory in Linux. These nine permissions are shown on the left side of the output of the `ls -l` command. Consider this sample output from the `ls -l` command:

```
-rwxr-xr-x    1 nwells    users    121024 Nov 18 14:36 newprogram
```

The far left character of the output (a hyphen in this example) indicates the type of item you are viewing. A hyphen indicates a regular file. The letter **d** indicates a directory. The next nine characters represent three permissions for the file's owner (user permissions), three permissions for members of the file's assigned group, and three permissions for all other users on the system. As a further example, consider a few common arrangements of Linux file permissions. A utility such as `fdisk` or `less` has the `root` user assigned as the file's owner and has file permissions that appear like this in a file listing using `ls -l`:

```
rwxr-xr-x
```

These indicate that the file's owner (`root`) can write to (alter) the file, and that everyone else on the system (both group members and other users) can read the file and execute it as a command. A common set of permissions assigned to files that you create is shown here:

```
rw-r--r--
```

You, as the owner of the file, can read and write to it. Others on the system can read the file's contents but cannot alter the file.

You can use the **chmod** command to change the permissions assigned to any file or directory that you own. If you are logged in as **root**, you can use chmod to change the permissions of any file or directory on the system. To use the chmod command, include the type of permissions you want to change (user, group, or other, entered as **u**, **g**, or **o**), followed by a plus or minus sign to add or remove permissions, followed by the permissions you want to add or remove (**r**, **w**, or **x** for read, write, or execute). For example, to add the write permission for other users to the file **test**, use this command:

```
chmod o+w test
```

You can also set specific permissions using an equal sign. For example, to set the permissions for members of the group assigned to the file **test** to read and write, use this command:

```
chmod g=rw test
```

System administrators often use a different syntax with the **chmod** command. This alternative syntax is easier to use once you are familiar with it, but it's more challenging to learn. In this alternative syntax, each of the sets of three permissions (for user, group, and other) is represented by a number from 0 to 7. The three possible permissions (read, write, and execute) are assigned values of 4, 2, and 1, respectively. Now suppose that a system administrator wanted to grant read (4) and write (2) permission for the user, read (4) permission to the group, and no permissions to other users. The first digit used in **chmod** is 6, the sum of 4 and 2; the second digit is 4; the third digit is 0 (no permissions are granted). So the command would look like this:

```
chmod 640 test
```

Using the same method, if the system administrator wanted to assign read (4), write (2), and execute (1) permissions to the user, read (4) and execute (1) permissions to the group, and the same to other users, the command would look like this:

```
chmod 755 test
```

Although this method may appear strange at first, you should become familiar with it because you will see it used often by experienced system administrators on all UNIX systems. You will also discover that only a few combinations of file permissions are commonly used. Once you are familiar with the three-digit code for those commonly used sets of permissions, using the three digits is easier than entering all the letters with a plus, minus, or equal sign.

Conversely, using a graphical environment like Gnome or KDE provides a much easier method of setting file permissions. Within the Properties dialog box described previously, the Permissions tab includes check boxes in which you can activate or remove any of the nine permissions described in this section. Figure 4-5 shows the Permissions tab in the Properties dialog box of the Gnome file manager.

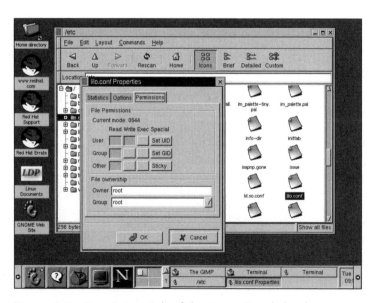

Figure 4-5   Permissions tab of the Properties dialog box

> **TIP** The Permissions tab includes additional security information that is beyond the scope of this book.

Each time you create a new file, a default set of file permissions are assigned to the file. On most Linux systems, the permissions for a newly created file look like this:

rw-r--r--

The permissions above assign you as the file's owner, and give you permission to read and write to the new file. Others can only read the file. The **umask** command determines the file permissions assigned when you create a new file. The umask command is executed automatically when you log in to Linux. You can alter the default permissions assigned to a new file by executing the **umask** command again at any time. The umask command uses three-digit codes similar to the **chmod** command. Assume that the default permissions without using umask would look like this:

rw-rw-rw-

The value provided with the **umask** command disables one or more of these standard permissions, using the same numbers assigned to each permission as the chmod command (4 for read, 2 for write, and 1 for execute). Thus, a standard **umask** command like this will disable the write permission for the group and other categories:

umask 022

This results in the default file permissions shown here.

rw-r--r--

MANAGING SOFTWARE PACKAGES

To run any program in Linux, you simply enter the program's name at a command-line prompt. The shell then loads and executes the command. This is true for command-line utilities, such as **cp** and **ls**, and also for programs, such as WordPerfect for Linux (whose program file is named **xwp**) or Netscape Communicator (whose program file is named **netscape**). Some programs allow you to add parameters or options along with the command to run the program. A **command-line parameter** is an additional piece of information (besides the name) that is included on the command-line when a program is started. The shell passes the command-line parameter to the program to control how the program operates. In the previous section you learned about one example of a command-line parameter: the **ls -l** command. The **-l** command-line parameter is passed to the **ls** program to instruct it to print a long-format list of files. Command-line parameters are also called **command-line options**.

To execute a program, Linux must be able to locate it within the Linux directory structure. For example, when you enter the command **cp**, Linux must be able to locate the **cp** program file in the directory where it is stored: **/bin**. To do this, Linux uses an environment variable called **PATH**. A **variable** is a memory location used by a program to store a value, such as a number or a word. Each variable is assigned a name so that the program can access the value by referring to the name. **Environment variables** are variables that are defined by the Linux shell so that all programs can access their values. The `PATH` environment variable includes a list of all the directories where programs on the system are normally located, such as `/bin`, `/usr/local/bin`, and others. When you enter a program name to execute, the shell searches each of the directories named in the `PATH` environment variable until the program name is found. Then the program is loaded and executed. If the program cannot be found in any of the directories listed in `PATH`, the shell returns an error. For example, attempting to execute a nonexistent program called `makedir` (the real command is `mkdir`) causes the shell to print the following error message:

```
bash: makedir: command not found
```

You can view the value of the `PATH` environment variable (and thus see where all the programs on your system are stored) by using the `echo` command. The **echo** command prints to the screen (that is, displays on the screen) text you specify. For example, the command `echo This is a test` displays this on the screen:

```
This is a test
```

Whenever the shell detects the name of an environment variable preceded by a dollar sign, such as `$PATH` , the shell replaces the name of the environment variable with the numbers or letters stored in memory under that variable's name. Using the `echo` command you can display on the screen the numbers or letters stored in an environment variable. Use the command `echo $PATH` to display on the screen the value of the `PATH` environment variable. Sample output of the command `echo $PATH` is shown here:

```
/usr/bin:/bin:/usr/local/bin:/usr/bin/X11:/usr/X11R6/bin:/home/nwells/bin
```

The value of the `PATH` environment variable differs slightly based on which version of Linux you are using, though the value will always be similar to the preceding output. Notice in the output above that each of the directories where programs are stored is separated by a colon (:).

To run a program stored in a directory that is not named in the `PATH` environment variable, use the full pathname of the program. For example, if you have a new program called `kpacman` stored in your home directory (which is not part of the `PATH` variable), use a command like this to start the program:

```
/home/nwells/kpacman
```

You can also use a single period to refer to the current directory. (Remember, use two periods to refer to the parent directory.) So to run a program called `kpacman` that is stored in your current directory (whatever directory you happen to be working in), the command would look like this:

```
./kpacman
```

In Chapter 6 you learn more about creating and using `PATH` and other environment variables.

Function Libraries

Many Linux programs require the same underlying functionality to complete tasks. For example, most programs need to open files on the hard disk. Many programs also need to read information from the keyboard or write results to the screen. Each of these tasks is called a function in computer programming jargon. A function is a small task that a computer program performs. The average programmer could probably list hundreds of functions commonly required by his or her programs.

Rather than having to include all of these functions in every program, programmers can assume that the necessary functions are already included in a Linux system, in the form of a function library. A **function library** is a file that contains a collection of commonly used functions for any program to use as it runs. Dozens of these libraries are installed when you install Linux. Function libraries help a Linux system conserve system resources (such as memory), because one function library can be used by multiple programs at the same time.

The directories /lib and /usr/lib contain most of the libraries used by Linux programs. A few of the commonly used libraries are listed in Table 4-3. As you explore the directories /lib and /usr/lib, notice that the library files all begin with the name lib and end with the file extension .so, followed by a version number. (The version number is not included in Table 4-3.) The file extension .so stands for *shared object*, because the libraries can be shared among many programs. When you install new libraries on your system, they are normally placed in the /usr/lib directory. Some parts of the Linux system, however, such as the KDE Desktop or the X Window System, have separate directories for dedicated library files. For example, /opt/kde/lib for KDE and /usr/X11R6/lib for the X Window System are two standard locations.

Table 4-3   A Few Common Function Libraries

Library	Purpose
libc	Standard programming functions in the C programming language
libm	Mathematical functions
libext2fs	Functions to access an ext2-format (native Linux) hard disk
libtermcap	Functions for working with terminals (controlling the character format and output on character-mode screens)
libcrypt	Functions to encrypt passwords for managing user logins
libgif	Functions used when processing gif-format graphics

As you work with new programs in Linux, sometimes the libraries needed to run a program are not included on your Linux system. To fix this you must determine which libraries are needed and add them to your system. The **ldd** command lists the function libraries that a program uses. For example, to view the libraries used by the **ls** command, use this command:

```
ldd /bin/ls
```

This command results in only two lines displayed on the screen, indicating that the **ls** command uses only two libraries. Larger, more complex programs (such as graphical programs) will use many more libraries. For instance, **gtop** (a Gnome system administration utility described in Chapter 10) uses a number of libraries. Consider the output of the command **ldd /usr/bin/gtop**.

```
libgnomeui.so.32 => /usr/lib/libgnomeui.so.32 (0x40019000)
libart_lgpl.so.2 => /usr/lib/libart_lgpl.so.2 (0x400d1000)
libgdk_imlib.so.1 => /usr/lib/libgdk_imlib.so.1 (0x400de000)
libSM.so.6 => /usr/X11R6/lib/libSM.so.6 (0x40102000)
libICE.so.6 => /usr/X11R6/lib/libICE.so.6 (0x4010b000)
libgtk-1.2.so.0 => /usr/lib/libgtk-1.2.so.0 (0x40122000)
libgdk-1.2.so.0 => /usr/lib/libgdk-1.2.so.0 (0x40235000)
libgmodule-1.2.so.0 => /usr/lib/libgmodule-1.2.so.0 (0x40266000)
libXext.so.6 => /usr/X11R6/lib/libXext.so.6 (0x40269000)
libX11.so.6 => /usr/X11R6/lib/libX11.so.6 (0x40276000)
libgnome.so.32 => /usr/lib/libgnome.so.32 (0x4031a000)
libgnomesupport.so.0 => /usr/lib/libgnomesupport.so.0
libesd.so.0 => /usr/lib/libesd.so.0 (0x40332000)
libaudiofile.so.0 => /usr/lib/libaudiofile.so.0 (0x40338000)
libm.so.6 => /lib/libm.so.6 (0x40345000)
libdb.so.2 => /lib/libdb.so.2 (0x40362000)
libglib-1.2.so.0 => /usr/lib/libglib-1.2.so.0 (0x40370000)
libdl.so.2 => /lib/libdl.so.2 (0x40390000)
libgtop.so.1 => /usr/lib/libgtop.so.1 (0x40393000)
libgtop_sysdeps.so.1 => /usr/lib/libgtop_sysdeps.so.1
libgtop_common.so.1 => /usr/lib/libgtop_common.so.1 (0x403a4000)
libgdbm.so.2 => /usr/lib/libgdbm.so.2 (0x403a9000)
libc.so.6 => /lib/libc.so.6 (0x403af000)
libz.so.1 => /usr/lib/libz.so.1 (0x4049d000)
/lib/ld-linux.so.2 => /lib/ld-linux.so.2 (0x40000000)
```

In the next section you learn how to add missing libraries to a Linux system using the **rpm** command.

Adding and Removing Software Packages

In Chapter 3 you learned that a single software package file can contain all of the files and configuration information needed to set up a new application or collection of utilities. You also learned that the Red Hat Package Manager (rpm) data format is the most popular type of software package for Linux. Files in rpm format (each with a file extension of **.rpm**) are copied to the system during the Linux installation process. After the installation is complete, you can use the **rpm** command to manage all of the rpm software packages on a Linux system.

The many options of the **rpm** command allow you to maintain a database of all the software installed on the Linux system. You can query this database to learn about what software is installed, what version of a software package you are using, and other information. You can also use the **rpm** command to install new software packages or remove software packages from the system.

To see if a package is installed on the system, use the **-q** option. To use this option you must know the name of the package. For example, to see if the Apache Web server is installed, use the command **rpm -q apache**. The response tells you either the complete name and version number of the installed package or that the package is not installed. The command **rpm -qa** lists all the packages installed on the system. You can use this command with the **less** command to browse through the list. The command would look like this:

```
rpm -qa | less
```

You can install new packages in rpm format using the **rpm** command. Linux CDs that are based on rpm-format packages will contain hundreds of rpm files that you can use to install additional software on your system. For example, the installation option that you selected when installing Linux might not have included the graphical program called Gimp. Once you have mounted your Linux CD-ROM drive with a command such as **mount /mnt/cdrom** (Chapter 9 provides details on this step), you can change to the directory containing the rpm files and use the **rpm** command to install **Gimp**. On Red Hat Linux, the necessary commands are as follows. (The directory in the second command and the version number in the final command will be different on other Linux systems.)

```
mount /mnt/cdrom
cd /mnt/cdrom/RedHat/RPMS
rpm -Uvh gimp-1.0.4-3.i386.rpm
```

After the last command shown here is executed, a list of hash marks (#####) appears on the screen, indicating that the files in the software packages are being installed. The **-U** option on the **rpm** command line indicates that you want to upgrade the package. Thus, if a package of the same name is already installed on the system, the **-U** option updates the package using the newer package's files.

You can also delete a package from the Linux system using the **-e** option (for *erase*). Note that all information about a package is completely erased when you use the **rpm -e** command. This means that once you delete a package, you can only reinstall it using the original rpm file from the Linux CD (or from the Internet). For example, the following command erases the Gimp program from the Linux system:

```
rpm -e gimp
```

TIP

When using `rpm` to install a package, you must specify the complete filename (ending with `.rpm`). Otherwise `rpm` will not be able to locate the software package in the directory structure. When using the `–q` or `–e` option, you only need to specify the package name, without a version number or `.rpm` extension, to locate the package within the internal rpm database.

The `rpm` command includes dozens of more complex options, which you can review by entering `rpm` without any command-line parameters after the command.

Several graphical programs are available to help you manage rpm software packages. These programs use the `rpm` command in the background as you select menu items and work in dialog boxes, which provide an easy-to-use interface to the many functions of the command. For example, you can list a description of a package by using the command `rpm –qi`, or list all the files in a package by using the command `rpm –ql`, or show which package contains a certain file by using the command `rpm –qf filename`. But rather than memorize all of these commands immediately, you can use the menu items and dialog boxes provided by one of the rpm graphical tools.

One such graphical tool is the `GnoRPM` package management utility. To open it from the Gnome Desktop, click the footprint icon, point to `System`, and then click `GnoRPM` (see Figure 4-6). The left side of the window shows a list of categories into which packages have been divided for easy reference. The right side of the window displays an icon for each software package included in the category that you select. You can right-click on a package icon to display a list of options related to that package.

The KDE Desktop also includes a package management tool called `kpackage`. You can start this program from the `System` menu on most KDE Desktops. (Some systems use a different location for `kpackage`; for instance, Caldera OpenLinux places `kpackage` on the `COAS` submenu.) Within `kpackage`, categories are displayed on the left. Click on a category to open a list (also on the left side of the window) of the packages in that category. Click a package name to display information about that package in the right side of the window. A description of the package and a list of every file contained in the package are available on two tabs on the right side of the window. Figure 4-7 shows the `kpackage` utility displaying information for one software package.

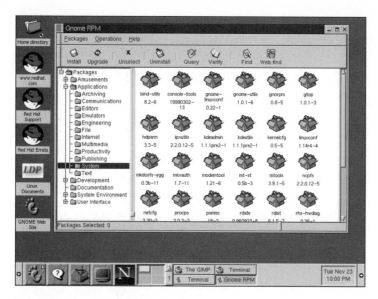

Figure 4-6   The GnoRPM package management utility

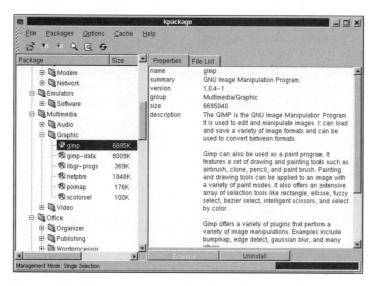

Figure 4-7   The kpackage utility for software package management

Both GnoRPM and kpackage provide menu items that let you search for a package with a certain name, search for a package containing a certain file on the system, or install and uninstall software packages. They do not provide access to all the features of the rpm command, but they handle most tasks that you are likely to need as a system administrator. The kpackage utility also lets you manage different types of software packages, such as those in .deb format used by the Debian Linux distribution.

> **TIP**   Both GnoRPM and kpackage can be started from the command line as well. Within a terminal window, enter the command gnorpm (or kpackage).

Using tar Archive Files

Although many Linux systems use rpm software packages, another common format, a tar archive, is used for much of the Linux software that you might see on the Internet. The **tar** command is used to create a single file that contains many other files, often compressed to save space. A **tar archive** is a file created by the **tar** command and has a file extension of .tar. When a tar archive has been compressed using the standard Linux compression utility, **gzip** (pronounced gee-zip), the file is sometimes called a *gzipped tarball*. These compressed tar archives have the file extension .tgz or sometimes .tar.gz.

A tar archive does not provide the functionality of an rpm software package. The tar archive is simply a collection of files within one directory tree. No database of installed tar archives is maintained, and no special tools support the features of rpms when using tar archives. But tar archives are supported on virtually every UNIX and Linux system in the world, so they make a convenient method of sharing files across the Internet. As you explore Internet sites containing Linux programs, such as *ftp://metalab.unc.edu/pub/Linux*, you will see many tar archives. After you have downloaded a tar archive, you can extract its contents using the **tar** command. For example, to extract the contents of an archive file named **program.tgz**, use this command:

```
tar xvzf program.tgz
```

The **tar** command is used extensively in Linux for creating backups of files on the system. The name **tar** comes from *tape archive*, because data backups were formerly always written to a tape back-up device. (Now devices such as writeable CD drives are also used.) Chapter 14 describes how to use the **tar** command to create and manage backups on Linux.

A tar archive is not the only type of file that can be compressed on Linux. You can also use the **gzip** command to compress any file on the system. For example, to compress the file **large.doc**, use this command:

```
gzip large.doc
```

The preceding command transforms the file **large.doc** into a compressed file called **large.doc.gz**. The **gunzip** command uncompresses a file that you have compressed using **gzip**. For example, to uncompress the **large.doc.gz** file, use the command **gunzip large.doc.gz**. The resulting file is named **large.doc**.

TIP When you use the `tar` command to extract the contents of a tar archive, the tar archive remains intact. When you use the `gzip` or `gunzip` command to compress or uncompress a file, the original file is altered (compressed or uncompressed), and its name is changed accordingly.

4

The amount that the `gzip` program compresses a file depends on the type of data contained in the file. Text files and some types of graphics files may be compressed by 70 to 90%. That is, a file of 1 MB may be compressed to only 100 KB to 300 KB. Other types of data may only be compressed by 10 to 20%.

The `gzip` utility is the most commonly used compression tool on Linux systems, but it is not the only one available. All of the compression utilities are listed in Table 4-4.

Table 4-4   Compression Utilities in Linux

Compress/uncompress utility	Description
`gzip` and `gunzip`	Provides good compression ratios. Use this tool for most cases; it is the most commonly used compression tool on Linux. Compressed files have the extension `.gz`.
`zip` and `unzip`	Compresses multiple files into one file, much like a compressed tar archive. Compatible with `pkzip` and `WinZip` on other operating systems. Use this program to share files with users on non-Linux systems. Compressed files have the file extension `.zip`.
`compress` and `uncompress`	Provides poor compression compared to `gzip` (files are not as small when compressed with the `compress` command). It is an older utility supported on almost all UNIX systems. Compressed files have the extension `.z`.
`bzip` and `bunzip`	Provides excellent compression (creates very small files), but it is a newer utility that is not widely used yet. Limit your use to sharing files with those you know have `bzip`. Compressed files have the extension `.bz2`.

THE LINUX KERNEL

In Chapter 1 you learned the definition and function of an operating system kernel. In this section you learn more about how to manage the Linux kernel. The Linux kernel continues to be managed by Linus Torvalds, the original creator of Linux. New features are regularly added to the Linux kernel, which is then integrated into new versions of Linux products such as SuSE Linux, Turbo Linux, and Red Hat Linux. As new features are added to the kernel, Linus Torvalds (and the developers with whom he works) assign new version numbers to the kernel.

You can learn more about the current status of Linux kernel development by visiting the Web site *www.linuxhq.com*. The latest Linux kernel is always available for download from this site, or from the FTP site *ftp.funet.fi* in Finland.

Learning About Your Kernel

After installing Linux you can use the `uname` command to learn about the kernel that is running your particular system. The `uname` command provides the kernel version, as well as additional information about the operating system. Two useful options of the `uname` command are `-r` and `-v`. The `-r` option (for *release*) displays the Linux kernel version number, followed by a release number. The **release number** is a number assigned by the company that prepared the Linux product. The release number allows the company to track how many times the kernel has been altered before shipping the final product. For example, using the `-r` option on your system might result in something like:

```
2.2.10-15
```

Here the kernel version is `2.2.10`, and the release number is `15`.

Each kernel also has a timestamp associated with it, which indicates the date and time when the kernel was created. As you begin to create your own Linux kernels (later in this chapter), you will need to use the `uname  -v` command to check the timestamp of the kernel that is currently controlling the system. For example, after installing a new Linux system, the `uname -v` command might show something like this:

```
#1 Fri Nov 19 10:25:20 PST 1999
```

After you have created a new kernel with different features enabled, and rebooted the system to start the new kernel, the `uname  -v` command would show a different date and time, letting you know that the new kernel was active.

You can also use the command `cat /proc/version` to print the kernel version to the screen. Sample output from this command is shown here. It includes both the version number and the timestamp.

```
Linux version 2.2.5-15 (root@incline.xmission.com) (gcc ver-
sion egcs-2.91.66 19990314/Linux (egcs-
1.1.2 release)) #1 Fri Nov 19 10:25:20 PST 1999
```

Kernel Modules

One of the most useful features of Linux is its ability to add and remove features of the kernel without restarting the computer. Linux **kernel modules** are files containing computer code that can be loaded into the kernel or removed from the kernel as needed. Some features of the kernel are built in, but many others are available by adding modules to a Linux kernel. For example, you can add kernel modules to provide any of the following:

- Support for a network adapter card
- Support for a SCSI hard disk controller card
- Networking features such as firewall capability
- The ability to access other types of file systems, such as data stored in Windows NT
- Support for a sound card

Some kernel modules may be automatically loaded into the kernel based on the configuration you set up during the Linux installation. The `lsmod` command lists the modules that are installed in the Linux kernel. The names of modules are often very cryptic, but some are recognizable. For example, the `sound` module is used for sound card support, and the `scsi` module is part of the support for SCSI hard disk controllers. Sample output of the `lsmod` command is shown here:

```
Module                   Size      Used by
nfsd                     150936       8   (autoclean)
lockd                    30856        1   (autoclean) [nfsd]
sunrpc                   52356        1   (autoclean) [nfsd lockd]
pcnet_cs                 7456         1
8390                     5920         0   [pcnet_cs]
ds                       5740         2   [pcnet_cs]
i82365                   21956        2
pcmcia_core              39720        0   [pcnet_cs ds i82365]
```

Each kernel module is stored as a file on the hard disk. When the module is added to the kernel, it is copied from the hard disk to memory as part of the kernel. Figure 4-8 shows how kernel modules relate to the Linux kernel.

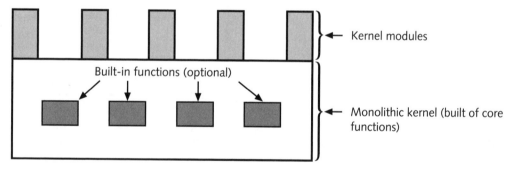

Figure 4-8   Linux kernel modules and the kernel itself

Adding and Removing Modules

If you need to add a feature to the Linux kernel (such as support for a sound card or a networking feature), you can use the `insmod` command. The `insmod` command copies a module file from the hard disk and adds it to the Linux kernel running in memory. For example, the command `insmod  sound` adds the `sound` module to the kernel.

Sometimes one module requires another module in order to function correctly. For example, to use the `sb` module to support a SoundBlaster card, you must first load the `sound` module. The **modprobe** command loads a module with all of its required supporting modules. For example, you use the command `modprobe  sb` to load the SoundBlaster module and all the modules that it requires to function correctly. Using `modprobe` is the preferred method of adding kernel modules.

The **rmmod** command removes a module from the kernel. The module remains available on the hard disk so that you can insert it again later using `insmod` or `modprobe`.

Some modules require specific hardware information in order to function correctly. For example, when you add a module to support a network adapter card, you may need to include information about the card's IRQ. (This information might have already been supplied during the Linux installation.) **Module parameters** provide information needed by a module to locate system resources. When using the `insmod` or `modprobe` command, you should add module parameters after the module name. For example, to add a kernel module for an NE2000 network adapter (which requires a module called `ne2`), the following command would specify the hardware's IRQ and I/O port address:

```
modprobe ne2 irq=11 io_port=0x330
```

 The `0x` at the beginning of the last number in the preceding example indicates a hexadecimal value.

When you execute the `insmod` or `modprobe` command, the module attempts to communicate with any related system hardware as it is being loaded. If the module loads successfully, you see no feedback on the screen. If a problem occurs, you see a message stating that the module could not be loaded or could not be initialized. Such a message means that the module parameters were either incorrect or inadequate.

Locating Modules

When you see a module name (something like `sb` or `aic7xxx`), it's difficult to know which devices or kernel features that module provides support for. In addition, the module parameters that are supported by each module are difficult to find. You can always experiment with different modules until you finally locate the correct module for hardware that is not working correctly. However, it's more efficient to contact the vendor of your Linux system and ask the technical support representative which module and parameters to use. (You will still need to determine the values for the required parameters based on your computer's hardware configuration.)

The source code for the modules contains detailed information about what devices are supported by each module and what parameters are supported by the module, but reading the source code of a module (not to mention simply locating the correct module in the first place) can be tedious and time consuming. However, if you do want to review a module's source code, simply load any of the files from the following directory into a text editor: `/usr/src/linux/modules`.

The modules that are available on your system are stored in the directory `/lib/modules/version`, where `version` is the version number of the Linux kernel on the system. For example, `/lib/modules/2.2.12` is one possible directory name. Within this directory are several subdirectories, each of which contains dozens of modules. Example subdirectories include `ipv4` for networking features, `net` for network adapter card support, and `video` for Linux video support. The `insmod` and `modprobe` commands automatically search these directories for the correct module file.

Automatically Loading Modules

You can use the `insmod` or `modprobe` command to load kernel modules into memory as part of the Linux kernel after the Linux system has started. But it is more convenient to have the necessary modules loaded automatically as the system starts. You can do this using several configuration methods. Before you automate module loading, you need to verify that you can add the module successfully using `insmod` or `modprobe`.

The first method for automating the process of loading a module is to add the appropriate `insmod` or `modprobe` command (with any needed module parameters) to the end of the `/etc/rc.d/rc.local` file. This file is executed each time the system is started (as described later in this chapter). When you add a command, such as the following `modprobe` example, to the end of the `rc.local` file (using any text editor program), the command is executed automatically as the system boots.

```
modprobe ne2 irq=11 io_port=0x330
```

The second method for installing modules is to let the `kerneld` program attempt to load modules automatically when they are needed. Red Hat Linux is designed so that system administrators can easily use this method to automate module loading. The `kerneld` program watches for programming requests that cannot be handled without a new module. It then loads the required module automatically. Keep in mind, however, that the `kerneld` program may not be able to determine the module you need. In this case, you can add a module name to the file `/etc/conf.modules` in Red Hat Linux. This causes the module to be automatically loaded by the Linux start-up process.

Yet a third method relies on a list of modules that are needed for the system to operate. All the modules in the list are loaded at start-up time. Caldera OpenLinux is designed to have system administrators use this method. (OpenLinux includes scripts that a system administrator can modify to easily implement this method of module loading.) The file containing the list of modules is stored in the directory `/etc/modules/version`, where *version* is the kernel version number, such as `2.2.10`. The file containing the list of modules is named for the timestamp of the kernel. For example, suppose the output of the `uname -v` command gives the following output:

```
#1 Fri Nov 19 10:25:20 PST 1999
```

In this case, the list of modules to load for that kernel is located in the following file (using the example kernel version of 2.2.10):

```
/etc/modules/2.2.10/#1 Fri Nov 19 10:25:20 PST 1999
```

Because this filename contains spaces, you need to enclose it in quotation marks when using it in a command. For example, to view the list of modules to be autoloaded in OpenLinux, use this command:

```
cat "/etc/modules/2.2.10/#1 Fri Nov 19 10:25:20 PST 1999"
```

Modifying the Linux Kernel

Although the Linux kernel provides many features and support for many types of hardware, you may discover situations that make it necessary to recompile the source code of the Linux kernel. Examples of when this might be necessary include the following situations:

- You need to add a feature to your system that Linux supports but which is not activated in the kernel that you installed by default. For example, you may need to add support for multiprocessing systems (such as dual-Pentium computers).

- You need to add built-in support for a hardware device that is currently supported only by adding a module to the kernel. For example, some types of SCSI hard disks require built-in kernel support in order to boot the Linux system from those hard disks.

- You want to use an updated version of the Linux kernel to add new features or fix a problem that was discovered with your current version.

In any of these cases, you can recompile the Linux kernel from its source code into a new kernel. The file `vmlinuz` contains the Linux kernel. It is usually located in the / directory or in the `/boot` directory. Before you can work with the kernel source code, you must verify that it is installed on your system. If you are using Red Hat Linux, you should find the source code in a single rpm package named `kernel-source`. You can use the `rpm` command with the `-q` option to see if this package is installed, or use the `rpm` command with the `-Uvh` options to install the package from CD if needed. Other versions of Linux may use different names for the source code package. For example, the source code on Caldera OpenLinux is stored in two files named `linux-source-common` and `linux-source-i386`.

Once the source code is installed, you can explore the source code files in the directory `/usr/src/linux`. When you install the kernel source code from the CD that you used to install Linux, and then recompile the source code to create a new kernel file, you are not changing the version of the kernel. You are only changing the features that are activated in the kernel. For example, if the kernel installed with a Linux system is version 2.2.10, the version after recompiling the kernel remains 2.2.10, but the timestamp of the new kernel will be different because it was compiled at a different time.

Before you can recompile the kernel, you must configure the features you want to include in the kernel by using a menu-based utility provided with all Linux systems. To start this utility, first verify that the kernel source code is installed on your system. Then enter these two commands:

```
cd /usr/src/linux
make menuconfig
```

Figure 4-9 shows the menu-based kernel configuration tool. Use the arrow keys and other keys as directed in this interface to select features of the kernel that you want to activate. Each item in the initial screen leads to a submenu of options. Over 1000 configuration options are available. A default setting based on your current kernel is used for any settings that you do not alter. When you have made all the changes that you want to make in the kernel configuration, choose the `Save and Exit` option on the main menu. A hidden configuration file is then created based on your selections.

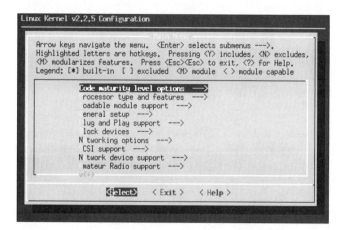

Figure 4-9   The menu-based kernel configuration screen

 TIP A graphical configuration tool is also provided with the Linux kernel. You can start that tool by entering the command `make xconfig`. You can execute the `make menuconfig` command from any command line.

After completing the configuration, you must compile the kernel source code based on the new configuration. To do this, verify that the `/usr/src/linux` subdirectory is the current directory, and then enter the following command:

`make dep; make zImage`

This command begins the compilation process, which can take from 5 minutes to several hours, depending on the speed of your system. A typical Pentium-class system should take 15 minutes or less. As parts of the kernel are compiled, you see hundreds of lines of text scroll on the screen.

Other compilation options are available. The commands shown in this section are the simplest means of creating a new kernel file. The file is called `zImage` and is located in the subdirectory `/usr/src/linux/arch/i386/boot`. You can copy this file to the `/` or `/boot` directory of the system and set up the LILO boot manager to use the new kernel when you restart your system. You must set up LILO to use the new kernel because the LILO program determines which kernel file is loaded when you boot the system. Configuring the LILO boot manager is discussed at the end of this chapter.

 TIP Sometimes a Linux vendor such as Red Hat Software will prepare updated kernels as rpm packages. In this case you can use the `rpm` command to update the kernel without following the steps in this section. Check the instructions from your Linux vendor carefully before attempting to install a new Linux kernel using the `rpm` command.

THE INITIALIZATION PROCESS

When you turn on a computer, many things must occur before the operating system is loaded and ready to accept commands and execute programs. The following sections describe the main steps that Linux takes to initialize the system each time you turn it on. Some of the details of this process vary among Linux distributions, but most Linux systems use a process very similar to the one described here for Red Hat Linux.

Booting the Kernel

When you first turn on the computer, the LILO boot manager displays a prompt that reads `boot:`. At this prompt you can choose which operating system to load. (If the computer has only Linux installed, you can only choose Linux.) Normally, you can enter the label `linux` to start the Linux system.

In addition to simply entering `linux`, you can add boot parameters to control how Linux is started. **Boot parameters** are codes similar to module parameters that instruct the Linux kernel how to operate or how to access parts of the computer system's hardware. (Chapter 3 mentioned boot parameters briefly in relation to helping Linux work with hardware components that could not be recognized.)

Besides helping Linux recognize hardware, boot parameters can be used to activate features of Linux. For example, by entering this command at the LILO boot prompt, you start Linux in a special single-user maintenance mode:

```
linux S
```

The Linux kernel supports dozens of boot parameters. Most are used either to help Linux find hardware or to assist with troubleshooting and system administration work. The BootPrompt-HOWTO document describes all of these boot parameters. You can find this document in the directory `/usr/doc/HOWTO`.

On some systems you will be required to add boot parameters each time you start Linux. For example, on many systems you must add a line specifying the amount of memory on the system so that Linux can recognize and use all available RAM. This command would look like this for a system with 128 MB of RAM:

```
linux mem=128M
```

You can configure the LILO program to use certain boot parameters automatically so that you don't have to enter them each time you start the system. The last section of this chapter describes how to change the configuration of LILO.

Initializing System Services

After the LILO boot manager starts the kernel, the kernel initializes all of the computer's hardware. You see messages scroll by as each piece of hardware is initialized. When the boot process is complete and you have logged in to Linux, you can execute the **dmesg** command to view the messages printed by the kernel during the boot process.

4

After the kernel has completed the hardware initialization, the kernel launches a program called init. The **init program** is a master control program that starts many other processes on the system, such as the login prompts. The init program also runs many scripts that initialize the system services you have configured during the installation of Linux. (A **script** is a collection of commands, similar to a macro, that are stored in a text file and executed without user intervention.)

The init program is controlled by the /etc/inittab configuration file. This file contains pointers to the scripts that init will run to initialize the Linux system each time it is turned on. The /etc/inittab file is slightly different in each version of Linux, but after reviewing the file on one system, you should be able to recognize which features work on other Linux systems. Almost all of the files referred to by the /etc/inittab configuration file are located in the /etc/rc.d subdirectory. The main configuration files referred to by the /etc/inittab file in Red Hat Linux are described in the list below. (Each is located in the directory /etc/rc.d.)

- rc.sysinit: this is the main system initialization script for Red Hat Linux. It includes commands for setting up how the keyboard is used, which environment variables are needed, and many other hardware-specific configuration details that are not handled by the Linux kernel.

- rc: this script starts system services such as networking, a Web server, an e-mail server, and many others. The specific services that are started depend on how the system is configured (you may have set this up during the Linux installation). The rc script is used to set up runlevel-related services, as described in the next section.

- rc.local: this script is executed after other initialization scripts. It is initially empty or almost empty. Rather than containing commands by default, rc.local is the script in which you can place commands that you want to have executed each time the system is turned on. Examples include loading modules using the insmod or modprobe command, or executing a special program that you want to have running all the time.

Although a detailed explanation of the contents of each initialization script is beyond the scope of this book, by knowing where the scripts are located, you can research the initialization process yourself to learn more.

Runlevels

A **runlevel** is a mode of operation that provides a particular set of services. Table 4–5 shows the standard runlevels for most Linux systems, with a brief description of how each is used. (The numbers associated with each runlevel's functionality may vary somewhat from one Linux distribution to another.)

Table 4-5   Runlevels in Linux

Runlevel	Name	Description
0	Halt	Used to shut down all services when the system will not be rebooted.
1	Single-user mode	Used for system maintenance. Does not provide networking capabilities.
2	Multiuser mode without networking enabled	Rarely used except for system maintenance or testing.
3	Regular multiuser networking mode	Most systems start in this runlevel.
4		Not used.
5		Identical to runlevel 3, except a graphical login screen is provided; the system remains in graphical mode at all times.
6	Reboot	Used to shut down all services when the system will be rebooted.

The runlevel used when starting the Linux system is defined in the `/etc/inittab` file. The `init` program launches the `rc` script located in the `/etc/rc.d` directory with a parameter that includes the runlevel to use. The `rc` script then starts the appropriate system services based on the selected runlevel.

Each runlevel is associated with a subdirectory. These subdirectories are located in the `/etc/rc.d` directory. For example, the directories `/etc/rc.d/rc3.d` and `/etc/rc.d/rc6.d` include files that control which system services are used in runlevel 3 or 6, respectively.

The runlevel subdirectories, such as `/etc/rc.d/rc3.d`, contain files that indicate which services are to be started or stopped when using that runlevel. Each file in these directories begins with a K or an S, followed by a two–digit number. The number indicates the order in which services are started or stopped. Services that begin with a K are stopped (*killed*); services that begin with an S are started. For example, the contents of a typical `/etc/rc.d/rc3.d` directory are shown here:

```
K15gpm          S11portmap      S60nfs
K20rstatd       S15netfs        S75keytable
K20rusersd      S20random       S80sendmail
K20rwhod        S30syslog       S85httpd
K45named        S40atd          S85sound
```

```
K55routed           S40crond            S90xfs
K60mars-nwe         S45pcmcia           S91smb
K92apmd             S50inet             S99linuxconf
S10network          S601pd              S991ocal
```

Here you can see that as Linux begins to use runlevel 3, the `rc` script will start the network services, the HTTP server, the Samba server, and many other services that are marked with an `S`. The contents of the `/etc/rc.d/rc6.d` directory shown below indicate a similar list of services that will be stopped when the system is being rebooted. Notice that the numbers in this case are in approximately the reverse order. The first services (network access, for example) form a foundation for the entire system and are therefore the last services to be stopped.

```
K00linuxconf        K20rwhod            K80random
K05keytable         K30sendmail         K85netfs
K10xfs              K45named            K89portmap
K15gpm              K50inet             K90killall
K15httpd            K55routed           K90network
K15sound            K60atd              K92apmd
K20nfs              K60crond            K96pcmcia
K20rstatd           K601pd              K99syslog
K20rusersd          K60mars-nwe         S00reboot
```

The initialization of each of these services includes another level of complication. The files you see in the runlevel subdirectories (such as those just shown) are not regular files—they are pointers to scripts that stop and start the services. Looking at a single example of this should clarify the point. If you use the `ls -l` command to see a long listing of the HTTP service in the `/etc/rc.d/rc3.d` subdirectory, you see that the `S85httpd` file is actually a pointer to another file: `/etc/rc.d/init.d/httpd`. Because the file (the pointer) in the `/etc/rc.d/rc3.d` subdirectory contains a leading `S`, the `rc` script executes this script with the word `start` after it. Thus, the `rc` script is actually executing this command to start the HTTP service:

```
/etc/rc.d/init.d/httpd start
```

> **TIP** The pointers described here are called symbolic links. A symbolic link allows one file to refer to another file on the system. You'll learn much more about symbolic links in Chapter 6.

Figure 4-10 shows how the initialization components described in this section relate to each other. Each file in the various runlevel directories operates in the same manner as the S85httpd pointer just described. All of them point to scripts stored in the /etc/rc.d/init.d directory. The scripts in this directory provide an organized method of starting and stopping system services. Although most of the services listed pertain to networking, which is not discussed in detail in this book, you need to understand the concept because these scripts make it easy for you to change almost anything on a Linux system (short of using a new Linux kernel) without restarting the computer. For example, suppose you had reconfigured all of the networking information on a Linux system. Rather than restart the system, you could simply execute these two commands to reinitialize networking:

```
/etc/rc.d/init.d/network stop
/etc/rc.d/init.d/network start
```

Some systems support the use of this single command:

```
/etc/rc.d/init.d/network restart
```

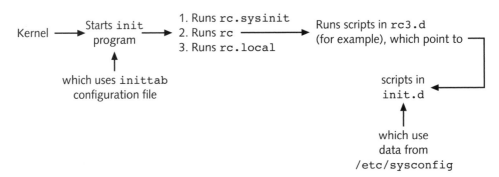

Figure 4-10   The Linux initialization components

Different Linux systems provide various utilities to manage which services are started using this runlevel directory system. One example is the **ksysv** program for KDE, shown in Figure 4-11. Using this utility, you can drag and drop icons representing services to determine which services are started or stopped in which runlevels. The **ksysv** program is not included with all versions of the KDE Desktop; you can look for it on the **System** menu in KDE. The **LinuxConf** utility in Red Hat Linux also provides a capability similar to **ksysv**.

The name **ksysv** may seem odd. The initial **k** simply means that the program is designed to run on the KDE Desktop. The reason for the **sysv** designation is historical. The initialization system just described for Linux is the same basic system that has been used for a long time in UNIX System V (a major version of the UNIX operating system). That system was adopted for Linux, and experienced system administrators know it as a standard System V (pronounced "system-five") initialization process—thus the name **ksysv**, for a KDE utility used to configure *system 5*-style initialization.

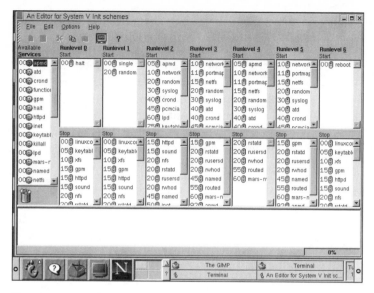

Figure 4-11   The `ksysv` utility

The initialization scripts located in `/etc/rc.d/init.d` are provided for you when you install Linux. In addition, if you install a new software package using the `rpm` command, a script will be placed in the correct directory if the package you install requires one to start a service. Of course, relatively few software packages are used for system services such as a Web server or e-mail server. The point is simply that you don't need to prepare these scripts yourself.

The initialization scripts in `/etc/rc.d/init.d` usually rely on a set of configuration information located in the `/etc/sysconfig` directory (and its subdirectories). Each file in `/etc/sysconfig` is named for a service, and each file contains name-value pairs that define for the initialization script how the service should be configured. For example, the `/etc/sysconfig/network` file on Red Hat Linux looks like this:

```
NETWORKING=yes
FORWARD_IPV4=false
HOSTNAME="incline"
```

These lines are used by the script `/etc/rc.d/init.d/network` to control how networking is set up. (Specific network information is located in the `network-scripts` subdirectory of `/etc/sysconfig`, but a further explanation of networking is beyond the scope of this book.)

Although you can edit the files in `/etc/sysconfig` directly, it is often best to try using the standard configuration tool provided with your Linux distribution. For example, use **COAS** on OpenLinux, **YAST** on Suse Linux, **LinuxConf** on Red Hat Linux, and so forth. Consult your Linux system documentation if you have questions about which utility to use.

Shutting Down Linux

In addition to being familiar with the initialization process of Linux, you need to know how to properly shut down a Linux system. The most important reason for properly shutting down a Linux system is because Linux caches hard disk data in memory. All modern operating systems use caching to improve system performance. **Caching** is the process of storing data from the hard disk in RAM so that it can be accessed more rapidly (because RAM is much faster than a hard disk). But caching data in RAM instead of writing it immediately to the hard disk entails a risk: if you turn off the computer suddenly, data in RAM may never be written to the hard disk and will then be lost.

For this reason, it is important to shut down Linux in an orderly, or graceful, way. The term **graceful shutdown** means stopping all Linux services and shutting down all file access in an orderly way before turning off or rebooting the computer. You can use the following methods for performing a graceful shutdown:

- Enter the command **reboot**. This will shut down all services and then restart the computer.

- Enter the command **halt**. This will shut down all services and then stop the computer with the message "System halted." This message indicates that you can safely turn off the computer.

- Use the **shutdown** command with a parameter to indicate how long to wait before shutting down the system and a parameter to indicate whether the system should be rebooted or halted. For example, to halt the system, beginning in five minutes, use the command **shutdown -h 5**.

- Press Ctrl+Alt+Del. This executes a shutdown command immediately. (The command the system will execute when you press Ctrl+Alt+Del is configured in the **/etc/inittab** file.)

- Enter the command **telinit 0** to halt the system, or the command **telinit 6** to reboot the system (shutting down all services first in both cases). The **telinit** command switches the system to a different runlevel: 0 or 6 in this case.

If you are working in a graphical desktop, you should log out before shutting down the system. This allows your graphical setup to be stored for use the next time you start the desktop. After logging out, you will either return to a character-mode prompt (if you are in runlevel 3) or a graphical login screen (if you are in runlevel 5). The graphical login screen usually includes a button that you can select to shut down the Linux system.

Although it's important to know how to shut down Linux, many Linux systems are left running for weeks or months (or years) between reboots. Unless you are working on a machine in a computer lab, or you need to change to a new kernel, or install new hardware, you can leave the system running a very long time without any fear of the system crashing or requiring a reboot.

Only the system administrator should be allowed to shut down a Linux system. By using boot parameters or starting the system from a floppy disk, a user could disrupt the system's security by rebooting. Thus, a system administrator should watch for evidence of unauthorized system reboots to be certain that nothing improper has been done to the system. Chapter 11 describes how to read system log files, which always include information about when the system was rebooted.

Configuring LILO

As you installed Linux you learned about setting up the LILO boot manager in order to launch Linux and, if necessary, other operating systems located on the same computer. In this section you learn how to update the configuration of LILO after the installation is completed. As with other system administration tasks, you must be logged in as **root** to update the LILO configuration.

The configuration of LILO is stored in the file /etc/lilo.conf. This file is created during the installation process, but you can use a standard text editor to alter the file as needed at any time. The lilo.conf file contains global configuration options as well as a configuration for one or more operating systems. A sample lilo.conf configuration file is shown here and described in detail in the paragraphs that follow:

```
boot=/dev/hda
map=/boot/map
install=/boot/boot.b
prompt
timeout=50

image=/boot/vmlinuz-2.2.5-15
      label=linux
      root=/dev/hda3
      read-only
other=/dev/hda1
      label=dos
      table=/dev/hda
```

The **boot=** line identifies where the LILO boot manager should be installed. If this line indicates a partition name, such as /dev/hda1, then LILO is stored on the boot sector of that partition. If a hard disk device is named, without a partition number, such as /dev/hda, then LILO is stored on the Master Boot Record of that hard disk. The next few lines in lilo.conf define the boot manager program that will be stored at the indicated location and, possibly, a message file to print as LILO starts.

The **prompt** keyword is normally included on systems that support more than one operating system. This allows you to choose which operating system to launch. The **timeout** field provides a waiting time in increments of 1/10 of a second. For example, the line **timeout=50** causes LILO to pause for five seconds before starting the default operating system.

The first few lines in lilo.conf (through the **timeout=50** line) are called the global section. These lines define how LILO behaves overall. After the global section, additional sections are defined for each of the operating systems that LILO can launch. In the output above, two types of systems are defined. In order for LILO to boot a Linux operating system you must use the keyword **image** followed by the name of the kernel image file (such as **vmlinuz** or zImage). Additional options below the `image` line define how Linux is loaded. The configuration options for a non-Linux operating system are indicated by the keyword `other`. The existence of an `other` section within this file indicates that LILO should pass control to another partition. For example, if you want LILO to start a Windows system, the `other` section should indicate the partition number where Windows is stored, like this:

```
other = /dev/hda1
```

The `other` partition must have some method of starting the operating system located on that partition. (Windows partitions are able to start Windows by default.)

For both Linux and an `other` operating system, you can specify additional parameters. You can only use a few of these parameters in the `other` sections. One that you can use is `password`, which requires the user to enter a password before LILO will cede control to the other operating system. The `password` parameter looks like this:

```
password=mypassword
```

The `image` sections (used to start a Linux operating system) support many options. One of these options is `append`, which is used to add boot parameters to Linux:

```
append="mem=128M"
```

The line beginning with `label` names the `image` section or the `other` section within the `lilo.conf` file. The values of all the `label` fields are displayed when you boot the system and press Tab to display operating systems that LILO can start.

You can review the documentation for the `lilo.conf` configuration file to discover all of the possible options that apply to the global section (the first part of the file) and to the `image` and `other` sections. To view the documentation, enter the command `man lilo.conf`.

Because LILO loads the Linux kernel as a file when the system is started, LILO can choose among several Linux kernels. When you recompile the kernel as described previously in this chapter, you can update `lilo.conf` so that LILO can start either your previous (existing) kernel or the new kernel that you just created. It is wise to provide configuration options for both in case the new kernel that you created has an unexpected problem—you can still reboot the system and have LILO start the old kernel that works. The following lines show how the two `image` sections of `lilo.conf` would look if you wanted to configure LILO so that it could start one of two different Linux kernels stored on the hard disk.

```
image=/boot/new_vmlinuz
     label=new_kernel
     root=/dev/hda4
     read-only

image=/boot/vmlinuz-2.2.5-15
     label=linux
     root=/dev/hda4
     read-only
```

After you have set up the `lilo.conf` file to support all of the operating systems and options needed, you must update the information on the hard disk. Saving the `lilo.conf` file records the configuration data, but it does not activate it on the boot sector or Master Boot

4

Record. To do that, you must run the `lilo` command. The `lilo` command reads the `lilo.conf` configuration file and updates the hard disk boot information based on the configuration you set up. Using this command is simple:

`/sbin/lilo`

If you update the `lilo.conf` file but do not run `lilo`, the configuration of LILO remains unchanged when you reboot the system. When `lilo` runs successfully, it displays the name of each operating system label for which you have defined a section.

 In rare instances, you will only see part of the word `LILO` when you boot the system (for example, you may see just `LI`), and the system then stops responding without booting an operating system. This indicates that LILO cannot locate information to start an operating system. In this case you must start the system from a boot disk or rescue disk and change the `lilo.conf` file. See Chapter 9 for more information on using these disks.

CHAPTER SUMMARY

- All files in Linux are stored in a single directory structure beginning with /, the root directory. You can use standard commands as well as graphical tools to move around the directory structure and manage files. All Linux files and directories have file permissions assigned based on the user assigned as owner and an assigned group name.

- Software packaging schemes, especially rpm, are used to install and manage applications on a Linux system. Graphical and command-line utilities are available to manage software packages. The `tar` command—one of many ways that files can be compressed and combined in Linux—is also popular on Linux systems.

- The Linux kernel uses modules to extend its functionality. Linux version numbers are significant in denoting the status of a particular version of the kernel. The kernel can be recompiled from source code after setting up a configuration for the new kernel using a menu-based tool. A new kernel must be configured in LILO so that it can be launched.

- Linux uses a standard System V–style initialization process in which the `init` program starts many configuration scripts to configure the system and launch system services. Using a complex system of subdirectories, the `rc` script and the default runlevel define which services are started. Linux must be properly shut down. The LILO boot manager can be configured with many different options to manage how Linux is started.

KEY TERMS

boot parameters — Codes similar to module parameters that are used to instruct the Linux kernel how to operate or how to access parts of the computer system's hardware.

caching — The process of storing data from the hard disk in RAM so that it can be accessed more rapidly (because RAM is much faster than a hard disk).

cat — Command used to print the contents of a file to the screen.

cd — Command used to change the directory you are working in (the current working directory).

chmod — Command used to change the file permissions assigned to a file or directory.

chown — Command used to change the ownership of a file or directory.

command-line option — A command-line parameter.

command-line parameter — An additional piece of information (besides the program name) that is included on the command line when a program is started.

command-line window — A window within a graphical environment that permits you to enter commands at the keyboard.

cp — Command used to copy a file or directory from one location or name to another.

current working directory — The directory in which you are working.

dmesg — Command used to view the messages printed by the kernel during the boot process.

echo — Command used to print text to the screen, converting variable names to their corresponding values.

environment variables — Variables that are defined by the Linux shell so that all programs can access their values.

execute permission — A file permission that allows a user to launch a file as a program or see a file within a directory. Represented by a letter **x**.

file — Command used to print a summary of the type of data contained in a file.

file extension — The last part of a filename after a period.

file manager window — A graphical window that displays the contents of a directory (usually as a collection of icons) and lets you work with the files and directories using menus, mouse clicks, and dialog boxes.

file permissions — Codes that define the type of access that a user has to a file or directory on the Linux system.

function library — A file containing a collection of commonly used functions that any program can use as it runs.

graceful shutdown — The technique of stopping all Linux services and shutting down all file access in an orderly way before turning off or rebooting the computer.

group — A named account that consists of a collection of users. Each member of a group has access to files owned by that group.

group permissions — A set of three file permissions (**r**, **w**, and **x**) that apply to members of the group assigned to a file or directory.

gunzip — Command used to uncompress a file that has been compressed using **gzip**.

gzip — Command used to compress any file on a Linux system.

halt — Command used to shut down all services and then stop the computer with the message "System halted."

home directory — The location where all of a user's personal files are stored.

init — Command used to switch the system to a different runlevel.

init program — A master control program that starts many other processes on the system, such as the login prompts.

insmod — Command used to copy a module file from the hard disk and add it to the Linux kernel running in memory.

kernel modules — Files containing computer code that can be loaded into the kernel or removed from the kernel as needed.

ldd — Command used to list the function libraries that a program uses.

less — Command used to print the contents of a file one screenful at a time. It allows you to move around in the file and otherwise control the command by using the keyboard.

lilo — Command used to read the `lilo.conf` configuration file and update the hard disk boot information based on the configuration.

ls — Command used to list the files in a directory.

lsmod — Command used to list the modules that are installed in the Linux kernel.

mkdir — Command used to create a new directory.

modprobe — Command used to load a module with all of its required supporting modules.

module parameters — Information needed by a module to locate system resources. The parameters are added after the module name when using the `insmod` or `modprobe` command.

more — Command used to print the contents of a file one screenful at a time. The `more` command is similar to the `less` command but with fewer keyboard control options.

mv — Command used to rename a file or move it to a new location.

other permissions — A set of three file permissions (`r`, `w`, and `x`) that apply to all users on the Linux system who are not the owner of the file or directory in question and are not members of the group assigned to the file or directory.

parent directory — The directory that is one level above the current directory.

pwd — Command that displays the current working directory.

read permission — A file permission that allows a user to read the contents of a file or browse the files in a directory. Represented by a letter `r`.

reboot — Command used to shut down all services and then restart the computer.

release number — A number assigned by the company that prepares a Linux product. It allows the company to track how many times the kernel file has been altered before the final product is shipped.

rm — Command used to delete a file.

rmdir — Command used to remove (delete) an empty directory.

rmmod — Command used to remove a module from the kernel.

root directory — The starting point for all access to Linux resources. It is indicated by a single forward slash: `/`.

rpm — Command used to manage all of the rpm software packages on a Linux system.

runlevel — A mode of operation that defines which Linux system services are started and which are shut down. The standard Linux runlevel of 3 includes networking and other common services such as system logging and task scheduling.

script — A collection of commands, similar to a macro, that are stored in a text file and executed without user intervention.

shell — The program in Linux that captures and handles commands entered in a command-line environment.

shutdown — Command used to shut down Linux gracefully.

tar — Command used to create a single file that contains many other files, often compressed to save space.

tar archive — A file created by the **tar** command.

telinit — Command used to switch the system to a different runlevel.

terminal emulator window — A command-line window (also called a terminal window) within a graphical environment.

timestamp — A record of the date and time when an event occurred.

touch — Command used to create a new file with no data in it or update the access timestamp of an existing file.

umask — Command used to set the file permissions assigned when you create a new file.

uname — Command used to provide information about the operating system, including the kernel version.

user permissions — A set of three file permissions (**r**, **w**, and **x**) that apply to the owner of a file or directory.

variable — A memory location used by a program to store a value, such as a number or a word. Each variable is assigned a name so that the program can access the value by referring to the name.

write permission — A file permission that allows a user to add or change information in a file or create files within a directory. Represented by a letter **w**.

xterm — A program within a graphical environment that provides a command-line window.

zcat — Command used to print the contents of a compressed file to the screen.

REVIEW QUESTIONS

1. The _____ directory is the beginning of the Linux directory structure.

    a. /

    b. /root

    c. /home

    d. /dev/hda

2. The **pwd** command is used to:

    a. Process writeable domains on the network

    b. Control power used by a Linux system

    c. Print the current working directory to the screen

    d. Print a summary of the writeable devices on the system

3. As with a DOS system, the command **cd..** can be used to change to the parent directory at any time. True or False?

4. Name three commands that can be used to view the contents of text files.

5. The command `Ls -l` is invalid because:

   a. Linux commands cannot contain hyphens.

   b. Linux commands are case sensitive.

   c. The `ls` command is not a real command.

   d. The `-l` option is not supported by the `ls` command.

6. The command `chmod 652 test` grants _____ execute permission to the `test` file.

   a. user

   b. group

   c. other

   d. all users on the system

7. The owner and group assigned to a file are shown by which of the following commands?

   a. `chown`

   b. `ls -l`

   c. `modprobe`

   d. `useradd`

8. Execute permission on a file is required to

   a. Launch that file as a program

   b. Create a directory with a matching name

   c. Allow other users to read the file

   d. Use the `insmod` command to add the file as a module

9. Describe the purpose of function libraries and name two directories where they are commonly located.

10. The command `rpm -q packagename` does the following:

    a. Determines whether `packagename` is installed on the system

    b. Locates `packagename` on a CD-ROM

    c. Erases `packagename` if it is currently installed

    d. Summarizes the disk quota for users of `packagename`

11. The `tar` command creates archive files that are commonly compressed by the _____ command.

    a. `bzip`

    b. `compress`

    c. `zip`

    d. `gzip`

12. Contrast the advantages of `rpm` and `tar` formats.

13. Which of the following represents a development release of the Linux kernel?

    a. 1.2.13

    b. 2.1.42

    c. 2.0.10

    d. 2.2.5

14. Name two methods of determining the version and timestamp of the kernel currently running on a Linux system.

15. The module files loaded by the `insmod` command are located in a subdirectory of `/etc/modules`. True or False?

16. Red Hat Linux uses a program called _____ to automate loading of kernel modules as they are needed.

    a. `modprobe`

    b. `kerneld`

    c. `find`

    d. `/lib/modules`

17. Name four commands used to work with kernel modules.

18. The terms *module parameter* and *boot parameter* refer to the same basic thing. True or False?

19. The process of recompiling the Linux kernel does *not* include:

    a. Creating a configuration file

    b. Making certain the kernel source code is installed

    c. Running the `make` command

    d. Inserting kernel modules that provide support for recompiling the kernel

20. After creating a new kernel file you must reconfigure LILO so that:

    a. The new kernel can be started by the LILO program when the system is rebooted

    b. The older kernel version is gracefully unloaded from memory

    c. Existing kernel modules do not cause a memory conflict when loaded

    d. Security enhancements remain in force

21. The _____ program displays kernel hardware configuration messages from the system boot process.

    a. `init`

    b. `chmod`

    c. `dmesg`

    d. `uname`

22. Why is `modprobe` preferred over `insmod` as a tool for adding modules to the kernel?

23. The init program uses the following configuration file:

   a. /etc/lilo.conf

   b. /etc/inittab

   c. /etc/modules/inittab

   d. /etc/rc.d/rc

24. Name the two runlevels normally used to run a Linux-based computer, and describe the difference between those two runlevels.

25. Files in the runlevel subdirectories, such as /etc/rc.d/rc3.d, are actually pointers to scripts in /etc/rc.d/init.d. True or False?

26. The files in /etc/rc.d/init.d can be used to:

   a. Automatically insert kernel modules

   b. Stop and restart most standard services in Linux

   c. Reconfigure the LILO program after recompiling the kernel

   d. Set default file permissions for the root user

27. The scripts in /etc/rc.d/init.d are provided by:

   a. The system administrator who installs Linux

   b. The rc script, which runs before any of the init.d scripts

   c. The rpm that installs the service that the script controls

   d. The kernel itself

28. The configuration data stored in files within the /etc/sysconfig directory can be modified using many different configuration utilities. True or False?

29. Name three commands that can be used to begin a graceful shutdown of Linux.

30. Describe why the LILO program must be executed after making changes to the lilo.conf file.

HANDS-ON PROJECTS

Project 4-1

In this activity you practice using Linux commands for managing files and directories. To complete this activity you should have available an installed Linux system on which you have a valid user account (one for which you know the password).

1. Log in to Linux using your user account name and password.

2. If you logged in using a graphical login screen, open a terminal window by opening the main menu of your desktop environment, pointing to the **Utilities** menu, and then clicking on **Gnome Terminal** (in the Gnome Desktop) or **Terminal** (in the KDE Desktop).

3. Enter the **pwd** command to display your current working directory. Because you have just logged in, this should display your home directory.

4. Create a new subdirectory within your home directory using the command **mkdir archive**.

5. Change to the new subdirectory you just created by entering **cd archive**.

6. Create a new file named **report** using this **touch** command: **touch report**.

7. Enter **ls -l** to view a long-format listing of the files in the **archive** subdirectory. Can you identify your username in the command output as the owner of the file **report**?

8. Notice the file permissions in the output of the **ls -l** command from the previous step. What default file permissions were assigned? Use this **chmod** command to remove all permissions for the group and other users: **chmod go-rwx report**. How could you reset the file permissions using a three-digit code in the **chmod** command?

9. Enter **ls -l** again to review the file permissions with your changes.

10. Change the name of the **report** file to **oldreport** using this **mv** command: **mv report oldreport**.

11. Use the **ls** command to verify that the file **report** is no longer there—it has been replaced by **oldreport**.

12. Copy a system file from the **/etc** directory by entering: **cp /etc/termcap .** (Remember to include the period to indicate that you want to copy the file to your current directory.) Do you see any feedback when a command is successful?

13. Use the **cat** command to view the contents of the file that you copied in the previous step: **cat termcap**. Can you read the contents?

14. Use the **less** command to view the contents of the file: **less termcap**. Use the Page Up and Page Down keys to scroll through the file. Press **q** to exit the **less** command.

15. Enter the **ls -l** command. Note the size of the **termcap** file.

16. Compress the **termcap** file using the **gzip** command: **gzip termcap**.

17. Use the **ls -l** command to view the directory contents. How has the filename changed? How has the size of the file changed?

18. Use the **file** command to display the type of data contained in the **termcap.gz** file: **file termcap.gz**.

19. Erase the **termcap.gz** file using the **rm** command: **rm termcap.gz**.

20. Change back to your home directory by entering **cd ..** (don't forget the space before the two periods).

21. Erase the **archive** directory using the **rmdir** command: **rmdir archive**. Why won't the command work? How could you make it work?

Project 4-2

In this activity you use several commands to learn about the Linux kernel running on a computer. To complete this activity you should have available an installed Linux system on which you have a valid user account (one for which you know the password).

1. Log in to Linux using your user account name and password.

2. If you logged in using a graphical login screen, open a terminal window by opening the main menu of your desktop environment, pointing to the **Utilities** menu, and then clicking on **Gnome Terminal** (in the Gnome Desktop) or **Terminal** (in the KDE Desktop).

3. Enter the command **uname -r** to see which version of the Linux kernel is running on the computer. Do you see a release number in the output?

4. Enter the command **uname -v** to see the timestamp of the Linux kernel.

4

5. Enter the command **cat /proc/version**. How does the information displayed compare to the output of the **uname** command?

6. Review the contents of the **lilo.conf** file by entering the command **less /etc/lilo.conf**.

7. Locate the section of the **lilo.conf** file beginning with the line **image=**, and note the directory and filename listed.

8. Press **q** to exit the **less** command.

9. Change to the directory indicated on the **image=** line in **/etc/lilo.conf**: **cd /boot**.

10. Enter the **ls -l** command to see the files in the **boot** directory. Can you locate the file named in the **image** section of **lilo.conf**? That file is the Linux kernel. How large is the file?

11. Enter the command **dmesg | less** to review the kernel boot messages. What parts of the system hardware do you recognize in the output? How might this output help you manage the system's hardware?

Project 4-3

In this activity you review the initialization information on the Linux system. To complete this activity you should have available an installed Linux system on which you have a valid user account (one for which you know the password).

1. Log in to Linux using your user account name and password (not the **root** account).

2. If you logged in using a graphical login screen, open a terminal window by opening the main menu of your desktop environment, pointing to the **Utilities** menu, and then clicking on **Gnome Terminal** (in the Gnome Desktop) or **Terminal** (in the KDE Desktop).

3. Enter the command **cat /etc/sysconfig/network**. What configuration options do you recognize in the output?

4. Change to the **rc.d** initialization directory: **cd /etc/rc.d**.

5. Enter the **ls** command. What filenames do you recognize from the discussion in the chapter?

6. List the files in the **init.d** subdirectory: **ls init.d**. Can you recognize any network or other services that match the names of the files in this directory?

7. List the files in the **rc3.d** subdirectory: **ls rc3.d**. How do the files in this directory correspond to those in the **init.d** subdirectory?

8. Change to the `init.d` subdirectory: **cd init.d**.

9. View the `syslog` script using the `ls -l` command: **ls -l syslog**. Notice the file permissions assigned to the script. Who is permitted to read the script? (The `syslog` script controls the system logging programs described in Chapter 11.)

10. Execute the `syslog` script using the command **./syslog restart** (don't forget the **./** at the beginning to indicate that the file is located in the current directory). Wait a few moments for all of the messages to appear on screen and the command prompt to return. What can you conclude about the file permissions allowing everyone to read the script?

11. Use the `less` command to look at the contents of the script: **less syslog**. You can learn about creating scripts by reviewing existing scripts on the system. (Chapter 12 describes how to create your own scripts.) Press **q** to exit the `less` command.

12. Change back to your home directory using the command **cd** with no parameters. (This always returns you to your home directory.)

13. Enter **pwd** to verify that you are in fact in your home directory.

CASE PROJECTS

1. You are helping a local company set up a research lab containing several Linux-based computer systems that will be used for various scientific experiments. The experiments require high performance from Linux. Each computer system includes a fast hard disk attached to a SCSI controller, a high-speed networking card, and 512 MB of RAM. As you install Linux on the system, you notice that the SCSI card is not supported by the default kernel. A kernel module is required to support the SCSI cards in the lab. What problems might come up if Linux were installed on a SCSI hard disk, but the SCSI hard disk could not be accessed without first loading a module into the kernel?

2. Given what you know about the Linux kernel, does it seem possible that you could create a software package containing a new Linux kernel that included built-in support for the lab's SCSI device, and then add that package to each system in the lab? Do you think this would be worth the time required to prepare such a package?

3. Each computer in the lab is slightly different, though all have the same type of SCSI controller card installed. After installing Linux on each computer, one of the computers will not boot to Linux. What could you check to identify differences in the computer's hardware or configuration? Could using a boot parameter help? Could using a boot disk help?

5

USING GRAPHICAL SYSTEMS WITH LINUX

After reading this chapter and completing the exercises, you will be able to:

♦ Discuss concepts related to the X Window System

♦ Install and configure the X Window System

♦ Start up and use the most popular graphical interfaces on Linux

♦ Use a graphical login

In the previous chapter you learned basic commands for working with the Linux file system. You also learned how to manage software packages and make modifications to the Linux kernel by using kernel modules or by recompiling the Linux kernel. In addition, you learned how a Linux system is initialized through a series of scripts that are started by the `init` program.

In this chapter you will learn how to work with a graphical environment in Linux and how to configure access to graphics hardware. You will also practice using the most popular graphical interfaces available for Linux. In addition, you will learn how to set up a graphical login screen so that the users on a Linux system can work continuously in a graphical environment.

LEARNING ABOUT THE X WINDOW SYSTEM

When you installed Linux in Chapter 3, you attempted to configure the X Window System, the graphical system in Linux that is often called, simply, X. Because the graphical system can be challenging to configure, you may need the additional information provided in this chapter to successfully set up the graphical environment. Before exploring additional configuration details, however, you should take a moment to become familiar with the history of the X Window System.

A Brief History of X

The rise of graphical environments on computer systems began in the early 1980s. The seeds of this trend were planted at the Palo Alto Research Center of Xerox Corporation, where researchers did the earliest work on graphical user interfaces (GUIs) and devices for interacting with them (including the mouse). But Xerox was not the company that made GUIs popular. That honor fell to three different groups, each working independently toward the goal of making its computer system easier to use. The first GUI to be made widely available was an early version of Windows from Microsoft—Windows 1.0. However, this version and the later version, Windows 2.0, were not functional enough to be anything more than technological curiosities. Conversely, the Apple Macintosh, which began shipping in 1984, made full use of GUI technology, such as menus and dialog boxes, all within a functional and stable environment. At Microsoft, developers continued working on versions of Windows until, by the 3.1 release, the product was functional and stable enough to gather a following in the market.

The third group working on graphical environments was made up of developers bent on creating a useful GUI for UNIX. At the time Windows was establishing its place in the market (the mid-1980s), UNIX had already been in widespread use for years. To make the operating system easier to use and to encourage the development of graphical standards, people at the Massachusetts Institute of Technology (MIT) and Digital Equipment Corporation (DEC, now part of Compaq Computer Corporation) began working together on a graphical environment for UNIX. This development process was initially dubbed **Project Athena**. The new graphical environment was eventually called the X Window System, with the assumption that X would be replaced with something more descriptive. But the X appellation stuck and is used to this day.

The X Window System, or X, as it is commonly known, was released as public domain software in 1985. This allowed many UNIX vendors to begin creating products based on X, and it rapidly became the default graphical system for the entire UNIX market. The GPL (the license under which Linux was released) was not developed by Richard Stallman of the Free Software Foundation until 1992, so X was released under a different legal arrangement. By placing the software in the public domain, the developers (MIT and DEC) gave up their copyright to the software, leaving all others free to create derivative works and copyright them. The result was a somewhat fragmented market, in which users could choose from various graphical systems based on X. Because the UNIX market was already fragmented and did not rely on the mass-market economies that are associated with computers today, the availability of many varieties of X was not considered problematic.

In 1988 the Open Software Foundation, or OSF, took over work on the development project (Athena) that created new versions of X. The not-for-profit OSF (now called the Open Group) continues to maintain X to this day. Because X is public domain software, however, the source code is available to anyone, much like the source code to the Linux kernel or the GNU utilities. Figure 5-1 shows the Open Group's Web site, at *www.opengroup.org*, where you can find more information about X. For additional background, visit *www.x.org*.

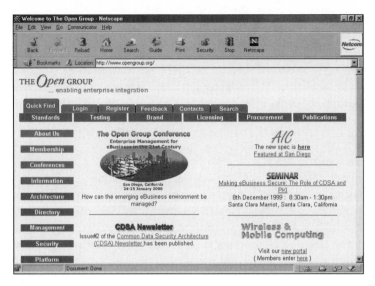

Figure 5-1   The Open Group's Web site

As long as the Open Group controlled the core development of the X Window System as public domain software, there was no freely available version of X; it was included only as part of expensive UNIX systems from vendors such as IBM and Hewlett-Packard. These versions of X ran on specialized hardware such as the RS/6000 and PA-RISC microprocessors. The XFree86 Project was started as a nonprofit organization dedicated to creating a version of X that could be used on UNIX systems running on Intel-based computers. The XFree86 Project software was welcomed by Linux developers because it provided the foundation for a graphical interface similar to that used by all other UNIX-like operating systems. X was soon incorporated into most major Linux distributions. You can read more about the XFree86 Project at *www.xfree86.org*.

Concepts Related to X

The success of both the Macintosh and Windows graphical environments was made possible by the fact that the developers of these GUIs had access to detailed information about video graphics hardware. To ensure sales of their products, video card manufacturers needed to ensure that their video cards were compatible with Windows or Macintosh software. To this end, manufacturers agreed to give video card specifications to the software developers. The developers then embedded these specifications in Macintosh and Windows software, thus allowing the operating systems to control the video card.

The developers of X took a different approach. Instead of embedded video card specifications in the operating system kernel, they employed a text-based configuration file whose job was to send controlling information to the video card. By adjusting the information in the configuration file, X could theoretically work with any video card without relying on information from video card manufacturers and constant updates to the X software.

In fact, this system worked well, and continues to work, so long as you want only the minimum level of functionality in your graphical display. This minimal level provides 640×480 screen resolution with 256 colors. But every modern computer system is capable of displaying 1024×768 screen resolution, often with millions of colors. Hence, the developers of X had to continue developing software to take advantage of the advanced features of newer graphics cards. This process continues to this day. Few standards exist among video card manufacturers, who are all hard at work creating faster, more powerful video cards.

Most of these video card manufacturers were not very forthcoming in providing specifications to the developers at the XFree86 Project, because the largest market for video cards was for Windows-based PCs. This is changing, however. As manufacturers begin to see Linux as a large and growing market, they are more willing to provide information to XFree86 developers. As a result, XFree86 is in a position to create better software for newer video cards, and to do it soon after the video cards are released. Not all vendors provide this information, of course, but the lack of video card specifications is becoming a problem of the past for XFree86 developers.

Components of the X Window System

The original developers of X were very insightful in the way they designed the system, and that early insight has allowed X to continue as a viable technology 15 years after it was first released. This design separates the control of the video card (the computer hardware) from the display of information on the screen. The following components show the further modularization of the parts of the X Window System design, which are incorporated into modern Linux distributions:

- **X server:** this is the program that communicates with the video card to create images on the screen. In software produced by the XFree86 Project, separate X server software packages are used for different types of video cards. For example, one software package, called XFree86_S3, is the X server on computers that have an S3 video chip on their video cards. Several default X servers can be used for less specialized graphics modes. For example, the monochrome, VGA, and SVGA graphics modes are standard on all graphics cards and are managed by X servers that do not rely on a chip-specific X server program. The X server alone does not provide any display on a monitor. A window manager (described later in this list) controls the X server.

- **X client:** this term refers to any kind of graphical application. Essentially, a graphical application runs in the background on a Linux computer and does not in itself have a direct effect on the screen display. Instead, as the application runs, it sends requests to the X server regarding keyboard and mouse input; the X server collects these messages and translates them into images on the screen. The windows and dialog boxes associated with a graphical application are the output of the X server, which is in turn controlled by the X client (the actual application that you are running). The important point here is that X clients do not communicate directly with either your graphics card or your monitor. Although you might find this terminology confusing at first, you should become familiar with it so that you can use the remote features of X, as described later in this section. An X client is also referred to as an X application.

- **Window manager:** this component is a special-purpose graphical application (that is, a specialized X client) that controls the position and manipulation of the windows within a graphical user interface. Other graphical applications (such as system administration utilities or word processors) rely on the functionality provided by a window manager to direct how the X server displays dialog boxes and performs other standard GUI operations. The window manager gives the X server the ability to draw windows and track mouse movement so that every graphical application does not have to reimplement these functions. At the same time, the window manager provides a library of functions that programmers can use when developing graphical applications.

- **Graphical libraries:** these are collections of programming functions that an X client application can use to more efficiently manage the elements of a graphical environment.

- **Desktop environment:** also known as a desktop interface, this graphical application provides a comprehensive interface, including system menus, desktop icons, and the ability to easily manage files and launch applications. Gnome and KDE are two examples of desktop environments.

Figure 5-2 shows how these components are arranged to interact with each other. The next section explains how these components are actually used in Linux.

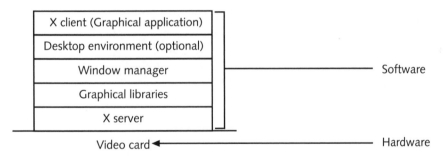

Figure 5-2   Components of the X Window System

How X Components Interact

When you install Linux, the installation program selects which XFree86 server to install based on the computer's video card. The XFree86_SVGA server may be installed, or the XFree86_S3 server, or another server. You can use the **rpm** command to install several X servers if you want to experiment with different servers to see which works best with your video card. Only one X server will be used at a time (as you will see later in the discussion of configuration). Commercial servers from companies such as Xi Graphics (*www.xig.com*) and MetroLink (*www.metrolink.com*) combine X server functionality for all video cards into a single X server program, so you don't need to select among servers when using these products. Future releases of XFree86 will also use this single-server model.

Unlike with Macintosh and Microsoft Windows systems, each user of the X Window System is free to select the interface type he or she prefers. This flexibility is made possible by the numerous window manager programs included with X, each providing a different set of functionality and different look and feel to the graphical environment, and requiring different levels of system resources and expertise to use.

One popular Linux window manager, **fvwm**, is shown in Figure 5-3. When only the window manager is running, you see a blank screen with a color pattern and a mouse pointer. (When you actually open a window manager, you'll see that it alone doesn't provide much of a display on screen, because the window manager is designed mostly to provide services to other programs.) Pressing a mouse button opens a menu from which you can start programs or other functions that control the graphical environment.

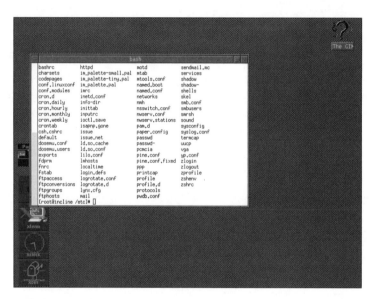

Figure 5-3 The **fvwm** window manager

A few of the window managers available for Linux are described in the following list.

- **twm** (Tab Window Manager): this is a classic UNIX window manager that has been used for many years.

- **fvwm** (Feeble Virtual Window Manager): developed by Robert Nation, this program was the most common window manager for Linux until desktop environments became popular. It includes many of the same characteristics of **twm**, but it requires only about half the memory required to run **twm**. The latest version of **fvwm** is called **fvwm2**. A special version of **fvwm** known as **fvwm95** is designed to emulate the Windows 95 desktop, though tools to emulate the Windows Explorer and other Windows features are not included with **fvwm95**. You can find more information about **fvwm** at *www.fvwm.org*.

- **AMIwm** (Amiga Window Manager): this window manager emulates the look and feel of the old Amiga computers of the late 1980s, specifically the Amiga Workbench.

- **wm2**: a minimal window manager requiring little memory and allowing little configuration.

- **Window Maker** and **AfterStep**: both of these window managers simulate the interface of the NeXT computer.

- **mwm** (Motif Window Manager): a commercial window manager commonly included with commercial UNIX workstations.

- **Enlightenment**: this window manager, sometimes called simply **E**, was based on **fvwm2**. It is used primarily as the window manager for the Gnome Desktop (which is discussed later in this chapter).

- **olwm** (OpenLook Window Manager): the OpenLook interface style was created by Sun Microsystems and is still used primarily by developers wishing to emulate the look and feel of a Sun UNIX workstation.

Why would you choose one window manager over another? The choice is a matter of personal preference based on the appearance of the window manager and the features that it offers. A hallmark of Linux is that it allows the flexibility to configure components (such as the window manager) according to your personal preferences.

Many different graphical libraries are also available for X. For the most part, each of these libraries was originally created to simplify the development of a specific application. The particularly useful libraries were used by developers of other applications. A graphical library consists of a few files containing programming commands that graphical applications can access. A graphical library is installed on a Linux system just like any other application (using an **rpm** command, for example). But a graphical library is not launched directly—it only provides tools for other applications. The two graphical libraries that are most widely known for Linux at this time are listed here:

- The Qt library was developed by a company in Norway called Troll Tech. Qt was used as the foundation of the KDE Desktop, which is the most popular graphical environment used on Linux. (See *www.kde.org* for more information.) KDE is described in more detail later in this chapter.

- The GTK+ library was developed by Spencer Kimball and Peter Mattis at the University of California at Berkeley as the foundation of the Gimp graphics application. (Gimp is a program similar to Adobe Photoshop.) Subsequently, GTK+ was used to create the Gnome Desktop, which is the second of the two major graphical environments used on Linux systems today. (See *www.gnome.org* for more information.) Gnome is described in more detail later in this chapter.

Using X Remotely

Although X supports many features (described in the configuration sections that follow), the remote capabilities of X deserve special mention. With X, you can display graphical applications remotely; that is, you can launch an application (an X client) on one computer, but specify that the application should be displayed on a different computer. For example, suppose you have WordPerfect for Linux installed on one computer (call it computer A). Many different users can log in to computer A and start a copy of WordPerfect at the same time. All of the copies of WordPerfect are running on computer A, but the WordPerfect program appears on computers B, C, D, and so forth, where all of the users are physically located.

Each computer (B, C, D in this example) must be running an X server program. The X server receives requests from the X client (WordPerfect) to display windows and collect keyboard and mouse input. Figure 5-4 illustrates the arrangement of the X server and X client.

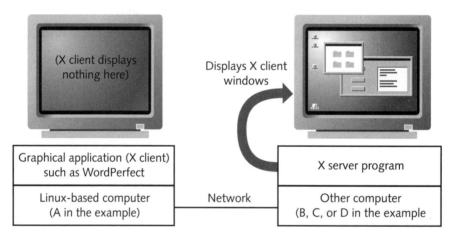

Figure 5-4   An X client running on a remote X server

The X server used to provide the screen display for an X client can be located on any type of computer. For example, X server programs are available for Microsoft Windows computers. By installing one of these programs, you can launch an application on a Linux computer system and have that application displayed on a Windows computer, as shown in Figure 5-5. You can learn about two companies that sell X servers for Windows by visiting *www.starnet.com* (look for the X-Win product) and *www.hummingbird.com* (look for the Exceed product).

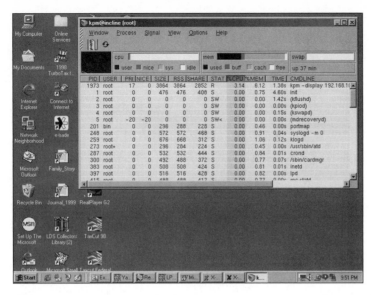

Figure 5-5   An X server displaying a Linux program within Windows

RUNNING THE X WINDOW SYSTEM

Though the flexibility and features of X are impressive, they come at a price: the X Window System can be difficult to configure. The following list explains some of the issues that make setting up X such a challenge:

- Video card manufacturers do not focus on creating X software for their hardware devices, so you must make adjustments to fit the video hardware's requirements.

- The various components of X (such as window managers and graphical libraries) are interchangeable, developed by separate groups, and based on completely different configuration models, requiring that you learn multiple versions of each component in order to support a variety of user preferences and application needs.

- X supports a multiuser, networked environment, which means you may need to set up and maintain numerous configuration files. (These configuration files are described later in this chapter.)

You learned the basics of configuring X in Chapter 3. The following sections provide additional guidance on getting X installed and working.

Installing and Configuring X

When you installed Linux, at least one X server from the XFree86 set of X servers was probably installed, along with the supporting packages needed to run graphical applications. You can review the packages that are installed on your system by using the command rpm -qa | grep XFree. The output of this command for a typical Red Hat Linux installation is shown here:

```
XFree86-75dpi-fonts-3.3.5-3
XFree86-SVGA-3.3.5-3
XFree86-libs-3.3.5-3
XFree86-xfs-3.3.5-3
XFree86-3.3.5-3
XFree86-devel-3.3.5-3
```

If a list similar to this does not appear on your system, you should use the **rpm** command with the **-Uvh** options (as described in Chapter 4) to install these packages from the Linux CD (or other installation source files available to you). If you cannot successfully configure X following the steps in this section, you should consider trying to upgrade the XFree86 server to a later version to add support for the video card you are configuring. Visit the Web site *www.xfree86.org* to learn the version number of the latest release of the software. If the output of the **rpm** command shows an older version of XFree86, you may need to upgrade to the latest version. (In the sample **rpm** output above, the version number of XFree86 is 3.3.5.) You can do this by downloading software from the *ftp.xfree86.org* Internet site or, in most cases, by visiting the Web site of your Linux vendor (such as *ftp.redhat.com*) and obtaining updated software packages for the XFree86 software. In some cases, you will not need a completely new set of XFree86 packages; you may simply be able to add a new X server program to support the video card. Again, you can locate new X servers on the XFree86 Web site or on the Web site of your Linux vendor.

 TIP You can learn about configuration options for X by reviewing the X online manual page (enter the command man X). Additional manual pages are available for each X server (for example, enter the command man XFree86_SVGA).

The X software is normally located in the directory `/usr/X11R6`. This directory is sometimes called the X-root directory. The filename `X11R6` refers to the fact that the features of X used in current X servers are based upon X version 11, release 6. You will hear people who work with many types of Linux and UNIX systems refer to "ex-eleven-are-five" or "ex-eleven-are-six" when describing their version of X. The developers of X have stopped advancing the version number (it stays at 11), but the release number does change occasionally (every few years).

In addition to the XFree86 software, you need at least a window manager program, and perhaps other software packages, depending on what software you want to run on the system. All general-purpose Linux distributions install these components by default. For example, you can enter the command **rpm -q fvwm** to see if the **fvwm** window manager is installed. Using the command **rpm -qa | grep kde** will list all of the packages related to the KDE Desktop. You can use similar commands to check for the Gnome Desktop or for any graphical libraries or window managers.

Some specialized Linux distributions, such as the Linux Router Project (see *www.linuxrouter.org*), do not include X. On any Linux system, you can choose not to run X to save system resources (both memory and CPU processing time).

5

Chapter 3 mentioned several utilities you can use to set up X. The configuration described in Chapter 3 and in this section is only for configuring the X server to access the video card. After the X server is configured, the window manager or desktop environment that you use will work without additional configuration. You can also make changes in the configuration of a window manager or desktop environment. These changes are relatively simple and straightforward because they do not require that you know any additional information about the computer's hardware. But before these other components can work, you must first properly configure the X server.

You normally configure the X Window System when you install Linux. But as this is sometimes not possible because of problems identifying the video card or configuring its use, you may need to set up the X configuration file after installing the rest of the system.

It's sometimes useful to launch X several times with different configurations until you find one that works. If the display is garbled or the screen simply goes blank when you launch X (using the commands given later in this chapter), try pressing the key combination Ctrl+Alt+Backspace to exit X and return to character mode. If the keyboard does not respond but the computer is connected to a network, you should be able to log in to the system from another computer and use the `kill` command to end the X server program. (See Chapter 10 for details on using the `kill` command.)

The Configuration File

The configuration file for XFree86 is located either in the `/etc` directory, in the `/etc/X11` directory, or in the `/usr/X11R6/lib/X11` directory. The configuration file is called `XF86Config`. (Note the use of upper- and lowercase.) A sample configuration file is shown here:

```
# See 'man XF86Config' for info on the format of this file
#

Section "Files"
    RgbPath "/usr/X11R6/lib/X11/rgb"
    FontPath "/usr/X11R6/lib/X11/fonts/Type1"
    FontPath "/usr/X11R6/lib/X11/fonts/Speedo"
    FontPath "/usr/X11R6/lib/X11/fonts/misc"
    FontPath "/usr/X11R6/lib/X11/fonts/75dpi"
EndSection


Section "ServerFlags"
EndSection
```

```
Section "Keyboard"
    Protocol "Standard"
    XkbRules "xfree86"
    XkbModel "pc101"
    XkbLayout "us"
EndSection


Section "Pointer"
    Protocol "microsoft"
    Device "/dev/ttyS0"

    Emulate3Buttons
EndSection


Section "Monitor"
    Identifier "Primary Monitor"
    VendorName "Typical monitors"
    ModelName "800x600, 60Hz"
    HorizSync 31.5-37.9
    VertRefresh 55-90
    Modeline "800x600/60Hz" 40 800  840  968 1056
        600   601  605  628
+HSync +VSync
EndSection


Section "Device"
    Identifier "Primary Card"
    VendorName "Unknown"
    BoardName "None"
    VideoRam 2048
EndSection


Section "Screen"
    Driver "VGA16"
    Device "Primary Card"
    Monitor "Primary Monitor"
    SubSection "Display"
        Depth 4
        Modes "640x480/60Hz"
    EndSubSection
EndSection


Section "Screen"
    Driver "SVGA"
    Device "Primary Card"
    Monitor "Primary Monitor"
```

```
        DefaultColorDepth 16
        SubSection "Display"
            Depth 8
            Modes "800x600/60Hz"
                Virtual 800 600
        EndSubSection
        SubSection "Display"
            Depth 15
            Modes "800x600/60Hz"
                Virtual 800 600
        EndSubSection
        SubSection "Display"
            Depth 16
            Modes "800x600/60Hz"
                Virtual 800 600
        EndSubSection
        SubSection "Display"
            Depth 24
            Modes "800x600/60Hz"
                Virtual 800 600
        EndSubSection
        SubSection "Display"
            Depth 32
            Modes "800x600/60Hz"
                Virtual 800 600
        EndSubSection
EndSection

Section "Screen"
        Driver "accel"
        Device "Primary Card"
        Monitor "Primary Monitor"
        DefaultColorDepth 16
        SubSection "Display"
            Depth 8
            Modes "800x600/60Hz"
                Virtual 800 600
        EndSubSection
        SubSection "Display"
            Depth 15
            Modes "800x600/60Hz"
                Virtual 800 600
        EndSubSection
        SubSection "Display"
            Depth 16
            Modes "800x600/60Hz"
                Virtual 800 600
        EndSubSection
        SubSection "Display"
            Depth 24
```

5

```
       Modes "800x600/60Hz"
            Virtual 800 600
    EndSubSection
    SubSection "Display"
        Depth 32
        Modes "800x600/60Hz"
            Virtual 800 600
    EndSubSection
EndSection

# End of automatically generated file
```

Notice that the `XF86Config` file contains specifications for display fonts, instructions for using the keyboard and mouse, details about the monitor and video card capabilities, and information on combining the video card and monitor details to create a specific view (such as 1024×768 resolution with 256 colors).

The sample file shown above does not include comments, which you will find in many `XF86Config` files. These comments can help you understand the different sections of the configuration file, and they provide examples of alternative configurations.

Commercial X servers do not rely on the `XF86Config` file. Each uses a different configuration file with a different format. For example, the Accelerated-X server from Xi Graphics uses the configuration file `/etc/Xaccel.ini`. To make the task of configuring them easier, commercial X servers include configuration tools similar to the XFree86 configuration tools described later in this chapter. One such tool, which provides configuration options for Accelerated-X, is shown in Figure 5-6. In general, when working with a commercial X server, you should review documentation accompanying the product to learn how to use the product's configuration utility before preparing a configuration file.

Figure 5-6 The configuration utility for Accelerated-X

Using Xconfigurator

The **Xconfigurator** program is a utility for creating an **XF86Config** file for your XFree86 X server. It was developed by Red Hat Software and is executed automatically as part of the installation of Red Hat Linux. You can also run this program after completing the installation in order to complete or redo the X configuration. To start the program, enter the program's name on a command line (note the capital **X**):

Xconfigurator

The interface to **Xconfigurator** will be familiar to you if you have installed Red Hat Linux. **Xconfigurator** lets you select a video card from a list and then gives you the option of manually setting additional options or having **Xconfigurator** probe the video card to determine the best settings. Figure 5-7 shows a sample screen from **Xconfigurator**, where you can select the screen resolutions to use with different color depths. Detailed steps for using **Xconfigurator** are provided as part of the installation instructions in Chapter 3.

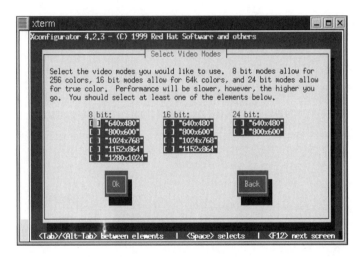

Figure 5-7   Selecting screen resolutions in Xconfigurator

Although **Xconfigurator** is a helpful tool, it is not always the best way to set up X, because it may not provide all the options you need. As a result, you may find that after choosing the video card in your system and selecting the options that seem correct, X still will not function. (See the section "Launching X" later in this chapter.) The problem with **Xconfigurator** is that it does not provide sufficient configuration detail to let you select the options that would result in a correctly functioning X server; neither does it have the ability to set up the video card without asking you numerous questions. If **Xconfigurator** does not successfully set up X, try using one of the other tools described in the following sections.

Using xf86config

The XFree86 software comes with a command-line configuration utility called **xf86config** (all lowercase). After launching this utility you must read detailed information presented on screen for each option and then answer questions as you are prompted. The **xf86config** utility provides complete access to the features of the XFree86 software. If you take the time to read the information presented on screen and you know the hardware details of your video card (such as the video chipset and the amount of video RAM), **xf86config** is very likely to correctly configure any video card supported by an XFree86 X server.

The **xf86config** utility is included on a standard Red Hat Linux system. Many other Linux distributions also include this utility. To launch **xf86config**, enter the utility's name at any Linux command line (note that it is all lowercase):

```
xf86config
```

Figure 5-8 shows one of the questions asked by **xf86config**, along with with a list of options to choose from and detailed instructions about how to select the correct option.

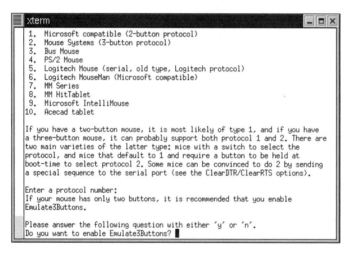

Figure 5-8   The xf86config utility

The following list summarizes the information that **xf86config** requests during the configuration process. The exact questions posed and the order of those questions depends on your answers (which in turn depend on which video card you are configuring).

- Mouse protocol
- Mouse device
- Keyboard settings
- Monitor scan frequencies
- Video card description

- XFree86 server to use

- Amount of video memory

- The clockchip setting

- Resolution and number of colors to use on screen

Using XF86Setup

Although the `xf86config` utility is an effective means of configuring X, it requires you to read a lot of information and answer many questions that may not be relevant to your video configuration. As an alternative, XFree86 also includes a graphical configuration utility called **XF86Setup**. This utility is not included with Red Hat Linux 6.0, but it is found on many Linux distributions and is available through the XFree86 Web site. **XF86Setup** uses the VGA graphics mode, which is a low-resolution mode supported by virtually all video cards. This mode provides a screen with 640 × 480 resolution on which you can use a mouse to select items to configure the X server for higher resolutions.

To start **XF86Setup**, enter the utility's name on any Linux command line. A series of text-mode messages prompt you for confirmation before switching to the VGA mode in which the configuration options are displayed. The first screen, used for configuring the mouse, requires you to use the keyboard (the Tab, Spacebar, and Enter keys) to select the correct mouse configuration. This configuration screen is shown in Figure 5-9. After you have configured the mouse and chosen the **Apply** button to activate it, you can use the mouse to select other configuration options.

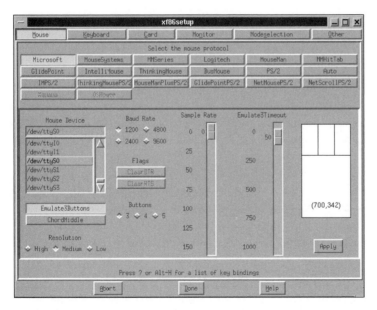

Figure 5-9   The Mouse configuration tab in XF86Setup

On the `Monitor` tab of `XF86Setup`, which is shown in Figure 5-10, you select the monitor scan values, as described in Chapter 3. Recall that if you select a higher scan rate or resolution than your monitor supports, you risk damaging your monitor.

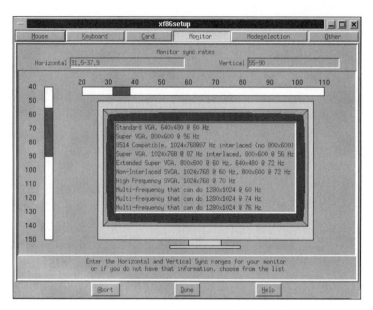

Figure 5-10   The `Monitor` tab in `XF86Setup`

The most challenging part of using `XF86Setup` is selecting the correct settings on the `Card` tab. You can view this tab two different ways: in Card List view, or in Detailed view. You only need to complete one of these views to finish the video card configuration.

In Card List view, shown in Figure 5-11, you see a long list of video cards arranged by manufacturer and model. (If necessary, you can choose the `Card List` button to switch to this view.) If the video card you are configuring is included in this list, simply select it. If the video card is not listed, choose the `Detailed Setup` button to switch to the `Card` tab's Detailed view, which is shown in Figure 5-12. In Detailed view, you must define the characteristics of the video card by selecting options such as the amount of video memory. Fortunately, many of these fields include the `Probed` option; selecting this option tells the `XF86Setup` program to attempt to determine the correct value for you. If the program is not able to do this correctly, however, you may need to enter an explicit value to get the X server to function.

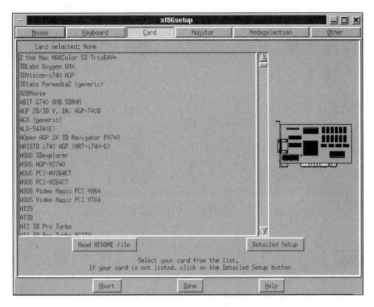

Figure 5-11   The Card List view of the `Card` tab

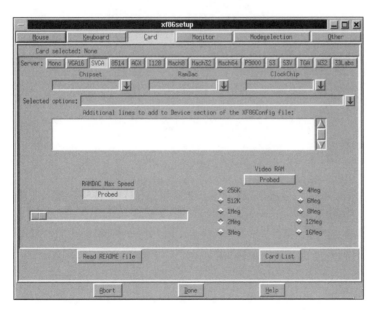

Figure 5-12   The Detailed view of the `Card` tab

To complete the configuration using XF86Setup, choose the Mode tab and select a screen resolution. The most commonly used screen resolution is 1024 × 768. Unless you have special instructions from another source (such as your video card manufacturer), you don't need to set any of the options on the Other tab, though you can explore them if you wish.

When you choose the Done button and confirm that you are ready to exit XF86Setup, the utility creates a temporary XF86Config file for you and starts the X server to test the configuration. If the server starts successfully, you see the xvidtune program's graphical screen. You can use the options in this program to adjust the position of the picture on your monitor, but this is usually not necessary. (You can generally use the controls located on the front of most monitors to control the position of the screen.) Figure 5-13 shows a view of the xvidtune program. When you have finished exploring the options in xvidtune, choose Save and Exit to exit the X server and save the new XF86Config file.

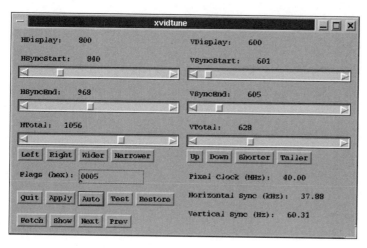

Figure 5-13   The xvidtune program

Occasionally the XF86Setup program appears to work correctly (that is, the test screen at the end of the process displays correctly), but then when you launch X, as described later in this chapter, the window manager screen or desktop environment does not appear as it should. In this case you can exit X and restart the XF86Setup program to try a different set of configuration options.

Using `lizardx`

The easiest method of configuring X is to use the **`lizardx`** program from Caldera Systems. This program, like the **`XF86Setup`** program, provides a graphical interface in which you select a few simple options. But `lizardx` (short *for Linux installation wizard for X*) doesn't require you to know anything about your video card. Its autoprobing features are the best available for Linux.

`Lizardx` was taken from the installation program for Caldera System's OpenLinux product. But `lizardx` is a separate program that you can execute from a command line in any Linux distribution (after you have downloaded the free `lizardx` program from the Caldera Systems FTP site at *ftp.calderasystems.com*). Start the program using this command:

`lizardx`

When the first screen of `lizardx` appears (as shown in Figure 5-14), move the mouse around slowly to autoconfigure it. Then choose the **Next** button to proceed to another screen where you can select a keyboard model and layout. Most users can accept the default settings and simply choose **Next** to continue.

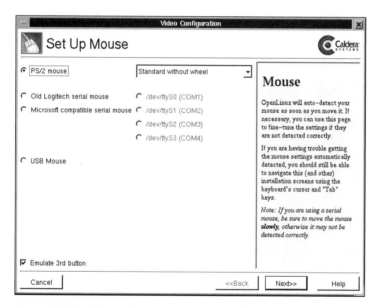

Figure 5-14   The `lizardx` mouse configuration screen

The next screen is where the wizardry of `lizardx` is evident. In this **Select Video Card** screen, you'll find that the video card has already been autodetected and appears in the drop-down list at the top of the screen (see Figure 5-15). To finish the configuration of the video card, choose the **Probe** button; then confirm that the probing can begin by choosing OK in the message box that appears. The screen goes black, then returns after a moment with the message `Probing is complete and apparently successful`. Choose the **Next** button to continue.

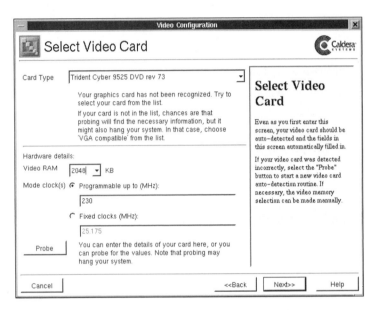

Figure 5-15   The `Select Video Card` screen in `lizardx`

In the next configuration screen you select a monitor model from a list of thousands of models, all arranged by manufacturer. A short list of standard or default monitor types is included at the top of the list in case the monitor you need is not listed. When you select **Next**, the `Select Video Mode` screen appears, as shown in Figure 5-16. On this screen, `lizardx` presents a list of video modes that are available based on your video card and monitor. First, choose the number of colors you want to include by selecting an item in the drop-down list in the lower-left part of the screen. (The number of colors you select may change the list of available screen resolutions, depending on the amount of video memory on the video card.) Then choose one of the screen modes that looks appealing (based on the screen resolution). Finally, choose the **Test** button, and then choose **Yes** in the message box that appears. If you see a functional desktop screen after a few moments, the graphics are configured, and you can choose the **Finish** button to complete the configuration. If you do not see a desktop interface displayed, wait a moment until the `lizardx` screen reappears; then choose another mode in the list and select the **Test** button again. Repeat this process until you find a mode that works well.

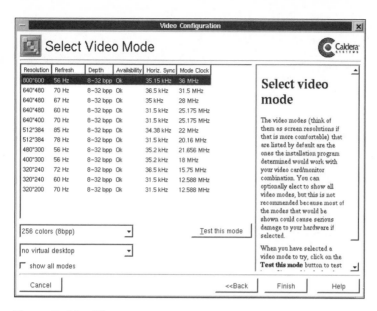

Figure 5-16   The `Select Video Mode` screen in `lizardx`

Configuring X Using Other Resources

Just as you likely consulted your system administrator or Internet Service Provider when gathering information about your network, you may need to contact knowledgeable people to help you set up a video card to work in Linux. To get help configuring X, try the following:

- Ask another person who has successfully installed Linux several times to help you configure X. Sometimes options that are unfamiliar to you will be well known to a person who has already configured a similar system.

- Visit the XFree86 Web site and search for information about the video card you are trying to configure.

- Visit the Web site of your Linux vendor and search for information about configuring X.

- Use a newsgroup reader to explore messages on the *comp.os.linux* newsgroups and related newsgroups for X. Some of these are dedicated to discussions of the X Window System. Read a few messages; then post a brief, polite message asking for guidance. Include as much detail about the computer system and video card as you have available.

- Buy a commercial X server (after checking that support for the troublesome video card is included). Contact the vendor for support if you have trouble installing the product.

- Visit Web sites dedicated to using Linux. In particular, try the Linux on Laptops page at *www.cs.utexas.edu/users/kharker/linux-laptop/*. This page has links for hundreds of laptop models, where owners of those laptops have posted suggestions (and often sample `XF86Config` files) for making X work with specific models of laptops.

- Visit the Web site of the computer vendor and search for information in the technical support database. As more vendors add support for Linux, you are more likely to find helpful information from computer system vendors.

If you have easy access to any of these resources, you might choose to consult them before trying the different programs outlined earlier in this chapter.

Launching X

The standard method of starting X is to log in to Linux on a character-mode console and then execute the `startx` command. This command automatically executes a number of other commands that launch the X server and run the programs that make up the graphical environment. In this section, you will learn how all those programs interact.

 TIP Depending on how your Linux distribution is configured, you may see a graphical login screen when the computer starts. The graphical login screen is called the X display manager, or xdm. The last section of this chapter describes how to use and configure xdm.

The `startx` program is actually a small script located in `/usr/X11R6/bin`. This script launches another program called `xinit`, which looks for several scripts in various locations in the Linux directory structure, including `~/.xinitrc`, `~/.Xclients`, `/etc/X11 /xinit/xinitrc`, and `/etc/X11/xinit/Xclients`. A system administrator can place scripts in a user's home directory (`~/.xinitrc` and `~/.Xclients`) to define a unique graphical configuration for that user. All of the scripts listed here specify which programs should start along with X. For the most part, these programs are X clients. (As explained earlier in this chapter, an X client is an application that runs in X.) Each X client is started as a background application. A **background application** is an application that does not prevent the program that started it (the `xinit` program in this case) from going on to other tasks (launching other X clients). In this case, the `xinit` scripts can start an X client and then go on to start another (and another, and another, and so on) without waiting for the first one to finish execution. The X clients that `xinit` starts from the initialization scripts include programs such as a file manager, an on-screen clock, and a toolbar. These X clients provide a minimal set of graphical tools as the window manager is started.

The last X client started is the window manager, which is responsible for controlling the graphical screen. The window manager features are used by all of the X applications that are started before the window manager; the other X applications wait until the window manager is started before trying to display information on screen.

A very simple script that `xinit` uses to launch one X client and a window manager might look like this:

```
xterm &
fvwm
```

If this script were used by xinit to start X, a single xterm (command-line window) would appear on a blank background. (The background is provided by fvwm, which also manages the keyboard and mouse, as described previously.)

In practice, Linux vendors create complex scripts that check for the availability of default window managers, look at a variety of configuration files, and start numerous X clients to provide a convenient working environment for users. The standard start-up process is outlined in the following list and illustrated in Figure 5-17. Details about the last few items in the list are provided later in this section.

1. The user executes the startx command to launch the graphical system.

2. The startx command initiates the xinit command.

3. The xinit command starts the X server program (such as XFree86_SVGA or XFree86_S3).

4. The xinit command attempts to launch a script called .xinitrc located in the user's home directory.

5. If the file is found, the commands in .xinitrc are executed by xinit. This script normally executes commands in other scripts, particularly the .Xclients script, which can also be located in each user's home directory, if the system administrator implements a different graphical configuration for each user.

6. If the .xinitrc file is not found in the user's home directory, the xinit program looks for the file /etc/X11/xinit/xinitrc. (Notice that this filename does not begin with a period as do those in a user's home directory.)

7. If the /etc/X11/xinit/xinitrc file mentioned in Step 6 is found, the commands in it are executed by xinit. The /etc/X11/xinit/xinitrc script normally executes commands in other scripts, particularly the /etc/X11/xinit/Xclients script. (Again, the filename has no initial period.) These two scripts (located in /etc/X11/xinit) are systemwide graphical configuration scripts, which are used for any user who does not have files in his or her home directory as described in Steps 4 and 5.

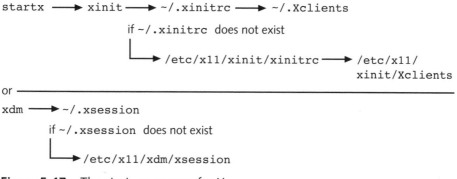

Figure 5-17 The start-up process for X

The scripts `xinitrc`, `.xinitrc`, `Xclients`, and `.Xclients` often include calls to execute other scripts, such as `Xclients_default`. The names and arrangement of these additional scripts vary by Linux distribution, but you can learn more about them by reviewing the contents of the `xinitrc` or `.xinitrc` file. All of the standard scripts (such as `xinitrc`), and the additional scripts that may be used by a particular Linux distribution, are shell scripts, which are discussed in Chapter 12.

Notice in the steps above that employing a separate configuration file in each user's home directory results in a different graphical configuration for each user. One user might choose to use `fvwm` as a window manager; another user might select Gnome or KDE as a graphical environment. A sample `.xinitrc` configuration file is shown here. Notice that the last item executed is a window manager, `twm`.

```
xrdb -load $HOME/.Xresources
xsetroot -solid gray &
xclock -g 50x50-0+0 -bw 0 &
xload -g 50x50-50+0 -bw 0 &
xterm -g 80x24+0+0 -bw 0 &
xterm -g 80x24+0-0 -bw 0 &
twm
```

In Step 3 of the procedure above, the `xinit` program starts the X server. To do this, the `xinit` program looks for the file named `X` in the directory `/usr/X11R6/bin`. This file is a pointer to the actual X server or similar program that helps the system choose an X server. You can see what file it points to by using the `ls` command. For instance, the command `ls -l /usr/X11R6/bin/X` displays an arrow character indicating that the file `X` refers to another file. The file X will refer to either the `XFree86_SVGA`, or the `Xwrapper` file, or another X server program (depending on which X server is needed for the video card). If you use a commercial X server, the file `X` will point to an X server such as `Xaccel` (the Accelerated-X server). This type of pointer is called a symbolic link. (You will learn about symbolic links in Chapter 6.) The sample output of the command `ls -l /usr/X11R6/bin/X` is shown below. You see that the `X` file refers to a file called `Xwrapper`, which is used to launch an X server program.

```
lrwxrwxrwx 1 root root   8 Nov 18 02:45 /usr/X11R6/
     bin/X -> Xwrapper
```

A user's home directory can contain a file named `.xserverrc` that defines which X server to start for that user. All users on a system are likely to employ the same X server, however, because all users on the system rely on the same video card. Thus, you will rarely see this configuration file used.

X Resources

Each graphical application uses a number of separate screen elements, such as scroll bars, text fonts, mouse pointers, and title bars for windows or dialog boxes. Each of these elements is called an **X resource**. This is a term used mostly by programmers; however, you should be familiar with it, because as a system administrator you can configure the appearance of the X resources used in each application.

A collection of default X resource settings applies to all X applications. These default settings govern how windows in the application are displayed, which colors and fonts are used, and which features of the application are active when the application starts. You can also set up additional X resource settings that apply only when a specific user runs a specific application. These resource settings are compiled into a **resource database** file. Collectively, the information in this file defines how an X resource should appear on screen.

The main resource database file is called `app-defaults`. It is located at `/usr/X11R6/lib/X11`. In addition to this set of resource information, each user's home directory can contain additional settings that will override the default appearance of specific applications. A file named `.Xresources` or `.Xdefaults` contains this information. For example, the following sample lines in an `.Xresources` file define how an `xterm` window will appear and what features it will include. These same features can be set or changed once the `xterm` program is running, but when a user creates an X resource database, the application is started with the user's preferences already active.

```
XTerm*cursorColor: gold
XTerm*multiScroll: on
XTerm*jumpScroll: on
XTerm*reverseWrap: on
XTerm*curses: on
XTerm*Font: 6x10
XTerm*scrollBar: on
XTerm*scrollbar*thickness: 5
XTerm*multiClickTime: 500
XTerm*charClass: 33:48,37:48,45-47:48,64:48
XTerm*cutNewline: off
XTerm*cutToBeginningOfLine: off
XTerm*titeInhibit: on
XTerm*ttyModes: intr ^c erase ^? kill ^u XLoad*Background: gold
```

X resource database files are activated within one of the start-up scripts such as `.xinitrc` or `.Xclients` by using the command `xrdb`. The **xrdb** command loads an initial X database resource file or adds resource configuration details from files such as `.Xresources`. The following `xrdb` command was included in the resource database given earlier:

```
xrdb -load $HOME/.Xresources
```

When there are additional resource settings to be loaded, the **-merge** option is used instead of the **-load** option. You will rarely need to set up the **xrdb** command, because it is part of the default configuration when you install X. But you may want to add information to an `.Xresources` file to configure the appearance of an application. The online manual page for a graphical application will tell you about options you can configure via X resources.

 Linux desktop environments (such as KDE) include an X resource database that is designed to assign a standard look and feel to all programs that you launch. The desktop environments do not depend on using configuration files such as `.Xresources`. Rather than trying to use an `.Xresources` file to configure the appearance and options of a desktop such as KDE or Gnome, use the configuration tools in these environments.

USING DESKTOP INTERFACES

Not all Linux users want a graphical interface, but for those who do, the latest developments in the field of graphical desktops for Linux provide a number of impressive features. A desktop interface is a graphical environment that provides a collection of functions and utilities to make using the computer easier for those who do not have many commands memorized. You can use a desktop interface to:

- Place icons on the screen's background (where no other windows are visible). Clicking on these icons launches applications or displays data files that the user commonly accesses.

- Manage multiple applications efficiently using toolbars, keyboard controls, and so forth.

- Use menus to access frequently used utilities and applications. You can customize these menus to meet your specific requirements.

- Use a collection of basic applications provided along with the desktop, such as a text editor, calculator, calendar, note-taking application, music player, and so forth.

- Use a convenient, integrated file management utility to view and manipulate files.

- Use applications created specifically for the desktop interface. These applications rely on a common set of functions that create a single look and feel for the environment, reduce the system resources required (because of shared functionality), and interact with other applications via drag-and-drop features (or some other type of application linking feature).

Powerful window managers such as **fvwm** include some, but not all, of the features discussed above. If you encounter all of these features on an **fvwm**-based system, it's because your Linux vendor or system administrator has combined numerous Linux applications into a working graphical environment. But this cobbling together of pieces does not result in an integrated environment in which applications have the same look and feel, can share data, and can be easily managed from a central set of desktop utilities. A complete desktop interface does provide all of these benefits. The advent of complete desktop interfaces is likely to be a primary reason for increased use of Linux in the coming years.

The KDE Interface

In 1996 Matthias Ettrich began creating a full-featured graphical environment for Linux. He dubbed the project the K Desktop Environment (KDE). KDE is now the most widely used graphical environment on Linux systems. When you install most Linux distributions, KDE is installed by default with a complete set of KDE applications. KDE applications use the same graphical toolkit as the desktop itself and can thus share functionality such as common dialog boxes and drag-and-drop capability.

KDE includes a suite of applications for Internet access, system maintenance, personal productivity (organizers, calculators, music players), and many other basic tasks. KDE includes a set of icons at the bottom of the screen known as the Panel. You can use the icons in the Panel to start common applications such as Netscape Communicator or a terminal window. Each application that you start in KDE appears as a button in the taskbar (which is normally at the top of the KDE screen). You can switch between applications or open a minimized application using the corresponding button on the taskbar. A few standard icons are included on the KDE default desktop; each user can add others. Figure 5-18 shows a basic KDE desktop.

5

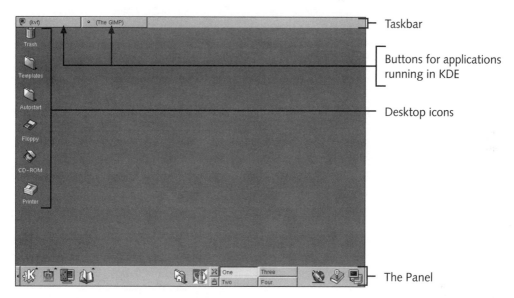

Figure 5-18   The KDE Desktop interface

KDE includes a powerful file manager program called **kfm** that provides several views of files (such as an icon view and a detailed view) and also doubles as a Web browser (much like the Microsoft Explorer program). The file manager in KDE is designed to assign icons to files automatically, based on the file's type (such as text file, program, or graphics file). Based on the type of file, the file manager also assigns default capabilities that allow a user to perform appropriate actions. For example, you will be able to click on a text file to view that file, or you can drag and drop a graphics file onto a desktop icon to view that graphics file in the program represented by the icon. You can right-click on a file and choose Properties from the pop-up menu to open a dialog box in which you can adjust the file's properties (including the file's name and access rights). Figure 5-19 shows a file manager window with a dialog box showing properties for one file.

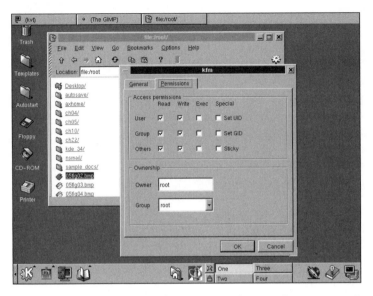

Figure 5-19   The KDE file manager window, with properties for one file

KDE includes several system administration utilities (described in later chapters), which you can use to manage your Linux system. At the same time, KDE includes a complete Control Center in which you can configure KDE itself. Via the Control Center, you can configure color schemes, screen savers, fonts, languages used (KDE supports over 30 languages, including Chinese and Russian), and the position of each part of the KDE screen (such as where the Panel and taskbar are positioned). Advanced options in the Control Center let you decide what information should be included on the title bar of each application window and which keystrokes should switch between applications. Many other options are available. Figure 5-20 shows the KDE Control Center with some of the configuration options for desktop appearance. Each user's configuration choices are stored separately.

The left side of the KDE Control Center window displays a list of sections, such as `Desktop`, `Applications`, and `Network`. By clicking the plus sign next to any section name, you will see a list of items within that section. Clicking on one of these items displays configuration options on the right side of the Control Center window.

Although a default set of desktop icons is included with KDE, each user can create additional icons, assign icons to applications, and add items to menus as desired. Applications created for the KDE Desktop can interact via drag-and-drop and other methods. Non-KDE graphical applications cannot interact in this way. Although non-KDE applications cannot use all KDE features (such as drag-and-drop), you can add any application to a KDE menu or assign it to an icon on the KDE Desktop.

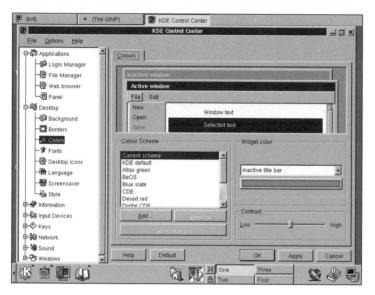

Figure 5-20   The KDE Control Center

Development of KDE continues, pushed forward by a worldwide staff of volunteer programmers, designers, writers, and translators. To learn more about the KDE project, visit the Web site *www.kde.org*.

When KDE is installed on a Linux system, the KDE components are integrated into the standard X Window System configuration files, so that the KDE window manager (called **kwm**) and related KDE programs are launched when you execute the **startx** command. Some distributions create special commands that you should use to start KDE. Caldera OpenLinux uses the command **kde** to start the KDE desktop. (The **startx** command in OpenLinux starts a simple **fvwm**-based display.) In Red Hat Linux, you can use the **switchdesk-kde** utility to select KDE as the default desktop environment.

The standard KDE installation places all KDE files in the directory **/opt/kde**. Some systems (Red Hat Linux) place KDE in a different directory, such as **/usr**. In addition, the home directory of each user who runs KDE contains a subdirectory named **.kde**. This subdirectory contains configuration files specific to that user for any KDE applications the user has reconfigured (that is, the user has selected settings other than the default KDE settings). You can alter the KDE configuration using the standard KDE graphical tools such as the KDE Control Center, although advanced KDE users may choose to edit the configuration files directly.

The Gnome Desktop

At about the time that the KDE project was first becoming popular, a group of developers within the Linux community became concerned about the fact that KDE was based on a graphical library that was not licensed using the GPL. Troll Tech, the makers of the Qt graphical library used by KDE, permitted the graphical library to be freely distributed with KDE, but the license for commercial users was stricter than the GPL used by Linux itself. Because of this concern, a new desktop project was founded. This project, the Gnu Object Model Environment (GNOME, usually written as Gnome) resulted in a complete desktop environment similar to KDE, but governed by licensing terms of the GPL.

> **TIP** Because the Gnome project is associated with the GNU project, the name of the desktop interface is pronounced with a hard letter *g*. Pronounce it as "Gh-nome," like GNU.

While Gnome was being developed, Troll Tech decided to change its licensing agreement to mirror the terms of the GPL. Thus, Linux now boasts two completely free, open source desktop environments.

Gnome is very similar to KDE. It includes a Panel with an integrated taskbar (containing a button for each running application). Icons on the desktop let you launch commonly used applications or data files. A main menu provides quick access to dozens of applications written to take advantage of the look and functionality of Gnome. The applications included with Gnome are similar to those provided with KDE. They include a powerful file manager, personal productivity applications, and system maintenance utilities. Figure 5-21 shows the Gnome Desktop with a file manager window and the main menu open for viewing.

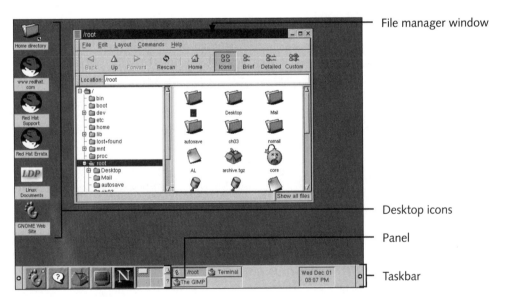

Figure 5-21   The Gnome Desktop with a file manager window

From the beginning, the Gnome project received encouragement and financial support from Red Hat Software. As a result, Red Hat is currently the only major Linux distribution that includes Gnome. Granted, Red Hat is the largest Linux distributor, so Gnome enjoys a large following of supporters. But the Gnome Desktop is not as far along in development (and hence is not as stable or complete) as the KDE Desktop.

Gnome includes a Control Center similar to the one in KDE, in which you can set up the appearance of the desktop. This tool is shown in Figure 5-22.

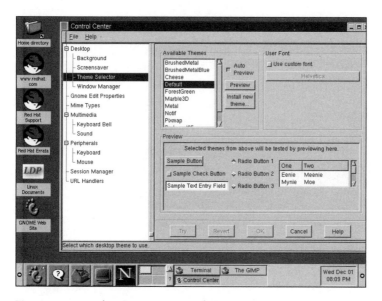

Figure 5-22   The Gnome Control Center

Although Red Hat Linux favors the Gnome Desktop, Red Hat also recognizes the prominence and features of KDE. The Red Hat Linux installation provides an option to select KDE as the default desktop, or to install KDE in addition to Gnome. When KDE is installed as part of a Red Hat Linux system, you can execute the `switchdesk-kde` program to open a dialog box in which you can choose the desktop interface you prefer to use: Gnome or KDE.

USING A GRAPHICAL LOGIN SCREEN

If the installation of Linux is successful, most Linux distributions will start the system in runlevel 5 rather than runlevel 3. As explained in Chapter 4, runlevel 5 is equivalent to the standard operating mode (runlevel 3) except that runlevel 5 always provides a graphical interface. After Linux starts and initializes, it switches immediately to graphics mode. A graphical login screen similar to the one shown in Figure 5-23 appears. This screen is equivalent to the character-mode login screen in that it requires you to enter a valid username and password before using the system. Once the username and password have been entered, a standard graphical system such as **fvwm**, Gnome, or KDE is launched.

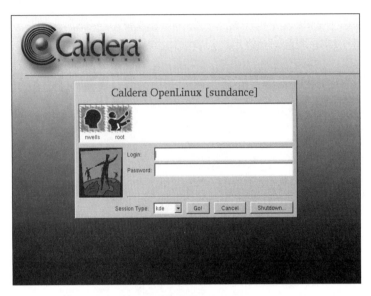

Figure 5-23   Graphical login screen

 To change the runlevel used by default as the Linux system starts, set the value in the `initdefault` line of the `/etc/inittab` file, as outlined in Chapter 4.

The graphical login screen shown in runlevel 5 is provided by the X display manager, or **xdm** program. **Xdm** is started by the `init` program as Linux boots. Any time a user exits the graphical environment, **xdm** is restarted automatically to provide a graphical login screen. Thus the user never encounters a character-mode screen—a fact that can make new users much more comfortable with Linux. The **xdm** program is installed as part of the X Window System.

When a user logs in using an **xdm** graphical login screen, **xdm** selects which programs to start based on the session chosen by the user. A **session** defines a set of graphical programs to run when a user logs in. Sessions are often named after window manager or desktop choices, such as KDE, **fvwm**, or Gnome. Another common session name is **failsafe**. The **failsafe** session opens a single terminal window and is used by the **root** user when troubleshooting the system.

A configuration file called **xsession** specifies which programs are started by a particular session name. When **xdm** starts X (after a user logs in), it executes the file `/etc/x11/xdm/Xsession` to determine which X clients to launch. The **Xsession** file contains a set of instructions that match the names of sessions defined for **xdm**. For example, if the user selects the **failsafe** session, the **Xsession** script will only launch an **xterm** program; if the user selects a KDE session, `Xsession` starts all of the standard KDE components. A per-user configuration file named `.xsession` (all lowercase, beginning with a period) can be placed in a user's home directory to control which sessions that user has available. The available session types are normally common to all users, however, so using an `.xsession` file in a home directory is unusual.

Different versions of `xdm` have been created for different environments. For example, the KDE Desktop uses a program called `kdm` (the KDE display manager). The `kdm` program is basically identical to `xdm` in functionality, but `kdm` can be graphically configured within KDE. The `xdm` program must be configured using a series of complex options within the files of the `/etc/X11/xdm` directory. Figure 5-24 shows a sample configuration screen for `kdm` within the KDE Control Center. (The `kdm` program is configured by the `Login Manager` item in the `Applications` section of the Control Center.)

5

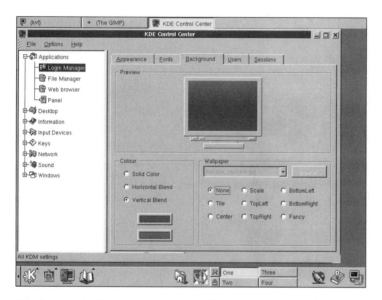

Figure 5-24   Configuring kdm in KDE

Similarly, other Linux distributions provide graphical tools you can use to configure `xdm` (or a similar program supplied by the Linux vendor as a graphical login display manager). The `LinuxConf` utility in Red Hat Linux, for example, provides this capability.

CHAPTER SUMMARY

❑ The X Window System is a powerful and flexible graphical system. A window manager or desktop interface is required to provide a user interface to X. Many different utilities can be used to configure an X server, but it remains a challenging process.

❑ The X Window System is launched by the `startx` command. This command relies on a number of scripts to control which graphical programs are started, including which window manager or desktop interface is used. By editing these scripts, or configuration files, a user controls how the graphical environment appears.

❑ Desktop interfaces include many features to promote ease of use in Linux, such as menus, toolbars, desktop icons, and convenient file management utilities. The two primary desktop interfaces on Linux are KDE—which is used on almost all Linux distributions in the world—and Gnome, which is included with Red Hat Linux, the most widely used Linux distribution in the world. The two desktop interfaces are quite similar in design and functionality.

❑ A graphical login screen is provided in Linux by the **xdm** program. This program uses a configuration file containing session definitions to determine what programs to launch after a user has entered a valid username and password at the graphical login screen.

KEY TERMS

background application — An application that does not stop the program that started it from going on to other tasks.

desktop environment — A graphical application that provides a comprehensive interface, including system menus, desktop icons, and the ability to easily manage files and launch applications.

graphical libraries — Collections of programming functions that an X client can use to more efficiently create and manage the elements of a graphical environment.

lizardx — A graphical utility used for configuring the X Window System.

Project Athena — The project sponsored by DEC and MIT to create a graphical environment or windowing system for UNIX.

resource database — A file that defines how an X resource should appear on screen.

session — A configuration that defines a set of graphical programs to run when a user logs in.

window manager — A special-purpose graphical application (X client) that controls the position and manipulation of the windows within a graphical user interface.

X client — A graphical application.

X resource — The separate screen elements of a graphical application, such as scroll bars, text fonts, mouse pointers, and title bars for windows or dialog boxes.

X server — The program that communicates with the video card to create images on the screen.

Xconfigurator — A utility in Red Hat Linux for configuring the X Window System.

xf86config — A standard text-based utility for configuring the X Window System.

XF86Setup — A graphical utility for configuring the X Window System.

xrdb — A command that loads an initial X database resource file or merges additional resource configuration details.

REVIEW QUESTIONS

1. The historical beginnings of the X Window System originated with:

   a. Project Athena

   b. Early versions of Microsoft Windows

   c. The Apple Macintosh computer

   d. The XFree86 Project

2. The X Window System was released under the same license (the GPL) as Linux. True or False?

3. Describe the function of an X server within the X Window System.

4. A(n) _____ is another name for any graphical application running in the X Window System.

   a. window manager

   b. X client

   c. `xinit`

   d. X resource

5. Name four window managers that can be used with the X Window System on Linux.

6. A window manager is best described as:

   a. A special-purpose X client that provides core graphical functionality for other X clients

   b. The management tool that administers the underlying X server

   c. The program that communicates directly with a video card in order to create windows on a computer's screen

   d. An optional component used to improve the appearance of some graphical applications

7. Name the two graphical libraries used by the two major desktop environments of Linux.

8. A graphical library is best described as:

   a. The functions that control the video card

   b. A collection of functions that any graphical program can use to create a common look and feel

   c. The configuration program used to set up X

   d. The X client that draws all windows and handles mouse and keyboard input

9. To view an X application remotely on a Windows-based computer, you must add a(n) _____ to the Windows computer.

   a. X client

   b. `xinit` program

   c. X server software

   d. Qt library package

10. The X Window System files are normally located in which subdirectory in Linux:

    a. `/x`

    b. `/usr/graphics`

    c. `/opt/kde`

    d. `/usr/X11R6`

11. On any Linux system you can choose not to run the X Window System in order to conserve system resources. True or False?

12. The `Xconfigurator` program is a standard X configuration tool in which Linux distribution?

    a. SuSE Linux

    b. TurboLinux

    c. Debian Linux

    d. Red Hat Linux

13. Name four programs that you can use to configure the XFree86 X server programs.

14. Explain why configuring the X server is challenging, but configuring other components of X is fairly straightforward.

15. The _____ program is considered the easiest, most effective tool for configuring XFree86 servers.

    a. `lizardx`

    b. `xf86config`

    c. `XF86Setup`

    d. `xdm`

16. Which is *not* considered during a standard X configuration process?

    a. The mouse

    b. The video card

    c. The graphical fonts used

    d. The screen resolution

17. Besides the standard configuration programs available for Linux, describe four other methods of obtaining information to help you configure X.

18. The _____ command is normally used to launch the X Window System.

    a. `xinit`

    b. `startx`

    c. `xdm`

    d. `xinitrc`

19. The `xinit` program searches for a variety of configuration files, including which of the following?

    a. `/etc/startx`

    b. `/etc/X11/xinit/xinitrc`

    c. `/opt/kde/share/config/kdmrc`

    d. `/tmp/xsession`

20. Explain the steps used by `xinit` to launch X, name four configuration files that `xinit` checks for, and describe the types of alterations or additions that a Linux distribution might make to the default steps.

21. To function correctly, the `startx` and `xinit` programs require that:

    a. A symbolic link named `/usr/X11R6/bin/X` is created to point to an X server program

    b. The `xdm` program has been properly configured

    c. All of the X client scripts have the 644 file permission assigned

    d. X resources have not been modified by the root user

22. Name four features associated with a modern desktop environment.

23. Describe the history of the Gnome project as it relates to the KDE project, including naming the graphical library on which each project is based.

24. The `xrdb` command is used to manage:

    a. X resources using X resource database files

    b. Automatic execution of X applications

    c. The configuration of a screen saver application

    d. The display manager `xdm`

25. The `xdm` program is started by the _____ program (or script).

    a. `init`

    b. `startx`

    c. `xinit`

    d. `xrdb`

26. A session used in `xdm` refers to:

    a. A set of applications to be started, as defined by the system administrator or Linux vendor

    b. One login and logout event by a user

    c. The time spent running a single graphical application

    d. The resources assigned to X by the Linux system

27. An **xdm** session is normally defined by information in:

a. An **Xsession** file

b. The resource database

c. The KDE login manager screen

d. An **Xclients** file

HANDS-ON PROJECTS

Project 5-1

In this activity you search the Web for information on video card compatibility. To complete this activity you should have a computer with a Web browser and an Internet connection.

1. Go to the XFree86 Project Web page at **www.xfree86.org**.

2. Scroll to the bottom of the page, reviewing the information on the page as you do so. Near the bottom of the page, in the section on XFree86 documentation, locate the link to the XFree86 video card/server list. Click on that link.

3. Review the list of video cards. What does the X server name on the right side of the list correspond to? How would you make use of this information or check that it was used correctly on the Linux system you are configuring? What steps are recommended at the top of this Web page if the video card you are searching for is not listed?

4. Check another source of information by entering the following URL in your Web browser: **www.calderasystems.com**. When the Web page appears, click the **OpenLinux 2.3** link.

5. When the OpenLinux 2.3 page appears, click the **Hardware Compatibility** link. A list of compatible hardware appears.

6. Click the **Video** link. What is this link titled? Although you are viewing the Caldera Systems Web site, what information do you see that would make you comfortable using this list for other Linux systems?

7. When a list of compatible video cards appears, review its contents. Why do you think this list is longer than the list of cards at the XFree86 Project Web site? How could the information at the bottom of the page about additional X servers help you? How would you make use of it?

8. Suppose you needed to configure an Intel Real3D Starfighter AGP card with an i740 video chipset. Click the link at the bottom of the page that would tell you more about how to support that video card.

9. Go to the Linux Documentation Project site at **www.metalab.unc.edu/LDP**.

10. Click **HOWTO** at the top of the page. A list of available formats for the HOWTO documents is presented. Click **plaintext**.

11. An index of HOWTO documents appears. Scroll down and click **Hardware-HOWTO**. This large file takes a few moments to load. Scroll down to section 6, which is titled "Video Cards." Does this information resemble the information on the Caldera Systems Web site?

Project 5-2

In this activity you continue researching video card information using commercial X server products. To complete this activity you should have a computer with a Web browser and an Internet connection.

1. Go to the Xi Graphics site at **www.xig.com**.

2. Click **Hardware Support Library** at the top of the page. A hardware information page appears. Click the link leading to the list of supported graphics cards.

3. After a moment a list of card manufacturers appears. Scroll down, reviewing the list.

4. Review the information for the Intel chips supported by the Xi Graphics product. Based on what you learned in Project 5-1, do you think the Xi Graphics product will support the Starfighter video card?

5. Click on the link to display benchmark data. Review the information in the Web page that appears. Why might you choose to purchase a commercial X server from Xi Graphics rather than use the free X servers included with a Linux distribution?

6. Go to the MetroLink home page at **www.metrolink.com**. Click the **Products** link. The Products page for the MetroLink X servers (and other related products) appears.

7. Click the link that displays video cards supported by the Metro-X product.

8. Review the list of supported graphics cards that appears. If the list seems shorter than the XFree86 and Xi Graphics lists, explore the MetroLink Web site to determine why a person might purchase the MetroLink products rather than use the XFree86 servers. Are some graphics cards listed on the MetroLink site that are not listed on the other two sites?

Project 5-3

In this activity you explore the X Window System configuration files that are included in a Linux system. To complete this activity you must have an installed Linux system with a valid user account (root access is not required, however).

1. Log in to the Linux system using a valid username and password.

2. If you logged in using a graphical login screen and are now viewing a graphical desktop, open the **main** menu of the desktop, and then choose **Terminal** from the `Utilities` submenu. A terminal window opens, where you can enter commands.

3. Change to the `/etc/X11/xinit` directory with this command:
`cd /etc/X11/xinit`.

4. Enter `ls` to list the files in this directory. What files do you see that were discussed in the chapter? Can you describe which user or users will use these files? What additional information do you need to determine whether a user will access these files when starting X?

5. Change to your home directory by entering the **cd** command without any parameters.

6. List all the files in your home directory, including hidden files, by entering the command **ls -a**.

7. What files can you see that were mentioned in the chapter? Do you see additional files that appear to be related to the X Window System?

8. If you see an **.Xdefaults** file, review its contents using the command **cat .Xdefaults** (include the period at the beginning of the filename). What effects do the contents of this file have when you log in and start X? Could you add information to this file if you had proper documentation on an X application?

9. Change to the **xdm** directory using the command **cd /etc/X11/xdm**.

10. List the files in this directory with the **ls** command. Do you see a file in which the sessions available on the system are defined?

11. Use the following **more** command to view the **Xsession** file a page at a time: **more Xsession**. Can you identify any familiar items in this script file, such as the name of a window manager or desktop environment? (Remember that this file is only used if you are using a graphical login screen.)

CASE PROJECTS

1. The Starwood movie studio has decided to create a movie using computer animation and wants to use Linux on the computers to help with some of the graphical work required. You have been asked to help set up the Linux graphics workstations that the studio will use. As you might expect, the studio is in a big hurry to finish the production. Fortunately, money is not a limiting factor in your decisions. The studio wants to use a new graphics card that provides high-resolution images and high-speed preparation of computer animation. You are concerned that the card is not yet supported on Linux versions of the X Window System. How will you determine whether the card is supported? If the standard XFree86 software does not support the card, what steps could you take to locate or create support among those who work with X and Linux?

2. Once you have installed Linux and configured the new video cards successfully, the studio asks you to adjust the features of the system to display a nonstandard resolution of 1420×865 pixels. You know that X is flexible enough to do this, but the configuration tools don't provide this screen resolution as an option. How will you learn more about the video card capabilities and X configuration in order to grant this odd request?

3. As the movie winds down production, and all the graphics work is done, the studio asks you to prepare the Linux systems to be used as regular desktop workstations in the studio. How will you configure the graphical portion of Linux to be used by the inexperienced workers in that section of the studio? What components of X will you include? How will you seek to make the systems easy to use for common daily computing tasks?

6

THE SHELL AND TEXT FILES

> **After reading this chapter and completing the exercises, you will be able to:**
>
> ◆ Describe how a Linux shell operates
>
> ◆ Customize a shell environment
>
> ◆ Use common text editors to create or modify text files
>
> ◆ Describe popular text-processing methods and tools used on Linux

In the previous chapter you learned about using a graphical system on Linux. You learned how to locate and configure the X Window System programs using a variety of utilities. You also learned how the X Window System is launched and how to modify the corresponding configuration files. You learned about the desktop environments that are commonly used on Linux and the graphical login application that can be used to start a graphical environment.

In this chapter you learn about how the Linux command-line environment—the shell—operates and how you can customize it to fit your preferences or those of other users on the Linux system. You learn about working with common Linux text editors to modify text files, and you are introduced to the more advanced programs used for complex text manipulation tasks.

UNDERSTANDING THE SHELL

In previous chapters you learned that the shell is the command interpreter, or command-line environment, for Linux. You learned a few basic commands such as `ls` to list files and `cp` to copy files. In the first part of this chapter you learn more about how the shell operates and how it interacts with the Linux kernel.

In many operating systems, a command interpreter is always running. A **command interpreter** is a program that accepts input from the keyboard and uses that input to launch commands or otherwise control the computer system. The most well known command interpreter is the `COMMAND.COM` program that is always running in DOS or Windows 95/98. This command interpreter is always available to receive input from the user via the keyboard or via programs that are running on the system. The command interpreter in DOS or Windows is integrated with the kernel of the operating system and provides functions that no other program can provide.

In Linux (or any UNIX-like system), the command interpreter (called the **shell**) has a very different relationship with the kernel and with users compared to the DOS/Windows model. The following list describes the major differences:

- The shell is only loaded when a user logs in or otherwise requests that a shell be launched.

- The shell is like any other program running on Linux. It has no special privileges, no special relationship with the Linux kernel, and no special capabilities.

- Different types of shells are available for Linux. A user can choose which shell best suits his or her preferences or environment.

As you learned in Chapter 4, when you first boot a Linux-based computer, the kernel starts the `init` program, which launches all of the system services that have been configured by the installation process or by the system administrator. The `init` program displays a login prompt (text based or graphical), but does not start a shell. Two reasons for the lack of a shell initially are:

- Linux is often used as a network server. Because no user is directly using the system (entering commands to launch programs), a shell is not needed in this situation. Instead, network services such as a Web server watch for incoming network requests and handle those requests appropriately.

- Linux security requires that no one can access the system until a valid username and password have been entered. Because a user cannot enter any commands until first logging in, no shell is required until a user has logged in.

TIP Network services such as Web servers can be used to access files on Linux through a regular user account. This means a network service is governed by the permissions assigned to its user account. For example, suppose you are using a Web browser to request a particular file from the Web server. The Web server can only retrieve the requested file if its user account has permission to access that file. As a result, the Web server controls what the Web browser can access; you are not free to explore the files on the server as if you were logged in to the server.

After a user logs in from a character-mode screen, a default shell is started, which in turn provides a shell prompt where the user can enter commands. After the user logs in from a graphical login screen (using `xdm` or a similar program), the user does *not* see a shell prompt, because it is not strictly necessary. Instead, the user can manipulate the graphical environment (started by `xdm`) to access the same core functionality (launching programs and viewing files) that is provided by a shell. If you want to access the shell from a graphical environment, you need to use the appropriate menu command.

The Shell Prompt

Figure 6-1 shows a standard shell prompt that appears after logging in to Linux using a character-mode login prompt or after starting a shell from a graphical environment. The **shell prompt** is a set of words or characters indicating that the shell is ready to accept commands that you enter. The default shell prompt includes four components:

- The user account name that you used to log in (the first `nwells` in Figure 6-1).

- The hostname of the computer that you logged in to (`incline` in Figure 6-1).

- The last part of the full directory path for your current working directory (the second `nwells` in Figure 6-1, which is the last part of the full directory path `/home/nwells`).

- A prompt character (the ending `$` in Figure 6-1).

6

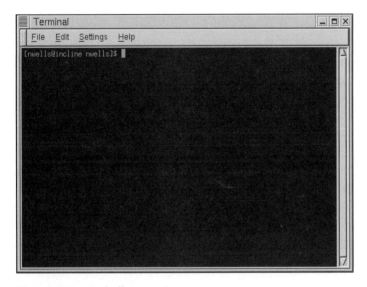

Figure 6-1   A shell prompt

Although you can alter the information provided in the shell prompt, the default setting shown here is usually an appropriate choice. The username and hostname help you keep track of your location within a networked environment involving many computers. The last part of your current working directory helps you keep track of your location within the directory structure. Although seeing the full path might be helpful in some cases, an extremely long directory path would be unwieldy; thus it makes sense to include only the last part of the path in the shell prompt.

The prompt character used in the standard Linux shell is a dollar sign, `$`. Other shells may use different prompt characters, such as a percent sign, `%`. On all shells, when you log in as `root` (the superuser), the prompt character changes to a hash mark, `#`. This makes it easier for you to determine as you work whether you have `root` permission or not. Remember that you should not use the `root` account unless you are completing system administration tasks.

The Functions of a Shell

The purpose of a shell is to make it easy for users to launch programs and work with files on the Linux system. That simple definition doesn't entirely capture the features of the shells you use in Linux, but it explains the basic rationale behind their design.

A shell's primary purpose is to launch programs. When you use the `ls` command to view the files in a directory, or use the `mv` command to rename a file, or use the `more` command to view a file, you are actually launching a program that performs those tasks. The shell processes the information entered at the keyboard and uses it to launch the program. In many cases, the information you enter on a command line includes parameters, such as the name of the file to copy and the location to copy it to. The shell passes these parameters to the program being launched. For example, entering the following command line at a shell prompt causes the shell to launch the `cp` command, handing it the two parameters `report.doc` and `report.doc.bak`. In this command, the `cp` command must decide what to do with the parameters, or return an error message if it cannot determine how to process the parameters.

```
cp report.doc report.doc.bak
```

If you enter the following command at a shell prompt, the shell will try to start a program called `report.doc` and hand that program the parameters `report.doc.bak` and `cp`. Because no program named `report.doc` exists, the shell will return an error message stating that it could not locate the requested command.

```
report.doc report.doc.bak cp
```

Besides the ability to start programs, the shell has many other built-in features that make it convenient to work with numerous files and commands on a Linux system. For example, from the shell, you can use keyboard shortcuts to enter long commands quickly, and you can control multiple programs that you have started from the shell prompt. In addition, you can define variables (assign numbers or strings to a name) to make your shell environment easier to use or to provide information (the values of variables) that other programs besides the shell can access when needed. Many of these features are described in this chapter; others are described later in the book.

A particularly important feature of a Linux shell is that it gives users the ability to write scripts (or programs) that the shell can execute. As you will learn in Chapter 12, a script is essentially a list of commands stored in the form of a text file. Instead of entering each of these commands, one by one, at the command line, you can use a script to automate the execution of a series of commands. Chapter 12 is dedicated to teaching you how to write shell scripts.

Different Types of Shells

When UNIX was first created decades ago, the original developers decided that the shell (the command interpreter) should be separated from the operating system so that it could be changed or improved later without affecting the operating system. As described in the previous section, the shell is just a regular program whose purpose is to launch other programs. The original shell for UNIX, written by Stephen Bourne, is called the **Bourne shell**. The Bourne shell program is called `sh` (for *shell*). Although the Bourne shell is standard on all UNIX and Linux systems, it is an old program with limited functionality (it was first written nearly 30 years ago).

True to the foresight of the developers of UNIX, other developers started with the Bourne shell and altered or enhanced it to provide new functionality. These later-generation shells are used on all UNIX and Linux systems today. Table 6-1 shows the commonly available shells for Linux.

Table 6-1 Linux Shells

Shell name	Program name	Description
Bourne shell	sh	The original UNIX shell. The sh program on Linux usually refers to the bash program. bash contains all sh functionality, plus interactive features such as history and tab completion (described later in this chapter) and shell programming via shell script files.
C shell	csh	A shell developed by Bill Joy in the 1970s. He focused on adding easy-to-use features for interactive work at the shell prompt. The C shell was the first to contain features similar to history and tab completion; these features were later added to the bash shell and other shells as well. The C shell uses a more complex syntax for shell programming than the Bourne and bash shells. Because of this, it is not popular for shell programming, though its interactive features make it popular with users who are not creating shell programs.
TENEX/TOPS C shell (also called the **TC shell**)	tcsh	An enhancement of the C shell. This is the version of the C shell that is commonly used on Linux systems.
Korn shell	ksh	A proprietary (not freely available) shell written by David Korn. The Korn shell is a revision of the Bourne shell that includes the interactive features of the C shell but maintains the Bourne shell programming syntax, which is considered easier to use than C shell programming syntax.
Public Domain Korn shell	pdksh	A version of the Korn shell that is freely available. (This shell is often accessed using the program named ksh on Linux systems.)
Bourne Again shell	bash	An enhanced and extended version of the Bourne shell created by the GNU project for use on many UNIX-like operating systems. Commonly referred to as the bash shell, rather than by its full name, bash is the default Linux shell.
Z shell	zsh	A recently developed shell that combines Korn shell interactive features with the C shell programming syle (for those who prefer the more complex syntax of the C shell).

6

The default shell for all Linux systems is **bash** (pronounced as the word looks, "bash"). Users on a Linux system are normally content to use the **bash** shell exclusively. The exception occurs when a user has experience with another type of shell from working on other UNIX systems, or the user writes a lot of shell scripts and needs the features of another shell. (The C shell and TC shell both use different shell programming methods than **bash**.)

Shells can be roughly divided into two groups based on the type of shell programming commands used. The two groups are:

- Those that follow the Bourne shell programming style (which is based on a very old programming language called ALGOL)

- Those that follow the C shell programming style (which is based on the widely used C language)

Further shell derivatives have combined features from different shells to make this grouping less distinct. For example, the Z shell includes many popular features of the **bash** shell but with C shell–style programming. But the overall distinction between these two groups is still valid.

 Not all of the shells in Table 6-1 will be installed by default or even included on the CD for all Linux distributions. Contact your Linux vendor or an Internet download site such as *www.linuxberg.com* to obtain a particular shell that is not included on your Linux CD.

In Linux, the shell started for each user is determined by the settings in the user account configuration file. Chapter 8 describes how you can set up or modify this configuration file. If the shell you want to use is installed on the Linux system, changing to a new default shell is very easy using the **usermod** command described in Chapter 8. Each user on the system can select a preferred shell independent of all other users.

To immediately run a different shell that is installed on the Linux system you are using, enter the name of that shell program. For example, if you are working in the standard **bash** shell but you want to run the C shell instead, enter this command and you are immediately switched to the C shell:

```
csh
```

Entering Commands

Modern shells like the **bash** and the Korn shell include features designed to simplify the process of entering commands and command parameters. Two of the most useful features are tab completion and history, which are described in the following sections.

Using Tab Completion

Tab completion is a shell feature that lets you enter part of a file or directory name and have the shell fill in the remainder of the name. Using tab completion makes it easier to enter long or complex directory paths and filenames. This is often helpful because Linux filenames can be very long, and they sometimes include punctuation, multiple digits or periods, and mixed upper- and lowercase. Because tab completion is a feature of the shell, it works whenever you are entering text at a shell prompt, no matter which command you are entering. Anytime the shell determines that you are trying to enter a command name, a filename, or a directory name, you can use tab completion.

To see how tab completion works, consider this example. Suppose you want to use the `rpm` command to install a new software package that you have downloaded and placed in the `/tmp` directory. The filename of the package is shown here:

```
desktop-backgrounds-1.1.2-6.noarch.rpm
```

To install this package, you enter the `rpm` command followed by the path and filename of the package. But for this example, suppose you just enter the following:

```
rpm -Uvh /tmp/deskt
```

To take advantage of tab completion at this point, you press the Tab key. The shell then looks at the contents of the `/tmp` directory for a file or subdirectory matching the first few letters you typed (`deskt`). Once it finds the package name, the shell fills in the remaining filename; thus, immediately after pressing Tab, you see this at the command line:

```
rpm -Uvh /tmp/desktop-backgrounds-1.1.2-6.noarch.rpm
```

Now suppose the `/tmp` directory contains another file named **desktop**. Instead of filling in the full filename when you press Tab, the shell beeps to indicate that a unique matching name is not available. You can then press Tab a second time to have the shell display all of the matching names, like this:

```
rpm -Uvh /tmp/deskt
desktop    desktop-backgrounds-1.1.2-6.noarch.rpm
```

After reviewing this list of available files with similar names, you can type enough of the name to make it unique, and then press Tab again to fill in the complete filename. In this case, because the hyphen is the first character that distinguishes the two filenames, you would need to enter the following:

```
rpm -Uvh /tmp/desktop-
```

When you first use tab completion, you may think it's more work than it's worth to keep pressing Tab and entering a few more letters if the filename is not unique. But after some practice, using tab completion to enter long filenames or paths becomes almost automatic—much easier than entering the complete file or directory name manually.

When the first part of the name that you enter is a directory, tab completion fills in the directory name, ending with a forward slash. This means you can immediately begin typing the name of a subdirectory or file within that directory. You will have a chance to try using tab completion in Project 6-1, at the end of this chapter.

Using the History Feature

A second shell feature designed to make launching commands easier is the history feature. The **history feature** records a list of each command that you enter at the shell prompt. You can quickly call up and repeat any command from this list without entering the command again.

The simplest method of accessing the history list of commands is to press the Up arrow key. This displays the most recently executed command on the command line. To use the command, press Enter. Pressing the Up arrow key repeatedly displays in turn each of the previously entered commands (the commands in the history list). Hold down the Up arrow key to see dozens of commands flash by at the shell prompt (the full contents of the history list). Press the Down arrow key to execute commands farther down in the history list (those more recently entered).

When the command you want to repeat was entered some time ago, using the Up arrow key to locate it in a large history list can be tedious. In this situation, the `history` command is useful. The `history` command displays the entire **history list**, which contains the most recently executed commands. (Normally at least 100 commands are included in the history list.) The following shows the last few lines of a history list. (Of course, the commands and numbers in the history list on your system will differ from this sample output.)

```
33   who
34   vi /etc/passwd
35   gimp
36   cd /etc
37   cd X11/
38   cd xdm
39   more Xsession
40   rpm -qa |grep XFree
41   mount -t ext2 /dev/hda3 /mnt/openlinux/
42   mcopy /mnt/openlinux/etc/XF86Config A:
43   file Xwrapper
44   umount /mnt/cdrom
45   type fvwm
46   exit
47   clear
48   mv ch05/ch04fig.zip ch04/
49   mv ch04/ch04fig.zip course_ch04/
50   cd course_ch04/
```

The length of this list can make it difficult to quickly locate the command you want to reuse. Thus you may prefer to use one of the following three methods for locating previously executed commands:

- Use the history number
- Use the beginning of a command
- Search the history list

The term *history number* refers to the number to the left of each item in the history list. For example, in the history list above, the first item has a history number 33.

You can execute any of the commands in the history list by entering the number of that command prefixed by an exclamation point. An exclamation point is sometimes called a **bang** in UNIX and Linux. So to execute the most recent `mount` command, you would enter `!41` (pronounced "bang-forty-one").

The shell displays the command matching that number and immediately executes it. You don't need to view the history list before using this technique if you already know the number of the command you want to execute. But be aware that the numbers change as you enter new commands.

To use the command name to repeat a command, use an exclamation point followed by the first part of the command you want to repeat. In the sample `history` output shown, you could execute the most recent `mount` command using this command:

```
!mou
```

When you execute this command, the shell searches for the most recent command that begins with the letters "mou" and executes it.

> When executing a command from the history list using any of the three methods described, remember that the commands are executed from your current working directory, which may be different from the directory where they were originally executed. If a command does not include a full pathname, you might see unexpected results. Be especially careful when using the partial command name method to reexecute a command without checking the full text of the command.

You can also search the history list without reexecuting a command to see what the command parameters were or how you completed a task. This method requires the use of a pipe symbol and the `grep` command, both of which are discussed in detail in Chapter 7. To use this method, enter the `history` command followed by the `grep` command and the command name you want to locate. For example, in the sample `history` output shown previously, suppose you want to search for a `mount` command to see what parameters it contains. The following command will display all items in the history list that contain the `mount` command. You can then review the displayed output to learn about the previously executed command.

```
history | grep mount
```

The `bash` shell supports additional techniques for executing commands. But the examples shown here for using tab completion and the `history` command should help you enter commands much more efficiently in Linux. To learn more about these features, review the online manual page for the `bash` shell by entering `man bash`.

The Shell Start-up Process

You learned in Chapter 5 that certain scripts are executed each time the graphical system of Linux is launched. In a similar manner, several scripts are executed when you log in to Linux or start a new shell. These scripts initialize (or configure) various parts of a user's environment, as described in the next section of this chapter.

When a user first logs in to a Linux system, the script **/etc/profile** is executed. The **/etc/profile** script contains configuration information that applies to every user on the Linux system. Each user's home directory can contain another start-up script called **.profile** (with an initial period). The **.profile** script in a user's home directory is also executed when the user logs in, but the **.profile** script is specific to a single user. Each user's home directory can contain a different **.profile** script. Only the root user can change the **/etc/profile** script; any user can change the **.profile** script in his or her home directory.

On some systems, additional scripts are executed when a user logs in. For example, on Red Hat Linux, a set of scripts located in the **/etc/profile.d** directory is started by the **/etc/profile** script. The scripts in **/etc/profile.d** add specific configuration information for KDE, a language selection, or other system features set up by the installation program. Red Hat Linux also uses a file called **.bash_profile** rather than the standard **.profile** script in each user's home directory. The operation of the file is the same as the **.profile** script.

The **profile** scripts are executed when a user logs in; additional scripts are executed when a user starts a shell. Because a shell is started immediately when a user logs in at a character-mode screen, these additional scripts are generally executed immediately after the profile scripts. A user working in a graphical environment can start multiple **bash** shells without logging in to Linux again. When a new shell is started by a user who is already logged in, the additional scripts described next (such as **/etc/bashrc**) are executed; however, the **profile** scripts are not executed again.

Some Linux distributions, including Red Hat Linux, provide an **/etc/bashrc** script that is executed for all users on the system each time a **bash** shell is started. Other Linux distributions rely on the **/etc/profile** script for configuration settings that should apply to all users, though this script is only executed at the time a user logs in.

Each user's home directory contains a script called **.bashrc**. The **.bashrc** script is executed each time the user starts a **bash** shell. Any configuration information that a user wants to add to his or her environment can be placed in the **.bashrc** file. Additional scripts with similar names are sometimes used on a Linux distribution. Examples include the following:

- **.bash_default**, which is executed each time a **bash** shell is started
- **.bash_login**, which is executed each time a **bash** shell is started
- **.bash_logout**, which is executed each time a user closes a **bash** shell

You may find scripts on your Linux distribution. In general, the names of these files provide a good description of when they are used. Consult your Linux vendor or try placing test commands in each file (see Chapter 12 for directions) if you are unsure of how the files are used. Figure 6-2 shows how a typical start-up script works when a user logs in to Linux.

```
/etc/profile ──▶ ~/.profile ──▶ /etc/bashrc ──▶ ~/.bashrc
                     or
               ~/.bash_profile
```

Figure 6-2   A typical series of start-up scripts when logging in to Linux

TIP When the user logs in or starts a shell, the systemwide script file is executed, followed by the corresponding file in the user's home directory. When starting the X Window System (see Chapter 5), the system default file /etc/X11/xinit/xinitrc is executed *only* if the xinit program does not find an .xinitrc file in the user's home directory.

The scripts described here apply when a **bash** shell is started. Similar files are executed when a user chooses to work with a C shell, Korn shell, or other shell. For example, a user's home directory may contain a file called .cshrc or .kshrc. These scripts would be executed each time a C shell or Korn shell was started, respectively. Because the script format is different for each type of shell, different script files are needed to initialize each shell. These configuration scripts can coexist in a user's home directory (and in the /etc directory, for systemwide configuration files), each one being executed only when the corresponding shell is launched.

CUSTOMIZING THE SHELL

The configuration scripts that Linux executes when a user logs in, or that **bash** executes when a shell is launched, provide a place where users can customize the Linux environment in which they work. The following sections describe several methods of customizing the shell environment. These features are separate from any customization that a user or system administrator may choose to do within a graphical environment.

Using Aliases

An **alias** is a string of characters that is substituted for another string of characters at the shell prompt. The general format of the alias command looks like this:

```
alias <string entered by user>=<string substituted by the shell>
```

For example, suppose that you are accustomed to entering the **COPY** command in DOS to copy files. Rather than enter the correct Linux command (**cp**) each time you want to copy files in Linux, you can create an alias that allows you to use the DOS command. You create the alias as follows:

```
alias copy=cp
```

With this alias in effect, each time you enter the string **copy** at the shell prompt, the shell replaces it with the string **cp**. In effect, you can now enter a command like this:

```
copy /tmp/download.tgz /home/nwells/
```

Because of the alias created earlier, the preceding command would then execute the following command:

```
cp /tmp/download.tgz /home/nwells/
```

After you create an alias, each time you enter text at a command prompt, the shell substitutes one string of characters for the other that you defined. You must be careful when you create an alias that uses an existing command name. For example, entering the command **alias more=less** would render the **more** command inoperative, because every time you entered **more**, the shell would substitute the string **less**.

To see a list of aliases that are in effect as you work, enter the **alias** command without any text after it. Many Linux distributions include a few aliases such as the following ones. These are defined for all users in a start-up script, such as **/etc/profile** or **/etc/bashrc**. Notice that when the string substituted by the shell contains a space, it must be enclosed in quotation marks.

```
alias ll="ls -la"
alias rm="rm -i"
alias cp="cp -i"
```

The **alias** command is useful in several circumstances, including those listed here:

- Aliases can shorten long commands. For example, if you regularly enter a command with many options, create an alias so you can enter that command with just two or three characters.

- Aliases can correct typing or spelling mistakes. For example, if you always enter **sl** instead of **ls**, you can create an alias that makes **sl=ls**. Aliases can help people new to Linux use the system without knowing all of the commands perfectly.

- Aliases can protect you from erasing files by automatically inserting options with commands that are used to delete files. For example, the **alias** command shown previously for the **cp** command (**alias cp="cp -i"**) causes the shell always to execute the **cp** command with the **-i** option, which prevents overwriting files when copying files.

- Aliases can add command names that you prefer to use, but that are not part of Linux by default. For example, you can use an alias to substitute the string **mv** for **ren**. (The DOS command **ren** does not exist in Linux; the **mv** command is used instead.)

Of course, when you use aliases for these purposes, you won't master Linux commands, nor will you improve your typing skills. But used wisely, aliases can make tasks proceed more quickly as you work at a Linux command line. Entering the **alias** command causes that alias to be active only as part of the current shell. Once you have decided on several **alias** commands that suit your needs, add those commands to the **.bashrc** file in your home directory so that they are executed each time you start a shell.

Symbolic Links

Symbolic links are a feature of the Linux file system. They are not part of the shell, but they can make working in the shell easier. Symbolic links are also sometimes confused with aliases in the shell, so they are presented here to avoid that confusion. Chapter 9 describes symbolic links in more technical detail.

A **symbolic link** is a file that refers to another filename rather than to data in a file. For example, suppose several employees in a company want to work on the same file. The system administrator can place the file in a directory and then create a symbolic link in each user's home directory to access the real file. If the real file is **/tmp/report.doc**, the symbolic links might be **/home/nwells/report.doc**, **/home/davis/newreport.doc**, and **/home/laura/report.doc**.

All three users can access the same physical file, /tmp/report.doc, by opening the respective files in each home directory. The file system follows the symbolic link to the file that it points to and opens that file. When users make changes after opening the file in their home directory, they are all changing the same file. Figure 6-3 illustrates a symbolic link.

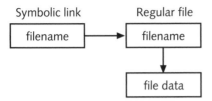

Figure 6-3 Symbolic link referring to another file

Symbolic links are used when the same data must be accessed from two locations in the directory structure, or by two (or more) different names. Using a symbolic link takes only a few bytes of hard disk space—enough to store the filename that the link refers to rather than a copy of the file. Symbolic links are commonly used in directories such as /lib and /usr/lib, where a system file must be referred to by several names in order for programs to find it.

You can view any symbolic links in a directory by using the ls -l command. For example, part of the output from the command ls -l /lib is shown below. Within the first column, a symbolic link is indicated by the letter *l*. In the last column, the filename preceded by an arrow (—>) is the file to which the symbolic link points.

```
-rwxr-xr-x   1 root     root      4016683 Apr 16   1999 libc-2.1.1.so
lrwxrwxrwx   1 root     root           13 Nov 18 02:35 libc.so.6 -> libc-2.1.1.so
lrwxrwxrwx   1 root     root           17 Nov 18 02:36 libcom_err.so.2 -> libcom_err.so.2.0
-rwxr-xr-x   1 root     root         7889 Mar 21   1999 libcom_err.so.2.0
-rwxr-xr-x   1 root     root        63878 Apr 16   1999 libcrypt-2.1.1.so
lrwxrwxrwx   1 root     root           17 Nov 18 02:35 libcrypt.so.1 -> libcrypt-2.1.1.so
-rwxr-xr-x   1 root     root       787688 Apr 16   1999 libdb-2.1.1.so
lrwxrwxrwx   1 root     root           15 Nov 18 02:35 libdb.so.2 -> libdb1-2.1.1.so
lrwxrwxrwx   1 root     root           14 Nov 18 02:35 libdb.so.3 -> libdb-2.1.1.so
-rwxr-xr-x   1 root     root       219002 Apr 16   1999 libdb1-2.1.1.so
lrwxrwxrwx   1 root     root           15 Nov 18 02:35 libdb1.so.2 -> libdb1-2.1.1.so
-rwxr-xr-x   1 root     root        73486 Apr 16   1999 libdl-2.1.1.so
lrwxrwxrwx   1 root     root           14 Nov 18 02:41 libdl.so.1 -> libdl.so.1.9.5
-rwxr-xr-x   1 root     root         5388 Mar 21   1999 libdl.so.1.9.5
lrwxrwxrwx   1 root     root           14 Nov 18 02:35 libdl.so.2 -> libdl-2.1.1.so
lrwxrwxrwx   1 root     root           13 Nov 18 02:36 libe2p.so.2 -> libe2p.so.2.3
-rwxr-xr-x   1 root     root        14519 Mar 21   1999 libe2p.so.2.3
lrwxrwxrwx   1 root     root           16 Nov 18 02:36 libext2fs.so.2 -> libext2fs.so.2.4
-rwxr-xr-x   1 root     root        84999 Mar 21   1999 libext2fs.so.2.4
-rwxr-xr-x   1 root     root       538944 Apr 16   1999 libm-2.1.1.so
lrwxrwxrwx   1 root     root           13 Nov 18 02:35 libm.so.6 -> libm-2.1.1.so
lrwxrwxrwx   1 root     root           15 Nov 18 02:42 libncp.so -> libncp.so.2.2.0
lrwxrwxrwx   1 root     root           15 Nov 18 02:42 libncp.so.2 -> libncp.so.2.2.0
-rwxr-xr-x   1 root     root        96737 Apr  6   1999 libncp.so.2.2.0
```

Graphical file manager windows (such as those in Gnome and KDE) also indicate a symbolic link using a special icon. Figure 6-4 shows a Gnome file manager window containing the /lib directory. The small arrow in the lower-right corner of the file's icon marks a file as a symbolic link.

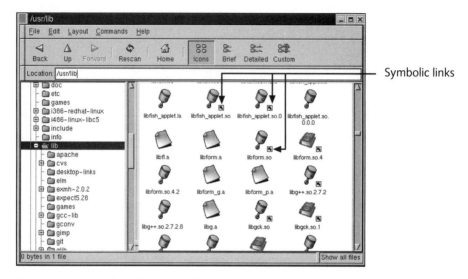

Figure 6-4   Symbolic links in a Gnome file manager window

You use the **ln** command with the **-s** option to create a symbolic link. The syntax of this command is as follows:

```
ln -s <existing file> <symbolic link to create>
```

For example, if you have a file called **report.doc** in your home directory and you want to create a symbolic link to the /tmp directory named **newreport.doc**, you would use the following command:

```
ln -s /home/nwells/report.doc /tmp/newreport.doc
```

In the command above, you could use relative pathnames depending on your current working directory.

 Don't confuse aliases and symbolic links. An alias causes the shell to substitute a different string in text that you enter. A symbolic link causes the file system to pass a request for one file to a different file in the directory structure.

Environment Variables

Environment variables are settings, or values, available to any program launched by a particular user. Each user has a separate set of environment variables available to programs launched by that user. In Linux terminology, an environment variable is assigned a value. For example, the value of the HOME environment variable is the path to a user's home directory.

6

The USER environment variable is assigned a value of the current user account. The OSTYPE environment variable is assigned a value of the operating system type, Linux.

Environment variables define the environment in which a user works. For example, the HOME variable contains the value of the user's home directory path, such as /home/nwells. When the cd command is executed without a parameter, the shell changes the current working directory to the value of HOME.

The initialization scripts or start-up scripts (that are run when Linux is booted or when a user logs in) create many environment variables and assign values to them. Each time a user starts a program, the environment of that new program is taken from (inherited from) the program that launched it, which is normally the shell that the user is working in. The shell has many environment variables defined. These variables are created by various scripts that are executed during system boot and when a user logs in. When you start a new program, all of those environment variables become part of the environment in which the new program runs. This means that the new program you launch can access the values of all those environment variables. For example, any program can request the value of the USER environment variable to see which user launched the program.

The **set** command displays a list of all environment variables defined in your current environment. The output of the **set** command on a Red Hat Linux system is shown below. Many variables listed by **set** are used by system processes with which you are not yet familiar, but you will recognize some of them. For example, the PWD=/home/nwells line indicates the current working directory. When you execute the **pwd** command, the value of this environment variable is printed to the screen. When you use the **cd** command, the value of this variable is updated to a new directory name.

```
BASH=/bin/bash
BASH_ENV=/root/.bashrc
BASH_VERSION=1.14.7(1)
COLUMNS=80
EUID=0
HISTFILE=/root/.bash_history
HISTFILESIZE=1000
HISTSIZE=1000
HOME=/root
HOSTNAME=incline
HOSTTYPE=i386
IFS=
INPUTRC=/etc/inputrc
KDEDIR=/usr
LINES=25
LOGNAME=root
MAIL=/var/spool/mail/root
MAILCHECK=60
OPTERR=1
OPTIND=1
OSTYPE=Linux
PATH=/usr/bin:/sbin:/bin:/usr/sbin:/usr/bin:/usr/X11R6/bin:/root/bin
```

```
PPID=604
PS1=[\u@\h \W]\$
PS2=>
PS4=+
PWD=/root
SHELL=/bin/bash
SHLVL=1
TERM=linux
UID=0
USER=root
USERNAME=
_=set
```

You can also view the value of a single environment variable using the **echo** command, which prints text to the screen. You can include an environment variable name after the **echo** command to print the value of that variable. The variable name is preceded by a dollar sign so that the value of the variable is substituted by the shell. For example, to print the value of the HOME variable to the screen, use the following command:

```
echo $HOME
```

Many programs use environment variables to obtain information about your environment or about how the program should function. For example, a program may use the HOME variable to determine where to look for a user's data files. A program may also expect that certain environment variables have been set up specifically for the use of that program. For example, the documentation for a database program may state that before launching the program, you must define an environment variable named DB_DIR that defines the directory where the database files are located. If you execute the database program without first setting this environment variable, the program will not function correctly. (In such a case, the program usually displays an error message indicating that you must set a certain environment variable.) When programs need certain environment variables set, you should include a command to set those variables either in the systemwide start-up scripts or in a specific user's start-up scripts (if only one user runs the program in question).

You use the **export** command to make a newly created environment variable available to other programs running in the same environment. For example, you can define a new environment variable for the example database program just mentioned, and then make that variable available to the database program, using these two commands:

```
DB_DIR=/usr/local/db_data
export DB_DIR
```

> **TIP** Most environment variables are all uppercase letters, but they are case sensitive. If a program requires that you set up an environment variable, follow the format given in the program's documentation.

An excellent example of a program that uses environment variables is the shell itself. The online manual page for the **bash** shell lists dozens of variables that the shell uses (or can use, if you set them) to control or select features of the shell. Two of these variables deserve mention here as examples.

The **PATH** environment variable contains a list of directories on the Linux system that the shell searches each time a command is executed. When you enter a program name to launch at the shell prompt, the shell searches in each directory listed in the value of the **PATH** variable. If the program is not found in the first directory, the second is searched, and so forth. The command to view the value of **PATH** is `echo $PATH`. Sample output of this command on a Red Hat Linux system is shown below. (The value of **PATH** varies depending on whether you are logged in as root or as a regular user. The output here is for a regular user account.)

```
/usr/bin:/bin:/usr/bin:/usr/local/bin:/usr/bin/X11:/usr/X11R6/
  bin:
/home/nwells/bin
```

When you want to execute any program or script that is not located in a directory that is part of the **PATH** variable, you must provide the shell with the file's complete pathname. For example, you must give the full pathname to execute any program in your home directory. If the program is named **newprogram** and your current working directory is `/home/nwells`, either of these commands will run the program:

```
/home/nwells/newprogram
./newprogram
```

If you simply enter **newprogram** alone, the shell will look in the **PATH** directories and be unable to find the **newprogram** program. An interesting exercise is to press the Tab key twice on an empty shell prompt line. The shell then attempts to use tab completion, but because you have entered no characters, the list of possible matches is very large, and the shell requests confirmation with a message like this one:

```
There are 1599 possibilities. Do you really
wish to see them all? (y or n)
```

Pressing the Y key for yes causes the shell to list all of the executable programs that it can find in the **PATH** directories.

Another example variable used by the shell is called **PS1**. This variable defines the shell prompt for **bash**. The command `echo $PS1` produces the following output:

```
[\u@\h \W]\$
```

The \u, \h, and \W parameters refer to the username, hostname, and working directory, respectively. You can alter the shell prompt by changing the value of this variable. You will have a chance to try using this command in Project 6-1, at the end of this chapter.

USING TEXT EDITORS

The most often-used tool of a Linux system administrator is a text editor. As you have probably already noticed from the discussion so far, most of what happens on a Linux system is controlled by a text configuration file. Graphical configuration utilities are sometimes available to assist with configuration, but a competent Linux system administrator can also modify the configuration files using any text editor. This provides the flexibility to update or repair a Linux system without having access to special configuration utilities.

A Variety of Editors

Linux supports numerous text editors; at least three are included with every popular version of Linux. Some of these text editors are graphical, such as the KDE text editor shown in Figure 6-5. You don't need any special training to use graphical text editors because a menu bar and dialog boxes guide you through any editing tasks you need to perform. The disadvantage of a graphical editor is that it requires you to be in the X Window System, which is not always available. (You may also choose not to use X because it consumes a lot of system resources.) At those times when a graphical environment is not available, you must use a text-based editor.

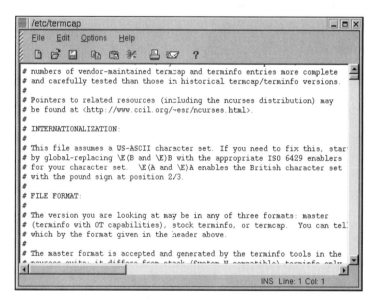

Figure 6-5   The KDE text editor

The following list shows some of the better-known character-mode text editors included with various Linux distributions. Not all are included with every version of Linux, but several are probably available on the Linux system you are using.

- `vi`: the name stands for *visual editor*, though you may wonder if this title is appropriate the first time you interact with `vi` because it doesn't provide any visual clues about how to use the editor's functions. This is the most widely used editor on UNIX and Linux systems. It is discussed in detail in the next section. Different versions of `vi`, such as `vim` and `elvis`, are usually launched with the command `vi`.

- **emacs**: this powerful editor provides macros, programming tools, customization, and hundreds of keyboard shortcuts. A graphical version called **xemacs** is available.

- **pico**: this simple editor includes on-screen information about which Control key sequences perform which functions.

- **ed**: because this is a line editor, you can only work with one line of text at a time, instead of viewing an entire screen full of information at once as you can in other text editors.

- **joe**: this is another simple text editor with on-screen command help.

Figure 6-6 shows the **pico** editor with a text file loaded for editing. Notice the commands at the bottom of the screen. Each item indicates a control character that you can use to control the editor. For example, the text **^X Exit** indicates that you can press Ctrl+X to exit **pico**.

Figure 6-6 The **pico** text editor

Using the **vi** Editor

Because the **vi** editor is a powerful program that is available on all Linux systems, it is important that all system administrators have at least a basic familiarity with it. **vi** is not easy to learn, however, because it requires you to memorize strange key sequences to perform even basic commands. Once you have learned a few commands, the patterns used by **vi** start to emerge, and learning new commands becomes easier.

To launch the **vi** editor, enter the command **vi** at any Linux shell prompt. You can include the name of a file you want to edit after the program name, such as **vi /etc/lilo.conf**, or just use the program name to begin creating a new file. When you open a new file, you see tilde characters (~) down the left side of the screen. These indicate lines that are not part of the file (because a new file is empty). Figure 6-7 shows **vi** after starting it without specifying a file to edit.

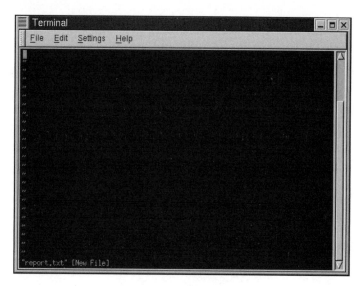

Figure 6-7 A new file in the **vi** editor

vi is a modal editor. In a **modal editor**, your keystrokes are interpreted differently depending on the task at hand. Different modes (such as command mode and edit mode) determine how keystrokes are interpreted by the editor. For example, if you are in command mode and press a key, the key is interpreted as a command; if you are in edit mode and press a key, the key is interpreted as data entry and is added to the document. **vi** has several modes. The most important ones are listed here:

- Command mode: keystrokes are interpreted as commands to edit the file, such as deleting lines or searching for text.

- Insert mode: keystrokes are inserted into the document you are creating.

- Replace mode: keystrokes are added into the document you are creating, over-writing any existing text at the place where you begin typing.

When you open **vi**, you begin in command mode. You can always return to command mode by pressing the Esc key. When you are in command mode, **vi** displays only the document you are editing. When you are in insert mode or replace mode, you see a message line at the bottom of the screen with the text **--INSERT--** or **--REPLACE--**. (You'll learn how to switch to another mode later in this section.)

Many commands in **vi** require you to enter a series of keystrokes. The following tables use the notation "Ctrl+X" to indicate "hold down the Ctrl key while pressing the X key." The notation "1, Ctrl+g" indicates "press the 1 key, then hold down the Ctrl key while pressing the g key." All **vi** commands are case sensitive. The notation "Ctrl+g" indicates a lowercase *g*. The notation "Ctrl+Shift+G" indicates an uppercase *g*.

You can use the arrow keys and the Page Up and Page Down keys to move around the screen as you edit a document. These keys normally work if you are in insert mode or replace mode as well. Table 6-2 shows additional commands you can use to move around a large document while you are in command mode.

Table 6-2   `vi` Commands Used for Moving Around a Document

Keystroke	Description
j	Move the cursor one line down.
k	Move the cursor one line up.
h	Move the cursor one character left.
l	Move the cursor one character right.
w	Move the cursor one word forward.
b	Move the cursor one word backward.
Shift+G	Move to the last line of the file.
1, Shift+G	Move to the first line of the file.
Ctrl+g	Display a status line at the bottom of the screen to indicate the line number where the cursor is positioned and the name of the file being edited.

Caution

If you are working on Linux over a network connection (for example, with the Microsoft Windows telnet program), `vi` may have trouble displaying text correctly. The first indication of a problem is usually that the arrow keys do not work correctly. You can still use the commands in Table 6-2 to move around the document, but you may want to investigate getting a different terminal program for the Windows system, such as PowerTerm Pro. (See *www.powerterm.com*.)

You can enter the insert or replace mode using several different commands, depending on where you want to begin entering text. Table 6-3 shows the most commonly used commands of this type. When you enter any of these commands (in command mode) you see the `--INSERT--` or `--REPLACE--` indicator at the bottom of the `vi` screen.

Table 6-3   `vi` Commands to Enter Insert or Replace Mode

Keystroke	Description
i	Begin inserting text to the left of the current cursor position.
a	Begin inserting text to the right of the current cursor position.
I	Begin inserting text at the beginning of the current line.
A	Begin inserting text at the end of the current line.
o	Insert a blank line after the line that the cursor is on, place the cursor on the new line, and begin inserting text.
O	Insert a blank line above the line that the cursor is on, place the cursor on the new line, and begin inserting text.
r	Replace one character with the next character entered.
R	Enter replace mode; all text entered will overwrite existing text beginning at the current cursor position.

Table 6-4 shows a few common editing commands that you can use in **vi**'s command mode. From the commands given here, you can deduce other similar commands. For example, if the command 10,y,y copies 10 lines into the clipboard, the command 20,y,y will copy 20 lines into the clipboard.

Table 6-4   Standard **vi** Editing Commands

Keystroke	Description
x	Delete one character to the right of the cursor.
5,x	Delete five characters to the right of the cursor.
d,w	Delete one word to the right of the cursor.
5,d,w	Delete five words to the right of the cursor.
d,d	Delete the current line.
D	Delete from the cursor position to the end of the current line.
u	Undo the previous command (use repeatedly to undo several commands).
y,y	Copy the current line into a buffer. (A **vi** buffer is like the Windows clipboard, but **vi** has many different buffers; this command uses a standard buffer.)
p	Paste the line(s) from the standard buffer below the current line.
J	Join the next line to the end of the current line (remove the end-of-line character at the end of the current line).

All of the commands shown so far affect the document you are editing but do not display anything as you enter the command characters. Many **vi** commands do display the text that you enter, making it easier to enter these commands. Table 6-5 shows a few of these commands, most of which begin with a colon or a forward slash. After you enter the colon or forward slash, you see the remaining characters in the command at the bottom of the screen. For each of these commands, you must press Enter to indicate that you have finished entering the command.

Table 6-5   Additional **vi** Commands

Command	Description	Example
:, w, Enter	Save the current document.	:w
:, w, *filename*, Enter	Save the current document as *filename*.	:w report
:, q, Enter	Exit **vi**.	:q
:, q, !, Enter	Exit **vi**, discarding any changes to the current document.	:q!
:, w, q, Enter	Save the current document and exit **vi**.	:wq
Z, Z	Save the current document and exit **vi**.	
/, *searchtext*, Enter	Search for *searchtext*.	/annual
/, Enter	Search again for the most recent *searchtext*.	/
:, !, *commandname*, Enter	Execute *commandname* and return to **vi**.	:!dir

Although the commands in the preceding tables may seem too numerous to memorize, you will quickly become familiar with at least the basic commands required to add or delete text and then save your changes and exit from `vi`. Other powerful `vi` features, such as complex search-and-replace tasks and integration with other Linux commands, are not discussed in detail here.

TEXT PROCESSING

The text editors presented in the previous section are used only to create or edit basic text files. These files do not contain any type of formatting, such as you would see in a word processor. To create documents that include formatting, such as bold text and multiple fonts, you must use additional utilities.

The methods that you can use to create formatted documents are of two types:

- **Graphical**, or **WYSIWYG** (pronounced "whiz-ee-wig") programs show documents on the computer screen much as they will look when printed on paper or in a Web browser (depending on the type of document you are creating).

- **Mark-up languages** define a series of codes to indicate how you want a document formatted. You can create a document using a mark-up language in any text editor, but you see the results (the effect of the codes you entered) only when you view the document in another program or print it on paper.

Mark-up Languages

The mark-up method of creating documents is older than the graphical programs that are now available. Mark-up languages are still popular with many Linux and UNIX enthusiasts. Although graphical programs may be easier to learn, they require many more system resources and often lack the flexibility of mark-up systems. If part of a document created with a mark-up language is incorrect, it is usually easy to repair or add the mark-up code that makes the document correct; in graphical systems, the user must locate a menu option that performs the needed alteration of the underlying document structure.

The best-known mark-up language is HTML, the hypertext mark-up language. HTML is used on the Web as the format for all the documents downloaded for viewing on a browser. You can choose from many different graphical programs for creating HTML documents, but

6

you can also use a text editor like `vi` to create an HTML document. Figure 6-8 shows an HTML document in a text editor. The figure shows the format of the mark-up codes, with each enclosed in angle brackets—for example, `<TITLE>` and `<P>`.

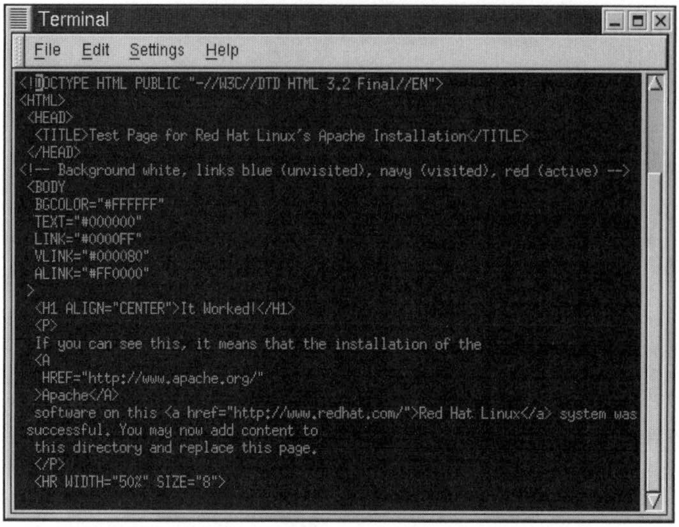


```
<!DOCTYPE HTML PUBLIC "-//W3C//DTD HTML 3.2 Final//EN">
<HTML>
 <HEAD>
  <TITLE>Test Page for Red Hat Linux's Apache Installation</TITLE>
 </HEAD>
<!-- Background white, links blue (unvisited), navy (visited), red (active) -->
 <BODY
  BGCOLOR="#FFFFFF"
  TEXT="#000000"
  LINK="#0000FF"
  VLINK="#000080"
  ALINK="#FF0000"
 >
  <H1 ALIGN="CENTER">It Worked!</H1>
  <P>
  If you can see this, it means that the installation of the
  <A
   HREF="http://www.apache.org/"
  >Apache</A>
  software on this <a href="http://www.redhat.com/">Red Hat Linux</a> system was
 successful. You may now add content to
  this directory and replace this page.
  </P>
  <HR WIDTH="50%" SIZE="8">
```

Figure 6-8 An HTML document in a text editor

The most widely used mark-up language in the UNIX and Linux world is called TeX (pronounced "tek"). **TeX** is a document-processing system that writers use to create documents—or even books—on UNIX or Linux systems. TeX is complex and requires training to use effectively, but it has a long list of features that allow it to be used effectively for projects as complex as creating scientific textbooks and software manuals.

TeX includes the capability to create macros. A **macro** is a set of commands that can be executed at one time by referring to the name of the macro. To make their work with TeX easier, writers often prefer to use a version (or package) that includes many macros. The most popular of these versions are LaTeX and TeTeX. Because of the popularity of TeX, you will often find it included on a Linux system. If you don't intend to do text processing, you can remove the TeX-related packages.

Figure 6-9 shows a **LaTeX** document in a text editor. You can see that the mark-up codes in a LaTex document begin with a backslash. As with HTML documents, you can create a LaTeX document in any text editor. You can print the resulting document on paper to see the results of the mark-up codes. You can also view the document in a graphical program called `xdvi`. The **`xdvi`** program displays a LaTeX-coded document as it will appear on paper. Figure 6-10 shows the `xdvi` program viewing a document that was originally created in a text editor using LaTeX mark-up codes.

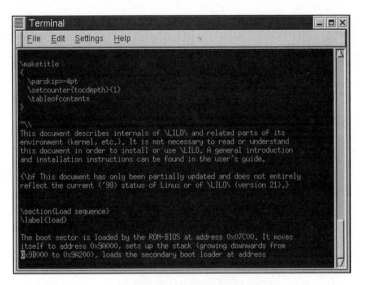

Figure 6-9   A LaTeX document in a text editor

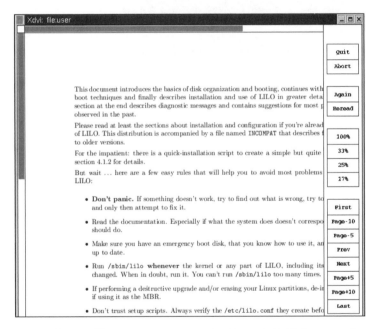

Figure 6-10   The xdvi program viewing a LaTeX document

Although LaTeX is a popular format for creating books and reports, it is not used much for formatting text to be displayed on a computer screen. Another mark-up language called roff is commonly used for online documents such as the online manual pages. You can use the **troff** and **groff** programs to format and display documents that are created with roff mark-up codes. (Roff rhymes with "cough." **Troff** is pronounced "t-roff" and **groff** is pronounced "g-roff"—again, with "roff" rhyming with "cough.") Figure 6-11 shows an online Linux manual page for the `ls` command as it appears in a text editor. Notice that the roff mark-up codes begin with a period; they are different from the HTML or LaTeX codes. The `man` command converts the roff codes to formatting, such as indented lines and bold text, when a manual page is displayed on screen.

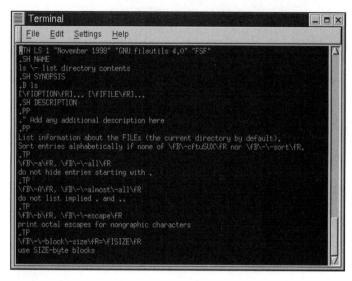

Figure 6-11   The `ls` man page file in a text editor

Some systems allow you the best of both worlds by combining a graphical system with a mark-up language. The WordPerfect for Linux product uses a WYSIWYG system for creating documents, so you don't need to learn any mark-up codes to create complex documents. But you can view the codes used internally by choosing Reveal Codes on the View menu. Figure 6-12 shows a document in WordPerfect for Linux with the Reveal Codes option selected so that the internal mark-up codes are visible at the bottom of the screen.

Controlling Fonts

A large part of formatting documents in Linux relates to fonts. This section describes several methods of controlling the fonts used on a Linux system.

The LILO program that launches the Linux kernel can control which video mode is used for the text-based display. Only a few options are available, but this flexibility is useful when you want to control the size or style of the display. The image section of the `lilo.conf` file that you learned about in Chapter 4 can contain a `vga` parameter that defines which video mode is used when the system starts. Table 6-6 shows the possible video modes and the corresponding value of the `vga` parameter.

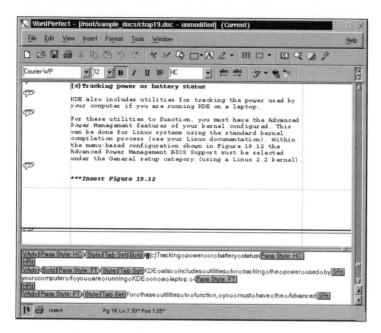

Figure 6-12 A WordPerfect for Linux document with mark-up codes visible

Table 6-6 Screen Resolutions for the vga Parameter

vga parameter value	Resolution (lines × characters per line)
0	80×25
1	80×50
2	80×43
3	80×28
4	80×30
5	80×34
6	80×43
7	40×25
8	40×28
9	132×43
a	132×43

Not all screen resolutions will be supported on all video cards. Before setting a mode, you may want to use the parameter **vga=ask** so that you can enter different values from Table 6-6 to test each until you find an appropriate choice for your system and preferences. The image section of the **lilo.conf** file with a video mode of 2 is shown in the following list:

```
image=/boot/vmlinuz-2.2.5-15
      label=linux
      root=/dev/hda3
      read-only
      vga=2
```

More important than the **vga** option for setting a character-mode font size is the ability to work with many fonts in the X Window System. Each font used in the X Window System is stored in one of the font directories named in the **XF86Config** file (described in Chapter 5). The common location for the font files is **/usr/X11R6/lib/X11/fonts**. This directory contains subdirectories for different types of fonts, such as Type1 for PostScript fonts. You can review the fonts available on the system by using the **xfontsel** program. **xfontsel** is a graphical program that lets you choose each aspect of a font definition (such as the font family and typeface). It then displays the corresponding font for your review. Figure 6-13 shows the **xfontsel** program with a font selected and displayed in the bottom portion of the program window.

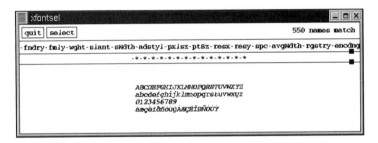

Figure 6-13   The xfontsel program

You can use the **xfontsel** program to select a font for a graphical program. The font that you choose can be added to a resource database file such as **.Xdefaults** (see Chapter 5), or it can be selected within the graphical program (if that option is provided by the program). Not all X fonts are appropriate for all displays. Some are very small and cannot be enlarged; others are poorer quality, suitable only for older computer systems with limited video display capabilities.

When you use Gnome, KDE, or other graphical desktop you can select the font for many applications; you can also select a default font for the desktop itself. The Gnome Control Center and the KDE Control Center both provide access to a standard font selection dialog box in which you can choose the font you want to use. (In the Gnome Control Center, use the Themes item; in the KDE Control Center, use the Fonts item.) Many graphical applications allow you to select fonts using the same standard dialog box. The font selection dialog box for the Gnome Control Center is shown in Figure 6-14.

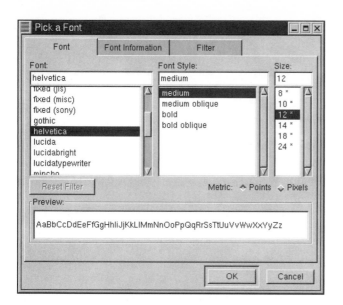

Figure 6-14   The Gnome font selection dialog box

> **TIP** KDE provides a Font Manager application in which you can set up the X Window System fonts that will be available in the KDE font selection dialog box. Because some X fonts may not be appropriate for your system, limiting the display of these fonts using the font manager makes it easier for you to select a font in the font selection dialog box.

Adding new fonts to a Linux system requires several steps, as outlined here:

1. Obtain the file for a new font from an Internet site of a font vendor such as Adobe. The preferred file format is `pcf`, but other formats such as `snf`, `pfa`, `pfb`, `spd`, and `bdf` are also supported by XFree86. Check the file extension of the font file to be certain that the format of the font is supported.

2. Go to the font directory specified in the `XF86Config` file, which is normally `/usr/X11R6/lib/X11/fonts`. Copy the font file into the correct subdirectory based on its type (such as `Type1`, `Speedo`, or `100dpi`). Ask the font vendor for this information if it is not apparent from the font's name.

3. Within the subdirectory where you copied the font file, locate the `fonts.scale` file. Load it into a text editor and add the font file that you copied into this directory, following the format of the other lines in the `fonts.scale` file. Increase the number on the first line of the file by one (this is the number of fonts in the file). If the font you have installed is not scalable, you can skip this step.

4. Activate the new font immediately by using the following command. (The font will also be activated automatically if you exit and restart the X Window System.)

```
xset fp rehash
```

Altering Text Files

The mark-up languages presented previously let you create complex, professional-looking documents using a Linux text editor. Many times you'll want to modify part of a plain text file by adding, removing, or altering data in the text file based on complex rules or patterns. This kind of modification, known as **filtering**, is not possible in even a powerful text editor such as `vi` or `emacs`. To filter text files, you need to use some special Linux commands.

Linux provides many commands for filtering text files. A simple example is the `sort` command. You can use the `sort` command to sort all of the lines in a text file, writing them out in alphabetical order or according to an option you provide to the command. A simple example is the following, which prints a list of all users on a Linux system, sorted by the username.

```
sort /etc/passwd
```

Other options for the `sort` command allow you to merge multiple files, sorting the contents of all files; to sort based on different fields within each line of a file; and to check whether a file is already sorted.

More complex commands for altering text include a complete programming syntax to let you define how to filter a text file. The simplest of these complex commands is the `sed` command. The `sed` command (for *stream editor*) processes each line in a text file according to a series of commands provided by the user. The following command prints to the screen all lines of the `/tmp/names` file that contain the text `wells`.

```
sed -n '/wells/p' /tmp/names
```

The pattern between the two forward slashes (`wells` in the above example) can be very complex. In Chapter 7 you will learn about regular expressions, which you can use in a `sed` command to match complex patterns. As another `sed` example, the following command prints to the screen all lines of the `/tmp/names` file except those containing `wells`. (The d after `wells` indicates "delete matching lines from the output.")

```
sed '/wells/d' /tmp/names
```

A final example shows how to replace all occurrences of the pattern `wells` in the file `/tmp/names` with the string `welles`:

```
sed 's/wells/welles/' /tmp/names
```

The syntax of the `sed` commands can become very complex. Other programs such as `awk` and `perl` are also often used to filter text. Both `awk` and `perl` are full programming languages that developers use to create scripts for working on text files. (Both `awk` and `perl` are also used for many other types of tasks besides filtering text files.)

CHAPTER SUMMARY

❑ The Linux shell operates like any other programs on a Linux system. Many types of shells are available, such as **bash**, the Korn shell, and the C shell. All shells are used primarily for launching other programs, including system administration utilities. All shells also provide ease-of-use features such as a history list and tab completion. Many different scripts are used to initialize a shell when it is launched.

❑ You can customize a shell by using aliases to assign new strings to information that you enter at the shell prompt. Environment variables provide values that any program can access. You can view the value of an environment variable or set up a new environment variable from the shell prompt.

❑ Linux systems include numerous text editors. The most widely available is called **vi**. The **vi** editor is powerful, but requires that you memorize a series of commands to use it. Graphical editors are included on modern Linux desktops, but knowledge of **vi** remains a critical system administrator skill.

❑ Text files can be created using WYSIWYG word processors or mark-up languages such as LaTeX and roff. Files that use a mark-up language can be created in any text editor. To see the effect of the mark-up codes, you must use another program or print the file to paper. Several programs are available to filter lines in text files based on simple or complex rules. The **sed** command is one example of a text-filtering program.

KEY TERMS

.bashrc — A configuration script that is executed each time the user starts a **bash** shell.

.profile — A configuration script that can be located in each user's home directory. A script that is executed each time any user on the system starts a **bash** shell. This script is not included by default on all Linux distributions, but can be created if needed.

/etc/profile — A script containing configuration information that applies to every user on the Linux system.

alias — A string of characters that the shell substitutes for another string of characters when a command is entered.

awk — A programming language that developers use to create scripts for working on text files and completing other complex tasks.

bang — In Linux jargon, an exclamation point character

bash — Short for *Bourne Again shell*, an enhanced and extended version of the Bourne shell created by the GNU project for use on many UNIX-like operating systems. **bash** is the default Linux shell.

Bourne shell — The original shell for UNIX, written by Stephen Bourne.

C shell — A shell developed by Bill Joy in the 1970s. He focused on adding easy-to-use features for interactive work at the shell prompt. (Most of these features were later added to the **bash** shell as well.) The C shell is not popular for shell programming because its syntax is more complex than that of the Bourne, **bash**, and Korn shells.

command interpreter — A program that accepts input from the keyboard and uses that input to launch commands or otherwise control the computer system.

echo — Command used to print text to the screen.

environment variables — Settings, or values, available to any program launched by a particular user. Each user has a separate set of environment variables available to programs launched by that user.

export — Command used to make a newly created environment variable available to other programs running in the same environment.

filtering — The process of adding, removing, or altering data in the text file based on complex rules or patterns.

groff — A command used to format and display documents that are created using roff mark-up codes.

history — A command used to display all of the stored commands in the history list.

history feature — A feature of the shell that records in a list (the history list) each of the commands that you enter at the shell prompt.

history list — A list that contains the most recently executed commands. (Normally at least 100 commands are included in the history list.)

Korn shell — A revision of the Bourne shell that includes the interactive features of the C shell but that maintains the Bourne shell programming style. The Korn shell was written by David Korn.

LaTeX — A version of the mark-up language TeX that includes numerous macros for easy document creation.

ln — Command used to create a symbolic link.

macro — A set of commands that can be executed as one by referring to the name of the macro.

mark-up languages — Computer languages that define a series of codes indicating how to format a document.

modal editor — A text editor that uses multiple modes for editing text and entering commands to apply to that text.

PATH — An environment variable containing a list of directories on the Linux system that the shell searches each time a command is executed.

perl — A programming language that developers use to create scripts for working on text files and completing other complex tasks.

sed — A command used to process each line in a text file according to a series of commands provided by the user.

set — Command used to display a list of all environment variables defined in the current environment.

shell — The command interpreter in Linux.

shell prompt — A set of words or characters indicating that the shell is ready to accept commands at the keyboard.

sort — A command used to sort all of the lines in a text file, writing them out in alphabetical order or according to options provided to the command.

symbolic link — A file that refers to another filename rather than to data in a file.

tab completion — A feature of the shell that lets you enter part of a file or directory name and have the shell fill in the remainder of the name.

TENEX/TOPS C shell (TC shell) — An enhancement of the C shell. This is the version of the C shell that is commonly used on Linux systems.

TeX — A document processing system that writers use to create large and complex documents on UNIX or Linux systems.

`troff` — A command used to format and display documents that are created using roff mark-up codes.

WYSIWYG — A characteristic of programs that show documents on the computer screen much as they will look when printed on paper or in a Web browser (pronounced "whiz-ee-wig").

`xdvi` — Program used to display a LaTeX-coded document as it will appear on paper.

`xfontsel` — Program that lets the user choose each aspect of a font definition (such as the font family and typeface) and then displays the corresponding font for review.

6

REVIEW QUESTIONS

1. The default shell used by Linux cannot be altered. True or False?

2. When logged in as `root`, the shell prompt normally changes to display:
   a. A % character
   b. A # character
   c. The root directory
   d. A $ character

3. The main function of a shell is to:
   a. Track kernel resources for `root`
   b. Provide a convenient programming environment
   c. Complement desktop interfaces
   d. Launch programs entered at the shell prompt

4. Name four different shells and briefly describe the differences between them.

5. Tab completion is useful when you need to:
   a. Repeat a previously used command
   b. Reinitialize the X Window System font list
   c. Enter long filenames or directory names at the shell prompt
   d. Create a brief shell program

6. The `history` command is used to
   a. Display a list of previously entered commands
   b. Execute a previously used command
   c. Change the environment variable controlling tab completion
   d. Edit an existing text file

7. Entering the command `!fr` would do the following in the `bash` shell:

    a. Cause an error because the command name is incomplete

    b. Execute the most recently executed command that began with `fr`

    c. Execute the `free` command to display system memory

    d. Search for the pattern `fr` in the `vi` editor

8. To have a command executed each time any user logged in to the Linux system, you would place the command in which one of these files:

    a. `/etc/profile`

    b. `/etc/.profile`

    c. `~/.profile`

    d. `/etc/bashrc`

9. If a `.bashrc` file is found in a user's home directory, the systemwide `/etc/bashrc` script is not executed. True or False?

10. If a directory contains the filenames `micron` and `microscope`, and you enter `micro` and press Tab, what happens?

    a. The shell prints all matching names, `micron` and `microscope`.

    b. The shell fills in the first alphabetical match, `micron`.

    c. The shell beeps.

    d. The `micron` command is executed.

11. Describe the difference between an alias and a symbolic link.

12. Which of the following is a correctly formed alias for executing the `mv` command?

    a. `alias ren mv`

    b. `alias ren=mv -i`

    c. `alias mv=ren`

    d. `alias ren="mv -i"`

13. Which command is used to create a symbolic link?

    a. `sh`

    b. `ln`

    c. `set`

    d. `sed`

14. The command `echo $HOME` will display:

    a. The word `HOME`

    b. The current user's default shell

    c. The value of the `HOME` environment variable

    d. A prompt requesting a home directory path

15. Describe the purpose of the **PATH** environment variable.

16. The **export** command is used to make an environment variable available to other programs. True or False?

17. Name at least three nongraphical text editors that may be included with a Linux distribution.

18. Knowledge of the **vi** editor is considered an essential skill because:

    a. Memorized **vi** commands correspond to other Linux command options.

    b. The **vi** editor is virtually always available to complete system administration tasks.

    c. Other editors are not as reliable or easy to use.

    d. The developer of **vi** also developed part of Linux.

19. Describe the result within **vi** of pressing the following keys:

    `itest<Esc>yyp:wq<Enter>`

20. To view the formatted appearance of a LaTeX document, you would use the following command:

    a. **xdvi**

    b. **groff**

    c. **TeTeX**

    d. WordPerfect for Linux

21. Describe the difference between a WYSIWYG program and a document containing mark-up codes.

22. The **lilo.conf** file can contain the **vga** option, which controls:

    a. Whether the X Window System is available after the system boots

    b. Which display mode is used on the character-mode console

    c. The action of the virtual **grep** archive

    d. How many colors can be displayed on the system

23. Fonts for the X Window System are normally stored in which directory?

    a. **/usr/X11/xdm/fonts**

    b. **/usr/X11R6/fonts**

    c. **/etc/X11/xinit/fonts**

    d. **/usr/X11R6/lib/X11/fonts**

24. Filtering text files refers to removing lines matching a certain pattern. True or False?

25. Name three programs that can be used to filter text files in Linux.

6

HANDS-ON PROJECTS

Project 6-1

In this activity you use tab completion to explore the Linux file system and alter an environment variable within the shell. To complete this activity you should have a working Linux installation with a valid user account. The filenames described in this activity are taken from a Red Hat Linux installation, but the steps will work on other Linux versions as well.

1. Log in to Linux using your username and password.

2. If you are using a graphical environment, open a terminal window so you have a shell prompt.

3. Change to the directory /bin using the command **cd /bin**.

4. List the shells that are installed on the system using the command **ls *sh**. Can you recognize all of the shells listed?

5. Change to the directory /etc using the command **cd /etc**.

6. Type the command **ls -l host** but don't press Enter.

7. Press the **Tab** key twice. The first time you press Tab the shell beeps. The second time it displays a list of files in /etc that begin with host.

8. Type **s.** (so that the command line contains **ls -l hosts.**), but don't press Enter.

9. Press the **Tab** key twice. The shell beeps and then displays all the files in /etc that begin with **hosts.** (including the period). The list is shorter than the output of Step 7 because you added more characters to search for.

10. Type the **a** and press **Tab**. The shell fills in the full filename so that the line reads **ls -l hosts.allow**.

11. Press **Enter** to complete the **ls** command that the Tab key finished filling in.

12. Change to your home directory by entering the command **cd**.

13. Enter the command **!ls** to execute the most recently used **ls** command, which you entered in Step 11. Why does the command display an error now?

14. Enter the command **echo $PS1** to display the format of the standard shell prompt.

15. Enter the command **man bash** to view the manual page for the **bash** shell.

16. Enter the text **/\\W** to search for the string \W, which is part of the **PS1** definition you saw in Step 14.

17. Use the arrow keys to review the list of parameters that you can use to redefine the **PS1** environment variable. Locate the \d option.

18. Press **q** to exit the man page viewer.

19. Enter the command **export PS1="\d$PS1"**. What happened? What does the $PS1 at the end of the command indicate?

20. Enter the command **bash** to start a new shell. How does the shell prompt change? Why?

21. Enter the **exit** command to leave the new shell you started in Step 20. How does the shell prompt change? Can you explain this?

Project 6-2

In this activity you work with the **vi** editor to make a change to a shell start-up script. To complete this activity you should have a working Linux installation with a valid user account.

1. Log in to Linux using your username and password.
2. If you are using a graphical environment, open a terminal window so you have a shell prompt.
3. Enter the **pwd** command to make certain you are in your home directory.
4. Enter **vi .bashrc** to display the **.bashrc** file in the text editor window.
5. Press **Shift+G** on the keyboard to move to the end of the file.
6. Press the **o** key to start inserting a new line of text.
7. Type the text **TEST_VAR="This is a test"** and press **Enter**.
8. On the next line type the text **export TEST_VAR** and press **Enter**.
9. On the next line type the text **alias tv="echo $TEST_VAR"**.
10. Press **Esc** to return **vi** to command mode.
11. Hold down the **Shift** key while you press **Z** two times to save the file and exit **vi**. (You can also use the other methods shown in the chapter if you prefer.)
12. Type **tv** and press **Enter**. What is the result?
13. Start a new shell by entering the command **bash**.
14. Type **tv** and press **Enter**. What is the result? Why?
15. Enter the **exit** command to exit the additional copy of **bash** that you started in Step 13.
16. Enter the command **vi .bashrc** to begin editing the same file as in previous steps.
17. Press the **j** key repeatedly until the cursor is located on the line containing TEST_VAR="This is a test".
18. Type **3**, then press **d** twice to delete the three lines that you entered.
19. Type a colon (**:**), type **w**, type **q**, and then press **Enter** to save the file and exit.

Project 6-3

In this activity you explore various font issues on the Linux system. To complete this activity you should have a working Linux installation with a valid user account and the X Window System running (using any window manager or desktop interface). The commands described in this activity are included in Red Hat Linux; other versions of Linux may not have all of the same utilities installed by default.

1. Log in to Linux using your username and password.
2. If you are using a graphical environment, open a terminal window so you have a shell prompt.

6

3. Enter the command **sed –n '/vga/p' /etc/lilo.conf** to see if the LILO configuration on your system includes any preset video modes for the console character display.

4. Enter the command **vi /etc/lilo.conf** to review the LILO configuration file. The file appears on screen.

5. If anything was output by the command given in Step 3, can you locate that line in the **lilo.conf** file within **vi**? If nothing was output, can you identify where the **vga** parameter would go (within an **image** section)?

6. Enter the command **:q!** to exit **vi** without saving any changes that you inadvertently made.

7. Change to the X **fonts** directory using the command **cd /usr/X11R6/lib/X11/fonts**.

8. Use the **ls** command to list the subdirectories within the **fonts** directory.

9. Change to the **75dpi** subdirectory using the command **cd 75dpi**.

10. Review the list of fonts included in this directory using the command **more fonts.dir**. Press the **Spacebar** to advance the list of fonts; press **q** to exit the listing.

11. Start the **xfontsel** program by entering **xfontsel**.

12. Explore the buttons and drop-down lists provided in **xfontsel**. How do they correspond with the information in the font listing you saw in Step 10?

CASE PROJECTS

1. You are the system administrator for a large travel agency where you manage Linux workstations for about 70 employees. The employees use the workstations to access several types of text-mode reservations systems. They also use a browser on the Linux systems to review Web sites related to travel and travel destinations, and to exchange e-mail with clients. Jill, one of the more technically inclined employees, approaches you. She has some requests and recommendations.

Some of the programs used by the employees require that certain environment variables be set. Jill suggests that the environment variables be set up in some type of automatic way so that users don't have to enter the values each time they start the program in question. Jill heard about aliases from a friend and asks if that might be a good option. Is it? What other options would you consider? Would you consider placing something in each user's home directory, or would a file that applied to all users on the system be preferable?

2. Jill has used `vi` for several different tasks, but she doesn't use it often. She asks if you could install another text editor of some type so that she can edit files without using `vi`. How do you respond? Do you see any reason not to grant her request? Given that all of the users are working in a graphical environment (with a Web browser as well as text-based applications), what text editors might you consider recommending to Jill? Should other users be informed about text editor options if they don't already know about them?

3. Jill confides that one of the older travel agents has trouble reading the small characters on the terminal windows that are displayed in the graphical environment. You know that these can be changed. Research how to make these changes in a terminal window for the desktop interface on the Linux systems you work with, and then determine how to make the change permanent (so that large characters are always used). (The steps required depend on which Linux distribution or desktop interface you are using.)

6

CHAPTER

7

THE ROLE OF THE SYSTEM ADMINISTRATOR

After reading this chapter and completing the exercises, you will be able to:

- ♦ Explain the work of a system administrator
- ♦ Discuss the responsibilities of a system administrator
- ♦ Use basic system administration commands in Linux

In the previous chapter you learned about the Linux command-line environment (the shell) and how to use different text editors and text-processing tools to create scripts and work effectively at the command line.

In this chapter you will look at the role of a Linux system administrator. The topics in this chapter lay the foundation for the rest of this book, which covers in detail the separate tasks performed by a system administrator.

WORKING AS A SYSTEM ADMINISTRATOR

The job of a system administrator is to make technology work and continue to work. While others may develop programs or devices with great potential, the system administrator ties them into complete, operational systems that can increase productivity, lower costs, or otherwise benefit those who use the technology. The system administrator keeps these systems running efficiently as new pieces are added, changes occur, and reconfigurations and failures alter the face of the original systems. The job of the system administrator is primarily practical. It requires perseverance, patience, curiosity, creativity, and technical knowledge. To be truly successful as a system administrator, you must continue to increase both the breadth (number of subjects) and depth (expertise in a subject) of your technical knowledge. If you don't, new problems will come along that you won't know how to solve. At the same time, you will lack the ability to integrate new technologies into your systems or to determine how they apply to your environment.

A system administrator generally works as part of the **Information Systems (IS)** or **Information Technology (IT)** Department of an organization. In a large organization, this group reports to a **chief information officer (CIO)**. In smaller organizations, a group of system administrators might consult other company officers to make decisions about information technology. The IS or IT Department is concerned only with internal information systems. In technology organizations (such as companies that develop software or sell computers or telecommunications equipment), the team that develops software and hardware for sale to others is not generally part of the IS or IT Department. Figure 7-1 shows the position of a system administrator in a typical small or large company.

In addition to working with technology, system administrators also work with people. They may work primarily with a group of technical colleagues in their department, but they also are likely to interact with most of the organization as they answer questions, solve technical problems, train users, install software, and so forth. In larger organizations, the tasks of working with end users and maintaining the systems are divided into different areas. For example, the IS team may manage the servers, while the **Help Desk** team directly solves problems for **end users** (those who use computer systems to accomplish their daily work). In such an environment, you, as a system administrator, can focus on the particular area that best suits your interests. The same technical knowledge and problem-solving ability are required for both types of work.

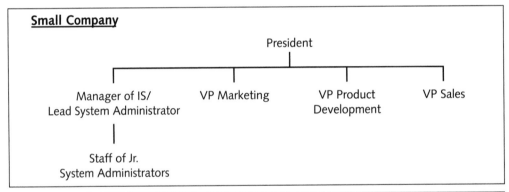

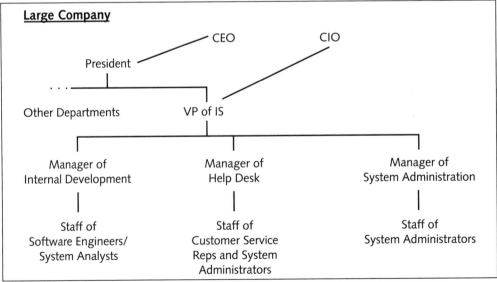

Figure 7-1   Role of the system administrator within large and small companies

Tasks of a System Administrator

As a system administrator, the tasks for which you are responsible can vary considerably based on factors such as:

- Your expertise and specific job position
- Your seniority in an organization
- The size of the organization

The following list describes in detail some of the common tasks a system administrator performs.

- Creating new user accounts and making changes in user accounts, such as granting new access permissions as assignments change.

- Maintaining system hardware, including installing new hardware as part of increasing system capacity, replacing damaged systems, or upgrading obsolete components.

- Training end users to effectively use new systems, software, or procedures.

- Performing other occasional or recurring tasks that keep the system running smoothly. Some of these are routine, such as backing up files; others require more creativity, such as determining why system response time has slowed, or tracking down an intruder from the Internet.

- Documenting the system so that other system administrators can understand your work. This might include informing others of how applications are configured, where back-up files are stored, and which users have had specific problems with certain hardware or applications. This task is often related to the next one.

- Defining procedures and policies related to how systems are administered at your site. Among other things, a system administrator might need to define back-up procedures, privacy and security policies, user guidelines, or a disaster plan. (All of these topics are discussed in future chapters.)

- Recovering from emergencies to get a system running again after a power outage, hardware failure, employee problem, or natural disaster.

- Planning a system. When working within small organizations or departments, or as you gain experience in a large organization, you may be asked to decide on new hardware purchases or plan for future system components or designs to meet anticipated needs.

In addition to the core tasks listed above, you may be asked to:

- Inform management of potential technical needs for upgrades.
- Watch for security threats and implement remedies when possible.
- Keep yourself up-to-date regarding new developments in your field. Staying current allows you to take advantage of new developments that could benefit the employer's information technology strategy and increase your value to your employer (and to future employers).

7

Ethics and the System Administrator

Working as a system administrator involves many ethical issues that may not be evident at first. As a system administrator you have control—full or partial—over an organization's computer systems. Implicit in this responsibility is a great deal of trust on the part of both the company (its officers, managers, and owners) and the individual employees who use the systems that you manage. The way you view this trust will likely determine how effective you are as a system administrator.

Employers pay you to maintain their systems in a way that contributes to the success of their organization. Your role also has an important effect on individual users. Although you may be working behind the scenes most of the time (and probably should be if things are running smoothly), remember that your fellow employees count on your work in order to do theirs. A lack of preparation or accuracy on your part can lead to companywide downtime, corrupted or lost files, malfunctioning printers, and so forth. As a result, none of the other employees can be productive. Everyone in a modern office relies on the work of a good system administrator every workday.

Along with this control over the working lives of others comes the potential for abuse of this power. For example, as the system administrator with root privileges on the Linux server, you have the power to:

- Read people's e-mail and the files in their home directories
- Alter company or personal files
- Send falsified messages as if they came from other users
- Erase ("lose") any files on the system
- Delay fixing a system problem or helping an employee with a simple question
- Neglect security measures that would protect sensitive data

These actions are unethical because they invade others' privacy and impede the work of your employer. Many are also illegal and would make an unscrupulous system administrator subject to prosecution. But as you may realize, many unethical actions are likely to go undetected, especially if you are the sole person in a company with expertise in Linux. You should decide at the outset on a few rules that can guide you in your relationships with employers and fellow employees whose systems you manage. Your rules might include statements like these:

- I realize that I know more about the systems I manage than others, but I also realize that they know more about their job functions and what they need from their computer systems.
- I will never read files that do not belong to me personally unless required to do so as part of a legal order or to comply with a publicly acknowledged company policy.
- I treat other employees as my clients. Success as a system administrator depends on their satisfaction regarding how I meet their needs for information technology.

Occasionally, a system administrator may decide to configure systems in such a way that no one else can figure out how the system is configured or used. This is sometimes done in the name of job security: "They can't fire me," this kind of system administrator reasons, "or the entire company will have to shut down."

In fact, however, your best route to success as a system administrator (not to mention peace of mind) will come through making your employer successful. This allows you to grow professionally, with additional responsibility and technical opportunities. If you train yourself well, you need never feel compelled to make implied threats of holding your employer "hostage" because you are the only person who can maintain the computer systems. Remember these two rules:

- Good jobs are always available for well-trained technical people; hence job security should not depend on work at a single company. Build a reputation as both a technical expert and a personable employee to make future employers eager to hire you and past employers sorry they lost you.

- If you haven't trained yourself well, you're not worth keeping as an employee. Your employer can then replace you with someone who is not being territorial under the guise of "job security." The true expert will always be able to set up efficient, standardized, well-documented systems and have a solid career based on managing those systems.

To read more about working as a system administrator, you should also visit the System Administrators Guild (**SAGE**) at *http://www.usenix.org/sage/*. SAGE is part of the USENIX group, an organization for people who work with advanced computing systems that provides tremendous resources to system administrators. The SAGE Web site contains information about:

- Jobs and salary profiles

- Local user groups

- Technical information

- Events where system administrators gather for technical conferences

PRINCIPLES OF MAINTAINING A LINUX SYSTEM

Compared to the other types of technical work demanded of a system administrator, learning about Linux is especially rewarding. Whereas some technical topics relate to mastering a specific graphical tool or proprietary method, knowledge that you gain about Linux is generally applicable to a wide range of systems and situations. Although learning Linux well can be a challenge, that knowledge carries over to other systems. For example, if you learn about the Domain Name Service (DNS) on Linux, you will find that the knowledge applies to DNS servers on practically any system in the world. Knowledge of Linux also forms a strong foundation for learning about related topics such as TCP/IP routing or NIS+. Or suppose you learn about configuring an Apache Web server on Linux. Other Web servers may have graphical interfaces that are easier to configure, but the concepts relating to how a Web server operates and the options you learn about in detail as you work in Linux will apply to nearly every Web server available.

As you become familiar with the Linux tools used for system administration, you may notice that they are different in fundamental ways from tools used on non–UNIX-like operating systems such as Windows NT. The history of UNIX (and thus of Linux development by association), followed a very different path from Windows NT. The result is that certain methods of solving problems have been developed on Linux and UNIX systems. As you learn about these methods, you will be better able to use the tools that Linux provides to keep your Linux systems running efficiently with the least amount of work and the fewest headaches.

Many of the principles outlined in this chapter have been developed over the 30-year history of UNIX and Linux technology. Thirty years ago, computers were much slower, more expensive, and more difficult to use (no graphical interfaces were available until fairly recently). UNIX (and Linux) were originally designed for these systems. As a result, Linux is generally more efficient in using limited system resources.

When designing an operating system for these early computers, UNIX and Linux developers were forced to create extremely efficient operating systems. For example, special files known as shared libraries allowed multiple programs to use the same set of functions stored in memory. The goal of efficiency in Linux is reflected in the way the various system administration tasks are organized. Some key facts to notice about Linux system administration are the following:

- Plain-text files configure the system. Individual files control each program or service.

- Everything on the Linux system is accessed as if it were a file, including devices and remote computer systems.

- The entire system is designed to be used by multiple users.

- Linux command-line utilities are usually small and simple in function, being designed to do just one task very well. They have the capacity, however, to be connected with other commands to complete more complex tasks.

The sections that follow describe some of these traits in more detail.

Linux Configuration Files

A full-featured Linux system may support hundreds of users and include thousands of programs on its hard disks. Many of these programs are system or network services, such as a Web server, an e-mail server, or a Samba server (to allow SMB clients like Windows 98 to connect to Linux). Other programs might include a graphical **utility** (a program used for system administration) on a Linux desktop such as Gnome or KDE, or an end-user program such as WordPerfect for Linux or ApplixWare for Linux.

Each of these programs and system services creates and maintains its own set of configuration information. The configuration files for programs run by the system administrator (and available to all users), such as a Web server, are normally stored in the /etc directory. Configuration files for programs that are used by only a single user are stored in that user's home directory. Programs that are used by all users on a system often include default configuration information that is applied when any user runs the program, plus user-specific options that are stored in a user's home directory.

Configuration files for Linux programs and services do not follow a well-defined pattern or naming convention. Some configuration files end with the word conf, for *configuration*. Others end with rc, for *run control*. The names of some configuration files show no indication of what the file is used for—as the system administrator, you must simply know which file to look for. Some of the configuration files used by Linux are listed in Table 7-1. The exact location of these files varies slightly depending on the version of Linux that you use—most are located in the /etc directory or one of its subdirectories.

7

Table 7-1   Configuration Files Used by Linux

Filename	What the file configures
XF86Config	XFree86 graphical system
smb.conf	Samba server
httpd.conf	Web server
resolv.conf	DNS name resolver (selects a Name server to access)
hosts	Hostnames and IP addresses used for networking access
xinitrc	Programs that start along with the graphical system
ftpaccess	FTP server
lilo.conf	LILO boot loader
bashrc	Configuration script that runs when starting a shell
passwd	User account names and configuration information

 TIP   You can immediately begin learning about the content and format of any of the configuration files in Table 7-1 by entering the command man 5 *filename*.

Advantages of Multiple Plain-Text Configuration Files

The historical forces that have made Linux so powerful have also resulted in numerous and diverse configuration methods: software developers are not required by any authority to follow a specific pattern. In fact, UNIX systems have always used text-based configuration files. Using **plain-text configuration files** has the following advantages:

- You can easily write a program to manipulate the configuration of a program or service, because this involves basic text string manipulation.

- Each configuration file is small and independent, which can create a more efficient use of resources to update or query the configuration of a program.

- If one configuration file becomes corrupted, other configuration information is not affected—Linux configuration has no single point of failure or vulnerability.

- Developers creating programs can create new configuration designs to meet their needs, without being constrained to fit an existing configuration architecture.

- You can use a single tool (any text editor) to configure the most complex features of any program or system service.

Disadvantages of Multiple Plain-Text Configuration Files

Using text-based configuration files also has the following disadvantages:

- The system administrator must learn multiple configuration formats, some of which are highly complex, in order to set up and maintain a Linux system.

- New programs cannot take advantage of an existing configuration method or architecture to speed development.

- Text-based configuration files can be organized according to extremely complex rules, which often allow for many possible methods of expressing a configuration. These rules vary for each configuration file (and for possible new programs coming out all the time). These factors make it very difficult to create graphical configuration tools to make Linux configuration easier to learn or manage.

Despite the difficulty involved, many serious efforts have been made to create graphical configuration tools to ease the task of learning to configure Linux, much as many UNIX systems have an overall system administration interface. Some of these development efforts are aimed at configuring a single program, such as the Apache Web server. The Comanche project is one example of this. Figure 7-2 shows Comanche, a graphical utility for configuring many parts of the Apache Web server.

The Samba suite is another example of a service that you can configure using a graphical configuration tool for configuring Linux. Many graphical tools are available to help you set up Samba, including Ksamba and GTKSamba, which sets up a Samba file and print server. GTKSamba is illustrated in Figure 7-3.

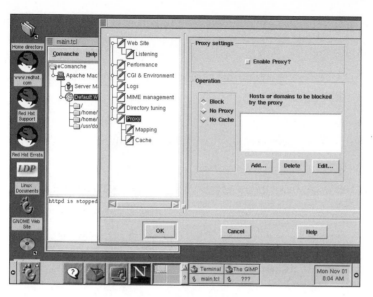

Figure 7-2   The Comanche graphical utility

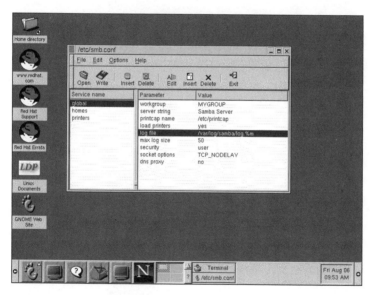

Figure 7-3   GTKSamba

Other tools have been designed to provide a framework for all Linux configuration and maintenance. At least three of these programs have been sponsored by Linux vendors in an effort to make Linux easier to use. These three are:

- **COAS**, the Caldera Open Administration System, sponsored by Caldera Systems (shown in Figure 7-4)

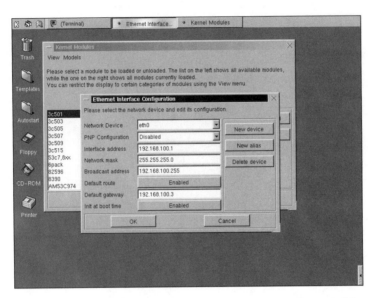

Figure 7-4   COAS, a graphical administration tool from Caldera Systems

- **LinuxConf**, sponsored by Red Hat Software (shown in Figure 7-5)

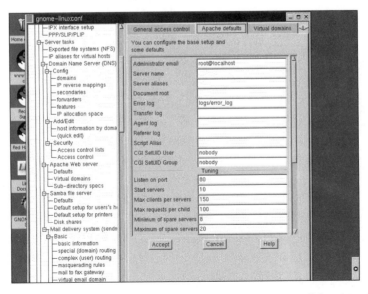

Figure 7-5   LinuxConf, a graphical administration tool from Red Hat Software

- **YAST**, sponsored by SuSE (shown in Figure 7-6)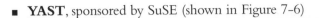

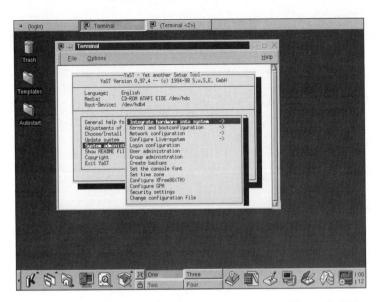

Figure 7-6   YAST, a graphical administration tool from SuSE Linux

Success in these efforts to create graphical configuration tools has been hampered because Linux configuration options are too varied and complex to allow a simplistic tool to be of much use in real life. Complete tools require substantial development time; but because Linux programs don't remain static for long, any developer who did invest the necessary time and money to create a truly comprehensive administration tool would find that the tool was out of date upon its release. In addition, many Linux administrators prefer to work directly in text files, feeling that they have more control over the configuration without the system overhead of a graphical interface.

This introduces the question: Why not use graphical utilities to configure Linux where possible, especially while learning Linux, since more advanced features won't be immediately needed?

The answer is perhaps more philosophical than practical at this stage: because someone has to know how the system *really* works. As the system administrator for a Linux-based server or network, you will often be called on to solve problems that cannot be solved by even advanced graphical tools. These problems may cross boundaries between different programs, and they may involve networking activity that you have no control over, or require making minor adjustments to configuration files that would not be available in a graphical tool. If you can't get "under the hood" of the system, as the saying goes, and adjust all possible program parameters, your ability to keep a system running smoothly is much reduced. You are left instead clicking buttons, wondering what is really happening on a system that continues to have a problem you cannot diagnose or repair.

TIP Linux and most Linux programs provide the added benefit of allowing you to review the program source code. Using this method of last resort, you can fix anything, given enough time. But before you can take advantage of this option, you must start by learning *how* things work, not simply which buttons to click in order to complete rote or simple tasks.

The numerous plain-text configuration files in Linux provide access to all features of Linux programs; once you are familiar with these files, you can use them to solve any problem. Other operating systems put information about system services and resources into a single configuration file. An example of such a file is the Windows Registry. Figure 7-7 shows how the Windows Registry differs from the multiple configuration files used by Linux.

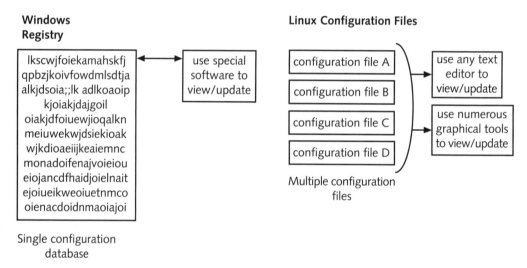

Figure 7-7   Registry vs. multiple configuration files

Understanding Files, Devices, and Processes

Managing a Linux system includes managing all of the resources of the system: the file system, the devices, and the processes. As you learned in Chapter 4, the default Linux file system is large and complex, with predefined locations for most types of files. The task of locating, creating, moving, and deleting files is part of every system administrator's day. The later section "Using Basic System Administration Tools" describes many of the utilities you can use to manage the Linux file system. The following sections define the terms *devices, processes, programs,* and *thread*.

Devices

Devices are an important part of your system maintenance responsibilities. All of the resources at your disposal in Linux—the hard disk, modem, mouse, system memory—must be accessed using the appropriate Linux method. Linux accesses devices by assigning them a filename in the /dev subdirectory, as described in Chapter 4. Later chapters, such as Chapter 14, describe many tools that interact with the physical devices that are part of your computer.

Some of these devices are accessed directly. For example, when you configure a printer as described later in this book, you may refer to the `/dev/lp0` device name. This pathname indicates your computer's first parallel port. Other devices are accessed indirectly. For example, to use a hard disk, you configure access to the file system on that hard disk by referring to the device, such as `/dev/hda1`, and linking it to a standard directory path, such as `/usr` or `/home`. Linux users do not access the disk via the `/dev/hda1` device name, but by referring to the standard directory path (the `/usr` or `/home` directory in this example) to which access has been configured.

Processes

Processes are the individual programs running on a Linux system. Because Linux is a multitasking operating system, many programs can be running on a Linux system at the same time. Chapter 10 describes in detail how you can manage multiple processes to make the most efficient use of system resources for all users. The section "Using Basic System Administration Tools," later in this chapter, describes a few common utilities that provide information about the processes running on Linux at any moment.

Although process is a precise term used to describe a task that the Linux kernel is running, several other terms are commonly used to refer to various types of processes. To avoid confusion, review the related terms in the sections that follow.

Program

The word **program** is a vague term for a piece of software that executes on the Linux system. A program may be composed of many different processes or tasks that Linux manages in concert to accomplish an overall goal, or a program may have just one process. The terms program, utility, tool, and software package are all used interchangeably when discussing software that runs on Linux. All of these terms are imprecise compared to using the term process, but they serve the purpose of outlining what is being described.

Daemon

A **daemon** is a background process. It normally runs continually, but it does not have any visible output. An example of a daemon is an FTP server. It processes incoming requests, sending back files as needed, but it never displays anything on the Linux screen. Instead, information on the activities of a daemon is normally recorded in a log file (`/var/log/xferlog` in the case of the FTP daemon). Many daemons are usually running on a Linux system at any moment. The name of a daemon program usually ends with the letter *d*. Some of the daemons you can expect to see running on your Linux system after a default installation include those listed in Table 7-2.

Table 7-2   Daemons Running on Linux

Daemon name	Description
`crond`	Runs scripts at scheduled times (as described in Chapter 12).
`httpd`	Responds to Web browser requests using the HTTP protocol.
`inetd`	Watches for incoming requests of many types and starts the appropriate daemon to respond to the request. (Requests to Internet services such as FTP, Telnet, Finger, Talk, and Gopher are normally handled through `inetd`.)
`syslogd`	Records information from running programs to the system log file `/var/log/messages`.

Thread

A **thread** is a piece of a process (or a piece of a daemon, since a daemon is a type of process). Threads are most commonly used in multiprocessor environments (computers with more than one CPU installed). A single task normally performed by a process in sequential fashion can be split into multiple threads, or subtasks, that can be accomplished in parallel by multiple CPUs working at the same time. The distinction between processes and threads is not important for most system administration work. Instead, the term process is used in most cases that don't involve programmers developing software for multiprocessor computers.

Multiple Users, Multiple Processes

Linux was designed from its initial stages to be a multiuser operating system. As you have already seen, during the installation of Linux, you must create user accounts before any user can log on to use the system. No one can enter commands at a Linux command line without first entering a valid username and password to log on.

Each user account can execute multiple programs (start many processes). Each of these processes is associated with the user that started it and can be managed by the system administrator accordingly. For example, in Chapter 10 you will learn how to assign a higher priority to all of a user's processes so that they are executed faster. You will also learn how to stop (kill) a single process that might be consuming too many system resources or that has stopped working correctly.

Because a Linux system often supports many users and each user runs many processes, the management of users and processes forms an important part of system administration.

Using Small, Efficient Utilities

Linux utilities (most of which are based on UNIX utilities that have been used for decades) usually perform only a single task. The design goal for these system utilities is to do a single task, offer flexibility in how to perform the task, and do it very quickly (with the most efficient use of system resources—CPU time and disk space).

To provide flexibility, Linux commands often have numerous options that you can add to modify the basic operation of the command. For example, the ls command used to list files (described in the next section) supports over 40 options. You can select these options by including them after the command name.

Almost all Linux commands use the same format for including options. Each option is represented by either a hyphen followed by a single letter or two hyphens followed by a word describing the option. If single letters are used to select options, they can be combined after a single hyphen. If full-word descriptions are used to select options, each must be written out separately. In both cases, the options are listed before any filenames or other parameters to the command.

 TIP   Some Linux utilities, such as ps and tar, described later in this chapter, use single-letter options without a hyphen preceding them.

Table 7-3 lists 10 common ls command options.

Table 7-3   Common Options of the ls Command

Single-letter format	Full-word format	Description
-a	--all	Lists all files in a directory, including hidden files (files that start with ".")
-l Note: Use a lowercase letter *L* for this option.	--format=long	Prints not only the names of items in a directory, but also their sizes, owners, dates of creation, and so forth
-C	--format=vertical	Displays items in sorted columns
-r	--reverse	Reverses the sorting order of the items being listed
-t	--sort=time	Sorts items being listed by their timestamp rather than alphabetically
-S	--sort=size	Sorts items being listed by their size rather than alphabetically
none	--color	Displays files color coded according to type
none	--help	Displays help text with an abbreviated options list
-I Note: Use an upper-case letter *i* for this option.	--ignore *pattern*	Does not display items matching the pattern given
-R	--recursive	Lists the contents of all subdirectories as well as the current directory, showing the entire directory tree
-i	--inode	Prints the index number for each file to the left of the filename

7

Both the names of Linux commands and their options are case sensitive. The −r option and the −R option are both valid and have very different meanings.

You can combine options in several ways, as the examples in Table 7-4 show.

Table 7-4   Combining Command Options

Command example	Description of results
ls −laSr	Lists the contents of the current directory, including all files (−a), in long format (−l), sorted by size (−S), in reverse order (−r).
ls −l −a −S −r	Same as the previous example.
ls −R −−color	Lists the contents of all subdirectories (−R), color coding each item shown (−−color). In this example, no single character option for −−color is supported, so the two options cannot be combined.
ls −−format=vertical −−sort=time −ai	Lists all files (−a), including their index numbers (−i), in a vertical column, sorting them by their creation time and date.

Standard Input and Output

Most input and output in Linux is done using standardized channels. Normally input comes from the keyboard and output goes to the screen. These channels can be redirected, however, using **redirection** operators. The redirection feature gives you great flexibility in using Linux utilities.

When a program expects input such as a line of text, it reads that information from the **standard input** channel (abbreviated STDIN). Normally, the STDIN data comes from the keyboard. But you can redirect input so that the program reads data from a file or from another program instead of the keyboard.

When a program writes output, it normally writes to the **standard output** channel (abbreviated STDOUT). This information is normally written to your console screen in the window where the program was launched. The STDOUT data can be redirected, however, so that it is written directly to a file or sent to another program.

A third standard channel, called **standard error**, is also used. Error messages are written to standard error (abbreviated as STDERR) separately from STDOUT in case STDOUT has been redirected. Of course, the output of STDERR can also be redirected to a special location such as an error log file.

A special tool related to redirecting communication between programs is called a pipe. A **pipe** connects the output channel of one command to the input channel of another command. Pipes are used to connect the output of one application to the input of another application. Figure 7-8 shows how this works conceptually.

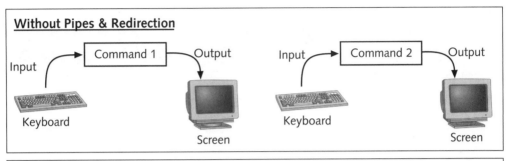

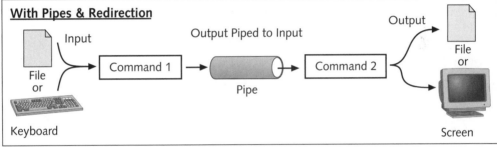

Figure 7-8   Diagram of a pipe between applications

To see a pipe in action, consider two commands: `ls`, which lists the contents of a directory; and `sort`, which sorts all the lines in a file. The `ls` command normally writes output to the screen, whereas `sort` normally requires a filename as a parameter. But you can combine the `ls` and `sort` commands by entering the following at a Linux command prompt:

```
ls -l | sort
```

The output of this `ls` command is not written to the screen. Instead, it is sent (piped) to the `sort` command. Although the `sort` command normally requires a filename, in this case it receives the names of the files it needs to sort from the `ls` command. The result is that `sort` writes to the screen the lines from `ls`, sorted according to the first word in each line.

By combining the features of STDIN, STDOUT, and STDERR with the ability to redirect these communication channels and use pipes, each Linux utility can interact with other utilities and files to meet the needs of users and system administrators. Table 7-5 shows how input and output can be redirected.

Table 7-5　Redirecting Input and Output

Symbol to use in a command statement	Description	Command-line example
`> filename`	Writes STDOUT output to the given filename	`ls -l > savelisting`
`>> filename`	Appends STDOUT output to the given filename (adding it to the end of any existing file contents)	`cat newfile >> existing_data`
`< filename`	Sends data from the given filename as the STDIN, rather than reading from the keyboard	`my_script < input_codes`
`|`	Creates a pipe between two programs, so that the STDOUT output from the command on the left of the pipe symbol is used as the STDIN input for the command on the right of the pipe symbol	`ls -l | sort`

A savvy system administrator knows command options and useful techniques for combining a few basic commands to provide all sorts of useful information. The next section describes some of these utilities and explains how to combine them.

USING BASIC SYSTEM ADMINISTRATION TOOLS

A good system administrator has a mental "toolbox" of methods for solving problems. A large part of this toolbox is knowing about a number of basic Linux commands that can provide information about the current state of a Linux system and tune the system as needed. This section describes some of these basic utilities. As described in the previous section, these tools are simple in their function, but when combined, they can be powerful and extremely useful.

In later chapters you will learn about many other utilities that are specific to certain tasks, such as backing up files or formatting new hard disks. This section focuses on tools that are useful in a variety of circumstances. If you have worked at a command line in another operating system, some of these tools will be familiar to you. Other tools are unique to Linux and UNIX environments.

Case Sensitivity in Linux

Nearly everything in Linux is case sensitive. This can be a big change for users of other operating systems. It means that typing a command in all capital letters is different from using all lowercase. In fact, each of the items in this list would be a different, distinct command in Linux:

- `find`

- `FIND`

- `Find`

- `FiNd`

Linux commands are all lowercase and must be entered without capital letters.

Filenames and File Extensions

Some operating systems use the last part of a filename as an indication of what type of data the file contains. For example, a file ending in `.gif` is a certain type of graphics file, while a file ending in `.wpd` is a certain type of word processing document. The ending part of a filename is often called the file extension, from the days when a filename consisted of a maximum of eight letters and a three-character extension.

Linux does not use file extensions in this way. Instead, it examines the contents of a file to determine its type. A file may have an extension that indicates its type, but this information should be regarded as a convenience for the user, not a requirement for the operating system. For example, if you create a program using the Perl language, it can be named `myscript.pl`, using the conventional `.pl` file extension, but it can also be named `myscript_written_in_perl` or just `myscript`. None of these filenames will affect whether the script functions correctly.

This leads to another point. Filenames in Linux can be very long—up to 256 characters. They can also contain nearly any character except a forward slash (/). Linux filenames do not have shortened versions; they only exist as the complete filename that you see in a file listing. If you use unusual characters in a filename, such as a space or punctuation marks, you should enclose the filename in quotation marks so that the characters are not interpreted as special commands.

Learning About Linux Commands

In the following sections (and in future chapters), you will learn about many Linux commands. Because most of these commands have numerous options and sometimes complex **syntax** (formatting) rules, you may need to refer to additional information as you work in Linux. The Linux system provides several methods of learning about a command as you work:

- Use the online manual page. These are called man pages in the Linux world. Each **man page** contains a description of the command's syntax and all options supported by the command, along with descriptions of how the command can be used, related commands, and additional information. The man pages rarely contain examples of command usage, however. To view the man page, use the `man` command followed by the command you wish to learn about. For example, to learn about the `ls` command, enter `man ls`.

- Use the `help` option for the command. Most commands will print a summary of options and syntax when you enter the command with `--help` as a parameter. This information is less complete than the man page, but may provide more accessible help, especially if you are already familiar with the command and only need a quick reminder about an option. For example, to learn about the `ls` command, enter `ls --help`.

- Use the `info` command. For some commands, the man page is not updated regularly. Instead, an info file is maintained with instructions on the command. For example, to learn about the `ls` command, enter `info ls`.

- Use the `apropos` command when you don't know the name of the command to use for a task. The `apropos` command returns a list of man pages that contain a keyword that you enter. For example, to see a list of all man pages that contain information about the LILO boot manager, enter `apropos lilo`. On some systems you must generate a database for the `apropos` command to use before `apropos` will return any helpful results. On a Red Hat Linux system, the command `/usr/sbin/makewhatis` will create such a database.

 TIP   You must already know the name of the appropriate command before you can use man or the `help` option. If you don't know which command to use to solve a problem, use the `apropos` command or try to find a related word in the index of this book and see which commands that section of the book covers.

Using Regular Expressions

Many times, system administration tasks involve working with patterns of information. These patterns might apply to filenames, information on a Web server, information within database files, or in many other locations and situations. Linux and UNIX use a system of expressing patterns called regular expressions. A **regular expression** provides a flexible way to encode different types of patterns. Regular expressions are used with many of the Linux commands you will learn in this chapter and in later chapters. They are also used in writing shell scripts and other types of scripts and programs that provide system administration functionality. A single regular expression can be used to describe each of the patterns in the following sentences:

- Lines containing the word *President* or *president* (upper- or lowercase *P*)

- Filenames with the digits 18 followed by any other digits

- Text at the beginning of a line that starts with *Cruise* or *cruise* and includes the word *ship* later in the same line

- Filenames that end with TIFF, TIF, Tif, Tiff, tif, or tiff

Regular expressions are similar to using wildcards to define filenames. In DOS or Windows, for example, you can indicate a set of all Word files by using a wildcard statement like this: `*.doc`. Regular expressions can be as simple as `*.doc`, but they can also include more complicated statements. Table 7-6 summarizes parts of a regular expression. It would take an entire book to cover all the nuances of creating regular expressions, but mastering the items listed here will let you take advantage of the power of regular expressions in the Linux commands you will be learning.

Table 7-6   Common Regular Expressions in Linux

Expression syntax	Meaning of syntax
`*`	Match zero or more characters
`?` or `.` (a period)	Match one character
`^`	Match text at the beginning of a line
`$`	Match text at the end of a line
`[abc]`	Match one of the characters in brackets
`[^abc]`	Exclude all of the characters in brackets

To better understand the syntax of regular expressions, study the examples in Table 7-7.

Table 7-7   Sample Regular Expressions

Example regular expression	What it matches
`[iI]tal*`	Any word starting with *I* or *i* followed by *tal*, such as Italy, italy, Italian, italian, Italianate, italianate, and so forth.
`^[mM]us??m`	Text at the beginning of a line that begins with *m* or *M*, followed by *us*, two characters, and *m*. (The two characters are intended to allow misspelled versions of the word *museum* to be found.)
`180[0..9]$`	Text at the end of a line that begins with 180 and ends with a digit from 0 to 9 (any of the years from 1800 to 1809 will match).

Using File and Directory Management Utilities

If you have used other computer systems, the basic file operations needed to access and maintain a system are probably familiar to you. For example, in every operating system, you move and copy files, view the contents of directories, and create new directories. This section describes the utilities that Linux provides for these basic tasks. You can access all of these utilities from any Linux shell (any command-line interface).

Table 7-8 describes each of the basic file system management commands used by Linux. An equivalent command from the DOS/Windows command line is shown for reference. Most of these commands have many options that you can learn about by viewing the man page for the command.

Table 7-8   File System Management Commands in Linux

Command name	Description	Example of command usage	DOS equivalent command
ls	List the items in the current directory (or other directory given as a parameter)	ls	DIR
cd	Change the current working directory to the directory given as a parameter	cd /home	CD
pwd	Print working directory (show the current working directory)	pwd	CD (with no directory name parameter)
cat	Dump the contents of a file to the screen	cat textfile	TYPE
cp	Copy files to a new filename and/or location	cp file.txt file_old.txt	COPY
rm	Remove (delete) a file or files given as a parameter	rm *.txt	DEL
rmdir	Remove an empty directory	rmdir datadir	RMDIR or RD
mv	Move a file or directory to a new location, effectively renaming it if moved to the same directory	mv report reportold mv report /archive/report	REN or MOVE
mkdir	Make a new subdirectory	mkdir archive	MKDIR or MD

TIP Most Linux commands are separate programs that start when you enter their names at a command line. But some commands are built into the shell (the command-line interpreter). These commands do not have a man page—you must read the man page for the shell (enter man bash) to learn more about how to use them. The only built-in command from the table of file system commands is cd.

Deleting Files in Linux

To delete files in many popular operating systems, you drag or move them to a trashcan or recycle bin. The deleted file remains on your system until you "empty" the trashcan or recycle bin. In effect, when you delete a file in this way, you are not really erasing the file, but simply marking it for deletion when the trashcan is emptied. This serves as a protective system against accidentally deleting files that you discover you need soon after you delete them.

In many cases, even after you have emptied the trashcan or recycle bin, you can use special utilities to "undelete" the erased file, reassembling the contents of the file from your hard disk so that it is a complete file again.

In Linux, files cannot be undeleted except in very rare circumstances. When you use the `rm` command to remove (delete) a file, the file is immediately deleted from your hard disk. Because of the way Linux arranges file information on the hard disk, recovering the pieces of a deleted file is rarely successful. How then can you protect yourself and users on your system from accidentally erasing files that are later needed? Here are a few methods used by some system administrators:

- Always use the `rm` command with the `-i` option, which prompts you for confirmation before deleting a file. This reminds you to reconsider any need for the file you are about to erase.

- Use a **safedelete** utility, which compresses and stores files in a hidden directory when they are "deleted." From this directory, they can be undeleted later if needed. Using this type of utility requires additional maintenance and disk space for the compressed files, but it provides a back-up copy in case deleted files are needed.

- Use the trashcan on one of the popular Linux graphical desktops, such as KDE or Gnome. These act like the trashcan or recycle bin in other popular operating systems: files are not truly deleted until you empty the trash.

- Use a special disk tool that attempts to reassemble the pieces of a deleted file based on their location on your hard disk. Using these tools rarely gives complete success, but can often recover at least part of an important file that was accidentally deleted.

Finding What You Need

Once you know some basic utilities for working with the file system, you can use more complex tools to help you locate information in files and directories. This section describes three such tools: `locate`, `find`, and `grep`.

Use the `locate` command to search an index of all files on your Linux system. If Linux finds any directory or filename that matches your `locate` query, it prints the full pathname of that item to the screen. For example, suppose you need to locate the Web server configuration file on a Linux system and can't remember where it is stored. By using the following command, you see a list of all occurrences of `httpd.conf` in the entire Linux file system:

`locate httpd.conf`

If you are not certain of the complete name, you can use part of it. If that partial name occurs anywhere in a directory or filename, the `locate` command lists it on screen. For example, you could use the following command to locate the `httpd.conf` file:

`locate tpd.conf`

The `locate` command has the advantage of being very fast, because it searches an index of your file system rather than searching the entire file system each time you make a query. Using `locate` has two disadvantages, however. First, if you haven't updated the index since you changed your file system, you may not see the results you need (the item you're looking for may not be listed). Second, if you don't know much about the name you're searching for, the list printed by `locate` can be so large that it's not very useful. You can't use special patterns (regular expressions) to make a more precise query using the `locate` command.

 If you leave your Linux system running, the file system index used by `locate` is automatically updated in the middle of the night. Otherwise, you can run the `updatedb` command to update the index (a process that can take several minutes).

The **find** command also provides a list of files that match a query string, but it provides many more options than `locate`, so it can be used for much more in-depth and powerful system administration work. The **find** command operates on your file system at the time you run a command; it doesn't use a prebuilt index. This means that other processes might slow down if you run a complex **find** query. The results can also take a few seconds to appear with **find**.

The simplest use of **find** is to search for files that match a specific name pattern and print them to the screen. In this example, the path where the search should begin is given as /home, followed by the name of the file to search for and the action to take with each filename found (print it to the screen).

```
find /home -name report.doc -print
```

The **find** command uses full words as options, but preceded by only a single hyphen instead of two. These nonstandard formats can make learning each of the Linux commands a challenge.

The options supported by **find** enable you to perform complex searches for information on your Linux system. For example, using a single (complex) **find** command, you could do any of the following tasks:

- Create an archive file of all the files that have been modified in the last 24 hours
- Delete all files owned by a certain user on the Linux system
- Create a list of all files that are larger than a certain size
- Create a list of all files that have specific access permissions
- Create a list of all files that do not have a valid owner

In later chapters you will see **find** used in examples for specific tasks like those listed here.

The `locate` and `find` commands help you locate a file with specific characteristics. To search within a file, use the **grep** command. Grep can rapidly scan numerous files for a pattern that you specify, printing out the lines of text that include the pattern. These lines of text can then be processed according to the system administration task at hand. For example, suppose you need to see the shell used by a certain user account. Rather than open a user management tool or look at the `/etc/passwd` file in a text editor, you can enter this command and immediately see the line of `/etc/passwd` that contains the information you need:

```
# grep nwells /etc/passwd
nwells:x:564:564::/home/nwells:/bin/csh
```

The last item in the response line indicates that the current default shell for user `nwells` is the C shell (`csh`).

> **TIP** The `grep` command is intended for use with text files, not with binary-format data such as program executables.

You can also perform much more complex searching. Suppose you have a directory full of text files and you want to see all occurrences of a string pattern that starts with `ThomasCorp`. The following command lists all of those occurrences, showing the filename containing the string and the complete line of text containing the string:

```
grep ThomasCorp  *txt
```

The first parameter—`ThomasCorp`—is a regular expression. In this case, a specific string is the pattern to search for, with no special characters. When using the `grep` command, an asterisk is never needed at the beginning or end of the string pattern (such as `ThomasCorp*`), because `grep` will locate the string wherever it occurs. For example, `grep` would find instances of the following strings during the search:

- `ThomasCorp`
- `ThomasCorporation`
- `ThomasCorps`

But these strings would not be included:

- `Thomas Corporation`
- `Thomascorporation`
- `Thomas Nast`

The second parameter to `grep` is also a regular expression that defines which files to search. The asterisk in the command indicates that all files in the current directory that end with the letters `txt` should be searched.

The results of the `grep` command might include lines like these:

- `Annual_report.txt: As news of ThomasCorporation reaches customers around the world, we are pleased to…`
- `memo0518.txt: that Rachel and I think ThomasCorp should be looking seriously at acquiring an interest in…`
- `meetingsummary.txt: Discussed needs of ThomasCorp to diversify plastics manufacturing capacity for…`

7

The `grep` command is often used with a pipe to search the output from another command. For example, you can pipe the output of the `locate` command through the `grep` command to refine a search. A sample command might look like this:

```
locate tif | grep airframe
```

In cases like this, `grep` uses only a single parameter—the pattern to search for. Rather than include a filename to define the text to be searched, the output of the `locate` command is searched. The results are printed to STDOUT—the screen.

Reviewing System Processes

Linux includes many tools that you can use to track and interact with the many processes that may be running at the same time on your system. Two of these commands are introduced here. These and others are covered in detail in Chapter 10.

The `ps` command lists the processes that are currently running on your Linux system. The process list can contain a great deal of information. Selecting various options for the `ps` command lets you control which pieces of information are included in a listing of processes and how that information is organized. The basic format of the `ps` command uses no parameters and produces a listing of programs that you have started in your current session (this is generally a short list, as shown here):

```
$ ps
PID     TTY       TIME         CMD
576     tty1      00:00:00     login
584     tty1      00:00:00     bash
741     tty1      00:00:00     ps
```

In this list, you see a PID (**process ID**) number (a unique number identifying a process); the terminal that the process is using for output (`tty1` is the first main console screen); the CPU time that process has used so far; and the command that started the process.

Other `ps` commands include information such as the user that started (owns) the process, the process priority, current status, and the PID number of the parent process (the process that started this one).

An important command related to processes is the `kill` command. You can use the `kill` command to end a process. Chapter 9 explains more about how this occurs within the Linux operating system, but the simplest example of `kill` is shown here, with the PID number of the process you want to end:

```
kill -9 873
```

CHAPTER SUMMARY

- ❏ The role of the Linux system administrator is to keep Linux-based computer systems running efficiently, usually for the use of a group of co-workers.

- ❏ A system administrator holds a position of great trust within an organization and must use ethical practices to protect the integrity of the systems being managed.

- ❏ Linux systems incorporate many different plain-text configuration files used to set up system services. These files each use a different format. Various graphical tools can be used to configure some services by automatically modifying the appropriate text files.

- ❏ Linux administration is built on a collection of single-task utilities that can be combined to achieve the desired results. Understanding these tools and their options is the basis of the toolbox that a system administrator has available to solve problems.

7

KEY TERMS

apropos — Linux command used to show all man pages that contain a keyword.

chief information officer (CIO) — The executive in an organization who determines how information systems are used within the organization to further its goals or mission effectively.

COAS (Caldera Open Administration System) — A set of graphical utilities developed by Caldera Systems and used to manage many aspects of a Linux system.

daemon — A background process that runs on Linux to handle tasks, such as responding to network traffic, without any visible screen output.

end user — An individual who uses the computer systems in an organization to accomplish assigned tasks, but relies on a system administrator to keep those systems running smoothly.

find — Linux command used to search the file system for files matching certain characteristics.

grep — Linux command used to search within files for lines containing a certain pattern.

Help Desk — A service in many organizations that assists end users in solving problems related to information technology.

info — Linux command used to access online command reference information.

Information Systems Department (IS) — The area of an organization in which the staff are responsible for maintaining computer and information systems that support the employees in their work (also called the IT Department in some organizations).

Information Technology Department (IT) — *See* Information Systems Department.

kill — Linux command used to end a process.

LinuxConf — Graphical configuration and administration utility for Linux, developed and supported by Red Hat Software.

locate — Linux command used to search an index of the file system for items matching a given pattern.

man page — An online reference documenting a Linux command.

pipe — A connection between two Linux commands (indicated by the | character) that causes the output of one command to be used as the input of a second command.

plain-text configuration file — A file containing human-readable instructions that are used by a program to set its configuration information.

process — A task running on a Linux operating system, managed by the Linux kernel.

process ID (PID) — A number from 1 to 65,000 that is associated uniquely with a process running on a Linux system.

program — An imprecise term used to refer to any process running on a Linux system.

ps — Linux command that provides information about processes running on Linux.

redirection — The concept of changing the location where a Linux program receives its input and sends its output in order to increase flexibility and interaction with other Linux programs.

regular expression — A system of expressing patterns using special characters that can be interpreted by many Linux programs.

safedelete — A type of utility that makes files appear to have been deleted but actually saves a compressed copy of each one in case it is needed later.

SAGE (System Administrators Guild) — A professional organization for system administrators.

standard error (STDERR) — The channel used by most Linux programs to send information about errors in program execution.

standard input (STDIN) — The communication channel used by most Linux programs to collect input (normally from the keyboard).

standard output (STDOUT) — The communication channel used by most Linux programs to write output (normally to the screen).

syntax — A formalized arrangement of information to allow a Linux command to understand parameters, options, and so forth.

thread — A piece of a process (or a piece of a daemon, since a daemon is a type of process). The distinction between processes and threads is not important for most system administration work. Instead, the term *process* is used in most cases that don't involve programmers developing software for multiprocessor computers.

utility — An imprecise term referring to a program used to administer a computer system rather than do work for an end user.

YAST — A graphical configuration utility developed by the makers of SuSE Linux.

REVIEW QUESTIONS

1. Why are nontechnical skills like curiosity and creativity important to being a successful system administrator?

2. Name one key advantage of using multiple plain-text configuration files in Linux.

   a. They are compatible with configuration files from other operating systems.

   b. Several system administrators can access the same configuration file at the same time.

   c. If one configuration file becomes corrupted, none of the other system services are affected.

   d. Special utilities are required to change system configuration settings.

3. Which of these tasks is not likely to be assigned to you as a system administrator?

   a. Develop a new cash register system using C programming.

   b. Install new hard disks in Linux servers.

   c. Teach new users how to access their e-mail accounts.

   d. Attend a conference on improving system security.

4. A _____ runs a subtask as part of a larger task, often on a multi-processor system.

   a. daemon

   b. process

   c. thread

   d. utility

5. Name two disadvantages to using any of the current graphical Linux configuration/administration tools.

6. Name three graphical tools that are used either for general system administration or for administration of a specific service (such as a Web server).

7. Which of the following does not have correctly formed options?

   a. `ls --help`

   b. `ls --color -R`

   c. `ls -il -aX --reverse`

   d. `ls -sort=time`

8. A pipe is a method of connecting processes with daemons. True or False?

9. The command `ls | sort` causes the following to occur:

   a. The output of the `ls` command is sent to the `sort` command. The results are printed to the screen.

   b. It cannot be determined without information about the next command to be executed.

   c. The output of the `ls` command is written to a file named `sort`.

   d. The output of the `ls` command is filtered based on the regular expression contained in the file `sort`.

10. A regular expression is used to:

   a. define a list of threads that a process can execute

   b. assign values to variables

   c. define a complex pattern used for searching

   d. build filenames from component parts

7

11. When you run a program called `gather_data`, it normally reads lines entered at the keyboard. If you use the command `gather_data < input_text` to run the program, the following occurs:

    a. The `gather_data` command is executed followed by the `input_text` command.

    b. The input that the `gather_data` program would normally read from the keyboard is taken from the `input_text` file instead.

    c. The `input_text` program runs first, collecting data, which is then passed through a pipe to the `gather_data` program.

    d. Both `gather_data` and `input_text` run as concurrent processes reading from the keyboard as STDIN.

12. Describe the difference between `find` and `locate`.

13. The regular expression `[cC]hapter0[12345]*` will *not* match which of the following files:

    a. `chapter01`

    b. `Chapter03.doc`

    c. `Chapter1.doc`

    d. `Chapter02`

14. The `find` command should be used instead of the `locate` command when:

    a. your locate index has not been updated recently

    b. the number of processes on the system is large

    c. you prefer to use `grep` at the same time

    d. the file system appears to be unstable

15. The `grep` command is *not* useful for which of the following:

    a. Searching for all filenames that match a pattern

    b. Determining which directories are currently in use

    c. Finding lines of text that contain a certain word

    d. Locating specific information in the output of another command

16. The `locate` command uses a prebuilt index of your file system to search for file information. True or False?

17. Describe the difference between `ps` and `kill`.

18. Linux filenames can be eight characters with a three-character extension, but a longer filename is also stored for reference. True or False?

19. The **rm** command is used in Linux to:

    a. remove special characters from a filename

    b. delete files from a hard disk

    c. remove case-sensitivity settings

    d. manage regular expressions

20. Only command names are case sensitive in Linux. True or False?

21. Name three methods of learning about Linux commands as you work at a command line.

22. All Linux systems use a trashcan facility to save deleted files. True or False?

23. Describe the errors in this command: `Ls   /help`

24. The **ps** command does *not* provide information about:

    a. who started a process

    b. the number assigned to a process

    c. the current status of the process

    d. when the threads of the process expire

25. The **kill** command is used to end:

    a. a process

    b. a thread

    c. a user account

    d. a locate query

HANDS-ON PROJECTS

Project 7-1

In this activity you access the SAGE Web page to learn about conference events for system administrators. As you learn about the events, you can see what topics are presented to system administrators seeking to improve their skills. To start the exercise, you should be at a computer with an Internet connection and a Web browser.

To find information about system administrator conferences:

1. Enter **http://www.usenix.org/sage/** on the Location or Address line of your browser. The SAGE Web page appears, as shown in Figure 7-9. The SAGE Web page contains information for professional system administrators.

2. Click the **Events** link on the SAGE Web page. A list of recent and forthcoming events is displayed. (The events listed change over time.)

3. Click the link for one of the listed events near your area. (You may also choose to select a conference event with a topic that is of special interest to you, such as security or the Web.)

4. Locate a link on the page for the event that you have chosen that describes the program for the conference. The name of this link varies with each event. You may also choose a link that shows information about past conferences and their topics.

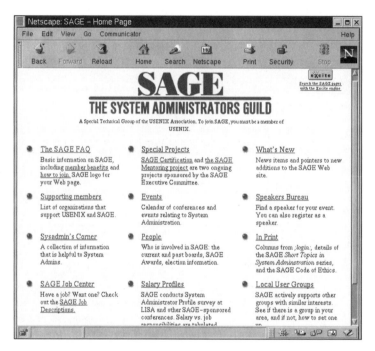

Figure 7-9 SAGE Web page

Project 7-2

In this activity you practice using some of the commands described in this chapter. To complete this project, you should be logged on to a standard Linux system using a regular user account.

To practice Linux commands:

1. Type **cp /etc/termcap ~/testfile** to create a practice file. This copies a system file to your home directory.
2. Type **ls -l** to list the files in your home directory. Make certain the test file is listed. Note the file's size and the date it was created.
3. Type **mkdir archive** to create a subdirectory to hold the file.
4. Type **mv testfile archive** to move the sample file to the new directory.
5. Type **cd archive** to change your working directory to the new directory.
6. Type **pwd** to check which directory you are working in.
7. Type **ls -l** to list the contents of the new directory.
8. Type **grep Linux testfile** to search the test file for the string **Linux**.
9. Type **grep Linux testfile > results** to repeat the search, but this time write the results to a file.
10. Type **cat results** to review the contents of the results file.
11. Type **rm -i testfile results** to delete the test file and results file. What does the **-i** parameter do? How would you now delete the archive directory?

Project 7-3

In this project you view information about the processes running on your Linux system. To complete this project, you should be logged on to a standard Linux system using a regular user account.

To view information about Linux processes:

1. Type **ps** to list the processes that you have started in your current Linux session.
2. Type **ps ax** to list all of the processes running on your Linux system for all users.
3. Type **ps ax | more** to view the **ps** output one screen at a time. Note that this command uses a pipe to combine the **ps** command with the **more** command.
4. Type **ps ax | grep httpd** to search the output of the **ps** command. This command uses **grep** to find out the number of Web servers (**httpd** daemons) running on your Linux system.

CASE PROJECTS

1. You've been working at Tyson Electronics as a system administrator for about three months. Most of the employees are highly trained in technical topics and use their computers for all of their daily work, which includes sending e-mail to colleagues around the world.

   One of the product managers approaches you with a belligerent tone and insists that you improve the system response time so he can download large e-mail messages faster. You realize that increasing the speed of the company's Internet connection involves a substantial cost. How could you respond to the product manager's request while maintaining a good relationship with all employees? Describe the probable effects on your relationships with all employees and the company's success if you were to retaliate against the belligerent manager by slowing down his connection or creating other technical problems on his account. What if your actions were discovered?

2. The CIO of Big Brother Corp. is concerned that some employees are spreading rumors about the company's financial status to colleagues in other companies. She asks you to collect all the e-mail messages sent by two employees who are under the most suspicion so they can be reviewed by management. The messages are archived and available to you as system administrator; you also have the ability to capture new messages as they are sent. The company has a policy stating that e-mail is subject to review, but no one really expects that others will read their mail. What is your reaction to the demand of the CIO? Do you feel you have an ethical obligation to remind employees of the corporate policy so they are more careful in their use of company resources? If the company didn't have a policy about reading employees' e-mail and you left the company because of an incident such as this, what would you tell your next potential employer about why you left?

3. While checking the available free hard disk space on the server, you notice an employee using an inordinate amount of disk space. On examining a few of the employee's numerous files, you discover that the majority contain offensive material. What action might you take towards this employee? How will the company's stated policies regarding employee privacy and use of company resources affect your actions? Are your own actions subject to review?

# CHAPTER 8

BASIC ADMINISTRATION TASKS

> **After reading this chapter and completing the exercises, you will be able to:**
> ♦ Create and manage Linux user accounts
> ♦ Install and maintain diverse types of Linux file systems
> ♦ Manage processes on Linux using basic commands

In the previous chapter you learned what it means to be a system administrator. You also learned the role ethics and nontechnical skills play in a system administrator's daily duties. In addition, you learned about some basic concepts related to Linux system administration and became familiar with some of the most popular administrative utilities.

In this chapter you look at basic administration tasks, such as working with users, processes, and file systems. You will also learn about the utilities used to manage users, processes, and file systems in Linux.

ADMINISTERING USER ACCOUNTS

In order to complete any operation in Linux, the user must first log in to a valid user account. The task of setting up and maintaining these user accounts is a large part of the work of a system administrator. In Chapter 4 you learned how to manage the initialization files for a user account. This section provides more details on how to configure and manage user accounts. In general, the more user accounts you have on your Linux system, the more work is required to keep them all running smoothly. More users also means more security risks—thus proper management and tracking of user accounts is crucial to keeping the system running securely and efficiently.

Before you can thoroughly understand the nature of user accounts, you need to understand the situations in which user accounts are *not* used. As a rule, a user account is not required when accessing a network service provided on the Linux server. For example, when a person connects to a Linux system using a Web browser, the remote Web browser does not have (or need) a user account. In fact, the remote Web browser never actually logs in to the Linux system. Instead, the Web server daemon watches for incoming requests and responds over the network without allowing the browser to have full access to a Linux user account. The Web server runs as a certain Linux user (usually as user **nobody**, to increase security) and uses the access privileges of this user account to read files that are passed back over the network to the Web browser. Some types of network services (like telnet or FTP) require an account on the Linux system to which a client wishes to connect. Other services, such as those that send e-mail messages or request Web documents, do not.

Types of User Accounts

You are probably familiar with the process of logging in to Linux with a user account that looks like your own name. It's important to keep in mind, however, that Linux has many user accounts with strange names that serve special purposes on the system. All of these user accounts are part of the same "system," but they have different characteristics according to how they are used by the various Linux programs. Three types of user accounts are described in the following sections.

The root Account

As you know, the administrative account (the **superuser**) on a Linux system is named root. The root user account is created when you install Linux, at which time you normally assign a password to that account as well. The root user has authority to complete any operation on the Linux system, including changing any configuration information or deleting the entire operating system with a single command. The root user on Linux is similar to the admin user on a NetWare server. The administrative user account on Windows NT does not have access to all system files and resources; Windows NT does not have a user account that is truly equivalent to the Linux root user.

Because of the power of the root user, you must not log in as root for your normal work. Even though you are the system administrator, root is not intended to be your main account. Always create a separate account (normally based on your name) and log in using this account for normal work. When you need to do administrative tasks that require superuser privileges (such as creating new user accounts), you need to temporarily change to root account privileges, complete the administration task, and then return to your normal user account. You can temporarily change to root account privileges using the su utility.

The **su** utility (for substitute user) changes any user account's permissions to the permissions assigned to another user account. This is like logging in as a different user. If you simply type su, without any parameters, you change to the root account. If you type su followed by a username, you change to that user's account. This utility is useful when you need to temporarily assume the privileges of another user account for administrative purposes. For example, to assume the permissions of a user named lizw, you would type:

```
su - lizw
```

This command places you in the home directory of user lizw, with all environment settings as they would be for that user. If you omit the hyphen, you are not placed in a new directory with new environment settings. Because the root user has all power over the system, no password is required to use the su utility when logged in as root. Regular users must supply a password when using the su utility.

You must be especially careful with the root password. If an intruder obtains this pass word, he or she could inflict severe damage to your Linux system, including creating many security holes that will allow the intruder access to the system even if the root password is changed later.

Regular Users

A regular user account is intended for a person who needs to log in and use the Linux system. Although a regular account can be associated with a role in an organization (you could name a user account "manager" or "designer"), user accounts are commonly associated with individuals. The name of the account reflects the name of the individual. For example, Chris Lee might have any of the following as a user account name:

- `chris`
- `lee`
- `clee`
- `chrisl`
- `cl`

User account names should be no more than eight characters. The example user account names for Chris Lee, in the preceding list, are not predefined, but depend on how you decide to set up your user accounts. It's common practice to define a standard method of converting real names to usernames. For example, an administrator might decide to combine the user's first name and last initial to create the person's username. In another scheme, the username might consist of the first initials of a user's first and last names. Some duplicate usernames may require variation from the standards you define.

Non-Regular Users

In addition to the `root` user and the regular user accounts, Linux includes several default user account names that might appear strange to Linux newcomers. These user accounts are employed only by Linux programs and are referred to as special, or non-regular, accounts. By using a special user account, programs can better control file permissions and therefore ensure the security of the system. Most non-regular user accounts are created during the installation of Linux; others may be created by programs that you install. The non-regular user accounts created during installation of your Linux system vary depending on the services you have installed. For example, if you have installed the PostgreSQL database package, your system contains a `postgres` user; otherwise your system will not include this user. The special user accounts you are likely to see on your system are shown in Table 8-1. Although these user accounts allow programs to control system access in their respective areas, these accounts do not have passwords or default shells defined. This means that a person cannot log in using these accounts.

Table 8-1   Non-Regular User Accounts Created by Default on Most Linux Systems

User account	Description
bin	Can be used by any program
daemon	Used by daemons
adm	Used for administrative purposes
lp	Used by the printer control daemon
sync	Used to synchronize disk updates
shutdown	Used during system shutdown
halt	Used when the system is being halted
mail	Used by the e-mail server
uucp	Used by programs related to the UUCP protocol
news	Used by the newsgroup server
operator	Can be used for system administration work
ftp	Used for anonymous FTP access
nobody	Used as a restricted access account
games	Used by game programs to control system access

Linux Groups

Like most other operating systems, Linux allows the administrator to organize user accounts into groups. A **group** is a collection of user accounts that can be granted access to the system collectively. Assigning users to groups makes it easier to give each user access to areas of the system that match his or her specific work requirements. Permissions to use directories and files on Linux are granted to the owner of a file or directory or to the group assigned to a file or directory. Each user in Linux is assigned to a primary group. Information regarding a user's group assignment is stored with the user's account information. Users can also be assigned as members of additional, secondary groups. Information regarding a user's secondary groups is stored in the group configuration file (described in the next section). Groups can be assigned permissions, just like individual user accounts.

Many Linux systems employ User Private Groups to increase security on the system. A **User Private Group** system creates a group with a single member for each new user account that is created. The new user is the only member of the group. When a user creates a file or directory, that user's private group is assigned as the group for that file or directory; thus no other users have access to the file or directory by virtue of belonging to the same group as the user that created it. This prevents inadvertent security mishaps from making a user's files accessible to others that are part of the group assigned to a file that the user created.

To understand the nature of groups, suppose you have created a new user account called `chrislee`. Because your system employs User Private Groups, the primary group for this user is the group named `chrislee`. User `chrislee` is also assigned to the following groups: `projectleads`, `salesteam`, and `hrcommittee`. Now suppose you want to give all members of the sales team access to a particular directory or group of files. Rather than having to assign permissions to each user account individually, you can simply assign the necessary permission to the `salesteam` group. In the process, user `chrislee` will also be granted permission. (This example is illustrated in Figure 8-1.)

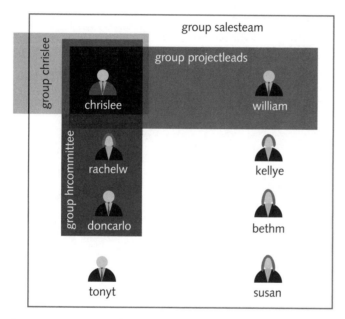

Figure 8-1   Example of groups and users

User and Group Files

User account information is stored in the file **/etc/passwd**. In earlier releases of Linux, password information for each user was also stored in this file, hence the file's name. Because of security problems in the past, this is no longer the case. Other basic information about each user is contained in the file, however. A sample **/etc/passwd** file from a new Linux installation is shown below, followed by a description of each of the file's colon-separated fields.

 The exact list of users created on a new Linux system depends on which version of Linux you are using and which features you have selected to install or activate.

```
root:x:0:0:root:/root:/bin/bash
bin:x:1:1:bin:/bin:
daemon:x:2:2:daemon:/sbin:
adm:x:3:4:adm:/var/adm:
lp:x:4:7:lp:/var/spool/lpd:
sync:x:5:0:sync:/sbin:/bin/sync
shutdown:x:6:0:shutdown:/sbin:/sbin/shutdown
halt:x:7:0:halt:/sbin:/sbin/halt
mail:x:8:12:mail:/var/spool/mail:
news:x:9:13:news:/var/spool/news:
uucp:x:10:14:uucp:/var/spool/uucp:
operator:x:11:0:operator:/root:
games:x:12:100:games:/usr/games:
gopher:x:13:30:gopher:/usr/lib/gopher-data:
ftp:x:14:50:FTP User:/home/ftp:
nobody:x:99:99:Nobody:/:
gdm:x:42:42::/home/gdm:/bin/bash
xfs:x:100:233:X Font Server:/etc/X11/fs:/bin/false
nwells:x:500:500:Nicholas Wells:/home/nwells:/bin/bash
```

The following list describes the fields in the list above. The last line of the file (the user nwells) is used as an example.

- User account name (nwells): the name used by a person to log in to Linux.

- Password (x): the password for each user was formerly stored in this field in encrypted form. An *x* in this field indicates that the shadow password system is in use, in which case the password information is stored in the file /etc/shadow. You will learn more about shadow passwords later in this chapter.

- User ID number, or UID (the first 500): a number from 0 to 65,535 that uniquely identifies this user on this Linux system. The number is arbitrary and normally is automatically assigned by the utility used to create a new user account.

- Group ID number, or GID (the second 500): a number from 0 to 65,535 that uniquely identifies the primary group for this user account. The GID must correspond to a group defined in the /etc/group file (described below).

- The user's real name (Nicholas Wells): a complete name (or a comment for non-regular users). Spaces are permitted in this field. If the user account was created for a certain role in the organization, other text can be placed here instead, such as "Database Administrator."

- Home directory (/home/nwells): the position in the Linux file system that will be used as the current working directory when the user first logs in.

- Default shell (/bin/bash): the program that runs automatically when the user logs in. The default setting for this field is /bin/bash, which runs the bash shell. If a user prefers a different shell (such as the **Korn shell** or **C shell**), this field can be changed to accommodate that. This field can also be used to start a nonshell program to restrict the user's actions in the system.

Although you can edit the /etc/passwd file directly in a text editor, this is not a good idea. Advanced security measures that have been added to your distribution of Linux may make any alterations to the **passwd** file invalid. In addition, there is a small risk that another program might be trying to edit user information at the same time and create a conflict. Instead of a text editor, use the programs described in the following sections to update the user account file. If you need to use a text editor to correct a problem in the file, try the special editing program **vipw**. (This program is basically a copy of the **vi** editor that automatically loads the **passwd** file.)

Groups on a Linux system are defined in the **/etc/group** file. A sample of this file is shown here, with the fields in the file (again separated by colons on each line) described in the following list.

```
root::0:root
bin::1:root,bin,daemon
daemon::2:root,bin,daemon
sys::3:root,bin,adm
adm::4:root,adm,daemon
tty::5:
disk::6:root
lp::7:daemon,lp
mem::8:
kmem::9:
wheel::10:root
mail::12:mail
news::13:news
uucp::14:uucp
man::15:
games::20:
gopher::30:
dip::40:
ftp::50:
nobody::99:
users::100:
floppy:x:19:
console:x:101:
gdm:x:42:
utmp:x:102:
pppusers:x:230:
popusers:x:231:
slipusers:x:232:
slocate:x:21:
xfs:x:233:
nwells:x:500:
rsolomon:x:501:
authors:x:502:rsolomon,nwells,jsmith
```

8

- The name of the group: this field cannot contain spaces. Avoid names more than eight letters long.

- Group password: this field is either blank or *x* (meaning the password is stored in another location). Group passwords are rarely used.

- Group ID (GID) number: this number uniquely identifies this group within the Linux system. Group numbers are automatically assigned when you create a new group, though you can specify a number if you prefer.

- Members of the group: This field identifies members of the group. Note in the sample file that many groups do not have member users defined. A program may be able to assume the permissions of the group using system calls (programming instructions), but no user is part of the group by virtue of logging in. Some of the groups (such as `sys` and `adm`) have a comma-separated list of users as the last field. In addition to the two User Private Group items (for `nwells` and `rsolomon` in this sample file), a standard group named `authors` has been added to this default installation.

> TIP   Some UNIX and Linux systems employ a special group called `wheel`, which has special administrative powers; it is essentially a reduced version of the `root` account. On some systems a user must be a member of the `wheel` group in order to use the `su` command to change to the `root` account permissions. Although Linux includes a `wheel` group by default (with `root` as the only member), no special features or privileges apply to the `wheel` group in Linux.

Shadow Passwords

All programs and users may need to access the list of users on the system stored in the `/etc/passwd` file. However, if the encrypted password text is readable by many users, it may be subject to attack, allowing unauthorized use of someone's account.

To counteract this problem, the passwords for Linux user accounts are no longer stored in the `/etc/passwd` file. Instead, they are commonly stored in a file called **`/etc/shadow`**. Systems that make use of this file are said to be using the **Shadow Password system**. This file can only be read by the `root` user (and special programs such as the `login` routine). This tighter security protects all user passwords from the open access formerly allowed with the `/etc/passwd` file.

A sample `/etc/shadow` file is shown below. Fields on each line are separated by colons, as in the `/etc/passwd` file. The first field is a user account name that must correspond to a user account in `/etc/passwd`. The second field is the encrypted password text. Additional fields configure password security information for the user account on that line. For the many non-regular user accounts (such as `bin` and `daemon`), an asterisk in the second field indicates that the account has no password. No user can log in to an account with no password.

```
root:$1$xlo5lRMK$oklXHuoBjHH7JmiVdk/fQ.:10815:0:99999:7:-1:
    -1:134538444
bin:*:10815:0:99999:7:::
daemon:*:10815:0:99999:7:::
adm:*:10815:0:99999:7:::
lp:*:10815:0:99999:7:::
sync:*:10815:0:99999:7:::
shutdown:*:10815:0:99999:7:::
halt:*:10815:0:99999:7:::
mail:*:10815:0:99999:7:::
news:*:10815:0:99999:7:::
uucp:*:10815:0:99999:7:::
operator:*:10815:0:99999:7:::
games:*:10815:0:99999:7:::
gopher:*:10815:0:99999:7:::
ftp:*:10815:0:99999:7:::
nobody:*:10815:0:99999:7:::
gdm:!!:10815:0:99999:7:::
xfs:!!:10815:0:99999:7:::
nwells:$1$3gWKUouQ$L7XUsJWpIwtqLUoWlmVvN1:10816:0:99999:7:-1:
    -1:134538436
rsolomon: 1J42Wuip3dYAh8$1pvNMAVK$UsrD6O90:10817:0:99999:7:-1:
    -1:134538412
```

On some Linux systems, user password security goes even further, with various systems available that can hide and encrypt passwords. These systems are beyond the scope of this book, however.

Creating New User Accounts

New user accounts can be created using any of several methods. The most rudimentary is to edit the /etc/passwd file and then use the mkdir command to create a new home directory. This has several disadvantages, however:

- Editing the /etc/passwd file can create a conflict with another program trying to edit the file, as already stated.

- Hand editing can introduce syntax errors. The new user account may not work, and the errors might make other user accounts invalid as well.

- Advanced security systems that store user information in nonstandard locations may not be affected by direct changes to the /etc/passwd file.

- Using one of the other methods is easier and can be included in system administration scripts.

User administration is one of the main tasks of a system administrator, so many graphical tools are available. For instance, you may choose to use one of the graphical user configuration tools shown in Figure 8-2. You had an opportunity to use the `LinuxConf` graphical utility in Chapter 4, when you created a user account for yourself after installing Linux. These utilities all work with the same core configuration files. Some may allow group and password management in addition to user account management.

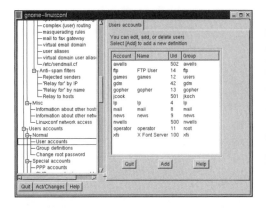

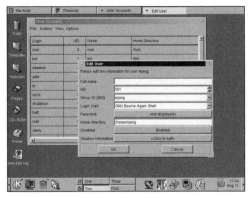

Figure 8-2   Graphical user account configuration tools

The most secure method of managing user accounts, however, is the `useradd` command. You will have a chance to practice using the `useradd` command in the hands–on projects at the end of this chapter.

The **useradd** command allows you to automate user creation, update user accounts, and take advantage of various options when creating users. If additional security is added to your Linux system, an updated version of `useradd` is normally included as the preferred method of adding new user accounts.

On some Linux systems, a script named adduser is available. Using a script to create new users is less secure than using the useradd command. On the latest Linux systems (such as Red Hat 6), the adduser command merely points to the `useradd` command.

To add a user with `useradd`, you must be logged in as `root`. Along with the command name, include the name of the new user account as a parameter. For example, to add a new account called `rsolomon`, you would use this command:

```
useradd rsolomon
```

The default user account settings are used to create the account and a home directory. These defaults are stored in the `/etc/login.defs` file and in the `/etc/default/useradd` file.

Specific options can be added to the `useradd` command. These options override any default settings for the user account that you are creating. For example, if you want to include the user's full name in the command field (generally a good idea), you can use the `-c` option. The `-g` option defines the primary group for the new user. A command incorporating these two options would look like this:

```
useradd -g sales -c "Raley Solomon" rsolomon
```

In this example, the value of the `-c` parameter is `Raley Solomon`. Because this value includes a space, it must be enclosed in quotation marks so the `useradd` command does not interpret the part after the space (`Solomon`) as the next command parameter.

Table 8-2 shows the options for the useradd command.

Table 8-2   Useradd Command Options

Option	Description	Example
-c	Defines a user's full name or other comment for this account	useradd -c "Jose Carrera" josec
-d	Specifies the home directory path (useful mostly for special user accounts that use a nonstandard home directory location).	useradd -d /usr/home/ josec
-e	Specifies the date this user account will expire (and be disabled automatically). Used for temporary accounts.	useradd -e 03/15/01 josec
-f	Specifies the number of days after the password expires until the account is disabled.	useradd -f 7 josec
-g	Specifies the primary group for the new user (either the group's name or its unique GID number can be used).	useradd -g ops josec

8

Table 8-2   Useradd Command Options (continued)

Option	Description	Example
-G	Adds a list of additional groups that the new user should be made a member of (this information is stored in the /etc/group file, not in /etc/passwd).	`useradd -G teamlead,party,emt josec`
-m	Forces creation of the user's home directory, even if the default settings do not include creating a home directory.	`useradd -m josec`
-M	Does not create a home directory, even if the default is set to include one.	`useradd -M josec`
-n	Disables the User Private Group feature so that a group matching the new username is not created.	`useradd -n josec`
-s	Sets the user's login shell. The default shell in Linux is bash. The complete path to another shell program can be used with this option.	`useradd -s /bin/zsh josec`
-u	Sets a specific numeric value for the user ID of the new user. (Normally a UID is selected automatically—use this option if you need to force the use of a specific UID number.)	`useradd -u 509 josec`

To display the default settings for the useradd command, use the -D option. Typical output of the -D option is shown here:

```
# useradd -D
GROUP=100
HOME=/home
INACTIVE=-1
EXPIRE=
SHELL=/bin/bash
SKEL=/etc/skel
```

The information returned by the -D option is described in the following list:

- GROUP: the group ID number for the group that all new users will be placed in (as a primary group) if no other is indicated when the user is created.

- HOME: the path in which home directories for new users will be created.

- **INACTIVE**: the number of days after the password for the new account expires that the account will be disabled. Using a value of –1 for this field disables this option (the user account will *not* be disabled).

- **EXPIRE**: the expiration date for a new user account.

- **SHELL**: the path and program name for the default shell (command-line interpreter) to be used by a new user account.

- **SKEL**: the path to the skeleton directory used to fill a new home directory with basic files (this directory is discussed later in this section).

You can also use the **–D** option to update the defaults that will be used in the future for all new user accounts. For example, to change the default shell so that all new users will use the C shell instead of the **bash** shell, use this command:

```
# useradd -D -s /bin/csh
```

 TIP   If you prefer, you can edit the /etc/default/useradd file directly in a text editor.

The items you are most likely to need to update in the default user creation settings are the login preferences—that is, the settings for how long a password can be used, how many days after expiration before the account is disabled, and so forth. Because all of these options are part of Linux security, they are not described in detail here. They are documented in the /etc/login.defs file and in the man page for useradd.

After adding a new user account, check that the user's home directory has been created. For example, after creating a user with the command useradd jsmith, you should check that the directory /home/jsmith exists. Depending on how you have set up e-mail accounts on your network, each user may also need a file to hold incoming e-mail in the /var/spool/mail/ directory. For example, after creating a new account with the command useradd jsmith, you may need to also create the mail file for this user with the **touch** command (which creates an empty file or updates the access time of a file). In this example, the touch command would be: touch /var/spool/mail/jsmith.

Changing User Passwords

Before anyone can log in using a new account, the account must be assigned a password. After the password is assigned, the account is ready for normal use. A password is not defined by useradd when a new user account is created.

 TIP   Some of the graphical tools shown in Figure 8-2 can be used to create a password for the new user account. It is not possible to create passwords with the command-line utility useradd.

The `passwd` command is used to change (or initially set up) a password on a user account. (This command has the same name as the `/etc/passwd` file.) To use this command as `root`, include the name of the user account whose password you need to configure. You must then enter the new password twice to be certain you have not made a typing error.

Suppose you have already created a new user named `lizw`, and you want to set this user's initial password or change this user's password. For either task, you must do the following:

1. Make sure you're logged in as `root`.

2. Enter the command **passwd lizw**. The following text then appears on the screen:

```
Changing password for lizw
New UNIX password:
```

(Note that the word *UNIX* indicates the type of password system Linux is using.)

3. Type the new password for the Linux user account and press **Enter**. Nothing appears on screen as you type, so work carefully. The following text appears when you press Enter:

```
Retype new UNIX password:
```

4. Type the new password a second time, exactly as you typed it the first time. This verifies that the password was entered as you intended to type it, without any typing mistakes. When you press Enter the second time, the following text appears:

```
passwd: all authentication tokens updated successfully
```

If you enter a password that is a poor choice (such as *password*, the username, or a simple word from the dictionary), you see a message stating **BAD PASSWORD**. Although this message should cause you to reconsider the password, the password is still changed. For a temporary password on new accounts, almost anything will do. Popular choices include the user's account name (`lizw` in this example), the word *password*, *change.me*, or something similar.

The standard procedure is for a system administrator to assign an initial password to a new account using the steps just given, thus enabling the user account for regular use. The administrator should communicate the password to the new user, who should then immediately select a new password that is unknown to the `root` user or to any other users.

The user can change his or her password by using the `passwd` command without any parameters. Thus, after `lizw` has logged in, she can change her own password as follows:

1. Type the command **passwd**. The following text then appears on the screen:

```
Changing password for lizw
(current) UNIX password:
```

(Note that the word *UNIX* indicates the type of password system Linux is using.)

2. Type the current password for the `lizw` account and press **Enter**. Nothing appears on screen as you type, so work carefully. The following text appears when you press Enter:

```
New UNIX password:
```

3. Enter a new UNIX password, typing carefully (nothing appears on screen as you type). When you press Enter, the following text appears:

```
Retype new UNIX password:
```

4. Type the new password a second time, exactly as you typed it the first time. This verifies that the password was entered as you intended to type it. When you press Enter, the following text appears:

```
passwd: all authentication tokens updated successfully
```

Although the root user can use any word as a password, the default settings do not allow regular users to change their passwords to something like *password* or their user account name. A message stating BAD PASSWORD will appear if a poor password choice is entered, and the password will not be updated. The **root** user can change the **root** password by using the **passwd** command without including a user account name.

As the system administrator, you must explain to users the importance of changing their passwords immediately after a new account is created for them. Passwords should be changed monthly, even if the Linux system does not enforce frequent changes. This lessens the danger that someone may discover a user's password and be able to continue using it. Good passwords have these characteristics:

- They are at least 5 characters long, though a 7- to 10-character password is *much* more secure.

- They include digits or punctuation marks. A common trick is to substitute the number 1 for the letter *l* and the number 0 for the letter *o*, but this is too well known to add much security.

- They mix upper- and lowercase letters in nonstandard ways.

- They are easy for the account owner to remember, but hard for anyone else to guess—even someone who knows the account owner well.

- They are not created from a simple manipulation of a word found in a dictionary or the name of a person or place.

A password that is hard to remember is probably hard for someone else to discover, but it doesn't help security much if the password is written on a note taped to the computer monitor. Creating a password that is pronounceable (with punctuation added in the middle) will help you to remember it. Three good examples of passwords are:

- miCru%norMouse@

- BLAST-!t-ALL

- call=9LL&nOw

As you choose a password for your account, especially the **root** account on the Linux system, remember that you will be dealing with many different passwords. These include the root password, a personal account password, plus passwords for other parts of your life, such as bank accounts, Web pages, and voice mail codes. If these passwords and codes are identical or even similar, discovery of one of your passwords could jeopardize the security of many different areas.

8

Creating New Groups

Although modifying the /etc/group file in a text editor does not pose as great a danger as editing /etc/passwd, the preferred method for adding a new group is to use the **groupadd** command. This command is used much like the **useradd** command, but it supports fewer options.

 TIP Graphical tools designed for creating users often allow you to create groups as well. These tools are useful if you prefer to work in a graphical environment. However, you should learn about the groupadd command as a backup and for troubleshooting, because the graphical tools rarely allow you to do much besides simply creating and deleting groups.

To add a new group, include the group name as a parameter, as follows:

`groupadd managers`

If you need to use a specific GID number for the new group, you can include it with the **-g** option. For example:

`groupadd -g 919 managers`

Modifying User Accounts

After setting up user and group accounts as described in the preceding sections, you will find occasions when you need to modify or update the account information. To do this, use the **usermod** (for *user modify*) command or **groupmod** (for *group modify*) command. The **usermod** command uses the same options as the **useradd** command, but it operates on an existing user account. To use the **usermod** command to update a user's account information, type **usermod** followed by one of the **usermod** parameters and a value for that parameter. For example, suppose **lizw** gets married and wishes to have her full name changed from Liz Wells to Liz Osowski on her employment records and user account. Using the **-c** option, as with the **useradd** command to change the Comment field of the user account, the command to update the **lizw** account to include the new name would be:

`usermod -c "Liz Osowski" lizw`

You can change the user's login name from **lizw** to **lizo** with the **-l** option:

`usermod -l lizo -d /home/lizo lizw`

Using the **-l** option alone leaves the home directory as it was before (/home/lizw). By using the **-d** option shown above, the home directory path for the user account is updated as well (to /home/lizo). Note that the **usermod** command cannot be used to change the directory name. After using the **usermod -d** command, you must change the actual directory name as follows:

`mv   /home/lizw   /home/lizo`

As another example, suppose you created an account for a new employee, using the default settings, and then discovered that the new employee prefers to use a different login shell and needs to be part of several additional groups to accommodate her job responsibilities. The command to update the user account would be something like this:

```
usermod -G taskforce,marketing -s /bin/tcsh srubenst
```

Automating Home Directory Creation

When you create a new user account, it's very useful to include basic configuration files in the new user's home directory. This information might include:

- Company document templates and calendars

- Environment settings to access department printers and servers

- Terminal settings to make Linux work well with desktop PCs

- Commands (scripts) to automate basic tasks and set up the user's system each time the user logs in

By using the **/etc/skel** directory, you can automatically copy files and thus apply settings to each new user account as you create the account. When you use **useradd** (or most graphical user creation utilities), all of the files in the **/etc/skel** directory are copied into a new user's home directory when the account is first created. As the system administrator, you should place files in **/etc/skel** when you first install Linux so that those files are automatically placed in each user's home directory that you create later with the **useradd** command. Because these are likely to be configuration files, many of them are hidden. By using the **ls -la** command, you can list the contents of the **/etc/skel** directory. Here is one version:

```
$ ls -la /etc/skel
total 12
drwxr-xr-x  4 root    root    1024  Jun 10  08:12  .
drwxr-xr-x 31 root    root    3072  Aug  9  14:13  ..
-rw-r--r--  1 root    root    1422  Mar 29  09:08  .Xdefaults
-rw-r--r--  1 root    root      24  Jul 13  1994   .bash_logout
-rw-r--r--  1 root    root     230  Aug 22  1998   .bash_profile
-rw-r--r--  1 root    root     124  Aug 23  1995   .bashrc
drwxr-xr-x  3 root    root    1024  Jun 10  08:12  .kde
-rw-r--r--  1 root    root     966  Apr 16  14:45  .kderc
drwxr-xr-x  5 root    root    1024  Jun 10  08:12  Desktop
```

The files shown here are used for the X Window System (graphical interface), the **bash** default shell, and the KDE Desktop (which was installed on this system). If you want to have other files included in each user's home directory, simply copy those files to **/etc/skel**.

TIP The files from /etc/skel are copied to a user's home directory when the account is created. When you add files to /etc/skel, they are not added automatically to the home directories of all existing user accounts; only user accounts created after the new files are added will include them. For existing accounts, you must copy any additional files to the home directories manually.

Creating Aliases to Ease User Angst

As you add files to the /etc/skel directory in order to prepare an environment for new users, you may also want to edit the existing startup files to add functionality or ease the transition to Linux. One of the best ways to do this is by adding aliases to the **.bashrc** startup script. The commands in this script are executed each time a user starts a session (logs in or opens a new command-line window). By adding aliases to this file, you can define pseudo-commands that may make it easier for users to work with Linux (you may even want to add some to your own environment).

By using the **alias** command, you can give any Linux command another name—an alias. For example, you can create an alias named **copy** for the **cp** command. Then whenever you enter **copy** on a command line, the **cp** command is executed. To use the **alias** command to define another name for a command, you include the new command name (the alias) followed by an equal sign and the real command (which can include command options if you wish). The real command should be enclosed in quotation marks if it includes spaces. For example, this alias command makes the **copy** command (which doesn't really exist in Linux) execute the real command **cp**:

```
alias copy=cp
```

You can execute this **alias** command on any command line. By adding it to the **.bashrc** script, the **alias** command is executed automatically as every command-line session starts. After you enter this **alias** command, the **copy** command will always be interpreted as **cp**. How is this done? The shell (**bash**) actually substitutes the string **cp** whenever you enter the string **copy**. As with the rest of Linux, these strings are case sensitive, so entering **COPY** won't have the same effect as entering **copy**. As a rule, adding a few of these aliases can make it easier for users to become comfortable with Linux commands.

 TIP   Don't confuse the text substitution aliases described here with other types of links or substitutions that may also be called aliases or links. Examples include symbolic links in the file system and e-mail aliases used by an e-mail server.

If you add aliases to the **.bashrc** file, they are only in effect if the user runs the **bash** shell. Similar startup files can be created for other shells, such as **.kshrc** for the Korn shell and **.cshrc** for the C shell. Each of these is a hidden file (and thus the filename begins with a period).

Aliases serve many purposes. In addition to making DOS commands available, as in the example for **copy**, you might add aliases to do the following:

- To shorten commonly used commands. For example, if you must regularly use the command **cd /mnt/samba/datafiles/project/**, you could create an alias that allows you to simply type **cdp**. This command sets up the alias:

  ```
  alias cdp="cd /mnt/samba/datafiles/project/"
  ```

- To fix typing errors. For example, if you habitually type **sl** instead of **ls**, create an alias that changes **sl** to **ls**. This command sets up the alias:

  ```
  alias sl=ls
  ```

- To make operations safer by including options to confirm file deletions. A common feature is to have an alias named `rm` that refers to `rm -i`, so that you must confirm each file that is removed. This command sets up the alias:

```
alias rm="rm -i"
```

To see a list of the aliases that are active in your environment at any time, use the alias command without any parameters, as follows:

```
$ alias
```

You can also review the `.bashrc` file in your own home directory or in `/etc/skel` to see the default aliases configured on your system. (On some Linux systems, aliases are configured in the systemwide files `/etc/bashrc` or `/etc/profile`.)

Setting Up Environment Variables

In addition to aliases, many users will require environment variables that make it possible to access various programs and services. **Environment variables** are named values that any program can access. For example, when a database program is executed, it may expect an environment variable named `DB_DIR` to indicate the path where the database files are located. If that environment variable is not specified, the database will not be able to operate. In such a situation, each user's environment must include a definition of the `DB_DIR` environment variable.

Many Linux programs rely on environment variables to store configuration information. Rather than maintain a configuration file, a program's documentation may specify several environment variables that the user can set to alter how the program operates. The `bash` shell is a good example of this. The `bash` shell uses many environment variables to determine how features of the shell are used. For example, to change the prompt used at each command line, a user simply alters the environment variable `PS1`. To alter how often the shell checks for new e-mail messages, a user changes the value of the `MAILCHECK` variable. The manual page for `bash` lists over 50 environment variables that a user or program can use to learn the status of `bash` or to affect how `bash` operates.

To set an environment variable from the command line, use the `export` command with the variable name and value. For example:

```
export DB_DIR=/opt/database/
```

However, to avoid the need to enter this command each time a user logs in, this command can be added to the configuration files described previously: `.bashrc` in the home directory, or `/etc/bashrc` if the environment variable is needed by all users.

Disabling User Accounts

At times you will need to disable a user account—either temporarily or permanently. Reasons for disabling a user account include:

- An employee has left the organization (permanent deletion of the account)
- An employee is on vacation (temporary disabling as a security precaution)

- A guest user has not paid for the account or for computer time (temporary, perhaps permanent later on)

- An employee is under disciplinary action and is not allowed to access company information (temporary, perhaps permanent later on)

To temporarily disable a user's account, you can simply change the password so that the user can no longer log in. This can be done with the **passwd** command as described previously. However, be sure to use a password that is not easy to guess, rather than a simple password like change.me.

If you are concerned about having an active account with only a new password as security, you can edit the /etc/shadow file in a text editor and place an asterisk before the encrypted password. This saves the password (because you can simply remove the asterisk later to reenable the account). But while the asterisk is part of the password, Linux will not allow anyone to log in to the user account. The line in /etc/shadow before the edit might look like this:

```
nwells:$12$tJhxVO2kUgVU2/o0434jj0:10799:0:99999:7:-1:-1:134538468
```

And after the edit it looks like this:

```
nwells:*$12$tJhxVO2kUgVU2/o0434jj0:10799:0:99999:7:-1:-1:134538468
```

TIP   The other fields of the /etc/shadow file are described in the manual page for this file but are not described here because they relate explicitly to system security.

If you decide to permanently delete a user's account, use the **userdel** command with the user account name. For example:

```
userdel lizo
```

This command removes the user named lizo from the user database (/etc/passwd or a similar secure file). As a result, the user will no longer be able to log in because the user account no longer exists. However, keep in mind that the **userdel** command does *not* remove the user's home directory or its contents. As a result, it is possible for the administrator to review or save the information contained in the home directory of a disabled user account. Be aware, however, that if an employee is leaving the organization, friends may be able to access part of the former employee's home directory (because of common group membership, for example) and pass files to that person. It's generally a very good idea to archive or otherwise remove or relocate the home directory of a deleted user account as soon as possible after deleting the account.

MAINTAINING FILE SYSTEMS

When you install Linux, you create the `root` file system in which the operating system is stored. The term **file system** refers to an organized set of data that can be accessed via the standard Linux directory structure. The command-line instructions (such as `cd /home/nwells`) that refer to the directory paths in Linux provide access to data stored in an underlying file system located on a hard disk or other physical device.

The `root` file system within which Linux is installed is normally located on one of the computer's main hard disks. Even a basic Linux system uses many other different file systems, however. Each one provides access to a different set of information. In some operating systems, file systems are accessed using drive letters or special network access tools, but as you have seen in previous chapters, all Linux file systems are accessed as part of a single directory tree, starting with the root directory. The root directory is always indicated by a forward slash /.

To access a file system in Linux, it must first be mounted into the root directory structure. Even the `root` file system must be mounted—although this occurs during the initialization of Linux at boot time. Other special file systems (listed in Table 8-3) are also mounted during initialization. You can set up additional file systems to be mounted during initialization, or you can mount them manually after the system has booted. The Linux directory structure always provides access to multiple file systems; each one is accessed via a different directory path. The sample setup in Figure 8-3 shows how different parts of the directory structure can be located on different physical devices.

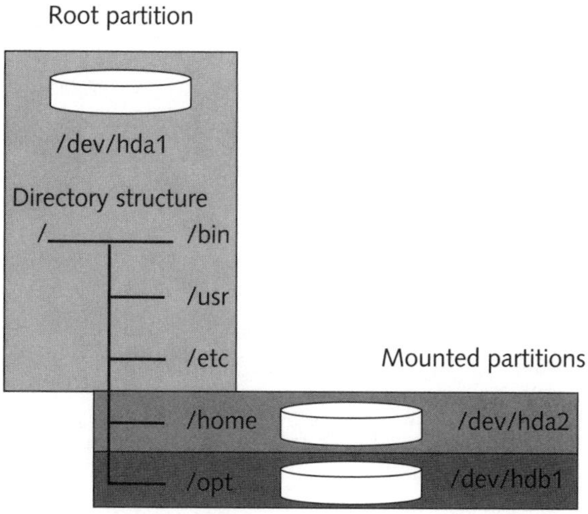

Figure 8-3   File systems mounted in the directory structure

Some of the special file systems that Linux mounts automatically after a standard installation are shown in Table 8-3. The term **mount point** refers to the path in the directory structure where the data in a file system can be accessed. The data stored within some of these file systems can be viewed using the **cat** command. This command dumps the contents of a file to STDOUT (which normally appears on the screen). For example, you can use the following command to view information within the **proc** file system:

```
cat /proc/meminfo
```

Table 8-3   Automatically Mounted File Systems

File system	Mount point	Description
swap	No mount point. This is a special file system used only by the Linux kernel.	Used to create virtual memory, allowing the Linux kernel to work as if the amount of system memory available is the sum of RAM and the swap file system.
proc	/proc	Provides up-to-date information about the kernel and all processes running on Linux.
auto	/auto	Automatically mounts a device when a request is made to the device. (This is called the automounting file system or the automount daemon—amd. It is installed automatically with most Linux systems.)
root	/	Serves as the base of a running Linux system. The root file system cannot be unmounted unless you first shut down Linux.

You use the **mount** utility to view all of the file systems currently available to the system. Using the **mount** command without any parameters displays a list of the currently mounted file systems, as follows:

```
$ mount
/dev/hda4 on / type ext2 (rw)
/dev/hda2 on none type swap (rw)
/proc on /proc type proc (rw)
brighton:(pid455) on /auto type auto
intr,rw,port=1023,timeo=8,retrans=110,indirect,map=/etc/amd.local
    dev)
```

The output from the **mount** command includes fields, from left to right, as described in the following list:

- The device where the file system is located (such as **/dev/hda4** on the first line of the output above, which refers to a hard disk partition)

- The path in the directory structure where the file system can be accessed (such as **/** on the first line of output above)

- The type of the file system, which indicates the format of data stored on the file system (**ext2** is the type on the first line above)

- The options that apply to the file system. These are described in detail in Table 8-5. The options on the first line of output above are **rw**, indicating that the file system is mounted for both reading and writing of data.

Managing Linux file systems is critical to running a successful Linux system. Although file systems as a rule don't require much day-to-day maintenance, the more people using a Linux system and the more crucial the data stored on that system, the more important it becomes to track and maintain the file systems.

The next sections describe how to manage file systems to provide disk space and stability for all Linux users. Additional information on safeguarding file systems is provided in Chapter 9. Chapter 14 describes how to back up file system data.

Checking File System Status

File systems that are used regularly tend to become disorganized and to fill up with data as users create new files. If the **root** file system of Linux becomes full, the Linux kernel cannot function and the system will crash. If the space where users' files are stored becomes full, users will not be able to complete their work.

By using the **df** utility at a Linux command line, you can display the file systems that are mounted in Linux and see the space used on each one. The **df** utility only displays regular file systems, not special file systems like /proc. The following sample output from **df** shows two file systems that are dangerously full.

```
$ df
File system     1024-blocks   Used       Available  Capacity  Mounted on
/dev/hda4       956173        895614     11160      99%        /
/dev/hda3       1018329       901074     64643      93%
/opt
sundance:/a     2017438       1210459    806979     60%        /a
```

The fields output by the **df** command, from left to right, are described in the following list:

- The device where the file system is stored. This is normally either a hard disk device name or a networked location (as in the last line of the sample output).

- The number of 1 KB blocks on the device. This indicates the file system's overall size. For example, in the sample output, the size of the three devices currently mounted are approximately 1 GB, 1 GB, and 2 GB, respectively.

- The number of 1 KB blocks that are used on the device.

- The number of 1 KB blocks that are free on the device.

- The percentage of capacity reached so far (percentage full) for the device. This is the critical number. If this value is approaching 100%, action needs to be taken.

- The location in the directory structure where this device is accessed.

If a file system is becoming full, you probably won't have the luxury of shutting down the Linux system while you figure out what to do. The busier your Linux system, the quicker a file system can fill up as multiple users download files, create new documents, and so forth.

8

To understand how quickly the Capacity percentage can increase, consider this example: If the hard disk partition where a file system is located is only 1 GB in size, one percent of the file system is 10 MB, not even enough for one large application to be downloaded. If you have a 100 GB file system, one percent is 1 GB, which may be enough space to continue running for a short time. Of course, if you need 100 GB of storage, you can probably use 1 GB quite rapidly. The df command run on a major ISP might look more like the following example. After reviewing this, you should be able to see why larger systems require more careful maintenance procedures to keep them running smoothly.

File system	1024-blocks	Used	Available	Capacity	Mounted on
/dev/dsk/c0t3d0s0	229610	110187	119423	48%	/
/dev/dsk/c0t3d0s6	306954	245175	61779	80%	/usr
/dev/dsk/c0t0d0s0	5783718	3378119	2405599	58%	/var
/dev/dsk/c0t1d0s7	2663048	1983612	679436	75%	/space1
/dev/dsk/c0t1d0s6	533992	232744	301248	44%	/usr/local
nfs.isp.com:/home	69837128	42182931	27654197	60%	/home
mail.isp.com:/var/mail	10766840	8172635	2594205	76%	/var/mail

If you see that a file system is nearing capacity, you can immediately free space by performing one of the actions in the following list. Remember, however, that you must free space in the directories where the file system is mounted. For example, if you have a separate device such as a hard disk partition mounted at the /home directory and the partition is almost full, you must free space in /home or its subdirectories. Freeing space in /tmp won't help.

■ Look for large or numerous files in the /tmp directory that can be deleted.

■ Look for large or numerous files in the /var subdirectories, especially in tmp/ and spool/.

■ Move the system log file (/var/log/messages) to another file system that isn't as full.

■ See if any of the user subdirectories are using an inordinate amount of disk space.

■ Consider deleting unused archive files that are backed up or even applications that you can reinstall later when space is not critically short.

While you need to be very careful as you delete files, you may have to act quickly in response to an overly full file system. In using the techniques just listed, the du utility can be a big help. The du utility provides disk usage information on a directory tree. When you run du at a Linux command line, you see a summary report of the space used by that directory and each of its subdirectories. A few sample lines from the output of du are shown here:

```
$ du
22          ./public_html
2228        ./Public/shell_programming
2229        ./Public
2           ./Desktop/Autostart
2           ./Desktop/Trash
8           ./Desktop/Templates
13          ./Desktop
1           ./.kde/share/apps/kfm/tmp
1           ./.kde/share/apps/kfm/bookmarks
6           ./.kde/share/apps/kfm
1           ./.kde/share/apps/kppp/Rules
1           ./.kde/share/apps/kppp/Log
3           ./.kde/share/apps/kppp
10          ./.kde/share/apps
15          ./.kde/share/config
1           ./.kde/share/icons/mini
2           ./.kde/share/icons
1           ./.kde/share/applnk
1           ./.kde/share/mimelnk
30          ./.kde/share
31          ./.kde
1           ./archive
2337        .
```

The number at the far left indicates how many 1 KB blocks are used by the subdirectory. Every subdirectory is shown separately, with totals for the parent directory. For example, the line showing 13 KB for the Desktop directory includes the sum of the /Desktop/Autostart directory, the /Desktop/Trash directory, and the /Desktop/Templates directory, as well as any files located in the Desktop directory itself. So by looking at the last line (the period indicates the current directory), you can see how much space is used by the entire directory tree. More importantly, if you need to manage how space is used on a file system, you can see which subdirectories are consuming space, even if they are buried deep in the directory structure.

Suppose you wanted to see if any single home directory consumed more than 10 MB of space. The output of the du command is given in KB, so we calculate that 10 MB is equal to roughly 10,000 KB of space. The following commands would change you to the home directories (on most Linux systems—the location is configurable) and list any large directories for you:

```
$ cd /home
$ du | grep ^....[0-9]
```

If any line of the output of du starts with a number with more than four digits, `grep` will print that line, showing you the oversized subdirectory. The output of the above command might look like this:

```
72529   ./nwells/images/NASA_mars/
10218   ./nwells/database/archive/
21749   ./rsolomon/doc/HTML/
```

Running du on the root directory of a large system can take some time (and slow down everyone else's work). Any directory that contains thousands of files or hundreds of subdirectories requires some time for the du command to process.

To avoid drains on the system, consider using the du command in the middle of the night or at some other time when no one is using the system. Make it a practice to update a file containing the output of du each night. Then you can quickly search that file for overly large directories—directories that may require your attention (in the form of deleting or archiving files) if space becomes scarce.

In addition to using the du command, you can employ various graphical tools and system administration scripts that will automatically alert you to a file system that is approaching a threshold you specify. In Chapter 12, you will learn how to schedule tasks (such as running du) for the middle of the night, using simple programs called shell scripts.

Creating New File Systems

As a Linux system grows, it will usually require additional storage space. As you will learn in Chapter 14, you can use archive systems to remove unused information and then store this data on compact disc, streaming tape, or other devices. Nevertheless, the amount of "live" storage needed often grows to exceed the administrator's original expectations. In fact, part of planning a Linux system in an organization is knowing in advance what steps will be taken when the system must be expanded. If these steps are outlined in advance, a system administrator is less likely to make choices that create obstacles to efficient system upgrades later on.

Adding a file system generally means adding a hard disk device to your system and making that hard disk available to Linux by formatting and mounting it. This process is similar to part of the Linux installation process. Because the installation utility takes care of some details described in this section, however, the steps described here may not be familiar to you. In this section you will learn how to make additional file systems stored on a hard disk, CD-ROM, or other device into active parts of your Linux directory structure.

You can install new file systems that are permanent (loaded each time you boot Linux) or temporary (loaded only occasionally as needed). File systems can be stored on a device with removable media (such as a cartridge) or fixed media (such as a hard disk). Some of the devices you might install on your computer are listed below. Data can be stored on any of these devices:

- CD-ROM drives

- CD writers

- DVD compact disc drives

- Tape drives
- Hard disks
- Iomega Zip and Jaz drives
- Other special removable cartridge devices

These devices can be connected to the computer's system board via an IDE interface, a SCSI interface, or by other proprietary expansion cards.

 Linux can use the Network File System (NFS) to access file systems on other computers (that is, to access hard disks located on remote systems). It can also use NFS to mount such remote file systems as part of the local root file system. Many techniques described in this section apply to managing remote file systems. However, the details of using NFS are beyond the scope of this book.

The steps involved in installing a new hard disk in your Linux-based computer are beyond the scope of this book. You should consult your hardware manual for detailed guidelines. Once the hard disk is installed, you can use the Linux `fdisk` command to examine its partitions, creating new partitions for use by Linux if needed. Before any hard disk can be used as a native Linux file system, it must have Linux partitions defined. You learned about using the `fdisk` utility to create Linux partitions as you installed Linux. The `fdisk` utility can be used in the same way to prepare new devices installed on your system.

 Devices with removable media such as Iomega Jaz disks and CD-ROM drives cannot have multiple partitions. With such devices, you can proceed directly to formatting the device for use by Linux.

Almost all file system devices use either an IDE or SCSI interface to communicate with your computer. Devices connected to these interfaces use standardized device names in Linux. Table 8-4 provides some examples designed to help you determine the correct name for a device. All IDE and SCSI devices are accessed via the /dev subdirectory.

Table 8-4   Example Linux Device Names

Device	Description
/dev/hda	The first IDE device
/dev/hdb	The second IDE device
/dev/hdc	The third IDE device (often a CD-ROM drive)
/dev/hda1	The first partition on the first IDE device
/dev/hdb3	The third partition on the second IDE hard disk
/dev/sda	The first SCSI device
/dev/sdb	The second SCSI device
/dev/sda4	The fourth partition on the first SCSI hard disk
/dev/sdc1	The first partition on the third SCSI hard disk

For example, you can use the `fdisk` utility to set up partitions on a standard SCSI hard disk using this command:

```
/sbin/fdisk  /dev/sdb
```

Once the `fdisk` utility has started, the `p` command in `fdisk` shows you the existing partition table; the `n` command starts the process of defining a new partition if you need to create a Linux partition on the new device. As you'll recall from installing Linux, the partition number is added to the device name. For example, if you create two partitions on the second SCSI hard disk, they are accessed as devices `/dev/sdb1` and `/dev/sdb2`.

If your device uses a special interface (not IDE or SCSI), Linux may already provide support for the device. In some cases you will need to contact the manufacturer to ask about Linux support. Alternatively, you can query a Linux mailing list or newsgroup to see if others have successfully used the device on a Linux system.

The extended file system 2 (`ext2`) is the default or native file system used by Linux. Once you have created the Linux partitions, you need to format the partition with the `ext2` file system. The command to create a new `ext2` file system is **mke2fs** (for *make ext2 file system*). This command formats the partition, erasing all information on it, and organizes space for data to be recorded so that the partition can be used by Linux. The command is as simple to use as adding the device name as a parameter:

```
/sbin/mke2fs /dev/sdb2
```

To format a hard disk partition, you may also use the **mkfs** program. This program requires a parameter to indicate the type of file system being created. The `mkfs` command simply starts the `mke2fs` command. This is an example of using the `mkfs` command to format a Linux file system:

```
/sbin/mkfs -t ext2 /dev/sdb2
```

When you format an `ext2` file system, you see many lines of output on the screen as the program lists all of the structure information that is being written to the device. In any case, formatting even a large hard drive is quite fast. On a Pentium system, using `mke2fs` on a 4 GB partition normally takes less than one minute to complete.

 You can use a special command called **fdformat** to format floppy disks. This command is rarely used, however, because all floppy disks are preformatted; the man page provides detailed information.

Mounting File Systems

After a new file system has been created (that is, formatted), it can be mounted as part of the Linux directory structure and accessed just like the existing Linux partitions. To add a new file system, you must create a directory as a mount point, which is a place in the directory structure where the file system can be accessed. Once you have created a directory to use as a mount point, use the mount command to activate the file system.

To create a directory, use the `mkdir` command and define the directory that you have chosen as an access point for the new file system. For example, if the new hard disk is intended as a document archive for your office, you could create a directory called `/archive`. If the new file system will be used for a database system and all applications are currently stored in the `/opt` directory, you might define the `/opt/db` directory as a mount point. The command would be:

```
mkdir /opt/db
```

After you create the directory, it is empty—it's just another directory on your root file system. The next step is to use the `mount` command to instruct Linux to access the new file system whenever you go to the `/opt/db` directory. The `mount` command can be complex. This is how the command would look using the example values used so far:

```
mount -t ext2 /dev/sdb2 /opt/db
```

This command says: mount a file system of type `ext2` (Linux native) located on the device `/dev/sdb2`, and make it accessible on the directory `/opt/db`.

Now when you go to the `/opt/db` directory, you'll find that it is no longer empty. Instead, it contains a directory with a strange-looking name: `lost+found`. The `lost+found` directory is placed in the beginning of all new `ext2` file systems. This directory is initially empty, but when you use disk–checking utilities (described in Chapter 9), files may be created in the `lost+found` directory. You will very rarely see anything in this directory, but don't delete it. The presence of the `lost+found` directory indicates that the new file system has been mounted successfully.

You can also use the `mount` command without any parameters to display a list of all mounted file systems, as shown earlier in this chapter. If you used the `mount` command alone in the previous example, the list of mounted file systems would include the `/dev/sdb2` device mounted on `/opt/db`.

The standard devices that are included when you install Linux generally have a mount point directory already created for them. For example, the floppy disk drive and CD-ROM drive are normally mounted to `/mnt/floppy` and `/mnt/cdrom`, respectively. These directories are created when Linux is installed. You can mount a CD-ROM by using this command, including the mount point as a parameter:

```
mount /mnt/cdrom
```

You can mount a floppy disk with this command:

```
mount /mnt/floppy
```

Why don't these commands include the information in the `mount` command given previously, such as a file system type and device name? You'll learn the answer shortly, in the section "Automating File System Mounting."

Once you have mounted a floppy disk or CD-ROM, you should not eject the disk or CD-ROM until you have unmounted the file system. If you do, Linux may not be able to access that device for a time.

Unmounting File Systems

To unmount a file system, use the **umount** command with the device name or mount point. For example, to unmount a floppy disk, you might use this command (depending on the mount point defined on your Linux system):

```
umount /mnt/floppy
```

To unmount a CD-ROM, the command might be:

```
umount /mnt/cdrom
```

Similarly, to unmount a hard disk partition such as the one described in the previous section, the command would be:

```
umount /opt/db
```

 TIP The command name is umount, not unmount. If you see errors when you attempt to unmount a file system, look for an extra n in the command.

Keep in mind that a file system cannot be in use when you unmount it. If any users on the Linux system are working with a file on the file system, or if any user's current working directory is located on that file system, the **umount** command will fail, and it will indicate that the file system is busy. The Linux kernel stores information about each mounted file system that includes the number of files currently being accessed. All users must stop using files on the file system and change their current working directory to a location outside the file system before you can unmount that file system.

Automating File System Mounting

As a system administrator, you'll want to automate everything that you can. Ideally, your systems should be as self-sustaining as possible, leaving you free for tasks that require new analysis and problem-solving skills. As you saw earlier, several types of file systems are mounted automatically when you start Linux. The new file systems that you create from additional hard disks or other devices can also be automatically mounted at boot time. Thus, you never need to enter the **mount** command after rebooting.

The key to automounting file systems is the **/etc/fstab** configuration file. This file contains a line for each file system that you want to have automounted when Linux boots. It also contains a line for file systems that you want to mount later on without providing all of the file system information in the `mount` command. A typical default `fstab` configuration file is shown here:

```
/dev/hda3     /              ext2      defaults          1  1
/dev/hda4     /archive       ext2      defaults,noauto   1  0
/dev/hda2     swap           swap      defaults          0  0
/dev/fd0      /mnt/floppy    ext2      noauto            0  0
/dev/cdrom    /mnt/cdrom     iso9660   noauto,ro         0  0
none          /proc          proc      defaults          0  0
```

The fields of this configuration file, from left to right, are described in the following list:

- The device where the file system is located. Most of the devices in this example file are IDE hard disks; the floppy drive and CD-ROM drive have other device names; the `proc` file system has none.

- The mount point in the directory structure where the device will be accessed after being mounted. Each file system has a mount point directory except the `swap` file system, which is only used by the Linux kernel.

- The file system type. Most of the examples shown are `ext2`, the Linux native file system. `iso9660` is the CD-ROM standard; `proc` and `swap` are special file system types.

- Options that apply when this file system is mounted. You will learn more about these options later in this section.

- Whether the file system can respond to the `dump` command (this command is called `dumpe2fs` in Linux). A `1` in this field indicates that the `dumpe2fs` command can be used to print information on the structure of the file system. Only standard `ext2` hard disk partitions should have this field set to `1`.

- The order used to check file systems when Linux is booted. Each time Linux starts, it checks the file systems in `fstab` before mounting them. The `root` file system (`/dev/hda3` above) should be numbered 1; other `ext2` file systems should be numbered 2. If 0 is used, the file system is not checked. All file systems that are not automounted can have 0 in this field.

8

The most powerful part of this configuration file is the options field. The options used to mount file systems are an effective way to increase security and ease system administration work. Key settings for the options field are described in Table 8-5.

Table 8-5   Important Option Field Settings

Mount option	Description
`async`	Specifies that all reads and writes to the file system should be asynchronous—in other words, that information will be buffered (stored in memory) to improve access speed.
`auto`	Specifies that the file system should be automatically mounted at boot time or when the `mount` command is used with the `-a` option.
`dev`	Designates the file system as a special device in the `/dev` directory.
`exec`	Permits programs stored on the file system to be executed.
`noauto`	Indicates that this file system should not be automatically mounted. Instead, the file system must be mounted by an explicit `mount` command.
`noexec`	Indicates that programs stored on the file system cannot be executed.
`nouser`	Specifies that no regular users can mount the file system; instead, only `root` can mount it.
`ro`	Mounts the file system as read-only, which means no data can be written to it.
`rw`	Mounts the file system as read/write—the standard mode in which data can be written to the file system.
`suid`	Allows special user ID permissions to be used on this file system.
`user`	Allows a regular user to mount the file system. This is useful if you are running a desktop Linux system and don't want to switch to the `root` user account to mount a floppy or CD-ROM.
`users`	Functions the same as the `user` option except that any user can unmount the device.
`defaults`	Includes the options `rw`, `suid`, `dev`, `exec`, `auto`, `nouser`, and `async`.

TIP

> When removable media such as a CD-ROM is mounted, the Eject function of the drive is disabled (until the device is unmounted). Keep in mind that this is not true of floppy disk drives, which means it is possible for a user to eject a floppy disk while it is still mounted. This can cause problems, resulting in lost data. For example, files will still be marked as open even though they cannot be accessed. Although the `user` option in Table 8-5 is appropriate for some situations, it may create the problem noted here if users are not aware of the need to unmount devices before ejecting media.

Additional (less commonly used) options are described in the manual page for the `mount` command. Two important additional points about the options in the `fstab` file must be mentioned. First, the last options listed on each line of the `fstab` file override any earlier options used on the same line. For example, if the options list includes `defaults, user`, the `user` option overrides the `nouser` option that is part of `defaults`. Second, the options can be added to the `mount` command by using the `-o` parameter. For example:

```
mount -t ext2 -o defaults /dev/sdb2 /opt/db
```

Let's walk through two examples of how you might add a line to the `fstab` file to automate file system mounting. As a first example, suppose you had set up a large SCSI hard disk to hold a database application. You want the database file system to be mounted automatically when you start Linux. Users should not be able to run programs or modify the file system configuration. For this situation, the `fstab` line might look like:

```
/dev/sdb2   /opt/db     ext2   defaults,noexec,nosuid  1   2
```

As a second example, suppose you are using Linux as your desktop workstation and have installed a new DVD drive. The device shouldn't be mounted at boot time because you don't normally keep a DVD disk in the drive, but you want to be able to mount the device without changing to the `root` user account. You also want to protect any writeable DVD disks from having any data damaged. You might use this line in the `fstab` file:

```
/dev/hdd /mnt/dvd  iso9660    ro,noauto,user    0 0
```

Once you have the `fstab` file set up, you can use the `mount` command with only the device name or mount point. The `mount` command looks in the `fstab` file for all of the additional information needed to mount the file system. For example, the CD-ROM device is normally configured in `fstab` after a Linux installation. The CD-ROM can thus be mounted with this command:

```
mount /mnt/cdrom
```

No additional information is needed on the command line because `mount` retrieves everything else from the `fstab` file. If you use the `mount` command without sufficient information (and the information is not contained in the `fstab` file), an error message is displayed and the file system is not mounted.

The `mount` command does only minimal checking when a file system is first mounted. This means that Linux may allow you to proceed with a `mount` operation that appears to provide access to a file system, when in fact the file system is not supported. As you begin using the file system, Linux may discover the problem, and display an error message such as **not a valid block device**.

8

Nevertheless, Linux supports many different file systems. If you have partitions on your computer's hard disks that use any of the file system types listed in Table 8-6, you can access them directly from Linux by mounting them. Support for each of these file system types may be built into your Linux kernel, or you may need to load a kernel module to enable support for a specific file system type. The module you load provides back-end support in the kernel for a specific file system type.

Table 8-6   File System Types Supported by Linux

File system	Description
ext2	The native Linux file system type.
minix	File system used by the Minix operating system.
msdos	File system used by DOS and older Microsoft Windows systems. Note that this file system is also called the FAT file system, but the msdos name must be used with the mount command and with the fstab file.
hpfs	The High Performance File System used by OS/2.
iso9660	File system used on CD-ROMs.
nfs	The Network File System, used to allow networked computers to access remote hard disks as part of a local directory structure.
smbfs	File system used to mount SMB network devices such as networked Windows computers. This file system type is part of the Samba suite. (For more information, see www.samba.org.)
vfat	File system used by Windows 98; also known as the FAT32 file system. Provides long filename support when reading Windows partitions from Linux.
ntfs	File system used by Windows NT. This file system requires kernel configuration that is normally not enabled by default.
sysv	A standard UNIX System V file system.
qnx4	File system used by the QNX operating system.
coherent	File system used by the Coherent UNIX operating system.
ufs	A UNIX file system type.
xenix	File system used by the Xenix operating system, a variant of UNIX.

TIP   The msdos file system type provides access to DOS or Windows file systems. Because these file system types do not provide the same features as more robust file systems such as ext2, the back-end to the msdos file system within the kernel maps features between msdos file systems and Linux. For example, the end-of-line characters are different in DOS files and Linux files. Linux also has additional file attributes compared to DOS. The msdos file system back-end maps between these differences to make msdos files usable in Linux.

Managing Swap Space

As mentioned in Table 8-3, the `swap` file system (often called the swap space) is a special file system type used by the Linux kernel for virtual memory. **Virtual memory** is a kind of memory that is used like standard RAM; however, information in virtual memory is stored on a hard disk instead. The swap file system is set up during Linux installation and activated (via the `fstab` file) each time Linux boots.

The swap space is normally a separate hard disk partition. This allows the most efficient access by the Linux kernel. For systems without an available partition for the swap space, a file on the regular `ext2` file system can be designated as the swap space instead. However, this technique degrades performance and should only be implemented on a system set up for testing Linux.

In some Linux systems, the maximum size of a swap partition is 128 MB. With today's large Linux systems, this may be insufficient. On some new Linux systems (running Linux 2.2 kernels or later versions), a swap partition can be 2 GB or larger, depending on the platform on which Linux is running.

You use the **mkswap** command to create a swap partition. This is similar to using the `mke2fs` command to create an ext2-formatted partition. If you have set up a swap partition using `fdisk` or another partitioning tool, the command would be something like this (depending on the partition you need to format as swap space):

```
mkswap /dev/hda2
```

Once you have formatted a partition as swap space, you need to add a line to the `fstab` file that tells Linux to use the swap automatically. The example file shown previously includes this line:

```
/dev/hda2        swap  swap  defaults    0 0
```

Swap space is activated by system initialization scripts during the system start-up phase. The **swapon** command is used in these scripts to activate swap space.

With large or busy systems, the swap partition should be located on a separate hard disk from the root partition or other key data partitions. If the system is large enough, a separate hard disk might even be used just for swap space. By placing the swap space on a separate hard disk, you ensure that information can be read from and written to the root or other data partitions without interfering with the kernel's efforts to move data to and from the swap area. The two (or more) hard disks can act in parallel instead of completing one operation after another. For the same reason, some Linux system administrators set up multiple swap partitions to take advantage of parallel hard disk accesses. Multiple swap partitions were sometimes needed in older versions of Linux to overcome the 128 MB limit, but they may still be used to achieve speed increases by having the kernel access multiple hard disks in parallel. Linux supports up to eight distinct swap areas. Each one can be created using the **mkswap** command and included in the `fstab` file to be activated at boot time.

8

The status of swap space (or virtual memory) can be viewed using the **free** command. Following is a typical example of output from this command:

	total	used	free	shared	buffers	cached
Mem:	30820	28768	2052	16852	11860	7104
-/+ buffers/ cache:		9804	21016			
Swap:	130748	1248	129500			

Note the `total` and `free` columns. `Mem` refers to RAM memory; `Swap` refers to swap space. On the small system shown here, a total of about 32 MB of RAM and 130 MB of swap space are available on the system. Very little of the swap space is used, and most of the RAM is free also (21 MB). As the system becomes busy, the free memory will drop to zero, and the swap space will be used.

Because swap space is located on a hard disk, it is significantly slower to access than the RAM on your system board. Because of this, you may at first want to avoid using it by installing enough RAM so that the Linux kernel never needs to save information in the swap space. In truth, both RAM and swap space are useful. A typical system should have at least as much swap space as RAM. The reason for this is that the Linux kernel will attempt to cache (store) in RAM as many files and programs as possible in order to increase the system speed. But if many users on a system are working with many programs, it's likely that not all programs will be active at the same time. Rather than have these programs use RAM, they can be placed in the swap space while they are inactive. On a well-tuned system, the kernel can quickly bring these programs back into memory when a user needs them—so quickly that most users won't notice any delay.

Another reason to make wise use of swap space is cost. Swap space (that is, hard disk space) is so much cheaper than RAM that in many situations adding more swap space is more cost effective than adding RAM.

However, while swap space is an important part of your system, its advantages diminish on systems with insufficient RAM. On systems with too little RAM, the swap space will be overused. This means that a single program might be moved to the swap space and back into system memory several times per second, as it competes with other programs for processor time. The time required to move information to and from the swap space greatly reduces the efficiency of the system. This problem is called **thrashing**. To solve this problem you need to reduce the system load or add more system RAM.

To see detailed information about how the swap space is used, try the **vmstat** command (for *virtual memory statistics*). The output of this command is cryptic and requires careful study of the relevant manual page. (See also Chapter 10.) The output of **vmstat** provides information on which processes are using swap space, how much space they are using, what is waiting to happen when RAM is available, and so forth.

If the Linux kernel runs out of swap space (in which case it runs out of memory), the kernel may crash. This very rarely happens, but the possibility is reason enough for monitoring swap space use.

SIMPLE TASK MANAGEMENT

In Chapter 7 you learned that the **ps** command can be used to list the processes running on Linux. In the sections that follow, you will learn more about how to control those processes. Additional detail on managing the CPU load via other utilities is provided in Chapter 10.

Job Control in the Shell

Often you will want to start multiple programs from the command line at the same time. These might include an editor, a script you have written, an e-mail reader, and perhaps other programs as well. Although Linux can easily run many applications (processes) at the same time, you must learn to control all of these processes from a single command line. Most of the tools for doing this are part of the **shell**, or command interpreter. Because the default shell for Linux is **bash**, commands described in this section apply to the **bash** shell. Other shells such as ksh, csh, tcsh, and zsh support similar features.

You may choose to work in command-line windows within a graphical display, in which case you can open multiple windows to start multiple programs. You may also use the virtual consoles described in the next section. On occasion, however, you will need to manage multiple programs from a single command line. This discussion also helps you understand how processes are managed and how the shell operates.

Processes

When you start a program, that program takes control of the command line where you are working. For example, if you enter the command

```
man ps
```

the man page appears, and you no longer see a prompt where you can enter additional commands. Some commands don't display screen output like the man page viewer, but they still leave you without an active prompt to enter additional commands.

If you type an ampersand after the name of a command, the shell places the process in the background—in other words, the process continues to run, but it doesn't control the command line. You can then start another command immediately. Multiple processes started from a single shell are called jobs.

Jobs

A job is simply a process that is associated with a single shell or command-line environment. You can use the command **jobs** to list all jobs or processes that are running from the current shell.

Use the Ctrl+Z key combination to suspend a job. This key combination is useful if you have started a command that is controlling the command line and you want to interrupt it so that you can use the **bg** command to place it in the background. A suspended job is not ended, but it stops running normally. It waits for further instructions before beginning normal execution again. You can use the `jobs` command to see which processes are currently suspended, as in the following output:

```
$ jobs
[1]+  Stopped (signal)           top
```

The output of the jobs command shown above includes a job number at the left of the line (1 in the output above). The process ID number is not shown by the `jobs` command. When a job is suspended, you can either place it in the background (restart it without displaying output to the current console) or place it in the foreground (allow it to take control of the screen again). Figure 8-4 shows how a single command-line window can start and manage multiple processes (or jobs).

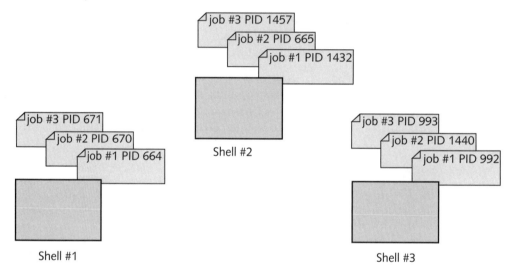

Figure 8-4 Multiple jobs running from one shell

The commands used to place a job in the background or foreground after it has been started are **bg** and **fg**. To use the **bg** or **fg** command, you must know the job number assigned by the current shell. You can find this number by using the `jobs` command.

The following steps show how the **bg** and **fg** commands work:

1. At any Linux command line, enter the command **man ls**. The manual page for the `ls` command appears.

2. Press **Ctrl+Z** and then **Enter**. You see the following message (the number at left may be different on your system):

```
[4]+  Stopped                man ls
```

3. Enter the command **man ps**. The manual page for the **ps** command appears.

4. Press **Ctrl+Z** and then **Enter**. You see the following message (the number at left may be different on your system):

```
[5]+  Stopped                man ps
```

5. Enter the command **jobs**. You see output like the following:

```
[4]+   Stopped              man ls
[5]+   Stopped              man ps
```

6. Enter the command **fg %4**. (Use the number at the left of the first output line from the jobs command—on your system it may not be 4.) The `ls` manual page appears again.

7. Press **q** to end the man `ls` command.

8. Enter the `jobs` command again. You see that the man `ls` command is no longer listed.

> **TIP** Some commands (including the `man` command) are only used to display information. Placing a command-line `man` in the background with the `bg` command automatically suspends the command. It only runs in the foreground.

8

You can also use the process ID number in the **fg** or **bg** command. Just use the number without the percentage sign. For example, suppose a process you have started is job number 3 in the current shell and has a PID of 725. You can bring the process to the foreground with either of these commands:

```
fg %3

fg 725
```

Using Virtual Consoles

As you learned in Chapter 4, you can open multiple command-line windows within a graphical environment. When you are not working in a graphical environment, you can use virtual consoles in Linux to start multiple command-line sessions at the same time. A **virtual console** is a separate login screen that you access by pressing a combination of keys on your keyboard. A virtual console allows you to start several separate login sessions in Linux from the same computer.

> **TIP** Networked Linux systems allow many users to log in using a network connection. Virtual consoles provide the same type of login functionality without a network connection.

When the graphical mode is not active, you access a new virtual console by pressing Alt+F2. This displays a new login prompt, where you can log in using any valid username and password. Any commands that you start from this virtual console run independently of those on other virtual consoles. Each console starts a separate copy of the **bash** shell, so the **jobs** command will only list jobs started in one virtual console, even if you have logged in using the same username.

To switch back to your first virtual console, press Alt+F1. Most Linux systems have six virtual consoles. They can be accessed by pressing Alt+F1 for the first virtual console, Alt+F2 for the second, and so on, to Alt+F6 for the sixth virtual console. A graphical system normally appears on a seventh virtual console, which you can display by pressing Alt+F7.

When the graphical environment is running, you can switch to the nongraphical virtual consoles by pressing Ctrl+Alt+F1 for the first virtual console, and so on, to Ctrl+Alt+F6 for the sixth virtual console.

Learning About Processes

The **ps** command that was introduced in Chapter 7 includes many additional options to help you learn about what is happening on your Linux system from moment to moment. A simple **ps** command shows you only the commands that you have started in the current command-line environment (also called the current terminal):

```
$ ps
PID TTY          TIME CMD
  576 tty1     00:00:00 login
  584 tty1     00:00:00 bash
  946 tty1     00:00:00 top
  951 tty1     00:00:00 ps
```

Although this is useful, it doesn't provide much more information than the **jobs** command. As a system administrator, you need access to the details provided by the **ps** command options. For instance, the **a** and **x** options show you the processes started by all users, as well as those that were started by the system at boot time (or other processes that have no controlling **tty** where they were started).

This is a much longer list than that provided by the **ps** command without any options, and it includes all of the system-level daemons that are running in the background as you work on Linux. For example, the **login** command running on other virtual consoles, the Web server (called **httpd**), the system logging daemon, and possibly an e-mail server will all appear in the list. By adding the u option to the **ps** command, you can also see information about how each process is using your Linux system. This command is shown here with its output sent to the **less** command. By using the **less** command, you can use the Page Up and Page Down keys to view the many lines of output. The first few lines of output are shown after the command:

```
$ ps aux | less
USER       PID %CPU %MEM  SIZE   RSS TTY STAT START   TIME COMMAND
bin        381  0.0  0.9   840   300  ?  S    13:32   0:00 rpc.portmap
daemon     451  0.0  1.9  1156   596  ?  S    13:32   0:00 lpd
daemon     471  0.0  1.0   828   324  ?  S    13:32   0:00 atd
nobody     845  0.0  2.5  1384   784  ?  S    13:32   0:00 httpd -f
nobody     846  0.0  2.5  1384   784  ?  S    13:32   0:00 httpd -f
root         1  0.0  1.0   828   332  ?  S    13:31   0:04 init
root         2  0.0  0.0     0     0  ?  SW   13:31   0:00 (kflushd)
root         3  0.0  0.0     0     0  ?  SW   13:31   0:00 (kpiod)
```

In the first lines of the output shown above, you see column headings indicating which user started the process, the percentage of CPU time and memory used by the process, the terminal that the process is running on, status, and other information. The most important part of this information is the process ID number, or PID. With this number, you can control the process using other Linux commands.

You can use the **f** option to display the relationship between different processes, showing which process started which other processes. The following command uses the **f** option along with the **a** and **x** options, in order to display all the processes on the system (the output has been shortened to save space here, however):

```
$ ps axf
PID TTY         STAT    TIME COMMAND
    1 ?         S       0:04 init
    2 ?         SW      0:00 [kflushd]
    3 ?         SW      0:00 [kpiod]
  535           S       0:00 sendmail: accepting connections: p
  550 ?         S       0:00 gpm -t ps/2
  564 ?         S       0:00 httpd
  568 ?         S       0:00  \_ httpd
  571 ?         S       0:00  \_ httpd
  577 ?         S       0:00  \_ httpd
  594 ?         S       0:00 xfs
  638 tty2      S       0:00 login -- root
  664 tty2      S       0:00  \_ -bash
  676 tty2      T       0:00       \_ man ls
  677 tty2      T       0:00       |   \_ sh -c /bin/gunzip
  678 tty2      T       0:00       |       \_ /bin/gunzip
  679 tty2      T       0:00       |       \_ /usr/bin/less -is
  680 tty2      T       0:00       \_ top
  686 tty2      R       0:00       \_ ps axf
  639 tty3      S       0:00 /sbin/mingetty tty3
  642 tty6      S       0:00 /sbin/mingetty tty6
  644 ?         S       0:00 update (bdflush)
```

As you can see, the processes are presented in a tree diagram. This output shows which processes were started by other processes. For example, process ID (PID) 638 (see the left column of the output above) is the **login** command, where a user has logged in as **root**. The login process started a **bash** shell (the next line in the output, process 664). The **root** user started several commands within the shell, including **man ls** (PID 676), **top** (PID 680), and the **ps** command (PID 686). The **man** command started other commands to uncompress the manual page file. Many processes were started by the Linux kernel when the system was booted. These processes appear without any tree structure.

Before you can successfully control process operation and manage your Linux CPU and memory resources, you need to understand how processes are related to one another. Each process has a parent process—that is, the process that started it. A parent process can have many child processes. The first process started on a Linux system is called **init**. This process is the parent to all processes and has a PID number of 1.

Controlling Processes

You can use the **jobs**, **fg**, and **bg** commands to control processes (jobs) that were started within a single shell. By using the **kill** command, you can control all processes on the system. The name of this command is a little unfortunate. Although it is often used to kill, or end, processes, it actually is used to send signals to processes. Some of those signals end the process; others serve different purposes, such as suspending a process or causing a program to reread its configuration file.

 TIP   You must be logged in as the **root** user to control processes that you didn't start.

Signals are messages that are sent to a process. The full list of signals contains about 30 messages, but most of these are not used regularly. Each signal has a name and a number associated with it. To see a cryptic list of all the signals, use the **kill** command with the **-l** option (for list), as follows:

```
kill -l
```

When writing a program, the developer decides which signals the program will respond to. Some programs only respond to one or two signals. Others may respond to more signals, depending on the purpose of the program. For example, a program designed to control your computer in the event of a power failure will respond to the signal from a power supply indicating that the main power is out. Other programs wouldn't respond to this signal.

Almost all programs respond to the SIGTERM signal (signal number 15). This signal requests that the program end. Another special signal is SIGKILL (signal number 9). The SIGKILL signal is not handled by the program itself. Instead, if you send a SIGKILL using the **kill** command, the Linux kernel shuts down the process automatically. Any unsaved data in a program will be lost when the SIGKILL signal is used to end the process. As a rule, you should use the SIGTERM signal (rather than the SIGKILL signal) to shut down processes, because SIGTERM requests that a program close itself, giving the program a chance to clean up its work, close any open files, and so forth, before ending. When you use a SIGKILL, the process is cut off before it can do any of those things. However, SIGKILL is very useful when a process is not responding to the SIGTERM signal.

To see how the **kill** command is used, suppose a user on your Linux system had started a program called **myeditor**. The program appears to have stopped working but is still running in the background. You would use the following **ps** command to see that state of the process:

```
ps ax | grep myeditor
```

The single-line output of this command includes only the process for the **myeditor** program with the PID number for the process. Using this information, you can send a signal to the process (because the user in question started the process, he could also use the **kill** command to send the signal):

```
kill -15 1482
```

By sending the SIGTERM signal in this way, you send a request to the **myeditor** program to close. The command could also be written using the name of the signal:

```
kill -SIGTERM 1482
```

If the program does not respond to the request to terminate (you still see it in the list of processes from the **ps** command), you can send a SIGKILL signal that will cause the Linux kernel to end the process immediately:

```
kill -9 1482
```

 Before you can send a process a signal, you must obtain the correct process ID for the process by using the ps command.

A special form of the **kill** command is the command named **killall**. This command is used to send a signal to all processes that were started by commands of the same name. This is useful when a program is starting copies of itself faster than you can locate the PIDs and use **kill** to end them. If the **myeditor** program were doing this, you could use this command:

```
killall -9 myeditor
```

Always be careful using **killall**. If you are running multiple programs of the same name and only one needs to be sent a signal, do not use **killall** because it will end all of the processes. Instead, determine the PID of the specific copy of the program that needs to be ended. Then use the **kill** command rather than **killall**.

This section has provided only an introduction to the concepts and commands used to control processes in Linux. In Chapter 10 you will learn how to manage the load on your Linux system by allocating time and disk space to processes and tracking how busy your Linux system is to see if additional hardware resources may be required to handle the load.

CHAPTER SUMMARY

- ❏ A Linux system administrator must perform some basic tasks regularly to keep the system running smoothly. These tasks include user management, file system management, and process management.

- ❏ User management involves defining user environments, creating user accounts, and managing modifications to those accounts as required by the system or requested by the user. Maintaining user accounts is an important part of system security.

- ❏ File system management provides stability and performance for your Linux system. Each file system must be tracked to see how it is being used and when new hardware resources need to be added to handle the system's load. Working with file systems must be done carefully to avoid damaging data.

- ❏ To manage processes, you use commands to examine all the processes on the Linux system and send various signals to control how those processes behave. The **root** user can control all processes, suspending or stopping any process.

KEY TERMS

alias — Command used to create a text substitution in a command-line shell, effectively giving any Linux command a new name.

bash — Short for Bourne again shell. It is the default command-line interpreter for Linux.

bashrc — Configuration file containing commands that are executed each time a user starts a new command-line environment.

bg — Command used to place a job (process) in the background (either by suspending it or by preventing its output from appearing in the current shell's terminal window), thus allowing the shell prompt to become active again.

C shell — A shell designed for ease of use more than for programming features.

cat — Command used to dump the contents of a file to STDOUT.

command interpreter — (More commonly called a shell in Linux.) A command-line environment in which a user can enter commands to be launched.

default shell — The default command-line interpreter used in most Linux systems (**bash**).

df — Short for display file systems. Command used to display file system summary information such as device, mount point, percentage used, and total capacity.

du — Short for disk usage. Command used to display disk space used by a directory and each of its subdirectories.

environment variables — Set of named values (name-value pairs) that provide information to programs running in a user's environment.

/etc/fstab — Configuration file that contains a file system table with devices, mount points, file system types, and options. Used by the mount command.

/etc/group — Configuration file in which group information (group names and membership lists) is stored.

/etc/passwd — Configuration file in which user account information is stored.

/etc/shadow — Configuration file in which encrypted user passwords and password configuration data are stored.

/etc/skel — Directory containing files that will be used to populate a new user's home directory at the time it is created.

fdformat — Command used to format a floppy disk.

fg — Command used to bring a job (process) running in a shell to the foreground so that the job controls the shell's terminal window.

file system — A collection of data, normally stored on a device such as a hard disk partition, which can be accessed in Linux via the directory structure.

group — A collection of user accounts that can be granted access to the system collectively.

groupadd — Command used to add a new group to a Linux system.

init — Linux process that initiates other key processes as the system is booting.

jobs — Command used to list jobs (processes) started in the current shell environment.

kill — Command used to send signals to processes, often to end them via a SIGTERM or SIGKILL signal.

Korn shell — A revision of the `bash` (or Bourne) shell that is popular on some UNIX systems and available in Linux as the Public Domain Korn shell, `pdksh`.

`mke2fs` — Command used to format a device such as a hard disk partition with an `ext2` file system.

`mkfs` — Command used to format devices using various file system types. The `ext2` default type for Linux file systems can be indicated as an option. *See also* `mke2fs`.

`mkswap` — Command used to format a partition as a swap space for the Linux kernel.

`mount` — Command used to make a logical or physical device available as a file system in the Linux directory structure.

mount point — The place or path in the Linux directory structure where a file system is accessed.

`ps` — Command used to obtain detailed information about processes running on Linux.

`root` — Superuser account name in Linux.

Shadow Password system — Security system used to restrict access to encrypted password text.

shell — A command-line interpreter, providing a command-line interface.

signal — A message (one of a fixed set determined by the Linux kernel) that can be sent to any process and responded to according to how that program is written.

`su` — (Short for substitute user.) Command used to take on the identity of a different user account.

superuser — The root user account, which has supervisory privileges throughout the Linux system.

`swapon` — Command used by Linux initialization scripts to activate the swap partition defined in the `/etc/fstab` file.

symbolic link — A pointer in the file system to another file.

thrashing — Excessive movement of processes between RAM and swap space, resulting in reduced system performance and excessive wear on the hard disk.

`touch` — Command used to create an empty file or to update the access time of an existing file.

`umount` — Command used to unmount a file system that is accessible as part of the Linux directory structure.

User Private Group — Security system that creates a new group containing one user when that user is first created.

`useradd` — Command used to create (add) a new user account in Linux.

`usermod` — Command used to modify or update an existing user account.

virtual memory — Memory available to the Linux kernel for running programs but which is actually located on a hard disk. Data that the Linux kernel stores in virtual memory is placed in the swap file system, or swap space.

`wheel` — Special system administrative group, not used officially in Linux.

REVIEW QUESTIONS

1. Name two reasons why you shouldn't log in as **root** unless you are doing system administration work.

2. A user's primary group can be a User Private Group. True or False?

3. The `/etc/passwd` file does *not* contain which of the following fields:

   a. The name of the user account

   b. The file privileges for the user

   c. The user's default shell

   d. A UID and GID for the user

4. Explain the meaning of this line in the `/etc/group` file:
   `webmasters:x:710:rthomas,cyang`

5. To create or change a password on any user account, the following is used:

   a. The `useradd` utility

   b. The file `/etc/shadow` with a text editor

   c. The `passwd` command

   d. The UID and GID of the user

6. The `useradd` command can be used to modify or update account information. True or False?

7. When you add a file to the `/etc/skel` directory, the file is automatically added to the home directory of all existing users. True or False?

8. A _____ defines a string of text to be substituted whenever another string of text is used on the command line.

   a. link

   b. substitution string

   c. alias

   d. symbolic link

9. The Linux command used to format a Linux `ext2` hard disk partition is:

   a. mke2fs

   b. fdisk

   c. fsck

   d. Linux does not use formatted partitions

10. List two ways in which regular user accounts differ from nonstandard user accounts that are used only by Linux programs.

11. If you enter a new password for a user account that can be easily guessed, the message **BAD PASSWORD** appears and the password is not updated. True or False?

12. Environment variables are used by nearly all users to:

    a. Provide system or user information to the programs that the user executes

    b. Make it easier to use DOS commands in a Linux environment

    c. Track system resources used by each user

    d. Record environment information as users work with system administration tools

13. Describe one simple method of temporarily disabling a user account without using a graphical utility.

14. A mounted file system is one that:

    a. Has been included as part of the Linux directory structure

    b. Has been correctly formatted for use in Linux

    c. Allows any user to run programs located on it

    d. Includes at least a `root` user account

15. Describe the value of multiple virtual consoles in Linux.

16. The Shadow Password system enhances Linux security by:

    a. Validating members of the `wheel` group as they log in

    b. Hiding encrypted passwords in a file that only `root` can read

    c. Checking that new passwords entered for users are not easily guessed

    d. Stopping unauthorized users from accessing the `root` account

17. Which of the following is *not* a good way to create a new user account:

    a. Use the `useradd` command.

    b. Use the `LinuxConf` utility in Red Hat Linux.

    c. Add a line to `/etc/passwd` with appropriate information.

    d. Start the Shadow Password system.

18. Which of the following is *not* a valid reason to use aliases in a user's environment settings:

    a. They save processing time as commands are executed.

    b. They protect against accidental erasure of files.

    c. They correct typographical errors as you work.

    d. They make non-Linux commands behave in a familiar way.

19. The `df` utility provides information about which one of the following:

    a. Which users have mounted the file system

    b. The virtual memory usage as stored on all mounted file systems

    c. File system capacity, device name, and percentage used status

    d. Per-directory usage and file system mount point

8

20. Describe the actions of the `defaults` options in a configuration line of the `/etc/fstab` file.

21. Which of the following is a valid `alias` command?

    a. `alias cp copy`

    b. `alias copy=cp`

    c. `alias DOS COPY to Linux cp`

    d. `export alias=copy,cp`

22. Describe the key advantage to having swap space located on a hard disk separate from the root Linux partition.

23. List two reasons why a user account might need to be disabled.

24. If you attempt to unmount a mounted file system and receive an error message, the most likely cause is:

    a. The file system was not mounted correctly in the first place.

    b. The `df` command is in the process of computing file system statistics.

    c. An error on the physical media that Linux cannot interpret.

    d. One or more users are working in the file system.

25. By starting multiple jobs in one command-line session, you can

    a. Conserve resources for each process you start

    b. Prevent the swap space from thrashing

    c. Manage those jobs with the `jobs`, `fg`, and `bg` commands

    d. Kill any unneeded process quickly

26. Signals are used by the `kill` command to manage processes. True or False?

27. Describe at least four fields of information provided by the command `ps auxf`.

HANDS-ON PROJECTS

Project 8-1

In this project you will create a new group and a new user account using the `groupadd` and `useradd` commands. Then you will update the user information on that account using `usermod`. To complete this project you need to have Linux installed. You should be at a Linux command-line prompt and have **root** access in order to perform these steps.

1. Enter the following command: **groupadd webmasters**. This creates a new group named webmasters.

2. Enter the following command: **cat /etc/group**. This displays the group file, with the new group in the last line of the output.

3. Enter the following useradd command: **useradd -g webmasters -e 06/30/01 -c "Hailey Mendez" hmendez**. This creates a new user account with an expiration date, full name in the comment field, and primary group assignment.

4. Enter the following command: **cat /etc/passwd**. This displays the user file (**/etc/passwd**), with the new user account information in the last line of the output.

5. Determine whether a home directory was created by the command in Step 3 by entering the following command: **ls /home/hmendez**. If you see a list of files, the home directory was created in Step 3; if you see an error message, the home directory was not created. If the home directory was not created, create it with this command: **mkdir /home/hmendez**.

6. Set a password for the new user account using this command: **passwd hmendez**.

7. Enter a new password twice as prompted.

8. Change to the new user account using the following substitute user command: **su - hmendez**. (Note that no password is required because you are logged in as **root**.)

9. Enter the following command: **alias**. This displays the aliases that are in effect for the new user. (Note that this command displays your system's defaults, unless you have changed the configuration files.)

10. Enter the following command: **exit**. As a result, you exit from acting as the new user and return to the **root** user account.

11. Now suppose you have been asked to change the login shell used by this user. Change the shell with the following usermod command: **usermod -s /bin/tcsh hmendez**.

12. Enter the following command: **cat /etc/passwd**. This displays the user file, where you can see the effect of the **usermod** command. Specifically, note **/bin/tcsh** in the last field of the line defining the **hmendez** account.

Project 8-2

In this activity you will explore how a signal sent with the **kill** command affects a Web server running on your Linux system. Most Linux systems have an **httpd** daemon (a Web server) that runs automatically after installation. You should have a completely installed Linux system to complete this task. Ideally, the Linux system should have a Web server installed by default. If you have not selected this installation option, you may be able to start a Web server using the command **httpd**. Log in to Linux and open a command-line window to complete the steps that follow.

1. Filter the **ps** command output through the **grep** command as follows: **ps aux | grep httpd**. This lists all of the Web server processes running on your computer.

8

2. Look at the output and notice the **owner** field on the far left (see Figure 8-5). Why is one copy of `httpd` owned by `root` and the others owned by a user named `nobody`?

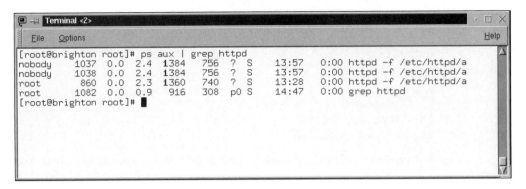

```
[root@brighton root]# ps aux | grep httpd
nobody    1037  0.0  2.4  1384   756  ?   S    13:57   0:00 httpd -f /etc/httpd/a
nobody    1038  0.0  2.4  1384   756  ?   S    13:57   0:00 httpd -f /etc/httpd/a
root       860  0.0  2.3  1360   740  ?   S    13:28   0:00 httpd -f /etc/httpd/a
root      1082  0.0  0.9   916   308  p0  S    14:47   0:00 grep httpd
[root@brighton root]#
```

Figure 8-5 Output from `ps aux | grep httpd`

3. Use the same command again with the **f** option, as follows: `ps auxf | grep httpd`. This displays the parent-child relationship of the Web servers. You can see that the copy owned by `root` started the other copies.

4. Note the start-time field (third field from the right) for each of the Web server daemons.

5. Note the PID of the Web server daemon owned by `root`. (The PID is the number nearest the far left column.) (The following steps will use the number 515, but you should replace this number with the PID that appears when you run the `ps` command on your system.)

6. Send a restart signal to the parent Web server process using the following `kill` command: `kill -HUP 515`. This signal causes the Web server to reread its configuration and restart all child processes.

7. Use the following `ps` command again: `ps aux | grep httpd`. Notice the start-time field. All of the processes owned by **nobody** (the child processes of the main Web server daemon) have been restarted and have a new start time. The main process owned by `root` does not have a new start time.

CASE PROJECTS

1. You have been asked to help design the file systems to be used for a large new Linux system in your research lab. The Linux system will support about 50 researchers who will log in each day to run scientific applications and access relevant Internet resources. The Linux system will also act as a news server, receiving about 1 GB of newsgroup messages each day over the Internet. A large database application runs on the Linux server to provide research data. As the system administrator, you expect to upgrade the Linux operating system about once per year; you will also maintain complete backups on a writeable CD-ROM drive.

Design a structure for the file system of the new Linux server, showing how you would set up partitions or separate hard disks and devices to accommodate each of the needs mentioned above. Prepare sample entries for an **fstab** file showing the options that you would likely use for each mounted file system. Include information about how you would configure the swap space on the devices you choose to use.

2. After using the system for several months, you notice that the **df** command shows that one file system is at more than 95% capacity. Describe some steps you might take to remedy this problem. How would your actions vary depending on which of the file systems was at 95%?

3. After running smoothly for about a year, one of the hard disks fails. Fortunately, you have backups of all data. How does the file system arrangement that you have designed assist in getting the system running again?

8

CHAPTER

9

HARDWARE REDUNDANCY AND FAULT TOLERANCE

> **After reading this chapter and completing the exercises, you will be able to:**
> ♦ Prepare for emergencies that can cause system downtime
> ♦ Manage the power supply to your Linux computer
> ♦ Check the integrity of your Linux file systems
> ♦ Understand how redundant disk systems can protect data

In the previous chapter you learned how to set up and manage user accounts and multiple file systems in Linux, which included creating new user accounts and new file systems. You also learned basic information about how to view and manage processes in Linux.

In this chapter you learn how to protect the data on your Linux system from downtime. This involves planning for potential trouble before it occurs and understanding how to manage key aspects of a Linux computer to avoid downtime. As you will learn in this chapter, the power supply and hard disks are key potential causes of downtime.

PREPARING FOR EMERGENCIES

As you probably know by now, computer systems are not infallible. For all the dependence society places on computers, they continue to break down, leading to crises for customers, managers, and system administrators. These crises loom largest for system administrators, the people everyone else looks to for immediate guidance and resolution when an organization's computer systems malfunction. These are the times when a system administrator who has prepared for emergencies really shines. Although handling crises is part of the system administrator's job description, those who excel in this area are on the path to promotions or raises when the proverbial sky falls. Conversely, those who have not prepared to handle difficult situations are likely to be looking for work elsewhere.

Creating a Disaster Plan

The first step in preparing for emergencies is to do everything possible to avoid them. A "disaster" somewhere else doesn't have to mean an emergency for your systems. Rather than sending out a distress call, how much better to send the following sort of message to management: "You may have heard that a tornado ripped through downtown Salt Lake City last night—I just wanted you to know that our systems are all backed up, with full power, running smoothly and without interruption." The preparation that allows such a message begins with a **disaster plan**—a written document stating how you have prepared your systems and what you will do in the event that various problems occur. A disaster plan should cover a wide range of potential problems. Your plan may include guidelines regarding some of the following problems:

- A hard disk crash.

- An employee or intruder destroying data on the system or attempting to crash it.

- A fire in the server room.

- A natural disaster that wipes out all backups in the office, destroys the server, and blocks anyone from getting near the office.

A disaster plan should outline policies and procedures to guide the actions of the system administrator and other staff members in preparing for and reacting to many types of emergencies. Information in a disaster plan should include the following:

- Detailed system specifications for all hardware

- A list of software installed on the server

- Location of software masters, manuals, and licensing information for each application

- Information about the server's power supply

- Steps required to start the server using a boot or rescue disk (described later in this chapter)

- Steps required to reinstall critical applications and data archives for those applications

- Names and contact information for those to be informed of server emergencies

- Names and contact information for those who can be called to help in case of emergencies (including key technical support numbers for hardware and software vendors)

The exact steps outlined in the plan depend on the nature of your organization. For example, a company that provides credit card services to customers around the world could not even allow a natural disaster that wiped out an entire office to stop customers from accessing the network. In such a situation, millions of dollars are at stake; as a result millions should be spent in preparing systems that will prevent a problem in one area from blocking access to the entire system. A study done by Oracle, the largest database software company, estimated that for its key customers, every *hour* of system downtime resulted in a loss of $80,000 to $300,000.

On the other hand, a small company with a server or two is not subject to such losses, though it may be just as dependent on its computer systems. Small firms can take some simple precautions that will greatly help in nearly all situations. A critical difference is the amount of time that the organization is willing to be without data.

By performing all the tasks on the following checklist, you could get any office up and running again in 24 hours after most emergencies, at much less cost than keeping duplicate servers in cities around the country.

- Keep a replacement hard disk and possibly other parts (power supply, network cards) in storage.

- Back up the system each night to a rotating set of archive media (as described in Chapter 14).

- Take copies of the back-up media off-site once per week (to another office, a bank vault, or even someone's home in the case of a small company).

As you draft a disaster plan in consultation with management teams and others involved with the information systems at your organization, consider the monetary value of time. Can you calculate the dollar value of each minute that data is inaccessible to employees or customers? Many companies can; they should then spend accordingly to keep systems up and running.

Depending on your organization's requirements, you should consider all of the following components as potential points of failure, setting up redundant systems when possible:

- Hard disks

- Memory chips

- Network cards

- Power supplies (within a computer)

- Incoming AC power (wall socket)

- Software failure (kernel or application crash)

Preventing Downtime

The term **downtime** refers to occasions when an organization's computer systems cannot respond to requests for information. For example, a Web server that doesn't respond to browser requests, a database server that can't respond to queries, or a print server that can't accept print jobs are all experiencing downtime. In computer parlance, these devices are down. It's important to remember that a computer can be down without being powered off. If software or hardware problems prevent a computer from responding as intended, it is effectively down— because users can't perform tasks as they need to. The rest of this chapter describes techniques that you can use to protect your Linux system from excessive downtime. Before you can successfully prevent downtime, you need to understand a few key concepts:

- **Redundancy:** A state of readiness in which a duplicate component can take over if the primary component fails. A completely redundant system is a replicated system. Most computer systems are not completely redundant. Because of cost considerations, only those components that are most likely to fail or that cause the greatest problems if they fail are supported by redundant systems.

- **Fault tolerance:** The ability of a system to deal effectively with problems (also known as faults). Faults can include hardware failure, power failure, stolen data, and many others. The more fault tolerant a system is, the more unexpected problems it can handle without going down.

- **Points of failure:** Weakness or vulnerabilities in the information system. Looking for the possible points of failure is a good way to strengthen the fault tolerance of your system. Work to eliminate any **single point of failure**—a single highly vulnerable part of a system whose failure will bring down the entire system. If a single (or most dangerous) point of failure cannot be eliminated entirely, try to make that part of the system redundant.

Understanding High Availability

Fault tolerant computer systems that run continuously are said to provide **high availability**. A high availability computer system is able to serve data as much of the time as possible. The availability of a system may be measured as a percentage. For example, a system may have a statistical availability (uptime) of 99.99%. Most standard Pentium-class systems running Linux would probably have an availability of 95% or higher, depending on the environment in which they are running. (For example, if the municipal power supply was subject to frequent outages, the availability might be lower.) But improving system availability becomes increasingly difficult as you approach 100%. To achieve 100%, all possible causes of downtime must be eliminated through redundant systems, elimination of points of failure, and so forth.

It's important to keep in mind that while achieving 100% uptime is an admirable goal, it is only a theoretical goal. All systems will necessarily experience some degree of downtime. To understand the difficulty implied in attempting to achieve 100% availability, think of a graph in which a curve approaches a line (an asymptote). The curve of availability never actually touches the line of 100%, but as it gets closer and closer, the costs rise to infinity. Thus, companies are forced to set more practical availability goals, based on the amount of downtime the organization can realistically tolerate. One way a company can accommodate unavoidable downtime is to schedule it in the form of maintenance or upgrades. A network that is carefully maintained and upgraded in this way is far less likely to experience costly, unexpected downtime.

Downtime is generally measured as a percentage. For example, suppose your organization can tolerate one hour of downtime per year. In other words, out of the 8760 hours in a year, 1 can be allocated to downtime (scheduled, if all goes well). Dividing 1 by 8760 gives a value of 0.0001142. Multiplying by 100 gives the percentage of downtime: 0.01142%. Put another way, this organization requires 99.989% uptime. Once you have calculated this goal, you can more easily determine the amount of time and resources required to achieve it.

Within the realm of high availability systems, the term **resource groups** is used to refer to an application, the data that it requires to operate, and any other resources the application requires to complete its computing tasks. The term **high availability cluster** is used to refer to a group of servers that have high availability features and are dedicated to handling a common set of tasks. Each high availability cluster is devoted to handling a set of tasks or resource groups. Several methods are used to control how the servers in a cluster respond to problems. The two most widely used of these methods are:

- One or more servers sit idly waiting to take over a resource group (a task) in the event that a main server fails. When the main server is restored to activity, the back-up server becomes idle again as the main server takes over. This method requires additional hardware equivalent to the main server to provide redundancy, which may be costly.

- Each server in a cluster may handle various tasks. If one server goes down, the other servers take over the resource groups of that server. This doesn't require costly hardware to sit idly waiting for a failure, but performance may be seriously degraded if all servers are already busy when one fails.

Linux supports some high availability features. These include UPS devices and both hardware and software RAID (these subjects are discussed later in this chapter). However, Linux does not support some high availability features, such as software control of high availability clusters and mainstream applications that are aware of high availability features. Many people in the Linux community are working on getting Linux to support additional software tools and hardware components. In the future these will allow Linux to compete better with UNIX vendors that have been working on high availability systems for decades. These systems, from vendors like Oracle, IBM, and Hewlett-Packard, may cost millions of dollars. They include all of the redundancy features described in this chapter, as well as others that Linux does not yet support. By increasing its high availability features, Linux can be used in more business critical computing environments.

Creating Rescue Disks

One of the most common system failures is a hard disk problem. This can take the form of a complete crash, in which case you may have to restore all of the data to a new hard disk from a back-up archive. In other cases, part of the disk may be corrupted so that the system cannot boot correctly. Sometimes a hard disk problem can even be caused by something that the system administrator has done to the system. In the case of many hard drive failures, you cannot boot the system normally from the hard disk; you must boot the Linux system from a floppy disk before you can access the hard disk to try to solve the problem. This disk is called a rescue disk.

A **rescue disk** is a floppy disk that includes the files needed to run a minimal version of Linux without using the hard disks on your system. After booting the system from such a disk, you can mount the hard disks of your system (as described in Chapter 8) and edit files (including the LILO boot information) to correct problems. A rescue disk is only one type of floppy disk you may use with your Linux system:

- A rescue disk allows you to run Linux without relying on data stored on your system's hard disk. It contains a text editor such as `vi`, a few command-line utilities such as `ls` and `cat`, and a few utilities for managing hard disks such as `fdisk`. A rescue disk is used only for emergencies.

- A **boot disk** is used to launch the operating system stored on your hard disk. It is used in normal operating situations to start the Linux system.

- An **install disk** is used when you first install Linux. Its contents are similar to a rescue disk, but it is not designed to assist you in recovering damaged data.

- A **root disk** is used in conjunction with an install disk during some Linux installations (depending on the Linux distribution you are using).

Some system administrators always boot their servers from a boot disk. This takes more time than booting from a hard drive, but because a server is rebooted only rarely, speed of booting is not really a concern. By using a boot disk, the system administrator can control how the system boots and easily maintain a backup of the boot disk in case of problems. A rescue disk is used when the boot disk or hard disk fails.

Ideally, you would create a rescue disk for your system when installing Linux. This guarantees that the rescue disk and the information on the computer's hard disk are compatible, which may help as you attempt to fix system problems.

As an example, the Red Hat 6.0 Linux CD provides copies (or images) of the two disks needed to start the installation program: a boot disk and a root disk (the root disk contains a minimal root file system). Once you create these disks, you can use them to start your Red Hat Linux system at any time. The images for these disks are located in the `images/` subdirectory of the installation CD. You can copy these images to a floppy disk using the `rawrite` utility in DOS or Windows (which is also on the Red Hat CD). Alternatively, you can use the Linux `dd` utility by combining the `dd` command with the name of the image file (`rescue`, `boot`, or `root`). For example:

```
dd if=rescue.img of=/dev/fd0 bs=72k
```

 TIP   To start a Red Hat 6.0 system in emergencies, you must first boot the system using a boot disk, then insert the rescue disk to begin the process of dealing with problems on the system's hard disks. Red Hat refers to this process as entering **rescue mode**. You can also create a boot disk in Red Hat 6.0 using the `mkbootdisk` command.

Other Linux distributions require similar techniques for creating a boot disk or rescue disk. Many installation programs also provide multiple virtual consoles that you can use to diagnose or repair problems after booting the system from an installation disk. By switching from one virtual console to another, you may be able to mount a hard disk and diagnose or repair a problem. Press the Alt key and then a function key (F1 to F6) to switch between virtual consoles. When using an installation disk rather than a rescue disk for this task, keep in mind that the installation disk may not have the tools you need to diagnose and fix a problem.

Maintaining Software Masters

As you will learn in Chapter 14, most back-up strategies focus on backing up user data—that is, the information created by your organization, for use only within your organization. System administrators are often careless about backing up the software tools and operating system files used to create and work with that data because they think these items can be purchased in any computer store. However, this is not always the case. Consider the following problems that can occur after a system failure, when you attempt to reacquire your company's software tools:

- The company that created the software may be out of business. Note that this is most likely to happen when the software is specific to one industry, such as a video store software package, chemical plant software, or medical office software.

- The particular version used by the company may no longer be available from the vendor. A costly upgrade would then be required, with new training for all employees.

- The vendor may not be able to ship the replacement application software immediately. For instance, if your system goes down on a Friday, the vendor probably wouldn't be able to ship the software until Monday, for delivery on Tuesday. Thus, the process of reconstructing the system data from backups could not begin until five days after the initial failure.

In all of these situations, a system administrator would be better served if he or she had carefully and securely stored the **software masters** (such as the installation CD) originally provided by the vendor. Unfortunately, software masters are often discarded along with the unread user manuals as soon as the products are installed. Instead, they should be stored along with backups of other system data and mentioned prominently in your disaster plan. When using complex applications such as client/server databases or customized business software, application data sometimes cannot be restored properly until the application is first installed. If you can immediately locate software masters for all important applications used on your server, you can then rebuild a system as follows:

- Rebuild or repair hardware components such as hard disks.

- Install the operating system and applications used by the company.

- Restore user data files.

 If you can afford the additional capacity, it's a good idea to back up the operating system and applications as well as user data. This safeguards your custom configurations as well as the applications themselves. But keep track of the software masters and documentation nevertheless. You may need them to retrieve license information or activation keys for your applications.

MANAGING THE COMPUTER'S POWER SUPPLY

The power supply is one of the easier components to protect within a Linux server. This component converts the **AC power** from a wall socket to the low-voltage DC power used by computer chips, disk drives, and other accessories. As shown in Figure 9-1, the **power supply** is usually the single largest component inside your computer. It rarely fails if it is properly cooled by an internal fan or room air conditioner. For occasions when the power supply does fail, two possible remedies can be part of your disaster planning:

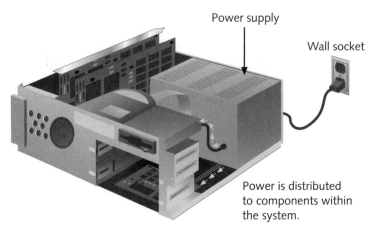

Power supply

Wall socket

Power is distributed to components within the system.

Figure 9-1   The power supply component inside a computer

- Keep a second power supply on hand. If the power supply inside a computer fails, you should be able to replace the part and have the system running again within an hour. Spare power supplies are not overly expensive.

- Purchase a server with a built-in back-up power supply. This is similar to having an uninterruptible power supply (described in the next section) within the computer. It allows you to schedule a time to shut the server down when it is not being used so you can replace the failed power supply component. Servers with dual power supplies are generally quite expensive because of the control circuitry required to switch to the back-up supply in case of a failure.

A power supply is a single component in your computer. Don't ever try to disassemble and repair it, or you risk receiving a powerful electric shock. Replace it as a complete unit. Opening a power supply unit is very danger-ous. A power supply contains components such as capacitors that can hold a large electric charge even when the power to the system is shut off.

Connecting a UPS to a Linux System

In most parts of the world, failure of or an unexpected irregularity in the AC power (the wall socket power) is much more likely than a failure of the computer's power supply. You can ameliorate the effects of irregular power by using devices known as surge suppressors. **Surge suppressors** provide a regular power signal to the computer's power supply. These devices remove voltage spikes, brownouts (moments of reduced voltage), and other irregularities (such as changes in the frequency of the signal—normally 60 cycles per second) that don't affect your refrigerator or office lights, but can damage sensitive electronic equipment. Figure 9-2 illustrates how a surge suppressor removes irregularities so that the computer's power supply can rely on a consistent level of incoming power.

Figure 9-2   A surge suppressor removes power irregularities

When the power actually fails, however, a surge suppressor doesn't help. For these cases, an **uninterruptible power supply (UPS)** is needed. A UPS contains batteries that are continually charged by the main AC power when it is active. During a power outage, the batteries in the UPS take over, delivering power to the computer as if the outage had not occurred. Figure 9-3 shows a computer connected to a UPS.

9

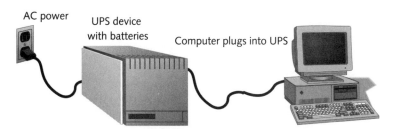

Figure 9-3   Computer connected to a UPS

 A UPS also includes surge suppressor features. Thus when the main AC power is active, the power reaching the computer is filtered by the UPS; a separate surge suppressor is not necessary.

Because batteries are expensive (and heavy), a low-cost UPS typically provides only 5 to 30 minutes of battery power to a computer. Systems that require high availability may have a UPS costing thousands of dollars, that provides power for several days. Such high-end UPS systems may be integrated with gas-powered generators that recharge the UPS batteries. In most situations, however, a UPS is intended to provide power during momentary power outages, which generally last less than five minutes. In the event of a long-term outage due to weather or utility company problems, a UPS allows computer systems to be shut down gracefully. This is especially important for a Linux computer system, in which data is cached in memory rather than being written immediately to hard disk. If the system is not shut down properly, such data will be lost. What's more, when the Linux system is turned on again, the system may require a few minutes (or several hours) to check the integrity of the hard disk files and perform other checks. A UPS prevents these problems by giving the Linux system administrator time to shut down Linux properly, inform users that the server will be shut down, and exit system services without any loss of data.

Automating Linux Shutdown

Although a UPS allows time for a system administrator to shut down a Linux system gracefully, the system administrator may not be present when the power outage occurs. For this reason, UPS devices typically have a serial communications port (similar to the connection used by a printer or external modem) that signals the Linux system in the event of a power outage. The Linux system then executes simple scripts to determine what actions to take. UPS devices can generally recognize three events, as described in Table 9-1.

Table 9-1   Events Tracked by a UPS Device via a Serial Port

Event recognized by UPS	Linux system response	Notes
Power failure	Begin a system shutdown	The shutdown process may take 5 to 30 minutes, depending on the capacity of the UPS device and the type of work and number of users supported by the Linux server.
Power is out and the UPS battery is low	Shut down quickly	In this situation, Linux usually executes an immediate `halt` command to write cached data to files and unmount file systems before the UPS battery fails. Users logged in to the system may have very little warning about closing their files, but typically no data is lost.
Power has been restored	Cancel any pending shutdown	When a nonemergency shutdown (taking 5 to 30 minutes) is in process, the shutdown can be canceled before any services are shut down.

Each item in Table 9-1 corresponds to a signal number (similar to those used with the `kill` command, as described in Chapter 8). When a UPS is connected to a computer running Linux, the system administrator also installs a software daemon to monitor the serial cable that the UPS uses to communicate with the computer. Figure 9-4 shows a UPS connected to a Linux system via a serial cable.

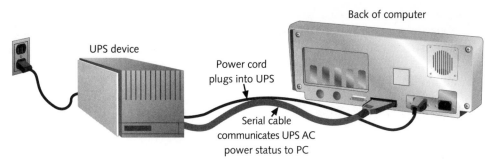

Figure 9-4   Serial connection between UPS and Linux system

Many different programs are available to monitor a UPS. One popular UPS manufacturer, American Power Conversion (APC), has Linux-specific programs designed to provide access to special control features of its UPS devices. Because most UPS devices employ common communications systems, however, the standard Linux UPS daemon, known as **powerd**, can be used with any UPS. The **powerd** software package may be included on your Linux CD-ROM. You can also acquire the **powerd** software package from Linux FTP sites such as *metalab.unc.edu* in the `/pub/linux/system/ups` subdirectory. The package on this FTP site is in `.tar.gz` format, so the command to prepare it on your system would look like this:

```
tar xvzf powerd-2.0.tar.gz
```

After installing the **powerd** software package, the system administrator must activate it by performing the following three steps:

1. Add **powerd** to the start-up scripts so that it is started each time the Linux system boots. (This step is described in the following section.)

2. Set up the **powerd** configuration file. This file controls how the **powerd** program monitors the serial communications line connected to your UPS.

3. Check the `/etc/inittab` file to see what actions Linux will take based on the instructions sent from the **powerd** program.

Autostarting the `powerd` Daemon

Before the **powerd** daemon can start automatically each time you boot Linux, you must add it to the system initialization scripts described in this section. The exact method required to accomplish this depends on your version of Linux, though the variations between Linux versions are small. This section describes a typical Linux configuration.

The **powerd** software package includes a script used to start the **powerd** daemon. The **powerd** installation process copies this script to the `/etc/rc.d/init.d` directory. In some cases you may need to manually copy the script to the correct directory. For example, if you stored the **powerd** package in the `/tmp` directory, the command to copy the script would look like this:

```
cp /tmp/powerd-2.0/powerd /etc/rc.d/init.d/
```

Once this script is installed in the correct directory, you can execute it (and start the **powerd** daemon) with the following command:

```
/etc/rc.d/init.d/powerd start
```

To stop the **powerd** daemon, use this command:

```
/etc/rc.d/init.d/powerd stop
```

This **powerd** start-up script should also be added to your system initialization directories so that **powerd** starts automatically each time you boot your Linux system.

To have Linux run the **powerd** start-up script automatically when the system is booted, add a pointer from a run level directory to the **powerd** start-up script.

The run level directories define which services Linux starts when using a given run level. Run levels 3 and 5 are most often used for standard systems. The run level directories are located in `/etc/rc.d`. For example, the directory used to initiate services for run level 3 is `/etc/rc.d/rc3.d`.

To add the **powerd** script to the run level 3 directory, create a link, or pointer, in that directory that refers to the start-up script. Each link in this directory begins with a letter S followed by a two-digit number. The numbers indicate the order in which services will be started.

The **powerd** daemon should be started before most other system services, so a value of 03 is a good choice. To create this link, use the following command:

```
ln -s /etc/rc.d/init.d/powerd /etc/rc.d/rc3.d/S03powerd
```

A similar link (using a filename beginning with K for **kill**) is used to indicate that the **powerd** daemon should be shut down when run level 0 (halt) or run level 6 (reboot) is initiated by the system administrator. These two commands create links within the run level 0 and run level 6 directories that point to the **powerd** script. Services are shut down in the reverse order of how they are started up, so the number used for these links is 90. The **powerd** daemon will be shut down after almost all other system services are shut down. To create this link, use the following command:

```
ln -s /etc/rc.d/init.d/powerd /etc/rc.d/rc0.d/K90powerd
ln -s /etc/rc.d/init.d/powerd /etc/rc.d/rc6.d/K90powerd
```

 The exact numbers used on your Linux system, the directories where these files are contained, and the specific daemons started in each run level will vary depending on your Linux distribution. The numbers that you select are somewhat arbitrary. They should simply be between the numbers used for other services on the system. You can review these other services by examining the contents of the run level directories (such as `/etc/rc.d/rc3.d`).

Configuring the powerd Daemon

The configuration file used by the **powerd** daemon, named **powerd.conf**, is located in the `/etc` directory. By default, most of the options in this file begin with a hash mark (#), indicating that they are commented out (marked as comments and thus inactive). By reviewing the comments, you can learn how each feature is used. Then you can select the features you want to use and activate them by deleting the hash mark. Although the **powerd** daemon supports many features, the configuration available to you depends on your UPS device. The remainder of this section describes a generic configuration for signaling a power failure.

In order to be a successful system administrator, you don't need to understand everything about serial communications, but you will need to learn about how your UPS device signals a power failure or low battery condition. Specifically, to understand how the UPS informs the **powerd** daemon of a failure, you must understand the structure of a serial connection. A standard serial cable contains either 9 or 25 pins, as shown in Figure 9-5. These pins can be referred to by number, as indicated in the figure. A small number of these pins (wires inside the cable) are named for the functions they perform, such as carrying a bit of data or signaling that a bit of data was received successfully. (The exact names are abbreviations of the pin's function. For example, the pin that indicates "ready to send data" is known by the label RTS.)

9-pin serial connector (cable end)

25-pin serial connector (cable end)

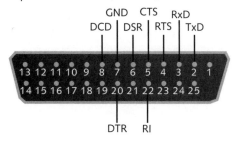

Figure 9-5   Standard serial cable connections

As one example, a Blackout Buster UPS from PK Electronics uses pin number 1 on a 9-pin cable to signal a low battery condition. When the UPS sets the voltage on pin number 8 to low, this indicates that the main AC power has failed. By contrast, a non-low voltage on that pin indicates that the power outlet is working. On any 9-pin serial cable, pins 1 and 8 are referred to, respectively, by the names DCD and CTS. The /etc/powerd.conf file contains information about the pin numbers and corresponding names for 9-pin and 25-pin cables, but you must learn the specifications of your UPS to determine which pins or names to use in configuring the **powerd** daemon. The technical support number or Web site of the UPS manufacturer generally has all of this information readily available.

> UPS vendors' software packages are usually designed to provide automatic shutdown for NetWare or Windows servers. Note that this software will not work with your Linux system. Very few UPS vendors currently support Linux. American Power Conversion (see *http://www.apcc.com*) is one exception.

The `powerd` program can be configured by making a few changes to the default configuration file. Within the `/etc/powerd.conf` file, update the following lines using a text editor of your choice:

1. Look for the line containing the word `disabled`. This line indicates that the `powerd` program should not actively monitor the serial port. By default, the `powerd` configuration is disabled to prevent it from listening to a serial port before it has been configured properly. An improperly configured `powerd` daemon might listen to the wrong serial port and attempt to shut down the computer, even though the power supply is fine. If necessary, add a hash mark (#) to the beginning of this line to make it a comment.

2. Use the search feature of your text editor to locate the phrase `debug yes` in the `powerd.conf` file. This statement indicates that the `powerd` program should not run in the background but should stay active on the command line after being started. This allows you to immediately end the `powerd` program by pressing Ctrl+C as you test that `powerd` works correctly. Change the line `debug yes` to `debug no`. You may want to do this step after testing the UPS configuration as described in the next section, but you should not reboot your system unless you have set this line to `debug no`. Otherwise, your system may pause while waiting for a response on the serial port.

3. The section labeled `serialline` includes three lines of text that define how the `powerd` program will monitor the serial port. The three lines define which serial port to monitor, the wire within the port to monitor, and the status of the line to look for (watch for either high voltage or low voltage). Uncomment these lines and set the correct values that you have determined by reviewing the documentation for your UPS device. For example:

```
serialline        /dev/ttyS1
     monitor          DCD
     failwhen         low
```

These values indicate that the second serial port (`/dev/ttyS1`) should be monitored, that the DCD line within the port should be monitored, and that a failure signal should be sent when the DCD line goes to low voltage.

4. Save your changes to the `/etc/powerd.conf` file and restart the `powerd` daemon using the following two commands so that the configuration file is reloaded by `powerd`:

```
/etc/rc.d/init.d/powerd stop
/etc/rc.d/init.d/powerd start
```

You may see device names (such as `/dev/cua0` or `/dev/cua1`) within the `powerd.conf` configuration file. Formerly, the serial port devices on a Linux computer were known by the names `/dev/cua0` for the first port, `/dev/cua1` for the second port, and so forth. The preferred names for serial port devices in Linux have been changed to `/dev/ttyS0` for the first port, `/dev/ttyS1` for the second port, and so forth. You may still see the `/dev/cuax` device names—and they will still work on most Linux systems— but try to use the newer `/dev/ttySx` device names where you have a choice.

Although a UPS has only one serial communications cable attached to it, every UPS has several power outlets; thus several Linux servers can be plugged into one UPS. Each Linux server that is powered by an outlet on the UPS should run a copy of **powerd**, even though the serial cable is not connected to each of the Linux servers. Thanks to additional features of the **powerd** daemon, it can use a network connection to inform a copy of **powerd** running on other Linux servers of a power outage. Thus, **powerd** on those other servers can watch for a message on the network from another copy of **powerd**. When this message is received, each copy of **powerd** can shut down the server on which it is running. The **remoteserver** line in the `/etc/powerd.conf` file is used to configure this remote mon- itoring feature. Figure 9-6 shows how several servers can be plugged into one UPS device. A single serial cable allows the UPS to inform one server of a power outage. That server then informs other servers via the network. (All of these messages are communicated between copies of the **powerd** daemon.)

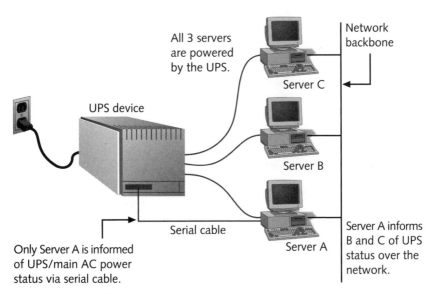

All 3 servers
are powered
by the UPS.

Network
backbone

Server C

UPS device

Server B

Serial cable

Server A

Only Server A is informed
of UPS/main AC power
status via serial cable.

Server A informs
B and C of UPS
status over the
network.

Figure 9-6   Multiple servers connected to one UPS with remote server shutdown

Responding to a Power Outage

The **powerd** daemon doesn't shut down your Linux system. Instead, it watches the serial port for information from the UPS device. When it receives information indicating the power is out, the UPS battery is low, or the power has been restored, it communicates a signal to the `init` program. The `init` program is a control process that starts the first processes on Linux, such as the login screens.

The `init` program is configured by a file called `/etc/inittab`. When the `powerd` daemon sends a signal to the `init` daemon, `init` checks the `/etc/inittab` configuration file to determine what action to take. The file `/etc/inittab` normally includes two or possibly three lines indicating how Linux should respond when a power outage occurs, the UPS battery is low, or the power is restored. The exact content of these lines (that is, the exact actions they specify) depends on your Linux vendor and version, but these lines taken from Red Hat 6.0 Linux are good examples:

```
pf::powerfail:/sbin/shutdown -f -h +2 "Power Failure; System
  Shutting Down"
```

```
pr:12345:powerokwait:/sbin/shutdown -c "Power Restored; Shutdown
  Cancelled"
```

The first part of the line (`pf` or `pr` in these two example lines) is a label chosen by Red Hat. The second part, `powerfail` and `powerokwait`, indicates to the `init` daemon what is being configured: either power failure or power restored. Only two possible signals are represented here. (Testing for a low battery condition is not part of the `/etc/inittab` configuration in Red Hat 6.0.) In another distribution, the configuration line for a low battery would look something like this:

```
p1:powerfailnow:/sbin/shutdown -h now "Battery Low…"
```

All three of these signals make use of the `shutdown` command. In each of the three relevant lines in `/etc/inittab` (monitoring signals for power failure, UPS battery low, and power restored), different parameters are included after the `shutdown` command to determine how `shutdown` operates. Each of the three commands is described in the following list. In each case, the message in quotation marks is part of the `shutdown` command and appears immediately on the screen of every user who is logged in to the Linux system.

- `shutdown -f -h +2 "Power Failure; System Shutting Down"`: Initiates a timed shutdown that warns all users on the system that the server will be halted (shut down and not automatically rebooted, using the `-h` option) in two minutes. No system services are actually shut down until the end of the two minutes. If your UPS can supply power for a longer time, you could change the `+2` parameter to another number—for example, to `+10` for 10 minutes.

- `shutdown -c "Power Restored; Shutdown Cancelled"`: Cancels an existing shutdown. This command is useful after a timed shutdown has been announced to users but before the time has expired. If power is restored, there is no need to shut down the system, so another announcement is sent to all users that the shutdown has been canceled and they can continue working normally. This would be used if a short power outage causes the `init` program to announce a shutdown in 2 to 10 minutes (or more, depending on your UPS), but the power was restored after a short time.

- `shutdown -h now "Battery Low"`: Initiates an immediate shutdown (halt and do not automatically reboot, using the `-h` parameter with `now`), disconnecting any users that are connected via the network and ending all applications. When the UPS battery is failing, the time left before the power is cut to the computer cannot be determined, so this rather impolite command is used. Though it is unpleasant for users because it ends their Linux session without warning, it is better to preserve the file system integrity than to risk losing data because the battery fails before a shutdown has been completed. As a rule, you can avoid low battery conditions by careful planning. Ideally, your UPS device would be adequate for your Linux system, which means this command would never be necessary.

You can update the information in the `/etc/inittab` file so that the `init` daemon executes any command that meets the needs of your system. The `shutdown` command is effective for unmounting file systems and preventing data loss, but you might also want to create a script (see Chapter 12) that completes a set of tasks related to shutting down the system. These tasks might include:

- Writing an incident to a log file

- Sending an e-mail message to another system

- Signaling a back-up server to take over a critical task

- Writing information to a networked hard disk so it can still be accessed

- Starting the `shutdown` command to halt the system

9

CHECKING FILE SYSTEM INTEGRITY

Maintaining the integrity of file systems is a key part of protecting data on your Linux systems. In order to maintain the file system, it's useful to understand some basics about the information stored on a file system and the arrangement of that information. The definitions in the following paragraphs apply to all Linux `ext2` file systems.

The **superblock** is a set of information about the entire file system. It includes items such as the following:

- Maximum number of times the file system can be mounted between complete file system checks (using the `fsck` utility described in the next section)

- Size of the file system in blocks (the standard block size is 1024 bytes)

- Number of free blocks on the file system

- Number of reserved blocks (reserved blocks can only be used by the root user or another user or group that the root user specifies)

- Amount of time since a complete integrity check was performed on the file system

If the superblock is corrupted, the entire file system is unusable. Copies of the superblock are stored in multiple locations across the hard disk during the formatting of an `ext2` file system to protect against a superblock problem rendering the system unusable. Some parameters stored in the superblock, such as the maximum number of times the file system can be mounted between integrity checks, can be configured during formatting or reset using the `tune2fs` utility described later, in "Tuning a Linux File System." Some features of the file system, such as the size of a data block, cannot be changed without reformatting the entire file system.

An **inode** (pronounced eye-node) is a file information record. A **file record** contains a filename and the inode that holds information needed to access the file. The file record is an indirect pointer to the file's data: it points to an inode, which in turn points to the data in a file. A **directory record** is a file containing a list of files and corresponding inode numbers used to access data in those files.

Each inode contains all of the information about a file except the file's name. This information includes the following:

- The file access permissions
- The owner and group of the file (noted as a user ID and group ID number)
- The time and date of the last access, last modification, and file creation
- Number of blocks used by the file on disk and the precise size of the file in bytes
- A pointer to the blocks of data in which the file's contents are stored

Because of the way inodes are arranged on an `ext2` file system, a file system can have only a limited number of inodes and thus a limited number of files. The number is large, and you're never likely to run out of inodes for creating new files. But you will notice as you use the `fsck` utility in the next section that the utility displays messages indicating the maximum number of files that the file system can hold. For example, the utility output reading `43686/247808 files` indicates that of 247,808 possible files on this 1 GB hard disk, 43,686 have been created thus far.

The brief explanation of inodes provided in the previous paragraph should help you understand how links are used in the Linux file system. A **link** allows two or more file records to refer to the same physical data stored in a file system. Among other things, a link makes it possible for two users to have two different filenames listed in their home directories, but actually be working with the same data when they edit those two files. Links are of two types: symbolic and hard. A **symbolic link** is a file record that includes a path and filename, but not an inode. When a user refers to a symbolic link, Linux looks at the path and filename mentioned in the file record—sort of like an internal URL pointing to another filename. The file record for that second path and filename includes an inode. That inode is used to access the file data for the symbolic link.

A **hard link** is a file record that includes a filename and inode, just like a regular file record. But a hard link refers to an inode that already has a file record pointing to it. The hard link is a second file record pointing directly to the same physical data. A single inode can have numerous file records (hard links) pointing to it. After a hard link is created, it is equal to the first file record that points to the same inode. If the first file record is deleted, the second file record (created as a hard link) is unaffected—it still refers to the same file data.

Both symbolic and hard links are used often in a Linux file system. Whenever you use the `ls -l` command, any symbolic links are indicated as extra filenames in the right column of the output. An example of a symbolic link in Red Hat Linux is the `view` command. This output shows how you can use the `ls -l` command to show the `view` command:

```
$ ls -l /bin/view
lrwxrwxrwx    1  root root 2    Aug 12 13:36  view  ->  vi
```

The arrow in the right column indicates that the file named `view` is a symbolic link to the file named `vi` (located in the same directory, because no pathname is included). The letter `l` in the far left column of the screen output also indicates that the file is a symbolic link.

The number in the second column from the left (in this case, 1) indicates the number of file records that refer to the same inode as this file record.

The `zcat` filename (also in Red Hat Linux) is an example of a hard link. The `zcat` file record refers to an inode that two other file records also refer to. The `ls -l` command again shows this:

```
$ ls -l /bin/zcat
-rwx-r-xr-x    3  root root   50384    Mar 25 13:28 zcat
```

In this sample screen output, the number 3 in the second column from the left indicates that the file record holding the filename `zcat` refers to an inode that two other files also refer to (for a total of three). Figure 9-7 shows the difference between a symbolic link and a hard link. In this figure, a programming language named Perl is stored in a file called `perl5.003`, where the `5.003` indicates a precise version number. Other file records also point to the same information (inode) using different filenames. This allows users who might not know the precise version number to access the Perl programming language file.

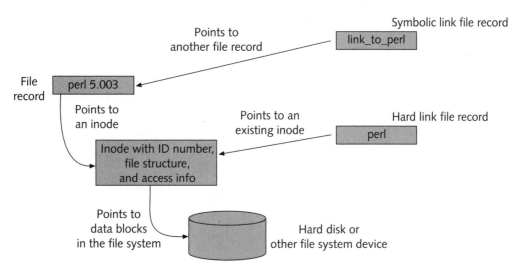

Figure 9-7   Hard link vs. symbolic link

To see the inode numbers associated with the filenames in a directory, use the -i option of the ls command. Only the first few lines of the output for this directory are shown in this listing:

```
$ ls -i /bin
22549 arch
22497 ash
22498 ash.static
22507 awk
22514 basename
22475 bash
22499 bsh
22495 cat
22477 chgrp
22478 chmod
22479 chown
22502 consolechars
22480 cp
22504 cpio
```

Using the fsck Utility

You can run the fsck utility at any time to check the integrity of a Linux file system. The fsck utility can quickly determine whether any file system problems are evident. If none are apparent, fsck runs very quickly. You can, however, force fsck to execute a full suite of file system tests even when the utility would otherwise exit quickly because no errors are apparent. This is called forcing the fsck utility.

Each time you boot Linux, the fsck program runs automatically to check all mounted file systems. Under normal circumstances, this automatic check takes only a few seconds. Two situations will cause the fsck utility to spend more time checking the file systems:

- Linux was not shut down gracefully (all system services were not shut down in an orderly way). Data was therefore not written correctly or fully to the file system.

- The file system has been mounted numerous times. After a certain number of mount operations, Linux forces the fsck utility to go through a complete check of the file system even if no problems are evident.

When the second condition occurs, Linux displays a message like the following as you boot the system:

```
Maximal mount count reached: check forced.
```

Just as Linux occasionally does a thorough (forced) file system check automatically, you can also use the fsck utility to manually check each of your Linux file systems. Such a complete check is wise before any disk-intensive operations, including the following:

- Backing up the system completely before a hardware upgrade

- Defragmenting the file system (as described in the next section)

- Attempting to repair data in a corrupt (damaged) file system

To force a complete check of a file system, use the `fsck` command with the `-f` option, followed by the name of the device on which the file system is located. The following example of the `fsck` command checks the file system located on the first partition of the second IDE hard disk:

 You can only use the `fsck` command on file systems that are *not* mounted. Using it on a mounted file system will damage the file system.

```
fsck -f /dev/hdb1
```

You can also use the mount point in the directory structure. For example, if the first partition of the second IDE hard disk (`/dev/hdb1`) is mounted as `/database`, you could also use this command:

```
fsck -f /database
```

Multiple file systems can be checked at the same time by listing them. For example:

```
fsck -f /dev/hdb2 /dev/hdb3 /dev/hdc1
```

The `fsck` program runs all the file system checks at the same time, querying you as questions arise about file system information. If a file system you are checking is fine, you see only a brief output after running `fsck`, as follows:

```
Parallelizing fsck version 1.14 (9-Jan-1999)
e2fsck 1.14, 9-Jan-1999 for EXT2 FS 0.5b, 95/08/09
/dev/hdb2: clean, 43686/247808 files, 906478/987997 blocks.
```

Launching `fsck` with the `-f` option provides more detailed information. Sample output is shown here:

```
Parallelizing fsck version 1.14 (9-Jan-1999)
e2fsck 1.14, 9-Jan-1999 for EXT2 FS 0.5b, 95/08/09
Pass 1: Checking inodes, blocks and sizes
Pass 2: Checking directory structure
Pass 3: Checking directory connectivity
Pass 4: Checking reference counts
Pass 5: Checking group summary information
/dev/hdb2: clean, 43686/247808 files (0.3% non-contiguous),
   906478/987997 blocks.
```

Note that running a complete file system check using the `-f` option takes several minutes. A 1 GB Linux file system that is almost full of data may take three minutes to check. Larger file systems take considerably longer. What's more, using `fsck` to perform file system repairs on a Linux system with multiple or large file systems may take up to an hour to restart the Linux system. You can avoid time-consuming file system checks by shutting down Linux properly every time.

> **TIP**   A proper system shutdown in Linux is often referred to as a "graceful shutdown." An ungraceful shutdown does not allow Linux to store information to files, stop system services, and cleanly unmount file systems.

The screen output of the `fsck` utility shown above contains five complete passes through the file system. The `fsck` utility will automatically correct any problems detected during each of the five passes. If an automatic correction is not possible, a query will appear on screen. These queries are simple questions asking you whether to save or delete unidentified pieces of information, or to provide some other piece of information that the file system requires. It is rare to have `fsck` ask a question during a file system check unless a serious disk problem occurred, such as the power to the Linux system being cut off during a complex disk operation.

When Linux is booted, the `fsck` utility is run with the `-a` option, which automatically corrects any minor errors. These minor errors might include such things as a missing timestamp on a file if the system was not shut down properly.

In some cases it may be necessary to indicate to the `fsck` utility the type of file system being checked. This is done with the `-t` option. For example:

```
fsck -t ext2 -f /dev/hdb2
```

Defragmenting a File System

All file systems are divided into units of storage called **blocks**. A standard block contains 1024 characters (bytes). All of the files stored in a file system are broken into pieces and stored in these file system blocks. On many operating systems, the information stored in a file system becomes fragmented. That is, the blocks that make up individual files are spread all over the surface of a hard disk or other device. Reading an entire file on a fragmented hard disk requires much more time and movement of the hard disk mechanism than reading nonfragmented files, which are stored in sequential sections of the hard disk. Windows NT is particularly noted for the need for frequent disk **defragmenting**. (Defragmenting is also called **disk optimization** because it optimizes access time to files and reduces wear on the hard disk.)

Fortunately, the `ext2` file system used by Linux is not subject to much file fragmentation. When new files are written to a Linux hard disk, the files are stored at locations spread across the entire hard disk. This allows space for each file to grow in size without becoming fragmented. In contrast, most file systems used by other operating systems begin storing a new file at the first available location on the hard disk. As new files are added, they fill up the space immediately next to existing files. As a result, if an existing file increases in size, the operating system cannot simply squeeze more information into a space adjacent to the file. Instead, it must allocate the necessary space from a different part of the hard disk. As more and more files become broken into pieces in this way, the disk becomes fragmented. Figure 9-8 illustrates the difference between an `ext2` file system and most other file systems in this regard.

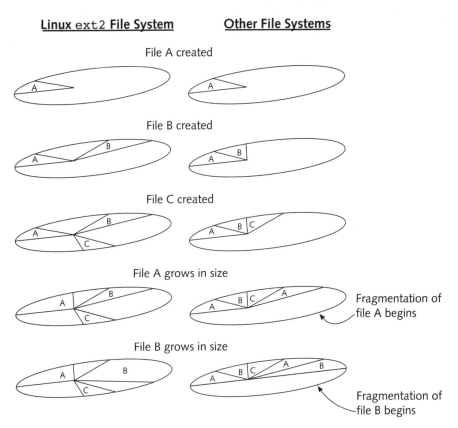

Figure 9-8   Creation of new files in ext2 and in other file systems

When you run the **fsck** utility (or watch it run automatically as Linux is booted), the screen displays the percentage of files on each file system that are fragmented. This percentage is normally less than 3%.

Hard disks that are becoming very full, however, are likely to experience more file fragmentation as space for new or expanded files becomes scarce. In this case, it can be helpful to defragment your Linux hard disk. Because this operation is rarely done in Linux, the utility used to defragment a Linux hard disk is not included with most Linux products. You can download it from the Internet using an FTP site such as *metalab.unc.edu*. Multiple utilities are provided in the defragment package to allow you to work with various types of file systems. The utility used to defragment a standard Linux **ext2** partition is called **e2defrag**.

 When you need to defragment a Linux file system, begin by unmounting the file system. Then be certain to run **fsck** to check the hard disk's integrity. To complete these tasks on the **root** file system, you must boot Linux from a floppy disk so the root partition on the hard disk is not mounted.

Tuning a Linux File System

The **dumpe2fs** command provides many pages of information about a Linux **ext2** file system. This command can be used on any Linux file system, whether mounted or not mounted. It provides details about the options set in the superblock of the file system and information about the data blocks. A paging program such as **less** should be used to view the output of **dumpe2fs**, as it runs to many pages. A sample command is shown here:

```
# /sbin/dumpe2fs /dev/hda3 | less
```

You can use the **tune2fs** utility to specify how an **ext2** file system acts in certain situations. When you format an **ext2** file system, the **mke2fs** command described in Chapter 8 uses default options for the items described in this section. You can add parameters to the **mke2fs** command to set those options as you format a new file system, or you can use the **tune2fs** command after the file system is formatted. Most of these options are stored as part of the superblock on the file system.

The **tune2fs** command should never be used on a file system that is mounted. Unmount the file system that you need to adjust, booting Linux from a floppy if the **root** file system must be tuned.

The tunable parameters for an **ext2** file system affect the file system's stability and, to a lesser degree, its performance. Some configuration options of a file system, such as the block size, cannot be changed without reformatting the file system and using a parameter on the **mke2fs** command. The primary options available with the **tune2fs** command are described in the following paragraphs.

You can set the maximum number of times the file system can be mounted without having a complete integrity check using the **fsck** utility. A lower number will check for errors more often, but will also slow down system startup more often as the system is being checked. You can use the **dumpe2fs** command to see what the current maximum mount count value is set to. A sample command to set this value is shown here:

```
# /sbin/tune2fs -c 10 /dev/hda3
```

The number of times the file system has been mounted since the last time it was checked is recorded in the superblock. You can change this value using the **-C** option. By lowering or raising this number in relation to the maximum mount count parameter, you can control when the next forced automatic integrity check will occur.

You can determine the Linux system's response when a file system error is detected. The response is normally **continue**. However, you can choose to stop the Linux kernel when an error is detected, or remount the file system as read-only instead of read/write. (Note that mounting the file system as read-only may make the operating system unusable, although safe for examination and repairs.) A sample command is shown here:

```
# /sbin/tune2fs -e remount-ro /dev/hda3
```

Part of each Linux file system is set aside as reserved space. This space cannot be used by any regular system users for normal file storage. Instead, it is generally only available to the **root** user when the hard disk becomes full so that `root` can continue to operate the system in order to free space for other users. If the entire `root` file system (including this reserved space) becomes full, the system is basically unusable.

This reserved space on a file system is normally 5% of the total file system space. However, you can configure this amount as a percentage of the total file system size or as a number of data blocks on the file system. You configure these options using the `-m` or `-r` option with the `tune2fs` command. The `root` user can always access this reserved space, but you can also allow another user ID number or group ID number to access it by using the `-g` and `-u` options of `tune2fs`. This might be useful, for example, if you have a file system dedicated to a database application and wish to reserve some space for the database administrator's group.

In addition to the `dumpe2fs` command, you can use the `-l` option of `tune2fs` to list the contents of the superblock. Because the `tune2fs` command sets options within the superblock, viewing the current settings with the `-l` option can be helpful.

UNDERSTANDING REDUNDANT DISK SYSTEMS   9

One of the most vulnerable parts of a computer system is the hard disk. It contains many moving parts, and it may be subjected to constant heavy use. Its health is crucial to the health of the entire system and to users' productivity, because the hard disk contains the data that the computer system was designed to provide. For these reasons, a great deal of effort has gone into making hard disks redundant—so they don't form a potential single point of failure in a system. Although redundant hard disks have long been available on mainframe systems costing millions of dollars, most users now rely on groups of hard disks, known as **redundant arrays of inexpensive disks**. More commonly, these groups of disks are called **RAID** subsystems or RAID arrays.

The idea behind RAID is this: rather than attempting to create a single expensive hard disk that never fails (a technological impossibility), it makes more sense to use a group, or **array**, of standard (inexpensive) hard disks. The assumption is that if one disk fails, the others can take over its duties until the failed disk is replaced. The safety of a RAID system lies in the extreme improbability of all the disks in the array failing at the same time. Of course, this assumes that high-quality components are used—an important assumption for RAID.

The management or control of a RAID system can be implemented in hardware or software. It can contain as many disks as necessary to reach the storage capacity needed. A RAID system does not have a specific number of hard disks, a specific storage capacity, or even a specific platform. RAID systems are used by all operating systems. Instead, the different forms, or levels, of RAID are distinguished by the techniques used to store data, as explained in the following sections.

Defining RAID Levels

RAID can be implemented in many forms, or levels. The levels differ in the amount of fault tolerance they provide and the cost of implementation. The next sections introduce the different RAID levels and define the terms and techniques associated with RAID.

 Vendors occasionally differ in the features they associate with the different RAID levels. When reviewing RAID technologies or products, look for specific features rather than just a level number.

RAID-Linear

RAID-Linear is a technique that makes it possible to combine multiple physical devices into a single logical device. This allows one logical file system (as mounted in Linux) to span multiple disk drives or partitions. This is useful when you want a file system to be larger than a single hard disk. For example, suppose you need a huge file system for the /home directory. By storing this file system on multiple disk drives, you avoid buying one very large (and very expensive) hard disk. Instead, you can purchase multiple disks of a more common size. But the /home directory can still be managed as a single file system because of RAID-Linear.

By itself, this system doesn't provide any fault tolerance or data protection. RAID-Linear is not a true RAID level because it does not provide any fault tolerance, nor does it improve system performance as some RAID levels do. In fact, RAID-Linear reduces fault tolerance because if any one of the disks in a RAID-Linear array fails, the entire file system is unusable. RAID-Linear is illustrated in Figure 9-9.

RAID-0 (Striping)

RAID-0 makes use of a data storage technique known as striping. With **striping**, a single piece of data is divided into pieces and stored on more than one hard disk. This technique allows the system to access data faster, because two disk drives work together to gather parts of any requested information at the same time. The performance gain is increased if each hard disk uses a separate hard disk controller, such as having two SCSI cards; the multiple hard disk controllers prevent a bottleneck in communicating with the CPU via a single data channel. However, if either hard disk fails in a RAID-0 setup, the entire file system is unusable. Hence, using RAID-0 without other measures described in this chapter reduces fault tolerance significantly. Figure 9-10 illustrates the use of striping.

Without RAID-Linear

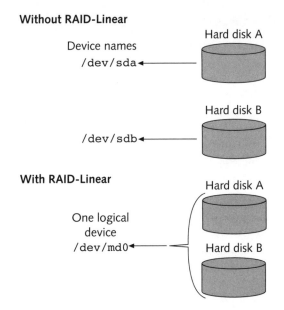

Device names
/dev/sda

Hard disk A

/dev/sdb

Hard disk B

With RAID-Linear

Hard disk A

One logical
device
/dev/md0

Hard disk B

Figure 9-9   RAID-Linear

Without RAID-0 Striping

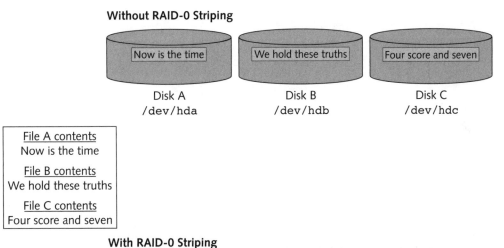

| Now is the time | We hold these truths | Four score and seven |

Disk A
/dev/hda

Disk B
/dev/hdb

Disk C
/dev/hdc

File A contents
Now is the time

File B contents
We hold these truths

File C contents
Four score and seven

With RAID-0 Striping

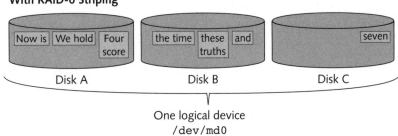

Now is | We hold | Four score   the time | these truths | and   seven

Disk A   Disk B   Disk C

One logical device
/dev/md0

Figure 9-10   RAID-0, or disk striping

RAID-1 (Disk Mirroring and Duplexing)

RAID-1 mirrors data across multiple hard disks. The term **mirroring** is used to describe a system with two or more hard disks that contain identical information. Each time one hard disk is updated, the copy or copies are also updated. If one hard disk fails, the mirrored hard disks continue to respond to data requests without interruption. **Duplexing** is identical to mirroring except that the hard disks are on separate controller cards. The separate controller cards provide increased performance and reduced vulnerability to a hardware failure. Duplexed hard disks are sometimes referred to casually as mirrored disks, though in fact the use of multiple controller cards makes the two techniques distinct. Duplexing is the preferred technique when possible.

Mirrored and duplexed hard disks provide both increased performance (because multiple hard disks respond to data requests at the same time) and increased fault tolerance (because if one hard disk fails, the duplicate disks continue to work without interruption). Mirroring or duplexing disks does have two downsides. First, the time required to write files to a hard disk is increased because data must be written to each disk instead of just one. Second, these techniques require extra hard disks that are used only for mirroring—they don't provide extra storage capacity. For example, if you want to mirror a 10 GB hard disk, you must pay for 20 GB of hard disk space. With the low price of hard disks today, this is generally a very good investment, though it can be a limiting factor when planning a system that includes large amounts of storage (hundreds or thousands of GB of data). Figure 9-11 shows a mirrored hard disk system.

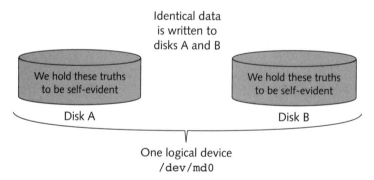

Figure 9-11   RAID-1 with mirrored hard disks

RAID-3 (Striping with Parity)

RAID-0 (striping) improves performance but makes a system more vulnerable to failure. **RAID-3** combines the performance advantages of striping data across multiple hard disks but provides additional protection against the failure of one of the hard disks in the form of parity. The term **parity** refers to a technique that allows corrupted data to be reconstructed using an extra piece of information that is created as the data is stored. The parity information provides redundancy to the piece of data. In RAID-3, this extra information regarding how files are divided up is stored in a **parity stripe**. If one of the hard disks fails, the system can use the parity information to reconstruct the data stored on that disk. Figure 9-12 illustrates a RAID-3 system.

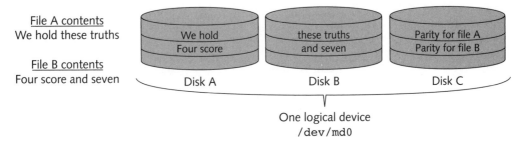

Figure 9-12 RAID-3, striping with parity

RAID-3 provides good fault tolerance because of the parity stripe. If a hard disk fails, data is still usable; when the disk is replaced, the data is rebuilt without any intervention by the system administrator. RAID-3 also improves performance on systems that read a lot from the disk. All the hard disks in a RAID-3 array can work in parallel to respond to multiple requests at the same time. Instead of waiting for a single disk, the chances are good that a hard disk that is not busy can immediately begin to service a read request. Also, unlike disk mirroring, with RAID-3 only one hard disk (the one containing the parity information) is unavailable for data storage. For example, to have 80 GB of storage space in a RAID-3 system, you only need to purchase 90 GB of hard disks. The write performance of RAID-3 does suffer because the parity information must be computed and several hard disks must store information for each write operation.

 Although RAID-2 and RAID-4 are listed in some definitions of RAID, they are not used in production systems and so are not presented here. These two RAID levels simply use different combinations of the technologies implemented by other RAID levels.

RAID-5 (Striping and Parity)

RAID-5 is similar to RAID-3 except that with RAID-5 both the parity information and the stored data are striped across multiple hard disks. This has the advantage of making read performance better, but it makes write performance even worse than RAID-3. As with RAID-3, if a hard disk fails, the parity information allows the information to be reconstructed once the disk is replaced. In the meantime, data remains available.

Figure 9-13 illustrates how RAID-5 spreads information across multiple hard disks. Many vendors who sell RAID-5 hardware systems (see the next section) use built-in **write caching** to store new information in memory until it can be written to the multiple hard disks without degrading performance overall.

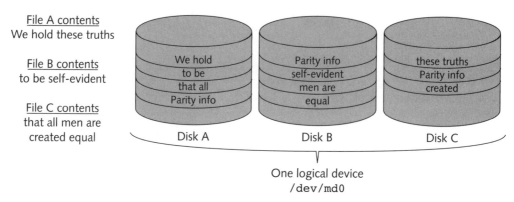

Figure 9-13 illustrates:

File A contents
We hold these truths

File B contents
to be self-evident

File C contents
that all men are
created equal

Disk A: We hold / to be / that all / Parity info

Disk B: Parity info / self-evident / men are / equal

Disk C: these truths / Parity info / created

One logical device
/dev/md0

Figure 9-13   RAID-5, parity and striping over multiple disks

Using Hardware-Based RAID

A RAID system can be implemented as a separate device that connects to your Linux computer like an external printer or CD-ROM drive. This type of RAID is known as **hardware-based RAID** because the control and management of the disk array relies on a hardware system (called a **RAID subsystem**) that is separate from the main computer. Hardware-based RAID devices include separate memory, a CPU, and other components besides the array of hard disks. A hardware-based RAID system contains a separate microprocessor and control circuits; it is practically a separate computer with the sole purpose of providing data to your main system. The main advantage of using a hardware-based RAID system is that all of the special technology is contained in the RAID device. The operating system itself cannot differentiate between a RAID device and any other hard disk. This eliminates the need for any special software or configuration on the Linux system.

Another advantage of hardware RAID systems is that they can provide features that are rarely duplicated without a separate device to house the hard disk array. The most prominent of these features is **hot-swapping**, which makes it possible to pull out and replace a failed hard disk without ever turning the system off. The hot-swapped hard disk is gradually reintegrated into the array as data is written to it; as a result, the failed hard disk entails no downtime. This feature obviously adds to the expense of a RAID system.

A hardware RAID system may include utilities that run on the host operating system and that are designed to manage or configure the RAID device. You must be certain that such utilities can be used on a Linux platform. See the Linux HOWTO document "DPT-Hardware-RAID HOWTO," which explains how to use hardware RAID devices on Linux. The end of the next section describes where to find HOWTO documents.

The main disadvantage of hardware-based RAID is the cost. Because the RAID system has a complete suite of electronics to manage the hard disks, plus a separate case and software utilities, hardware-based RAID is much more expensive than the software-based RAID described next.

Using Software-Based RAID

The term **software-based RAID** refers to RAID that is controlled and managed by software on the computer system that uses the hard disk array. A software-based RAID array includes only the hard disks; the CPU and memory of the computer system to which the array is attached control how the disk array is used. The software used to control this type of RAID array consists of the operating system (the Linux kernel) and additional special device drivers or file system management tools. Because those who use Linux systems are often concerned about the high cost of proprietary computing hardware, software-based RAID is an attractive way for Linux users to achieve the fault tolerance and performance improvements associated with RAID.

To implement software-based RAID on Linux, you can purchase a commercial product designed to support Linux. One such program is the TwinCom duplexed hard disk product (see *www.twincom.com*). Commercial products have the advantage of being fairly easy to install; in addition, the vendors usually provide technical support either for configuration or problem solving.

It is not necessary to choose a commercial version of software-based RAID. The features built into the Linux kernel for support of software-based RAID devices are less expensive and more flexible. However, most system administrators choose not to use these features because they are fairly new and difficult to use. Because these features add fault tolerance without excessive cost (only the extra hard disks and the system administrator's time), you should familiarize yourself with them.

RAID support in the Linux kernel is called Software-RAID. Linux support for softwarebased RAID uses a set of kernel modules called multiple device drivers, which are identified in the /dev directory by the designation md. After enabling the multiple device drivers in the Linux kernel, you can use the RAID software utilities (called `raidtools`) to configure multiple hard disks in accordance with one of the RAID levels described previously. RAID-Linear, RAID-0 (striping), RAID-1 (mirroring/duplexing), and RAID-5 (striping with parity) are supported in the Linux version 2.2 kernels. (This is the kernel shipped with Linux versions

9

such as Red Hat 6.1, SuSE 6.2, and OpenLinux 2.3.) Figure 9-14 shows the screen from which you can configure RAID options.

A complete discussion of setting up RAID using these kernel features is beyond the scope of this book, but the `raidtools` package and copious additional documentation are available to guide the system administrator in this task. You'll find a great deal of helpful information in the mini-HOWTO called "Software-RAID" (though named "mini," this HOWTO is long and thorough). Regarding the specialized task of using RAID for the root partition of a Linux system, see the HOWTO document called "Root-RAID." These documents are available at many Internet sites where the Linux HOWTO documents are stored, such as *ftp://metalab.unc.edu/pub/Linux/docs/HOWTO/*. Most Linux distributions also include a copy of the HOWTO documents. For example, Red Hat 6.1 includes these files on the first CD-ROM in their package at `/doc/HOWTO` and `/doc/HOWTO/mini`.

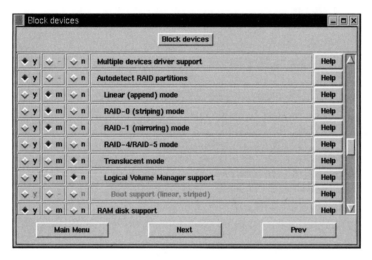

Figure 9-14   Screen used to configure Software-RAID

REDUNDANT SERVERS

The first part of this chapter mentioned using duplicate servers located in different cities as a method of providing a highly fault tolerant information system. However, Linux does not yet have the ability to accommodate redundant servers in the same way that some operating systems can. A redundant server requires very high speed data communications lines and special software to both mirror information and inform each system of when the other is responding to requests and when it should respond because of an outage of some sort. Figure 9-15 shows how two redundant servers might be connected after additional hardware and software support is added to Linux. The connections include:

- A serial cable over which a brief repeating signal (known as a heartbeat) informs each system of the status of the other system. This signal allows special software on each server to know when to take over functions because the other server is down. (In some server configurations, a high-speed network connection is used instead of a serial cable.)

■ A hardware RAID subsystem with a "twin-tailed" cable. The twin-tailed cable allows one RAID subsystem to be connected to two computers. Both computers can access information simultaneously. If either server goes down, the other server still has complete access to the same data.

■ Dual network cards in each server, so that if one network card were to fail, the server could still communicate with clients on the network.

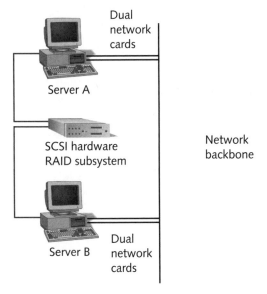

Figure 9-15   Redundant servers

Although standard Linux does not yet support true redundant servers, you can use several technologies to improve the fault tolerance of your Linux systems. Consider the following ideas for improved fault tolerance of Linux systems in large organizations:

■ You can use a commercial product such as the TwinCom Linux disk mirroring software mentioned previously to mirror hard disks across a network link. Though this doesn't create a true redundant server that can automatically take over if the other server fails, it does replicate data in two different locations.

■ By configuring your router and Domain Name Service appropriately, you can ensure that two or more computers are available to respond to requests for Web pages, FTP information, or other Internet services. Special routers are available to spread incoming requests among several servers that contain identical information. Thus if one server goes down, another server will respond to the incoming requests. This arrangement isn't appropriate for a small system used by only a few people (such as a departmental database server), but it is very helpful (though expensive) for Web sites that cannot tolerate downtime. By using a product like the network-based mirroring in the previous item, you can position these different servers in different offices or cities.

- Some Linux products support a set of multiple servers working in tandem to run Web servers or other network services that require constant uptime. (One notable vendor of such products is Turbo Linux; see the company's Web site at *www.turbolinux.com.*) These additions to a standard Linux distribution manage the transfer of control between systems to handle large numbers of incoming requests. Figure 9-16 illustrates how a DNS name server can route incoming requests for a Web page among a set of Web servers. This setup allows the set of Web servers to handle a large traffic volume with redundancy among the Web servers.

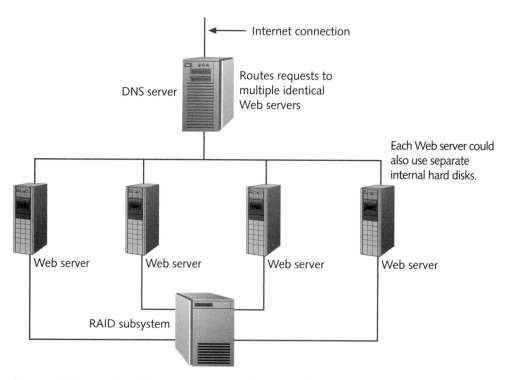

Figure 9-16   A set of Web servers responding to Web page requests

- The high-end server systems sold by the major hardware vendors (such as IBM, Toshiba, Compaq, Dell, and Acer) now support Linux. These servers support features like hot-swap hard disk bays for use with RAID software, redundant power supplies and cooling fans, and other fault tolerant hardware features.

> **TIP** You may have heard of a Linux development called **Beowulf**. This technology allows multiple Linux-based computers to be tied together in a parallel-processing architecture to simulate a supercomputer for work requiring massive amounts of computation (such as calculating weather patterns or world economic models). Beowulf is not intended to create redundancy for a single server, however, because each server in a Beowulf cluster takes on a specific portion of the computing task.

CHAPTER SUMMARY

❑ Maintaining high availability of a Linux system is increasingly important for many organizations. A disaster plan and an understanding of the hardware and software options available can help reduce downtime for a Linux system. Creating a disk from which a failed system can be booted and maintaining a software master for all server applications are two easy steps that help a system administrator to prepare for possible emergencies.

❑ The power supply to a computer is a key point of possible failure. By using surge suppressors, maintaining back-up power supply parts, and installing a UPS, the power to a Linux system can be safeguarded.

❑ Hard disks are the most vulnerable failure point in most computer systems. By checking file systems regularly and using redundant systems such as RAID, information on hard disks can be protected against costly system failures. RAID systems can be controlled by separate hardware devices or directly through software support in the Linux kernel. Several levels of RAID are defined, according to how information is arranged on a set of hard disks. Different RAID levels provide various performance, reliability, and cost trade-offs.

9

KEY TERMS

AC power — The standard alternating current power coming into a building from a public utility; the power from a wall socket.

array — A collection of multiple hard disks. *See* RAID.

Beowulf — A cluster of multiple Linux servers operating in parallel as a supercomputer to solve complex problems.

block — A unit of storage on a file system. A standard block contains 1024 characters (bytes).

boot disk — A disk used to launch the Linux operating system stored on your hard disk. It can be used in normal operating situations to start the Linux system.

defragmenting — The process of rearranging the files on a file system so that all the parts of a file are located next to each other on the physical hard disk. Defragmenting a hard disk increases system performance and reduces wear on the storage device.

directory record — A file containing the names and inode numbers of other files.

disaster plan — An organized written plan that describes how to respond to various threats to an information system such as Linux.

disk optimization — *See* defragmenting.

downtime — Occasions when an organization's computer systems cannot respond to requests for information.

dumpe2fs — A utility used to display technical statistics and parameters about a Linux `ext2` file system.

duplexing — Term used to describe a system in which the contents of two file systems, that are located on different hard disk controllers, contain identical information. Compare to "mirroring," a technique that provides identical information on two file systems but without redundant disk controllers.

e2defrag — The utility used to defragment a standard Linux **ext2** partition.

fault tolerance — The condition of being able to tolerate errors or events that might otherwise cause system failure.

file record — An information item within an **ext2** file system that includes a filename and an inode number. The inode itself contains detailed information about the file.

fsck — A utility used to check the integrity of an **ext2** file system.

hard link — A pointer to an inode that is already pointed to by at least one other file record.

hardware-based RAID — A RAID array that is contained in a separate hardware device (a RAID subsystem) and is controlled by a CPU and other components separate from the CPU of the Linux system.

high availability — Term used to refer to the processes, products, or programs involved in ensuring that a system experiences as little downtime as possible. The goal for all high availability systems is 100% uptime.

high availability cluster — A group of servers that process the same tasks (resource groups) and take over each others' functionality in the event of an outage or failure.

hot-swapping — The process of removing and replacing a failed hard drive from a RAID hardware device or specialized server without turning off the power to the device.

init — A daemon that acts as a control process to start the first processes on Linux, such as the login screens.

inode — A file information record, identified by a unique number within a file system, which contains detailed information about a block of data commonly called a file.

install disk — A disk used when you first install Linux. Its contents are similar to a rescue disk, but it is not designed to assist you in recovering damaged data.

link — A special file record that refers to the same physical file data as another file record.

mirroring — Term used to describe a system in which the contents of two file systems contain identical information. Mirroring improves data access speed and provides fault tolerance in the event that one of the file systems fails.

parity — A technique that allows corrupted data to be reconstructed using an extra piece of information (the parity information) that is created as the data is stored. Parity information provides redundancy for a piece of information.

parity stripe — Parity information stored as part of a RAID-3 or RAID-5 system.

points of failure — Parts of an information system that are subject to failure.

power supply — The component within a computer system that converts the incoming AC power from a wall socket or UPS device to the correct voltage for use by components in a computer.

RAID — A system using multiple inexpensive hard disks arranged in a predefined pattern (an array) to improve performance, increase fault tolerance, or both.

RAID-0 — A RAID level that uses striping to improve disk performance but without adding any fault tolerance.

RAID-1 — A RAID level that uses disk mirroring to significantly improve fault tolerance. Disk read performance is also improved, but disk write performance suffers.

RAID-3 — A RAID level that uses striping with parity information to improve both performance and fault tolerance.

RAID-5 — A RAID level in which data striping with parity is spread across all disks in the RAID array (compared to RAID-3, in which the parity information is stored on a single hard disk).

RAID-Linear — A method of combining multiple physical devices into a single logical device.

RAID subsystem — A hardware-controlled RAID device containing a CPU and other components to control the array of hard disks.

redundancy — Term used to refer to a duplicate system component or piece of data. Many fault tolerant systems rely on the use of redundant components or data; in the event of a failure, the duplicate component or copy of the data would still be available.

redundant arrays of inexpensive disks — *See* RAID.

rescue disk — A disk created specifically to boot a Linux system in the event of a system failure. Contains the software tools most likely to be of help in diagnosing and repairing the problem with the failed system.

rescue mode — A mode of operation in Red Hat Linux that is initiated by starting the system using a rescue disk. Rescue mode is used to repair a system failure that blocks normal booting and operation.

resource groups — The tasks and their accompanying system resources that are defined within a high availability cluster. Each server in the cluster can take over a complete resource group if the server handling that resource group fails.

root disk — A disk used in conjunction with an install disk during some Linux installations (depending on the Linux distribution you are using).

single point of failure — A system component which, if it alone fails, renders a system unusable. Can be a hardware component or a piece of data.

software masters — Original copies of an application supplied by a software vendor or manufacturer, usually one or more CDs, tapes, or disks.

software-based RAID — A RAID array that is controlled or managed by software on the computer system that uses the hard disk array (the Linux system) rather than by a separate CPU or other hardware components.

striping — A technique in which parts of a file are written to more than one disk in order to improve performance. *See* RAID-3.

superblock — The master information record for a Linux file system.

surge suppressor — A device that prevents potentially damaging electrical irregularities from reaching a computer system's power supply.

symbolic link — A file record that includes a path and filename, but not an inode.

tune2fs — A utility used to view or adjust parameters within the superblock of a Linux file system.

uninterruptible power supply (UPS) — A device capable of providing power to a computer via batteries when the incoming AC power (wall socket power) fails. It also informs the Linux system of the status of the power.

write caching — A technique in which information to be written to a file system (particularly a RAID file system) is stored in system memory temporarily in order to improve performance of reading and writing information to the file system.

REVIEW QUESTIONS

1. A good disaster plan should consider _____ versus benefit.
   a. RAID level
   b. dangers
   c. cost
   d. availability

2. How does the amount of time that a company can be without data affect the contents of a disaster plan?

3. Why is it important to maintain software masters rather than rely on vendor support?

4. At a minimum, a rescue disk should contain which of the following:
   a. A virtual console option
   b. A text editor and disk repair utilities
   c. A Beowulf configuration
   d. The file system superblock

5. Points of failure in a system have a direct relation to the _____ of the system.
   a. fault tolerance
   b. redundancy
   c. cost
   d. write-caching

6. A built-in back-up power supply is the same thing as an uninterruptible power supply. True or False?

7. A surge suppressor protects against all of the following except:
   a. Power outages
   b. Voltage spikes
   c. Reduced voltage
   d. Brownouts

8. What program is used to monitor a UPS and send a signal indicating that Linux should shut down?

9. A `shutdown` command can be canceled if the main AC power is restored. True or False?

10. The configuration file for the `powerd` daemon includes the following:

    a. Scripts used when shutting down Linux

    b. The serial port and serial pin to monitor

    c. Debug information used to correct system flaws

    d. The call to the `shutdown` command

11. The `init` daemon does which of the following:

    a. Manages all processes and receives signals from the `powerd` daemon

    b. Monitors the UPS via a serial cable

    c. Manages the `powerd.conf` configuration file

    d. Creates a high availability server

12. Which condition is normally *not* monitored by a UPS or the `powerd` daemon?

    a. Main AC power failure

    b. UPS battery low

    c. Main AC power restored

    d. Telephone power failure

13. Redundant arrays of inexpensive disks (RAID) are used to provide:

    a. Lower-cost systems than single disks

    b. Redundant superblock information

    c. Fault tolerance and improved performance

    d. Beowulf clusters

14. Striping refers to which of the following?

    a. Spreading a single file across multiple hard disks

    b. Duplicating file information on multiple hard disks

    c. Adding error-correcting codes to a file

    d. Duplicating inode data

15. Define the advantages of using hot-swapped disk drives.

16. Linux does not yet support any high availability features. True or False?

17. A high availability cluster is a Beowulf cluster used for parallel processing. True or False?

18. Software-based RAID support in Linux is configured as part of which of the following?

    a. Both symbolic and hard links in the file system

    b. The write-caching configuration file

    c. The Linux kernel and related modules and drivers

    d. The `fsck` and `tune2fs` utilities

19. If data contained in a file system's superblock is unreadable, the file system cannot be accessed. True or False?

20. An inode contains information about a file, including all of the following except:

    a. The file's name

    b. The file's location on the hard disk or other device

    c. The file's inode number

    d. Dates and times of creation and last access

21. Symbolic links refer to inode numbers; hard links refer to paths and filenames. True or False?

22. Describe the purpose of reserving a percentage of the space within a file system for the **root** or other user account.

23. At boot time, the **fsck** utility does the following:

    a. Automatically checks each mounted **ext2** file system for errors

    b. Unmounts any damaged file systems

    c. Reads and resets key superblock parameters

    d. Calls the **tune2fs** utility to manage file system start-up

24. The maximum number of times a file system can be mounted between complete **fsck** integrity checks can be configured using **tune2fs**. True or False?

25. Disk fragmentation is not a problem in Linux **ext2** file systems because:

    a. New files are created at locations spread around the entire file system.

    b. Striping used by the Linux Software-RAID feature prevents fragmentation.

    c. The **fsck** utility defragments the file system each time the system is booted.

    d. Fragmentation is not a single point of failure for a high availability system.

HANDS-ON PROJECTS

Project 9-1

In this activity you create a floppy disk containing an **ext2** file system and work with that file system using the **fsck** and **tune2fs** commands. This allows you to experiment with concepts explained in this chapter without damaging the data on a hard disk. To complete this project you need a blank disk and an installed Linux system.

1. Insert a blank 3½-inch disk in the disk drive of your Linux computer.

2. Log in to Linux as **root** and open a command-line window.

3. Format the disk, creating an **ext2** file system, using this command: **/sbin/mke2fs /dev/fd0**. Study the information that appears on screen during the formatting process to see what items you recognize from the discussion in the chapter (such as inodes, blocks, and the superbock).

4. Dump the information from the floppy file system using this command:
   /sbin/dumpe2fs /dev/fd0. The listing is short because the floppy is a small file
   system. Review the information found on the superblock to see which fields you
   recognize from the chapter discussion. (Other fields are described in the **dumpe2fs**
   manual page.)

5. Change the maximum mount count for the floppy file system using this command:
   /sbin/tune2fs –c 5 /dev/fd0. (The default value when you created the file
   system in Step 3 was 20.)

6. Check that the new value for maximum mount count is stored on the disk by using
   the **–l** option of the **tune2fs** command to view the superblock (this is similar to
   the **dumpe2fs** command but only dumps the superblock parameters):
   /sbin/tune2fs –l /dev/fd0.

7. Check the integrity of the floppy file system using this command: **fsck /dev/fd0**.
   The results appear within a second or two because the file system is clean.

8. Mount the floppy disk so you can write a file to it, as follows: **mount –t ext2
   /dev/fd0 /mnt/floppy**. (The **/mnt/floppy** directory exists on most Linux
   systems. You can create this directory if necessary, or use a different mount point if
   you wish.)

9. Copy a system file to the floppy disk using this command: **cp /etc/termcap
   /mnt/floppy**. As the file is being written, eject the disk. (A large file is referred to in
   this example command to give you time to eject the disk while the copy operation is
   still in progress.) This simulates an error condition or power outage that may damage
   the file system.

10. Reinsert the floppy disk.

11. Unmount the floppy disk using this command: **umount /dev/fd0**.

12. Run the **fsck** command again as follows: **fsck /dev/fd0**. This time the command
    shows the message **/dev/fd0 was not cleanly unmounted, check
    forced**. Depending on what was in process at the moment you ejected the disk,
    fsck may ask you a question about the disk data, or it may automatically update and
    correct any damaged status information.

13. Mount the file system again as follows: **mount –t ext2 /dev/fd0 /mnt/floppy**.

14. View the file system contents to see if you copied the file successfully, using the
    following command: **ls –l /mnt/floppy**. Because the copy operation was
    interrupted, the file is probably not there.

15. Unmount the file system again and eject the disk using this command: **umount
    /dev/fd0**.

Project 9-2

In this activity you review information on the **root** file system. This is similar to the previous activity except that you work directly on your hard disk rather than on a blank floppy
disk. Follow the instructions carefully to avoid damaging your Linux hard disk. To complete
this project you need an installed Linux system.

1. Log in to Linux as **root** and open a command-line window.

2. Enter the **mount** command with no options to see which device contains your root file system. The first line of the output from the **mount** command includes this information. The line looks like the following sample output except that the first part (the device name) will be different on your system:

   ```
   /dev/hda3 on / type ext2 (rw)
   ```

3. Use the **dumpe2fs** command to review information about your **root** file system. Pipe the results through the **less** command so you can page through them one screen at a time. The necessary command looks like **dumpe2fs /dev/hda3 | less** (substitute the device name for your **root** file system where **/dev/hda3** is used).

4. Look for the line containing `File system volume name` in the output of the **dumpe2fs** command. Is a volume name defined on your system?

5. Look for the line containing `Mount count` in the output of the **dumpe2fs** command. What does this number represent? How does this number relate to the line labeled `Maximum mount count`?

6. Use the **tune2fs** command to list information from the superblock of your **root** file system. Use this command, substituting the device name of your **root** file system: **tune2fs -l /dev/hda3**. How does this information compare to the first part of the output from the **dumpe2fs** command?

7. The **tune2fs** command cannot be used to change parameters on a file system that is mounted. Because the **root** file system is always mounted when you boot your system normally, you must boot from a disk (such as a rescue disk) to change parameters on your **root** file system. View the man page of the **tune2fs** command to review what parameters can be changed using this command. Can you identify a hard disk parameter that cannot be changed with **tune2fs**?

Project 9-3

In this activity you review the Software-RAID HOWTO document. This document contains additional technical information about using RAID on Linux. To complete this project you need an Internet connection and a working Web browser.

1. Start your Web browser and go to the Linux HQ site at: *www.linuxhq.com*.

2. Click the link for the Linux Docs/Info section. (You can also explore other sections of this site to learn more about Linux kernel development.)

3. On the Linux Information page, click the link for HOWTOs. Additional documentation links are provided for many Linux-related subjects.

4. On the Linux HOWTO Index page, click **3.2 mini-HOWTOs**. The mini-HOWTOs cover more focused topics; they are not necessarily smaller documents.

5. When the long list of mini-HOWTO documents appears, scroll down and click **Software-RAID mini-HOWTO**. (You may also find many other interesting topics to study on the list of mini-HOWTOs.)

6. Review the sections of the Software-RAID mini-HOWTO document. Click on a section, read or skim some of it, then try the navigation links at the top or bottom of the section to switch to the previous or next section, or back to the table of contents for the Software-RAID mini-HOWTO. What warnings have you noticed about using RAID?

7. In section 1 of the mini-HOWTO, find the list of related Linux RAID documents. Select one that looks interesting and follow it to read more about RAID.

CASE PROJECTS

1. You have been asked to provide consulting services as an expert system administrator to Thompson Mutual Funds, a nationwide financial services company. Thompson employs customer service representatives who respond to customer inquiries about their accounts, via telephone, 24 hours per day. Thompson also maintains a Web site with information about mutual funds and access to stock market pricing information and individual accounts (where customers can view their balance, transfer funds between accounts, and so forth). Thompson has two main offices, one in San Francisco and another in Miami. All of the customer data is stored on Linux-based database servers. Without listing specific hardware and software requirements, what key measures would you use to try to protect Thompson's computer systems and provide high availability? Describe in general terms the features of your disaster plan, what it protects against, what risks it does not fully address, and how costly each part of the plan might be to implement.

2. Considering the strong financial position of Thompson Mutual Funds and the lost value caused by any system downtime, discuss which RAID level or levels you might use in setting up the storage systems on a Linux server within a single Thompson office.

3. The Thompson Web server is located in the San Francisco office. Because existing customers use the Web server to access account information, Thompson wants to avoid any downtime for the Web server. Web server uptime is not as important as keeping the main database servers running, because customers can always call a customer service representative if the Web site is down. Describe the relationship between the Web servers and the database servers. (Is one dependent on the other?) What high availability features would be appropriate for the Web server?

# CHAPTER 10

MANAGING SYSTEM RESOURCES

After reading this chapter and completing the exercises, you will be able to:

♦ Access the `/proc` file system to learn about system status

♦ Use the `ps` and related commands to control how processes use system resources

♦ Track physical and virtual memory usage

♦ Locate and relieve system bottlenecks

In the previous chapter you learned about safeguarding information on your Linux server by creating a disaster plan for your information systems. You learned about using an uninterruptible power supply and checking the integrity of your file systems using the `fsck` program. You also learned about several fault tolerance capabilities that you can add to Linux, such as RAID disk drives.

In this chapter you learn how to manage system resources so that users on your Linux system can complete their work effectively. Among other resources, you will learn about CPU time (processing capacity) and system memory. Once you are familiar with the commands that manage these resources, you will be able to locate and alleviate bottlenecks that restrict system performance.

ACCESSING THE `/PROC` FILE SYSTEM

In any operating system, many activities are taking place that are not visible on your computer screen. This is especially true of a Linux or UNIX system, in which multiple background processes (daemons) continue working even when users do not appear to be running applications. Background activities include managing network traffic, sending files to printers, logging Linux kernel activity, and managing system memory utilization (such as moving information to and from the swap partition).

When necessary, you can use the **`/proc` file system** to see what the operating system kernel is doing at any given time. This feature is called a file system because you access information in `/proc` the same way you do in any file system—by reading a file using a command such as `cat`. But the information in the `/proc` file system is not stored on a hard disk. When you view the contents of a filename in `/proc`, the Linux kernel responds with live information about the status of a process, memory, or other items related to the kernel or other system resources. This information changes from moment to moment inside the Linux kernel.

For example, `/proc` can provide a list of the amount of memory on your system and how it is being used. Execute the command `cat /proc/meminfo` to show memory information. Sample output for this command is shown here:

```
            total:      used:      free:       shared:    buffers:   cached:
Mem:        31559680   30765056   794624      45461504   782336     12251136
Swap:       133885952  1318912    132567040
MemTotal:   30820 kB
MemFree:    776 kB
MemShared:  44396 kB
Buffers:    764 kB
Cached:     11964 kB
SwapTotal:  130748 kB
SwapFree:   129460 kB
```

You can also write information to some filenames in `/proc`. For example, you can write a value to `/proc/sys/fs/file-max` to change the number of file handles that can be used at one time in Linux. (A **file handle** is an internal storage mechanism that allows a single file to be opened and used in Linux.) This command displays the number of file handles currently configured in the Linux kernel:

`cat /proc/sys/fs/file-max`

This command changes the number of file handles available in the Linux kernel to 2048:

`echo 2048 > /proc/sys/fs/file-max`

Most files in `/proc` are only used to display information about the kernel. The examples shown so far illustrate the types of information you can see by viewing files in the `/proc` file system. The next two sections explain how to use `/proc` to view a great deal of information about your system hardware and the processes running on Linux.

Viewing Device Information

The `/proc` file system provides information about many parts of your system hardware. This information can be useful as you configure devices or software services. Table 10-1 lists the paths in your Linux directory structure where you can access various hardware information.

Table 10-1   Hardware Information Accessible Through /proc

Hardware information	Path
Battery information for systems using advanced power management (APM) software	/proc/apm
CPU information	/proc/cpuinfo
Direct memory access (DMA) channels used by system devices	/proc/dma
Interrupts configured for system devices	/proc/interrupts
Ports (memory addresses) used to communicate with system devices	/proc/ioports
File systems currently available to the Linux kernel	/proc/mounts
Disk partitions known to the Linux kernel	/proc/partitions
Information on all PCI devices in your system, such as video cards and hard disk controllers	/proc/pci
Information on all SCSI devices in your system	/proc/scsi and its subdirectories
Information on the real-time clock in your system	/proc/rtc
Swap device information	/proc/swaps

10

To see the hardware interrupts used by your computer, use this command: `cat/proc/interrupts`. On a typical Linux system, this command would produce the following output:

```
            CPU0
   0:     149607         XT-PIC   timer
   1:       2589         XT-PIC   keyboard
   2:          0         XT-PIC   cascade
   4:       1431         XT-PIC   serial
   5:          1         XT-PIC   pcnet_cs
   8:          2         XT-PIC   rtc
  12:          2         XT-PIC   PS/2 Mouse
  13:          1         XT-PIC   fpu
  14:      78763         XT-PIC   ide0
  15:          4         XT-PIC   ide1
 NMI:          0
```

When you add devices to your system or configure existing hardware, you can use the output from the preceding command to verify that two devices are not configured to use the same interrupt number, or that a device such as a sound card is not configured to use an interrupt that is actually assigned to another device.

Keep in mind that you won't find all of the hardware information required for configuring Linux systems in /proc. For example, if your system includes a PCI video card, /proc/pci will not provide sufficient information to allow you to configure the X Window System and a graphical desktop. Video card details, such as the video chipset, are not used by the kernel, so they are not maintained in the /proc file system.

Many of the Linux system administration utilities rely on information from /proc. One example is the set of system information provided by the Control Center in the KDE Desktop, which is shown in Figure 10-1. Notice that the list of items under Information corresponds quite closely to the list of hardware information described in Table 10-1.

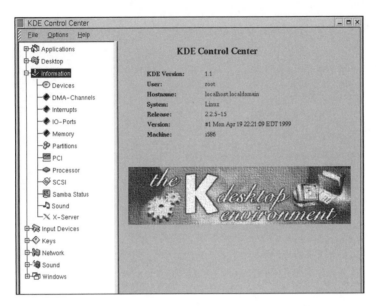

Figure 10-1   System information in the KDE Control Center

Other utilities such as free and ps, described later in this chapter, also obtain information from /proc and present it in a format that is easier to read than are the /proc files themselves.

Viewing Process Information

The /proc file system contains information for each process. This information is updated moment to moment, as the status of a process changes. Before you can access information in /proc regarding a specific process, you need to find the process's PID number. (As you learned in Chapter 9, every process running on Linux is assigned a process ID, or PID, number.) To find the PID for a running process (such as a program that you have started), you need to use the ps command.

Suppose that, using the ps command, you discover the PID for a particular process is 1066. You can then look for information about the process in a directory named /proc/1066. Much of this information is difficult to use directly because it consists of many numbers without explanations—hence the need for administrative utilities that can display process data in a meaningful way. One part of the process data that is readable, however, is the `cmdline` file, which tells you the command used to start the process. The following will tell you the command used to start the process with a PID of 1066: `cat /proc/1066/cmdline`. This produces the following output, which indicates that the enlightenment command with two parameters (`-clientId` and `default2`) was used to start the process.

```
enlightenment —clientId default2
```

You can explore other subdirectories of a process information directory like `/proc/1066` on your own Linux system to determine what types of information about a process are available to you and to Linux utilities.

MANAGING PROCESSES

In Chapter 9 you learned about using the **ps** command to send signals to processes running on Linux. In this section you will learn more about the output of the **ps** command. You will also learn how you can control the way processes use system resources on Linux.

To effectively manage your system, you need to select the processes you're interested in and then display various pieces of information about those processes. You can use several options in the **ps** command to select which processes are included in the command output. Table 10-2 summarizes these selection options.

10

Table 10-2 ps Options Used to Select Processes Included in Command Output

Command-line option	Description
-A	Selects all processes on the system.
T	Selects all processes running in the current terminal.
x	Selects all processes that were not started normally from a terminal (this list includes system initialization scripts and network services).
r	Restricts output to running processes (those that are not sleeping). This option is used in conjunction with another selection option.
-C	Selects processes by the command used to start the process. To use this option, you need to follow it with the name of the command.
-p	Selects processes by PID number. To view information on a single process, enter its PID number as a value after the option.
--user	Selects processes by username. To use this option, type the username after the option.
--group	Selects all processes belonging to users who are members of the group named after the option.

For example, **root** could employ the following command to list all processes owned by user **jsmith**:

```
ps --user jsmith
```

The **ps** command can provide many types of information about each process. You can select which pieces, or fields, of information **ps** includes in output by using command-line options. Table 10-3 shows the information available from the **ps** command for each process. Many of the terms used in the Description column (such as "nice level") are discussed at length later in this chapter, but a few are used only for special troubleshooting tasks and are beyond the scope of this book.

Table 10-3   Process Information Fields Available from **ps**

Display code (column heading in ps output)	Description	Command-line option
PID	Process ID	pid
PPID	Process ID of the parent process	ppid
PGID	Process group ID	pgid
SID	Session ID	sess
TTY	Controlling terminal	tty
TPGID	Process group ID of the owner of the terminal running the process	tpgid
USER	Owner of the process	user
PRI	Time left of a possible timeslice allocated to the process	pri
NICE	Nice level	nice
PLCY	Scheduling policy	plcy
RPRI	Real-time priority	rpri
MAJFLT	Number of major faults loading information from a file system	majflt
MINFLT	Number of minor faults (with no disk access involved)	minflt
TRS	Size of the text used by the program (in KB)	trs
DRS	Size of the data used by the program (in KB)	drs
SIZE	Virtual image size of the process (in KB)	size
SWAP	Space used on swap device by this process (in KB)	swap
RSS	Kilobytes of the program resident in memory	rss
SHARE	Shared memory size in KB	share
DT	Number of pages of information that are dirty (not yet updated to hard disk)	dt
STAT	State of the process	stat
FLAGS	Process flags	f
WCHAN	Kernel function at the point where the process is sleeping	wchan
UID	User ID of the owner of this process	uid

Table 10-3   Process Information Fields Available from ps (continued)

Display code (column heading in ps output)	Description	Command-line option
%WCPU	Weighted percentage of CPU time consumed	wpcpu
%CPU	Percentage of CPU used since last update	pcpu
%MEM	Percentage of memory used	pmem
START	Time that the process was started	start
TIME	Total amount of CPU time (cumulative) that the process has used since it was started	time
COMM	Command line that started the process (abbreviated)	comm
CMDLINE	Command line that started the process (complete)	cmd

The options from Table 10-2 are generally combined with output selection options from Table 10-3. To use a command-line option from Table 10-3 to view selected process information, use the arguments given in the third column of the table after the **o** option. For example, to display all processes (option -A), including processes without controlling terminals (option **x**), and display only the command line for each of those processes (option **comm**), use this command:

`ps -A xo comm`

You can use additional **ps** options to display a predefined set of process information. Table 10-4 describes these options.

Table 10-4   Predefined Sets of Process Information Displayed by the ps Command.

Command-line option	Description
j	Show fields related to controlling jobs in a shell
s	Show fields related to signals that each process handles
u	Show fields that define how the owner of each process is using system resources
v	Show fields detailing how each process is using virtual memory
l	Show numerous fields considered by system administrators to be of interest in tracking processes but not otherwise related (as the above groupings for job control, virtual memory, and so forth, are groups of related fields)
o or --format	User-defined format (display all of the fields listed after the option; each field to be included in the output is defined by using a code from the right column of Table 10-3)

TIP   The man page for the **ps** command contains additional details about how to use **ps** command options.

As a system administrator, you have the task of managing numerous processes started by numerous users. You need to track how these processes consume system resources—particularly CPU time. The %CPU and TIME fields of the ps command output are especially useful in tracking how processes are using CPU time.

The %CPU field compares the amount of CPU time used by a process with the total time elapsed since the previous computation of the %CPU field in the form of a percentage. The Linux kernel tracks a small slice of time (such as one second) and then determines for how much of that one second a process was using the CPU. That computation creates a percentage used for the %CPU field of the ps command output. The %CPU field does not show the average amount of CPU time used by the process since it was started. The %WCPU field is weighted to show a 30-second average of the percentage of CPU time used by a process. This field is more helpful for showing the overall usage pattern for a process.

The TIME field provides a cumulative measure of the amount of CPU time consumed by a process. Processes that have been running since the system was booted may still have a TIME value of 0:00 because they are background processes with very little activity to monitor. But some processes that are only recently started may show a large TIME value (for example, 5:30 to indicate five and a half minutes), indicating that they are using a lot of the CPU's time. The START field tells you when a process began running. When a process has a large TIME value after running for only a short time, you may need to change the priority of that process to prevent it from slowing down other processes. The next section describes how to do this.

Process Priorities

Each process is assigned a **priority** when it is started. This priority determines how much CPU time is granted to the process to complete its tasks. Normally, all processes have the same priority—that is, all processes are assigned an equal portion of CPU time for processing. Another name for the priority of a process is **nice level**.

> TIP   PRI in the ps command output is short for *Priority*, but this field actually indicates how a process is using the CPU time allocated to it. You will notice that this field changes regularly for a given process as the process works, using CPU time at different moments.

The NICE or NI field in the output of the ps command indicates the nice level, or priority level, assigned to a process. The nice level is a fixed value for a process. This value determines whether a process receives extra CPU processing time or less CPU processing time (compared to other processes running on the system). Thus the nice level can be set to change the relative priority of a process running on Linux. The idea behind the name "nice" is that if a user on the system decides a certain program is not time sensitive, the user can make the program "nicer" to other users' programs by giving up some of its CPU time.

Changing Priorities with `nice` and `renice`

You can alter the priority of a process by using the `nice` command or the `renice` command. The standard nice level is 0, meaning that all processes start with equal priority. Any user can raise the nice level of a process that he or she has started (and thus owns), making it nicer to other programs. The highest nice level, which makes a program run the slowest, is 20. The `root` user can make any process nicer, but `root` can also make programs less nice by lowering the nice level. The `root` user can lower the nice level of a process to -20, which gives that process a lot of extra CPU time. The current nice level of a process is shown as the `NI` or `NICE` field in the output of the `ps` command.

The `nice` command is used when launching a process to assign a nonstandard priority to that process—to make it nicer (or less nice if you are `root`). The parameters used with the `nice` command include a nice level and the name of the program to launch. For example, to start a script named `analyze` with a nice level of 10, use this command:

```
nice -10 analyze
```

The `renice` command is used to change the nice level of a process that is already running. Regular users can change the nice level of processes that they own; `root` can change the nice level of any process. The `renice` command requires at least the PID of the process you want to affect. The `root` user can perform more complex tasks using `renice`. These tasks require additional information such as the user ID (UID) of the owner of a process. For example, suppose you start a complex script named `analyze`. After starting the script, you decide you can wait for the results of the script, allowing other programs to run more efficiently. You can change the nice level of the process by using the PID of the running script with the `renice` command. For example, if the PID of the `analyze` script is 1776, this `renice` command will change the script's priority.

```
renice +10 1776
```

Suppose that as the system administrator you discover that a certain user is running several computationally intensive programs that are slowing down system response for other users. After checking with this user, you learn that the programs are a valid use of the system resources, but they are not time critical. To make things run more smoothly for other users, you change the priority of all processes run by that user so they run more slowly. When the intensive programs are finished running, you can reset the user's priority level back to a default value (0). This command changes the priority of all processes owned by user `jsmith`:

```
renice +5 -u jsmith
```

Examples of possible uses for `renice` include:

- The system administrator requests that all noncritical processes be run at higher nice levels while certain intensive system administration tasks are being completed.

- A user has started several processes; some are time sensitive, some are not. By raising the nice level of the processes that are not time sensitive, the other processes should be completed sooner. (The status of processes owned by other users affects the results of this effort, however.)

10

Viewing Processor Usage with `top`

The `top` utility is a standard command-line utility included with all versions of Linux. You can use `top` to display a list of processes on your Linux system similar to the list shown by `ps` with the `aux` options. But the output of `top` is arranged by how much CPU time is being used by a process. The process that is consuming the greatest amount of CPU time is shown at the top of the list, and so forth, to the bottom of the list. The output of `top` is also updated regularly (every five seconds by default, although you can configure the update interval yourself).

Running `top` and then leaving it visible on your screen allows you to watch the activity of different processes to see which ones are using a lot of CPU time. If one process begins to take more than its fair share of CPU time (in your judgment as system administrator), you can immediately take corrective action by changing the nice level of that process within the `top` command, as explained later in this section.

`Top` is normally launched without any options, like this:

```
top
```

As `top` starts running, it takes over the text window that you are working in. You cannot run `top` in the background (using the symbol `&` after the command), because `top` sends its output immediately to the screen. You can, however, use redirection (such as the `>` operator) to send the output of `top` to a file. Figure 10-2 shows how the output from `top` appears in a terminal window.

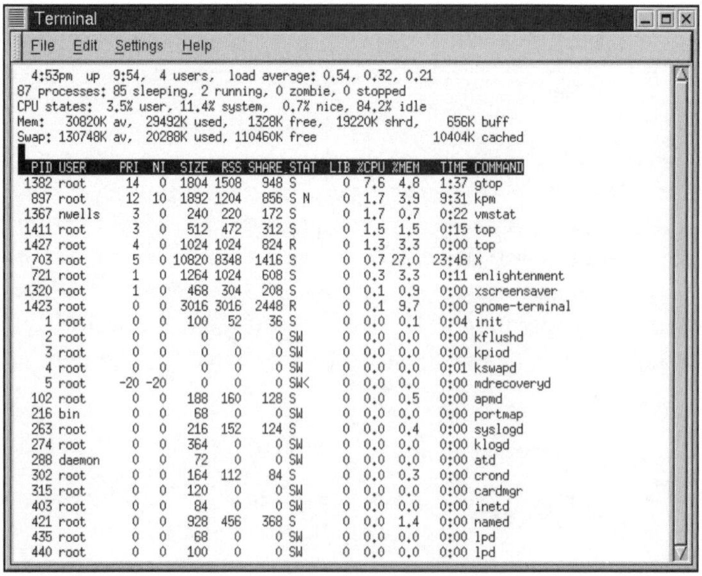

```
 Terminal                                                            _ □ ✕
 File   Edit   Settings   Help

  4:53pm  up  9:54,  4 users,  load average: 0.54, 0.32, 0.21
 87 processes: 85 sleeping, 2 running, 0 zombie, 0 stopped
 CPU states:  3.5% user, 11.4% system,  0.7% nice, 84.2% idle
 Mem:   30820K av,  29492K used,   1328K free,  19220K shrd,    656K buff
 Swap: 130748K av,  20288K used, 110460K free                  10404K cached

   PID USER     PRI  NI  SIZE  RSS SHARE STAT LIB %CPU %MEM   TIME COMMAND
  1382 root      14   0  1804 1508  948 S      0  7.6  4.8   1:37 gtop
   897 root      12  10  1892 1204  856 S N    0  1.7  3.9   9:31 kpm
  1367 nwells     3   0   240  220  172 S      0  1.7  0.7   0:22 vmstat
  1411 root       3   0   512  472  312 S      0  1.5  1.5   0:15 top
  1427 root       4   0  1024 1024  824 R      0  1.3  3.3   0:00 top
   703 root       5   0 10820 8348 1416 S      0  0.7 27.0  23:46 X
   721 root       1   0  1264 1024  608 S      0  0.3  3.3   0:11 enlightenment
  1320 root       1   0   468  304  208 S      0  0.1  0.9   0:00 xscreensaver
  1423 root       0   3  3016 3016 2448 R      0  0.1  9.7   0:00 gnome-terminal
     1 root       0   0   100   52   36 S      0  0.0  0.1   0:04 init
     2 root       0   0     0    0    0 SW     0  0.0  0.0   0:00 kflushd
     3 root       0   0     0    0    0 SW     0  0.0  0.0   0:00 kpiod
     4 root       0   0     0    0    0 SW     0  0.0  0.0   0:01 kswapd
     5 root     -20 -20     0    0    0 SWK    0  0.0  0.0   0:00 mdrecoveryd
   102 root       0   0   188  160  128 S      0  0.0  0.5   0:00 apmd
   216 bin        0   0    68    0    0 SW     0  0.0  0.0   0:00 portmap
   263 root       0   0   216  152  124 S      0  0.0  0.4   0:00 syslogd
   274 root       0   0   364    0    0 SW     0  0.0  0.0   0:00 klogd
   288 daemon     0   0    72    0    0 SW     0  0.0  0.0   0:00 atd
   302 root       0   0   164  112   84 S      0  0.0  0.3   0:00 crond
   315 root       0   0   120    0    0 SW     0  0.0  0.0   0:00 cardmgr
   403 root       0   0    84    0    0 SW     0  0.0  0.0   0:00 inetd
   421 root       0   0   928  456  368 S      0  0.0  1.4   0:00 named
   435 root       0   0    68    0    0 SW     0  0.0  0.0   0:00 lpd
   440 root       0   0   100    0    0 SW     0  0.0  0.0   0:00 lpd
```

Figure 10-2   Output from the `top` command

You can access many options from the keyboard as you view the output of top. One of the most useful is the ability to renice a process. To renice a process in top, press the r key and enter the PID of the process. For example, suppose the top few lines of the process list in top look like this:

```
PID   USER     PRI  NI  SIZE  RSS   SHARE STAT LIB  %CPU  %MEM  TIME   COMMAND
1066  jsmith   17   0   1012  1012  820   R    0    4.7   3.2   0:00   analyze
1     root     0    0   100   52    36    S    0    0.0   0.1   0:04   init
2     root     0    0   0     0     0     SW   0    0.0   0.0   0:00   kflushd
3     root     0    0   0     0     0     SW   0    0.0   0.0   0:00   kpiod
4     root     0    0   0     0     0     SW   0    0.0   0.0   0:00   kswapd
```

To change the nice level of process 1066 (the **analyze** command, as indicated by the far right column), you would follow these steps:

1. Press the r key. A message appears above the process list asking you to enter the PID of the process to be reniced.

2. Enter the PID of the process (1066 in this example).

3. A message appears asking you for the new value to assign to this process. For this example, the nice level is being raised to 10; it could also be lowered from 0 to a negative number if you are running as root. Enter 10.

4. Watch the NI column of the process listing to see the nice level value change. Because of the higher nice level, the process moves down in the process list after a moment as its CPU usage decreases.

 TIP You will often see the top command itself in the output of top. When the top program is listed near the top of the output, you can be sure that the system is not under a heavy load.

10

As you are viewing the output of the top command, you can use the keys listed in Table 10-5 to control top. Other command options can also be specified on the command line when you first launch top.

Table 10-5   Interactive Commands in top

Description	Press this key	Notes
Update the process list display immediately.	Spacebar	
Show a help screen with a command listing.	h or ?	
Kill a process.	k	You will be prompted for the PID.
Change the number of processes included in the display.	n or #	You will be prompted for the number of processes to include.
Quit the top program.	q	
Renice a process.	r	You will be prompted for the PID and new nice level.
Change the automatic update interval.	s	You will be prompted for a value (in seconds) for the update interval.

Additional options are available for sorting information in top, displaying or hiding certain information fields, and changing how some fields (such as %CPU) are calculated. See the man page for the top command for further details.

Using Graphical Process Management Tools

Several graphical process management tools are available for Linux. This section briefly describes where to find some of those tools and how to use them.

The **kpm** utility (for KDE Process Manager) is included with the KDE Desktop. It is a fairly new utility, so it may not be included on your Linux system if you are using an older version of KDE. In this case, you can download kpm from the KDE Web site at *ftp://ftp.kde.org*. On most KDE installations you can start the kpm utility by selecting Process Management from the Utilities or System menu. The main window of kpm is shown in Figure 10-3.

The process list in kpm is similar to the output of the top command. Fields of information are shown for each process. The list is updated every few seconds. Above the list of processes in kpm is a set of graphs that show the system's CPU load and memory usage. (Other CPU load utilities are described in the next section.)

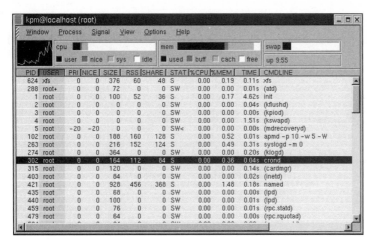

Figure 10-3 Main window of the `kpm` process management utility

Among other things, `kpm` allows you to:

- Click on system information graphs to change them to numeric data, and vice versa. Graphs are easier to read quickly, but numbers are more precise.

- Click on a process to select it, and then choose `Renice` from the `Process` menu to change the nice level of the selected process.

- Click on a process to select it, and then use the `Signal` menu to terminate, kill, or restart (that is, hangup) the selected process.

- Right-click on any process to open a menu of the most commonly used signals (such as Terminate and Kill). This menu also gives you access to the `Renice` option, which opens a dialog box in which you can change the nice level of the selected process.

- Use the `View` menu to select which fields of information to include in the list of processes. The `Select Fields` item on the `View` menu lets you choose exactly which information to include for each process.

- Click on a column heading (such as `PID` or `TIME`) to sort the list of processes by that field. You can click a second time on the same field to reverse the sorting order.

TIP   A program called **ktop** is included with some Linux systems. It runs on KDE and is similar in many ways to kpm.

The kpm utility is designed to run on Linux systems that employ the KDE Desktop. On systems (such as Red Hat Linux) that use the Gnome Desktop, you can use the **Gnome System Monitor utility**. The Gnome System Monitor, which is available on the Utilities menu, provides functionality very similar to the kpm program. Figure 10-4 shows its main window. To start the Gnome System Monitor from a command line, use the command gtop.

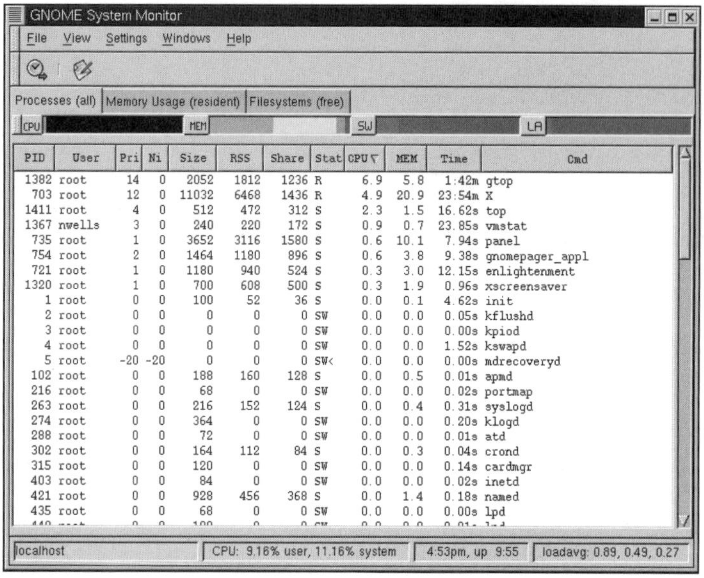

```
┌─────────────────────────────────────────────────────────────────────────────┐
│ ▤ GNOME System Monitor                                              _ □ ✕     │
│  File   View   Settings   Windows   Help                                      │
│ ─────────────────────────────────────────────────────────────────────────── │
│  ◔    ⏣                                                                       │
│ ─────────────────────────────────────────────────────────────────────────── │
│ Processes (all) │ Memory Usage (resident) │ Filesystems (free)                │
│ CPU▐███        MEM▐            SW▐            LA▐                              │
│ ─────────────────────────────────────────────────────────────────────────── │
│ PID    User   Pri Ni  Size   RSS  Share Stat CPU↑  MEM   Time      Cmd        │
│ 1382 root      14  0  2052  1812  1236 R     6.9   5.8  1:42m gtop            │
│  703 root      12  0 11032  6468  1436 R     4.9  20.9 23:54m X               │
│ 1411 root       4  0   512   472   312 S     2.3   1.5 16.62s top            │
│ 1367 nwells     3  0   240   220   172 S     0.9   0.7 23.85s vmstat         │
│  735 root       1  0  3652  3116  1580 S     0.6  10.1  7.94s panel          │
│  754 root       2  0  1464  1180   896 S     0.6   3.8  9.38s gnomepager_appl│
│  721 root       1  0  1180   940   524 S     0.3   3.0 12.15s enlightenment   │
│ 1320 root       1  0   700   608   500 S     0.3   1.9  0.96s xscreensaver    │
│    1 root       0  0   100    52    36 S     0.0   0.1  4.62s init           │
│    2 root       0  0     0     0     0 SW    0.0   0.0  0.05s kflushd         │
│    3 root       0  0     0     0     0 SW    0.0   0.0  0.00s kpiod          │
│    4 root       0  0     0     0     0 SW    0.0   0.0  1.52s kswapd         │
│    5 root     -20 -20    0     0     0 SW<   0.0   0.0  0.00s mdrecoveryd     │
│  102 root       0  0   188   160   128 S     0.0   0.5  0.01s apmd          │
│  216 root       0  0    68     0     0 SW    0.0   0.0  0.02s portmap        │
│  263 root       0  0   216   152   124 S     0.0   0.4  0.31s syslogd       │
│  274 root       0  0   364     0     0 SW    0.0   0.0  0.20s klogd         │
│  288 root       0  0    72     0     0 SW    0.0   0.0  0.01s atd           │
│  302 root       0  0   164   112    84 S     0.0   0.3  0.04s crond         │
│  315 root       0  0   120     0     0 SW    0.0   0.0  0.14s cardmgr       │
│  403 root       0  0    84     0     0 SW    0.0   0.0  0.02s inetd         │
│  421 root       0  0   928   456   368 S     0.0   1.4  0.18s named         │
│  435 root       0  0    68     0     0 SW    0.0   0.0  0.00s lpd           │
│  440 root       0  0   100     0     0 SW    0.0   0.0  0.01s lpd           │
│ ─────────────────────────────────────────────────────────────────────────── │
│ localhost        │ CPU: 9.16% user, 11.16% system │ 4:53pm, up 9:55 │ loadavg: 0.89, 0.49, 0.27 │
└─────────────────────────────────────────────────────────────────────────────┘
```

Figure 10-4　The Gnome System Monitor

The Gnome System Monitor display is very similar to those of the kpm utility and the top command. Graphs at the top of the window show CPU, memory, and swap space utilization. You can click on a process in the list to select it, then right-click to change the process priority or send a signal to the process.

The menu options in the Gnome System Monitor let you select which processes to display. To view or change settings for an individual process, right-click a process in the list, and then select a process option from the pop-up menu. Unlike the KDE Process Manager, the Gnome System Monitor provides details on how a single process is using CPU and memory resources. To view this information, click the process you want to display, right-click, and then click Details on the pop-up menu. This displays a details window like the one shown in Figure 10-5, which describes the CPU time consumed by the process with more precision than any of the programs discussed thus far in this chapter.

Figure 10-5 shows the **Process info** tab of the details window. Note that the details window also contains some additional tabs. Specifically, the **Raw memory map** tab shows memory usage numerically, while the **Graphical memory map** tab displays this information in graphical format. You will learn more about these two memory map tabs later in this chapter, when you learn about memory management.

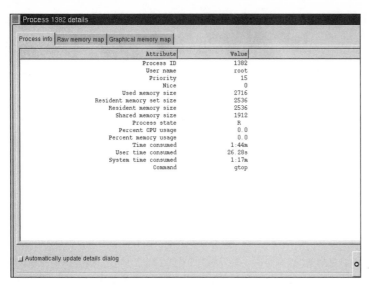

Attribute	Value
Process ID	1382
User name	root
Priority	15
Nice	0
Used memory size	2716
Resident memory set size	2536
Resident memory size	2536
Shared memory size	1912
Process state	R
Percent CPU usage	0.0
Percent memory usage	0.0
Time consumed	1:44m
User time consumed	26.28s
System time consumed	1:17m
Command	gtop

Figure 10-5   Details of a process in the Gnome System Monitor

Using Other Graphical CPU Status Tools

System administrators often use a simple graphical utility to track the CPU load of the Linux server. The KDE and Gnome utilities described in the previous section fill this need, but they also include other, sometimes unnecessary features. A basic utility called **xload** displays only a graph of the CPU load, with a higher line for heavy loads (during times of peak usage) and a lower line for light loads. Figure 10-6 shows the **xload** utility on a Linux desktop.

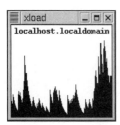

Figure 10-6   The xload utility

A system administrator can leave a window running **xload** open in order to see how the CPU is being used over time. This provides a graphical representation of potential problems when the load level in **xload** indicates that the CPU is continually under a very heavy load. By watching **xload**, the system administrator can decide when or if it is necessary to reduce the process load so that all users on the system experience better performance.

Utilities similar to **xload**, but designed specifically for KDE and Gnome, are also available. These utilities allow you to display a CPU load monitor graph in your tool panel or in a separate window. Many other CPU monitoring tools are available for Linux, though the tools described here (such as `xload`) are the most commonly employed and are likely to be included with any Linux product you might be using.

Actively Monitoring the CPU Load

So far you have learned about many tools available for viewing process information and update the status of one or more processes. This section discusses ways to apply your knowledge of Linux process management to your system.

First of all, it's wise to keep a CPU load monitor such as `xload` visible on your desktop as you work. When the CPU load is consistently high, begin checking for processes that may need attention. When you begin working on a new Linux system, you may need to judge what level of load on the CPU equates to slow response times for users based on their reactions to different load levels. A very fast CPU can tolerate a high load level with acceptable response times, whereas a slower CPU cannot.

When you decide to investigate the cause of a high load, begin by using `top` (or a similar graphical utility) to see if a single process is using an inordinate amount of CPU time. A "runaway process" started by a user may be the single cause of the heavy load. In this case you can change the priority of the process, talk to the user who started the process, and kill the process if necessary. As you become more familiar with the normal load on your Linux system, you will be able to tell from the output of `xload` whether a single process has suddenly run wild (for example, because of incoming network traffic or a programming bug), or the overall load has grown to a higher level because of work done by many processes or users.

When many processes are causing the heavy CPU load, the `ps` and `top` command options (or the graphical utilities) can help you determine whether one set of programs (such as the Web servers), one type of program (such as shell scripts), or one user's programs are causing the heavy load. In each case, when you know the details, you can take corrective action by renicing a set of processes based on the command name or the username.

In some situations, everything may appear to be normal, with no processes taking undue CPU time and no troublesome applications running anywhere on the system. Such a "normal" system may nevertheless be very busy. When this situation persists for several days or weeks (depending on the IT strategy of your organization), you may have to begin planning for increased capacity. As a rule, you will always need more of everything in the future. Tracking CPU usage and taking action to correct errant processes simply lets you delay spending money on additional computing power until you really need it.

The CPU load can be reduced in many ways. This list shows a few of them:

- Raise the nice level of numerous user processes so that they are not all competing at the same level. Of course, users will complain about the slowness of the system unless the CPU is fast enough to run their applications adequately. You must determine the importance of various tasks and then judge the performance levels that are allowable for different users and tasks.

- Add a microprocessor (creating a dual-processor system). This can significantly reduce the load on your server, but it may require a complex upgrade to both your hardware and your Linux kernel.

- Move some tasks to a separate computer. For example, separate the Web server or e-mail server from the system used to store users' home directories and applications. The NFS protocol can be used to remotely access users' directories stored on another server.

- Add memory. This will often reduce the CPU load on a busy system because it obviates the need for the CPU to spend time moving data to and from the swap space.

- Use devices with higher performance, which can reduce CPU load by eliminating waiting time in the applications that access those devices. Examples of devices that can improve system performance include SCSI hard disks or CD-ROM drives (in place of IDE devices), faster network cards, and accelerated video cards.

Improving system performance by lowering the CPU load while running a given set of applications is a continual quest for Linux system administrators. The sections at the end of this chapter provide some additional guidance for improving performance by locating and removing system bottlenecks.

MANAGING MEMORY

The previous section described how to track and manage a system's CPU time. This section describes how to manage another key system resource: physical and virtual memory. Physical memory, also called **random access memory (RAM)**, is the electronic storage used by your computer for all operations. **Virtual memory** is the swap space that the kernel uses to store inactive processes.

More memory—both physical and virtual—always leads to better performance. This is true because the Linux kernel and Linux programs can only interact with information stored in memory. Information stored on a hard disk must be loaded into memory before it can be manipulated or presented to a user. Because memory is so valuable, you must manage it carefully to provide the best performance for users on your Linux system.

You can't manage memory in the same way that you manage CPU time. After all, a Linux process must have a certain amount of memory to operate. You cannot take away memory from a process in the same way that you can slow down the process by taking away CPU time (that is, by using a higher nice level). Instead, you must watch how memory is being used on the system. If you find that the processes running on your Linux system consistently need more memory than is available, you should increase the amount of memory on the system or change how processes are used.

Changing how processes are used means moving some processes to a different system or running them at a different time. This is not the same as changing how a single process uses memory, which you cannot do as a system administrator except for rare occasions when an application provides configuration options for such things.

Understanding Shared Libraries

When a developer writes a program for Linux, he or she uses a collection of functions called **programming libraries**. These libraries provide functionality that is common to many applications. By using the library, a developer is freed from the burden of re-creating common functionality. Each library contains numerous programming functions that a developer can refer to within a new program. A standard Linux system contains dozens of library files, each one holding a set of functionality for other programs to draw on.

 TIP   Libraries in UNIX or Linux are similar to DLLs in a Windows program.

When you run a program that uses a library, the library must either be installed on your system or included with the program itself. Applications fall into one of two categories, depending on their relation to the library:

- **Statically linked applications** include the library functions in the main program. They require no additional library files on the Linux system. Each copy of an application loads a duplicate copy of all the library functions.

- **Dynamically linked applications** assume the library files are available on the Linux system. The library functionality is not included with the program itself. Dynamically linked applications use **shared libraries**. This means that several applications can use a single copy of the libraries that have been loaded into memory. (This also means that if the correct libraries are not loaded on the Linux system, a dynamically linked application cannot be used.)

Running multiple applications that are dynamically linked to the same libraries requires less memory than running multiple statically linked applications. To understand why, you first need to understand that the total memory allocated for a newly loaded application includes the memory required to store any shared libraries used by the application. This means that if you load one application and its attendant libraries, and then load a second application that is dynamically linked to those same libraries, the libraries will not be loaded a second time. Instead, the second application "shares" the libraries with the first application. If 10 applications were using one shared library, the library would still only load into memory once, rather than 10 times. Thus, dynamically linked applications save a great deal of memory in situations where applications use the same libraries.

Most Linux applications are dynamically linked, so they use a set of shared libraries that are installed on a Linux system by default. For example, if you start numerous KDE applications, most of the functionality of the application is contained in a single set of libraries shared by all applications.

Understanding Paged Memory

New Linux administrators sometimes have the mistaken impression that information is moved to and from swap space one application at a time. You may assume, for example, that as physical memory becomes full, an inactive application will be copied to the swap partition in order to free memory for a newly activated program. In fact, however, information is transferred to and from swap space in smaller units, known as pages. A **page** of memory is a block of 4 KB of RAM.

Whenever an application requires additional physical memory, the Linux kernel copies pages of memory to the swap partition. It does not copy an entire application; rather, it copies only enough pages to free the amount of memory needed by the newly activated application. The copied pages might be taken from the middle of the inactive application's memory. The kernel keeps track of which pages of memory are moved to the swap partition. The free space created by moving these pages to the swap partition is then made available for other programs that need physical memory immediately.

When a program that was inactive becomes active again, the kernel copies the swapped pages back from the swap partition to the same place within the memory space used by the application. Because the memory is restored by the kernel, the application cannot tell that its memory was used by another application for a time.

Swapping individual pages of memory (rather than complete applications) dramatically improves the performance of Linux on heavily loaded servers. If Linux swapped complete applications (rather than individual memory pages), system resources might be wasted copying a very large application to the swap partition when in fact only a small percentage of its memory was needed by another program.

Tracking Overall Memory Usage

Within the realm of memory management, your most important job is making certain that your Linux system has sufficient memory for the applications users want to run. To view the status of the memory, use the **free** command. A typical command would be as follows:

```
free
```

The output of the **free** command is shown here:

```
              total    used     free      shared    buffers   cached
Mem:          30820    30084    736       29960     656       10876
-/+
buffers/cache:         18552    12268
Swap:         130748   14144    116604
```

All the information displayed by **free** is in kilobytes. You can use command-line switches to change the display to bytes or megabytes. The following list describes each of the columns of information in the output of the **free** command:

- The `Mem` line refers to physical memory (RAM).

- The `Swap` line refers to swap space (located on your swap partition).

- The `total` column indicates the total amount of memory available to Linux. The sample output shows a system with about 30 MB of RAM and 128 MB of swap space.

- The `used` column indicates how much of the total memory is currently in use. Both RAM and swap space include an amount of used space.

- The `free` column indicates how much space is free. Both RAM and swap space include a free space amount.

- The `shared` column indicates how much of the used space is dedicated to shared libraries. Often this will be the majority of the used space.

- The `buffers` column indicates the amount of **buffers** memory, which is dedicated to data storage for the applications that are running. This number will be large if you are running applications that work with data files, such as word processors or spreadsheets.

- The `cached` column indicates memory that is being used by the Linux system for cached data (information from the hard disk that is stored temporarily in RAM, under the assumption that it will soon be needed by an application). If few applications are running, Linux will use most of the available RAM as a cache to improve performance. As more applications are launched, less memory is used for caching.

The following list describes some indicators to watch for in the output of the `free` command:

- If the value in the `shared` column is small on a busy system, you may be able to decrease memory consumption by using more applications that are dynamically linked. Check the documentation for large or critical applications to see if a dynamically linked version is available.

- If the last line of the `free` column (the `Swap` line) is small, you are in danger of running out of both physical and virtual memory. This situation can cause the system to crash under a heavy load. At the very least, it will decrease performance significantly as applications wait for memory to become available.

- If many applications are being run at the same time on a system with a small amount of physical memory, they will be continually moved to and from the swap space. This situation, called thrashing, wears out the hard disk mechanism and significantly decreases application performance. Thrashing indicates that you need more physical memory (RAM) to run the applications you intend to use.

- The first line of the `free` column (on the `Mem` line) is normally very small. This is because the Linux system tries to use all available RAM for caching hard disk information. If applications are launched, less information will be cached. Thus, if the `Mem` line of the `free` column indicates a value near zero, you may still start several applications without using a significant amount of swap space. Check the value of the `cache` column to see how much memory might be available for additional applications.

In addition to using the `free` command to learn the status of system memory, you can use fields in the `ps` command. Several fields in the output of the `ps` command provide information about a process's memory usage:

- The `%MEM` field shows the percentage of available system memory that the process is using.

- The `STAT` field (for Status) shows whether the application is sleeping (indicated by an `S`). Sleeping applications can be swapped to hard disk if the memory they occupy is needed by another process. The `STAT` field also shows a `W` if part of the process is already swapped to hard disk. The command line naming the process (the `COMMAND` field) will be enclosed in square brackets if part of the process has been swapped to hard disk.

- The `RSS` (Resident Set Size) field shows the amount of RAM currently used by the process. This value is given in kilobytes.

The Gnome System Monitor, mentioned earlier in this chapter, provides several helpful graphs that you can use to track system memory usage. The Gnome System Monitor is launched from the `Utilities` menu in Gnome (or by entering the command `gtop`).

After opening the System Monitor window, you display the middle tab by clicking `Windows` on the menu bar and then clicking `Memory Usage`. Figure 10-7 shows the resulting memory usage graph.

10

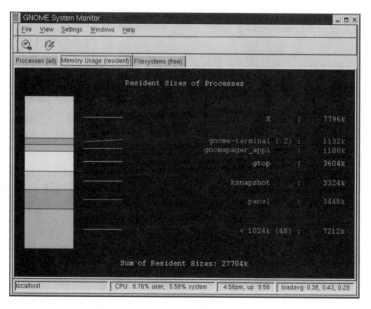

Figure 10-7   Memory usage displayed by the Gnome System Monitor

The process that uses the most memory is shown at the top of the graph. Additional applications are listed until the bottom of the window is filled. A summary of processes below the threshold value (1 MB by default) indicates the total memory used by those processes. A summary of the amount of memory used by all processes is shown below the graph with the label "Sum of Resident Sizes."

By default, this window shows the amount of RAM used by each process. With the `Memory Usage` tab displayed, you can use the `View` menu to display:

- Shared Sizes of Processes (usage of shared library memory space)

- Virtual Sizes of Processes (including the actual size of the program and the sum of all shared libraries the program uses)

- Swapped Sizes of Processes (the amount of space used by each process on the swap partition)

- Total Sizes of Processes (comprising the resident memory, or RAM, used and the swap space used)

> **TIP** In the `Preferences` dialog box (available via the `Settings` menu) you can also select the threshold level below which process names are not included on the graphs for each type of memory display.

Tracking Per-Application Memory Usage

You can use the graphs in the Gnome System Monitor to learn how a specific process is using memory. This information is included in the memory usage screen (see Figure 10-7) if the process is one of the larger memory consumers on the system. By viewing the details of one process, however, you can see exactly how that process uses memory, even if it is a small process consuming very little memory. Furthermore, by reviewing information about specific processes that are run frequently on your system, you may learn how to use your system resources more efficiently.

Within the Gnome System Monitor, view the process list by choosing `Windows` on the menu bar and then choosing `Processes`. Click on a process, and then right-click to display a pop-up menu of options. From this menu, choose `Details`. The `Details` dialog box for the process you selected appears. The `Process info` tab of this dialog box is shown in Figure 10-5. This tab contains information about the memory used by the process, including the resident memory size (amount of RAM the process is using) and the shared memory size (amount of memory used by shared libraries that this process relies upon to function).

Additional information about how a process uses memory is available on the `Raw memory map` and `Graphical memory map` tabs. The `Raw memory map` tab, as illustrated in Figure 10-8, shows all of the library files used by the process. A great deal of detailed information is provided on this screen. The information here can be used to diagnose problems with an application as well as to see how the application is using system memory.

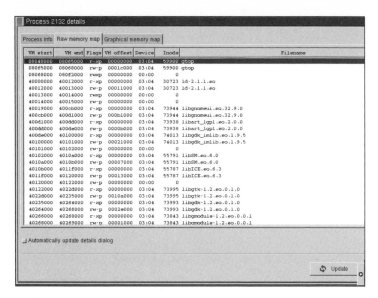

Figure 10-8   The Raw memory map tab in the Gnome System Monitor

The Graphical memory map tab, shown in Figure 10-9, provides information that is more useful to nonprogrammers. By reviewing the information on this tab, you can see the relative size of each section of the selected process. The program itself, as well as all of the libraries it uses, is divided into program code and data sections. The graph on the left of the window shows the relative sizes of each library used and any data files currently being used.

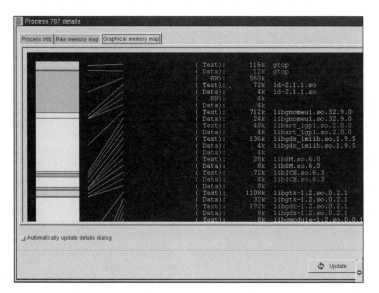

Figure 10-9   The Graphical memory map tab in the Gnome System Monitor

Viewing Virtual Memory Information

The general state of the swap space (the virtual memory) on your system is shown by the `free` command and by both graphs and numeric displays in several of the utilities described in this section (such as **kpm** and Gnome System Monitor).

You can use the **vmstat** command to examine detailed information about how the swap space on your system is being used. The output of the **vmstat** command is cryptic until you become familiar with the abbreviated labels for the fields that it displays. When **vmstat** is run as a regular command, its output is based on information averaged over time since the system was booted. You can also run **vmstat** as you would **top**, with updated information provided every few seconds. In this case the information is computed since the last update rather than since system boot time. To run **vmstat** as a regular command, simply type **vmstat**. Sample output is shown here:

```
procs  memory                      swap      io       system     cpu
r b w  swpd  free buff cache       si so     bi bo     in  cs     us sy id
0 0 0  11112 4108 700  11980       1  1      6  1       119 87     3  3  94
```

The fields displayed in the output of **vmstat** are explained in the following lists. Under the `procs` main heading:

- **r**: Number of processes waiting for run time

- **b**: Number of processes in uninterruptible sleep

- **w**: Number of processes swapped out but otherwise runnable

Under the `memory` main heading:

- **swpd**: Amount of virtual memory used (KB)

- **free**: Amount of idle memory (KB)

- **buff**: amount of memory used as buffers (KB)

- **cache**: amount of memory used to cache hard disk data (KB)

Under the `swap` main heading:

- **si**: Amount of memory swapped in from disk (Kbps)

- **so**: Amount of memory swapped to disk (Kbps)

Under the `io` main heading:

- **bi**: Blocks sent to a block device (the hard disk), measured in blocks per second

- **bo**: Blocks received from a block device (in blocks per second)

Under the `system` main heading:

- **in**: Number of interrupts per second, including the clock

- **cs**: Number of context switches (changes between active processes) per second

Under the **cpu** main heading each item indicates a percentage of total CPU time for three areas:

- **us**: User time
- **sy**: System time
- **id**: Idle time

To run the **vmstat** command in interactive mode as you would **top**, so that its output is periodically updated, you need to type a number after the command indicating the delay between updates. For example, the following command displays an updated line of information every two seconds:

```
$ vmstat 2
```

The information provided by **vmstat** is useful for locating bottlenecks on your system related to hard disk performance, lack of sufficient memory, or problems with specific applications. The next section discusses these issues in some depth.

LOCATING SYSTEM BOTTLENECKS

A **bottleneck** is the part of a computer system that significantly slows down completion of the task at hand. To understand the bottleneck metaphor, think of holding a bottle of soda pop upside down and trying to pour the contents out as rapidly as possible. Because the neck of the bottle (the bottleneck) is narrow, the liquid is restricted; it can't flow out as rapidly as it would if you cut off the top of the bottle, removing the bottleneck. Computer systems always have a bottleneck—a part that is slower than the other components of the system. Your goal as a system administrator is to make certain that the bottlenecks are large enough or hidden enough that they do not hamper the organization's computer system needs. When you discover that a computer system is not performing adequately, you must identify the bottleneck and improve the situation. Here are several examples:

- Many users on the network are accessing the Internet at the same time over a single dial-up modem connection. You all complain about slow service. The modem-based network connection is a bottleneck. To fix it, you could change to a higher-speed Internet connection using another technology.

- A large database index is created automatically each morning at about the time users are arriving for work. You notice that the system response is slow until the database task is completed. The CPU capacity is a bottleneck. You could add a separate CPU for the database to run on, add memory to improve database performance, or schedule the database task to begin earlier, so it does not compete with users' tasks each morning.

- A special-purpose server gathers network statistics and stores them on the server's hard disk. Because the server's hard disk is old and slow, and the network is very fast, the server generates statistics from the network faster than they can be written to disk, resulting in lost data. The hard disk speed is a bottleneck. To fix it, upgrade the hard disk to a newer, faster model with a faster interface, such as SCSI.

10

These three examples illustrate that bottlenecks in your computer systems can be inside your computer or outside—usually in the network infrastructure. Depending on the tasks your server is dedicated to, just about any part of your Linux server could become a bottleneck. In other words, possible bottlenecks include:

- Physical memory (RAM)
- Swap space (virtual memory)
- CPU time
- Hard disk space
- Hard disk access speed
- Video card speed
- Serial port speed
- Network card speed
- Internal bus speed

 TIP Internal buses such as ISA, EISA, MCA, and PCI determine how rapidly data can be moved between components of a single computer, such as from the system's RAM to its hard disk.

Identifying and Removing Bottlenecks

You can use the tools described in this chapter to identify and eliminate bottlenecks on your Linux system. Before you start, however, you must realize that improving the performance of a Linux system is to some degree more art than science. It is difficult to understand exactly what is happening in the system, but you must develop an understanding before you can make adjustments that will noticeably improve performance for yourself and for end users.

The only way to master this art is by working with Linux systems and related technologies for a long time. In the beginning, however, you will need to rely on science—that is, using various tools, testing many programs, and reviewing pages of numbers that indicate performance measurements and system status. These sometimes laborious steps will eventually lead you to a more intuitive understanding of the way events unfold within the system. At that point, you will probably use the commands described in this chapter to verify your own judgments, rather than to locate the source of a problem.

Because networking technologies are a major cause of bottlenecks on a Linux system, you will not be able to fully optimize your system until you have also learned something about networking with Linux. However, in the meantime, you can extract a great deal of helpful information about your system from the `free` command and from the various graphical monitoring tools. Even without extensive knowledge of networking, you can use these tools to locate problems related to poor system performance.

Using Benchmarks

One additional tool that can help you identify bottlenecks is a **benchmark program**, which provides a numeric measurement of a part of a system's performance. You can use the benchmark value to compare multiple systems that are working on the same task (for example, running the same program or responding to Web requests). A benchmark is also useful for showing you the speed at which events unfold within your system. If that speed is lower than expected, you can then look for the bottleneck that is slowing performance. The following list describes some benchmarks that you can use to test the performance of your Linux system:

- The values given in `/proc/cpuinfo` include a field called `bogomips`, which provides one measure of the speed of your processor. Note that this value is not a highly accurate measure of the CPU speed on your system (hence the name, which is short for "bogus measure of instructions per second speed"). This value on a single machine is not very useful, but comparing it among multiple machines can help you determine whether the CPU in your Linux system is slower than you thought it was.

- The **nbench** program measures CPU speed by running tests on tasks such as mathematical computations, sorting, and data compression. The **nbench** program is a Linux port of the benchmarks developed by now-defunct *BYTE* magazine. It is actively maintained at *http://members.xoom.com/Gavrilov_Con/nbench/index.html*.

- A hard disk benchmarking tool called **bonnie** provides throughput statistics in megabytes per second for various types of disk transfers, such as random and sequential reads. This program is an excellent way to identify bottlenecks in your system's performance. You can learn more about the **bonnie** package and link to the free download at *http://www.textuality.com/bonnie/*.

CHAPTER SUMMARY

- ❑ The Linux kernel makes a great deal of system information available via the `/proc` file system. This information is used by many Linux utilities that help system administrators manage processes and system memory in order to improve performance.

- ❑ To manage processes effectively, you must rely on information from programs like **ps** and **top** to identify how much CPU time a process is using. The utilities **nice** and **renice** can be used to change the CPU time that a process is allowed to consume. Graphical utilities can make process management more convenient.

- ❑ When managing memory, it's important to keep in mind that all applications must compete for a finite amount of system memory. But by watching the use of physical and swap memory (via utilities like **free**), a system administrator can determine whether memory in a Linux system is a bottleneck that degrades system performance.

10

□ Other standard graphical and text-based utilities, as well as benchmark programs, can be used to identify bottlenecks in a busy Linux system. Identifying and removing bottlenecks to increase system performance is a challenging task.

KEY TERMS

benchmark program — A program that provides a numeric measurement of performance for part of a system.

bonnie — A hard disk benchmarking program.

bottleneck — Part of a computer system that slows down completion of the task at hand.

buffers — Areas of memory dedicated to holding the working data associated with a running program.

cached data — Information from the hard disk that is stored temporarily in RAM, under the assumption that the data will soon be needed by an application. Caching data improves system performance, because data can be accessed faster from RAM than from the hard disk.

dynamically linked applications — Linux programs that do not include the library functions that they require in order to operate. The libraries must be installed (as shared libraries) on the Linux system on which the applications are executed.

file handle — An internal storage mechanism that allows a single file to be opened and used in Linux.

free — Linux command used to display the amount of free and used memory (physical and virtual), with basic information about how that memory is being used.

Gnome System Monitor — A graphical utility for the Gnome Desktop that is used to monitor and control processes running on Linux. Also called **gtop**. Similar to the **kpm** program for KDE.

kpm — The KDE process manager, a graphical utility for the KDE graphical environment that is used to control Linux processes. Similar to the Gnome System Monitor.

ktop — A KDE-based graphical utility used to manage Linux processes. Similar to the kpm program.

nbench — A benchmark program developed by *BYTE* magazine and ported to Linux.

nice — Linux command used to set the nice level of a Linux process as it is being launched.

nice level — The priority level assigned to a Linux task.

page — A block of 4 KB of memory. A page is the unit of memory in which the Linux kernel moves data to and from the Linux swap partition.

priority — A value assigned to a process running on Linux that determines how much CPU time is granted to the process to complete its tasks.

/proc file system — A method of viewing what the operating system kernel is doing at all times, using a section of the Linux directory structure and a file system interface (using the same commands used for regular files).

programming libraries — Collections of programming functionality that are common to many applications. *See also* shared libraries.

random access memory (RAM) — Electronic storage used by a computer as a work-ing space for all operations while the computer is turned on.

renice — Linux command used to change the nice level of a Linux process that is already running.

shared libraries — Programming libraries that are used by several dynamically linked applications running at the same time. Shared libraries are used to reduce memory con-sumption by providing a single copy of redundant functionality.

statically linked applications — Linux programs that include library functions in the pro-gram itself so that they are not dependent on the libraries loaded on the Linux system.

top — Linux command used to view the most CPU-intensive processes running on Linux at a given moment, along with related process information for those processes.

virtual memory — The swap space on a Linux system. Stored in a magnetic or other nonvolatile location, such as a dedicated hard disk partition.

vmstat — Linux command used to display detailed information about virtual memory usage.

xload — A graphical program that displays the CPU load over time on any Linux sys-tem's graphical interface.

10

REVIEW QUESTIONS

1. Although the /proc file system is not stored on a hard disk, it is called a file system because:

   a. It is accessed via a directory structure using standard commands that also apply to regular files.

   b. It contains information about partitions, mount points, and hard disk devices.

   c. The information from /proc can be stored on a hard disk using standard redirec-tion operators.

   d. Special utilities must be used to access the information contained in /proc.

2. For some system parameters, information can be written to the /proc file system. True or False?

3. The command cat /proc/partitions will display which of the following:

   a. A list of all swap partitions that the kernel is actively using

   b. A list of all partitions known to the Linux kernel

   c. The raw contents of the partition table for the root file system

   d. The equivalent of the Linux mount command output

4. Name five commands that rely on the information provide by the /proc file system to create their output.

5. Only the root user can view processes started by all users. True or False?

6. The command **ps -A xo comm** will display the following information:

   a. The command is invalid; it will display an error message.

   b. All processes started by the user who executes the **ps** command, with a standard set of fields pertaining to that user.

   c. All processes will be listed; a revised nice value will be requested for each one that matches the string **comm**.

   d. All processes running on the system, with the nice level and command-line fields displayed for each one.

7. The _____ field in the **ps** command output defines how much cumulative CPU time a process has used since it was launched.

   a. **TIME**

   b. **%CPU**

   c. **RSS**

   d. **START**

8. The **CMD** field of the **ps** command output displays:

   a. The command used to start the **ps** command (including all **ps** command options applied to the current output)

   b. The command used to start the process shown on each line

   c. The last signal sent to control the process on each line

   d. The equivalent output from the **vmstat** command

9. The **root** user can run the **renice** command to increase or decrease the priority level of any current process. True or False?

10. Which of the following commands is invalid if run by a regular user?

    a. **renice -10 1035**

    b. **renice 10 1035**

    c. **vmstat 5**

    d. **renice 5 1035**

11. Which of these programs allows you to change the nice level of a running process (choose all that apply)?

    a. Gnome System Monitor

    b. **free**

    c. kpm

    d. **top**

12. To update the process data displayed by the **top** command, you would press which key?

    a. r

    b. Spacebar

    c. u

    d. n

13. Name three graphical system management tools. Explain on which platforms they can be used and how to start each one.

14. Memory is not managed the same way that CPU time is managed because:

    a. Memory is a physical resource; CPU time is not.

    b. CPU time can be allocated restrictively among processes, slowing them down; memory cannot—a process must have its required memory allocation.

    c. The set of utilities available for managing memory is smaller and less effective than the toolset available for process management in Linux.

    d. Virtual memory is stored on a hard disk, which is a CPU-intensive activity that limits configuration options.

15. Shared libraries are commonly used in Linux applications. True or False?

16. Dynamically linked applications are preferred for their better memory usage unless:

    a. Statically linked applications are also available.

    b. Multiple users need to run the same application at the same time.

    c. The necessary libraries to run the application are not installed on the Linux system.

    d. The `free` command indicates that only virtual memory is available.

17. Contrast the output and use of the `free` and `vmstat` commands.

18. Explain why the amount of free RAM on a Linux system, as shown by the `free` command, is generally very small.

19. Thrashing occurs when:

    a. An excessive amount of information is moved to and from the swap partition in a short time.

    b. The `top` and `ps` commands both try to access process information at the same time.

    c. Physical and virtual memory are deadlocked over where program data should be stored.

    d. Multiple bottlenecks limit the speed of a Linux system.

20. A bottleneck occurs in a Linux system when:

    a. The system administrator is not able to respond to all end-user requests in a timely fashion.

    b. The `free` command indicates a shortage of physical memory.

    c. One part of the system restricts adequate system performance because it cannot keep up with the demands of other system components and applications.

    d. Multiple processes try to access the hard disk at the same time.

10

21. The `vmstat` command is useful for identifying bottlenecks because:

    a. It correlates precisely to the swapped process information given in the `ps` command output.

    b. In conjunction with the `bonnie` benchmarking tool, it provides detailed memory speed information.

    c. It can be used only by the `root` user, thus preventing interference by regular users consuming system resources.

    d. It provides detailed information about the number of processes waiting for access to physical memory.

22. Name seven parts of a Linux system's hardware that could become bottlenecks. For at least three of them, describe the situation in which that component would be a bottleneck.

23. Which statement best describes the process of improving performance on Linux systems?

    a. The art and science of it are best left to end users.

    b. It requires careful study of system details and user needs.

    c. It is only possible to make educated guesses about ways to improve system performance.

    d. With a Linux system, performance is usually fixed and cannot be affected by adjustments made by the system administrator.

24. The `bonnie` program is useful for determining which of the following:

    a. Hard disk performance data

    b. CPU speed benchmarks

    c. The balance of virtual and physical memory

    d. The status of information in the `/proc` file system

25. The command `vmstat 4` will do which of the following:

    a. List information on the process with PID of 4 if it is located in virtual memory.

    b. Set the default nice level for virtual memory processes to 4.

    c. Display continuous updates of the virtual memory status on a new line every four seconds.

    d. Start four instances of the virtual memory management module.

HANDS-ON PROJECTS

Project 10-1

In this activity you explore the /proc file system and see how your actions affect the information returned by queries to a filename in /proc. To complete this activity you need an installed Linux system.

1. Start a command-line window in Linux.

2. Change to the /proc directory.

3. Display the contents of the /proc/mounts file with the command cat /proc/mounts.

4. Insert a formatted floppy disk in the disk drive and mount it using this command: mount -t msdos /dev/fd0 /mnt/floppy. (The mount directory may be different depending on the configuration of your Linux system. You may also need to be logged in as root to mount the floppy disk. If the disk is a Linux-formatted disk, substitute the file system type ext2 for msdos.)

5. Execute the command cat /proc/mounts a second time. Is the floppy disk device shown?

6. Execute the command mount and compare its output with the output from Step 5. What additional information does the /proc file system include? Do you recognize that information from a system configuration file located in the /etc directory? What are the advantages of using mount instead of reading the /proc file system?

Project 10-2

In this activity you use the Gnome System Monitor to explore different ways of viewing process information on your Linux system. The tasks shown in this activity could also be done using the ps command on any Linux command line. The graphical interface provides a good way to interact with a large amount of system information without requiring you to memorize numerous command options. To complete this task you should have a copy of Linux with the Gnome Desktop installed (this would probably be a copy of Red Hat Linux).

1. Log in to Linux and start the graphical Gnome Desktop environment. Next, you need to start a program that you can monitor.

2. The Gnome Panel is the toolbar at the bottom of the Gnome screen. Click the footprint icon on the left end of the Gnome Panel to open the main menu, point to Utilities, then click Simple Calculator. Now you can use the Gnome System Monitor to monitor this program.

3. Click the Gnome Panel to open the Gnome main menu again. On the main menu point to Utilities, and then click System monitor. (You can also enter gtop in a terminal emulator window.) The main window of the System Monitor utility appears.

10

4. Click **View** on the menu bar, and then click **Only TTY Processes**. This limits the list of processes to those associated with one of the Linux terminals. Can you identify a few processes that are removed from the list when you choose this option?

5. Click **View**, then click **Only TTY Processes** to deselect that option. Click **View** again, then click **Hide System Processes**. How would you describe the process list now?

6. Select a process in the list by clicking it. Then right-click on that process and click **Renice** in the pop-up menu. Raise the nice level of that process to 20 with the slider bar and click **OK**. You see the new nice value in the **NI** field. Can you also see the CPU percentage field changing? (You will not notice a change in the CPU percentage field if the value of the CPU percentage field started as 0.0 before you changed the nice level of the process.) Change the process back to a nice level of 0 before proceeding.

7. The calculator process that you started in Step 2 is a program called **gcalc**. Locate that process in the list, right-click on it, and then click **Details** in the pop-up menu. The details window for the selected process opens. If necessary, click the **Process info** tab to display it.

8. Select the check box **Automatically update details dialog**.

9. Display the window for the selected process again. Begin using the process. Can you see the information on the **Process info** tab change as you use the process?

10. Click the **Graphical memory map** tab of the details window.

11. Switch back to the window of the application whose details you are viewing. What actions in the application cause the Graphical memory map to change?

Project 10-3

In this activity you track the status of the virtual memory usage (swap space) as you work with several applications. Normally you will not track virtual memory this carefully as you personally work with applications. Instead, you will have the easier job of watching the system-monitoring tools while other users are working with the programs. To complete this activity you should have an installed Linux system. The Netscape Communicator program is used in the steps that follow, but you can substitute any large program on your system.

1. Log in to your Linux system and start the graphical system.

2. Open a command-line window.

3. Use the following **vmstat** command in interactive mode to display an updated status line once every two seconds: **vmstat 2**.

4. Click the Netscape icon on your desktop (or open a second command-line window and enter the command **netscape**).

5. Watch the values in the **vmstat** output change as the Netscape program starts. Which fields do you see changing? Do you see any changes that indicate a potential bottleneck on your system if many copies of Netscape were started at the same time?

6. Open a second terminal emulator window and enter the following command to see the physical and virtual memory information, updated once every two seconds: **free -s 2**.

7. Start another large program, such as a second copy of Netscape, a spreadsheet, or a large system administration tool such as LinuxConf, the KDE Control Center, or the Gnome System Monitor.

8. Watch the values in the output of the `free` command change. Do the values in `vmstat` change as well? What additional information can you see in the `vmstat` output? If you opened a second copy of Netscape, how do the shared libraries used by the two copies of the same program affect the memory usage when you started a second copy?

9. Click on one of the command-line windows (where you are running `vmstat` or `free`) to activate the window. Then press **Ctrl+C** to end the output of the command displayed in that window. Enter the command **top** and review the output to see which processes are currently swapped out (stored on the swap partition). The letter `W` in the `STAT` column indicates that a process is swapped out.

10. As you read the output of these system administration tools, what can you conclude about how these tools affect system performance? What comments would you make about the value of using graphical system-monitoring tools such as those mentioned in this chapter?

CASE PROJECTS

10

1. You have been called in as a consultant to Home Care, an insurance company that runs a busy Web server for customers and numerous internal computers for employee use. You have been asked to solve a problem with the company's Web server. Although the company has a very fast Internet connection (T3 speed—45 Mbps) to service the thousands of customers who access the site, customers regularly complain about the slow speed of the Web server, particularly when requesting account information. You recall having installed very high performance SCSI hard disks on the Web servers. Considering the occasions when customers report the slowest service (during account inquiries), what might you conclude about the bottleneck that slows down Web server responses? How could you test your theory using some of the utilities you learned about in this chapter? How could you solve the problem using some of the methods described in this chapter? If the slow performance were a problem on all Web server requests, where might you look outside of the Home Care network infrastructure to identify potential problems?

2. Employees at Home Care access company data through a second Linux server that is unrelated to the public Web server. But they also complain about generally slow performance as they work. What tools could you use on the Linux server to determine where the drag on system performance originates? Keeping in mind that more than 100 employees access the Linux server during the day over a standard 10 MB Ethernet network, what are some possible bottlenecks in the network infrastructure or the server? Could the problem lie with each employee's Windows client? If so, how might you demonstrate this to management? Assuming the bottleneck was on the Linux server, how would your initial capacity planning (see Chapter 7) affect the ease and cost of upgrading the Linux server to handle employee needs with an acceptable level of performance?

11

SYSTEM LOGGING

After reading this chapter and completing the exercises, you will be able to:

♦ Explain the purpose of system log and other log files

♦ View the boot messages on your Linux system

♦ Configure the system logging daemons

♦ Maintain log files

In the previous chapter you learned about managing Linux resources (such as memory and CPU time) to keep processes running efficiently for all users. You learned about some command-line and graphical utilities that help you monitor the status of memory and all of the processes running on Linux. You also learned to control how individual processes use CPU time in Linux.

In this chapter you will learn how programs write messages to special Linux files, known as system log files, to help you track the activities of those programs. You will learn why log files are important, how to configure them to meet your needs, and how to maintain the log files to help keep your Linux system secure and running smoothly.

INTRODUCING SYSTEM LOGS

On any ship, the captain keeps a log of information about each day, including where the ship has traveled, its cargo, and any noteworthy events. The log serves as a record not only for the captain and crew, but also for others who may need detailed information about the ship.

In much the same way, Linux keeps detailed records of events within the system. These records, known as **log files**, are created by many programs. As the system administrator, you can refer to the log files to determine the status of your system, watch for intruders, or look for data about a particular program or event. Table 11-1 lists some commonly logged events and the location of the corresponding log files. This chapter describes the most important log files for general system administration.

Table 11-1   Commonly Logged Events and Their Log Files

Event	Path and filename of the log
Main system messages	`/var/log/messages`
Web server transfers	`/var/log/httpd/access_log`
FTP server transfers	`/var/log/xferlog`
E-mail server information	`/var/log/maillog`
Automatic script executions	`/var/log/cron`

The first log file in Table 11-1, **messages**, contains messages produced by the Linux kernel and most of the key programs running on the Linux system. It is stored in the same location on all Linux systems—in the `/var/log` directory. On your system, the other log files may have different default locations than those listed in Table 11-1. For example, Red Hat Linux stores the Web server transfer log (`access_log`) in the directory `/var/log/httpd`. Caldera OpenLinux stores the same file in the directory `/var/log/httpd/apache`. Later in this chapter you will learn how to configure log files to suit your own needs and preferences.

The Purpose of Linux Log Files

On any Linux system, many events go on in the background as users log in and do their work. **Daemons** are special-purpose background processes designed to watch for network activity, run other programs, and monitor user actions. The status information collected by daemons is not displayed on the screen. Instead, it is written to log files, which you can then review whenever you choose. Among other things, log files allow a system administrator to:

- Check for potential security problems, such as repeated login failures or a program that is stopped and restarted without the knowledge of the system administrator

- Review what was happening on the system in the moments before a major problem occurred

- Manage the system load by computing statistics based on the log file information

In the next section you will learn about the **messages** file. This is the main log file, where log messages from the Linux kernel and many important Linux programs are stored. For example, the **messages** file contains a record of login attempts, FTP server connections, and each occurrence of a daemon being stopped or started.

The messages File

The main system log for Linux is stored in the file `/var/log/messages`. Many different programs write messages to this file. A **message** is a description of what is happening within a program. The message may report information (someone has logged in), a warning (someone tried to log in unsuccessfully), or a serious error indicating that a program is about to crash.

Several sample messages are shown later in this section. A number of daemons, like the Web server, e-mail server, and login security programs, write to the file, as does the Linux kernel itself. The messages from the kernel tell you about low-level system activities such as when devices are first initialized and when daemons are started by the kernel.

The `messages` file uses a standard format. Each line of the file makes up an individual log message. Each message, in turn, contains the following information:

- The date and time when the event being logged occurred (often called the **timestamp**)

- The hostname (or computer name) of the system on which the event occurred

- The name of the program generating the log message

- The message text itself, which may be more than one line long

A few sample lines from a `messages` log file are shown here. Notice that the hostname for all of these messages is `brighton`, the name of someone's computer. Also notice that several different programs have generated the log messages shown here, including the Linux kernel, the `httpd` daemon (the Web server), the sound system, and other programs.

```
Oct 26 06:42:27 brighton kernel: parport0: PC-style at 0x378 [SPP,PS2]
Oct 26 06:42:27 brighton nfs: rpc.statd startup succeeded
Oct 26 06:42:27 brighton kernel: parport0: no IEEE-1284 device present.
Oct 26 06:42:27 brighton kernel: lp0: using parport0 (polling).
Oct 26 06:42:28 brighton nfs: rpc.rquotad startup succeeded
Oct 26 06:42:28 brighton kernel: lp0 out of paper
Oct 26 06:42:28 brighton nfs: rpc.mountd startup succeeded
Oct 26 06:42:29 brighton kernel: Installing knfsd (copyright (C) 1996 ok
Oct 26 06:42:29 brighton nfs: rpc.nfsd startup succeeded
Oct 26 06:42:29 brighton keytable: Loading keymap:
Oct 26 06:42:30 brighton keytable: Loading /usr/lib/kbd/keymaps/i386/qwe
Oct 26 06:42:30 brighton keytable: Loading system font:
Oct 26 06:42:30 brighton rc: Starting keytable succeeded
Oct 26 06:42:30 brighton gpm: gpm startup succeeded
Oct 26 06:44:57 brighton rpc.statd[451]: gethostbyname error for brighto
Oct 26 06:45:01 brighton httpd: Cannot determine local host name.
Oct 26 06:45:01 brighton httpd: Use the ServerName directive to set it
Oct 26 06:45:01 brighton httpd: httpd startup failed
Oct 26 06:45:01 brighton sound: Starting sound configuration:
Oct 26 06:45:01 brighton sound: sound
Oct 26 06:45:01 brighton rc: Starting sound succeeded
Oct 26 06:45:02 brighton PAM_pwdb[582]: (su) session opened for user xfs
Oct 26 06:45:03 brighton PAM_pwdb[582]: (su) session closed for user xfs
Oct 26 06:45:03 brighton xfs: xfs startup succeeded
Oct 26 06:45:04 brighton linuxconf: Linuxconf final setup
Oct 26 06:45:04 brighton rc: Starting linuxconf succeeded
Oct 26 06:45:05 brighton rc: Starting local succeeded
Oct 26 06:54:08 brighton PAM_pwdb[629]: check pass; user unknown
Oct 26 06:54:09 brighton login[629]: FAILED LOGIN 1 FROM (null) FOR
roopt, User not known to the underlying authentication module
Oct 26 06:54:11 brighton PAM_pwdb[629]: (login) session opened for user
```

Right now you don't have to understand everything in the preceding log file. But you should become familiar with the format of each line. As you learn about messages from a specific program, you can read that program's log messages to learn about what the program is doing on your system.

Not all messages are written to the **messages** log file. Many programs write information for system administrators in the **messages** file and other information to other log files. For instance, the Web server daemon generates information that would be useful to the **Webmaster** (the person who manages the content and functioning of the Web server program); this information is stored in separate log files called **access_log** and **error_log**.

The **syslogd** and **klogd** Daemons

Almost every program on a Linux system uses a set of common functions stored in system libraries. Programs share these libraries, as described in Chapter 10, so that the Linux system can use resources more efficiently. Each **function** in a shared library is a set of computer programming code that completes a certain task for any program that wants to use the function. To use a function in a shared library, a program calls the function, or transfers control to the function until the function completes the requested task. The shared system libraries include a function called **syslog**. Any program running on Linux can call this function, passing it a message. The **syslog** function then writes these messages to the **/var/log/messages** file. All of the calls to the **syslog** function are managed by a background program called **syslogd**, which stands for *system logging daemon*.

The purpose of **syslogd** is to watch for messages submitted by programs, while another daemon, **klogd**, watches for messages submitted by the Linux kernel. **klogd** (or the *kernel logging daemon*) logs kernel messages to the **/var/log/messages** file. Both **klogd** and **syslogd** write messages to the same log file. Figure 11-1 shows how these pieces work together to record log messages.

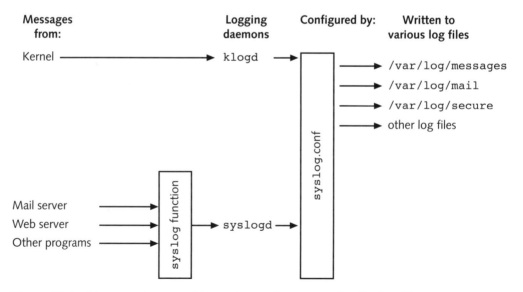

Figure 11-1   How **syslogd** and **klogd** accept messages for the log files

You can see the two logging daemons running on your system by using the `ps` command (which displays processes). The following command begins with a list of all processes (using the `aux` options), then searches the list of processes for those containing the string `logd` (using the `grep` command), and prints matching processes to the screen:

```
$ ps aux | grep logd

root  266  0.0  1.9  1264  592 ?     S  06:42  0:00 syslogd -m 0
root  277  0.0  2.4  1376  752 ?     S  06:42  0:00 klogd
root  690  0.0  1.2  1148  392 tty1  S  07:16  0:00 grep logd
```

In the sample output, you can see that the **START** field (the third from the right, with 6:42 in the first line) contains the time that each daemon was launched. This time matches the time you turned on your Linux system. The system logging daemons are started immediately after Linux is booted to ensure that all activities are logged.

In fact, the messages that are logged as the system is booting can be particularly useful to a student of Linux because they show how the operating system prepares for operation. The start-up messages are also useful for practicing system administrators who need to troubleshoot hardware problems, because the start-up messages show how the Linux kernel initializes each hardware device before use. Any problems related to accessing hardware are listed in the system log file.

The `syslogd` and `klogd` daemons are started by the **system initialization scripts** each time you boot your Linux system. These scripts start all the background processes that maintain Linux as you work. You should never need to start these programs manually after booting Linux.

11

VIEWING BOOT MESSAGES

When you turn on your computer system, the Linux kernel boots and initializes the computer hardware. The kernel then starts the `init` program, which in turn starts the system logging daemons `syslogd` and `klogd`. The system logging daemon `klogd` is therefore not available when the Linux kernel is initializing the computer hardware. The kernel writes messages to your screen during system start-up (before `klogd` is active). These kernel messages are also stored in a place within the kernel called the kernel ring buffer.

The **kernel ring buffer** is a small area of memory that holds internal kernel messages. If the kernel ring buffer becomes full, the first message written to it (the oldest message) will be discarded as new messages are received. This ensures that the most recent internal kernel messages can be found in the kernel ring buffer.

During system start-up, all of the messages displayed on screen are sent to the kernel ring buffer. However, if many messages are printed during start-up, the first few messages might be discarded to make room for the last few messages.

The exact number of messages or lines stored in the kernel ring buffer varies because each line is a different length. The default kernel ring buffer holds 8192 characters.

The **dmesg** utility shows you the contents of the kernel ring buffer. You can view this information on screen at any time. After you have Linux running, few messages are written to the kernel ring buffer, so it shouldn't change much. Instead, kernel messages are written to the system log file using klogd. However, keep in mind that some messages related to device status are still written to the kernel ring buffer after Linux is running. This allows the kernel to store information for viewing by a system administrator even if the system logging functions are not available for some reason. For example, if you insert a new floppy disk or change the PCMCIA cards in a laptop running Linux, the kernel will send a message about the change to the kernel ring buffer.

When you execute the **dmesg** program, use a pipe symbol with the `less` command so you can use the Page Up and Page Down keys to browse the multiple screens of information provided by **dmesg**. The command looks like this:

```
$ dmesg | less
```

Any user can execute the **dmesg** command; you do not need to be logged in as root. Some sample output lines from the **dmesg** command are shown here. Notice that the format of each line is very different from the lines in the `/var/log/messages` file. The lines output by **dmesg** sometimes start with a device name, such as hda when the first hard disk is detected, but the lines do not have a consistent format. You must read the entire line to see what information it conveys. Some messages fill multiple lines in the sample output that follows.

```
Linux version 2.2.5-15 (root@porky.devel.redhat.com) (gcc version
egcs-2.91.66 19990314/Linux (egcs-1.1.2 release)) #1 Mon Apr 19
22:21:09 EDT 1999
Detected 299946735 Hz processor.
Console: colour VGA+ 80x25
Calibrating delay loop... 598.02 BogoMIPS
Memory: 30760k/32832k available (996k kernel code, 412k reserved,
604k data, 60k init)
VFS: Diskquotas version dquot_6.4.0 initialized
CPU: Intel Mobile Pentium MMX stepping 02
Checking 386/387 coupling... OK, FPU using exception 16 error
reporting.
Checking 'hlt' instruction... OK.
Intel Pentium with F0 0F bug - workaround enabled.
POSIX conformance testing by UNIFIX
PCI: PCI BIOS revision 2.10 entry at 0xfd60a
PCI: Using configuration type 1
PCI: Probing PCI hardware
Linux NET4.0 for Linux 2.2
Based upon Swansea University Computer Society NET3.039
NET4: Unix domain sockets 1.0 for Linux NET4.0.
NET4: Linux TCP/IP 1.0 for NET4.0
IP Protocols: ICMP, UDP, TCP, IGMP
```

Because the output of the **dmesg** program contains much detailed information about how Linux recognizes your system hardware and how it is initialized, consider saving a copy of the **dmesg** output on a floppy disk for reference in case of hardware problems with Linux. If you are logged in as **root**, you can copy this information to a standard MS-DOS-format disk using these two commands:

```
# mount -t msdos /dev/fd0 /mnt/floppy
# dmesg > /mnt/floppy/dmesg_text
```

If you ask for Linux technical support from your Linux vendor or from another company, the technical support staff may request the output of the **dmesg** command to help them understand what is happening on your Linux system.

Because of the importance of this information, some Linux systems store the **dmesg** output in a file right after the system is started. By doing this, the original boot messages are preserved even if other messages are written to the kernel ring buffer later on. Red Hat Linux stores this information in the file **/var/log/dmesg**. You can view this file using any text editor or using a command such as this:

```
less /var/log/dmesg
```

CONFIGURING THE messages LOG FILE

The system log file **/var/log/messages** contains many types of messages from many different programs. Each Linux distribution has a default configuration for the system log files. However, you can specify what information you want to store in this file and what information you want stored in other files. Even if you decide not to change the log file's default configuration, learning about how the log file is configured will help you use the information in the **/var/log/messages** file.

Both **syslogd** and **klogd** are configured using the configuration file named **syslog.conf**, stored in the /etc directory. The /etc/syslog.conf configuration file determines where each type of message from different programs will be logged.

> **TIP** No graphical tools are available to set up the /etc/syslog.conf file. You will rarely need to change this file; but if you do, you must use a text editor.

The Format of syslog.conf

The **syslog.conf** file is one of the more difficult configuration files to set up. In this section you learn the format of this file and possible values that it can include. A sample line from **syslog.conf** is shown here. You can refer to this example line as you learn about each element of the **syslog.conf** syntax.

```
*.info;mail.none;authpriv.none                    /var/log/messages
```

To further help you get started understanding the `syslog.conf` configuration, Figure 11-2 shows the format of each line of the `syslog.conf` file. As with most configuration files, lines that begin with a hash mark (#) are considered comments. In other words, any line beginning with a # character is ignored.

```
facility.priority ;facility.priority      Action
```

    Selector   Optional additional
                          selectors

Figure 11-2   The format of each line in the `syslog.conf` file

Each line in the `syslog.conf` file contains two parts:

- A **selector** is a set of code words that selects what events are being logged.

- An **action** is a filename or username that determines either the file in which the message describing an event is written or which user's screen the message appears on. As you will learn later in this chapter, the action can also refer to a file on another (remote) computer.

The selector part of each line is composed of two parts:

- The **facility** is a code word that specifies which type of program is being selected (the category of program providing the log entry).

- The **priority** is a code word that specifies the type of messages being selected for logging.

Each of these items—selector, action, facility, and priority—is described in more detail in the following sections. But seeing an example at this point may be helpful. Consider the sample line shown here:

```
daemon.info                       /var/log/messages
```

The left part of the line contains a selector: `daemon.info`. The facility of this selector is `daemon`. The priority is `info`. Thus, messages from any daemon program with a priority of `info` or higher are selected by these code words. On the right, the line contains an action: `/var/log/messages`. This action is a filename, which specifies that messages selected by the `daemon.info` selector will be written to the file `/var/log/messages`.

The Facilities

When the time comes for a program running on Linux to write a message to the system log file, `/var/log/messages`, it issues a programming call to the `syslog` function. As part of that call, the program must indicate its type, or category. For example, when the `login` program records a message about a user logging into the system, the `login` program specifies that the message is coming from an authentication (security-related) program. The `syslogd` daemon uses this category information to determine where to write the message, based on the syslog.conf configuration. The actual name of the program (login, in this example), rather than the category (authentication in this example), is written to the log file.

You can configure where messages from each category of Linux program (each facility) are logged by how you set up the syslog.conf configuration file. Table 11-2 lists the different facilities, or types of programs, from which you can select system messages as you set up syslog.conf for system logging.

Table 11-2 Code Words Used to Specify Facilities in syslog.conf

Facility description	Facility name
Messages from user authentication utilities such as login	auth (formerly called security)
Special-purpose (private) user authentication messages	auth-priv
Messages from the cron program (used to control automated, scheduled tasks)	cron
Messages from all standard daemons or servers not otherwise listed by name here	daemon
Kernel messages (through klogd)	kern
Printer server messages	lpr
Mail server messages (from the Mail Transfer Agent)	mail
News server messages	news
Messages about the system logging process itself (such as starting the logging program)	syslog
Messages from programs started by end users	user
Messages from the uucp program (rarely used)	uucp
Eight special-purpose categories that a Linux vendor or programmer can define for specific needs not covered by the other categories	local0 through local7

11

You use the code words in the second column of Table 11-2 to specify which program's messages you are selecting on each line of the syslog.conf file. Remember, the facility is part of a selector that defines the messages for which you are configuring an action. For example, you might include the auth facility on a line in the syslog.conf file. Whatever action you include on the same line in syslog.conf will apply to the login program and other programs that are categorized as related to authentication (and thus specify the auth facility when logging their messages). If you indicate the mail facility on a line in syslog.conf, the action on that line will apply to the mail server and other programs related to processing electronic mail.

In many cases, multiple programs use the same facility. The daemon facility, in particular, is used by many programs.

The Priorities

All programs running on Linux generate different types of messages. Some messages are simply informational—about how the program is using system resources, for example. Other messages indicate a potential problem. Still other messages indicate a serious or critical problem that will corrupt data or shut down the program. Each program can generate messages with different priorities, depending on the seriousness of the event. You can configure your system so messages of different priorities are logged in different ways.

Table 11-3 shows the different priorities available, from lowest to highest, as you configure the system log files. A priority defines the seriousness of a message. As you would expect, the more serious messages are considered higher priority messages, with `emerge` being the highest priority.

Table 11-3 Message Priorities Supported by System Logging

Priority description	Priority name
Debugging messages used by programmers or those testing how a program works	`debug`
Informational messages about what a program is doing	`info`
Information about noteworthy events occurring as a program executes	`notice`
Warnings about potential problems with a program	`warning` (formerly called `warn`)
Notices about errors occurring within a program	`err` (formerly called `error`)
Critical error messages that will likely cause a program to shut down	`crit`
Error messages that will cause a program to shut down and may also affect other programs	`alert`
Messages about events serious enough to potentially crash the system	`emerg` (formerly called `panic`)

As a software developer writes a program, the developer decides which events are associated with which priority levels. For example, the developer might design a program so that a certain event generates a message with the priority of `warning`. Another programmer might decide that the same event would generate a message with the priority of `notice`. Thus, the programs themselves determine what facility they pertain to and what priority individual events or messages should have. As a system administrator, you simply determine where messages are logged based on their facility and priority.

The Actions

Once you set up a selector (consisting of a facility and a priority), you can assign an action to that selector. This action will determine what `syslogd` and `klogd` do with the messages defined by the selector—either write the messages to a file or display them on the screen of a user who is logged in to the system. Normally the action is simply the name of a local file.

Messages matching the selector are written to the file that you indicate by the `syslogd` or `klogd` daemon. The possible actions are listed here:

- Write the message to a regular file using the given filename.

- Write the message to the terminal indicated. This can be a standard virtual terminal name, from `/dev/tty1` to `/dev/tty6`, or the console device, `/dev/console`.

- Write the message to the screen of any users who are logged in, from a given list of users. For example, if the action is `root,lsnow`, the messages in the selector will be written to the screen of users `root` and `lsnow` if they are logged in.

- Write the message to the log file on a remote system. This is done using the symbol @ in the action. For example, you could specify the action as `@incline.xyz.com` to send log messages for the given selector to the `syslogd` daemon running on the system named `incline.xyz.com`.

Although it's wise to write all messages to a log file, it's also a good idea to send critical messages to the screen or to certain users. This can ensure that the `root` user, or the regular user account of the system administrator, is immediately informed when a very serious error occurs, such as the root file system running out of hard disk space, or a memory error causing a problem in the Linux kernel.

The option of writing messages to a remote system is useful in several circumstances:

- *To consolidate important messages:* many systems in an organization might send all log messages to a single system so they can be archived and studied as a group.

- *To safeguard information on a failed system:* when a system crashes because of a hardware failure, any system log files stored on the hard disk can be damaged, or at least rendered inaccessible until the system is restored. By storing log files on another system, you ensure that these messages can be reviewed even after the system that generated them fails.

- *To enhance security:* storing log files remotely makes it more difficult for intruders to delete records of their activities that may be stored in system log files. Remote log files can thus improve security management.

 TIP A network connection between two computers must be available before one computer can store log messages on another computer.

Setting up `syslog.conf`

Now that you understand something about facilities, priorities, and actions, you can review the default `syslog.conf` file on your Linux system to determine how messages are logged. You can also modify that configuration if necessary to suit your own needs.

The following list shows the default `syslog.conf` file from Red Hat Linux. Most of the lines are comments (beginning with a # character). The comments explain the purpose of each configuration line.

```
# Log all kernel messages to the console.
# Logging much else clutters up the screen.
# kern.*                                        /dev/console

# Log anything (except mail) of level info or higher.
# Don't log private authentication messages!
*.info;mail.none;authpriv.none                  /var/log/messages

# The authpriv file has restricted access.
authpriv.*                                      /var/log/secure

# Log all the mail messages in one place.
mail.*                                          /var/log/maillog

# Everybody gets emergency messages, plus log them on another
# machine.
*.emerg                                                 *

# Save mail and news errors of level err and higher in a
# special file.
uucp,news.crit                                  /var/log/spooler

# Save boot messages also to boot.log
local7.*                                        /var/log/boot.log
```

As mentioned previously, each selector includes a facility and a priority. As you refer to the preceding sample file, note the following points about formatting the selector and action in `syslog.conf`.

- The asterisk symbol (*) can be used to indicate "all," either for the facility or for the priority. For example, the sample file contains the selector `*.emerg`, which selects all emerg priority messages of any facility (coming from any program).

- When an asterisk (*) is used in the action field, it refers to users on the system, meaning that all users who are logged in will receive the message indicated in the selector for that line. The `*.emerg` selector in the sample file above uses * as the action field.

- The facility and the priority are separated by a period. The left side of each line in the sample file contains two items separated by a period.

- The keyword **none** is used as a priority to exclude all messages matching a certain facility.

- Multiple selectors can be included on the same configuration line (thus applying the same action to multiple selectors) by separating selectors with a semicolon (;). For example, one of the lines in the sample file contains `*.info;mail.none;authpriv.none`. Thus three selectors are given at one time.

- Multiple facilities or priorities can be selected at the same time using a comma-separated list. For example, `uucp,news.crit` appears in the sample file, indicating that messages of priority `crit` for either the `uucp` or `news` facility are being configured.

- Whenever a priority is specified in a selector, all messages of that priority and all *higher* priorities (more serious problems) are included in the configuration.

- The same messages can be logged to more than one place by including the same selector on multiple lines with different actions. For example, critical kernel messages might be displayed on the `/dev/console` device and also logged to a remote machine for later analysis. Configuration lines in `syslog.conf` do not override previous configuration lines; rather, each action configured by a line in `syslog.conf` adds to everything already configured in `syslog.conf`.

In addition to these basic rules of syntax for `syslog.conf`, several special symbols are also useful, as described in the following paragraphs. These symbols are not employed very often, but you need to understand them so that you can interpret any log configuration files you might encounter.

When a file is specified as the action (so that messages are written to the file), a hyphen (-) can be added before the filename to indicate that the file should not be accessed in sync mode each time a message is written to it. When a file is accessed in **sync mode**, all information cached in memory is written to the hard drive so that no data will be lost in case of a system crash. Normally, all log files are *synced* as each message is written. This ensures that no log messages are lost if the system crashes suddenly, but it also degrades performance by not taking advantage of the memory caching that Linux provides for optimized hard disk writing. You can choose to improve performance and increase the risk of losing log information by including the hyphen in the action field, for example:

```
*.info;mail.none;authpriv.none              -/var/log/messages
```

As stated previously, including a priority in the selector selects messages of that priority and all higher priorities. You can use the equal sign (=) to specify a priority without including all higher priorities. For example, using the selector `*.=crit` selects all messages from any program (all facilities) that have the priority `crit`, but not the higher priorities `alert` and `emerg`. (These should be configured on a separate line, however.)

You can use an exclamation point to exclude all priorities above a certain level. For example, the following combines these two selectors: `kern.info;kern.!err`. This configuration line selects all messages from the kernel (those with a facility of `kern`) above the priority of `info`, except those with a priority of `err` or higher. In effect, this selects messages of priority `info`, `notice`, and `warning`.

The equal sign and the exclamation point can be used together to exclude a single priority instead of excluding everything above that priority. For example, consider two selectors similar to the example in the previous paragraph: `kern.info;kern.!=err`. These selectors configure an action for all kernel messages of priority `info` and higher, excluding `err` messages, but including `crit` and `emerg` messages (the priorities above `err`).

11

Few system administrators will need the flexibility provided by using the = and ! symbols within the `syslog.conf` file, but they are available to make your configurations as precise as you decide they need to be.

Table 11-4 describes the effect of several sample configuration lines in `syslog.conf`. Some of these lines are taken from the sample file shown previously; others are taken from the `syslog.conf` file on other Linux systems.

Table 11-4   Sample `syslog.conf` Configuration Lines

Sample configuration line	Effect of the configuration line
`#kern.*     /dev/console`	None; this line begins with a comment character.
`kern.*     /dev/console`	Log all kernel messages (of any priority) to the console (the computer screen).
`*.info;mail.none;authpriv.none /var/log/messages`	Log all messages from any facility with a priority of `info` or higher to the file `/var/log/messages`. But exclude all messages with a facility of `mail` or `authpriv`, no matter what priority.
`authpriv.*      /var/log/secure`	Log all messages from the `authpriv` facility to the file `/var/log/secure`.
`uucp,news.crit /var/log/spooler`	Write any messages of priority `crit` or higher for the facilities `uucp` or `news` to the file `/var/log/spooler`.
`*.emerg            *`	Display any messages with a priority of `emerg` on the screen of all users who are logged in.
`mail.*         /var/log/maillog`	Log all messages from the `mail` facility to the file `/var/log/maillog`.
`*.emerg         @loghost`	Send all messages of priority `emerg` (from all facilities) to the `syslogd` daemon running on the computer named `loghost`.

You can view additional examples of `syslog.conf` lines in the manual page for `syslog.conf`. (Enter the command `man syslog.conf` to view this online documentation.) Be aware that the manual page includes instructions for all UNIX systems, so the example directories used to store log files will not match everything on your Linux system. The examples, however, are still instructive.

Restarting the System Logging Daemons

After changing the `syslog.conf` configuration file, you must tell `syslogd` and `klogd` to reread the configuration file, so that your changes to the file are implemented on your system. Rather than stop the logging daemons and miss some events that need to be logged, you can send a signal using the `kill` command. Remember from Chapter 8, the `kill` command doesn't always end a program. You can send a program different types of signals using the `kill` command. Some signals end the program; many do not. The signal that you send with `kill` (as described in this section) tells the logging daemons to reread the `syslog.conf` configuration file.

In order to send a signal using `kill`, you must know the process ID (PID) number for the logging daemons. Several important Linux programs store their PID in a file for occasions when you need to send a signal to the process. The following command shows you the PID of `syslogd`:

```
cat /var/run/syslogd.pid
```

The following command shows you the PID of `klogd`:

```
cat /var/run/klogd.pid
```

By inserting the value returned by these commands (the PID of the corresponding logging daemons), you can use the `kill` command to send a **SIGHUP** signal to each daemon. This signal tells the daemon to reread its configuration files. To send this signal using the `kill` command, you can use single backward quotation marks to execute the `cat` command and insert the resulting text as a parameter for the `kill` command. (Be sure to use single backward quotation marks rather than forward marks.) To summarize, the following command will cause `syslogd` to reread the `syslog.conf` configuration file:

```
kill -HUP `cat /var/run/syslogd.pid`
```

Similarly, you can have `klogd` reread the configuration file using this command:

```
kill -HUP `cat /var/run/klogd.pid`
```

11

Another acceptable method of restarting the logging daemons is to use the `killall` command with the name of the daemon, as these two commands show:

```
killall -HUP syslogd
killall -HUP klogd
```

You will have other occasions when you need to send the SIGHUP signal to the system logging daemons as you learn about rotating log files later in this chapter.

Using the `logger` Utility

The **logger** utility lets you send a message to the `syslog` function, just as programs do. You can use the **logger** utility from a command line or from a script file. As you will learn in Chapter 12, a **script** is a collection of commands that functions as a macro, executing commands as if you had executed them on the command line. Once you become proficient at creating scripts, you might want to log events to the system log files.

You can use the **logger** command with only a message. For example, suppose you created a script to compress files automatically. The script could include a simple **logger** command like this:

```
logger Compression utility started
```

This would log the message using a default selector of **user.notice**. Thus, the message would be logged wherever the `syslog.conf` file had configured messages matching that selector. (This would normally be in `/var/log/messages`.) Because no additional information is specified, the username of the user running the script is included in the log file as the program name providing the log message. The resulting log entry would look something like this (with the timestamp, machine name, and username varying):

```
Oct 26 11:42:25 brighton nwells: Compression utility started
```

You can also specify other selectors with the `logger` command. For example, to log a message to the `mail` facility with a priority of `info` and the name of the compression script as part of the log file, use this command:

```
logger -p mail.info -t compress Mail folders compressed
```

This would result in a message like the following being written immediately to the log file specified in `syslog.conf` for `mail.info` messages. (The date and machine name vary according to which system is used to execute the `logger` command.)

```
Oct 26 11:46:13 brighton compress: Mail folders compressed
```

MAINTAINING LOG FILES

Ordinarily, your Linux system should require little day-to-day maintenance. Although systems with a large number of users may require that you monitor hard disk and memory usage, most parts of Linux take care of themselves. Log files, however, require and deserve some extra attention. This is true for two reasons:

- Log files contain a valuable record of what has occurred on your Linux system. The information in the log files can be used to check for problems, watch for intruders, and compute statistics about your system.

- Depending on how you have set up `syslog.conf`, log entries can create very large log files. Over time on a busy system, these files will fill up your hard disk.

Checking Log Files for Problems

A system administrator should regularly check log files for indications of problems. By reviewing log files and locating problems before they become critical, you can save a great deal of time and expense troubleshooting and repairing problems that have resulted in security problems, program failure, or even crashed systems.

The busier your system is and the more users with access to the system, the more important the log files will become to your work as a system administrator. By reviewing log files regularly, you will become accustomed to what is normal and what is unexpected. Table 11-5 lists some sample log file entries, along with some possible interpretations. For the sake of brevity, only the program name and message text are shown in the table; the timestamp and computer hostname have been removed from the log entries.

Table 11-5   Interpreting Sample Log File Entries

Sample log entry	System administrator considerations
`login: FAILED LOGIN 3 FROM (null) for nwells, Authentication failure`	Someone has tried to log in as user nwells and entered the wrong password three times in a row. If this happens repeatedly in a short period of time, someone may be trying to break in using that user account.
`login: ROOT LOGIN ON tty1`	Someone has logged in as root, but the time-stamp (not shown here) indicates that the login occurred at 2 a.m. If no one is expected to be working at that time, an intruder may have access to the system.
`syslogd 1.3-3: restart`	The syslogd daemon was restarted. If you did not do this as system administrator, someone may have changed the logging configuration to try to circumvent a security check or cover a security break-in.
`kernel: eth0: NE2000 Compatible: port 0x300, irg 5, hw_addr 00:E0:98:05:77:B2`	The kernel successfully located the Ethernet card as the system booted. The parameters used to access the card are shown in the kernel log message.
`named[339]: Ready to answer queries`	The DNS server has successfully started and is able to respond to requests from clients to resolve domain names to IP addresses.
`modprobe: can't locate module block-major-48`	The modprobe command was unable to initialize a device. Some device on the system may not be configured properly.
`kernel: cdrom: open failed`	A user has tried to mount or access the CD-ROM device and either used an incorrect mount command or has made some other mistake. The user may need instruction in using the CD-ROM device.
`--MARK--`	The syslogd program has inserted a marker to indicate that a fixed amount of time has passed (20 minutes by default). This helps you determine how many messages are written to the log file in each period, but not all systems use this feature. (Red Hat, for instance, does not.)

11

You can use standard Linux tools like the `grep` utility to search for lines in the log files. For example, to search for all lines in the `/var/log/messages` file containing the program name `login:`, use this command:

```
grep login: /var/log/messages
```

You can also use special log file management utilities that watch your log files for certain conditions that you specify. These utilities notify you (usually via e-mail) about irregularities or potential problems in the log files. You can then take corrective action.

Numerous log analysis utilities are available for free download from sites like LinuxBerg. (Visit *http://xmission.linuxberg.com/conhtml/adm_log.html.*) Example programs available at this site include **logscanner** and **LogWatch**. Both allow a system administrator to configure specific items to watch for in system log files based on criteria such as username, security level, and time frame of the event.

Rotating Log Files

With so many programs writing messages, the log files on your system can become very large. Obviously, the busier your system is, the more messages will be written to your log files in a given period of time. But on every system there is a limit to how large the log files can become without using an undue amount of disk space. This varies depending on your system. If you are working on an older system with only 500 MB of disk space, you might not want to use 1 MB of disk space for log files. Conversely, if you are running a large Linux system for many users and have 50 GB of disk storage space, dedicating 500 MB (1%) of the disk to log files that help you track how the system is operating might be perfectly acceptable.

Over time, however, all log files become too large. Part of every system administrator's job is to regularly rotate the log files so they can be used appropriately. The process of **rotating log files** might mean any of the following:

- Discarding old log files to provide disk space for new log information
- Compressing log files and storing them on an archive medium as a long-term record of system activity
- Renaming and compressing the log files so they can be studied at some future time

You don't need to save most log files forever. It's common to use a rotation system for log files, so that at any time, the past few days, weeks, or months worth of log files are available for review, each in separate files. Your particular circumstances dictate whether you use a separate file for each day, each week, or each month, and how many of those files you maintain. Log files are normally moved to another directory and often to another file system (another hard disk or hard disk partition) to free up space on the root partition.

For example, suppose you want to maintain four weeks worth of archived data for the `/var/log/messages` log. You plan to maintain this data as four files: `week1`, `week2`, `week3`, and `week4`, with the newest data being written to the `/var/log/messages` file by `syslogd`. Each Monday morning you rotate the log files. The basic process for rotating log files looks like this:

1. Rename all old log rotation files. In this example, `week4` is discarded, `week3` is renamed to `week4`, `week2` is renamed to `week3`, and `week1` is renamed to `week2`.

2. Rename the `/var/log/messages` file to `week1`.

3. Create a new file named `/var/log/messages` (initially, it is empty).

4. Send the `syslogd` and `klogd` programs a SIGHUP signal so that they begin to use the new `/var/log/messages` file.

The last two steps might be confusing at first glance. Why do you need to create a new file named /var/log/messages and then issue a SIGHUP signal? The reason revolves around how Linux accesses files. As the syslogd and klogd programs are launched, they begin by locating the log files they will write to. The /var/log/messages file is identified by a number called an inode (which you may recall learning about in Chapter 9). If you change the name of the file /var/log/messages, the inode that refers to that data remains the same, so the two logging daemons continue writing data to the file that you have renamed week1. By creating a new file called /var/log/messages and sending a SIGHUP signal, the logging daemons look for the /var/log/messages file again by name, obtain the inode for the new (empty) file you have created, and begin writing messages to that new file.

The commands required to accomplish the steps given above might look like the following, depending on where you are storing your log files. (The numeric endings on the files shown in this example are commonly used to designate archived log files.)

```
cd /archive
rm -f messages.4
mv messages.3 messages.4
mv messages.2 messages.3
mv messages.1 messages.2
mv /var/log/messages /archive/messages.1
touch /var/log/messages
killall -HUP syslogd
killall -HUP klogd
```

Because a typical Linux system includes many log files—for the Web server, e-mail, security messages, kernel messages, and so forth—it is common to rotate many different log files each day, week, or month, depending on how rapidly the various log files are growing. For example, if you are running a busy Web server, the Web access log file (/var/log/httpd/access_log) might need to be archived each night, while on the same system the /var/log/messages file is rotated weekly or every two weeks.

In Chapter 12 you will learn how to create a script to automate commands like these. One very helpful program to include in your scripts is the logrotate command described in the next section.

Using the logrotate Utility

Red Hat Linux provides a utility called **logrotate** that you can use to help you rotate all of the log files on your system. To use logrotate, you must set up a configuration file that the logrotate command uses. The logrotate command is normally executed automatically on a regular basis (using methods described in Chapter 12). However, using this utility is much easier than creating and maintaining separate lists of commands for each of your system's log files.

The configuration file for logrotate can be stored anywhere you choose. You must provide the name of the configuration file when you launch the logrotate command. A sample configuration file is shown here. This file only manages rotation of two log files: /var/log/messages and /var/log/httpd/access_log (for the Web server).

```
# sample logrotate configuration file
errors root@mycompany.com
compress
/var/log/messages {
      rotate 4
      weekly
      postrotate
            killall -HUP syslogd
      endscript
}
/var/log/httpd/access_log {
      rotate 10
      size=10M
      mail webmaster@mycompany.com
      postrotate
            killall -HUP httpd
      endscript
}
```

The following list explains this sample configuration file:

- Any error messages generated during the log rotation process are e-mailed to root@mycompany.com.

- All archived log files are compressed using the `gzip` utility.

- The `/var/log/messages` file is rotated weekly (assuming that the `logrotate` command is executed at least that often). Four old files are saved (as in the previous manual example). After each rotation (once per week) the `killall` command is used to begin using the new log files (again as in the manual example given previously).

- The Web server log file `/var/log/httpd/access_log` is rotated whenever its size exceeds 10 MB. A message is sent to webmaster@mycompany.com to confirm each log rotation operation. As with the `/var/log/messages` configuration, the `killall` command is used to make all `httpd` Web server daemons use the new log files after rotation.

Supposing you had saved the above configuration file as `/archive/logrotate.conf`, you would execute the `logrotate` command using this syntax:

```
logrotate /archive/logrotate.conf
```

The `logrotate` utility provides additional functionality that you can learn about in the online manual page for the utility (using the command `man logrotate`).

 The `logrotate` command is not available on all Linux systems.

CHAPTER SUMMARY

❑ Log files are an important part of system maintenance because they track all important activities occurring on a Linux system. They can be used for tracking down hardware problems, computing statistics, and identifying security dangers.

❑ The `syslogd` and `klogd` daemons store log messages based on the contents of the `/etc/syslog.conf` configuration file. All programs can use this mechanism to save data to log files. You can also use the `logger` utility to write messages to the log file from any command-line interface. The main system message file is `/var/log/messages`.

❑ The `syslog.conf` configuration file defines categories of messages (called facilities), as well as priorities for each message. Different priorities define how serious a message is. A facility and a priority together make up a selector. In the configuration file, you assign actions to selectors to determine how information is logged on your Linux system.

❑ Because log files can grow rapidly, you must maintain them regularly. This is normally done by rotating log files, saving older information for review as appropriate. Some specialized utilities such as `logrotate` are available to help with this task.

KEY TERMS

action — A field in the `syslog.conf` configuration file that determines what to do with messages matching the selector on that line.

daemon — A background process that does not display status information on the screen. Instead, daemons normally write information to log files.

dmesg — Program that displays the contents of the kernel ring buffer. This buffer normally contains hardware configuration data generated during system start-up.

facility — A category assigned to a system message, identifying the type of program providing the message.

function — A set of computer programming code that completes a certain task for a program.

kernel ring buffer — A small area of memory that holds internal kernel messages. These messages can be viewed using the `dmesg` utility.

klogd — A background program (or daemon) used to log kernel messages according to the configuration given in the `syslog.conf` configuration file.

log file — File that contains detailed records of activity on a Linux system.

logger — A program that lets you send a message to the `syslog` function. Such messages are written to the log files according to the configuration in `syslog.conf`.

logrotate — A program that manages the rotation of multiple log files at regular intervals according to a configuration file created by the system administrator.

11

logscanner — A log analysis program available for download at *http://xmission.linuxberg.com/conhtml/adm_log.html*.

LogWatch — A log analysis program available for download at *http://xmission.linuxberg.com/conhtml/adm_log.html*.

message — A description of what is happening within a program.

messages — The main system log file in Linux, usually stored in the directory `/var/log`.

priority — A number indicating the severity of a message submitted for logging. Log configurations are often based on the priority of incoming messages.

rotating log files — The process of moving existing log files to another filename and location for archiving or review. Rotating log files frees hard disk space for new log messages.

script — A collection of commands that functions like a macro, executing commands as if you had executed them on the command line.

selector — A field in the `syslog.conf` file that determines what events are being logged. The selector is composed of a facility and a priority.

SIGHUP — A signal sent to a logging daemon to instruct the daemon to reread its configuration files and the log file it writes to.

sync mode — An option assigned to log files by which the data written to the log file is immediately written to the hard disk rather than being cached in memory to improve system performance.

syslog — A programming function used by Linux programs to submit messages for logging. The `syslog` function interacts with the `syslogd` daemon to write messages according to the `syslog.conf` file.

syslog.conf — The configuration file used to control how and where messages are logged by `syslogd` and `klogd`.

syslogd — The background program (or daemon) that manages all of the calls to the `syslog` function, writing log messages according to the `syslog.conf` configuration.

system initialization scripts — Instructions executed each time you boot your Linux system.

timestamp — The date and time when an event being logged occurred.

Webmaster — The person who manages the content and functioning of a Web server program running on Linux.

REVIEW QUESTIONS

1. All messages generated by standard Linux services and the kernel are logged in the `/var/log/messages` file. True or False?

2. Log files are generally *not* used for which of the following tasks?

   a. Watching for security problems

   b. Calculating system usage statistics

   c. Calculating memory usage for applications

   d. Determining the cause of system failures

3. Given the log entry,

```
Oct 26 06:45:01 brighton httpd: Cannot determine local host
name
```

the word `httpd` refers to which of the following?

   a. The system name on which the event being logged occurred

   b. The program that generated the event being logged

   c. The daemon handling the logging of the event

   d. The configuration file used to control logging of this event

4. Explain the differences between the `syslogd` and the `klogd` logging daemons.

5. A standard `/var/log/messages` log entry contains all of the following *except*:

   a. The hostname of the computer on which the event occurred

   b. The name of the daemon that processes the `syslog` function call

   c. A timestamp showing when the event occurred

   d. Message text describing the event

6. The `syslogd` and `klogd` daemons must be started by the `root` user as soon as the system is booted and `root` logs in. True or False?

7. The kernel ring buffer is:

   a. A holding area for messages generated by `klogd` before writing them to `/var/log/messages`

   b. An internal storage area used by the kernel for certain types of messages

   c. A disk cache area used by the kernel

   d. A symbolic link to the kernel source code

8. The `syslogd` and `klogd` logging daemons depend upon which configuration file?

   a. `logrotate.conf`

   b. `syslog.conf`

   c. They are internally configured and use no configuration file

   d. The `syslog` function called by individual applications

9. A configuration pair consisting of a facility and a priority is called:

   a. An action

   b. The timestamp

   c. A selector

   d. A SIGHUP signal

11

10. Name four types of actions that can be associated with a selector when configuring how messages are logged.

11. The `dmesg` utility is used to do which of the following?

    a. View the kernel ring buffer contents

    b. Sync the log files, writing them to disk

    c. View the most recently logged device messages

    d. Configure events logged to the `messages` file

12. Priorities associated with logged events determine how quickly the message is logged. True or False?

13. The selector `*.info` will log the following:

    a. Messages from all facilities with a priority of `info` or higher

    b. Messages without a facility assigned with a priority of `info`

    c. Messages with a facility of `info` and any priority

    d. Messages from the `info` command that will be posted on the screens of all users who are logged into the system

14. Which of the following is not a valid facility name?

    a. `auth`

    b. `httpd`

    c. `user`

    d. `mail`

15. This configuration line

    ```
    *.emerg     @brighton
    ```

    will cause which of the following to occur?

    a. All messages with a facility of `emerg` are logged to a file matching the system name (the hostname).

    b. All messages with a priority of `emerg` or lower are logged to the file configured as an alias to `brighton`.

    c. All messages with a priority `critical` are sent to the machine named `brighton` for logging.

    d. All messages of any priority but `emerg` are displayed on the screen of user `brighton`, if that user is logged in.

16. Describe briefly the special configuration characters !, =, and – as used in the `syslog.conf` file.

17. An asterisk in the action field of `syslog.conf` is equivalent to an asterisk in the selector field of `syslog.conf`. True or False?

18. This configuration line

    ```
    *.info:mail,news.none:authpriv.none      -/var/log/messages
    ```

    is invalid because:

    a. A colon cannot be used to separate multiple selectors.

    b. Each selector can only include one facility.

    c. The **none** keyword cannot be used as a priority.

    d. The hyphen can only be used in the action field when associated with a set of usernames.

19. Describe why the system logging daemons must be restarted in order to access new configuration files.

20. The command **cat /var/run/syslogd.pid** does which of the following?

    a. Causes the **syslogd** daemon to reread its configuration file

    b. Prints the PID of the currently running **syslogd** daemon

    c. Sends a SIGHUP signal to the logging configuration file

    d. Prints out the most recent logging messages

21. The **logger** utility does which of the following?

    a. Sends messages to the **syslog** function for logging according to the **syslog.conf** file

    b. Writes messages to **/var/log/messages**

    c. Rotates log files according to a predetermined configuration

    d. Restarts the logging daemons with a SIGHUP signal

22. Log file messages can be analyzed using standalone specialized tools or a basic text editor at the command line. True or False?

23. Describe how the **logrotate** command is configured.

24. Which of the following is a valid reason to rotate your log files?

    a. Leaving them open for long periods can cause file corruption.

    b. The files become too large to store on the **root** partition.

    c. System administrators cannot study live log files.

    d. Security-minded individuals feel rotated log files are safer.

11

25. If you saw the message

```
login: FAILED LOGIN 3 FROM (null) for nwells, Authentication
failure
```

you might reasonably assume any of the following *except*:

a. Someone is trying to break into your system using the `nwells` account.

b. User `nwells` has forgotten his password.

c. The `login` program has become corrupted.

d. A user on your system is trying to break into the files owned by `nwells`.

HANDS-ON PROJECTS

Project 11-1

In this activity you watch the system log file as new messages are written to it by the `syslogd` daemon. To complete this activity you need an installed and working Linux system with a graphical interface.

1. Log in to Linux as `root` and start the graphical environment.

2. Open two terminal emulator windows (command-line windows).

3. In one of the windows, enter **tail -f /var/log/messages** to display the last 15 lines of the system log file, updating the display every few seconds.

4. In the second window, enter **killall -HUP syslogd** to restart the `syslogd` daemon. Notice that a message is added to the first window stating that the `syslogd` program was restarted.

5. In the second window, enter **killall -HUP httpd** to restart any Web server daemons running on your system. Notice the messages that are added to the `messages` file in the first window.

6. Leave the first window open for a few minutes as you work on your system, opening other applications or browsing the Web. Are additional messages written to `/var/log/messages`? Can you interpret the messages?

Project 11-2

In this activity you use the `logger` command to send a message to the `/var/log/messages` system log file. To complete this activity you need an installed and working Linux system with a graphical interface.

1. Log in to Linux as `root` and start the graphical environment.

2. Open two terminal emulator windows (command-line windows).

3. In one of the windows, enter `tail -f /var/log/messages` to display the last 15 lines of the system log file, updating the display every few seconds.

4. In the second window, enter `logger -p user.info -t TESTING This is a logging test`.

5. Notice the message that is added to the `/var/log/messages` file shown in the first window.

6. Using the facility and priority names you learned in the chapter, try sending one or two other messages using the `logger` program. In particular, try sending a message with the priority `emerg`. For example, you might use this command: `logger -p user.emerg -t TESTING Emergency message test`. What do you notice about how this command is treated compared to the other `logger` commands you entered? Can you explain why, based on the information in the `syslog.conf` file?

Project 11-3

In this activity you explore the contents of the kernel ring buffer using the `dmesg` command. To complete this activity, you need an installed and working Linux system.

1. Log in to Linux.

2. Enter the command `dmesg | less` to display information on the screen.

3. Use the Up and Down arrow keys and the Page Up and Page Down keys to scroll through the information. How would you describe this information? How does the format compare with that of the `/var/log/messages` file you saw in the previous two projects?

4. Describe some of the Linux device names that you recognize in the output of `dmesg` that you are viewing. Can you see an Ethernet card, a SCSI device, a video card, or a CD-ROM drive? (Not all devices are part of every Linux system.)

5. Press the **q** key to exit the `less` command.

6. Enter `dmesg | grep hda` to search the output of `dmesg` for lines that include information about your first IDE hard disk (device `/dev/hda`).

11

CASE PROJECTS

1. The main Linux file server used by employees at Marcus Financial Group is accessed heavily every day by about 50 people who share applications, send files for printing, and store their documents on the server. The IT management is considering making the file server into a gateway for the Internet so that employees can also browse the Web from their desktops. You have many concerns about this, ranging from the increased load on the network to the security of your Linux server. What precautions might you take with the log files stored on the Linux server as you create an Internet gateway? Will remote storage be part of your solution? Do you anticipate needing additional hardware resources because of the log files? What tools might you try using to alleviate your security fears? Would your efforts in this project also be beneficial to all the employees before the creation of the Internet gateway? How?

2. After the Internet gateway has been up and running for two weeks, you receive a midnight call from an employee working late. You learn that the Linux server has "crashed," or stopped responding to the employee's Web browser requests. Assuming that the server did not have a hard disk failure (thus the log files are still readable), how could you use the log files to help determine the cause of the problem? What effect would your previous preparations (discussed in Question 1) have on your ability to track down the problem using the log file information? Does this problem lead you to change the way the log files are managed or configured?

3. As you implement the revised plan that you conceived in Question 2, do you see any reason to use the `logger` command in your administration scripts? What circumstances might make that utility useful to you at Marcus Financial Group? Will you use the `logrotate` command if it is available on the version of Linux that you are using?

12

CREATING SCRIPTS AND AUTOMATED PROCEDURES

After reading this chapter and completing the exercises, you will be able to:

♦ Create shell scripts using basic shell programming features

♦ Automate one-time and repetitive tasks using at and crontab

♦ Manage automated system administration tasks

In the previous chapter you learned about configuring system log files to record information about what is happening in the Linux kernel and with other programs running on the Linux system. You also learned how you can use those log files to get information about system status and to enhance security.

In this chapter you will learn how to create shell scripts that automate tasks you would normally complete at a Linux command line. You will also learn how to automate system administration tasks via shell scripts that execute automatically at predefined times.

WRITING SHELL SCRIPTS

As you have seen in previous chapters, working with Linux often involves entering a series of commands at the command line (using a shell such as bash). In many cases the commands you enter may be identical—or nearly so—to previously entered commands. You can automate the process of entering frequently used commands by creating a shell script. A **shell script** is an executable file containing lines of text as you would enter them at a command line, including special commands to control the order in which lines in the file are executed. Within a shell script you can store a series of commands that you would otherwise enter at a shell prompt. To execute the commands in a shell script, you simply execute the shell script.

TIP   A shell script is like a batch file in DOS or Windows. Batch files in DOS or Windows end with the file extension `.BAT`, for example, `AUTOEXEC.BAT`. The capabilities of shell scripts, however, go far beyond those of batch files.

Shell scripts can be used throughout a Linux system. The following list describes just a few examples of the shell scripts discussed in preceding chapters:

- The system initialization scripts in the `/etc/rc.d` subdirectory (such as `rc` and `rc.local`) are shell scripts.

- The scripts in `/etc/rc.d/init.d` that start system services such as a Web server are all shell scripts.

- The `/etc/profile` and `/etc/bashrc` scripts that Linux executes each time you log in are shell scripts.

- The scripts that the X Window System uses to launch initial graphical programs are shell scripts (for example, `/etc/X11/xinit/xinitrc` and `/etc/X11/xdm/xsession`).

Using shell scripts for all of these system functions has two great advantages. First, it allows you to study what is happening on the Linux system by reviewing the contents of the scripts that control various programs or system services. Second, you can change the way anything on the system occurs simply by altering the relevant shell script.

Before you continue reading this chapter, take time to locate some shell scripts on your Linux system (using the list above as a guide). As you learn about shell script features in this chapter, refer to these scripts to see how they are configured, what commands they include, and what each is designed to accomplish.

Interpreted and Compiled Programs

Before you can create shell scripts, you need to be familiar with some basic programming concepts. First of all, you should be aware that there are two different types of computer programs: interpreted programs and compiled programs. Both types of programs are written using a computer language. A **computer language**, or **programming language**, is a set of words and syntax rules that can be arranged in predefined ways to cause a computer to perform tasks defined by the person using the language. The words used in a computer language are often called **keywords**, because they have special meanings when used within a computer program. For example, later you will learn the keyword `for`, which defines certain actions when used in a shell script.

A software developer or programmer writes a computer program using a computer language, storing the keywords and related information in a file. This file is considered the program's **source code**. The keywords that make up the computer language are human readable, though you must be familiar with the computer language to understand what the program will do. The computer cannot act directly on the keywords of the computer language. The keywords must first be converted to numeric codes that the computer uses. This numeric code is called the **binary file**, or **executable file**. To run the program, the user must run the executable file.

The process of converting computer language keywords into computer-readable numeric codes can occur in two different ways:

- When the computer language is a compiled language, the source code is converted after the programmer writes the source code. The binary file is normally given to people who want to use the program. (Linux and related programs are unusual in that the source code is also available, but few people need to access it.) A **compiled language** is one for which the source code is converted to a binary file long before the program will be run by users. A **compiler** is a special program that converts the source code of a compiled language into a binary file.

- When the computer language is an **interpreted language**, the source code is converted into numeric codes at the instant a user runs the program. This conversion takes place each time the user runs the program. The source code is given to people who want to use the program. For this reason, interpreted languages are generally much slower than compiled languages. An **interpreter** converts the source code of an interpreted language into numeric codes.

A shell script is an example of an **interpreted program**, that is, a program written in an interpreted language. The commands that you learn in this chapter are part of the interpreted language for the `bash` shell. The shell is the interpreter that acts on the keywords that you include in shell scripts. All of these keywords can also be used at the shell prompt (at any command-line prompt). In general terms, a **script** is a text file that can be interpreted or executed by another program.

12

Programming Concepts

Writing a shell script, though not overly difficult, is really computer programming. In order to write effective shell scripts, knowledge of a few programming concepts is helpful.

A computer program is executed one command at a time. Execution normally proceeds from the first line of the program to the last line. Each command within the program is also called a **statement**. The statement is often a single keyword, but the term *statement* may also refer to a group of keywords that the computer language syntax requires or allows to be used together. One such keyword, described later in this chapter, is `if`. You can never use the `if` keyword without also using the `then` keyword and the `fi` keyword (also discussed later in this chapter). This means that any references to an `if` statement actually refer to the `if` command and its associated information. Or you might hear of an `if/then` statement, which refers to the combination of several keywords that are normally (or always) used together. As you begin to learn about shell scripts, you will begin to think of the terms *command* and *statement* as being synonymous.

The real power of a computer program lies in its ability to decide which parts of the program to execute based on factors that the program itself examines. For example, if the program has the ability to check a stock price on a Web site, the program could be designed to perform one set of commands if the stock price is over a certain price, and another set of commands if the price is below that price. This is done with a selection statement. A **selection statement** lets a computer programmer determine which parts of a program will be executed according to values that are calculated by testing as the program is executed. The use of a selection statement means that all lines in a computer program will not necessarily execute when the program is run—the results of the tests in the selection statements determine which steps run. Figure 12-1 illustrates a selection based on the results of a test.

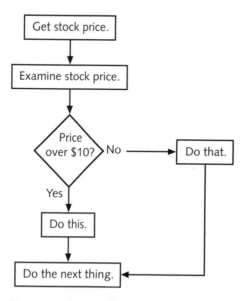

Figure 12-1   A selection statement choosing among alternative actions in a program

Most shell scripts include selection statements. They can be very complex, with many options, or very simple, with only a simple test such as "if this number is 4, do this; otherwise, don't." The tests performed in shell scripts (and in any computer programming language) only have two possible values: true or false. You must design your script to respond to these two possible values. Shell script tests are almost all related to checking the status of a file or the value of an environment variable. They are not designed for mathematical computations, though you can perform math functions using additional commands within a shell script.

A selection statement is used to determine whether part of a computer program should be executed. A **loop statement** is used to determine whether part of a computer program should be executed more than once. A loop statement has several parts:

- A counting variable, which is assigned a different value each time the loop is repeated. The counting variable is often called the **index** of the loop, because it tracks how many times the loop has executed a list of commands.

- A list of values that should be assigned to the counting variable.

- A list of commands that should be executed each time through the loop.

Figure 12-2 illustrates an example of a loop in which several files in a list are to be compressed. This example does not use shell script keywords, but only descriptive text to help you understand how a loop operates. Each of the files is named as part of the loop statement. The counting variable is assigned the value of a different filename each time through the loop.

Collect filenames (`file 1`, `file 2`, `file 3`).
Repeat block once per file.

Block  Compress file.

Counting variable updated on each repitition.

Figure 12-2   A loop statement repeats commands.

When using both selection statements and loop statements, you define a list of commands that are executed once, many times, or not at all depending on what happens when the selection or loop statement is executed. The list of commands (or statements) controlled by a selection or loop statement is often called a block, or a **statement block**. The statement block in Figure 12-2 is the single item, "Compress the file." Statement blocks usually contain many statements. They can even contain other selection and loop statements. **Nesting** is a programming method in which one selection or loop statement contains another selection or loop statement.

Components of a Shell Script

You can create a shell script in any text editor, including `vi`, `emacs`, or a graphical editor within KDE or Gnome. Any text file that adheres to these three basic rules is considered a shell script:

- The first line of the text file must indicate the name of the shell that should be used to execute the shell script.

- The text file must have the execute file permission set for the user, group, or other category (as you learned in Chapter 4).

- The text file must contain valid commands that could be executed at a command line.

 A shell script is sometimes called a shell program. The process of writing a shell script is also called shell programming because it involves using a shell's programming syntax.

When you execute a shell script, you are, in effect, launching a program. The program just happens to be contained in a human-readable text file rather than a standard binary file. But to the shell, both launching a shell script and launching a program such as WordPerfect require a similar process. In order for the shell to identify a text file as an executable script, the execute file permission must be set for the person attempting to execute the shell script.

For example, if you have created a text file in a text editor, the file permissions typically look like this (as viewed by the `ls -l` command):

`rw-r--r--`

To execute the shell script, you must activate the execute permission using this command. (Remember, you must be the file's owner or the `root` user to change file permissions.)

`chmod ugo+x filename`

You could also use the second form of the `chmod` command. This example grants a standard set of file permissions for a Linux program (using numeric codes for the `chmod` command):

`chmod 755 filename`

After using either of these `chmod` commands, the file permissions for the file look like this, indicating to the shell that the file can be executed as a program:

`rwxr-xr-x`

One difference between launching a shell script and launching a program like WordPerfect is that the shell must start another program to interpret (execute) the shell script. This is why the first line of the shell script must contain the name of the shell that will execute the script.

When a user executes a shell script (by entering the script name at a shell prompt), the shell examines the file to see what shell should execute the script. The shell then starts that shell and includes the shell script file as a parameter to be executed. If you are running the `bash` shell and launch a shell script that requires `bash`, the main shell starts a second copy of `bash` to execute the shell script.

The format of the first line of a shell script consists of a hash mark (#), followed by an exclamation point, followed by the shell name (with a complete path to the shell file). For example, the first line of a shell script written for the `bash` shell always looks like this, depending on the location of the `bash` shell program file within the Linux system (the location shown here is standard):

`#!/bin/bash`

Conversely, a shell script designed to be executed by the TC shell will have the following line as the first line in the script file:

`#!/bin/tcsh`

Many of the script examples in this chapter use the `echo` command. The **echo** command prints text (which you must enter after the `echo` command itself) to the STDOUT channel—to the screen unless output has been redirected. For example, to print the message "Hello world" to the screen, you would use the command `echo Hello world`. If the text after the `echo` command includes special characters, such as (or * you should enclose the text in quotation marks. Suppose you created a file named `testscript` containing the following lines (you could do this in any text editor):

```
#!/bin/bash
echo This is a sample shell script.
```

TIP It doesn't matter what filename you use for your shell scripts. You can use any filename and any file extension, so long as the contents of the file itself adhere to the three rules listed previously.

To test a new script, enter the name of the file as a command at a Linux command line. Use a period and a backslash (. /) before the filename to tell the shell that the file is located in the current directory rather than in a directory that is part of the PATH environment variable. For example:

```
./testscript
```

After you enter `./testscript` at the command line, the following steps will occur:

1. The shell you are working in looks at the first line of the `testscript` file and sees that it contains the line `#!/bin/bash`.

2. The shell you are working in launches a new **bash** shell with the filename `testscript` as a parameter. In effect, the shell executes this command for you:

   ```
   bash ./testscript
   ```

3. The new copy of **bash** loads the `testscript` file and executes each of the lines in the file as if they had been entered at a shell prompt, printing output from commands on the screen.

4. When the new copy of **bash** reaches the end of the `testscript` file, it exits, returning control of the screen to the shell from which the shell script was originally launched.

Figure 12-3 illustrates the execution of a shell script.

12

1. Script is launched in shell 1.	`$./testscript`	**testscript file**

2. Shell 1 reads first line of `testscript`.	`/bin/bash`	`#! /bin/bash`
		`command`
		`command`
		`command`

3. Shell 1 starts the script specified in the first line of `testscript`. This new shell is shell 2.	`/bin/bash testscript`	
4. Shell 2 executes each line of `testscript`.	`command` `command` `command`	
5. Shell 2 exits at the end of the script.		
6. Shell 1 is still running.		

Figure 12-3   Execution of a shell script

The sections that follow describe how to create shell scripts based on the `bash` shell programming syntax. As you will recall from Chapter 6, other shells use different programming syntax rules. Because `bash` shell programming is much more common than other types of programming in Linux systems, the information provided here should serve you well. But you should always keep in mind that the shell you are working in and the shell used to execute a script can be different.

Suppose, for example, that you preferred to work in the TC shell because of its interactive shell features, but that you wanted to write a shell script that used `bash` programming syntax. To do this, you would start the shell script file with the `bash` shell name, using the format `#!/bin/bash` shown previously. As described in Step 2 above, the TC shell would launch a copy of the `bash` shell in order to execute the shell script. At the end of the shell script (after the last line in the file had been executed), the `bash` shell would exit, and you would again be working in the TC shell.

Creating a Simple Shell Script

Some commands are generally used only within shell scripts. This section describes some of these basic commands and explains how you can use them to create simple shells scripts. For example, consider the following sample shell script:

```
#!/bin/bash
find /home -name core -exec rm {}\;
du /home >/tmp/home_sizes
```

The purpose of the second line of this script is to locate and remove all files named `core` within all users' home directories. In the third line, you use the `du` command to create a summary of the size of every subdirectory under `/home`, storing that information in a file named `home_sizes`. This script is not long, but the commands are somewhat complicated. By storing these lines in a script called `clean` (or any other name you select), you make it possible to execute both commands by entering this command:

```
./clean
```

 TIP The files named `core` that the preceding script example finds are produced when a Linux program ends unexpectedly. A developer can use the `core` file produced by a program to determine why a program ended. The `core` files can be quite large and are not needed unless someone is troubleshooting a recurring problem, so deleting them regularly can save a lot of hard disk space.

The `clean` script just shown doesn't produce any output on the screen. All of the commands in the script work directly with files. Other scripts write information to the screen or require input from the keyboard to process the commands in the script. The following script uses the `read` command. The `read` command causes the shell to pause for a user to enter information at the keyboard. The information entered is assigned to a variable provided with the **read** command.

```
#!/bin/bash
echo Enter a filename to process:
read THEFILE
echo The number of lines in $THEFILE is:
wc -l $THEFILE
echo The number of words in $THEFILE is:
wc -w $THEFILE
echo End of processing for $THEFILE
```

This script uses a programming concept known as a variable. A variable is a memory location where a program can store a value that it needs in order to complete a task. You normally define a variable by assigning a value to a variable name that you choose. For example, including this line in a script defines a new variable named **MYFILE** and assigns it a value of **index.html**.

```
MYFILE="index.html"
```

Another way you can define a variable is to use the **read** command followed by a variable name. This command causes a script to pause for keyboard input. The text that a user enters at the keyboard is assigned as the value of the variable given in the **read** command. You can see an example of this in the previous script, where the third line contains **read THEFILE**. This command causes the script to pause, awaiting input. Whatever data is entered by the user running the script is assigned as the value of the variable called **THEFILE**.

Once a value is assigned to a variable using either of these methods (a direct assignment or using a **read** command), the script can use the variable within any other commands. In the example script just referred to, the script references the variable **THEFILE** as it executes the **wc** command.

If the above script were stored in a file called **filesize**, any user with execute permission to the file could launch the script using this command:

```
./filesize
```

The output from the **filesize** script is shown here. The script pauses after displaying the first line of this output so that the user can enter a filename. The filename shown (**report.txt**) would be entered by the user running the script.

```
Enter a filename to process:
report.txt
The number of lines in report.txt is:
453
The number of words in report.txt is:
3215
End of processing for report.txt
```

Although the **read** command is useful for collecting input from a user, you should make sure your scripts test the validity of values entered by the user. For example, if the user running the **filesize** script entered a filename that did not exist on the system, the other commands in

12

the script (the wc commands in this example) would generate error messages. Later in this chapter, you will learn how to create scripts that can test values entered by the user.

Because scripts use standard Linux commands that write information to the screen, they can also use the Linux redirection operators to change the flow of information to and from commands. As you learned in Chapter 7, you can use redirection operators to change how the standard input and standard output for any command are treated. For example, suppose you start the `filesize` script using this command:

```
./filesize > /tmp/output
```

Because of the > redirection operator, all of the data that would normally be written to the screen is instead written to the file /tmp/output. When you view the contents of the /tmp/output file using the following command, you see exactly what you saw on screen when you ran the `filesize` command without a redirection operator.

```
cat /tmp/output
```

You can use any of the Linux redirection operators (<, >, >>, or |) when you run any shell script. By using these operators, you can treat a shell script as you would treat any regular Linux command, using pipes to connect scripts with other commands, and so forth. You will see other examples of using redirection operators later in this chapter.

Using Variables in Scripts

The `filesize` sample script shown in the previous section used a variable to store information entered by a user. A variable used in a shell script in this way is sometimes called a shell variable. Thus, a **shell variable** is a variable used within a shell script to store information for use by the script. You can work with shell variables and environment variables (which you learned about in previous chapters) in the same ways, though shell variables are usually defined by a person writing a new shell script, while environment variables are predefined by the Linux operating system scripts or programs running on Linux.

As you write shell scripts, you are likely to refer to many shell variables (which you define yourself by assigning a value within the shell script) and environment variables (which the shell defines by assigning them a value before executing the shell script). For example, a command in your shell script may need to copy a file into the home directory of the user running the shell script. To do this, you can refer to the HOME environment variable. The following sample command copies the file **report.txt** to a user's home directory:

```
cp /tmp/report.txt $HOME
```

Instead of the HOME environment variable, you could use the following command in the script, but this type of command only works if user **nwells** is running the script.

```
cp /tmp/report.txt /home/nwells/
```

By using the HOME environment variable, you ensure that the script works for any user who launches the script. As a system administrator, you should use techniques like this in order to create shell scripts that are as flexible as possible. This allows the scripts to be used safely by different system administrators and other users. Not all users can execute every script, however. Some scripts access parts of the system that only the root user can access. If another user runs such a script, an error will occur.

Shell scripts often use special shell variables called positional variables. Rather than taking on a value assigned to it within the script, a **positional variable** takes on a value based on the information that the user includes on the command line (along with the command to run the script itself). If the filesize script shown earlier incorporated a positional variable, the user could enter the filename at the command line at the same time he or she executed the script. For example, the user would enter the following command to process the file report.txt:

```
./filesize report.txt
```

Within a script, positional variables are indicated using a dollar sign and a number. The notation $0 indicates the first item on the command line (the script name, or in the example above, ./filesize). The notation $1 indicates the second item on the command line (in the example above, report.txt). The notation $2 indicates the third item on the command line, and so forth. (Although the example above only includes two items, you can create scripts that refer to numerous items entered at the command line.) Thus, to incorporate a filename entered at the command line into a script, you would write the script as shown below. As you compare this script with the one shown in the section "Creating a Simple Shell Script," you will see that in this script the read command is not used. Instead, the user executing the script must provide a filename on the command line. The shell will assign the filename to the variable $1 as it starts the script. The $1 positional variable is thus used in place of the THEFILE shell variable throughout the script.

```
#!/bin/bash
echo The number of lines in $1 is:
wc -l $1
echo The number of words in $1 is:
wc -w $1
echo End of processing for $1
```

Let's assume the preceding version of the filesize script is executed using this command line:

```
./filesize myreport
```

The shell assigns the value of myreport to the variable $1 before running the filesize script. The value of this variable is substituted in the script wherever you see a $1. So the commands that are executed when this script is run (as shown above) look like this:

```
echo The number of lines in myreport is:
wc -l myreport
echo The number of words in myreport is:
wc -w myreport
echo End of processing for myreport
```

Depending on the size of the `myreport` file, the output of the script might look something like this:

```
The number of lines in myreport is:
452
The number of words in myreport is:
3419
End of processing for myreport
```

 TIP As you've probably guessed, the term positional variable refers to the fact that the position of the items on the command line dictates the variable names to which they are assigned within the script.

As you work with positional variables, it's often helpful to know how many items the user running the script has included on the command line. For example, you may want to include commands to verify that the correct number of items is included on the command line before having the script proceed with execution. Each time you execute a script, the shell defines a special variable called `$#` that contains the number of items on the command line used to execute the script. Later you will learn about commands that enable your scripts to test the value of the `$#` variable to determine how many items a user provided on the command line when the script was launched. For example, suppose you created the following script to output information about several filenames entered at the command line:

```
#!/bin/bash
echo The script you are running is $0
echo The number of parameters you provided to process is $#
echo The number of lines in file $1 is:
wc -l $1
echo The number of lines in file $2 is:
wc -l $2
echo The number of lines in file $3 is:
wc -l $3
echo The number of lines in file $4 is:
wc -l $4
```

If the above script were stored in a file named `info`, you would launch it like this, with the names of four data files included on the command line:

```
./info data1 data2 data3 data4
```

The shell assigns the name of the script—the first item on the command line—to the positional variable `$0`. The shell also assigns the filenames included on the command line to the positional variables `$1`, `$2`, `$3`, and `$4`, respectively. Finally, the shell assigns the value of 4 to the `$#` variable (which you see on the third line of the script) because the command line used to execute this script contains four items besides the name of the script. Thus the commands executed when this script is run are as follows:

```
echo The script you are running is info
echo The number of parameters you provided to process is 4
echo The number of lines in file data1 is:
wc -l data1
echo The number of lines in file data2 is:
wc -l data2
echo The number of lines in file data3 is:
wc -l data3
echo The number of lines in file data4 is:
wc -l data4
```

The output of the script would then look like this (depending on the size of the data files):

```
The script you are running is info
The number of parameters you provided to process is 4
The number of lines in file data1 is:
123
The number of lines in file data2 is:
11241
The number of lines in file data3 is:
2321
The number of lines in file data4 is:
3159
```

Positional variables are a very useful way to provide information to the commands in a script. But a script such as this example requires that a user provide a precise number of filenames; if the user makes a mistake, the script will generate error messages. In the next section you learn how to test values in a shell script and act on the result of those tests.

Understanding Tests

In many scripts it is useful to determine whether a given condition is true or false. The following list provides a few examples of when such a test is useful.

- You need to determine whether a filename (that is entered by a user or included on the command line) actually exists.

- You need to see if two numeric values are identical.

- You need to determine whether a file is empty.

- You need to test whether the number of parameters on the command line is correct, thus allowing the script to function as intended.

A **test** is a method of examining something within a shell script such as a file or a variable. The script chooses which commands to execute according to the result of the examination (that is, according to the result of the test). For example, a script might test whether a filename referred to a valid file, or whether a certain variable value was too low for the needs of the script. The **if** command is used to introduce a test within a shell script. An **if** command is always followed by a **then** command. A **then** command identifies the other commands that should be executed if the test introduced by the **if** command succeeds (returns a value of true). The **fi** command marks the end of a set of commands that begin with an if/then command pair. If the test within an `if` command succeeds, all of the commands between `then` and `fi` are executed. Otherwise, none of those commands are executed. The **test** command evaluates the parameters that you include in the script after the `test` command and returns either true (a value of 1) or false (a value of 0). The results of the `test` command are then evaluated by the `if` command. An example of an `if` command used with a `test` command is shown here. (The parameters of the `test` command are described later.)

```
if test $1 -eq report
```

Instead of the `test` command shown in this example, square brackets are commonly used around the parameters that you would use with the `test` command. The shell uses the `test` command to evaluate the parameters in square brackets, and the result is used by the `if` command.

Figure 12-4 shows the format of the `if` command used with square brackets to test parameters as just described. This arrangement is called an `if/then` statement or an `if/then` block.

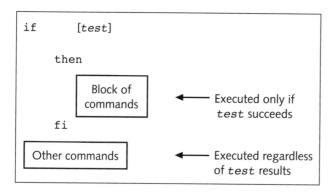

Figure 12-4   Structure of an `if/then` statement

To form a test in the `bash` shell, you include one or two items being tested along with a test operator that defines how you want to test the items. The items being tested and the test operator are like command parameters. All of the parameters are enclosed between square brackets. Table 12-1 shows the testing operators that are available in the `bash` shell.

Using `if/then/else` Statements

An **if/then/else statement** is another kind of selection statement. Such a statement specifies that *if* a test returns a value of true, *then* one set of commands should be executed; otherwise (*else*) another set of commands should be executed. Such a statement begins with an `if` command, such as the one shown below. In this example, the test being performed (that is, the item between the square brackets) could be described like this: "if the file /etc/smb.conf exists, return a value of true; otherwise, return a value of false."

```
if [ -f /etc/smb.conf ]
```

Table 12-1   File-Testing Operators in the bash Shell

Test operator	Description
-d	Test whether the item is a directory name.
-e	Test whether the filename exists.
-f	Test whether the file exists and is a regular file.
-h or -L	Test whether the file exists and is a symbolic link.
-r	Test whether the file exists and is readable
-w	Test whether the file exists and is writable
-x	Test whether the file exists and is executable.
-lt	Test whether the numeric variable on the left (of the operator) is less than the numeric variable or value on the right.
-gt	Test whether the numeric variable on the left (of the operator) is greater than the numeric variable or value on the right.
-le	Test whether the numeric variable on the left (of the operator) is less than or equal to the numeric variable or value on the right.
-ge	Test whether the numeric variable on the left (of the operator) is greater than or equal to the numeric variable or value on the right.
-eq	Test whether the numeric variable on the left (of the operator) is equal to the numeric variable or value on the right.
-ne	Return a value of true if the numeric variable on the left (of the operator) is not equal to the numeric variable or value on the right.

12

After this if command, you can add a block of commands that you want executed only if the test returns a value of true. (This is the *then* part of an if/then/else statement.) As a simple example, consider this partial script:

```
if [ -f /etc/smb.conf ]
    then
            echo The Samba server appears to be configured.
    fi
echo Processing the server configuration.
```

In the above example, the **-f** test operator used in the if command means that the echo command is only executed when the if command returns a value of true—that is, if the file /etc/smb.conf does indeed exist. If the file does *not* exist, the shell skips the statements between the if and fi commands, and proceeds to execute the next command after the fi command. In the above example, the next command would be the echo command with a message stating that the server configuration is being processed.

 The indentation of lines using tabs and spaces is a convention designed to make the script easier for a person to read. Tabs and spaces included in a program are called **white space**. White space between commands or lines has no effect on a shell script's operation.

The **else** command extends the capability of an `if/then` statement by adding a block of commands that are only executed if a test returns a value of false (that is, if the test fails). You can use an **else** command only after an `if/then` command. The structure of an `if/then/else` statement is shown in Figure 12-5. Notice especially that the **else** block of commands is skipped if the test returns a value of true.

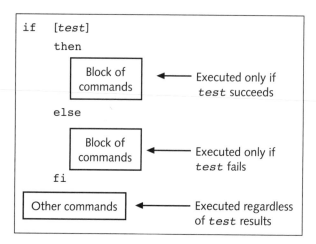

Figure 12-5 Structure of an `if/then/else` statement

The following sample script shows how the **else** command is used. As with the previous example, the **fi** command ends the entire statement. The commands between **then** and **else** are executed only if the test succeeds. The commands between **else** and **fi** are executed if the test fails.

```
if [ -f /etc/smb.conf ]
     then
          echo The Samba server appears to be configured.
     else
          echo The Samba server cannot be started.
     fi
```

The **exit** command stops the execution of a script immediately. The **exit** command is often included within an `if/then/else` statement, and it is then executed only if certain conditions exist (as determined by an `if` command).

 A **comment** is a line within a script that is not processed by the shell, but is only included to help someone reading the file understand the purpose of the script or how it functions. To include a comment, begin a line with a hash mark, #. (The first line of a script that begins with # ! is a special case and is not a comment.)

The following script includes a test in which the number of parameters included on the command line that launched the script is tested within an `if/then` statement. Specifically,

the test determines whether the $# variable has a value of 2 or not, using the **-ne** oper-
ator to test for "not equal to." Notice that the script includes several comment lines. You
should include numerous comments to help other system administrators understand the
scripts you write (and to remind yourself how and why you created a script when you
review it months later).

```
#!/bin/bash
#
#  Script to add a user to the database user's list
#  Requires a username and database table name on the command line
#     launching the script
#  Created 20 April 2000; Nicholas Wells
#
if [ $# -ne 2 ]
then
      echo You must provide a username and a database table name.
      exit
fi
# Begin processing: Store positional variables in new shell variables
DB_USER=$1
DB_TABLE=$2
```

Because Linux systems use many environment variables and complex test expressions involving multiple comparisons, you may have trouble understanding all of the shell scripts on your
Linux system until you have reviewed the test syntax thoroughly and seen many examples of
complex `if/then` statements. The `bash` shell supports several additional commands to extend
the capability of tests. Those additional testing commands are beyond the scope of this book.

Adding Loops to a Script

Recall that a loop is a block of commands that can be executed more than one time without the user having to restart a shell script. A loop can repeat a block of commands a certain
number of times or indefinitely until a condition is met (that is, until a test succeeds). The
`bash` shell supports several commands that you can use to define a loop within a shell script.

The **for** command repeats a block of commands one time for each item in a list. The block
of commands that is repeated is known as a **for loop**. You can include a list of items when
you write the script, or you can design the loop so that the list items are provided on the
command line when the script is executed. The syntax of a **for** command is shown below.
The parameters that you must include after the **for** command are a counting variable and
a list with each value that you want the counting variable to take. The commands between
the **do** command and the **done** command are executed one time for each item in the list.
The shell assigns a new value to the variable each time the loop executes—specifically, it
assigns each value in the list in turn. The **do** and **done** commands are keywords used to
begin and end a block of commands to be executed by a **for** command.

```
for variable in <list of items>
do
      block of commands
done
```

12

The list of items in a `for` command can be any of the following:

- Numbers
- Words
- A regular expression used to match filenames in the current working directory
- The special variable `$@`, described below

Each of these possible methods of defining a list of items in a `for` loop is shown in the following example script lines:

- `for COUNT in 1 2 3 4 5 6 7`
- `for NAME in george ali maria rupert kim`
- `for db_filename in *c`
- `for db_filename in $@`

When you use a regular expression (like `*c`) as the list of items in a `for` command, the shell replaces the regular expression with all matching names in the current directory. Using the example of `*c`, the shell will insert all the filenames in the current directory that end with the letter *c*. This occurs before the shell executes the `for` command itself.

The `$@` variable used in the last example above is a special variable that includes all of the parameters on the command line. This variable is often used when you create a script that processes any number of filenames given on the command line. The following example script shows how a loop processes each filename on the command line in turn:

```
#!/bin/bash
for i in $@
do
      gzip $i
done
```

Suppose the above script were stored in a file called **convert**. If you started the script using the following command line, the `for` loop would execute the commands between **do** and **done** (the `gzip` command in this example) three times, once for each filename on the command line.

```
./convert phoebe.bmp charon.bmp europa.bmp
```

Figure 12-6 shows how the value assigned to the `i` counting variable changes during each of the three times through the script. As you can see, Figure 12-6 uses the term iteration. Each time through the loop counts as one **iteration**. Programmers sometimes use the phrase "iterating through a loop," meaning that the block of commands within the loop is repeated, with new variable values assigned each time through.

for statement:	`for i in $@`
$@ replaced with file names:	`for i in phoebe.bmp charon.bmp europa.bmp`
Value of i:	First iteration, `i=phoebe.bmp` Second interation, `i=charon.bmp` Third iteration, `i=europa.bmp`

Figure 12-6   Iterations through a simple `for` loop

A second type of loop used in shell scripts does not include a list of items to use as variable values. Instead, this second type of loop includes a test like an `if/then` statement. As long as the test returns a value of true, the block of commands in the loop is executed again and again. As soon as the condition changes (the test returns a value of false), the loop exits. You use the **while** command to create such a loop. After a `while` command, you include a block of commands to execute as long as the test returns true. The syntax of the `while` command is shown here. It is similar to the `for` loop in that the block of commands constituting the loop is positioned between do and done.

```
while <test>
do
      block of commands
done
```

You can perform the same tests with a `while` command that you can with the `if` and `then` commands. For example, the following partial script requests a filename from a user. The loop repeats, asking for the filename again, until the filename entered is a valid file. The test in this example is a combination of the `-f` operator (which tests whether the file exists) and the `!` operator (which reverses the result of the test). The `!` operator is used because this script is designed to execute a block of commands if something is not true. Rather than have a separate set of operators such as "not a file," and "not a directory," you simply use a `!` operator with one of the other operators. You could read the test shown in the `while` command as "while not `DB_FILE` exists"—in other words, while the file `DB_FILE` does not exist—keep looping through the following commands (to try to collect a valid filename from the user). Notice that the programmer has assigned a value to the variable used within the test portion of the `while` statement *before* the `while` statement is executed. This lets the programmer be certain of the variable value (and thus the test result) the first time that variable is tested.

```
DB_FILE=" "
while [ ! -f $DB_FILE ]
do
      echo Please enter the database file to archive:
      read DB_FILE
done
```

The script will repeat the block of commands between **do** and **done** indefinitely unless a valid filename is entered. Note, however, that the user can generally exit any script by pressing Ctrl+C.

Other Scripting Methods

So far, you have learned about creating shell scripts, but many other types of scripts are also commonly used in Linux. The commands in a shell script must follow specific syntax rules for tests, loops, and so forth. Other types of scripts—which are written using different computer languages and which are executed by different interpreters (rather than the **bash** shell) —require you to follow different syntax. The specific syntax rules depend on the interpreter that will execute the script. Each interpreter (such as Perl or Python) enforces its own set of syntax rules to communicate a specific set of instructions to the computer.

Different types of scripts are used for different purposes. After you learn about the types of scripts available (or more precisely, about the programming languages that you can use to create scripts), you will be able to decide which type of script is best suited to helping you complete a given task. In every case, the three rules regarding shell scripts given at the beginning of the section "Components of a Shell Script" still apply. That list is shown again here.

- The first line of each script file identifies the interpreter that will execute the script.
- The script file must have the execute file permission set.
- The script file must contain commands that are valid for the interpreter that will execute the script.

Table 12-2 lists several popular scripting languages used in Linux. All of these languages are included in most standard Linux distributions. Many books are available to teach you how to write programs using any one of these scripting languages.

Table 12-2   Popular Scripting Languages

Language	Comments
Perl	Used extensively to process data on Web servers. Rarely used for graphical programs. Very popular and well known.
Awk	Used for system administration work, often processing text files in conjunction with the sed program (see Chapter 6). The most widely used version of the awk interpreter used on Linux is the gawk program from the GNU project.
Python	A fairly new scripting language that is rapidly gaining popularity. Excellent for creating graphical programs.
Tcl/Tk	A very popular language for developing graphical applications quickly.
Expect	Used by system administrators to interact with programs that normally require keyboard input.

As you have already learned, file extensions are not always used in Linux. Binary Linux programs such as `ls` and `cp` don't even include a file extension (like the `.EXE` or `.COM` used on Windows systems). Scripting languages are no different. By convention, however, script files often use standard file extensions to help users identify the information in a file. For example, Perl scripts often end in `.pl`, Python scripts in `.py`, and Tcl/Tk scripts in `.tcl`. You'll even see shell scripts that end with an `.sh` file extension. Just remember that these are conveniences for the user of the system, not requirements of the programs themselves. The next two sections describe some of these scripting languages in detail.

Perl Scripts and CGI

Working with Perl scripts is similar to working with shell scripts in many ways. One of the most widely used scripting languages is Perl. **Perl** is a programming language developed by Larry Wall initially to process strings of text and generate reports. Eventually Perl became very popular for creating powerful scripts that control the interaction between the Web server and a user running a Web browser.

When you launch a script by entering its filename at a shell prompt, the shell examines the first line of the script to determine which interpreter will execute the script file. The first line of a Perl script file would therefore look like this (depending on where the Perl interpreter is located on the Linux system):

```
#!/usr/bin/perl
```

> **TIP** The name Perl is actually an acronym for Practical Extraction and Reporting Language, but you will rarely hear this longer term used.

12

Web servers are designed to use the standards of the **Common Gateway Interface**, or **CGI**, which is a method of communication between two programs, such as a Web server and a Perl script. CGI employs the standard input and standard output channels to facilitate communications. Environment variables and other tools are also used to facilitate this communication. CGI is especially useful in situations where a user needs to submit information to a Web server by means of a form on a Web page. To understand the usefulness of CGI, consider the following scenario:

1. A user running a Web browser enters data (such as the user's name and e-mail address) in a form.

2. The browser sends the data from the form to a Web server running on Linux.

3. The Web server starts a Perl script designed to process the data in the form.

4. The Perl script retrieves the form data submitted by the browser and acts on it (perhaps adding it to a database).

5. The Perl script creates a customized response for the user based on the data that the user entered and writes that response text to standard output.

6. The Web server collects all the output of the Perl script and sends it back to the browser as a document.

The interaction between the Perl script and the Web server in Steps 5 and 6 unfolds according to the standards of CGI. By using CGI standards, the Web server can rely on standard communication channels as a type of gateway between two programs. To achieve higher performance, several other methods (such as using Active Server Pages or embedding a Perl interpreter within a Web server) are now commonly used for exchanging data between Web servers and customized programs. But CGI is still an important tool and one that a Linux administrator must understand. You need to be familiar with the way Linux programs (in particular Linux network services) incorporate the methods of CGI—that is, how these programs gather data from other programs using the standard Linux communication channels.

Scripts for Graphical Programs

You can use other types of scripting languages to create graphical programs that include dialog boxes and menus. A graphical program written in a scripting (interpreted) language performs much slower than one written in a compiled language (such as C or C++). This is because the interpreter must prepare everything for the graphical display the moment the program is run. By contrast, in a compiled program the many steps required to display a graphical interface are handled before the program is actually started. Using scripts to create graphical programs is often useful, nevertheless, because it normally takes much less time to write a script than to create a C or a C++ program.

Two of the most popular scripting languages for creating graphical programs are Tcl/Tk and Python. **Tcl/Tk** is a scripting language developed by John Ousterhout. The name Tcl/Tk stands for *tool control language/toolkit*. The word *toolkit* refers to the graphical toolkit, or set of programming functions that a programmer can use within Tcl/Tk scripts for creating graphical interfaces. (Note that Tcl/Tk is often referred to as "tickle-TK.")

Scripts written in Tcl/Tk rely on an interpreter called `wish`. Thus the first line of a Tcl/Tk script includes the name `wish` rather than the name Tcl or Tk. For example, the first line of a Tcl/Tk script might look like this:

```
#!/usr/bin/wish
```

The scripting language Python uses the same Tk graphical programming toolkit as Tcl. **Python** is an object-oriented programming language, meaning that Python programs are designed so that parts of one program can be reused in another program with minimal effort. Python was developed by Guido van Rossum. You can use either Tcl/Tk or Python to create powerful and complex graphical programs. Figure 12-7 shows an example of a graphical program written in Python.

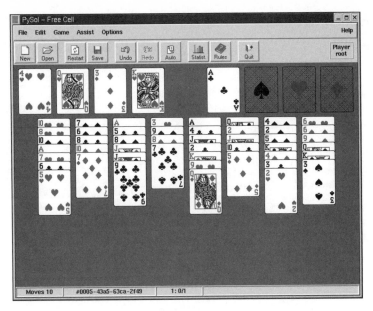

Figure 12-7   Sample graphical program written in Python

AUTOMATING TASKS WITH at AND crontab

Scripts are not the only means for automating a series of commands in Linux. This part of the chapter describes some other tools that let you define a task and have it execute automatically, either when you are doing other work on the system or when you are away from the system (such as in the middle of the night).

The **at** command lets you enter one or more commands that will be executed once at some future time. The **crontab** command lets you enter one or more commands that will be executed repeatedly at intervals that you designate. Both commands are included in all standard Linux distributions. The **at** command relies on a daemon called **atd**; the **crontab** command relies on a daemon called **crond**. Both of these daemons are started by the standard system initialization scripts located in **/etc/rc.d/init.d**. Each of these programs (**atd** and **crond**) checks once per minute for any scheduled tasks and then executes them.

A scheduled task is often called a job, and you will often hear of cron jobs. A **cron job** is a command or script that you have scheduled to be executed at a specific time. The term cron job is sometimes used to refer to tasks you have set up using the **at** command as well. Some scheduled tasks, or cron jobs, only need to be performed once. Others are repetitive. The next section describes how to use the **at** command to schedule cron jobs (or *at* jobs, as they are sometimes called) that only need to be executed one time.

12

Automating One-Time Tasks

Sometimes you may want to arrange for a single task to be executed once at some point in the future. The following list describes a few cases when this might be true:

- You need to start a back-up operation after all employees have left for the evening.

- You want to start a large database query during lunch, but you need to leave the office early.

- You need to remind several users on the network of a meeting occurring at 3:00 p.m., but you're afraid you'll forget it yourself as well.

In each of these cases, you can use the `at` command, as described in the next section.

The `at` command

To automate a task with the `at` command, you can either enter the commands you want to schedule for later execution directly at the command line, or you can include them in a file. For long lists of commands, it's best to include them in a file so you can check the accuracy of the commands before using the `at` command.

If you have created a text file containing the commands you want to enter, the format of the `at` command looks like this:

```
at -f filename <time specification>
```

For example, suppose you have stored the following `tar` command in a file called `archive_job`. (As described in Chapter 14, the `tar` command is used to back up a Linux system.)

```
tar cvzf /archive/home_dirs.tgz /home
```

Suppose further that you want to start the archive operation at 11:30 p.m. The following `at` command would execute the command for you:

```
at -f archive_job 23:30
```

As described previously, the `atd` daemon will check once per minute for any jobs that have been scheduled using the `at` command. At 11:30, the job scheduled by the above command will be executed. Any results from the command (that is, text that would normally be written to the screen) will be e-mailed to the user who entered the `at` command. If you prefer to have the output stored in a file, you rerun the `at` command after altering the `archive_job` file as follows:

```
tar cvzf /archive/home_dirs.tgz /home > /tmp/archive_listing
```

The time specification in the `at` command is very flexible. You can include a standard hour format, such as 23:30 in the previous example, but you can also include items such as the words `now`, `minutes`, `hours`, `days`, or `months`. You can include the words `today`, `tomorrow`, `noon`, `midnight`, and even `teatime` (4:00 p.m.). Table 12-3 shows several examples of specifying a time with the `at` command.

Table 12-3 Time Specifications in the at Command

Time specification	Description
at -f file now + 5 minutes	Execute the commands in file five minutes after the at command is entered.
at -f file 4pm + 5 days	Execute the commands in file at 4:00 p.m., five days from now.
at -f file noon Jul 31	Execute the commands in file at noon on July 31.
at -f file 10am 08/15/00	Execute the commands in file at 10:00 a.m. on 15 August 2000. (The at command has no problems with Year 2000+ dates.)
at -f file 5:15 tomorrow	Execute the commands in file at 5:15 a.m. tomorrow morning.

Note the following points about specifying times within the at command:

- Each item in the time specification is separated by a space.

- You cannot combine multiple phrases (such as 4 hours and 25 minutes).

- When you use the word **now**, it should be the first word of the time specification.

- When a time is specified (such as 23:30), the command file will be processed the next time the system clock reaches the indicated time. For example, if it is currently 9:00 a.m. and you want to schedule a task for 11:00 a.m. tomorrow, you must indicate **tomorrow** in the time specification or the task will be executed at 11:00 a.m. today (because 11:00 a.m. has not passed yet today).

- If the at command cannot understand the time specification, you see a message stating **Garbled time**, and the command is not accepted for processing.

When you enter an at command with both a valid file that contains commands and a valid time specification, you see a message like the following. (The job number and the time displayed depend on the state of the Linux system.) This message reminds you that the commands you enter will be executed using the /bin/sh program. (On most Linux systems this is another name for the bash shell.) It also indicates the exact date and time when the command file will be executed.

```
warning: commands will be executed using /bin/sh
job 9 at 2000-10-21 05:15
```

TIP   The filename that you include as a parameter to the at command can include a shell script that you have written. If you have already prepared a shell script for some task, referring to that shell script in an at command makes it easy to schedule a time to launch the script. In addition, you can create a shell script that relies on another shell (besides the /bin/sh shell used by default).

12

When you create a command file for the at command, you don't need to begin it with the line #!/bin/bash, as you would with a script. Commands in the file are executed by the /bin/sh shell as if you had executed them at the shell prompt.

Using at Interactively

The format of the at command shown in the preceding section requires you to prepare a file containing the commands that you want to execute. If you prefer, you can enter commands at the shell prompt so that you don't have to prepare a command file before using the at command. The disadvantage to entering commands interactively is that you cannot edit the commands after you enter each line; the advantage is that you don't need to create a separate file before scheduling a task.

To use the at command interactively, simply omit the −f *filename* portion of the at syntax. For example, you might enter a command such as this:

```
at now + 5 hours
```

When you press Enter after typing such an at command, you see a prompt that looks like this: at>. At this prompt you enter the command that you want the atd daemon to execute. You can enter multiple lines of text. You can also enter shell programming commands. For example, you can enter if/then statements or for loops, as described earlier in the chapter. Suppose, for instance, that you entered a for loop that uses the mail command to e-mail a short list of text files. The following would appear on your screen after you had entered all the lines of the for loop. (Press Enter after each line shown here.)

```
at now + 5 hours
at> for file in *.txt
at> do
at> mail -s "File $file" tomr < $file
at> done
at>
```

After entering all the commands that you want the atd daemon to execute, you must indicate that you have finished entering commands. To do this, you press the Ctrl+D key combination, which sends an end-of-input character to the at command. At this point, the text <EOT> is displayed on the last line containing the at> prompt, followed by a message indicating the job number and time that the atd daemon will execute the command. Then the shell prompt returns.

When you enter a series of commands at the at> prompt, the results of the commands are e-mailed to you, just as they are when you specify a command file using the −f parameter. The e-mail message that the atd daemon sends you has a subject such as "Output from your job 11," where the number at the end of the message (11 in this example) is the job number assigned when you entered the at command.

> For the specified task to be completed, the Linux system must be turned on at the time
> you specify in the `at` command. For example, if you indicate that a command should
> be executed in four hours, but the computer is not turned on in four hours, the com-
> mand will not be executed then, nor will it be executed when the system is turned on
> again. The `atd` daemon does not check for commands that could not be executed
> because the computer was turned off.

Sometimes you'll want the output from a command to appear on screen instead of being
e-mailed to you. For example, if you need to send yourself a reminder, having it sent to
e-mail won't be much help. If you remember to check for the e-mail message, you'll remember the event you were to be reminded of. As an alternative, you can use the `tty` command
to send output from a command (previously scheduled with `at`) to the location where you are
currently logged in. The `tty` command returns the name of the terminal device that you are
currently working in. For example, if you have logged in on the first virtual console of a Linux
system and you enter the command `tty`, you see the device name `/dev/tty1` displayed on
screen. You can use the output of this command to redirect output of a command that you submit to the `at` command. For example, suppose you submitted the following command to the
`at` command (either using a separate command file or directly at the `at>` prompt). Notice that
the `tty` command at the end of this command is enclosed in single backward quotation marks:

```
echo Go to your 401k meeting in conference room 6! > `tty`
```

When the `atd` daemon processes this line, the `tty` command is executed first, and the output from the `tty` command (such as `/dev/tty1`) is substituted for the `` `tty` `` text. The
`echo` command then sends the line of text to the terminal where you are working (such as
`/dev/tty1`). Any error messages will still be sent to standard output (and thus e-mailed to
you). You can also redirect the Standard Error channel using this format:

```
echo Go to your 401k meeting in conference room 6! 2>&1 > `tty`
```

The Standard Error channel is number 2. The above statement redirects channel 2 to channel 1, which is standard output. Standard output is then redirected to the device name output by the `tty` command, which will be the device where you are logged in.

> If you are working in multiple graphical terminal windows, the `tty` command may
> not allow the `atd` daemon to send the output to the precise window in which you
> are working. Don't rely on this method for sending critical, time-sensitive reminders
> to yourself.

Using the `batch` Command

A command similar to the `at` command, and which also relies on the `atd` daemon, is the
`batch` command. Rather than running commands at a specified time, the **batch** command
runs your commands when the system load average drops below 0.8. (You can see the system load by using the `top` command.) In addition, if you enter multiple commands at the
same time using the `batch` command, to avoid overloading the system, the `batch` command only starts one command at a time. The `batch` command is useful for times when
you want to run a CPU-intensive program but the system is currently very busy with other

tasks. In this case, you can use the `batch` command to enter the name of the program you want to run. As soon as the system is no longer so busy, the command will be executed. As with the `at` command, the results of commands run by `batch` are e-mailed to you.

For example, suppose you needed to start a time-consuming task such as reconfiguring the Linux kernel using the `make` command. You could enter the `batch` command as shown below. Notice that no time parameters are included; the commands run as soon as the system load permits. You can include the `-f` option with the `batch` command, or just use the command name and then enter commands at the `at>` prompt, as you would when using the `at` command.

```
batch
at> cd /usr/src/linux
at> make dep; make zImage
at><EOT>
```

As with the `at` command, you press Ctrl+D when you have finished entering the commands you want `batch` to process. The `<EOT>` designation then appears, and the command prompt returns. As soon as the system load was small enough, the `batch` command would execute the commands you entered.

> **TIP** The `make` command in the preceding example uses commands stored in a configuration file to compile source code into a binary program, or otherwise prepare a program to be executed. This command uses a file called `Makefile` (which acts like a control script) to determine what actions to take when you enter a command such as `make dep` or `make zImage`. To learn more about `make`, enter the command `man make`.

Automating Recurring Tasks

You can use the `crontab` command to prepare tasks that you want to have executed automatically at regular intervals. You might use `crontab` when you need to:

- Create a list of files that have not been accessed in a long time to check whether they can be deleted or archived

- Create a back-up copy of all active files (those recently accessed)

- Compile a list of all directories on the system, sorted by size, to help you identify areas that are using a lot of hard disk space

- Remove core files or other unused files that are using a lot of hard disk space

- Delete files in the `/tmp` directory that have not been used recently

- Rotate log files to keep them from becoming too large

- Run security scanning software (for example, check e-mail attachments for viruses or search system log files for multiple login failures)

- Store the results of the `ps` or `df` command to make a snapshot of the system's state at different times

Many Linux distributions include a simple method of automating tasks that doesn't require you to use the `crontab` command. In Red Hat Linux, the `/etc` directory contains subdirectories named `cron.hourly`, `cron.daily`, `cron.weekly`, and `cron.monthly`. You can place a script in any of these subdirectories. That script will be executed hourly, daily, weekly, or monthly, depending on which directory you place the script in. This method does not let you specify a precise time for your script, but most system administration tasks don't require a precise execution time; the important point is not to run them during the work day when most systems would be busy with many other tasks.

Every Linux system provides an `/etc/crontab` file, which shows the format of a standard entry for the `crontab` command. The `/etc/crontab` file in Red Hat Linux is shown here. This example file uses a special script from Red Hat Linux called **run-parts**.

```
SHELL=/bin/bash
PATH=/sbin:/bin:/usr/sbin:/usr/bin
MAILTO=root
HOME=/

# run-parts
01 * * * * root run-parts /etc/cron.hourly
02 4 * * * root run-parts /etc/cron.daily
22 4 * * 0 root run-parts /etc/cron.weekly
42 4 1 * * root run-parts /etc/cron.monthly
```

Notice the following about the example `/etc/crontab` file above:

- The **SHELL** variable defines which shell the **crond** daemon will use to execute the commands and scripts listed in the file.

- The **MAILTO** variable defines which user on the Linux system will receive an e-mail message containing the output from all cron jobs defined in the file.

- The **HOME** and **PATH** variables define a working directory and the directories where system commands are located. These variables will be used by all commands and scripts used in this file (and hence by all scripts in the `cron.daily` through `cron.monthly` subdirectories).

- The lines that end with the names of the subdirectories (such as `cron.daily`) include the username **root**. All of the cron jobs that you place in the `cron.daily` and related directories will be executed via the **root** user account.

The flexibility provided by the `crontab` command makes it challenging to use. For example, the preceding sample file includes numbers and asterisks that define when the commands and scripts will be executed. To use `crontab` effectively, you must learn well the format of the fields containing the numbers and asterisks. Each crontab specification begins with five fields, described in the following list as they appear on each crontab line from left to right:

- *Minute of the hour*: this field can range from 0 to 59.

- *Hour of the day*: this field can range from 0 to 23.

- *Day of the month*: this field can range from 0 to 31, but be careful about using the days 29, 30, or 31, because then nothing will happen in the month of February.

- *Month of the year*: this field can range from 0 to 12. You can also use the first three letters of a month's name (in upper- or lowercase).

- *Day of the week*: this field can range from 0 to 7 (0 and 7 are both Sunday; 1 is Monday). You can also use the first three letters of a day's name (in upper- or lowercase).

The `crond` daemon examines all five of these fields once per minute. If all five fields match the current time, `crond` executes the command on that line. When you use an asterisk in a field, `crond` ignores that field. In effect, placing an asterisk in a field means "execute this command no matter what the current value of this field is." For example, including an asterisk in the day of the month field means "execute this command no matter what day of the month it is." In order for the command to be executed, all five fields must match the current time and date. By placing an asterisk in four of the fields, the current time and date must only match the non-asterisk field. For example, the following entry specifies that a command should be run at 10 minutes after every hour, on every day of every month.

```
10 * * * *
```

The following example specifies that a command should be executed on the first day of every month at 2:15 in the morning.

```
15 2 1 * *
```

Fields can contain multiple values, either separated by commas (without spaces after the commas) or defined by ranges with a hyphen separating them. For example, the next entry specifies that a command should be executed on the 1st, 10th, and 20th of every month at 1:00 a.m.

```
0   1 1,10,20 * *
```

The time specifications can become very complicated if you need them to be. But by learning the meaning of the five fields and reviewing a few examples, you'll soon be able to construct any time specification you are likely to need.

 TIP To learn more about how you can form very complex time specifications for use with the `crontab` command, and to view more examples of time specifications, view the manual page for the `crontab` configuration file by entering the command `man 5 crontab`.

To use the `crontab` command to submit your own cron jobs (as opposed to placing scripts in the `/etc/cron.weekly` subdirectory, for example), you must create a file that has a time specification and a command to execute. Unlike the `at` command, you must create a file containing this information. You cannot enter cron job commands interactively. Suppose for example, that you wanted to run the du command on all home directories and sort the results every morning at 1:00 a.m. You would do this by following these steps:

1. Create a text file containing the time specification followed by the command you want to execute. For this example, the file would contain the following lines (assuming you are entering this cron job as the root user):

```
0 1 * * *  du | sort > /root/du_results
```

2. Submit the file to the crond daemon using the crontab command. Assuming that the file you created in Step 1 were called du_nightly, the command would look like this:

```
crontab du_nightly
```

You may notice that the file created in Step 1 does not include the #!/bin/bash information, as a shell script would. Also, the command shown in Step 1 fits on a single line.

Many times, you may need to do something more complicated with your scheduled administration jobs. Suppose, for example, that you had developed a series of shell scripts that checked the security of the Linux system by reviewing log files, checking network activity, and watching user login activity. If the script that performed all of these activities were called secure_system, you could run that script every morning at 1:30 a.m. by adding this line to your du_nightly file before submitting the file using the crontab command:

```
30 1 * * * /sbin/secure_system
```

The full pathname of the script is included so that the crond daemon will be certain to locate the script when it attempts to execute this job. The point of this exercise is that a cron job must be contained on a single line (though it can be a long line with several commands on it). For example:

```
du | sort > file
```

If you want to process more complex cron jobs, create a shell script and execute the script using a cron job.

In the example file /etc/crontab shown at the beginning of this section, you saw that some environment variables were defined. You can also include environment variables in the files that you create to define your cron jobs. For example, suppose you want the du_nightly cron job to be executed via the root user account so that it can access all home directories, but you want an e-mail message sent to your regular user account so it will be waiting in your regular e-mail account. (In other words, you won't have to log in as root to access the message.) To do this, you can include the following line in the du_nightly file (substituting your own username for nwells):

```
MAILTO=nwells
```

You can learn about a few other environment variables supported by the crontab command in the crontab manual page. You can also use the -u option to submit a cron job as

12

another user. (You can only do this if you are logged in as `root`.) For example, you could submit the `du_nightly` job as user `nwells` using this command:

```
crontab -u nwells du_nightly
```

You can check that the `atd` and `crond` daemons are running by using the `ps` command. For example, to see the `atd` daemon, use this command:

```
ps ax | grep atd
```

To see the `crond` daemon, use this command:

```
ps ax | grep crond
```

These two daemons are started using standard scripts located in `/etc/rc.d/init.d`. You can use those scripts to stop and restart the daemons if needed, but because these daemons carefully check the dates on files to see when new cron jobs have been submitted, you should never need to restart the daemons. The next part of the chapter contains additional information on managing the `cron` jobs that you have submitted.

MANAGING at AND crontab

Now that you have learned how to submit commands for future execution using the `at` and `crontab` commands, in this section you learn how to see what commands are scheduled for execution and how to alter those commands when necessary. As with other parts of Linux (such as file permissions and printing), you must be logged in as `root` to work with cron jobs that you have not submitted yourself. The `root` user can submit jobs as any user (using the `-u` option shown previously) and can also view or modify any cron jobs submitted by any user on the system.

Checking the Status of at and crontab

All of the commands that you submit using the `at` command or the `crontab` command are stored in a subdirectory of `/var/spool`. Jobs submitted using `at` are stored in the `/var/spool/at` directory; jobs submitted using `crontab` are stored in the `/var/spool/cron` directory. The two types of jobs are stored differently, however. Jobs for the `atd` daemon contain all the environment variables and related information so that the shell can execute the job independent of any other process. Jobs for the `crond` daemon store only a limited amount of information because they are executed in an environment that the `crond` daemon defines for the user who submitted the cron job.

Suppose you enter a single `du` command using the `at` command. When you enter this command, it might appear on screen like this:

```
at now + 10 minutes
at> du
at> <EOT>
```

When you change to the `/var/spool/at` directory, you will see a strange filename such as `a0000d00f08407`. This filename is generated automatically by the `at` command.

Looking inside this file using the less command (or a similar command), you will see a number of environment variables. These variables record the facts about the shell in which the command was entered via the at command, so that the same shell environment can be duplicated when the command is executed. The last line of the file is the command (in this example, du) that will actually be executed at the specified time. An example file from the /var/spool/at directory is shown here. The values in a file from your system will vary.

```
#!/bin/sh
# atrun uid=0 gid=0
# mail      root 0
umask 22
USERNAME=root; export USERNAME
ENV=/root/.bashrc; export ENV
HISTSIZE=1000; export HISTSIZE
HOSTNAME=localhost.localdomain; export HOSTNAME
LOGNAME=root; export LOGNAME
HISTFILESIZE=1000; export HISTFILESIZE
MAIL=/var/spool/mail/root; export MAIL
HOSTTYPE=i386; export HOSTTYPE
PATH=/usr/bin:/sbin:/bin:/usr/sbin:/usr/bin:/usr/X11R6/bin:/root/
bin; export PATH
KDEDIR=/usr; export KDEDIR
HOME=/root; export HOME
INPUTRC=/etc/inputrc; export INPUTRC
PS1=[\\u@\\h\ \\W]\\\$\ ; export PS1
USER=root; export USER
OSTYPE=Linux; export OSTYPE
SHLVL=1; export SHLVL
cd /root || {
        echo 'Execution directory inaccessible' >&2
        exit 1
}
du | sort > /tmp/du_listing
```

The information in the /var/spool/at directory does not, however, indicate the time when the command will be executed. Because of the complicated format of these files and their interaction with the atd daemon, you should not directly modify the /var/spool/at directory using a command such as rm. Instead, use the atq and atrm commands to view jobs submitted using at that are pending execution.

The atq command lists each of the jobs processed by the at command. For each job, this command lists a job number and the date and time when the job will be executed. To use the atq command, simply enter it at any shell prompt. No parameters are used. Sample output from the atq command is shown here:

```
6     2000-08-15 10:00 a
9     2000-12-21 05:15 a
12    2000-12-31 11:45 p
```

12

You can also use the `at` command with the `-l` option (for *list*) to see a list of jobs pending execution by `atd`. This command looks like this:

```
at -l
```

If you decide to cancel a command that you have submitted using `at`, use the `atrm` command. The **atrm** command deletes (removes) a job from the queue that `atd` uses to execute commands. (A **queue** is a list of commands or files to be processed.) You can also use the `-d` option (delete) with the `at` command to remove a job from this queue, so that it is not executed. Both `atrm` and `at -d` require you to include the job number, which you must obtain from the `atq` (or `at -l`) command. For example, to remove job 11, you could use either of these commands:

```
atrm 11
at -d 11
```

You can use a similar set of commands to manage jobs that have been submitted using `crontab`. To begin, you'll notice that the file stored in `/var/spool/cron` is different from the files stored in `/var/spool/at`. The `/var/spool/cron` directory contains a single file for each user who has submitted jobs using `crontab`. For example, if you have submitted a job using `crontab` while logged in as `root`, the file `/var/spool/cron/root` exists. If you submitted a job using `crontab` while logged in as `nwells`, the file `/var/spool/cron/nwells` exists. The file in `/var/spool/cron` that is named for your username contains a composite of all cron jobs that you have submitted. For example, when you have submitted a single cron job, the file looks something like this:

```
# DO NOT EDIT THIS FILE - edit the master and reinstall.
# (secure_cron installed on Mon Oct 20 18:12:16 2000)
# (Cron version — $Id: crontab.c,v 2.13 1994/01/17 03:20:37 vixie
Exp $)
30 1 * * * /sbin/security_scan
```

As with the contents of the `/var/spool/at` directory, you should not directly edit a crontab file in `/var/spool/cron`. Instead, use the options provided by the `crontab` command. These are summarized in the following list:

- `crontab -l` lists the contents of your `crontab` file (for the user account you are currently logged in to).

- `crontab -r` removes your `crontab` file. Use this option carefully, as it removes the entire file; so any cron jobs you have submitted are lost. Remember that you can store system administration scripts in the subdirectories such as `/etc/cron.daily` and `/etc/cron.weekly` to have them executed at regular intervals without creating a separate `crontab` file for the `root` user account.

- `crontab -e` opens your `crontab` file in a text editor, so you can make changes in the times or commands defined for your cron jobs. It's important that you use the `-e` option on the `crontab` command rather than using a regular editor session (such as `vi /var/spool/cron/nwells`) to change your `crontab` file. Using `crontab -e` prevents file locking conflicts that would cause problems with the `crond` daemon.

Controlling Access to `at` and `crontab`

The default settings on most Linux systems allow any user to submit commands for future execution using either `at` or `crontab`. You can create a set of configuration files that restrict access to the `at` and `crontab` commands so that only those users specified by the system administrator can use these commands. The files that enforce this control are as follows:

- `/etc/cron.allow`: contains usernames (one per line) that are allowed to use the `crontab` command

- `/etc/cron.deny`: contains usernames (one per line) that are not allowed to use the `crontab` command

- `/etc/at.allow`: contains usernames (one per line) that are allowed to use the `at` command

- `/etc/at.deny`: contains usernames (one per line) that are not allowed to use the `at` command

 On some Linux systems, the files listed above may be located in the `/var/spool/cron` and `/var/spool/at` subdirectories, in which case they will be named simply `allow` and `deny`, without the name `at` or `cron` as a prefix.

On most Linux systems, none of the four files just listed exist, meaning that any user can use both `at` and `crontab`. (On some systems, however, having none of these files may mean that only `root` can use `at` and `crontab`.) When you attempt to use the `at` or `crontab` command, the command checks the permission files in the following order:

- If the `/etc/cron.allow` file exists, a user must be listed in that file in order to use the `crontab` command. The same rule applies to `/etc/at.allow` for the `at` command.

- If the `cron.allow` (or `at.allow`) file does not exist, but the `cron.deny` file does exist, any user listed in `cron.deny` (or `at.deny`) cannot use the `crontab` command (or the `at` command).

By controlling access to the `at` and `crontab` commands on a busy Linux system, you can make it more difficult for regular users to consume system resources when you are completing (or scheduling for automatic execution) routine system administration tasks. In addition, users who have access to the `at` and `crontab` commands can create security hazards by automatically checking for and perhaps refreshing security loopholes that those users take advantage of on an insecure system.

CHAPTER SUMMARY

- Computer programs can be written using a compiled or an interpreted programming language. Each type has its own advantages. Shell scripts are interpreted programs, with the shell acting as the command interpreter. Using shell scripts is a powerful way to

12

automate many tasks on a Linux system. Shell scripts include commands that you would otherwise execute from a command line, as well as commands that are normally used only within script files, such as selection statements (`if`/`then`/`else`) and loop statements (`for` and `while`). Shell scripts can be executed by a variety of shells. Other types of scripting languages such as Perl, Tcl/Tk, Python, and Expect are also used for automating system administration tasks. All standard Linux systems have the capability to use these standard types of scripts.

❑ The `at` and `crontab` commands are used to automate one-time and repetitive tasks respectively. Both `at` and `crontab` permit you to use complex time specifications (though the two commands use different formats). Commands submitted for future execution using the `at` command can be entered interactively or using a file containing the commands. Commands to be executed using `crontab` must be placed in a file that also contains the execution time for those commands.

❑ Additional commands let you see what cron jobs are currently awaiting execution by either the `atd` daemon or the `crond` daemon. Both are normally running on Linux systems. The `atq` and `atrm` commands help you manage jobs submitted using `at`. The `-r`, `-l`, and `-e` options on the `crontab` command provide similar functionality for jobs submitted using `crontab`. Configuration files such as `/etc/cron.allow` let you control how regular users access the `at` and `crontab` commands.

KEY TERMS

`$@` — A special shell variable that includes all of the parameters on the command line.

`at` — A command that lets you enter one or more commands to be executed once at some future time.

`atq` — A command that lists each of the jobs that have been submitted using the `at` command, with a job number and the date and time when the job will be executed.

`atrm` — A command that deletes (removes) a job from the queue used by `atd` to execute commands.

`batch` — A command that executes scheduled tasks when the system load average drops below 0.8.

binary file — *See* executable file.

comment — A line in a script that begins with a # character. Comments are not processed by the shell, but are only included to help someone reading the file understand the purpose of the script or how it functions.

Common Gateway Interface (CGI) — A method of communication between two programs using the standard input and standard output channels.

compiled language — A computer language for which the source code is converted to a binary file long before the program will be run by users.

compiler — A special program that converts the source code of a compiled language into a binary file.

computer language — A set of words and syntax rules that can be arranged in predefined ways to cause a computer to perform tasks defined by the person using the language.

cron job — A command or script that you have scheduled to be executed at a specific time in the future.

crontab — A command that lets you enter one or more commands to be executed repeatedly at intervals that you designate.

do — A command used with the `done` command to enclose a block of commands to be executed by a `for` command.

done — A command used with the `do` command to enclose a block of commands to be executed by a `for` command.

echo — A command that prints text to the STDOUT channel—to the screen unless output has been redirected.

else — A command that extends the capability of an `if/then` statement by adding a block of commands that are only executed if a test returns a value of false (that is, if the test fails).

executable file — A file containing numeric codes that a computer can execute. Created from a source code file by a compiler, the executable file is the program that a user can run.

exit — A command that stops the execution of a script immediately.

fi — A command that marks the end of an `if/then` statement.

for — A command that repeats a block of commands one time for each item in a list that you provide.

for loop — A block of commands that is repeatedly executed according to the parameters provided with the `for` command.

if — A command used to introduce a test within a shell script. An `if` command is always followed by a `then` command.

if/then/else statement — A set of commands used to determine whether other commands in a script are executed. An `if/then/else` statement is one kind of selection statement.

index — A counting variable used within a loop statement. The index acts as a marker to count how many times the loop has executed a list of commands.

interpreted language — A language for which the source code is converted to numeric codes at the time a user runs the program. This conversion takes place each time the user runs the program. For this reason, interpreted languages are generally much slower than compiled languages.

interpreted program — A computer program that is converted from human-readable form to a format that can be used by a computer (numeric codes) at the moment you execute the program.

interpreter — A special program that converts the source code of an interpreted language into numeric codes that a computer can execute.

iteration — An occurrence of an event or process that can or must be done many times.

keywords — Words used in a computer language to define a specific task or meaning.

loop statement — A statement used to determine whether part of a computer program should be executed more than once.

12

make — A command that uses information stored in a configuration file to compile source code into a binary program, or otherwise prepare a program to be executed.

nesting — A programming method in which one selection or loop statement contains another selection or loop statement.

Perl — A programming language developed by Larry Wall initially to process strings of text and generate reports.

positional variable — A variable used within a shell script that contains data included on the command line when the script was launched.

programming language — *See* computer language.

Python — A scripting language developed by Guido van Rossum that is often used for creating graphical programs.

queue — A list of commands or files to be processed.

script — A text file that can be interpreted or executed by another program (an interpreter).

selection statement — A statement that lets a computer programmer determine which parts of a program will be executed according to values that are calculated by testing as the program is executed. The `if/then` statement is a selection statement used in shell scripts.

shell script — An executable file containing lines of text as you would enter them at a command line, including special commands to control the order in which lines in the file are executed.

shell variable — A variable used within a shell script to store information for use by the script.

source code — The file that a programmer writes using the keywords and syntax rules of a computer language.

statement — A command within a computer program. A statement is often a single keyword, but the term may also refer to a group of keywords that the computer language syntax requires or allows to be used together.

statement block — A list of commands (or statements) that are controlled by a selection or loop statement.

Tcl/Tk — A scripting language developed by John Ousterhout that is used to create graphical programs.

test — A command that evaluates the arguments provided after the command name and returns either true (a value of 1) or false (a value of 0).

test — A method of examining data within a shell script and acting according to the result of the examination (or test).

then — A command that identifies the commands to be executed if the test introduced by the `if` command succeeds (returns a value of true).

tty — A command that displays the name of the terminal device you are currently working in.

while — A command that creates a loop based on a test. The loop executes a block of commands as long as the test returns true.

white space — Tabs or spaces included in a program or script that make the script easier for a person to read.

REVIEW QUESTIONS

1. A shell script is similar to a DOS batch file in that both are used to automatically execute commands that would otherwise be entered manually. True or False?

2. Name four shell scripts that are included on a standard Linux system, and describe the use of each one.

3. The first line of a standard shell script must contain:

   a. A comment defining the username of the person creating the script

   b. A valid command as you would enter it from a command line

   c. The path and filename of the shell used to execute the script

   d. A time specification for when the script will be executed

4. In order to be executed by any user (including **root**), a shell script must have the _____ file permission set.

   a. Execute

   b. Write

   c. Other

   d. Owner

5. When you are working in the **bash** shell, all shell scripts that you execute must use **bash** shell syntax. True or False?

6. A shell variable is one that is:

   a. Restricted for use only by the shell itself

   b. Available to all parent processes

   c. Used to hold a value within a shell script

   d. Stored in virtual memory

7. Which of these statements contains a standard positional variable?

   a. `gzip $file`

   b. `gzip $1`

   c. `gzip /tmp/listing 2>&1`

   d. `gzip HOME`

8. Which two commands involve a test value of true or false?

   a. `if`

   b. `while`

   c. `for`

   d. `crontab`

9. The **test** command is equivalent to using square brackets around a test expression, but the **test** command is less frequently used. True or False?

12

10. Briefly explain why comments are an important part of any shell script.

11. Describe the difference in control methods between a `for` loop and a `while` loop.

12. A loop beginning with the command "`for i in 2 4 6 8`" will be executed how many times?

    a. Eight

    b. Four

    c. The preset value of `i`

    d. It cannot be determined without knowing what files are in the working directory.

13. Name three non-shell scripting languages. Include a statement on the use, characteristics, or author of each one.

14. CGI is popular for which of the following purposes?

    a. Creating Web servers

    b. Interfacing between scripts and Web servers

    c. Automating system administration work

    d. Creating graphical programs

15. Briefly explain the difference in time specification formats for the `at` and `crontab` commands.

16. The `crontab` and `at` commands both support an interactive mode in which you can enter commands to be scheduled for future execution at the command line. True or False?

17. The daemon(s) that manage(s) commands submitted using the `at` and `cron` commands is (are):

    a. `/etc/cron.allow`

    b. `crond`

    c. `atd` and `crond`

    d. `init.d`

18. When using the `at` command interactively to enter commands scheduled for future execution, you indicate that you have finished entering commands by pressing:

    a. Ctrl+D

    b. Ctrl+C

    c. Esc

    d. Ctrl+X

19. The `batch` command is used to schedule jobs so that:

    a. Jobs from the `at` and `crontab` commands are not executed at the same time.

    b. Commands used in a DOS environment can be executed by Linux.

    c. The system will not be overloaded with scheduled tasks.

    d. Regular users can schedule tasks.

20. A simple method for **root** to schedule recurring system administration tasks is to:

   a. Use the **at** command in interactive mode.

   b. Add a script to a directory such as **/etc/cron.daily** or **/etc/cron.weekly**.

   c. Create a graphical program using Python with Tk extensions.

   d. Debug existing shell scripts on the system.

21. The output of a cron job is normally sent via _____ to the user who submitted the cron job or to the user defined by the _____ variable within the file containing the cron job.

   a. e-mail, **MAILTO**

   b. e-mail, **USERLOG**

   c. tty, **MAILTO**

   d. standard output, **USERLOG**

22. Name in order from left to right the fields of the **crontab** time specification, giving the range of valid values for each one.

23. Output from a cron job cannot be redirected using standard redirection operators because the environment in which the cron job was created is unlikely to exist when the cron job is executed. True or False?

24. The _____ file can include a username in order to deny that user access to the **crontab** command.

   a. **/etc/cron.allow**

   b. **/etc/cron.deny**

   c. **/usr/local/bin/deny**

   d. **/etc/at.deny**

25. Name the two separate commands that can be used instead of **at -l** and **at -d**.

HANDS-ON PROJECTS

Project 12-1

In this activity you use the **vi** editor to create a simple shell script. Then you execute that script at the command line. To complete this activity you should have a working Linux installation with a valid user account.

1. Log in to Linux using your username and password.

2. If you are using a graphical environment, open a terminal window so you have a shell prompt.

3. Enter **vi fileinfo** to start **vi** and create a new file called **fileinfo**.

4. Press **i** to start insert mode in **vi**.

12

5. Enter the following lines in `vi`:

```
#!/bin/bash
if [ $# -lt 1 ]; then
        echo You must include a filename on the command line.
        exit
fi
echo Beginning to process files.
for i in $@
do
        echo Number of lines in $i
        wc -l $i
        echo Number of words in $i
        wc -w $i
done
```

6. Press **Esc** to return to command mode.

7. Press **Shift+Z**, **Z** to exit `vi` and save the file.

8. Enter **chmod 755 fileinfo** to change the file permissions on the file you created to include the execute permission. What would be the equivalent command using letters instead of the 755 code?

9. Enter **./fileinfo** to execute the command without any parameters. What happens? What result is returned by the test in the second line of the script? What other methods could you use to test for the presence of a command-line parameter? What would happen if you removed the `if/then` test but didn't include any filenames on the command line?

10. Enter **./fileinfo /etc/termcap** to execute the command with a parameter. What happens? How many times was the `for` loop executed?

11. Execute the command with the parameter shown here: **./fileinfo /etc/c*conf**. What happens? Do you see any error messages? Why? How could you alter the script to prevent those error messages from appearing on screen? How could you alter the script to test the validity of each filename before using the `wc` command to prevent the error code from being generated in the first place? (*Hint*: Use the **-r** file test from Table 12-1.)

Project 12-2

In this activity you submit a job for future execution using the `at` command. To complete this activity you should have a working Linux installation with a valid user account.

1. Log in to Linux using your username and password.

2. If you are using a graphical environment, open a terminal window so you have a shell prompt available.

3. Enter the `at` command with a time designation as follows: **at now + 15 minutes**. The at> prompt appears.

4. Enter the loop command **for i in /etc/*conf** at the first at> prompt.

5. Enter the **do** command at the next **at>** prompt.

6. Enter **wc -w $i** at the next **at>** prompt.

7. Enter **done** at the next **at>** prompt. Your screen should now look like this:

```
$ at now + 15 minutes
at> for i in /etc/*conf
at> do
at> wc -w $i
at> done
at>
```

8. Press **Ctrl+D** to finish entering the commands you want to automate. What message do you see? What time is specified? Is it a relative time or an absolute time based on the time specification that you entered?

9. Enter the **atq** command. What information do you see about the job you just entered? What is the job number? Where could you find the job information stored in the file system?

10. If you wish, use the **atrm** command to remove the job from the **at** queue, using the job number given by the **atq** command. For example, you might use the command **atrm 15**.

11. If you decided not to remove the **at** job you entered, what will happen at the time given by the **at** command (when you finished the entry with Ctrl+D)? Wait 15 minutes and then use a mail reader (such as mail, elm, pine, or Netscape) to view the output of your at job as an e-mail message.

Project 12-3

In this activity you submit a job for future execution using the **crontab** command. You then switch to the **root** account and modify a user's access to **crontab**. To complete this activity you should have a working Linux installation with a valid user account and access to the **root** account on the system. (If you don't have **root** access, you can complete all but the last few steps of the project.)

1. Log in to Linux using your regular username and password.

2. If you are using a graphical environment, open a terminal window so you have a shell prompt available.

3. Enter **vi du_job** to start the **vi** editor with a new filename of du_job.

4. Press **i** so that you can enter text in insert mode.

5. Enter **30 2 * * * du /home > /tmp/du_output** in **vi**.

6. Press **Esc** to return to command mode.

7. Press **Shift+Z**, **Z** to save the text you entered and exit **vi**. Describe the time specification that you entered in the du_job file. What problem could occur with the command entered in the du_job file because you are working as a regular user?

8. Enter **crontab du_job** to submit the file you created as a new cron job.

12

9. Enter **crontab -l** to review the contents of the **crontab** file for your regular user account. What do you see? How does it relate to the information you entered in the **du_job** file? Can you see an indication of the filename **du_job** and when it was submitted using **crontab**?

10. Enter **su** to change to the **root** account.

11. Enter the **root** password when requested.

12. Enter **vi /etc/cron.deny** to create a new file called **cron.deny** in the **/etc** directory.

13. Enter a single line in the **cron.deny** file that includes the regular user account name that you used to log in, in Step 1. For example, the file might include a single line like this: **nwells**.

14. Press **Shift+Z**, **Z** to save the text you entered and exit **vi**.

15. Enter **exit** to switch from the **root** account to a regular user account again.

16. Enter **crontab -r** to remove the **crontab** file for your regular user account. What happens? Why?

17. Enter **su** to change back to the **root** account, entering the **root** password when prompted.

18. Enter a command such as **crontab -u nwells -r** to erase the **crontab** file for the regular user account. (Substitute your own regular user account name for **nwells** in this example.)

19. Enter **rm /etc/cron.deny** to remove the **cron.deny** file so that in the future all user accounts will have access to the **crontab** command (unless you prefer to restrict it for some reason on this Linux system).

20. Enter **exit** to log out of the **root** account.

CASE PROJECTS

1. You are working as a senior system administrator at Image Makers, a large advertising agency and public relations firm in New York City. The office maintains a large Web site that contains advertising resources and samples of the agency's work for potential clients to review. The office also includes several servers and nearly 100 workstations that rely on those servers for data storage and Internet connectivity. Most of the servers are running on Linux. The desktop systems are Windows 2000 and Macintosh. The agency's management is concerned that the firm's Internet site is a potential victim of defacement by hackers because of some advertising the company has done for clients in the computer security business. Based on what you have learned so far about system administration and the tools described in this chapter, describe some of the most important system administration tasks you would like to automate using the **crontab** command. (Backing up the system would be one of these tasks, but that is the subject of a future chapter.)

2. Some employees at the agency want to use special Web browser programs to automatically retrieve large Web pages during the night. Are these types of programs compatible with the `crontab` command? Would you prefer that employees use the `crontab` command on the server? Why or why not? What issues would this bring up related to (a) security, (b) system load, and (c) end-user training?

3. After six months of continuous work at Image Makers, you finally have a day off scheduled for next Friday. During the four days before your day off, you come across several tasks that require action on Friday. You cannot do them before you leave because of the system load during work hours. Also, much of the data needed for the Friday reports will not be available until the end of the day on Friday. Describe the commands you would use to set up these one-time tasks for the time you are away from the office. Would you choose the `at`, `batch`, or `crontab` command? Why? How well do you need to know the company's systems and the Linux commands in order to perform this type of system administration feat?

12

13

THE PRINTING SYSTEM

After reading this chapter and completing the exercises, you will be able to:

♦ Explain how a Linux printing system operates

♦ Set up printing using standard utilities

♦ Manage printing on a busy Linux system

♦ Configure printing for remote computer systems

In the previous chapter you learned about creating shell scripts using `if/then` statements, `for` loops, and other commands. You learned how to execute these scripts from a command line and how to schedule a script or any command for later execution using the `at` and `crontab` commands.

In this chapter you will learn how to set up and manage printing on a Linux system. You will learn how printing occurs on Linux and what utilities are available for you to manage files printed by users. You will also learn how to set up and print to remote computers.

UNDERSTANDING LINUX PRINTING

The Linux printing system (which is usually referred to as LPRng) was originally designed to be similar to the one used in the BSD version of UNIX. For this reason, you'll sometimes hear that Linux uses a standard BSD printing system. This system allows many users to print files at the same time without interfering with one another. It also allows a system administrator to manage and track all printing activity. The next two sections explain the components and basic printing process in the Linux system.

The Printing Architecture

The printing architecture of Linux includes the following components. Each of these components is also shown in Figure 13-1, which illustrates how a file is printed. This process is described in detail following the list of components.

- **lpr**: a program that prepares files to be sent to a printer.

- **Print job**: a file submitted for printing via the lpr command.

- **Print filter**: a script used by the lpr program to prepare files to be sent to a printer.

- **lpd**: a daemon that sends files (previously prepared by lpr) to the printer.

- **printcap** (for *printer capture*): a printer definition file that specifies how and where files are stored and processed by lpr and lpd.

- **Print spool directory** (or print queue): directory where files are placed before being sent to the printer.

- Administrative utilities: programs used by a system administrator to manage files that have been printed or are in the process of being printed, the printer definition file (**printcap**), and the status of each printer. (These utilities are described in detail later in this chapter.)

lpr creates a print job using these components.

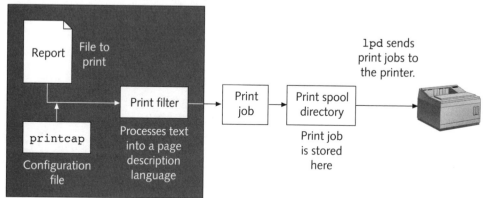

Figure 13-1 Printing a file in Linux

To print a file, you submit it to a print queue (or print spool directory) using the lpr command. Note that the terms *print spool directory* and **print queue** are used interchangeably to refer to a directory that stores files in the process of being printed. The lpd daemon retrieves files from the print spool directory one by one and sends them to the printer (for example, via the computer's parallel port).

TIP   A spool directory is a directory in which files are placed to await processing by another program. The print spool directory is only one of several spool directories within Linux.

The print spool directory is normally located within the `/var/spool/lpd` subdirectory. The print queue itself is often named for a printer. For example, you might define a print queue named `hplj` to store files that are destined to be printed on a Hewlett-Packard laserjet printer. If you define a print queue named `hplj`, the print queue directory, or print spool directory, would normally be `/var/spool/lpd/hplj`. Note, however, that the correlation between a print queue and a printer is not always one to one. That is, one print queue might be used to send print jobs to multiple printers. Conversely, several print queues might all specify the same printer.

To understand how this works, imagine a large network in which many users need to print files. All of the files might be submitted (by the `lpr` program on each networked computer) to a single print queue. The lines in the `printcap` file that define this single print queue might then list several printer devices (for example, the printers connected to parallel ports one and two). It is then the task of the `lpd` daemon to send each print job in order to maximize efficiency of the system (getting print jobs completed as rapidly as possible). Such an arrangement (shown in Figure 13-2) allows twice as many print jobs to be printed at the same time, without requiring that users decide which of two different print queues will be faster.

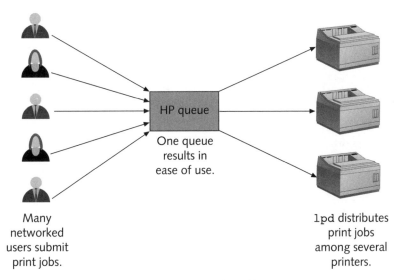

HP queue

One queue results in ease of use.

Many networked users submit print jobs.

`lpd` distributes print jobs among several printers.

Figure 13-2   A single print queue sending files to many printers

A small network might employ a different setup. For example, a system administrator might configure separate print queues for envelopes, color printing, legal-sized documents, and standard printing. Users on the network would submit files for printing depending on the type of document being printed. The person maintaining the printer would then activate the print queue for legal-sized documents (and disable all other print queues) only when legal-sized paper was inserted and ready to print. When envelopes were inserted in the single printer, the envelope queue could be activated, and so forth. This method requires that someone actively maintain the printer; it also requires users to wait while each queue is processed in turn. Figure 13-3 shows this arrangement graphically.

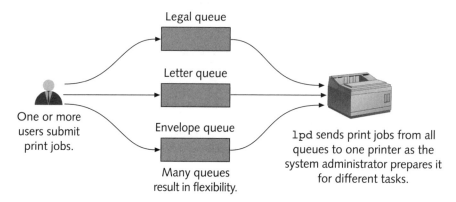

Figure 13-3   Many print queues sending to a single printer

Each print queue is configured by a series of lines in the `printcap` file. The information in this file that relates to a specific print queue is often called the printer definition. The `printcap` file, which is stored in the `/etc` directory, requires a complex format and can include dozens of options for each print queue that you define. For this reason, the `printcap` file is rarely configured manually (in a text editor). Instead, you can use one of the graphical tools (described later in this chapter) to set up the `printcap` file.

Although the `printcap` file defines print queues, system administrators refer to each print queue definition as a printer. When you refer to a printer (by a name such as `hplj`) in a Linux environment, you are actually referring to a print queue defined in the `printcap` file.

Print jobs are stored in the subdirectory assigned to a particular print queue. The `lpd` daemon watches for print jobs and then sends them one at a time to the physical printer device defined for that print queue. The `lpd` daemon also controls the actions allowed by the `lpr` command. For example, you could request that `lpd` disable a print queue so that users cannot submit new print jobs while you troubleshoot a printing problem.

The physical printer device is normally connected to a parallel or serial port. When you define the print queue, you specify which printer the files in that queue should be sent to; you do so by providing the name of the appropriate Linux device. For example, if the printer is attached to the first parallel port of the Linux computer, the device name is `/dev/lp0`. If the printer is attached to the third serial port, the device name is `/dev/ttyS2`. As you have learned in several previous chapters, these and other devices on Linux are accessed by referring to a filename in the `/dev` subdirectory. Device names accessed as filenames are sometimes called block special files or character special files. A **block special file** is a type of file (normally located in `/dev`) that refers to a physical device that transfers data in blocks of characters, such as a hard disk drive. A **character special file** is a filename that refers to a physical device that transfers data in single characters, such as a serial port.

The output of the `ls -l` command includes an indicator of whether a filename refers to a block or character special file. The leftmost column displays a **b** or a **c**, for block or character special file, respectively. For example, the command `ls -l /dev/hda1` produces the following output. (Note the **b** in the left column.)

```
brw-rw----   1 root      disk       3,   1 May  5  1998 /dev/hda1
```

The command `ls -l /dev/ttyS0` creates this output. (Note the **c** in the left column, indicating a character special file.)

```
crw-------   1 root      tty        4,  64 May  5  1998 /dev/ttyS0
```

The Role of Print Filters

In order to print different types of documents from Linux applications to a variety of printer devices, Linux uses special programs that prepare data for printing. You have complete control over how these programs operate. To understand these programs, you first must understand something about how printers process the data that is sent to them.

Printer Languages

Each printer uses a page description language to guide what it prints. A **page description language** is a special set of codes that determine the graphics elements, text font, and everything else about what appears on a printed page. The most widely used page description languages are called PostScript and Printer Control Language, or PCL.

The content of the document you want to print and the format of the page must be converted into instructions that match the page description language used by the printer. Each type of printer requires a different set of steps to convert a document into the correct page description language codes.

The PostScript page description language was developed by Adobe and is widely used in many types of printers. Printers that use the PostScript codes are expensive relative to non-PostScript printers. PCL, developed by Hewlett-Packard, is used by most Hewlett-Packard printers, although these printers often provide support for PostScript as well. When you send a print job to a PostScript printer, the print filter (described in detail in the next section) creates a PostScript document, which consists of special instructions that tell the printer what to print. The following shows an example of the first part of a PostScript document:

```
%!PS-Adobe-3.0
%%Creator: groff version 1.05
%%DocumentNeededResources: font Times-Bold
%%+ font Times-Italic
%%+ font Times-Roman
%%DocumentSuppliedResources: procset grops 1.05 0
%%Pages: 5
%%PageOrder: Ascend
%%Orientation: Portrait
```

13

```
%%EndComments
%%BeginProlog
%%BeginResource: procset grops 1.05 0

/setpacking where {
      pop
      currentpacking
      true setpacking
} if

/grops 120 dict dup begin

% The ASCII code of the space character.
/SC 32 def

/A /show load def
/B { 0 SC 3 -1 roll widthshow } bind def
/C { 0 exch ashow } bind def
/D { 0 exch 0 SC 5 2 roll awidthshow } bind def
/E { 0 rmoveto show } bind def
/F { 0 rmoveto 0 SC 3 -1 roll widthshow } bind def
/G { 0 rmoveto 0 exch ashow } bind def
/H { 0 rmoveto 0 exch 0 SC 5 2 roll awidthshow } bind def
/I { 0 exch rmoveto show } bind def
/J { 0 exch rmoveto 0 SC 3 -1 roll widthshow } bind def
/K { 0 exch rmoveto 0 exch ashow } bind def
/L { 0 exch rmoveto 0 exch 0 SC 5 2 roll awidthshow } bind def
/M { rmoveto show } bind def
/N { rmoveto 0 SC 3 -1 roll widthshow } bind def
/O { rmoveto 0 exch ashow } bind def
/P { rmoveto 0 exch 0 SC 5 2 roll awidthshow } bind def
/Q { moveto show } bind def
/R { moveto 0 SC 3 -1 roll widthshow } bind def
/S { moveto 0 exch ashow } bind def
/T { moveto 0 exch 0 SC 5 2 roll awidthshow } bind def

% name size font SF -

/SF {
      findfont exch
      [ exch dup 0 exch 0 exch neg 0 0 ] makefont
      dup setfont
      [ exch /setfont cvx ] cvx bind def
} bind def

% name a c d font MF -

/MF {
      findfont
      [ 5 2 roll
      0 3 1 roll % b
```

```
      neg 0 0 ] makefont
      dup setfont
      [ exch /setfont cvx ] cvx bind def
} bind def

/level0 0 def
/RES 0 def
/PL 0 def
/LS 0 def
```

PostScript instructions could be represented in English like this: "Start a new page. Go to this position on the page, draw a short line, then a small circle. Go to this position, draw a small graphic image." Taken as a whole, these instructions result in letters, images, and other parts of a printed page.

Page description languages are very complex. Some printers can interpret only basic instructions and as a result provide limited functionality. For example, the printer may simply print the characters that are sent to it, having only the ability to interpret a few special characters that mark the end of a line, the end of a page, or other special situations.

Drivers and Filters

The process by which a print filter converts a document into the appropriate page description language codes (such as PostScript codes) is comparable to what happens on a Windows-based computer when you print a document. However, the Windows-based computer uses a different system to accomplish the same work. On Windows-based computers, the operating system includes hundreds of drivers for different printers. A **driver** is a small software program that provides abstract services for a hardware component. For example, a hard disk driver allows the operating system to simply say "open this file." The driver contains the instructions for locating a file on a specific type of hardware device. In the same way, a printer driver contains instructions that convert data into the format needed for a specific printer.

Unfortunately, Linux does not use printer drivers because this method—which requires close cooperation between the operating system vendor and printer manufacturer—was not popular when UNIX was first developed. Linux inherited the UNIX printing model, which allows flexibility, but requires more effort by users (using print filters) to convert documents into the correct printer format.

A few commercial programs such as Corel WordPerfect for Linux and, to a lesser extent, StarOffice for Linux (from Sun Microsystems) include hundreds of printer drivers that let you create complex documents using all the advanced features of a printer. These printer drivers are not available to other Linux programs, however, because Linux has no standard system for interacting with the printer drivers, even if you have the drivers installed on your system as part of a program such as WordPerfect for Linux.

Instead of using printer drivers, Linux uses print filters. A print filter is a script that contains instructions for formatting all documents for a specific printer using the page description language that the printer requires. The concept of a print filter is the same as a printer driver; the difference is that a print filter is rarely as powerful. It does not provide access to advanced features of the printer. Print filters are also much more limited in the printer formats that they support. Print filters in Linux normally rely on a program that converts a text file into a page description language, including special printer codes for color printing, ejecting pages, and similar special functions. Examples of print filter programs include the following:

- `gs (GhostScript)`
- `enscript`
- `nenscript`

Each of these programs lets you provide the name of a printer device as a parameter. (This is done within the print filter.) The program then outputs data that `lpd` sends directly to the printer device. The output contains the correct page description language codes for the printer. Below you'll find a simple example of a print filter; this example illustrates how most print filters operate. A variable at the top of the script indicates the type of printer that the filter prepares data for. That variable is used later in the script when the `gs` or `enscript` program is executed. The output is stored in a file so that the `lpd` program can send the file directly to the printer.

```bash
#!/bin/bash
source /etc/sysconfig/printers/lp
if [ "$PAPERSIZE" = "a4" ]; then
   T=A4
else
   T=Letter
fi

enscript -M $T -Z -p - |

if [ "$DOUBLEPAGE" = "true" ]; then
   psnup -d -b0.6cm -p$PAPERSIZE -2
else
   cat -
fi |

if [ "$GSDEVICE" = "PostScript" ]; then
      cat -
elif [ "$GSDEVICE" = "uniprint" ]; then
      exec 3>&1 1>&2
      gs @$UPP.upp -q -sOutputFile="|cat 1>&3"
else
      gs -q $GSOPTIONS -sDEVICE=$GSDEVICE \
            -r$RESOLUTION \
            -sPAPERSIZE=$PAPERSIZE \
            -dNOPAUSE \
            -dSAFER \
            -sOutputFile=- -
fi
```

```
if [ "$SENDEOF" != "" ]; then
      printf "\004"
fi

exit 0
```

The print filter script is normally stored in the print queue subdirectory, along with the print jobs themselves. A separate print filter is used for each print queue. For example, if you defined a printer named `hplj`, the filter that processed documents going to that print queue would probably be `/var/spool/lpd/hplj/filter`. Because each print filter is located in the subdirectory of a specific print queue, all print filters are normally named `filter` or something similar. The `printcap` file specifies the location and script name for each print queue that is defined.

Normally your Linux distribution will be set up to use a magic filter. A **magic filter** is a filter program that automatically processes a file into the correct output format based on the file's type. For example, graphics files will be processed differently than plain text files. The most widely used magic filters that you will see mentioned in the `printcap` file or within a filter script file are called `APSfilter` and `magicfilter`.

SETTING UP PRINTING

When you install most Linux systems, the printing system is usually configured and running, except for the `printcap` file. (On some Linux systems, the printer is also configured as you install the operating system, so everything is ready for you to print files.) The Red Hat Linux installation allows you to configure a printer (create a `printcap` file). Note that the installation steps in Chapter 3 do not cover configuring a printer. Later in this chapter, you will learn how to use the Printer Tool program to configure a printer in Red Hat Linux. In general, the print configuration that you can perform during an installation is very basic. This part of the chapter describes how to define print policies and use various utilities to set up a robust printing system on a Linux-based computer.

13

The following list summarizes the steps required to get a printer working on Linux. These steps discuss editing a print configuration file in a text editor because this method works on all Linux distributions. In practice, however, you will almost always use a graphical utility specific to the Linux distribution you are using. (The Red Hat Printer Tool program described later is one example of this type of utility.) These steps are described in more detail in the following sections.

1. Connect a printer to the Linux computer using a parallel or serial cable.

2. Check the initialization scripts in the `/etc/rc.d/init.d` directory and the run level directories (such as `/etc/rc.d/rc3.d`) to be certain that the `lpd` daemon is started at boot time. Then use the `ps` command to be certain that the `lpd` daemon is in fact running.

3. Add an entry to the `printcap` file for the printer you have connected to the system.

4. Create the spool directory, filter, and accounting files, as appropriate. (This is normally done by the graphical utility that you use to configure the `printcap` file.)

5. Start the printer using the `lpc` command. (This is normally done by the graphical utility that you use to configure the `printcap` file.)

6. Test the printer by printing a small file.

Deciding on Print Policies

When overseeing a Linux system with many user accounts, the system administrator is likely to spend a great deal of time managing printing. Many of the other management tasks are either one-time tasks (such as creating user accounts or installing new software packages) or are necessary only when problems arise (and thus can be largely eliminated on a well-planned system). Printing, on the other hand, involves hardware (the printer) that is more subject to breakdown than almost anything inside a computer. Printing consumes resources such as paper and toner that must be replenished even when the system is working correctly. Finally, printers are a resource that is shared among all users, just as hard disk space is. What's more, printers are inherently hard to manage because they are slower, more expensive, and much more limited in capacity than hard disks.

To illustrate the differences between managing a hard disk used as a shared file server and a printer used by many users, consider these points:

- A single large hard disk will meet the needs of several dozen users on a standard system. Regular data backups and a redundant system such as disk mirroring provide protection against problems, but once users know where their data is stored and file permissions have been established, the system will generally run a long time without serious problems.

- Several dozen users probably require several printer devices, depending on the type of work they do. Each printer may cost as much as the single large hard disk. Supplies for the printers are a continuing cost.

- For users who print numerous reports, artwork sheets, or mechanical drawings, the printers become a bottleneck. If many users submit large print jobs at the same time, they must wait for the printer to finish each print job. Conversely, when a user saves data to a hard disk, the wait is never more than a second or two.

- The hard disk on which users store data is probably located in a locked closet. Only the system administrator has access to it. The printers, by contrast, are located where all users have access to them. Any user may try to adjust the printer features, cause a paper jam, or do other unexpected things. The actions of one user can make the printer unusable until the system administrator physically goes to the printer to solve the problem.

For all of these reasons, a printer policy is a helpful document for any organization with more than two or three users who rely on the same printer. A **printer policy** is a brief document that describes how print resources can be used and how the management of the printers will be conducted. Having a printer policy that everyone in the organization can review will help a system administrator avoid the headaches that come with multiple hardware failures and demands from users for special treatment. A typical printer policy would include statements about the following issues. (You will learn later in this chapter how to implement or manage the items mentioned.)

- Unless the system administrator is specifically authorized by a manager, no one's print jobs will receive priority over other print jobs. (The system administrator can move any print job to the top of the queue, but doing so invariably causes friction among users who have to wait longer because someone received special treatment.)

- Printers are to be used only for projects related to the organization (be it a school, business, or other type of organization). The policy may include a statement about using printers for personal work after certain hours with payment of a fee (such as five cents per page) to a fund for replenishing paper and toner.

- Each user's printer usage will be tracked and recorded. Any user found to be printing an excessive number of sheets may need to explain why. A specific page limit per week or month is sometimes stated. This feature, called print accounting, is especially useful for schools, where many users are using the printer.

- No one should alter the printer settings without instructions from the system administrator. This includes changing the default paper size or default paper tray, changing fonts, adding printer memory, and so forth.

Some of these statements might seem draconian or simply inappropriate within your organization. You can decide which will be helpful in maintaining the printers and the system administrators in good working order.

The `lpd` daemon can record the number of pages printed by each user on the system—a process known as print accounting. To implement print accounting, you need to add a single entry to the `printcap` file. (The following section explains how to add this and other entries.) Once the `lpd` daemon begins print accounting, you can use a simple command-line utility to print reports showing how many pages each user has printed to each printer.

13

 For most printers, page-based accounting is appropriate. If you use plotters on your Linux system, print accounting measures the number of lineal feet that a user has printed.

Creating a `printcap` Entry

The `printcap` file uses a format that is different from any of the Linux configuration files described so far in this book. You can edit this file in any text editor, or you can use one of the graphical utilities provided with your Linux distribution. The general format consists of a printer name (which is actually the print queue name), followed by a series of two-character option codes that apply to that printer. Each option is separated from the next by two colons. Many options are followed by specific parameters. For example, the parameter `lp=/dev/lp0` specifies that the line printer device (the `lp` option code) is `/dev/lp0`. The `lpd` daemon is designed to read the options defining a printer on a single line. To make the file easier for a person to read, however, each option code is often placed on a separate line of the file, with a backslash indicating that the line break should be ignored when processing the file. This creates a readable format in which many lines are effectively combined into a single line by lpd. A very simple `printcap` file from Red Hat Linux is shown below. The Printer Tool (described later) stores some information in the comment lines of the `printcap` file, which makes hand editing this file on Red Hat Linux somewhat problematic.

```
# /etc/printcap
#
# Please don't edit this file directly unless you know what you
are doing!
# Be warned that the control-panel printtool requires a very
strict format!
# Look at the printcap(5) man page for more info.
#
# This file can be edited with the printtool in the
control-panel.

##PRINTTOOL3## LOCAL cdj500 300x300 letter {} DeskJet500 3 {}
lp:\
        :sd=/var/spool/lpd/lp:\
        :mx#0:\
        :sh:\
        :lp=/dev/lp0:\
        :if=/var/spool/lpd/lp/filter:
```

Table 13-1 lists the two-letter codes you are most likely to use when creating a `printcap` file. Be careful about the formatting of this file if you create it manually in a text editor (rather than using a graphical utility as described in the next section). If a single colon, backslash, or equal sign is misplaced, printing may not function correctly. To see a list of all available option codes, use the command man 5 printcap to view the `printcap` man page.

Table 13-1 Useful Option Codes Within /etc/printcap

Option code	Description	Example
af	The print accounting file.	af=/var/adm/lp_acct/hplj_acct
bq	Define a remote system that should receive the print job, but filter the print job before sending it to the remote system.	bq=ps@192.168.100.67
ff	The form feed (start a new page) character.	ff='\f'
if	The print filter to use when printing to this printer.	if=/var/spool/lpd/hplj/filter
lp	The device name to open for printing (the first parallel port is shown in the example).	lp=/dev/lp0

Table 13-1 Useful Option Codes Within `/etc/printcap` (continued)

Option code	Description	Example
mx	The maximum file size for print jobs submitted to this printer (in 1024-byte blocks). The first example indicates a maximum print job size of about 2 MB; the second example (with #0) indicates that no maximum print job size is enforced.	mx=2000 mx#0
pc	Price per page (or foot for plotters) to use for print accounting, in hundreds of a cent. The example shows 15 cents per page.	pc=1500
pl	Page length, in lines.	pl=66
pw	Page width, in characters.	pw=80
rg	Restricted group; only members of the group named may submit print jobs to this printer.	rg=eng
rm	Hostname of a remote print server to which print jobs submitted using this printer name should be sent. (See the section "Remote Printing" later in this chapter.)	rm=ps.xyzcorp.com or rm=192.168.100.67
rp	Remote printer; the queue name to use on the remote print server (defined by rm).	rp=hplj5
rs	Restrict users trying to print from other machines to those with an account (or the same name) on this machine.	rs
sb	Use a short banner page of only one line.	sb
sc	Suppress multiple copies of the same print job even if they are specified in the lpr command submitting the job.	sc
sd	The spool directory where submitted print jobs will be stored by lpd.	sd=/var/spool/lpd/hplj
sh	Suppress printing of a banner or header page containing the username, filename, and other print job information. The banner page is helpful when many users use the same printer, but it uses a lot of paper.	sh

13

After creating an appropriate `printcap` entry for the printer you want to use, you should create the print spool directory and the print accounting files (if you have included the `af` option code). The print accounting file, described in detail later in the chapter, stores information about how many pages each user has printed. Assuming you have created a `printcap` entry for a printer named `hplj`, the following commands would create a print spool directory for that printer and set its ownership and permissions appropriately. The following commands assume you are logged in as `root` and that you have specified the directory shown here using the `sd` (spool directory) option code.

```
mkdir /var/spool/lpd/hplj
chown daemon.daemon /var/spool/lpd/hplj
chmod 755 /var/spool/lpd/hplj
```

If you are using print accounting and have indicated a print accounting file with the `af` option code, you can create the print accounting file using similar commands. You can create the file in any location that you choose, though it's best to place it somewhere in the `/var` directory to follow Linux conventions for file placement. You should create the accounting files before starting the printer with the `lpc` command or a graphical utility.

```
touch /var/adm/lp_acct/ hplj_acct
chown daemon.daemon /var/adm/lp_acct /hplj_acct
chmod 755 /var/adm/lp_acct/hplj_acct
```

Using the `lpc` Utility

The `lpc` utility is the printer control utility. (The name `lpc` stands for *line printer control*.) This command-line utility lets you control the actions of the `lpd` daemon, specifying how print jobs are accepted and processed. Because many Linux system administrators use one of the graphical utilities described in the next section, they don't regularly need to use the `lpc` utility. But `lpc` provides functionality that is not available in most of the graphical utilities. For example you can:

- Prevent new print jobs from being accepted into a print queue

- Prevent print jobs from being sent to a printer

- Cancel a print job that is currently being printed

- See the status of any printer (whether it is enabled, whether the corresponding print queue contains any print jobs, and so forth)

You can include an `lpc` command as a parameter on the command line, like this:

```
lpc status
```

You can also use `lpc` in an interactive mode in which you can enter multiple commands. To begin using `lpc` in interactive mode, enter the utility name without any parameters:

```
lpc
```

You then see a prompt like this:

```
lpc>
```

Table 13-2 lists the commands that you can use at the `lpc` prompt or as parameters to the `lpc` command (if you prefer not to use the interactive mode for some tasks).

Table 13-2   `lpc` Commands

Command	Description	Example (noninteractive mode)
help	Display a list of all `lpc` commands.	`lpc help`
status	Display status of the `lpd` printer daemon and the print queue indicated (or the default if none is indicated).	`lpc status`
abort	Cancel the print job currently being printed. (Use the `start` command to restart printing.)	`lpc abort`
stop	Stop sending print jobs to the printer after the current print job has finished printing.	`lpc stop`
start	Start sending print jobs to the printer (used after `abort` or `stop`).	`lpc start`
disable	Prevent users from submitting new print jobs.	`lpc disable`
enable	Allow users to submit new print jobs.	`lpc enable`
down	Stop sending print jobs to the printer and prevent new print jobs from being submitted (equivalent to using `stop` and `disable`).	`lpc down`
up	Begin sending print jobs to the printer and allow new print jobs to be submitted (equivalent to using `start` and `enable`).	`lpc up`
clean	Remove all temporary files used by `lpd` for the default (or named) printer.	`lpc clean`
exit or quit	Exit the `lpc` program.	Used only in interactive mode.
restart	Attempt to restart the `lpd` printer daemon (equivalent to using the command `/etc/rc.d/init.d/lpd restart`).	`lpc restart`
topq	Move a print job to the top of the named print queue. This command requires a printer name (where the print job will be placed) and the print job number (which you can obtain using the `lpq` command).	`lpc topq hplj 16`

13

For each of the commands shown, `lpc` acts on the default printer (the first one listed in the `printcap` file) unless you specify a printer name. For example, if the first printer in `printcap` is `lp`, using this command will bring down the `lp` printer:

`lpc down`

If the `printcap` file contains a definition of another printer named `hplj`, you can use this command to bring down the `hplj` printer:

`lpc down hplj`

When using any of the `lpc` commands (except `topq`), you can use the designation `all` to refer to all printers. For example, to completely shut down printing, so that no print jobs can be submitted and all printing stops after the current print jobs are finished, use this command:

`lpc down all`

 TIP The printing commands you will learn later in this chapter use a `-P` parameter before the printer name, without a following space, for example, `lpq -Phplj`. The `lpc` command does not use the `-P` parameter; you simply add the printer name as an additional parameter.

Figure 13-4 illustrates how some of the key `lpc` commands affect different parts of the printing process.

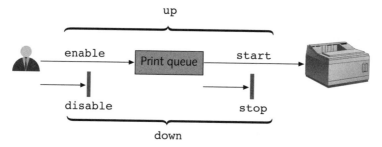

Figure 13-4   Effect of various `lpc` commands on print processing

Using Graphical Tools to Set Up Printing

After reviewing the long list of `printcap` entries in Table 13-1 and `lpc` commands in Table 13-2, you'll be glad to know that many system administrators rely on the graphical tools described in this section to set up and administer printing on their Linux systems. Several different tools are available, though the tools at your disposal depend on your Linux distribution. For example, only Red Hat Linux users are likely to have the LinuxConf and Printer Tool utilities; only SuSE Linux users will have the YAST utility, and only Caldera OpenLinux users will have COAS and LISA. This section describes how to use some of these popular utilities.

You'll note as you explore any of these utilities that they do not provide all of the options listed in Table 13-1 or in Table 13-2. As with much of Linux, if you need to use the full functionality of the Linux printing system, you will need to edit the configuration files yourself. However, many networks have very simple printing requirements, in which case the capabilities of the graphical utilities should be sufficient.

In this section you learn about utilities for setting up the `printcap` file so that users can begin to print files. Later in this chapter, in the section "Managing Printing," you learn about graphical utilities used to manage a print queue.

In Red Hat Linux, you can use the Printer Tool to set up multiple print queues in your `printcap` file. Though powerful, the Printer Tool program is not integrated with any of Red Hat's other system administration utilities. (In particular, you will not find the Printer Tool in the LinuxConf program.) This utility is located on the `AnotherLevel` menu's submenu, under `Administration`. You can also start this utility by entering `printtool` (all lowercase) in a graphical terminal emulator window. If you have started the Red Hat Control Panel (by selecting `Control Panel` from the `System` submenu), you can click on the printer icon to launch the Printer Tool program. Figure 13-5 shows the Red Hat Control Panel with the printer icon in the middle of the panel.

Click to start Printer Tool

Figure 13-5   The Red Hat Linux Control Panel

When you start Printer Tool, you see a main window with a list of all the printers that are configured on the system. To use the Printer Tool program, choose the `Add` button at the bottom of the main window. In the `Add Printer` dialog box that appears, select the type of printer you want to define. You can choose from the following four options:

- `Local Printer`: a printer connected to the Linux computer via a parallel or serial cable.

- `Remote UNIX`: a remote server that runs the `lpd` daemon and will accept standard UNIX or Linux print jobs over the network.

- `SMB/Windows 95/NT Printer`: a printer connected to a Windows system on the network. This option does not use `lpd`. It uses the Samba suite, which is not discussed in this book. (See *www.samba.org*.)

- `NetWare Printer (NCP)`: a printer connected to a NetWare server on the network. This option does not use `lpd`. It relies on the NCP protocol, which must be installed on your server. NCP networking is not discussed in this book. To learn more, visit the technical support pages at *www.redhat.com*.

13

Assuming you choose `Local Printer`, you see an informational dialog box listing the printer ports (parallel ports) detected on your system. Choose `OK` to close this dialog box. The `Edit Local Printer Entry` dialog box shown in Figure 13-6 appears. In this dialog box you define options for the printer. Figure 13-6 shows typical values for a local printer. When you use a graphical tool like Printer Tool, the print spool directory that you name in this dialog box is created for you by the utility.

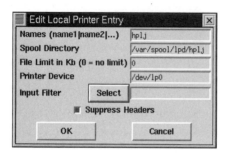

Figure 13-6   Selecting print options in the Red Hat Printer Tool program

As you can see in Figure 13-6, the Printer Tool program allows you to specify relatively few printer options. To add other options, you must edit `printcap` using a text editor. However, you have a powerful tool in the `Configure Filter` dialog box, which you open by clicking the `Select` button next to the `Input Filter` field. Figure 13-7 shows the dialog box, in which you select a printer type and then choose options for that printer. Although this dialog box doesn't include all printer models or options, it allows you to automatically create complex print filters for many popular printers. The options displayed for the printer type that you select reflect the current capabilities of the filtering programs (such as `gs` and `nenscript`), not the full capabilities of the printer model.

The `Configure Filter` dialog box uses the term driver because that term is more familiar to most users than print filter. But in fact, the Printer Tool program creates a print filter, not a driver as in Windows.

The Printer Tool program includes a few menu options that let you print a text page to the selected printer, restart the `lpd` daemon if you are having problems with the printing system, or reload the `printcap` file if you have changed it in a text editor. When you define a printer, the `printcap` file is immediately and automatically updated.

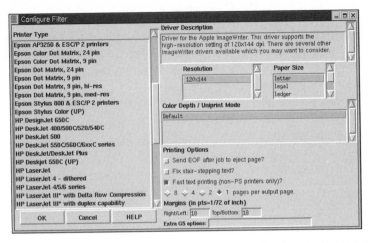

Figure 13-7   The `Configure Filter` dialog box in the Printer Tool

 After creating a new printer entry in the `printcap` file, you don't need to restart the `lpd` daemon. The `printcap` file is always read each time a print job is submitted, so the latest information in the file will always be used.

Caldera OpenLinux and SuSE Linux both include configuration utilities that let you define a `printcap` entry in text mode using a menu-style interface. The SuSE utility is called YAST. The Caldera utility is called LISA.

To use the LISA utility, you select `System Configuration`, then `Hardware Configuration`, then `Configure Printer`. Alternatively, you can start the LISA utility at the printer configuration screen using this command: `lisa --printer`. Figure 13-8 shows the LISA utility. After selecting a printer model, you respond to a few questions based on the model that you selected. The `printcap` file and spool directory are created for you.

13

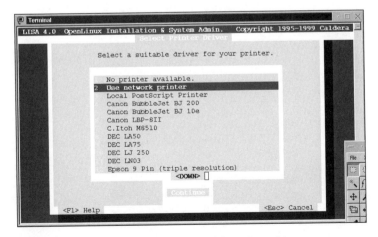

Figure 13-8   The LISA utility in Caldera OpenLinux

Caldera OpenLinux also includes a graphical printer configuration tool as part of its COAS administration system. On the main menu of the KDE Desktop, choose **COAS**, then choose **Peripherals**, then choose **Printer**. When the Printer configuration window appears, choose **Add** from the **Printer** menu. You can then select a printer model from the list and answer other questions about the printer and your preference settings to complete the configuration. The `printcap` file is updated when you confirm (in a pop-up dialog box) that you want your changes saved.

The most well integrated print configuration tool is in the Corel Linux distribution. Although Corel Linux is designed to be used as a desktop system rather than as a Linux server, its printing tools may find their way into other Linux distributions, so you should take time to become familiar with it. To manage printing from the Corel Linux KDE Desktop, open the main menu, choose **Control Center**, and then choose **Printers**. A list of configured printers displays, as in Figure 13-9. Using this dialog box you can do any of the following:

- Configure a local or remote printer using an interface very similar to a Windows wizard.

- Designate a default printer.

- Set advanced options for a printer, such as page size, resolution, and so forth. (You must still edit the `printcap` file to use advanced administration options, however.)

- View and manage the print jobs in any print queue. (Graphical utilities for managing print jobs in other Linux distributions are described in the next section.)

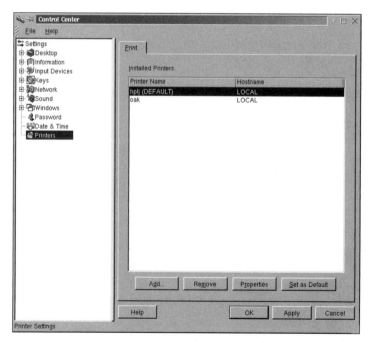

Figure 13-9   Managing printing in Corel Linux

Printing a File

After all of this configuration effort, users can begin to print files on Linux either from the command line or from applications. As mentioned earlier, the command `lpr` prints a file in Linux. The `lpr` command uses the information in the `printcap` file to submit a file to a print queue. From there the `lpd` daemon sends it, in its turn, to the printer. The `lpr` command requires only the name of the file to print. For example, to print a copy of the `printcap` file to the default printer, use this command:

```
lpr /etc/printcap
```

You can also use a pipe symbol to send information to a printer. The `lpr` command reads from the standard input if a filename is not supplied. For example, to sort a file and send the results to the default printer, use this command:

```
sort namelist | lpr
```

One disadvantage of using the `lpr` command in this way (with a pipe symbol rather than a filename) is that the print job information does not contain a filename. Thus you cannot identify what the print job contains after you have submitted it. Still, using the pipe symbol is sometimes useful. The `lpr` command includes many options to control how the print job is handled. Some of the more useful `lpr` options are shown in Table 13-3.

Table 13-3   `lpr` Command Options

Option	Description	Example
-C	Set a priority class for the print job. Priorities range from A to Z. The default is A. Print jobs of a lower priority are printed after all print jobs of a higher priority.	`lpr -C D stats.txt`
-h	Don't use a banner or header page for this print job, even if `printcap` specifies one.	`lpr -h stats.txt`
-i	Indent each line of the print job by this many spaces. This feature is not supported on all printers.	`lpr -i 5 stats.txt`
-J	Assign a name to this print job. The name appears on the banner page to help a user identify the print job.	`lpr -J "Weekly statistics" stats.txt`
-#	Specify the number of copies of the file to be printed. Note that there is no space between the # option and the numeric value.	`lpr -#3 stats.txt`
-m	Send an e-mail to the named user account if an error occurs during printing. If the user account is located on the same system, only the user's account name is needed, as in this example.	`lpr -m nwells stats.txt`

13

Table 13-3   `lpr` Command Options (continued)

Option	Description	Example
`-P`	Specify a nondefault printer using a printer name from the `printcap` file. Don't put a space between the `P` and the printer name.	`lpr -Phplj5 stats.txt`
`-w`	Specify the page width in characters.	`lpr -w132 stats.txt`

The `lpr` utility determines which printer to send a print job to using the steps outlined below. For most users, the default printer will simply be the first one listed in the `printcap` file, because none of the other items in this list are set up by default on most Linux systems. You can change that if you prefer. Note that this procedure also applies to the print queue management utilities (such as `lpq`) described in an upcoming section.

1. If the `-P` option is included with the `lpr` command, the printer named after `-P` is used.

2. If the `-P` option is not included, but an environment variable named `PRINTER` exists for the user printing the file, the value of the `PRINTER` variable is used.

3. If a `PRINTER` environment variable is not configured but a default_printer configuration line is included in the `lpd.conf` file (see the following tip), then that printer is used.

4. If none of the configurations in Steps 1 through 3 provide a printer name, the first printer in the `printcap` file is used.

> **TIP** A configuration file named `lpd.conf` is included with some distributions of Linux, usually in the `/etc` directory. The man page contains details about using this file for advanced configuration of the `lpd` daemon. For example, you can change the location where `lpd` looks for the `printcap` file and which network port `lpd` uses to connect to remote print servers. The configuration settings in this file are beyond the scope of this book. To learn more, contact your Linux vendor's technical support department.

Printing from a graphical program is straightforward. In most cases, you choose `Print` from the `File` menu, review the print options, and choose `OK` to print the current file. Because Linux programs don't have the advantage of full-featured printer drivers, the print dialog boxes are generally very simple affairs. You can occasionally select how many copies to print or select which printer to print to (with the list of available printers being drawn from the `printcap` file). Some print dialog boxes let you select which print command to use, with `lpr` or `nenscript` being the default command. Figure 13-10 shows this feature in the Print dialog box of the KDE text editor.

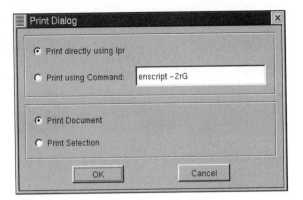

Figure 13-10   Printing a file in the KDE text editor

A few Linux programs such as StarOffice, WordPerfect, and FrameMaker for Linux include more substantial Print dialog boxes, though even these rarely have the depth of printer feature control that Windows users currently enjoy. Figure 13-11 shows the Print dialog box in Corel WordPerfect for Linux. Many additional features are available in this dialog box via the `Select` button in the Current Printer section of the dialog box.

Figure 13-11   The Print dialog box in Corel WordPerfect for Linux

13

MANAGING PRINTING

Once you have set up a `printcap` file and used the `lpc` program or a graphical utility to enable a printer, managing printing revolves around two tasks:

- Keeping the printers themselves stocked with paper, toner, ribbons, ink, cleared of paper jams, and online. (This book doesn't provide any guidance on these tasks.)
- Tracking print jobs in the print queues.

Linux includes both command-line and graphical utilities for tracking print jobs. Any user on the system can use these utilities, though their functionality is limited if you are not working as `root` because you can only change the status of print jobs that you have submitted.

Tracking Print Jobs

To view the print jobs in the default print queue, enter the command `lpq`. The `lpq` utility lists each of the print jobs in a print queue with the following information:

- Status of the print job (such as active, ready, or error)
- Owner (the user who submitted the print job)
- Class of the print job (this is normally `A`, unless the `-C` option was used with the `lpr` command)
- Job number assigned by the `lpd` print server
- Size of the file in bytes (characters)
- Time that the print job was submitted

Sample output from the `lpq` command is shown here:

```
lp is ready and printing
Rank    Owner     Job     Files           Total Size
active  nwells    308     stats.txt       2241 bytes
1st     cynthia   312     index.html      9617 bytes
2nd     alexv     323     userguide.ps    434898 bytes
```

If you are working on a server where the print queue contains many documents, you may either want to use the `-s` option, to display a shorter format for each print job, or add a job ID to the `lpq` command. The job ID refers to the print job number assigned by `lpd` and displayed under the `Job` field in the sample `lpq` output above. For example, to see information about all print jobs submitted by user `nwells`, enter this command:

```
lpq nwells
```

Or if you have previously used `lpq` to identify the job number of a large print job you submitted, use the number to query the status of that job, as in the following command. (The print job number would be different in each case, of course.)

```
lpq 572
```

As with the `lpr` command, you can include a -P option with the `lpq` command to view print jobs submitted to different print queues. For example, to view the print jobs in the `hplj` print queue, use this command:

`lpq -Phplj`

Once you know the number of a print job, you can remove it from the queue or, if you are logged in as `root`, move the print job to another print queue or to the top of a print queue so that it is printed next. The **lprm** command deletes a print job from a queue. It requires a job ID parameter, which can be a print job number or a username. For example, if you have determined (using `lpq`) that a print job with a number of 491 should be deleted before it is printed, use this command to remove it from the `hplj` print queue:

`lprm -Phplj 491`

You can remove all print jobs submitted by a user by referring to the user's name, for example:

`lprm -Phplj nwells`

You can also remove all of the print jobs in a queue by using the parameter –:

`lprm -Phplj -`

Obviously, you cannot remove another user's print jobs with a username parameter or the – parameter unless you are logged in as `root`.

Creating Print Accounting Reports

When you include the `af` option in the `printcap` file, each print job creates a print accounting entry in the file specified by the `af` option. You can use the **pac** (print accounting) command to display reports based on that accounting data.

Although a price per page or foot can be set using the `pc` option in the `printcap` file, the -p option of the `pac` command is a more convenient method of seeing a total cost of pages printed by a particular user. As an example of using the `pac` command with the -p option to specify a price, consider the command `pac -p0.15 -Phplj`, which will list all the accounting information for printer `hplj` and assign a value of 15 cents per page. Notice the unusual format: neither -p nor -P has a space after it. Because users will often be printing from multiple locations to a centralized print server (see "Remote Printing," later in this chapter), the -m option is commonly used to combine all of a user's print jobs from multiple servers into a single listing. For example, adding this option to the previous example

13

would yield: `pac -m -p0.15 -Phplj`. Sample output from a `pac` command is shown here, with some lines before the total removed for the sake of brevity:

Login	pages/feet	runs		price
nwells	23	4	USD	3.45
toma	490	17	USD	73.5
cynthia	134	6	USD	20.10
dalbis	88	2	USD	13.2
alexv	829	44	USD	124.35
...				
total	4319	213	USD	647.85

Because the `pac` command uses all of the information stored in the print accounting file that you specified with the `af` option in `printcap`, you may want to set up a script (perhaps a cron job) that periodically rotates the accounting files. Such a script could create a report of print activity, delete or archive the print accounting files for all printers, and then create new, empty files (using the `touch`, `chown`, and `chmod` commands discussed earlier in this chapter).

If you want to see print accounting information for a single user rather than wait for a weekly report to be generated by the script you created, add the user's name to the `pac` command. For example, to see the report for `nwells`, use this command: `pac -m -p0.15 -Phplj nwells`. When a username is not specified, `pac` creates a report line for each user who has printed anything to the specified printer.

Using Graphical Print Management Utilities

In addition to the `lpq` and `lprm` commands, a few graphical utilities are available to help you manage print jobs. Two examples are the `klpq` program (part of the KDE Desktop) and the printer management dialog boxes in Corel Linux. To start the `klpq` program from the KDE main menu, choose `Printer Queue` from the `System` menu. The main window is shown in Figure 13-12.

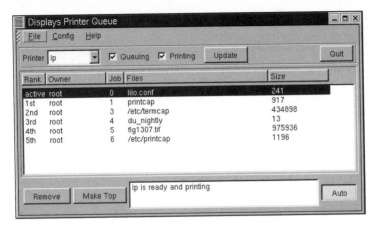

Figure 13-12   Available printers and queued print jobs listed in the KDE Printer
Queue Utility

The main window lists all the jobs for the print queue selected in the Printer list box. You
can choose which print queue's jobs are listed by selecting a print queue from the list. Each
printer in the `printcap` file is included in the list. The Queuing check box, when
checked, allows users to submit new jobs to the print queue (when unchecked, new jobs
cannot be sent). You check or uncheck the Printing check box to control the `lpd` daemon,
which sends print jobs to a printer device. These are equivalent to the `lpc` commands
`enable/disable` and `start/stop`, respectively. Remember to click the `Update` button after changing one of the check boxes.

If you are logged in as `root`, you can click on any print job listed and either remove it or
make it the next job to be printed. The list of print jobs is updated every few seconds. You
can set the update frequency using the `Auto Update` item on the `Config` menu.

Corel Linux takes a slightly different approach from `klpq`, integrating the print queue management into the same dialog box where new printers are defined. To see how this works in
Corel Linux, open the Control Center, and choose the `Printers` item; the list of printers

13

defined on the system (shown earlier in Figure 13-9) displays. Click a printer to select it, and then click the **Properties** button. A dialog box appears that contains a Job Queue tab (shown in Figure 13-13). On this tab you can see the owner, filename, and size for each print job. If you are the **root** user or the owner of a print job, you can use the **Remove** button to delete the print job from the queue.

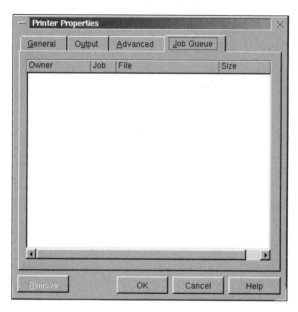

Figure 13-13   Print queue management in Corel Linux

REMOTE PRINTING

Though it's not apparent from what has been said so far, the **lpd** daemon is a network service much like other services that you're more familiar with: FTP servers, Web servers, and e-mail servers. Because security is less of a concern generally when printing files, little configuration is required to connect the **lpd** daemon running on one Linux-based computer to the **lpd** daemon running on another Linux-based computer and transfer a print job for remote printing. In fact, any UNIX system that uses the **lpd** daemon can accept print jobs from a Linux system, and vice versa.

Security is less of a concern with printing, but it may still be something you need to keep in mind. The /etc/lpd.perms file contains permissions for users who want to use the lpd daemon on a Linux system. This file is not used often, but you can use it to restrict printing activity based on usernames, hostnames, and other factors. To learn more about this feature, contact your Linux vendor's technical support department.

Other systems, such as NetWare and Windows NT, can use special `lpd` daemon software to share printers with UNIX and Linux systems. This software can be difficult to configure, however. You may prefer to use the facilities described below that let you configure native NetWare or Windows printing on Linux.

Printing to Remote Linux and UNIX Systems

Linux and UNIX systems that use the standard printing mechanism described in this chapter can share printers very easily. To print a file from one Linux system to a printer connected to another Linux or UNIX system, simply ask the system administrator of the other system for the print queue name and hostname (or IP address) of the computer. Add these to the `printcap` file as the `rp` and `rm` options, respectively, or use one of the utilities described earlier to define a new print queue for the remote printer. A simple `printcap` file that prints to a remote printer is shown here:

```
lp:\
        :sd=/var/spool/lpd/lp:\
        :mx#0:\
        :sh:\
        :rm=ps.xmission.com:\
        :rp=lexmark:\
        :if=/var/spool/lpd/lp/filter:
```

Figure 13-14 shows the process that `lpd` uses to print to a remote printer. This figure illustrates several important points, some of which are limitations in the Linux printing architecture that you should be aware of.

- The print job is not passed through a filter until it reaches the `lpd` program on the remote system. This allows the administrator of the remote system to control what data is sent to the printer at that location, but it may limit what you can do from your Linux system because your programs don't know how the remote printer is configured.

- Once a print job has been submitted to a remote system, the local `lpd` daemon has nothing more to do with it. You cannot query the remote print queue or learn more about the print job without first logging in to the remote system (which requires that you have an account on that system).

- Unless the default settings have been changed in the `printcap` or `lpd.perms` file, any user on the same network can connect to a printer and submit print jobs. This could be a problem in a large organization or one that is concerned about print usage.

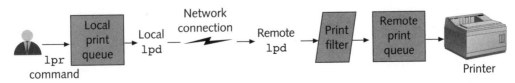

Figure 13-14 Processing a remote print job

Leaving print job filtering to be done on the remote server makes sense in most cases, but it causes a problem when the printer is attached directly to the network. This is a common situation. The printer is considered remote because it is not connected to a serial or parallel port on the Linux computer. Network printers in many companies have their own IP addresses, which makes it possible to send data directly to the printer without connecting it first to a computer's parallel or serial port. Because Linux applications do not preprocess a file based on a printer driver before submitting it for printing, the print filter must do this job. A network printer, however, does not have the ability to run a Linux-style print filter. To solve this problem, a bounce queue command is used.

A **bounce queue (bq)** is an option code in the `printcap` file that causes print jobs to be processed by the print filter before being sent to a remote printer. For example, if the `printcap` file includes the following lines, each print job will be processed by the filter, then sent to the print queue named `lexmark2` on the server 192.168.100.43:

```
lp:\
     :sd=/var/spool/lpd/lp:\
     :mx#0:\
     :sh:\
     :bq=lexmark2@192.168.100.43:\
     :if=/var/spool/lpd/lp/filter:
```

Note that no `rm` or `rp` lines are used here, because the `bq` option contains the remote printer information. In addition, no `lp` line is required, because no local printer port will be used to print files. However, as when using the `rm` and `rp` options to specify a standard remote `lpd`-based server, you should include the `sd` option to specify a print spool directory so that `lpd` has a location to store files between the time they are submitted and when they are processed.

Printing to Non-Linux Systems

When you configure a `printcap` file using utilities such as the Printer Tool in Red Hat Linux, you may see references to defining remote printers located on Windows or NetWare systems. The fact that several Linux vendors have integrated multiplatform printer configuration in this way is very helpful for system administrators. But the `lpd` daemon and the print management utilities that you have learned about in this chapter do not have anything to do with printing on these other platforms.

In order to print to a printer that is connected to a Windows-based computer (and not running a Windows version of `lpd`), you must install and configure the Samba suite of applications on your Linux system. This suite of applications provides SMB protocol support to Linux, so that files and printers can be shared between Linux and Windows systems. If you have the username and password required by the Windows security configuration, you can then use the `smbprint` command to send a file to a printer connected to a Windows computer. The Samba suite is included with virtually all Linux distributions, but Samba configuration is far beyond the scope of this chapter.

In order to use a printer that is connected to a NetWare-based computer, you must install and configure the `ncpfs` package or a similar NetWare client package developed by Caldera Systems under license from Novell. The `ncpfs` package is included with many Linux distributions, but it does not support Novell Directory Services—it operates only in NetWare's bindery mode. However, if you have an account on a NetWare server, you can use the `nprint` command to submit files to a NetWare print queue from Linux. Similarly, the NetWare client that Caldera Systems provides includes a utility called `nwprint` that allows you to print to any NetWare printer on your network for which you have access privileges. For more information, visit *www.calderasystems.com*.

CHAPTER SUMMARY

❏ Printing in Linux is based on the BSD UNIX system. It includes a print server daemon called `lpd` that processes print jobs, the `lpr` program used to submit print jobs, and several other utilities that manage print configuration and print queue management.

❏ Numerous graphical utilities are available to set up a `printcap` print queue configuration file. These are normally used instead of creating a `printcap` file in a text editor. The `printcap` file contains two-letter codes that define how `lpd` and `lpr` interact with each printer.

❏ The `root` user on a Linux system can use `lpq`, `lprm`, and `lpc` to manage printing activity and print queue contents. Regular users can manage their own print jobs using `lpq` and `lprm`, or they can use a number of graphical utilities designed for that purpose.

❏ The Linux printing system is designed for easy sharing of networked printers using one or two options in the `printcap` file. Printing to other systems such as Windows NT and Novell NetWare is also possible using additional Linux software.

13

KEY TERMS

block special file — A type of file (normally located in `/dev`) referring to a physical device that transfers data in blocks of characters, such as a hard disk drive.

bounce queue (bq) — An option code within the `printcap` file that causes print jobs to be processed by the local print filter before being sent to a remote printer.

character special file — A filename referring to a physical device (such as a serial port) that transfers data in single characters.

driver — A software program that provides abstract services for a hardware component, such as opening files or reading character input.

lpc — The Linux printer control utility. It stands for *line printer control*.

lpd — The line printer daemon, which sends files prepared by `lpr` to the physical printer device or remote print server.

lpq — A utility that lists each print job in a print queue and includes information such as the owner and size of each job.

lpr — A command that prepares files to be sent to a physical printer device, effectively "printing" files for Linux users.

lprm — A command that deletes a print job from a print queue.

magic filter — A print filter program that automatically processes a file into the correct output format based on the file's type.

pac — A command that displays reports based on print accounting data. It stands for *print accounting*.

page description language — A special set of codes that determine the graphics elements, text font, and everything else about how information appears on a printed page.

print filter — A script that contains instructions for formatting documents using the page description language required by a specific printer. The print filter is used by the **lpr** program to prepare files to be sent to a physical printer.

print job — A file submitted for printing via the **lpr** command.

print queue — A subdirectory where files are stored to wait for the **lpd** daemon to retrieve them one by one and send them to the printer. Also called a print spool directory.

print spool directory — *See* print queue.

printcap — The printer definition file used by the Linux printing system. This file specifies how and where files to be printed are stored and processed by **lpr** and **lpd**. It stands for *printer capture*.

printer policy — A brief document that describes how print resources can be used and how the management of the printers will be conducted within an organization.

REVIEW QUESTIONS

1. Name four components of the BSD UNIX printing architecture used by Linux.

2. A print queue is usually named for:

   a. The print accounting file

   b. A physical printer device

   c. The printer control program

   d. LPRng

3. Print queue definitions are stored in the _____ file.

   a. `/var/spool/lpd/lp`

   b. `/var/adm/acct`

   c. `/etc/printcap`

   d. `/etc/lpd.conf`

4. The relationship of print queue to physical printer can be one to many or many to one. True or False?

5. Print filters are used to:

    a. Convert graphics formats before printing images

    b. Prepare documents in a printer-specific format

    c. Remove unprintable characters from documents

    d. Compress print job files before transfer to a remote print server

6. Describe at least two purposes of having a printer policy in place.

7. Multiple options in the `printcap` file are separated by:

    a. An equal sign

    b. Two colons

    c. A carriage return/new line

    d. A tab

8. Define the meaning of the following option codes as used within the `printcap` file: `sh`, `mx`, `sd`, `if`, and `af`.

9. The `lpc` utility *should* be used to bring up a new printer *unless*:

    a. The graphical utility being used has taken care of this step.

    b. The `lpd` daemon has not been first restarted.

    c. The `printcap` file contains a `bq` option.

    d. The user is logged in as `root`.

10. Explain the difference between the `lpc` commands `up`, `enable`, and `start`.

11. Name four graphical tools that you can use to help set up or manage printing in Linux.

12. Graphical tools are *not* helpful for setting up printing when:

    a. You have only `root` account access.

    b. You require advanced printing security or accounting features.

    c. You are printing to a remote or non-Linux printer.

    d. You are using a standard Linux distribution.

13. You can use the `lpr` command to print a file using standard command-line redirection operators. True or False?

14. Explain the use of the `PRINTER` environment variable.

15. The _____ utility displays the owner, size, and submission time for print jobs.

    a. `lpq`

    b. `lprm`

    c. `lpc`

    d. `lpd`

16. The command `lprm -a kate` would do the following:

    a. Remove all print jobs from a printer called `kate`.

    b. Remove print jobs submitted by user `kate` from all print queues on the system.

    c. Remove the print job that will print the file `kate`.

    d. Remove the accounting files for printer `kate`.

17. The `pac` utility relies on files defined by the ————————— option in the `printcap` file.

    a. `ac`

    b. `pa`

    c. `af`

    d. `pc`

18. Graphical utilities are sometimes useful because they combine the functionality of numerous command-line utilities (such as `lpc`, `lpq`, and `lprm`) into a single graphical interface. True or False?

19. Describe two limitations of the remote printing architecture implemented by Linux using `lpd`.

20. The `lpd` daemon is a network service similar to a Web server. True or False?

21. The ————————— feature would be useful for printing to a departmental printer that was connected directly to the Ethernet network.

    a. bounce queue

    b. magic filter

    c. print accounting

    d. `ncpfs nprint`

22. Printing utilities such as the Red Hat Printer Tool are able to implement printing to Windows-based computers by relying on what additional software package?

23. Linux does not include a complete set of ————————— but instead relies on print filters and programs such as `gs` and `enscript`.

    a. printer drivers

    b. magic filters

    c. `lpd` permissions

    d. remote service packs

24. Contrast the interactive and command-line modes of `lpc`.

25. Linux print utilities commonly determine which print queue to act on by checking:

    a. The -P option, then the **PRINTER** environment variable, then the `printcap` file

    b. The **PRINTER** environment variable, then the -P option included with the command

    c. The order of print queues in the `printcap` file

    d. The systemwide printer configuration in `/etc/sysconfig`

HANDS-ON PROJECTS

Project 13-1

In this activity you create a `printcap` file with a printer definition, and then you use the `vi` editor to add an option to that printer definition. To complete this activity you should have a working Linux installation with `root` access. You don't need access to a printer.

1. Log in to Linux as the `root` user.

2. If you are using Red Hat Linux, start the graphical environment, and then follow the steps below. (If you are not using Red Hat Linux, skip to Step 3.)

   a. Open a terminal emulator window.

   b. Enter the command **printtool** to start the Printer Tool program.

   c. Choose the **Add** button.

   d. Select **Local Printer** and choose **OK**.

   e. Review the printer port autodetection notice, and choose **OK** to close the dialog box. The **Edit Local Printer Entry** dialog box appears.

   f. In the Names field enter the printer name **hplj**. (You can choose another if you prefer, but use it throughout this project wherever you see `hplj`.)

   g. In the Printer Device field enter **/dev/lp0**.

   h. Choose the **Select** button. In the **Configure Filter** dialog box select a printer model, explore the available options, and then choose **OK** to close the dialog box.

   i. Choose **OK** to finish the new print queue configuration.

   j. Choose **PrintTool**, then choose **Quit** to close the utility.

3. If you are not using Red Hat Linux, use another type of graphical utility to create a basic `printcap` file. You can choose any printer port or input filter that you like; you will not print anything to the printer in this project. You can also use a text editor such as `vi` to create or edit the `printcap` file. Enter this text in the `/etc/printcap` file:

```
hplj:\
        :sd=/var/spool/lpd/hplj:\
        :mx#0:\
        :sh:\
        :lp=/dev/lp0:
```

4. Enter `ls -l /var/spool/lpd/hplj` to check whether a spool directory was created for the printer. If you see a message stating that there is no such file or directory, create the spool directory by entering the following:

```
mkdir /var/spool/lpd/hplj
chown daemon.daemon /var/spool/lpd/hplj
chmod 755 /var/spool/lpd/hplj
```

13

5. Open the `printcap` file in a `vi` text editor (or another, if you prefer). Within the entry for the `hplj` printer that you have defined, insert the following line to restrict access to this printer to only those users who are members of the `eng` group:

   `:rg=eng:\`

6. Save your changes to `printcap` and exit the `vi` text editor.

Project 13-2

In this activity you use the `lpc` command to control the print queue that you created in Project 13-1. You also set up the group that is allowed to print (`eng`) and print a file to the newly created printer. To complete this activity you need a working Linux installation with `root` access, and you should have completed Project 13-1. You don't need access to a printer.

1. Log in to Linux as the `root` user.

2. Enter `lpc status hplj` to check the status of the `hplj` printer that you created in Project 13-1.

3. Enter `lpc stop hplj` to stop the `lpd` daemon from attempting to send any print jobs from the `hplj` print queue to a physical printer.

4. Enter `groupadd eng` to create the `eng` group (which is allowed to print to `hplj`). (On some Linux distributions you may be prompted to include a group ID number with the `groupadd` command.)

5. Enter `usermod -G eng username` (replacing *username* with your username) to add your regular user account to the `eng` group. (Be sure to use a capital *G* in the command.)

6. Change from `root` account access to your regular user account using the `su` command with your username (for example: `su - nwells`).

7. Enter `export PRINTER=hplj` to designate the printer assigned to the print queue named `hplj` as the default printer that you want to use. (Note that this change will only remain in effect until you exit the current `su` command; you would need to place this command in a start-up script such as `~/.bashrc` to make it permanent.)

8. Enter `lpr /etc/lilo.conf` to print a small file to the `hplj` printer. The `-P` option isn't needed because of the `PRINTER` variable that you just set. You can choose a different file than the one shown here if you prefer.

9. Enter `lpq` with no parameters to see the print job that you just submitted listed in the print queue.

10. Enter `exit` to return to the `root` account.

11. Enter `lpc disable hplj` to prevent more print jobs from being sent to the `hplj` print queue.

12. Change to your regular user account again using the command you used in Step 6.

13. Repeat the command you used in Step 8. What difference do you see? Use the `lpq` command. What do you see?

Project 13-3

In this activity you manage a print queue using command-line utilities. You can experiment with the graphical utilities that come with your Linux distribution if you prefer, but this activity relies on the `lpq`, `lpc`, and `lprm` commands. To complete this activity you should have a working Linux installation with **root** access. This project assumes you have completed Projects 13-1 and 13-2.

1. Log in to Linux as **root**.

2. Enter the commands **lpc enable hplj** and **lpc stop hplj** to allow print jobs to be placed in the `hplj` print queue but prevent `lpd` from trying to print the files.

3. Change to your regular user account using the **su** command.

4. Enter **lpr -Phplj /etc/printcap** to print a file. (Choose a different file if you prefer.)

5. Enter **lpr -Phplj /etc/hosts** to print a second file. (Choose any file if you prefer, but this file should be different from the one you printed in Step 4 so that you can identify which was first and which was second.)

6. Enter **lpq -Phplj** to list the print jobs in the `hplj` queue. Note the job number of the print job for the file **/etc/hosts** (or whatever the second file that you printed might be).

7. Enter **exit** to change back to the **root** account.

8. Use the `lpc` command with the print job number that you noted in Step 6. For instance, if the print job is number 415, enter **lpc topq hplj 415**.

9. Enter **lpq -Phplj**. What is different about the print queue contents?

10. Enter **lprm -Phplj 415**, substituting the number you noted in Step 6 for **415**.

11. Enter **lpq -Phplj** again. What has changed in the print queue?

13

CASE PROJECTS

The University Computer Lab

1. You have just obtained a coveted job as a system administrator at the university's computer lab. This job gives you experience with many technologies, but also plenty of time to do your homework between crises in the lab. The lab contains several Linux servers, many types of workstations where users work, and a bank of six laser printers. The task that takes up the largest part of your time is troubleshooting printing problems that users report when their print jobs don't come out on the printers. Describe some of the questions that you could routinely ask these users to help discover the problems they are having. As you begin this job, what problems would you anticipate having with numerous new users printing on a large computer lab network?

2. You discover over time that the software (print server) side of things is going fairly smoothly, but the printers themselves seem to be breaking down a lot under the heavy use. Assuming you can't charge the students for computer or printer usage, how could you use the features of Linux printing to help justify to your supervisor the expense of upgrading the printing equipment?

3. You occasionally discover a very large print job (over 300 pages) that appears to have been left on the printer when you finish your shift in the computer lab. But when you return the next day, someone has always returned to pick up the unclaimed papers. The print accounting reports don't seem to show any single user in the lab printing a large number of pages. You are suspicious that someone in another department of the university is sending large print jobs to the lab printers and picking them up later. Describe some of the steps you could take in the Linux printing configuration to watch for or prevent this unauthorized printing.

14

BACKING UP SYSTEM DATA

After reading this chapter and completing the exercises, you will be able to:

♦ Understand the issues surrounding backups and back-up strategies

♦ Discuss hardware and software issues related to backing up Linux data, such as back-up devices and storage media choices

♦ Use popular back-up utilities such as `tar`, `cpio`, and graphical back-up utilities

In the previous chapter you learned about managing the printing services on Linux. You learned how to create a printer configuration file and how to manage print queues using command-line or graphical utilities. You also learned how to print to remote print servers and to printers attached to computers running other operating systems.

In this chapter you will learn about backing up data stored on a Linux system. You will learn how to plan effective back-up strategies for different types of systems and environments. You will also learn about the hardware components, back-up media, and software utilities available to help you create and manage backups of your data.

BACK-UP STRATEGIES

As you learned in Chapter 9, no matter how many precautions you take, all computers are subject to failure. Thus, making backups of essential files is a form of insurance. In its simplest form, a **backup** is nothing but a copy of data on a computer system. However, backing up thousands of files owned by dozens or hundreds of users is not a simple process. But because the time and equipment needed to make backups are minimal compared with the costs associated with lost data, nearly all organizations regularly back up the files on their computer systems according to an established back-up plan. A **back-up plan** is a written document that outlines when, how, and, perhaps, why various files and file systems will be backed up, stored, and—when necessary—restored. As you might guess, implementing the back-up plan normally falls to the system administrator.

Among other things, the back-up plan should specify the type of back-up media to be used. The term **back-up media** refers to the device that stores the backed-up data, such as a tape cartridge (the most common format), writeable CD, or even a floppy disk. The back-up plan should also specify how lost data should be restored. The term **restore** refers to the process of copying data from a back-up location (for example, a tape cartridge) onto the file system where that data is normally used, and from which it was unintentionally lost.

Because of the complexities involved, developing a back-up strategy that works well in any organization is an ongoing process. As a system administrator, you can expect to work with numerous existing and new computer systems, a variety of applications and data storage needs, and computer users whose preferences and actions are rarely predictable. The following sections address some of the questions that you should consider when formulating a back-up plan.

Asking Initial Questions

Some of the initial questions that you'll want to consider as you formulate a back-up plan include the following:

- *What files should be backed up?* You might initially think that everything on the system needs to be backed up. Although that's an admirable goal, time and cost restrictions might make it impractical. You can evaluate various parts of your system to determine what data is easily restored from CD, such as the operating system or an application. If you are short on resources, these items can be re-created (and then reconfigured) from their original sources rather than from a backup that you create.

- *Who will back up files?* As mentioned previously, this normally falls to the system administrator. You may, however, decide that users on a networked system have some responsibility. Perhaps users should be informed that only data placed in a certain directory area will be backed up each night. Or a system administrator may share the responsibility for backups with a colleague, either to reduce the work burden on one person or to make backups more accessible in case they are needed for restoring data.

- *Where are files located?* You probably know offhand where most of the different types of data are located on your Linux system. A more thorough approach can help you see which specific directories on the system are being actively used, which contain data that is easily reconstructed, and which hold temporary files that don't warrant the effort of a regular backup. These are just three examples of the categories you might assign to parts of your system as you review the various file systems and devices that store data.

- *How should backups be performed?* The answer to this question may be determined by the equipment you purchase, as well as by how your organization operates its computer systems. Many system administrators must back up data during non-work hours. This process can be automated in most cases using a cron job (see Chapter 12). You might also want certain events to trigger a regular backup, or a different type of backup than would normally occur. For example, you might want to back up the entire system before installing new hardware devices such as SCSI adapters.

- *Must you be able to restore data within a specific period of time?* When a problem occurs (and it will), several factors affect how rapidly you can restore lost data to the system. These factors include the size and location of the lost files and the media format on which the back-up data was stored. Your backup plan should reflect the importance of timing in your organization. In some organizations, the ability to restore lost data immediately is essential. In others, speed may not be quite as critical.

A well-designed back-up plan will make it easy and convenient for you to regularly back up system data and restore files. Ideally, your back-up plan should prevent the headaches associated with having to locate files and figure out how to reconstruct damaged or lost data.

Determining the Value of Data

As with creating redundant systems, your back-up strategy should be based at least partially on the value of the data that you are backing up. The more expensive data is to create, acquire, or refine, the more you should spend to protect its integrity. Some data may only be valuable to one person in an organization, but if that person's time is required to re-create any data that is lost, the data still has value to the entire organization.

As an example, a study of the value of data held by an organization might determine that a given set of files required 4,000 hours of work by the employees of the firm to create. A different estimate might state that the data could be re-created given current experience and facts in about 2,000 hours. If the average wage of the employees involved in the project is approximately $40 per hour, the data would have a value of $80,000. But the study doesn't end there.

The estimate of 2,000 hours—about one work-year—is based on an experienced employee re-creating the data. If that well-trained employee spends time re-creating lost data, what current work will he or she not be able to do? This is called the opportunity cost. The employee might forgo a project worth many times $80,000 in order to re-create the lost data. Opportunity cost extends even further. How was the data that was lost going to be used? Was it part of a multimillion dollar advertising campaign? Or perhaps a financial merger? A great deal of money may be lost because the data is unavailable when needed. Even if $80,000 can be invested to re-create it, the moment of opportunity when the data was needed may be past.

14

 TIP This discussion doesn't address the anger or low morale of an employee who must re-create a project that was partially or completely finished. These are also key factors in any organization.

The following list summarizes questions to ask when determining the value of data:

- How many hours of effort were spent creating the data?

- How many hours of effort would be required to re-create the data?

- How much inherent value does the data contain for the operation of the organization?

- Is the data irreplaceable?
- Is the data time critical to a current project?

These considerations are similar to those raised in the discussion of hardware redundancy and fault tolerance in Chapter 9. The decisions you make as a system administrator are also similar to those you might make when evaluating your system's hardware: if data is worth millions of dollars to your organization, don't hesitate to spend $50,000 to $100,000 to protect that data. By answering the questions in the preceding list, you may be able to convince company officers or supervisors that the expense is warranted. With the right hardware and software tools, you'll be well prepared to secure the information that you safeguard as a system administrator.

Determining When to Back Up Data

Once you have created an initial backup or archive of important data, the question of how often to refresh the backup arises. Having at least one backup of data is better than having none at all, but data changes frequently in most organizations. Continually backing up the latest information stored on the system is a critical part of most system administrators' jobs.

The question of when to back up data is related to how valuable the data is to an organization. You need to start by asking, "How often does the data change?" Another good question to ask is this: "Do changes to the data affect the value of the data?"

The answers to these questions vary, depending on which part of your Linux system you are evaluating. The operating system itself probably changes very little after your initial configuration efforts. Applications installed on the system are also unlikely to change regularly. By contrast, user data, log files, and other items change rapidly and are normally the focus of back-up efforts. This data constitutes the daily work of others within your organization. By maintaining regular backups, no one is ever likely to lose more than a few hours worth of work, even if the entire system crashes or a hard disk is destroyed.

Several back-up strategies are commonly used. You can select a strategy based on how often data on your system changes and how valuable or critical each incremental piece of data is. The following discussion describes a widely used back-up strategy for Linux.

A Linux Back-up Strategy

Various strategies have evolved among Linux users to balance the need for a complete backup of data at all times with the need for convenience in creating and maintaining backups. The method described here is accepted as standard for most Linux and UNIX systems. You can adjust the time frame according to how often the data on your system changes.

Using Back-up Levels

To understand this back-up method, you need to understand the concept of a back-up level. A **back-up level** defines how much data is to be backed up in comparison with another back-up level. A back-up operation at a given back-up level copies all of the data that has changed since the last backup of the previous level. For example, a backup at level 1 stores all files that have changed since the last level 0 backup; a backup at level 2 stores all files that have changed since the last level 1 backup. A standard system might operate with three levels, as described here:

- Level 0 is a full backup. Everything on the system is backed up. Suppose for this example that a level 0 backup is performed on the first of every month.

- A level 1 backup is done once per week. Every file that has been modified since the last level 0 backup (on the first of the month) is included in the level 1 backup. This is referred to as an incremental backup.

- A level 2 backup is done each day. Every file that has been modified since the first of the week (the last level 1 backup) is included in the level 2 backup. Like a level 1 backup, this is considered an incremental backup.

Figure 14-1 illustrates the three-level backup just described.

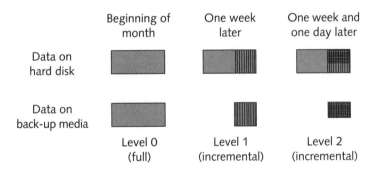

Figure 14-1   Back-up levels

The times associated with back-up levels are arbitrary, though a level 0 backup is normally a full backup in which every file is backed up. Beyond that, you can assign any time frame that you choose to each level; the point is simply that each level records all the changes since a backup of a previous level.

The advantage to using back-up levels is that you can back up data frequently—meaning very little work is lost if a system fails—but you don't have to back up the *entire system* each time you do a backup.

Restoring a File from a Three-Level Backup

Now consider how a system administrator would restore a file that a user had deleted and needed help recovering. The user can't recall when the file was last modified, but it was "recently." The system administrator follows these steps to locate the file:

1. Check the most recent level 2 backup. If the file is there, it was changed in the last day. This backup probably doesn't include very many files compared to the size of the entire system, so it's easy to search for a file. If the file isn't there, then it wasn't modified in the last 24 hours, so proceed to Step 2.

2. Check the most recent level 1 backup. If the file is there, it was changed sometime after the first of the week, but not in the last 24 hours. This backup contains more files, so it takes a little longer to search. If the file is not found, proceed to Step 3.

3. Check the most recent level 0 backup. The file will always be located on this backup because a full backup includes every file on the system. But searching through this backup may be time consuming because it is fairly large.

> **TIP**   Back-up media such as tape drives and optical disks always have directories of their contents to help you locate files as rapidly as possible, but a tape cartridge must be rewound to the place where the file is stored. As a result, restoring a single file from a tape cartridge can still be time consuming.

You may wonder why you shouldn't start searching for the file in the level 0 backup. You should always start with the most recent backup in order to find the most recent version of a file. If the file had been altered since the first of the month, the most recent copy of the file will not be on the level 0 backup. Hence you should start with the most recent backup (level 2) to see if the file is located there.

Advantages to the three-level back-up method include:

- Creating the level 2 daily backups requires little of the system administrator's time because few files are altered on any given day.

- No user will ever lose more than a single day's work because the changes in the file system from each day are recorded in a level 2 backup.

- Files that rarely change are still backed up and available, but don't require daily maintenance by the system administrator.

Some back-up utilities explicitly use the term back-up levels to refer to how data is backed up and how back-up media are tracked. The concept can be applied to any utility, however. For the system to work well, you need to keep careful records and label back-up media clearly.

In the event that an entire system must be restored using a set of back-up media that have been prepared using the three-level method, a system administrator would follow this procedure:

1. Restore everything from the latest level 0 backup.

2. Restore everything from the latest level 1 backup.

3. Restore everything from the latest level 2 backup.

Figure 14-2 illustrates how this procedure will result in all of the latest information being included in the restored file system. (Compare the back-up levels pictured in Figure 14-1 to the restore operation pictured in Figure 14-2.)

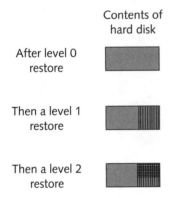

Figure 14-2   Restoring data from a set of back-up media with levels 0, 1, and 2

Managing and Storing Back-up Media

As you create a back-up plan that specifies back-up levels and times appropriate to your needs, you must determine how many back-up media you will need (disks, tapes, cartridges) for each level. That is, a level 0 full backup may require five tape cartridges, but a typical level 2 backup requires only a single cartridge (because relatively few files are modified each day). As an example, the three-level backup described previously might include the following:

- Three months of level 0 backups; each requiring 5 tape cartridges, for a total of 15.

- Five weeks of level 1 backups (some months have five weeks); each requiring 3 tape cartridges, for a total of 15.

- Five days of level 2 backups (you might need seven days if your organization runs seven days per week); each requiring 1 tape cartridge, for a total of 5.

14

You would therefore need a total of 35 tape cartridges. Figure 14-3 illustrates this arrangement. The importance of carefully labeling each tape cartridge cannot be overstated. If you can't identify which back-up media is the most recent of any given level, much of your back-up efforts will be useless when a serious problem arises.

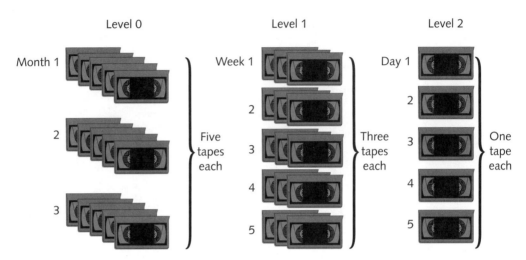

Figure 14-3   Multiple tapes used for a three-level back-up plan

Most organizations would store one set of the monthly (level 0) back-up media and perhaps the most recent weekly (level 1) back-up media off-site. The strategy for off-site storage depends on how critical data is and how often someone wants to take the responsibility of carrying the back-up media to the chosen secure location (such as a bank vault).

 TIP   Most back-up media are designed to be used repeatedly, like a floppy disk. For example, a rewriteable CD can be used about 1000 times, according to the manufacturer. But you should nevertheless plan on a scheduled life for back-up media, so that you avoid problems with deteriorating, outdated products.

Using the plan just outlined, you could reuse the same set of level 1 weekly tape cartridges each month, starting with the oldest one. The same applies to the level 2 tape cartridges. For example, on any Wednesday afternoon, you should have five level 2 tape cartridges containing the following:

- Last Wednesday's backup, which you will overwrite this evening with new data

- Last Thursday's backup, which you will overwrite tomorrow evening with new data

- Last Friday's backup

- Monday's backup (from two days ago)

- Tuesday's backup (from last night)

In addition to being fairly easy to manage, this system provides data redundancy. If you have a problem and need to restore a file on this particular Wednesday, you first check the Tuesday backup that you made last night. If a problem occurs with that tape cartridge, you can also check Monday morning's level 1 backup, Monday evening's level 2 backup, or even last Friday's backup. A user may lose more work if you cannot use the most recent backup, but the user is unlikely to lose everything, because many copies of the file exist, created at different times.

Backing Up the Root File System

The root file system requires special attention in your back-up plan because it contains the tools that you normally use to restore damaged data, such as a deleted file or data from a corrupted hard disk partition. You must therefore think about how to respond if the root file system is damaged, either by a hard disk failure or by corrupted configuration files that prevent you from booting the Linux operating system kernel.

Chapter 9 described how to create a rescue floppy or a boot floppy. That disk, which you can use to boot the system in an emergency, should contain the files necessary to restore the contents of the root file system from your back-up device. These files might include:

- The kernel modules needed to access the back-up device (such as SCSI modules)
- Other kernel modules needed to access the device where the root file system is stored
- Configuration files needed to set up access to the back-up device
- Information such as file indexes that are needed to locate the correct data and restore it from back-up media

As you prepare a back-up plan, you'll want to consider the hardware and software that you'll use to implement that plan. The next part of the chapter describes some key issues you face in making hardware and software choices.

14

HARDWARE AND SOFTWARE ISSUES

Once you have determined why, when, and how you want to back up your Linux system, you must determine the best tools to use to get the job done. Linux includes all the necessary software utilities for many back-up tasks. You can also purchase commercial back-up software. Both of these options are described later in this chapter.

Many different hardware devices are available for backing up data. The next few sections provide a review of the different options available to you.

Choosing Back-up Media

The size of hard disks in standard PCs is growing very rapidly. Whereas a 500 MB hard disk was considered huge just a couple of years ago, hard disks with 50 GB—100 times that amount—are now available for well under $1000. Storage space is often measured according to its cost per megabyte. For example, if a 16 GB hard disk costs $400, the cost per megabyte is about 2.5 cents. Similarly, if a tape cartridge used for backing up a system costs $79 and holds 20 GB, the cost per megabyte is 0.38 cents per megabyte.

When you back up your data, you will normally have multiple copies of the data that was backed up at different times. Back-up media such as tape cartridges generally cost much less than a hard disk or other similar device, but you must purchase multiple tape cartridges to back up the system.

Unfortunately, back-up devices have not kept pace with the growth in capacity of hard disks, though many different formats and devices are available for system backups, as described here. The following paragraphs review the different back-up media (and corresponding devices) that you might consider for backing up your Linux system.

Magnetic Media

Several types of magnetic media are occasionally used for specialized back-up needs.

- *Floppy disks:* although you might be surprised to see this item listed, floppy disks are a great way to back up small, sensitive pieces of information. For example, a boot disk, a rescue disk, a firewall or other server configuration, and other similar data can easily be copied to a floppy disk. The disk is inexpensive, easily transported, and easily stored. Just be certain to label the disk and move the write-protection tab over so you don't erase the floppy disk. An important disadvantage of floppy disks is that they are fragile. You should maintain multiple floppy disk copies of any critical data and check the integrity of the disks regularly.

- *RAID hard disks:* most of the data that you want to back up is already on a hard disk. It doesn't make sense to rely on long-term data storage located on another hard disk—even a RAID array—if the same vulnerabilities apply to that device as to your main hard disk. On the other hand, storing a back-up copy of crucial data from several locations on a centralized RAID array is a useful way to maintain an online backup—that is, a backup of the data that is still available if one of the hard disks becomes unavailable. In general, however, don't plan your back-up strategy around this sort of thing. Instead, look to removable devices such as tapes and removable cartridges.

- *Removable media:* many types of specialized cartridge storage devices are now available. These include Syquest cartridges, Floptical and similar devices that store a large amount of data on a small disk similar in size to a floppy disk, and various products such as the Zip and Jaz cartridges from Iomega. The data capacity of these cartridges continues to rise. The latest Jaz cartridges hold 2 GB each.

Removable media, the last item in the preceding list, have several advantages, including the following:

- Random, immediate access to any point on the media, similar to a hard disk

- The ability to expand storage by purchasing additional cartridges

- Relatively easy access to the back-up device—most are treated like a standard hard disk, formatted with the `ext2` file system, and mounted normally.

Removable media also have disadvantages, such as:

- High cost per megabyte of storage

- Proprietary formats (compared to most tape backups), which may mean difficulty obtaining new cartridges in the future and lack of support from other vendors

Optical Media

Optical media used by devices such as writeable CD drives and DVD drives are an attractive back-up choice. Advantages of optical media include:

- Their large storage capacity is sufficient for many needs.

- Storage media are very low cost.

- Storage media are widely available.

- Optical media are easily exchanged with vendors, customers, or other organizations.

Standard CDs, in particular, are a valuable method of exchanging large amounts of data with suppliers and also of easily creating data archives. Because a single writeable CD costs less than a dollar, it is cost effective to back up key data files regularly on a CD and to have a set of back-up CDs stored with snapshots at various times. Rewriteable CDs, which you can update in the same way that you update data on a hard disk, cost a little more but provide more flexibility. The capacity of a CD is only about 640 MB. That's not much compared with the data stored on an entire hard disk, but it's often sufficient for backing up an entire project directory, graphics archive, programming project, or operating system.

DVD drives, which are increasingly popular for watching movies on a computer, also come in a writeable format called DVD-RAM. A DVD-RAM cartridge (costing under $50) holds about 5.2 GB of data. Drives are inexpensive as well. For data sets too large for writeable CDs, the low cost and wide use of DVD make it an attractive choice.

14

Tape Cartridges

Tape drives are the workhorses of most computer back-up efforts. Tape drives are fairly inexpensive, as is the media (tape cartridges). Many formats are available, but in general, data capacities have kept pace with that of hard disks. Thus you can purchase a tape drive that will record 8, 40, or even 100 GB on a single tape cartridge. All such cartridges are priced under $100, with the smaller capacities costing far less. If you need to back up large amounts of data, such as hundreds or thousands of gigabytes, you should consider special tape cartridge jukeboxes or high-end digital tape formats available from major device manufacturers such as IBM and Hewlett-Packard. The term **jukebox** refers to a back-up device that holds multiple back-up media (such as multiple tape cartridges or writeable CDs) and can switch between them without assistance from a system administrator.

Tape drives are available in a variety of formats, and new formats seem to appear each year as manufacturers rush to keep up with growing capacities and speedier computers. Manufacturers of the latest tape drives claim storage capacities of up to 200 GB on a single tape cartridge; others claim data transfer rates in excess of 200 MB per minute. Explaining the features of a diversity of tape formats is beyond the scope of this book, but the information that follows provides enough basic details to familiarize you with the formats you're likely to see.

Keep in mind that tape cartridges can accommodate different methods for storing data, depending on the tape drive you use. This is similar to a regular 3.5-inch floppy disk, which can be formatted with either an MS-DOS, Macintosh, or Linux file system.

When reviewing the great number of tape devices on the market, you may feel overwhelmed by the alphabet soup of formats, companies, and product names. The following list describes some major tape cartridge device types and data formats.

- Digital Linear Tape (DLT) is a half-inch-wide tape inside a cartridge. The tapes store up to about 40 GB and are considered highly reliable. Quantum is considered the leader in DLT technology, but many others, such as StorageTek, also use DLT.

- Linear Tape-Open (LTO) is an open tape standard used by Hewlett-Packard, IBM, and Seagate (a prominent hard disk manufacturer). Many companies are currently planning devices based on this high-capacity format.

- Helical-scan tape drives write data onto a thin tape—either 4mm or 8mm. This storage format is the same method used by videotapes for recording movies. Figure 14-4 illustrates how a helical-scan device stores information by writing short, angled strips of data on the tape. Helical-scan tapes (usually the 8mm size) are used in several newer tape formats as described below.

- Advanced Intelligent Tape (AIT) is a format developed by Sony. Each AIT cartridge contains a memory chip that is used to increase the efficiency of data access. Sony plans to release a revised version of AIT every two years, with a doubled storage capacity and data transfer rate in each new version. AIT-3 tapes are expected to hold 100 GB and transfer data at about 720 MB per minute. (AIT-3 devices are not available at the time of writing.)

- VXA is a technology developed by the Ecrix company. The VXA format attempts to overcome some of the technical limitations that most other standard formats face. For example, VXA avoids stopping and starting the tape drive while waiting for the computer to send more data by using a variable speed tape drive and organizing data into packets rather than a single stream, as most formats use.

- Travan tape drives are widely used and are manufactured by many different companies. They do not have high capacities—10 to 20 GB is standard—but they have a longer history of reliability than many of the newer formats. Travan uses the QIC tape cartridge format.

Data tape

Stripes of information
written to tape

Spinning
read/write mechanism

Figure 14-4   Using the helical-scan method to write data on a 4mm or 8mm tape

After reviewing the available formats, media, and devices in this section, you can use the information in the next section to help you determine what factors to consider when choosing a back-up device.

Comparing Devices

Deciding among all of the available back-up devices and technologies is challenging. System administrators who are creating a new system from scratch and need to store large amounts of data may be able to focus on the latest technology for high-capacity, high-speed tape drives. Other system administrators may be more concerned with sharing copies of data between several existing computers using a CD drive, and so may opt for a low-cost CD recorder. Still other administrators may be forced to purchase new devices that use older technologies simply to keep costs low or maintain compatibility with existing systems, even though this means much more work to maintain numerous back-up media. These are just three examples of the varying requirements that have led manufacturers to develop so many different devices and formats.

In most cases, the cost of the back-up device and the back-up media is an issue, at least peripherally. Although you should keep in mind the discussion at the beginning of this chapter regarding the value of an organization's data, managers who control budgets will still expect you to be as frugal and wise as possible with an organization's money. The cost of the various back-up device options is affected by several factors, including the following:

- *What interface is used to connect the device to the computer?* The interface is usually SCSI (fast and expensive), IDE (common and inexpensive, but slower), or parallel port (great for special applications and inexpensive, but quite slow compared to IDE and SCSI).

- *How recent is the format?* The more recently developed formats are more expensive. They generally hold more data, however.

- *How much data can one disk or cartridge hold?* The same media may be able to hold slightly different amounts of data when used in different devices. The difference in storage is unlikely to be more than 20%, however.

14

- *Is the device from a name-brand manufacturer?* As with everything else in the computer industry, buying a product from a company such as IBM or Hewlett-Packard generally costs more than buying from a start-up or relatively unknown company. The start-up company may support newer technologies, however, and may actually have better products. New companies often must compete on price until their quality or technology is recognized.

- *Does the device have special features?* The most common of these is an automounting or jukebox feature, which allows you to load a number of disks or cartridges so that the device can create a multivolume archive without user intervention. These devices are always much more expensive than a device supporting a single manually inserted disk or cartridge. They are also more subject to breakdown because of the additional mechanisms required to automate media handling.

Among all the devices available, your decision may be guided by many things. The following list presents a summary of factors that you should consider in selecting a device to fulfill your back-up strategy. This list is not exhaustive, but it should give you a good start at considering which device will be best for your needs, and also understanding why so many different devices are available in the market.

- *How much does the hardware device cost to acquire?* A quick survey on a major hardware supplier site such as *www.warehouse.com* will show you prices ranging from $150 for a used 2 GB Iomega Jaz drive to more than $10,000 for a high-capacity, name-brand jukebox tape cartridge system.

- *How rapidly does data transfer from the computer system to the back-up media?* This is less important if you intend to back up using a scheduled cron job in the middle of the night. It may suddenly become important again if you need to restore a large amount of data with many people waiting while you do it. Data transfer rates are usually measured in megabytes per minute (MB/min). For example, a 14 GB tape drive might advertise a data transfer rate of 78 MB/min, meaning that an entire 14 GB tape could be filled in about three hours. Faster transfer rates generally cost more, but the data transfer rate that you actually achieve is based on many factors, such as the speed of your CPU, the quality of your system board components, and the type of interface used to connect to the back-up device.

- *Is data randomly accessible?* In other words, is it easy to back up a single file or set of files without restoring or going through an entire archive set?

- *Can the device you choose perform very large backups using an autoloader or jukebox mechanism?* If it can't, you may always need to be present during system backups to switch media when one is full.

- *How much does media for the device cost?* You can expect media costs to be greater in the long term than the hardware cost if you use a device for several years. Determine the media costs based on your planned back-up strategy, with replacement media purchased regularly as recommended by the manufacturer to avoid storage errors.

■ *Does the organization already own some back-up hardware?* Is the cost savings for not purchasing new hardware worth using the existing hardware if it relies on older or obsolete technologies? When dealing with this issue, you will often hear the term legacy systems. **Legacy systems** are systems that an organization already owns. Working with existing systems is a common concern when organizations plan new computer hardware or software acquisitions.

■ *How recent is the technology of the device?* Some older devices are still very viable and stable, but may be difficult to locate media for. If you have a nine-track tape reel in your office, you may have to work with a special service bureau to read the tape because these devices are rarely used now. On the other hand, very new technologies may not have proven themselves cost effective or technologically sound. For example, some tape formats had problems when first released to the public because magnetic material flaked off of the storage tapes.

■ *Does the device rely on an industry standard that many vendors support, or is it specific to one vendor?* If the device is only supplied by one vendor, can you rely on that vendor to be around for a while, or could that vendor change formats or discontinue a product, leaving you with outdated products or the prospect of retooling your back-up plans?

■ *How long is the media life?* This may not be a big issue if you are working with daily backups, but most organizations maintain some sort of archival backup of company financial records, personnel records, computer program source code, and other electronic assets. The media that these assets are stored on should last long enough so that you are not required to make an updated copy of massive amounts of data every two years. Table 14-1 shows the anticipated life of some key materials. (Paper and microfilm are included in the table for comparison, not because you would use them as back-up media.) Note that the industry's experience with these technologies does not extend past their supposed useful life. We *know* that paper can last 500 years. No one really knows if CDs can last 30 years, because they haven't existed that long.

14

Table 14-1 Comparison of Media Life

Media	Approximate useful life (before data loss potentially occurs)
Archive-quality acid-free paper	500 years
Microfilm	100 years
CD-ROM and similar optical media	5–30 years, depending on media quality
Hard disks and similar magnetic media	10–20 years, depending on media quality
Reel-to-reel data tapes	15–25 years, depending on media quality
Tape cartridges (QIC, 4mm, 8mm, etc.)	5–10 years, depending on media quality
3.5 inch disks	2–5 years

- *How robust is the media?* Can they be dropped? Can they handle the environmental conditions that are part of your working area (heat, humidity, dust)? Most media formats are quite robust, but if you work in a factory or outdoor environment, you should consider these factors.

- *Is the media easily transportable (if this is a requirement of your organization)?* Most system administrators keep the majority of back-up media near the systems that contain the original data. This makes it convenient to restore data if a problem occurs. But it's also a good idea to take at least one copy to another location in case a fire or other problem destroys the back-up media located nearby. Many organizations have a strict policy about regularly taking a data backup to a bank vault or other secure off-site location.

- *Do you need to exchange data with other organizations, or will you rely on service bureaus to help you process or recover data from archive media?* In this case you should consult several service bureaus and select a media format and device that are widely available.

- *How reliable is the hardware device?* An unreliable or faulty back-up device can corrupt back-up media so that no device can read them. Even if a hardware problem doesn't corrupt media, a breakdown can interrupt your scheduled back-up times or delay restoring data when a problem occurs.

Once you have selected a back-up device and media format, you are almost ready to implement your back-up plan. But a few additional issues still remain to be resolved. These are discussed in the next section.

Verification, Permissions, and Other Issues

As the saying goes, "Trust everyone, but lock your doors." The equivalent tactic when backing up your system is to verify your backups on a regular basis. Verifying a backup is sometimes done as part of a back-up utility, as described later in this chapter, but you can always perform your own verification using steps such as these:

1. Pick a back-up tape or disk, either at random or according to a reasonable plan. For example, you might decide to test a randomly chosen level 1 back-up tape once per week.

2. Check the file listing on the tape by querying for the contents of the back-up media. (This would be equivalent to using the `ls` command to see the contents of the back-up media. With some media you can actually use the `ls` command, with others you'll need to use a back-up utility.)

3. Restore a randomly selected file to the `/tmp` directory of your Linux system, just to be certain that the data in the file can be retrieved and reassembled without errors. If possible, do this step immediately after backing up data (on your regular schedule), and then compare the file you restored with the original file that you backed up to see that the size and contents match.

When you back up data, exactly what information is backed up? Does the backup include the contents of each file? What about the owner and file permissions associated with each file? Many times a system administrator will have problems after restoring a large number of files because the owner and group assigned to files and directories, or the file and directory permissions, are not stored as part of the backup. The consequences of this can range from no one being able to access his or her data once it is restored after a system shutdown, to everyone being able to access everyone else's data on the system, including the system configuration files. You'll have to decide which is worse in your organization.

Back-up utilities normally include options to maintain or ignore file ownership and permissions. Normally you will want to maintain this information and check it carefully when you verify your backups by restoring selected files.

Another issue related to how you choose to use back-up utilities involves the compression feature that most utilities provide. Tape drives typically list a standard capacity and a compressed capacity; back-up commands include options to compress data as it's being archived. Should you use these features? Probably so, but you should also be aware of their limitations. By definition, when you compress data you remove the redundancy from it. That is, compressed data can be re-created in its original form by adding back the redundant information using an established set of rules.

To understand compression better, consider this example. When you see the words "hllo my nm is Nchlas," you can probably understand their meaning even though part of the information is missing. The missing information is redundant—it's not needed for you to understand the sentence. You can also use standard rules (English grammar and spelling) to reconstruct the original sentence: "Hello my name is Nicholas."

The danger with using compression is that with all the redundancy removed from a set of information, all of the information and rules are needed in order to reconstruct the data. For example, if you don't speak English well, English words with missing letters are difficult to decipher. In the same way, if even a small part of some compressed data is lost, the original cannot be easily reconstructed. By leaving the redundancy in the data that you back up, you might make it easier to fix any problems that occur on back-up media.

All modern back-up media formats are highly reliable, but when age, environmental factors like heat and dust, and regular wear and tear are working against the data you have carefully saved, you should consider whether compression is always necessary.

USING BACK-UP UTILITIES

Many utilities are available to back up data from a Linux system in a secure and organized way. The most widely used of these utilities are the old UNIX standbys `tar` and `cpio`. Some of the other utilities use these programs in the background while they present a graphical interface to make configuration and selection of back-up options easier. Popular commercial back-up utilities include features such as tracking tapes for you, keeping online indexes of each backup that you have performed, and automating schedules for unattended backup (similar to the options provided by the `crontab` command).

The following sections outline basic information about using these back-up utilities. Although a complete discussion of tar, cpio, and commercial tools is not presented here, you should understand enough to use these tools for basic backups and to locate more exhaustive information when needed.

Using tar and cpio

The name **tar** stands for *tape archive*; it is the oldest of the back-up tools for UNIX. The **cpio** command (for *copy in and out*) is newer and includes additional features compared to tar. cpio also reads tar-formatted files. Both tar and cpio can create archive files, such as the .tgz format files that you may have seen when downloading Linux programs from Internet sites. But tar and cpio can also create an archive directly on a tape cartridge or other back-up device without first creating a file on your hard disk.

 In order to use a tape drive or other back-up device, you must first install and configure that device using the information presented in previous chapters. For example, see Chapters 2, 3, and 4 regarding the installation of Linux and the use of kernel modules for adding device support.

The tar and cpio commands operate differently. With the tar command you must specify files to be included in a back-up archive on the command line. By contrast, cpio always looks in the STDIN channel for the filenames to include in an archive. The tar command writes data to a filename or device that you provide; the cpio command always writes data back to STDOUT. To compare these two methods of operation, consider the following two examples for creating a full backup of the /home directory. You can assume for this example that the device /dev/tape is configured as a tape drive. (Notice that you refer directly to a tape drive device; you do not mount it first.)

```
tar cf /dev/tape /home
```

This command uses the c option of tar to create a new archive. The f option (for *filename*) followed by the device name indicates the location where the archived data will be stored. The last parameter, /home, indicates which files will be archived. Because the parameter is a directory name, tar will include all files located within that directory. A cpio command equivalent to the above tar command would be:

```
find /home -print | cpio -o > /dev/tape
```

To use cpio, you must use the **find** command to generate a list of files (one filename per line) for cpio to refer to. The **find** command with the **-print** option generates this list. Those filenames are sent to cpio using a pipe symbol because cpio reads the filenames in from STDIN. The > redirection operator then sends the archived files to the device /dev/tape. The **-o** option on cpio indicates that the archive is being output—that is, that data is being written out. A simpler example of cpio could archive the contents of a single directory to a local file using the **ls** command to generate the list of files to archive:

```
ls | cpio -o /tmp/archive.cpio
```

TIP You might have noticed that `tar` options do not normally include a preceding hyphen; those of the `cpio` command do.

The **v** option is normally added to both `tar` and `cpio` so that the output of the command is *verbose*, meaning that the command prints details of what it is doing to the screen. With that option added, the last example would look like this:

```
ls | cpio -ov /tmp/archive.cpio
```

Extracting files using `tar` or `cpio` is a similar operation, but using different options. If you had created an archive on a tape cartridge using `tar`, you could restore the contents of the tape into the current directory using this command (with the **x** option standing for *extract* and the **v** option included to see verbose messages about command progress):

```
tar xvf /dev/tape
```

The `cpio` command uses the **-i** option for input, again extracting the contents of the back-up media into the current directory. The **-d** option is also added here so that `cpio` will create subdirectories that existed in the data as required to re-create the original data organization. When using the `cpio` command with the **-i** option, `cpio` reads the STDIN channel to get the archived data; so the < redirection operator is used with the filename or archive device name.

```
cpio -idv < /dev/tape
```

These are very basic examples of `tar` and `cpio`. Each command supports dozens of options for features such as compressing files, preserving file attributes, controlling a tape device, setting timestamps on archived data, and many other things. You can review the manual and info pages for each command to learn more.

Both `tar` and `cpio` rely on other Linux commands to help you create an incremental or multilevel backup. The most useful of these is the `find` command. For example, the following `find` command will print a list of all files in the /home directory (and its subdirectories) that have been modified in the last day (note the **-mtime** parameter):

```
find /home -mtime 1 -print
```

By using the list of files generated by this command as the archive list for `cpio` or `tar`, you can easily create a level 2 backup, as described in the example earlier in the chapter, in which each level 2 backup contains all files modified since the last level 1 backup. (In this case, this command would be used on Tuesday; a different number of days would be used for each day of the week so that data changed since the beginning of the week was included in the backup.) The following two commands illustrate this:

```
find /home -mtime 1 -print | cpio -ov > /dev/tape
tar cf /dev/tape ` find /home -mtime 1 -print`
```

The options available with the `find` command make it a powerful companion to the `tar` and `cpio` commands. With `find` you can create a list of files owned by certain users, files modified or accessed within certain time limits, files with certain file permissions, or many other criteria.

14

Other Back-up Utilities

The `tar` and `cpio` commands can operate either with a tape drive or with back-up devices that rely on a standard `ext2`-style file system or standard mounting operation, such as a Jaz drive or a writeable CD drive. As mentioned earlier, tape drives are popular tools for back-ups, but they often require additional tools to manage tape indexes, tape rewinding and searching, and so forth. If you intend to use a tape drive, a freely available graphical utility worth reviewing is included with the KDE Desktop. The utility is called `kdat`, or the Tape Back-up Tool. It is included on the Utilities submenu under KDE menus in Red Hat Linux when using Gnome. Most other Linux distributions will include this program on the Utilities submenu of the KDE main menu.

The Tape Back-up Tool provides handy features like the following, all available from a graphical interface and menu structure (see Figure 14-5):

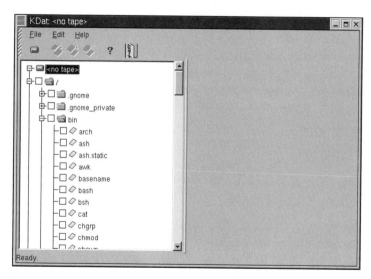

Figure 14-5   The Tape Back-up Tool in KDE

- Back up and restore files by dragging and dropping them between a list of the tape contents and a list of the hard disk contents
- Verify tape contents from the menu
- Manage mounting and unmounting of tape cartridges
- Create and maintain indexes of multiple tapes

- Set preferences from a graphical dialog box (see Figure 14-6)

- Format tapes

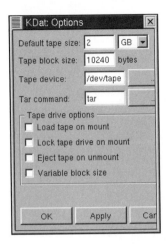

Figure 14-6   Setting preferences in the KDE Tape Back-up Tool

The Tape Back-up Tool is not intended to be compatible with all the high-end tape drives that you might consider using for your Linux servers, but it provides an easy-to-use method of tracking backups. It also makes it very simple to access data from a back-up tape.

Commercial Back-up Utilities

The complexities of maintaining large numbers of back-up media for large volumes of data led manufacturers long ago to create specialized software to help with the task. Fortunately, some of these tools have made their way to the Linux platform, and others appear to be forthcoming.

The best-known back-up utility with a strong following among Linux users is BRU, the back-up and restore utility, from Enhanced Software Technologies (see *www.bru.com*). The main

14

screen of BRU is shown in Figure 14-7, and the scheduling tool is shown in Figure 14-8. This product, which is included with some Linux distributions, provides features such as:

- Multiple levels of data verification

- Unattended operation with scheduled backups.

- Assistance in labeling large numbers of tapes, including backups that require multiple back-up media

- Support for numerous types of back-up devices

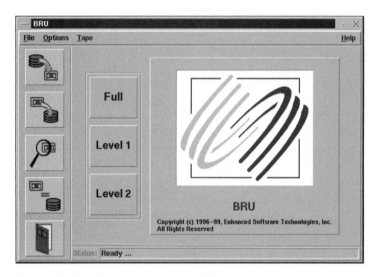

Figure 14-7   The main screen of BRU

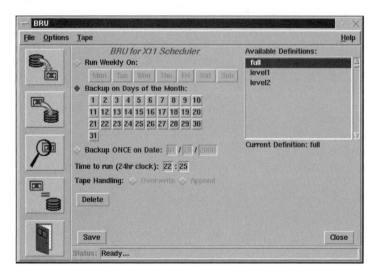

Figure 14-8   The scheduling tool in BRU

Another popular Linux back-up tool is Arkeia, from Knox Software (see *www.arkeia.com*). The Arkeia product is advertised as an enterprise network back-up solution and is considered a more full-featured tool than BRU. It is designed to control backup of multiple remote systems from a single location, saving or restoring data from anywhere on the network. Figure 14-9 shows a sample screen from the Arkeia program.

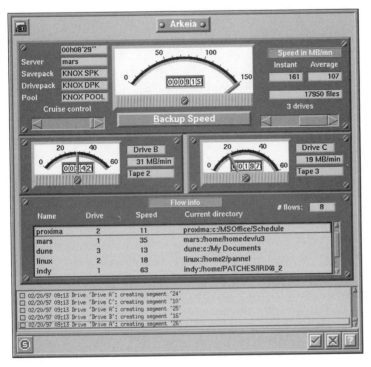

Figure 14-9   The Arkeia enterprise back-up program

Several additional back-up utilities are available for Linux or soon will be—some as part of high-end hardware platforms from companies such as MTI (*www.mti.com*) and Legato (*www.legato.com*).

CHAPTER SUMMARY

◻ Creating a back-up plan to safeguard an organization's data involves many considerations, such as the value of data, which devices and media formats are best suited to protecting that data, and how and when data should be backed up.

◻ Many types of back-up devices are available, with the most widely used being various tape cartridge formats. Optical devices have many advantages but lack the storage capacity of tape drives. Issues such as verifying data, compressing data, and restoring the root file system all must be considered when preparing the back-up plan.

❑ The `tar` and `cpio` utilities can be used to create simple backups, including incremental or multilevel backups. Numerous free and commercial graphical utilities are available to make back-up maintenance more convenient for a system administrator.

KEY TERMS

backup — A copy of data on a computer system.

back-up level — A definition of how much data is to be backed up in comparison with another back-up level. When performing a back-up operation at a given back-up level, all of the data that has changed since the last backup of the previous level is recorded.

back-up media — A device where data can be stored, such as a tape cartridge, writeable CD, or even a floppy disk.

back-up plan — A written document that outlines when, how, and, perhaps, why various files and file systems will be backed up, stored, and—when necessary—restored to prevent permanent data loss.

cpio — A Linux archiving program. The `cpio` command also reads archive files created by the `tar` command.

jukebox — A back-up device that holds multiple back-up media (such as multiple tape cartridges or writeable CDs) and that can switch between them without assistance from a system administrator.

legacy systems — Computer systems that an organization already owns. This term usually refers to systems that are no longer state of the art.

restore — To copy data from a back-up location (for example, a tape cartridge) onto the file system where that data is normally used, and from which it was unintentionally lost.

tar — A Linux archiving program.

REVIEW QUESTIONS

1. A back-up plan would normally not include the following:

   a. A list of tape drive prices

   b. Times when backups are performed

   c. The location of critical files on the system

   d. A recommended time to replace old tape cartridges with new ones

2. Explain how the speed with which files need to be restored affects a back-up plan.

3. It is important always to back up the operating system files as often as user data files. True or False?

4. Which of the following is part of measuring the value of data?

   a. The value of a project that cannot be done because data needed for the project was destroyed

   b. The cost of a complete set of back-up media to implement a three-level back-up plan

    c. The average data transfer rate of the chosen back-up device

    d. The average storage capacity of similar back-up devices

5. Name two parts of a Linux system that are likely to change daily.

6. Explain why a level 1 backup is called an incremental backup.

7. Using back-up levels has the advantage of:

    a. Reducing the time required to back up the entire file system

    b. Making it easier to recover a file that has not been changed in several weeks

    c. Allowing a system administrator to spend less time with backups but keep data backed up very frequently

    d. Causing all system backups to be available via a single file index

8. Using a standard three-level back-up plan with the time intervals described in the chapter text, a user would expect never to lose more than _____ worth of work.

    a. A week's

    b. A day's

    c. An hour's

    d. 20 MB

9. Explain in detail why a system administrator must use back-up media from three back-ups in order to completely restore a system that used three back-up levels.

10. Floppy disks are a useful back-up media in cases where:

    a. The cost of writeable CDs is prohibitive.

    b. Small amounts of critical data need to be backed up.

    c. Extreme durability is a key factor in the choice of media.

    d. A high data transfer rate is critical.

11. As a rule, tape cartridges can hold much more than optical media. True or False?

12. Describe two advantages of a back-up device with a jukebox feature.

13. Using a SCSI interface to connect a back-up device has the advantage of:

    a. Low cost

    b. Being proprietary (controlled by one company)

    c. High data transfer rates

    d. Limited availability

14. Name five factors to consider when selecting a back-up device and media type. Explain the circumstances in which each would be a controlling factor in the decision.

15. Name three tape cartridge formats and comment briefly on each.

16. You can expect a CD or other optical media to last about as long as high-quality microfilm. True or False?

14

17. The purpose of verifying your backups is to:

    a. Be certain that files are correctly recorded and can be restored

    b. Ascertain whether anyone has tampered with data contained in a backup

    c. Secure data from unauthorized use

    d. Compare data transfer rates among competing products

18. Explain how redundancy applies to compressed data.

19. The `tar` utility differs from the `cpio` utility in that:

    a. `cpio` always reads and writes to STDIN and STDOUT, while `tar` uses command-line parameters.

    b. `cpio` is a commercial utility, while `tar` is free software.

    c. `cpio` is widely used for Internet archive files, while `tar` is not.

    d. `cpio` is an older format that is not compatible with newer `tar` archives.

20. The _____ utility is a commercial back-up utility from Knox Software.

    a. BRU

    b. kdat

    c. Arkeia

    d. mke2fs

21. Describe why the `find` command is often used with `tar` or `cpio` for incremental backups.

22. The _____ option causes the `tar` command to extract files from an archive file or device.

    a. a

    b. x

    c. c

    d. e

23. Describe the special considerations that must be taken in order to restore the root file system of Linux after a hardware failure.

24. Name three removable media formats besides CD and tape cartridges.

25. In the long term, back-up media are likely to cost more than the back-up device used to access them. True or False?

HANDS-ON PROJECTS

Project 14-1

In this activity you learn more about the Arkeia and BRU commercial back-up utilities. To complete this activity you should have a Web browser with access to the Internet.

1. Start your Web browser and go to **www.arkeia.com**.

2. Review the Supported Platforms page. What comments would you make about this company's support of Linux? What advantages do you foresee if you choose to use this software in a large organization that uses many types of computers?

3. Review the Product Features pages. (There are many pages with different categories of features.) Locate three features that you understand, based on what you have learned in this chapter. (You will not understand all of the features after reading this chapter.)

4. Change to the section of the Web site containing white papers (technical reports). Select one of the reports and read it online.

5. If you are interested in experimenting with this software, download a copy.

6. Go to the BRU Web site at **www.bru.com**.

7. Explore the Products and Support pages. What comments do you have about the differences in the two products?

8. If you are interested in experimenting with this software, download a copy using the **Download** link.

Project 14-2

In this project you explore the Web site of a major computer sales company to learn more about what back-up devices are available. To complete this activity you should have a Web browser with access to the Internet.

1. Start your Web browser and go to **www.warehouse.com**.

2. Verify that the PC Products page is displayed, and then choose the **Drives/Storage** link.

3. Under the Removable Storage heading on the left side of the browser window, choose the **Tape** link.

4. Review the "best-selling" devices pictured. Do you recognize the formats from those mentioned in the chapter? Do you recognize some of the brand names of the manufacturers?

5. Under PC Tape Drives on the left side of the browser window, choose **Advanced Intelligent Tape (AIT)**.

6. Review the brands, capacities, and prices presented in this category of products.

7. Use the browser's Back button to return to the previous page.

8. Under PC Tape Drives on the left side of the browser window, choose **Travan**.

9. Review the brands, capacities, and prices presented in this category of products. How do they compare with the AIT devices?

14

10. In the banner at the top of the screen, click on the **Supplies** link.

11. Under the Supplies heading on the left side of the browser window, choose **Magnetic Media**.

12. Under the Magnetic Media heading on the left side of the browser window, choose **QIC 1/4" Tape**. (This is the tape used by Travan-format drives.) Note the prices of the tapes.

13. Use the Back button on your browser and explore the prices of other tape formats.

Project 14-3

In this activity you use the `tar` command to create a simple data archive file and then extract the contents of that file into another directory. To complete this activity you should have a working Linux system with `root` access.

1. Log in to Linux as `root`.

2. If you logged in using a graphical login window, open a command-line window.

3. Enter `cd /etc` to change to the `/etc` directory.

4. Enter `ls -l | less` and review the filenames and file permissions that you have to the various configuration files in this directory.

5. Create a `tar`-format archive of the configuration files in the `/etc` directory using the command `tar cf /tmp/testing.tar /etc`. Because you are including the pathname to both the `testing.tar` archive file and the directory containing the information you want to archive, you could execute this command from any location on the system.

6. Enter `tar cvf /tmp/testing2.tar /etc`, which is a similar command, this time including the v option. After you execute this command, you see a list of all the files in the `/etc` directory appear on the screen as each is added to the archive file.

7. Change to your home directory by entering the `cd` command.

8. Use the `ls` command to examine the contents of your home directory. Make certain you do not have a file called `lilo.conf` in your home directory. (You shouldn't, but if you do from a previous exercise, rename it to something else to complete this project.)

9. Enter `tar xvf /tmp/testing.tar etc/lilo.conf` to use the x option of the `tar` command to extract a single file from the `tar` archive that you just created. The file is placed in your current directory. Notice that because of the v option the filename is printed to the screen as it is extracted.

10. Use the `ls` command to review the contents of your home directory. Do you see a file called `lilo.conf`? Look for an item named `etc`.

11. Enter `cd etc` (without a forward slash) to change to the `etc` subdirectory of your home directory. The `tar` command created the subdirectory in which the requested file was located, starting with your current directory when you issued the command to extract the file from the archive.

12. Use the `ls` command again to see the `lilo.conf` file in the `etc` subdirectory of your home directory.

CASE PROJECTS

1. You are working for General Linux Corporation, a relatively new company focused on Linux products and services. The company has about 100 employees and has just become a publicly traded corporation. As news of the public stock offering becomes more widely known, the workload on all employees is increasing, but everyone is pleased with the opportunities provided by this step. The company's Web site is also extra busy as potential customers and investors review information about the company and its products. As a system administrator, do you think the three-level back-up strategy outlined in the chapter text is sufficient to protect the data stored on company servers? What changes would you make to that plan?

2. Given that the company considers itself an "Internet company," with many large Linux servers and all employees working with Internet resources each day, which of the back-up utilities you have reviewed would you consider using? Why?

3. What factors influence your decision about which devices and media to use for your back-up plan at General Linux? What factors do you consider in valuing the data that you are protecting via your back-up plan?

14

LINUX CERTIFICATION OBJECTIVES

This Appendix provides the most current information about the LPI and LCA certification objectives available at this writing. Both the LPI and LCA certification programs require you to take and pass multiple tests as explained in the Preface. To prepare for the LPI tests, you should master the material presented in this book and also in the companion book *Guide to Linux Networking and Security*. To prepare for the first two LCA tests, use this book; to prepare for the third and fourth LCA tests, use the companion book.

LINUX AND GNU EXAM OBJECTIVES

Items in bold text refer to Book II in this series, *Guide to Linux Networking and Security*. Although chapter numbers for material in that book are provided (for example, **Book II, 3**), they are subject to change. Please refer to the Table of Contents and Appendices of *Guide to Linux Networking and Security* for more detailed information. Complete exam objectives are available at *www.linuxcertification.com*.

Exam 1: Linux Installation and Configuration 3X01-101

Theory of Operation

Objective	Chapter
State the definition, origins, cost, and trade-off of free software.	1
Compare proprietary versus open source software licenses.	1
List the GNU public license (GPL) principles.	1
Describe how to sell free software.	1
Describe the structural components of Linux.	1, 4
Contrast multiuser multitasking versus single-sequential user multitasking.	1
Contrast command-line interpreters versus graphical user interfaces with trade-offs.	4, 6, 7
List PC system architecture configuration issues.	2, 3
Describe hard disk partitioning strategies.	2, 3
Contrast video adapter versus monitor capabilities.	2, 3, 5
List the network configuration parameters.	2, 3

Base System

Objective	Chapter
List and give the trade-off of installation media.	2, 3
Explain the Linux device driver lag and give examples.	2, 3
List the installation steps common to all distributions.	2, 3
Contrast high-volume Linux distributions and give trade-offs.	1, 2, 3
Install four Linux distributions.	1, 2, 3
Describe the configuration tools COAS, Linuxconf, and Yast.	7
List the boot up sequence, log-in, and shut-down sequence.	4
Define "package" and describe how to use it.	4
Describe basic file system principles.	4, 8
Explain the use of mounting versus the use of "mtools" for removable media.	8
List and describe the role of common directories.	4
List and describe the use of basic system navigation programs ps, kill, w, etc.	8, 10
Describe the use and misuse of the superuser account.	3, 8
List the steps in creating a user account.	8
Install, configure, and navigate two X11 window managers.	5

Shells and Commands

A

Objective	Chapter
Describe shell configuration files.	6
Compare and contrast environmental versus shell variables.	6, 12
Use commands that pass special characters among programs.	7
Use commands that allow programs to communicate.	7
Manipulate files and directories.	4, 6
Use the shell for multitasking.	8
Describe common shell editing commands.	8
Use the following commands in isolation or in combination with each other: ls, cd, more, less, cp, mv, mkdir, rm, rmdir, ln, head, tail, file, grep, du, df, and zcat.	4, 6, 7
Use the following vi commands i, ZZ, :w, :w! :q!, dd, x, D, J.	6

System Services

Objective	Chapter
List and describe seven tools that provide information on other tools.	1, 7
Describe and use LILO.	2, 3, 4
Install run-time device drivers.	4
Configure a printer capabilities file.	13
Configure a printer filter.	13
Use lpr, lpq, lprm, and lpc to control file printing.	13
List the sections of the X server configuration file.	5
Configure the X server video hardware.	5
Contrast xf86config, XF86Setup, Xconfigurator, and SaX.	5
Describe five components of the X Window System architecture.	5
List and give the trade-offs of Afterstep, KDE, Window Maker, FVWM95, Enlightenment, and Blackbox.	5

Applications

Objective	Chapter
Describe the general control of X11 desktops.	5
Describe Netscape functions, FTP functions, Telnet functions, and mail functions.	3, 5
Contrast WYSIWYG versus mark-up word processing.	6
Contrast ApplixWare, WordPerfect, and StarOffice	Appendix C
Contrast GIMP, X-Fig, and ImageMagick	Appendix C

Troubleshooting

Objective	Chapter
Describe the cause and solution to read errors.	3
Explain why FTP keeps missing certain files in group transfers.	4
Explain the problem and solution when LILO says LI.	4
Define rescue disk and describe three reasons for using it.	9
Explain how to get around a locked-up program.	8, 10
List eight steps to resolve an unresponsive printer.	13
Explain why Linux may report the wrong time and describe how to fix the problem.	2, 3
Describe how to reset the console screen, the keyboard repeat rate, and the Num Lock key.	4, 5
Describe the role of system logging and how to use it for troubleshooting.	11

Exam 2: Linux System Administration

Theory of Operation

Objective	Chapter
Describe the file system structure and hierarchy.	4
Describe the process of file system backup and `cron`.	12, 14
Describe printing and system tuning.	10, 13
Describe troubleshooting and emergency procedures.	9
List different system resources.	10
Describe the use of user profiles.	8
List different kinds of RAID and describe their uses.	9

Base System

Objective	Chapter
Describe the process of adding and removing a user.	8
List the different run levels and describe how they differ.	4
Describe `fstab` and volume remounting.	8
Describe the process of recompiling the kernel.	4
Describe performance and hard disk analysis.	8
The student will understand system shutdown techniques.	4

Shells and Commands

Objective	Chapter
Describe the role of the superuser.	2, 3, 4, 6, 7, 8, 9, 10, 12, 14
Describe motd and the issue with it.	4, 6
List and describe the MS-DOS tools.	4, 6
Describe the ARP/Route precedence.	**Book II, 1, 2**
Describe Bootp and DHCP.	2, 3; **Book II, 3, 4**
Describe the use of make and touch.	4, 12
Describe the use of CGI scripts.	12
Describe system status, system message logging, and performance analysis.	10, 11

System Services

Objective	Chapter
Describe "user" commands.	4, 6
Describe the archive utilities.	14
Describe using fsck and why.	8
Describe process management.	8
Describe printer settings and restarting.	13
Describe the background line printer daemon and the foreground line printer requester.	13
Describe software packages.	4

Applications

Objective	Chapter
Describe AMANDA, ORL's VNC, Mail Exchange, News, and the Apache Web server.	5, 8, 10
Describe XWindows desktops.	5
Describe benchmarks.	10

Troubleshooting

Objective	Chapter
Describe core dump control.	12

Exam 3: Linux Networking

Theory of Operation

Objective	Chapter
Describe the basic technology of Internet, Ethernet, and area networks.	Book II, 1, 2
Describe addresses and addressing.	Book II, 2
Describe the protocols.	Book II, 1, 2
Describe DNS, applications, and Internet access.	Book II, 5
Describe broadcasting, address assignment, and multicast.	Book II, 1, 2
Describe the UUCP subsystem.	Book II, 2
Describe SMB and IPX.	Book II, 5

Base System

Objective	Chapter
Describe networking interfaces.	2, 3; Book II, 1, 2
Describe the ARP and routing tables.	Book II, 1, 2
Describe firewalls.	Book II, 4, 5
Describe VPN and proxy servers.	Book II, 3, 4, 5
Describe IP multicast.	Book II, 1, 2, 3

Shells and Commands

Objective	Chapter
Describe basic network configuration.	2, 3; Book II, 2, 3
Describe how to access and the importance of system startup files.	4
Describe UUCP.	Book II, 1, 2
Describe network troubleshooting.	Book II, 6

System Services

Objective	Chapter
Describe DNS, FTP, and NFS.	Book II, 3, 4, 5
Describe the internet super server.	Book II, 3, 4, 5
Describe SAMBA.	Book II, 4, 5
Describe sendmail, smail, and qmail.	Book II, 4, 5
Describe POP3 and Imap.	Book II, 4, 5
Describe News, mail list servers, and the Apache server.	Book II, 4, 5

Applications

Objective	Chapter
Describe mail and pine.	Book II, 5
Describe browsers.	Book II, 5

Exam 4: Linux Security, Ethics, and Privacy

Theory of Operation

Objective	Chapter
Describe daemons as superusers and the buffer overflow problem.	Book II, 8, 9
Describe the protection scheme.	Book II, 7, 8, 9
Describe the access control list.	Book II, 8
Describe trojan horses, password weakness, and screening IPs.	Book II, 8
Describe CERT advisories, daily system check, and stealth filenames.	Book II, 7, 8, 9
Describe cert.org and rootshell.com.	Book II, 7
Describe intruder detection and removal.	Book II, 9
Describe user-mode viruses and worms.	Book II, 8, 9
Describe Ken Thompson on trusting trust.	Book II, 7

Base System

Objective	Chapter
Describe setting the superuser status from a shell script.	6; Book II, 8
Describe the importance of classification of user, group, and everybody.	8; Book II, 8
Describe UMASK.	4, 6; Book II, 7
Describe shadow passwords, host.allow, and host.deny.	Book II, 3, 5, 9
Describe the importance of files for logging in as superuser, file transfer as superuser, printer configuration, and system logging.	6, 8, 11, 13

Shells and Commands

Objective	Chapter
Describe the access control list and emulation.	Book II, 8

System Services

Objective	Chapter
Describe `checksecurity`, `rotatelogs`, `quotaon`, `quotacheck`, and `sa`.	Book II, 8, 9
Describe pluggable authentication modules.	Book II, 8
Describe TCP/UDP wrappers.	Book II, 1, 2, 9
Describe find, it's switches, important commands, and their significance.	4, 6, 7, 14; Book II, 8
Describe the importance of daily cron checks.	12; Book II, 8, 9

Applications

Objective	Chapter
Describe hidden logfile backup.	Book II, 9

Troubleshooting

Objective	Chapter
Describe why `setuid` shell scripts do not work.	Book II, 8

Linux Professional Institute (LPI) Exam Objectives

Final objectives for the LPI examinations were not finalized at the time of this writing and may differ somewhat from this list. The material covered is expected to remain consistent, however. The complete objectives are available at *www.lpi.org*.

Items in bold text refer to Book II in this series, *Guide to Linux Networking and Security*. Although chapter numbers for material in that book are provided (for example, **Book II, 3**), they are subject to change. Please refer to the Table of Contents and Appendices of *Guide to Linux Networking and Security* for more detailed information.

Exam 101: General Linux, Part 1

Topic 1.3   GNU and UNIX Commands

Objective	Chapter
Work effectively on the UNIX command line.	4, 6, 8
Process text streams using text-processing filters.	6
Perform basic file management.	4, 6
Use UNIX streams, pipes, and redirects.	6, 7, 8
Create, monitor, and kill processes.	8, 10
Modify process execution priorities.	10
Perform searches of text files making use of regular expressions.	7, 8

Topic 2.4   Devices, Linux File Systems, File System Hierarchy Standard

Objective	Chapter
Create partitions and file systems.	2, 3
Maintain the integrity of file systems.	8, 9
Control file system mounting and unmounting.	8
Set and view disk quota.	Book II, 3
Use file permissions to control access to files.	4
Manage file ownership.	4
Create and change hard and symbolic links.	4, 6, 9
Find system files and place files in the correct location.	7, 8

A

Topic 2.6   Boot, Initialization, Shutdown, Run Levels

Objective	Chapter
Boot the system.	3, 4
Change run levels and shut down or reboot the system.	4

Topic 1.8   Documentation

Objective	Chapter
Use and manage local system documentation.	1
Find Linux documentation on the Internet.	1
Write system documentation.	1
Provide user support.	1–14

Topic 2.11   Administrative Tasks

Objective	Chapter
Manage users and group accounts and related system files.	8
Tune the user environment and system environment variables.	6, 8
Configure and use system log files to meet administrative and security needs.	11
Automate system administration tasks by scheduling jobs to run in the future.	12
Maintain an effective data back-up strategy.	14

Exam 102: General Linux, Part 2

Topic 1.1   Hardware and Architecture

Objective	Chapter
Configure fundamental system hardware.	2, 3
Set up SCSI and NIC devices.	3, 4
Configure modem, sound cards.	2, 3

Topic 2.2   Linux Installation and Package Management

Objective	Chapter
Design hard disk layout.	2, 3, 9
Install a boot manager.	3, 4
Make and install programs from source.	12
Manage shared libraries.	4
Use Debian package management.	Book II, 3
Use Red Hat package manager (rpm).	4

Topic 1.5   Kernel

Objective	Chapter
Manage kernel modules at run time.	4
Reconfigure, build, and install a custom kernel and modules.	4

Topic 1.7   Text Editing, Processing, Printing

Objective	Chapter
Perform basic file editing operations using `vi`.	6
Manage printers and print queues.	13
Print files.	13
Install and configure local and remote printers.	13

Topic 1.9   Shells, Scripting, Programming, Compiling

Objective	Chapter
Customize and use the shell environment.	6
Customize or write simple scripts.	12

Topic 2.10   X

Objective	Chapter
Install and configure XFree86.	5
Set up XDM.	5
Identify and terminate runaway X applications.	8, 10
Install and customize a window manager environment.	5

Topic 1.12   Networking Fundamentals

Objective	Chapter
Fundamentals of TCP/IP	2; Book II, 1
TCP/IP troubleshooting and configuration	Book II, 1–6
Configure and use PPP	Book II, 3

Topic 1.13   Networking Services

Objective	Chapter
Configure and manage inetd and related services.	Book II, 3
Operate and perform basic configuration of sendmail.	Book II, 5
Operate and perform basic configuration of Apache.	Book II, 5
Properly manage the NFS, smb, and nmb daemons.	Book II, 5
Set up and configure basic DNS services.	Book II, 5

Topic 1.14   Security

Objective	Chapter
Perform security admin tasks.	4, 6, 7, 8, 9, Book II, 7-9
Set up host security.	4, Book II, 7-9
Set up user-level security.	8, Book II, 7-9

B

COMMAND SUMMARY

This appendix summarizes the command-line utilities presented in this book. Although all options are not included, the brief definitions in this quick-reference format should enable you to locate needed commands quickly.

To learn more about a command, use the **man** or **info** command with the command in question. For example, to learn about the **ls** command, enter **man ls** or **info ls**. Sometimes the man page will inform you that the info page is more up-to-date. If you are uncertain which command you need, try the **apropos** command with a keyword. This searches the man page database and reports all man pages (thus all commands) that include the keyword you entered.

LINUX COMMANDS

Command name	Description	Useful options
alias	Assign a new name to a command.	
apropos	See a list of man pages that contain a given keyword.	
at	Set up a one-time task for later execution by atd.	• −l lists all queued tasks (like atq). • −d removes a queued task (like atrm).
atq	See the list of jobs submitted to atd using the at command.	
atrm	Remove a scheduled job from the queue of jobs to be executed by the atd command.	
bash	The default Linux shell.	
batch	Set up a scheduled task for future execution by the atd daemon when the processor load falls below a certain level.	
bg	Make the current process a background process of the current shell.	
cat	Print the contents of a file or files to STDOUT.	−n displays line numbers.
cd	Change directory.	

Command name	Description	Useful options
chgrp	Change the group assigned to a file or directory.	
chmod	Change the permissions assigned to a file or directory.	
chown	Change the user (owner) and optionally the group assigned to a file or directory.	
clear	Clear the screen.	
cp	Copy files or directories from one location or filename to another.	• -i requests confirmation if the target file already exists. • -r copies directories to a new directory.
cpio	Back-up utility, similar to tar.	
crontab	Submit a script with assigned times for repeated future execution by the crond daemon.	-u allows the root user to set a cron job for a specific user.
date	Display the system date and current time.	
df	Display file system information for all mounted standard file systems (not swap and proc).	-l limits the listing of file systems to local file systems.
dmesg	Display the contents of the kernel ring buffer, where certain kernel messages are stored.	
du	Display usage information about the size of a directory and its subdirectories.	-s displays only a summary (total size).
dump	Back up data in a file system.	
echo	Display text to STDOUT.	-n prevents the standard new-line character at the end of the output.
emacs	A powerful text-mode editor.	
exit	Log out of a session or window.	
export	Make an environmental variable available to other processes.	
fg	Move a process to the foreground of the current shell, so that the output of the process is displayed.	
file	Display information about the content and file type of a file.	

B

Command name	Description	Useful options
find	Search for files with certain characteristics and list them or perform other actions on each one.	• -name filename finds files with the specified filename. • -print prints the pathname for each file found. • -type file type finds files with the specified access type. • -user username finds files owned by the specified user. • -perm permission code finds files with the specified file permissions.
free	Display the amount of free memory and swap space, with usage details on each.	-t includes a line with totals.
ftp	Access an FTP server using the file transfer protocol.	
grep	Search for a pattern using a regular expression within a file, group of files, or other input stream (using a pipe symbol).	• -c displays the count of matching lines. • -i ignores case in the matches. • -l lists only filenames. • -n displays line numbers. • -v displays lines that do not match the pattern provided.
gunzip	Uncompress a file that was compressed using gzip.	
gzip	Compress a file, adding the .gz file extension to it.	• -l lists statistical details for each file being compressed. • --fast compresses more quickly. • --best creates a smaller compressed file.
halt	Shut down all processes and halt the system so it can be powered off.	
head	Display the first 15 lines of a file.	-n displays the first n lines of the specified file.
history	Display recently used commands.	
hostname	Display the hostname of the system.	
ifconfig	Display or configure the networking interfaces that are part of the Linux kernel.	
joe	A full-screen text-mode editor.	
kill	Send a signal to a process; often used to end a process.	
killall	Send a SIGKILL signal to a process or processes started by the command name given as a parameter.	

Command name	Description	Useful options
less	Display STDIN (or a file) one page at a time.	
lisa	Caldera Systems' text-mode administration utility.	
ln	Create a link from one file or directory to another (both symbolic and hard links can be created).	
locate	Search an internal index of the file system for any files or directories matching the given string.	
login	Log in to the system using a user-name and password.	
logout	End a login session.	
lpc	Control the lpd line printer daemon, setting queuing and printing options for all defined printers.	
lpq	Display print jobs within a print queue.	-Pprinter defines the print queue to view.
lpr	Print a file.	• -Pprinter defines the print queue to send the print job to. • -# defines the number of copies to print. • -m sends an e-mail message to the user when the print job has been completed.
lprm	Remove a print job from a print queue.	-Pprinter defines the print queue from which the print job will be deleted.
ls	List the contents of a directory.	• -l lists additional (long) format information about each item. • -a displays hidden files. • --color attempts to list files and directories with color codes by type. • -i display the inode number of each file.
make	Compile or otherwise assemble the source code components of a program into a runnable binary file using a Makefile as instructions.	
makewhatis	Create a database of man pages for use by the apropos command.	
man	Display an online manual page for the given command.	

Command name	Description	Useful options
mcopy	Copy a file or files to or from the floppy disk drive.	
mdel	Delete a file or files from the floppy disk drive.	
mdir	List the files on a floppy disk drive.	
mkdir	Create a new subdirectory.	
mke2fs	Format a device with the ext2 file system.	
mkfs	Format a device with the file system included as a parameter.	
mkswap	Format a device as swap space (virtual memory).	
more	Display STDIN (or a file) one page at a time.	
mount	Allow access to a named file system via a named directory mount point.	• -r makes the file system being mounted read-only. • -t specifies the file system type (such as ext2).
mv	Rename or move one or more files or directories.	
passwd	Set or reset the password for a user account.	
pico	A full-screen character-mode text editor with on-screen help.	
pine	A text-mode e-mail reading program.	
ping	Send a data packet to a network address to test whether that address is reachable.	• -c count defines how many packets to send. • -s packetsize defines how many bytes should be in the packet.
printtool	Set up a printer in Red Hat Linux (this is a graphical utility).	
ps	Display information about processes running on Linux.	• -A displays information on all files. • u displays user-related fields. • x displays information on processes that have no controlling terminal. • f displays parent-child relationships of processes in a tree format.
pwd	Display the current working directory.	

Command name	Description	Useful options
rm	Delete one or more files or directories.	• `-i` requests confirmation before deleting each item. • `-r` deletes the contents of directories recursively. • `-f` forces deletion without confirmation.
rmdir	Delete an empty directory.	
route	View or configure the static IP network routing table within the Linux kernel.	
sed	Edit files or STDIN input using patterns and commands.	
shutdown	Shut down the system, optionally providing a message or delay for users working on the system.	• `-h` halts the system. • `-r` reboots the system. • `-c` cancels a previously scheduled `shutdown` command.
sort	Sort lines in a file according to various options.	
su	Change to a new user account.	
tail	Display the last 15 lines of a file to STDOUT.	`-n` displays the last *n* lines of the specified file.
tar	Create an archive file containing one or more files or directories, optionally compressing them all.	• `z` compresses the archive. • `f filename` gives the filename to work with. • `c` creates a new archive. • `x` extracts files from an existing archive file. • `v` gives verbose output (listing files).
telnet	Connect to a telnet server to create a console-like dumb-terminal connection.	
top	Display the processes running on the system sorted with the most processor-intensive task listed first.	• `-c` displays the command line that initiated each process. • `-i` ignores any idle processes. • `-s` runs top in secure mode, so no interactive keys function. • `-S` runs top in cumulative mode for the CPU time field.
touch	Update the last accessed time for a file, or create an empty file if the named file does not exist.	• `-a` updates the access time only. • `-c` prevents `touch` from creating a file that does not exist. • `-m` updates the modification time only.

Command name	Description	Useful options
umount	Unmount a file system that is currently mounted as part of the Linux directory structure.	
unzip	Uncompress a file that has been created using the zip command.	
updatedb	Create an index of the entire file system for use by the locate command.	
vi	A powerful full-screen text editor.	
vmstat	Display virtual memory (swap space) statistics.	-n delay specifies the number of seconds to wait between automatic updates.
wc	Display the number of characters, words, and lines in a file or STDIN input stream.	• -c displays only the number of characters (bytes). • -l displays only the number of lines. • -w displays only the number of words.
who	Display a list of users who are currently logged in.	
xload	Display the current processor load from 0% to 100% as a small graphic.	
xlsfonts	Choose from among installed fonts (this is a graphical utility).	
zip	Compress one or more files into a single archive (the resulting file is compatible with ZIP files on Windows systems).	

B

C

GRAPHICAL ADMINISTRATION UTILITIES

This appendix presents an overview of the graphical administration tools that accompany both the Gnome and the KDE Desktop interfaces. Although this appendix is not exhaustive—a nearly impossible goal given the rate of software development in these areas—the utilities described should give you a good idea of what is currently available on popular Linux distributions (nearly all of which use either Gnome or KDE). This appendix focuses on the Red Hat Linux distribution. Most of the KDE utilities are included with any product that uses KDE, such as SuSE Linux, Corel Linux, OpenLinux, or Mandrake Linux.

Many of the utilities described in this appendix have also been described to some extent within the main text of the book. Those discussions, however, have focused on using the utility for a particular task rather than providing an overview of the capabilities of numerous programs. This appendix does just that.

Updated versions of Linux distributions and of the Gnome and KDE Desktops are likely to include additional tools that are not mentioned here. In particular, many KDE system administration utilities that are currently in development are mentioned here only briefly or not at all. As these utilities become more stable, they will be included with standard KDE distributions, allowing administrators to rely on graphical configuration tools for more of their system management tasks. For details, you should visit the Web sites *www.gnome.org* and *www.kde.org* and browse the software listing (and download information) provided.

 Not all of the utilities mentioned on the Gnome and KDE Web sites are fit for general consumption. Many of them are still being developed. These utilities may crash your system or may not even run. Look for information about the status of a utility (such as a version number, or a designation of Alpha- or Beta-quality software) before risking any production system on a new administration tool.

Many excellent graphical utilities are available for the X Window System that do not rely on the Gnome or KDE Desktop. A few of these, such as `xload`, are mentioned in the main text of this book. The integrated nature of the Gnome and KDE utilities, as well as the continuing rapid rate of software development that they enjoy, makes them preferable in some ways to generic X Window System utilities. Nevertheless, if you are interested in locating a graphical utility that you do not see mentioned in this appendix, consult an online index or archive of Linux utilities. For example, search *www.freshmeat.net* for a subject or keyword, or browse in the FTP site *ftp.metalab.unc.edu* under the *pub/Linux* subdirectory.

GNOME UTILITIES

Gnome itself does not have numerous specialized graphical administration utilities, probably because it was developed with the idea of relying on the LinuxConf project, which was being developed at about the same time by the same group of developers (that is, developers sponsored by Red Hat Software). The LinuxConf program therefore deserves special consideration as a graphical administration tool.

LinuxConf is the main configuration platform for Red Hat Linux; other distributions that are not based on Red Hat have not adopted LinuxConf, but it is a powerful tool. LinuxConf is available on the Gnome `System` menu. One of its greatest strengths is its ability to work with configuration files via several interfaces:

- Text mode (in any character-mode screen)

- Graphical (standard X Window System in Gnome)

- Web based (via a remote browser)

A tool with design goals similar to those of LinuxConf is the Caldera Open Administration System, or COAS. This utility also aims to be accessible via text, graphical, and browser interfaces, and to provide numerous configuration options in a common interface. The development of COAS, intended as an OpenSource project and led by capable software engineers, has stalled to some degree, and COAS is not able to boast of the large list of configuration tools that LinuxConf can. COAS is not discussed in this appendix, but it is available on the KDE main menu of Caldera OpenLinux products.

Each time you select an item from the voluminous list of options on the left side of the LinuxConf screen, you see a panel appear on the right side of the screen with options to select from. When you have finished with one panel, you can choose `OK` or `Cancel` to close that panel. If you visit multiple panels without closing each one, they remain open. Therefore, when you close one, another that you had previously opened is visible. A set of arrows at the top right of the LinuxConf window lets you move between the panels that you have opened by clicking on items in the left side of the window.

LinuxConf provides an impressive list of configuration tools. But not all of these tools are completely stable or usable. Exercise caution when you first start using a LinuxConf feature until you have ascertained whether it works as you expect it to. Keep in mind that you must be logged in as `root` in order to access the system configuration files with LinuxConf; as always when logged in as `root`, you should be especially careful not to damage your system unintentionally.

The following list summarizes features included in LinuxConf menus. These are listed in the approximate order in which they appear in the left side of LinuxConf, though the sheer number of items and seemingly arbitrary arrangement of configuration tools makes locating any particular tool a challenge. Figures are provided for several representative screens.

TIP   Many of the topics listed here are related to networking and so were not discussed (or perhaps even mentioned) in this book.

- Network card configuration (see Figure C-1)

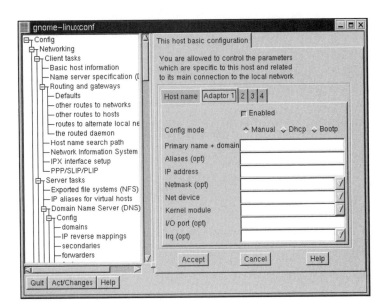

Figure C-1   Networking configuration in LinuxConf

- Network routing configuration
- NFS (remote UNIX file system access) configuration
- DNS (Domain Name Service) configuration

C

■ Apache Web server configuration, including several panels of options (see Figure C-2)

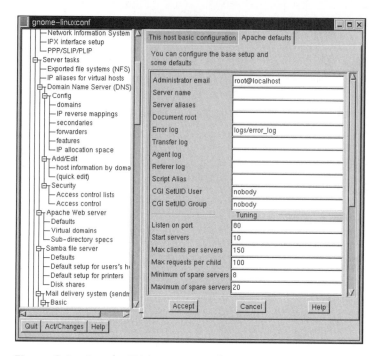

Figure C-2 Apache Web server configuration in LinuxConf

■ Samba (SMB) server configuration, including several panels of options

■ Sendmail e-mail server configuration, including several panels of options

■ FTP server configuration

■ User account setup and management (see Figure C-3)

■ Password policy configuration and enforcement (see Figure C-4)

■ File system management

■ System initialization script configuration and run level management

■ LILO boot loader configuration (several panels)

■ Default run level selection

C

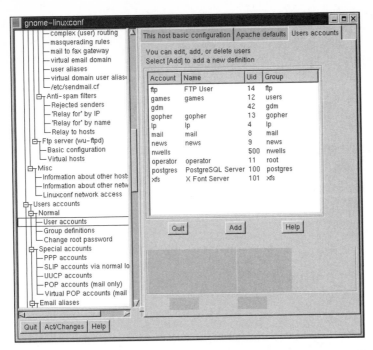

Figure C-3   User account creation and management in LinuxConf

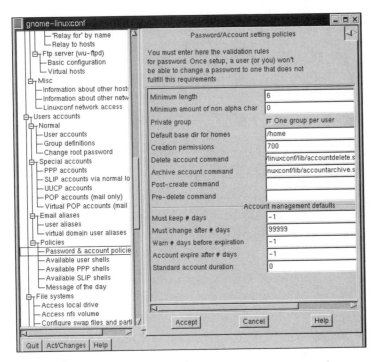

Figure C-4   Password policy configuration in LinuxConf

- LinuxConf network (Web browser) access control (see Figure C-5)

- Mounting and unmounting of file systems

- Superuser (`root`) access control

- System log configuration and tracking

- Date and time configuration

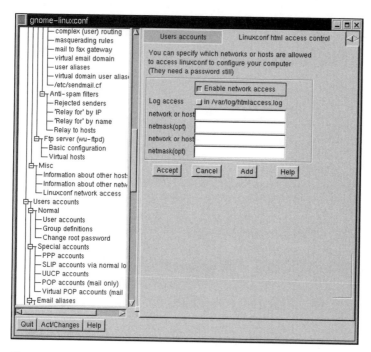

Figure C-5   LinuxConf network access configuration

In addition to the configuration options included with LinuxConf, Red Hat Linux provides several other configuration tools. Some of these tools are useful for nearly every Linux system, so it's unfortunate that they have not been incorporated into the LinuxConf program. Most of these tools are historical—they have been available in Red Hat Linux for several years. They are still included because no other tools have been implemented to replace their functionality. The most notable of these is the Control Panel, which you can access on the

`System` menu in the Gnome Desktop. The Control Panel is shown in Figure C-6. Its five buttons open windows that configure the following items:

Figure C-6   The Red Hat Linux Control Panel

- `Runlevel` directory contents (which services are started in each run level)
- Time and date configuration
- Printer configuration, using the Printer Tool program
- Network configuration, using the `netcfg` program (see Figure C-7)

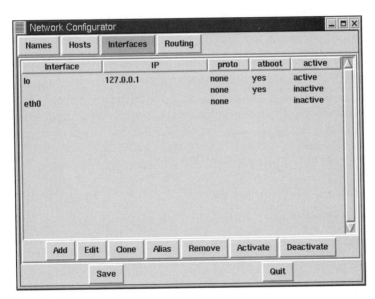

Figure C-7   The network configuration tool from the Red Hat Control Panel

■ Modem configuration (see Figure C-8)

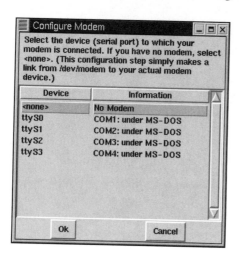

Figure C-8 The modem configuration tool from the Red Hat Control Panel

You can start any of these programs separately from other locations in the standard Gnome menu structure or from a command line (by entering the command `printtool`, for example).

A few additional Red Hat Linux utilities are also available from the `System` menu or from the menu labeled `AnotherLevel menus` under the `Administration` submenu. Some of these are standard X Window System utilities that, as with the Control Panel, have not been superseded by integrated utilities and so are still included somewhere in the convoluted menu structure. These include:

■ Disk management

■ Kernel configuration (see Figure C-9)

■ CPU load monitor

■ Font management (see Figure C-10)

■ User listing (showing all logged-in users)

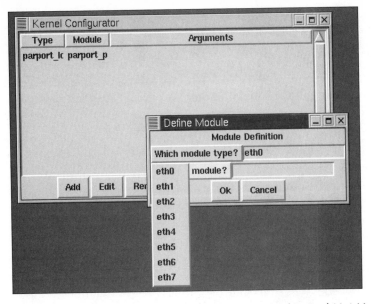

Figure C-9   The kernel module configuration tool in Red Hat Linux

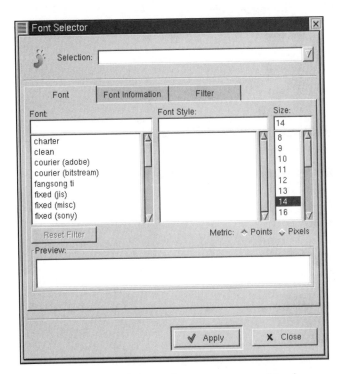

Figure C-10   The Gnome font management tool

Two excellent configuration utilities that are specific to Gnome are the Gnome System Monitor and the `GnoRPM` utility. The Gnome System Monitor is a process management utility. It is discussed at some length in Chapter 10. You can launch this utility from the `System` menu of Gnome or by entering the command `gtop` at a graphical command line. The `GnoRPM` command is used to manage RPM-format packages. While not as flexible as the multiformat `kpackage` utility described in the next section, `GnoRPM` provides a very nice interface for querying, installing, and deleting software packages.

The Gnome interface itself is configured mainly with the Gnome Control Center and the Menu Editor, both of which are available from the Gnome `Settings` menu. You use the Menu Editor to set up which applications and submenus are displayed in the Gnome menu. This task can become quite complex, so a graphical tool provides welcome assistance. The Control Center handles most other aspects of the configuration of Gnome. It includes the following configuration options:

- Background selection

- Screen saver configuration

- Theme selections (which include background, colors, and other display components)

- The default editor to use for text files

- The MIME data types that Gnome recognizes and how to respond to each (see Figure C-11)

- The keyboard bell

- Sound event associations

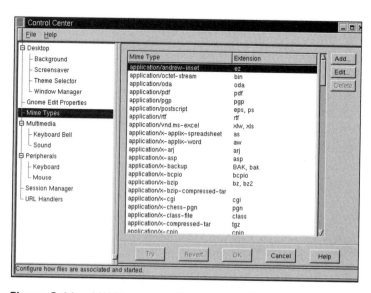

Figure C-11   MIME type configuration in the Gnome Control Center

- Keyboard and mouse configuration

- Session managers

- URL handlers

> **TIP** Don't confuse the Gnome Control Center, which configures the appearance of the Gnome Desktop, with the Red Hat Control Panel—a set of system administration tools such as Printer Tool.

A key item missing from the preceding list is the window manager configuration. By default, Gnome uses the Enlightenment window manager. From the Control Center you can launch the Enlightenment configuration tool. This tool alone is more complex than the rest of the Gnome Control Center. It allows you to configure the following:

- How to drag windows (see Figure C-12)

- How to resize windows

- How to apply focus rules when moving between windows

- How many virtual desktops to support and how to move between them

- When to use pop-up tooltip help windows

- Special effects for window animation

- Complex background manipulation settings

- Detailed desktop theme configuration

- Keyboard shortcuts

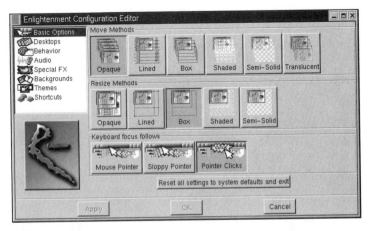

Figure C-12   Configuring window operations in Enlightenment

KDE Utilities

KDE is arguably farther along in development than the Gnome project. This fact is evident in the number of KDE-specific system administration tools. Sadly, no single, integrated system administration tool like LinuxConf is available for KDE, though you can easily run LinuxConf within the KDE Desktop on a Red Hat Linux system on which both are installed. (Using LinuxConf on a non–Red Hat system with KDE is a challenging task.)

KDE system administration tools are generally divided into two convenient locations: the System menu and the Utilities menu. The distinction is intended to be something like root user versus all other users, but it isn't that neat in practice. Still, having only the two locations to check makes it much easier for a new user to find programs in the KDE menus compared to Gnome menus.

Programs intended for the root user are located on the System menu. These include the following:

- Font management
- System V initialization script (run level service) configuration
- Task (process) management
- User creation and management

Programs intended for all users (to check system status or configure areas to which the user has access) are located on the Utilities menu. These include the following:

- Tape back-up tool
- Printer queue management
- Process management (very similar to the Task manager on the System menu)
- Menu editor (see Figure C-13)
- Archiver/compressed file manager
- RPM/deb/tar software package manager (not included with Red Hat Linux because the GnoRPM utility is provided instead)

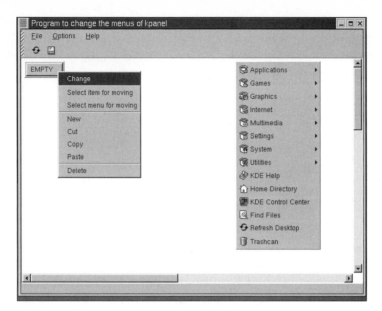

Figure C-13   Configuring KDE menus

A few additional network configuration and testing utilities are provided on the `Internet` menu of KDE. These are not nearly as complete as the LinuxConf network configuration tools, but they do provide some very useful functionality. These tools include:

- `kppp`, used to configure dial-up access
- Network utilities that allow you to run `ping`, `traceroute`, and others via a graphical interface (see Figure C-14)

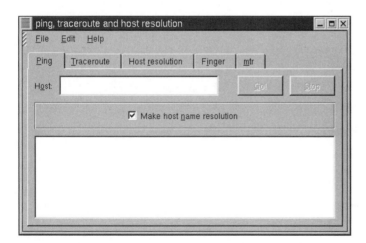

Figure C-14   Network testing utilities in KDE

In addition to the utilities mentioned thus far, KDE developers are working on numerous other programs that are not considered stable enough to include in a commercial Linux distribution. The following list includes some existing products that you can download and test; watch for their future stable release as part of a Linux product:

- `klilo` for LILO configuration

- `kcron` for graphically scheduling tasks using the `at` and `crontab` commands

- `kfstab` to manage file systems and mounting options

- `kdns` to set up and track a domain name service (DNS) server

- `ksamba` to set up and manage a Samba (SMB protocol) server that connects to Windows-based systems

The KDE Control Center is a one-stop interface for setting up the look and feel of the KDE interface. It also provides informational screens taken from the `/proc` file system for things like the interrupts, I/O ports, SCSI devices, PCI interfaces, and hard disk partitions. The following list shows the contents of the KDE Control Center. The Control Center interface operates much like the Gnome Control Center or the LinuxConf utility: you select an item from a hierarchical list on the left of the window; a panel with options appears on the right side of the window.

- Login manager configuration (`kdm` graphical login screen)

- File manager configuration

- Web browser configuration (as part of the file manager)

- Panel and main menu location, and related options

- Desktop background and wallpapers

- Desktop themes

- Screen saver

- Colors and fonts (see Figure C-15)

- Language to use for all applications

- Window styles

- Hardware information from the `/proc` file system (as described above)

- Keyboard usage and mouse configuration

- Keyboard shortcuts (global and per application)

- Mapping of system sounds to events

- Window appearance (title bar buttons, etc.)

- Results of various mouse actions in relation to window management (see Figure C-16)

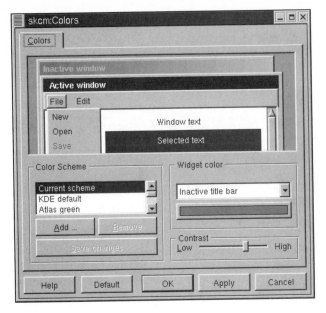

Figure C-15   Configuring colors in KDE

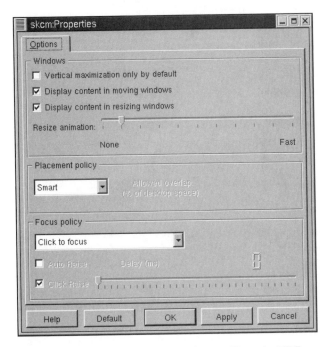

Figure C-16   Configuring window settings in KDE

Some Linux vendors—Corel in particular—are working to add system administration tools to the KDE Control Center so that a single unified interface for system administration can take root in the Linux community. Though licensing issues may affect the work of Corel, the results for users are very promising. For example, the Corel Linux product allows you to change passwords, configure printers, and set up all basic networking within a KDE Control Center panel.

With all of these graphical utilities available and many more being developed by talented individuals around the world, the prospects look bright for Linux to become easier to use for system administrators and more fully integrated into a single administrative interface in the coming years.

OTHER GRAPHICAL TOOLS

In addition to the system administration tools presented so far in this appendix, many other useful graphical programs are available to help make your work with Linux more productive. This section outlines a few of the most popular of these tools.

Office Productivity Suites

Although Linux is still used more as a network server than as a desktop workstation, several high-quality office suite packages are available for Linux. Three of these are described here.

ApplixWare is a collection of standard office productivity tools, including the following:

- A vector-based drawing program similar to Adobe Illustrator or CorelDRAW
- A word processor
- A spreadsheet
- A presentations package

ApplixWare has been available for many different UNIX platforms for many years. Applix, Inc., the developers of ApplixWare, created a Linux version of their popular suite. (See *www.applix.com.*) Although Applix is not as widely known as some other office suites, it is a full-featured, stable product that has been around for years. In fact, one of its strong points is that it was developed originally to run on UNIX, so it is very fast on Linux and doesn't rely on some of the more advanced graphical toolkits such as Qt or GTK that have only recently been used on Linux.

Another popular office suite for Linux is the StarOffice Suite. StarOffice was developed by StarDivision in Germany, but has since been purchased by Sun Microsystems. Sun makes the program available for free on their Web site (*www.sun.com/staroffice*). StarOffice is a very complete office suite, with an integrated desktop environment that attempts to provide everything you would need to work at a Linux-based desktop. The StarOffice environment features the following, all integrated into a single application:

- A word processor
- A spreadsheet

- Both vector and bitmapped drawing programs

- A presentations package with clip art

- A Web browser

- An HTML page editor

- A simple flat file database manager

- Internet newsgroup browsing

- FTP downloads

- The ability to send and read e-mail

StarOffice was written to run on many different platforms, including Microsoft Windows, OS/2, Solaris, and Linux. Because of this, it uses its own graphical libraries, allowing it to run on any version of Linux. However, this also makes StarOffice a large program. You should have a powerful system if you intend to run StarOffice on a regular basis. For example, 128 MB of RAM and a Pentium 400 MHz system would be appropriate.

The interface of StarOffice is designed to imitate Microsoft Office. If you are familiar with Microsoft products, using StarOffice should be very easy. Not all Microsoft features are represented in StarOffice, of course, but most are, and in the same menu structure found in Microsoft Office. Figure C-17 shows the StarOffice desktop.

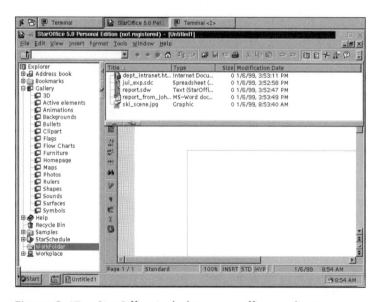

Figure C-17   StarOffice includes many office applications.

The Corel Office Suite is also available for Linux. Although the WordPerfect word processor has been available on Linux for years, the full office suite was only recently released. It includes:

- WordPerfect word processor

- Quattro Pro spreadsheet

- WordPerfect Presentations

- Central (a time-management tool similar to Microsoft Outlook)

- Paradox relational database management (available in some versions of Corel Office)

As with ApplixWare and StarOffice, the Corel Office applications are full-featured, commercial programs that you can use as desktop applications on Linux. Each of these tools also reads and writes files in Microsoft Office format. For example, if you have a friend who uses Microsoft Word, you can exchange files and read them using any of these three word processors (Applix, StarOffice, or WordPerfect).

Graphics Manipulation Tools

Creating bitmapped graphics such as icons, wallpapers, and illustrations is not a standard part of a system administrator's job description. But it's a task that you may nevertheless be asked to do often. Linux has a variety of tools to help you create and manage image files.

If you want to create new bitmapped images or edit existing images, you can use the popular Gimp program, which is similar in design to Adobe PhotoShop. Gimp includes advanced graphical filters, multiformat saves, layers, and other powerful features for professional designers. The creators of Gimp also developed the GTK+ graphical library on which the Gnome desktop was subsequently built.

Many other drawing programs are also available on Linux. Most of these have been used on UNIX systems for years and were simply converted to run on Linux. Examples include the X-Fig program and X-Paint. Gimp and X-Paint are included by default on Red Hat Linux. X-Fig is not, but is available for free download from various sites such as *www.metalab.unc.edu*. Figure C-18 shows Gimp with several image-editing tools.

You can manage existing images using other tools as well. These tools are not intended for designing new images but for organizing, studying, or presenting existing graphical files in many file formats. Examples of these tools include the graphical viewer XV and the format conversion package called netpbm. Both of these tools allow you to work with image files in dozens of formats.

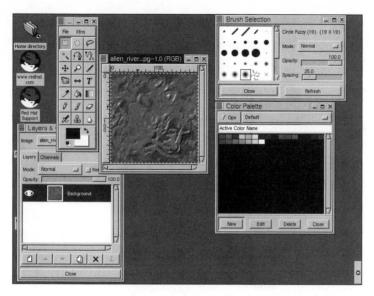

Figure C-18   Gimp includes many powerful image-editing tools.

Another image management tool that is included with Red Hat Linux is ImageMagick. This package includes commands that let you do all of the following:

- Animate a series of images
- Combine multiple images into one file
- Identify the format of an image file
- Convert an image to a different format
- Assemble multiple images into a montage
- Display images on screen
- Modify images, setting scale, rotation, etc.

GLOSSARY

$@ — A special shell variable that includes all of the parameters on the command line.

.bashrc — A configuration script that is executed each time the user starts a `bash` shell.

.profile — A configuration script that can be located in each user's home directory.

/etc/bashrc — A script that is executed each time any user on the system starts a `bash` shell. This script is not included by default on all Linux distributions, but can be created if needed.

/etc/fstab — Configuration file that contains a file system table with devices, mount points, file system types, and options. Used by the `mount` command.

/etc/group — Configuration file in which group information (group names and membership lists) is stored.

/etc/passwd — Configuration file in which user account information is stored.

/etc/profile — A script containing configuration information that applies to every user on the Linux system.

/etc/shadow — Configuration file in which encrypted user passwords and password configuration data are stored.

/etc/skel — Directory containing files that will be used to populate a new user's home directory at the time it is created.

/proc file system — A method of viewing what the operating system kernel is doing at all times, using a section of the Linux directory structure and a file system interface (using the same commands used for regular files).

AC power — The standard alternating current power coming into a building from a public utility; the power from a wall socket.

action — A field in the `syslog.conf` configuration file that determines what to do with messages matching the selector on that line.

active partition — The partition that receives control from the BIOS when the system is turned on.

alias — A string of characters that the shell substitutes for another string of characters when a command is entered.

alias — Command used to create a text substitution in a command-line shell, effectively giving any Linux command a new name.

application — A program (such as a word processor or spreadsheet) that provides a service to a person using the computer, rather than simply managing the computer's resources.

apropos — Linux command used to show all man pages that contain a keyword.

array — A collection of multiple hard disks. *See* RAID.

at — A command that lets you enter one or more commands to be executed once at some future time.

atq — A command that lists each of the jobs that have been submitted using the `at` command, with a job number and the date and time when the job will be executed.

atrm — A command that deletes (removes) a job from the queue used by `atd` to execute commands.

authentication — The process of identifying a user to a computer system via some type of login procedure.

awk — A programming language that developers use to create scripts for working on text files and completing other complex tasks.

backup — A copy of data on a computer system.

back-up level — A definition of how much data is to be backed up in comparison with another back-up level. When performing a back-up operation at a given back-up level, all of the data that has changed since the last backup of the previous level is recorded.

back-up media — A device where data can be stored, such as a tape cartridge, writeable CD, or even a floppy disk.

back-up plan — A written document that outlines when, how, and, perhaps, why various files and file systems will be backed up, stored, and—when necessary—restored to prevent permanent data loss.

background application — An application that does not stop the program that started it from going on to other tasks.

bang — In Linux jargon, an exclamation point character.

bash — Short for *Bourne Again shell*, an enhanced and extended version of the Bourne shell created by the GNU project for use on many UNIX-like operating systems. `bash` is the default Linux shell.

batch — A command that executes scheduled tasks when the system load average drops below 0.8.

benchmark program — A program that provides a numeric measurement of performance for part of a system.

Beowulf — A cluster of multiple Linux servers operating in parallel as a supercomputer to solve complex problems.

bg — Command used to place a job (process) in the background (either by suspending it or by preventing its output from appearing in the current shell's terminal window), thus allowing the shell prompt to become active again.

binary code — Machine-readable instructions used to execute a program.

binary file — *See* executable file.

BIOS (Basic Input/Output System) — Information stored in ROM that provides instructions to the operating system for using the devices on a computer.

block — A unit of storage on a file system. A standard block contains 1024 characters (bytes), or two sectors.

block special file — A type of file (normally located in `/dev`) referring to a physical device that transfers data in blocks of characters, such as a hard disk drive.

bonnie — A hard disk benchmarking program.

boot disk — A disk used to launch the Linux operating system stored on your hard disk. It can be used in normal operating situations to start the Linux system. A special version of the boot disk launches the Linux installation program.

boot manager — A program that lets you select an operating system to use each time you boot the computer.

boot parameter — A piece of information passed directly to the Linux kernel as the system is being booted. These parameters are normally used to affect how Linux recognizes hardware devices or to enable certain features of the operating system.

boot record — A small area on each partition that contains a program to launch the operating system on that partition.

bootable CD-ROM drive — A CD-ROM drive that can launch an operating system (or other program) directly from a CD without accessing the hard disk. (This feature of the CD-ROM drive must be enabled by the BIOS.)

bottleneck — Part of a computer system that slows down completion of the task at hand.

bounce queue (bq) — An option code within the `printcap` file that causes print jobs to be processed by the local print filter before being sent to a remote printer.

Bourne shell — The original shell for UNIX, written by Stephen Bourne.

broadcast address — A special IP address that sends a packet of data to all computers on the local network.

buffers — Areas of memory dedicated to holding the working data associated with a running program.

byte — Space within a computer system sufficient to store one character.

C shell — A shell developed by Bill Joy in the 1970s. He focused on adding easy-to-use features for interactive work at the shell prompt. (Most of these features were later added to the `bash` shell as well.) The C shell is not popular for shell programming because its syntax is more complex than that of the Bourne, `bash`, and Korn shells.

cached data — Information from the hard disk that is stored temporarily in RAM, under the assumption that the data will soon be needed by an application. Caching data improves system performance, because data can be accessed faster from RAM than from the hard disk.

caching — The process of storing data from the hard disk in RAM so that it can be accessed more rapidly (because RAM is much faster than a hard disk).

cat — Command used to dump the contents of a file to STDOUT.

cd — Command used to change the directory you are working in (the current working directory).

character special file — A type of file referring to a physical device (such as a serial port) that transfers data in single characters.

chief information officer (CIO) — The executive in an organization who determines how information systems are used within the organization to further its goals or mission effectively.

chmod — Command used to change the file permissions assigned to a file or directory.

chown — Command used to change the ownership of a file or directory.

COAS (Caldera Open Administration System) — A set of graphical utilities developed by Caldera Systems and used to manage many aspects of a Linux system.

command interpreter — (More commonly called a shell in Linux.) A command-line environment in which a user can enter commands to be launched.

command-line option — A command-line parameter.

command-line parameter — An additional piece of information (besides the program name) that is included on the command line when a program is started.

command-line window — A window within a graphical environment that permits you to enter commands at the keyboard.

comment — A line in a script that begins with a # character. Comments are not processed by the shell, but are only included to help someone reading the file understand the purpose of the script or how it functions.

Common Gateway Interface (CGI) — A method of communication between two programs using the standard input and standard output channels.

compiled language — A computer language for which the source code is converted to a binary file long before the program will be run by users.

compiler — A special program that converts the source code of a compiled language into a binary file.

computer language — A set of words and syntax rules that can be arranged in predefined ways to cause a computer to perform tasks defined by the person using the language.

cooperative multitasking — A technique in which an operating system kernel must wait for a program to yield control to other programs.

copyleft — An ironic term that refers to the GNU General Public License (the GPL), signifying a radical departure from standard copyright.

cp — Command used to copy a file or directory from one location or name to another.

cpio — A Linux archiving program. The **cpio** command also reads archive files created by the **tar** command.

cron job — A command or script that you have scheduled to be executed at a specific time in the future.

crontab — A command that lets you enter one or more commands to be executed repeatedly at intervals that you designate.

current working directory — The directory in which you are working.

cylinder — A set of tracks at the same location on all the platters of a hard disk.

daemon — A background process that does not display status information on the screen. Instead, daemons normally write information to log files.

default shell — The default command-line interpreter used in most Linux systems (**bash**).

defragmenting — The process of rearranging the files on a file system so that all the parts of a file are located next to each other on the physical hard disk. Defragmenting a hard disk increases system performance and reduces wear on the storage device.

desktop environment — A graphical application that provides a comprehensive interface, including system menus, desktop icons, and the ability to easily manage files and launch applications.

device drivers — Software that provides access to additional hardware, beyond core device support provided by the kernel.

df — Short for display file systems. Command used to display file system summary information such as device, mount point, percentage used, and total capacity.

direct memory access (DMA) channel — A communication method within a computer that allows a device to read and write directly to the computer's RAM, without going through the microprocessor first.

directory record — A file containing the names and inode numbers of other files.

disaster plan — An organized written plan that describes how to respond to various threats to an information system such as Linux.

disk image — A single file that contains an exact copy of a floppy disk.

disk optimization — *See* defragmenting.

dmesg — Program that displays the contents of the kernel ring buffer. This buffer normally contains hardware configuration data generated during system start-up.

DNS server — A computer that uses the DNS protocol to convert domain names and hostnames to IP addresses.

do — A command used with the **done** command to enclose a block of commands to be executed by a **for** command.

domain name — A name assigned to a network.

Domain Name Service (DNS) — A protocol that maps human-readable domain names and hostnames to IP addresses that correspond to networks and individual computers.

done — A command used with the **do** command to enclose a block of commands to be executed by a **for** command.

DOS — An operating system developed for personal computers in about 1980. It gained widespread acceptance when IBM introduced the first IBM PC.

downtime — Occasions when an organization's computer systems cannot respond to requests for information.

driver — A software program that provides abstract services for a hardware component, such as opening files or reading character input.

du — Short for disk usage. Command used to display disk space used by a directory and each of its subdirectories.

dual-boot system — A computer that allows a person to choose which operating system to start each time the computer is booted (turned on).

dumpe2fs — A utility used to display technical statistics and parameters about a Linux **ext2** file system.

duplexing — Term used to describe a system in which the contents of two file systems, that are located on different hard disk controllers, contain identical information. Compare to "mirroring," a technique that provides identical information on two file systems but without redundant disk controllers.

Dynamic Host Configuration Protocol (DHCP) — A protocol that allows a computer to obtain an IP address dynamically from a network server at the time the computer is turned on.

dynamically linked applications — Linux programs that do not include the library functions that they require in order to operate. The libraries must be installed (as shared libraries) on the Linux system on which the applications are executed.

e2defrag — The utility used to defragment a standard Linux **ext2** partition.

echo — A command that prints text to the STD-OUT channel—to the screen unless output has been redirected.

else — A command that extends the capability of an **if/then** statement by adding a block of commands that are only executed if a test returns a value of false (that is, if the test fails).

end user — An individual who uses the computer systems in an organization to accomplish assigned tasks, but relies on a system administrator to keep those systems running smoothly.

environment variables — Set of named values (name-value pairs) that provide information to programs running in a user's environment.

executable file — A file containing numeric codes that a computer can execute. Created from a source code file by a compiler, the executable file is the program that a user can run.

execute permission — A file permission that allows a user to launch a file as a program or see a file within a directory. Represented by a letter **x**.

exit — A command that stops the execution of a script immediately.

export — Command used to make a newly created environment variable available to other programs running in the same environment.

ext2 — The default file system type for Linux.

facility — A category assigned to a system message, identifying the type of program providing the message.

FAT32 — The default file system type for Windows 98.

fault tolerance — The condition of being able to tolerate errors or events that might otherwise cause system failure.

fdformat — Command used to format a floppy disk.

fdisk — A utility used to create hard disk partitions and configure how they are used.

fg — Command used to bring a job (process) running in a shell to the foreground so that the job controls the shell's terminal window.

fi — A command that marks the end of an **if/then** statement.

`file` — Command used to print a summary of the type of data contained in a file.

file extension — The last part of a filename after a period.

file handle — An internal storage mechanism that allows a single file to be opened and used in Linux.

file manager window — A graphical window that displays the contents of a directory (usually as a collection of icons) and lets you work with the files and directories using menus, mouse clicks, and dialog boxes.

file permissions — Codes that define the type of access that a user has to a file or directory on the Linux system.

file record — An information item within an `ext2` file system that includes a filename and an inode number. The inode itself contains detailed information about the file.

file system — A collection of data, normally stored on a device such as a hard disk partition, which can be accessed in Linux via the directory structure.

filtering — The process of adding, removing, or altering data in the text file based on complex rules or patterns.

`find` — Linux command used to search the file system for files matching certain characteristics.

FIPS — A program that creates two separate partitions from an existing Windows partition.

`for` — A command that repeats a block of commands one time for each item in a list that you provide.

for loop — A block of commands that is repeatedly executed according to the parameters provided with the `for` command.

`free` — Linux command used to display the amount of free and used memory (physical and virtual), with basic information about how that memory is being used.

Free Software Foundation (FSF) — An organization founded by Richard Stallman to promote his ideals of freely available software and to create and distribute that software.

`fsck` — A utility used to check the integrity of an `ext2` file system.

fully qualified domain name (FQDN) — The hostname of a computer and the domain name of the network to which the computer is attached.

function — A set of computer programming code that completes a certain task for a program.

function library — A file containing a collection of commonly used functions that any program can use as it runs.

gateway address — The IP address of the computer on a local network that can send packets of data outside that network.

`gcc` — A C language compiler. Probably the best known product of the GNU project.

gigabyte (GB) — A measure of space on computers equal to 1024 megabytes, or roughly enough space to store 1 billion characters.

Gnome System Monitor — A graphical utility for the Gnome Desktop that is used to monitor and control processes running on Linux. Also called `gtop`. Similar to the `kpm` program for KDE.

GNU General Public License (GPL) — The free software license that Richard Stallman of the Free Software Foundation developed for the programs created by the GNU project.

GNU project — An effort by the Free Software Foundation to create a free UNIX-like operating system. Much of a Linux distribution comes from the GNU project.

graceful shutdown — The technique of stopping all Linux services and shutting down all file access in an orderly way before turning off or rebooting the computer.

graphical interface — Software that provides mouse-driven applications with menu bars, buttons, and so forth.

graphical libraries — Collections of programming functions that an X client can use to more efficiently create and manage the elements of a graphical environment.

grep — Linux command used to search within files for lines containing a certain pattern.

groff — A command used to format and display documents that are created using roff mark-up codes.

group — A named account that consists of a collection of users. Each member of a group has access to files owned by that group.

groupadd — Command used to add a new group to a Linux system.

group permissions — A set of three file permissions (r, w, and x) that apply to members of the group assigned to a file or directory.

gunzip — Command used to uncompress a file that has been compressed using gzip.

gzip — Command used to compress any file on a Linux system.

halt — Command used to shut down all services and then stop the computer with the message "System halted."

hard disk — Magnetic storage space for data such as the operating system and data files.

hard link — A pointer to an inode that is already pointed to by at least one other file record.

hard wired — Computer functionality that is arranged in the wires and other components that make up a computer. Hard-wired functionality cannot be easily altered.

hardware-based RAID — A RAID array that is contained in a separate hardware device (a RAID subsystem) and is controlled by a CPU and other components separate from the CPU of the Linux system.

Help Desk — A department in many organizations that assists end users in solving problems related to information technology.

hexadecimal (hex) — A numbering system using base-16. Hex uses 0 to 9, plus the letters A through F (usually capitalized) to count the numbers 10 through 15.

high availability — Term used to refer to the processes, products, or programs involved in ensuring that a system experiences as little downtime as possible. The goal for all high availability systems is 100% uptime.

high availability cluster — A group of servers that process the same tasks (resource groups) and take over each others' functionality in the event of an outage or failure.

history — A command used to display all of the stored commands in the history list.

history feature — A feature of the shell that records in a list (the history list) each of the commands that you enter at the shell prompt.

history list — A list that contains the most recently executed commands. (Normally at least 100 commands are included in the history list.)

home directory — The location where all of a user's personal files are stored.

host — A computer attached to a network.

hostname — A single word used to name a computer.

hot-swapping — The process of removing and replacing a failed hard drive from a RAID hardware device or specialized server without turning off the power to the device.

HOWTOs — Documents within the Linux Documentation Project that cover specific topics.

IDE — A low-cost, easy-to-manage interface used by most new computers to connect hard disks and CD-ROM drives to the CPU.

IDE controller — A computer hardware component used to communicate between an IDE-compatible hard disk or other IDE device and the microprocessor.

if — A command used to introduce a test within a shell script. An `if` command is always followed by a `then` command.

if/then/else statement — A set of commands used to determine whether other commands in a script are executed. An `if/then/else` statement is one kind of selection statement.

index — A counting variable used within a loop statement. The index acts as a marker to count how many times the loop has executed a list of commands.

info — Linux command used to access online command reference information.

Information Systems Department (IS) — The area of an organization in which the staff are responsible for maintaining computer and information systems that support the employees in their work (also called the IT Department in some organizations).

Information Technology Department (IT) — *See* Information Systems Department (IS).

init — A daemon that acts as a control process to start the first processes on Linux, such as the login screens. Also, a command used to switch the system to a different run level.

inode — A file information record, identified by a unique number within a file system, which contains detailed information about a block of data commonly called a file.

insmod — Command used to copy a module file from the hard disk and add it to the Linux kernel running in memory.

install disk — A disk used to start the Linux installation program on some distributions of Linux. *See* boot disk.

installation source — The set of files from which Linux is installed. These files are normally stored on a Linux CD.

installation type — A specification indicating which Linux software to install; the correct installation type depends on how the Linux system will be used.

interrupt request (IRQ) — A numbered channel of communication allowing a device to inform the system that some action needs to be taken for the device.

interpreted language — A language for which the source code is converted to numeric codes at the time a user runs the program. This conversion takes place each time the user runs the program. For this reason, interpreted languages are generally much slower than compiled languages.

interpreted program — A computer program that is converted from human-readable form to a format that can be used by a computer (numeric codes) at the moment you execute the program.

interpreter — A special program that converts the source code of an interpreted language into numeric codes that a computer can execute.

I/O ports — Memory addresses used by a device for memory-mapped I/O.

IP — A networking protocol used to send packets of information across a network connection.

IP address — An identifying number assigned to a computer or device that uses IP to communicate across a network.

iteration — An occurrence of an event or process that can or must be done many times.

jobs — Command used to list jobs (processes) started in the current shell environment.

jukebox — A back-up device that holds multiple back-up media (such as multiple tape cartridges or writeable CDs) and that can switch between them without assistance from a system administrator.

kernel — The core of the operating system, which interacts directly with the computer hardware.

kernel modules — Files containing computer code that can be loaded into the kernel or removed from the kernel as needed.

kernel ring buffer — A small area of memory that holds internal kernel messages. These messages can be viewed using the `dmesg` utility.

keywords — Words used in a computer language to define a specific task or meaning.

kill — Command used to send signals to processes, often to end them via a SIGTERM or SIGKILL signal.

klogd — A background program (or daemon) used to log kernel messages according to the configuration given in the `syslog.conf` configuration file.

Korn shell — A revision of the Bourne shell that includes the interactive features of the C shell but that maintains the Bourne shell programming style. The Korn shell was written by David Korn. It is available in Linux as the Public Domain Korn shell, `pdksh`.

kpm — The KDE process manager, a graphical utility for the KDE graphical environment that is used to control Linux processes. Similar to the Gnome System Monitor.

ktop — A KDE-based graphical utility used to manage Linux processes. Similar to the `kpm` program.

LaTeX — A version of the mark-up language TeX that includes numerous macros for easy document creation.

ldd — Command used to list the function libraries that a program uses.

legacy systems — Computer systems that an organization already owns. This term usually refers to systems that are no longer state of the art.

less — Command used to print the contents of a file one screenful at a time. It allows you to move around in the file and otherwise control the command by using the keyboard.

LGPL — A special version of the GNU General Public License intended to govern both free and commercial software use of software libraries.

lilo — Command used to read the `lilo.conf` configuration file and update the hard disk boot information based on the configuration.

LILO (Linux Loader) — The boot manager included with Linux.

link — A special file record that refers to the same physical file data as another file record.

LinuxConf — Graphical configuration and administration utility for Linux, developed and supported by Red Hat Software.

Linux distribution — A Linux operating system product that includes the Linux kernel plus many software components, installation tools, documentation, and so forth.

Linux Documentation Project (LDP) — One of the first efforts to document how Linux is used. Started by Matt Welsh.

lizardx — A graphical utility used for configuring the X Window System.

ln — Command used to create a symbolic or hard link.

locate — Linux command used to search an index of the file system for items matching a given pattern.

log file — File that contains detailed records of activity on a Linux system.

logger — A program that lets you send a message to the `syslog` function. Such messages are written to the log files according to the configuration in `syslog.conf`.

logging in — The process of identifying yourself as a valid user who has been assigned a certain set of access rights.

logrotate — A program that manages the rotation of multiple log files at regular intervals according to a configuration file created by the system administrator.

logscanner — A log analysis program available for download at *http://xmission.linuxberg.com/conhtml/ adm_log.html*.

LogWatch — A log analysis program available for download at *http://xmission.linuxberg.com/conhtml/ adm_log.html*.

loop statement — A statement used to determine whether part of a computer program should be executed more than once.

lpc — Short for *line printer control*. The Linux printer control utility.

lpd — The line printer daemon, which sends files prepared by **lpr** to the physical printer device or remote print server.

lpq — A utility that lists each print job in a print queue and includes information such as the owner and size of each job.

lpr — A command that prepares files to be sent to a physical printer device, effectively "printing" files for Linux users.

lprm — A command that deletes a print job from a print queue.

ls — Command used to list the files in a directory.

lsmod — Command used to list the modules that are installed in the Linux kernel.

Macintosh — A computer developed by Apple Computer that integrated the operating system and the graphical interface.

macro — A set of commands that can be executed as one by referring to the name of the macro.

magic filter — A print filter program that automatically processes a file into the correct output format based on the file's type.

make — A command that uses information stored in a configuration file to compile source code into a binary program, or otherwise prepare a program to be executed.

man pages — Online reference pages for Linux commands. The man pages are accessed using the **man** command.

mark-up languages — Computer languages that define a series of codes indicating how to format a document.

Master Boot Record (MBR) — A small area of the first hard disk that contains a program to decide how to start an operating system.

megabyte (MB) — A measure of space on computers equal to 1,048,576 bytes, or enough space to store roughly 1 million characters.

memory-mapped input/output (memory-mapped I/O) — A technique that assigns a range of memory addresses in a computer as a place for a device to send and receive data.

message — A description of what is happening within a program.

messages — The main system log file in Linux, usually stored in the directory **/var/log**.

Microsoft Windows — The leading graphical interface for DOS.

mirroring — Term used to describe a system in which the contents of two file systems contain identical information. Mirroring improves data access speed and provides fault tolerance in the event that one of the file systems fails.

mkdir — Command used to create a new directory.

mke2fs — Command used to format a device such as a hard disk partition with an **ext2** file system.

mkfs — Command used to format devices using various file system types. The **ext2** default type for Linux file systems can be indicated as an option. *See also* **mke2fs**.

mkswap — Command used to format a partition as a swap space for the Linux kernel.

modal editor — A text editor that uses multiple modes for editing text and entering commands to apply to that text.

modprobe — Command used to load a module with all of its required supporting modules.

module parameters — Information needed by a module to locate system resources. The parameters are added after the module name when using the `insmod` or `modprobe` command.

more — Command used to print the contents of a file one screenful at a time. The `more` command is similar to the `less` command but with fewer keyboard control options.

mount — Command used to make a logical or physical device available as a file system in the Linux directory structure.

mount point — The place or path in the Linux directory structure where a file system is accessed.

multithreading — A technique used within multiprocessing operating systems to divide a larger task between multiple processors.

multiuser system — An operating system on which numerous users can log in to the same computer (usually over a network connection).

mv — Command used to rename a file or directory or move it to a new location.

nbench — A benchmark program developed by *BYTE* magazine and ported to Linux.

nesting — A programming method in which one selection or loop statement contains another selection or loop statement.

network mask — A set of numbers that tells the networking system in Linux how to identify IP addresses that are part of the local network.

nice — Linux command used to set the nice level of a Linux process as it is being launched.

nice level — The priority level assigned to a Linux task.

NTFS — The default file system type for Windows NT.

OpenSource — A trademarked name often used to refer to software licensed under the GPL.

operating system — Software that provides a set of core functionality for other programs to use in working with the computer hardware and interfacing with the user running the computer.

other permissions — A set of three file permissions (r, w, and x) that apply to all users on the Linux system who are not the owner of the file or directory in question and are not members of the group assigned to the file or directory.

pac — A command that displays reports based on print accounting data. It stands for *print accounting*.

page — A block of 4 KB of memory. A page is the unit of memory in which the Linux kernel moves data to and from the Linux swap partition.

page description language — A special set of codes that determine the graphics elements, text font, and everything else about how information appears on a printed page.

parent directory — The directory that is one level above the current directory.

parity — A technique that allows corrupted data to be reconstructed using an extra piece of information (the parity information) that is created as the data is stored. Parity information provides redundancy for a piece of information.

parity stripe — Parity information stored as part of a RAID-3 or RAID-5 system.

partition — A distinct area of a hard disk that has been prepared to store a particular type of data.

partition table — Information that defines the size and location of each partition on a hard disk.

PATH — An environment variable containing a list of directories on the Linux system that the shell searches each time a command is executed.

Perl — A programming language developed by Larry Wall initially to process strings of text and generate reports.

ping — A command used to test a network connection.

pipe — A connection between two Linux commands (indicated by the | character) that causes the output of one command to be used as the input of a second command.

plain-text configuration file — A file containing human-readable instructions that are used by a program to set its configuration information.

points of failure — Parts of an information system that are subject to failure.

positional variable — A variable used within a shell script that contains data included on the command line when the script was launched.

power supply — The component within a computer system that converts the incoming AC power from a wall socket or UPS device to the correct voltage for use by components in a computer.

preemptive multitasking — A technique used by the Linux kernel to control which program is running from moment to moment.

print filter — A script that contains instructions for formatting documents using the page description language required by a specific printer. The print filter is used by the `lpr` program to prepare files to be sent to a physical printer.

print job — A file submitted for printing via the `lpr` command.

print queue — A subdirectory where files are stored to wait for the `lpd` daemon to retrieve them one by one and send them to the printer. Also called a print spool directory.

print spool directory — *See* print queue.

printcap — The printer definition file used by the Linux printing system. This file specifies how and where files to be printed are stored and processed by `lpr` and `lpd`. It stands for *printer capture*.

printer policy — A brief document that describes how print resources can be used and how the management of the printers will be conducted within an organization.

priority — A number indicating the severity of a message submitted for logging. (Log configurations are often based on the priority of incoming messages.) Also, a value assigned to a process running on Linux that determines how much CPU time is granted to the process to complete its tasks.

process — A task running on a Linux operating system, managed by the Linux kernel.

process ID (PID) — A number from 1 to 65,000 that is associated uniquely with a process running on a Linux system.

program — An imprecise term used to refer to any process running on a Linux system.

programming language — *See* computer language.

programming libraries — Collections of programming functionality that are common to many applications. *See also* shared libraries.

Project Athena — The project sponsored by DEC and MIT to create a graphical environment or windowing system for UNIX.

protocol — An organized pattern of signals or words used to communicate efficiently.

ps — Command used to obtain detailed information about processes running on Linux.

pwd — Command that displays the current working directory.

Python — A scripting language developed by Guido van Rossum that is often used for creating graphical programs.

queue — A list of commands or files to be processed.

RAID — A system using multiple inexpensive hard disks arranged in a predefined pattern (an array) to improve performance, increase fault tolerance, or both.

RAID-0 — A RAID level that uses striping to improve disk performance but without adding any fault tolerance.

RAID-1 — A RAID level that uses disk mirroring to significantly improve fault tolerance. Disk read performance is also improved, but disk write performance suffers.

RAID-3 — A RAID level that uses striping with parity information to improve both performance and fault tolerance.

RAID-5 — A RAID level in which data striping with parity is spread across all disks in the RAID array (compared to RAID-3, in which the parity information is stored on a single hard disk).

RAID-Linear — A method of combining multiple physical devices into a single logical device.

RAID subsystem — A hardware-controlled RAID device containing a CPU and other components to control the array of hard disks.

random access memory (RAM) — Electronic storage used by a computer as a working space for all operations while the computer is turned on.

read-only memory (ROM) — Nonvolatile electronic storage within a computer. Used to store information about how the computer starts and how the devices in the computer are configured.

read permission — A file permission that allows a user to read the contents of a file or browse the files in a directory. Represented by a letter **r**.

reboot — Command used to shut down all services and then restart the computer.

redirection — The concept of changing the location where a Linux program receives its input and sends its output in order to increase flexibility and interaction with other Linux programs.

redundancy — Term used to refer to a duplicate system component or piece of data. Many fault tolerant systems rely on the use of redundant components or data; in the event of a failure, the duplicate component or copy of the data would still be available.

redundant arrays of inexpensive disks — *See* RAID.

regular expression — A system of expressing patterns using special characters that can be interpreted by many Linux programs.

regular user account — A user account that, unlike the **root** account, is not used for system administration work. A regular user account has a name similar to a person's name.

release number — A number assigned by the company that prepares a Linux product. It allows the company to track how many times the kernel file has been altered before the final product is shipped.

renice — Linux command used to change the nice level of a Linux process that is already running.

rescue disk — A disk created specifically to boot a Linux system in the event of a system failure. Contains the software tools most likely to be of help in diagnosing and repairing the problem with the failed system.

rescue mode — A mode of operation in Red Hat Linux that is initiated by starting the system using a rescue disk. Rescue mode is used to repair a system failure that blocks normal booting and operation.

resource database — A file that defines how an X resource should appear on screen.

resource groups — The tasks and their accompanying system resources that are defined within a high availability cluster. Each server in the cluster can take over a complete resource group if the server handling that resource group fails.

restore — To copy data from a back-up location (for example, a tape cartridge) onto the file system where that data is normally used, and from which it was unintentionally lost.

rm — Command used to delete a file.

rmdir — Command used to remove (delete) an empty directory.

rmmod — Command used to remove a module from the kernel.

root — Superuser account name in Linux.

root directory — The starting point for all access to Linux resources. It is indicated by a single forward slash: /.

root disk — A disk used in conjunction with an install disk during some Linux installations (depending on the Linux distribution you are using).

rotating log files — The process of moving existing log files to another filename and location for archiving or review. Rotating log files frees hard disk space for new log messages.

rpm — Command used to manage all of the rpm software packages on a Linux system.

run level — A mode of operation that defines which Linux system services are started and which are shut down. The standard Linux run level of 3 includes networking and other common services such as system logging and task scheduling.

safedelete — A type of utility that makes files appear to have been deleted but actually saves a compressed copy of each one in case it is needed later.

SAGE (System Administrators Guild) — A professional organization for system administrators.

script — *See* shell script.

SCSI — A high-performance interface used by many types of devices to connect to a computer.

sector — A unit of data storage on a hard disk. Normally a sector contains 512 bytes.

sed — A command used to process each line in a text file according to a series of commands provided by the user.

selection statement — A statement that lets a computer programmer determine which parts of a program will be executed according to values that are calculated by testing as the program is executed. The if/then statement is a selection statement used in shell scripts.

selector — A field in the syslog.conf file that determines what events are being logged. The selector is composed of a facility and a priority.

session — A configuration that defines a set of graphical programs to run when a user logs in.

set — Command used to display a list of all environment variables defined in the current environment.

Shadow Password system — Security system used to restrict access to encrypted password text.

shared libraries — Programming libraries that are used by several dynamically linked applications running at the same time. Shared libraries are used to reduce memory consumption by providing a single copy of redundant functionality.

shell — A command-line interpreter, providing a command-line interface.

shell prompt — A set of words or characters indicating that the shell is ready to accept commands at the keyboard.

shell script — An executable file containing lines of text as you would enter them at a command line, including special commands to control the order in which lines in the file are executed.

shell variable — A variable used within a shell script to store information for use by the script.

shutdown — Command used to shut down Linux gracefully.

SIGHUP — A signal sent to a logging daemon to instruct the daemon to reread its configuration files and the log file it writes to.

signal — A message (one of a fixed set determined by the Linux kernel) that can be sent to any process and responded to according to how that program is written.

single point of failure — A system component which, if it alone fails, renders a system unusable. Can be a hardware component or a piece of data.

software — Instructions that control the physical computer components, but which can be changed because they reside on a changeable media such as a hard disk.

software license — A legal definition of who can use a piece of software and how it can be used.

software masters — Original copies of an application supplied by a software vendor or manufacturer, usually one or more CDs, tapes, or disks.

software package — A single file that contains all the files needed to install and use an application or group of related applications. Special data formats are used to store many files in a single software package.

software-based RAID — A RAID array that is controlled or managed by software on the computer system that uses the hard disk array (the Linux system) rather than by a separate CPU or other hardware components.

sort — A command used to sort all of the lines in a text file, writing them out in alphabetical order or according to options provided to the command.

source code — The file that a programmer writes using the keywords and syntax rules of a computer language.

Stallman, Richard — Founder of the Free Software Foundation and the GNU project.

standard error (STDERR) — The channel used by most Linux programs to send information about errors in program execution.

standard input (STDIN) — The communication channel used by most Linux programs to collect input (normally from the keyboard).

standard output (STDOUT) — The communication channel used by most Linux programs to write output (normally to the screen).

statement — A command within a computer program. A statement is often a single keyword, but the term may also refer to a group of keywords that the computer language syntax requires or allows to be used together.

statement block — A list of commands (or statements) that are controlled by a selection or loop statement.

statically linked applications — Linux programs that include library functions in the program itself so that they are not dependent on the libraries loaded on the Linux system.

striping — A technique in which parts of a file are written to more than one disk in order to improve performance. *See* RAID-3.

su — Short for substitute user. Command used to take on the identity of a different user account.

superblock — The master information record for a Linux file system.

superuser — The `root` user account, which has supervisory privileges throughout the Linux system.

surge suppressor — A device that prevents potentially damaging electrical irregularities from reaching a computer system's power supply.

swap partition (also called swap space) — A designated area on a hard disk used as virtual memory by the Linux kernel.

swapon — Command used by Linux initialization scripts to activate the swap partition defined in the `/etc/fstab` file.

symbolic link — A file record that includes a path and filename, but not an inode. It refers to another filename rather than to data in a file.

symmetrical multiprocessing — A technique that allows an operating system to support multiple CPUs on the same computer.

sync mode — An option assigned to log files by which the data written to the log file is immediately written to the hard disk rather than being cached in memory to improve system performance.

syntax — A formalized arrangement of information to allow a Linux command to understand parameters, options, and so forth.

syslog — A programming function used by Linux programs to submit messages for logging. The `syslog` function interacts with the `syslogd` daemon to write messages according to the `syslog.conf` file.

syslog.conf — The configuration file used to control how and where messages are logged by `syslogd` and `klogd`.

syslogd — The background program (or daemon) that manages all of the calls to the `syslog` function, writing log messages according to the `syslog.conf` configuration.

system initialization scripts — Instructions executed each time you boot your Linux system.

tab completion — A feature of the shell that lets you enter part of a file or directory name and have the shell fill in the remainder of the name.

tar — Command used to create a single archive file that contains many other files, often compressed to save space.

tar archive — A file created by the `tar` command.

target hard disk partition — The location on the system's hard disk where Linux will be installed. Also known as *target partition*.

Tcl/Tk — A scripting language developed by John Ousterhout that is used to create graphical programs.

telinit — Command used to switch the system to a different run level.

TENEX/TOPS C shell (TC shell) — An enhancement of the C shell. This is the version of the C shell that is commonly provided on Linux systems.

terminal emulator window — A command-line window (also called a terminal window) within a graphical environment.

test — A command that evaluates the arguments provided after the command name and returns either true (a value of 1) or false (a value of 0).

test — A method of examining data within a shell script and acting according to the result of the examination (or test).

TeX — A document processing system that writers use to create large and complex documents on UNIX or Linux systems.

then — A command that identifies the commands to be executed if the test introduced by the `if` command succeeds (returns a value of true).

thrashing — Excessive movement of processes between RAM and swap space, resulting in reduced system performance and excessive wear on the hard disk.

thread — A piece of a process (or a piece of a daemon, since a daemon is a type of process). The distinction between processes and threads is not important for most system administration work. Instead, the term *process* is used in most cases that don't involve programmers developing software for multiprocessor computers.

timestamp — A record of the date and time when an event occurred.

top — Linux command used to view the most CPU-intensive processes running on Linux at a given moment, along with related process information for those processes.

Torvalds, Linus — Originator of the Linux kernel; formerly a student in Helsinki, Finland.

touch — Command used to create an empty file or to update the access time of an existing file.

tracks — The concentric circles on each platter of a hard disk.

troff — A command used to format and display documents that are created using roff mark-up codes.

tty — A command that displays the name of the terminal device you are currently working in.

tune2fs — A utility used to view or adjust parameters within the superblock of a Linux file system.

umask — Command used to set the file permissions assigned when you create a new file.

umount — Command used to unmount a file system that is accessible as part of the Linux directory structure.

uname — Command used to provide information about the operating system, including the kernel version.

uninterruptible power supply (UPS) — A device capable of providing power to a computer via batteries when the incoming AC power (wall socket power) fails. It also informs the Linux system of the status of the power.

UNIX — An operating system created at AT&T Bell Labs (now part of Lucent Technologies) about 30 years ago by Ken Thompson and Dennis Ritchie. UNIX is still widely used, and it provided the technical basis for Linux.

user permissions — A set of three file permissions (**r**, **w**, and **x**) that apply to the owner of a file or directory.

User Private Group — Security system that creates a new group containing one user when that user is first created.

useradd — Command used to create (add) a new user account in Linux.

usermod — Command used to modify or update an existing user account.

utility programs — Software that provides assistance in managing the hardware and operating system features (as opposed to doing other types of work such as word processing).

variable — A memory location used by a program to store a value, such as a number or a word. Each variable is assigned a name so that the program can access the value by referring to the name.

virtual memory — Memory available to the Linux kernel for running programs but which is actually located on a hard disk. Data that the Linux kernel stores in virtual memory is placed in the swap file system, or swap space.

vmstat — Linux command used to display detailed information about virtual memory usage.

Webmaster — The person who manages the content and functioning of a Web server program running on Linux.

wheel — Special system administrative group, not used officially in Linux.

while — A command that creates a loop based on a test. The loop executes a block of commands as long as the test returns true.

white space — Tabs or spaces included in a program or script that make the script easier for a person to read.

window manager — A special-purpose graphical application (X client) that controls the position and manipulation of the windows within a graphical user interface.

Windows NT — A business-oriented operating system product developed by Microsoft. Windows NT is not based on DOS as an underlying operating system.

write caching — A technique in which information to be written to a file system (particularly a RAID file system) is stored in system memory temporarily in order to improve performance of reading and writing information to the file system.

write permission — A file permission that allows a user to add or change information in a file or create files within a directory. Represented by a letter **w**.

WYSIWYG — A characteristic of programs that show documents on the computer screen much as they will look when printed on paper or in a Web browser (pronounced "whiz-ee-wig").

X client — A graphical application.

XFree86 Project — A free software project that creates software to provide X Window System functionality to Linux.

X resource — The separate screen elements of a graphical application, such as scroll bars, text fonts, mouse pointers, and title bars for windows or dialog boxes.

X server — The program that communicates with the video card to create images on the screen.

X Window System — A graphical software environment used by almost all UNIX and Linux operating systems.

Xconfigurator — A utility in Red Hat Linux for configuring the X Window System.

xdvi — Program used to display a LaTeX-coded document as it will appear on paper.

xf86config — A standard text-based utility for configuring the X Window System.

XF86Setup — A graphical utility for configuring the X Window System.

xfontsel — Program that lets the user choose each aspect of a font definition (such as the font family and typeface) and then displays the corresponding font for review.

xload — A graphical program that displays the CPU load over time on any Linux system's graphical interface.

xrdb — A command that loads an initial X database resource file or merges additional resource configuration details.

xterm — A program within a graphical environment that provides a command-line window.

YAST — A graphical configuration utility developed by the makers of SuSE Linux.

zcat — Command used to print the contents of a compressed file to the screen.

INDEX

Special Characters